G R A P H I S   P H O T O   9 3

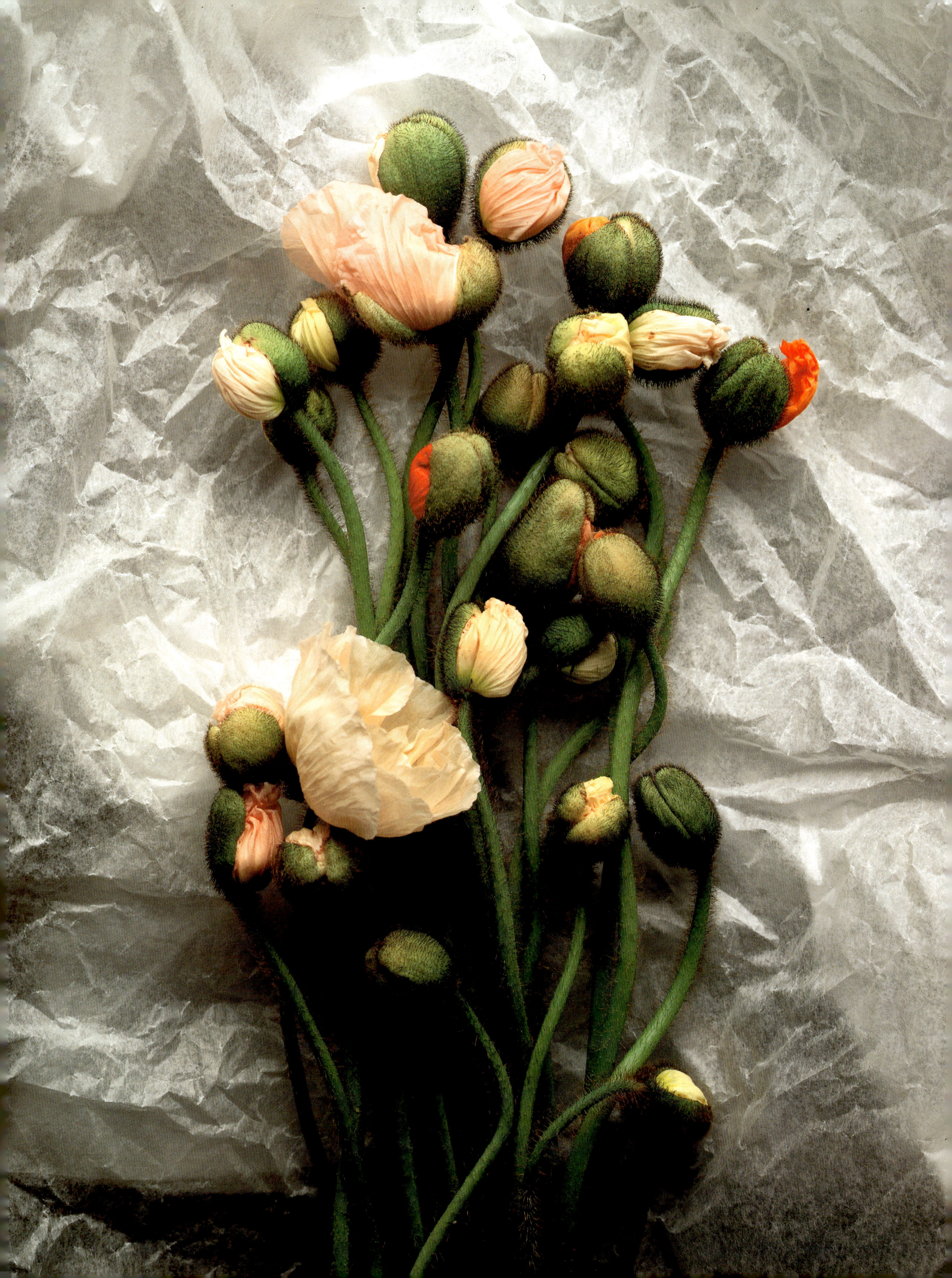

GRAPHIS PHOTO 93

···

THE INTERNATIONAL ANNUAL OF PHOTOGRAPHY

DAS INTERNATIONALE JAHRBUCH ÜBER PHOTOGRAPHIE

LE RÉPERTOIRE INTERNATIONAL DE LA PHOTOGRAPHIE

EDITED BY · HERAUSGEGEBEN VON · EDITÉ PAR:

B. MARTIN PEDERSEN

PUBLISHER AND CREATIVE DIRECTOR: B. MARTIN PEDERSEN

EDITORS: HEINKE JENSSEN, ANNETTE CRANDALL

ASSOCIATE EDITOR: KIMBERLY E. MORRIS

ART DIRECTORS: B. MARTIN PEDERSEN, RANDELL PEARSON

GRAPHIS PRESS CORP. ZÜRICH (SWITZERLAND)

OPPOSITE PAGE: JOHN PAYNE

PUBLICATION NO. 223 (ISBN 3-85709-293.9)
© COPYRIGHT UNDER UNIVERSAL COPYRIGHT CONVENTION
COPYRIGHT © 1993 BY GRAPHIS PRESS CORP., DUFOURSTRASSE 107, 8008 ZURICH, SWITZERLAND
JACKET AND BOOK DESIGN COPYRIGHT © 1993 BY PEDERSEN DESIGN
141 LEXINGTON AVENUE, NEW YORK, N.Y. 10016 USA
FRENCH CAPTIONS BY NICOLE VIAUD

NO PART OF THIS BOOK MAY BE REPRODUCED IN ANY FORM WITHOUT WRITTEN
PERMISSION OF THE PUBLISHER

PRINTED IN JAPAN BY TOPPAN PRINTING CO., LTD.

Contents · Inhalt · Sommaire

REMARKS

WE EXTEND OUR HEARTFELT THANKS TO CONTRIBUTORS THROUGHOUT THE WORLD WHO HAVE MADE IT POSSIBLE TO PUBLISH A WIDE AND INTERNATIONAL SPECTRUM OF THE BEST WORK IN THIS FIELD.

ENTRY INSTRUCTIONS MAY BE REQUESTED AT:
GRAPHIS PRESS CORP.,
DUFOURSTRASSE 107,
8008 ZÜRICH, SWITZERLAND

ANMERKUNGEN

UNSER DANK GILT DEN EINSENDERN AUS ALLER WELT, DIE ES UNS DURCH IHRE BEITRÄGE ERMÖGLICHT HABEN, EIN BREITES, INTERNATIONALES SPEKTRUM DER BESTEN ARBEITEN ZU VERÖFFENTLICHEN.

TEILNAHMEBEDINGUNGEN:
GRAPHIS VERLAG AG,
DUFOURSTRASSE 107,
8008 ZÜRICH, SCHWEIZ

ANNOTATIONS

TOUTE NOTRE RECONNAISSANCE VA AUX DESIGNERS DU MONDE ENTIER DONT LES ENVOIS NOUS ONT PERMIS DE CONSTITUER UN VASTE PANORAMA INTERNATIONAL DES MEILLEURES CRÉATIONS.

MODALITÉS D'ENVOI DE TRAVAUX:
EDITIONS GRAPHIS,
DUFOURSTRASSE 107,
8008 ZÜRICH, SUISSE

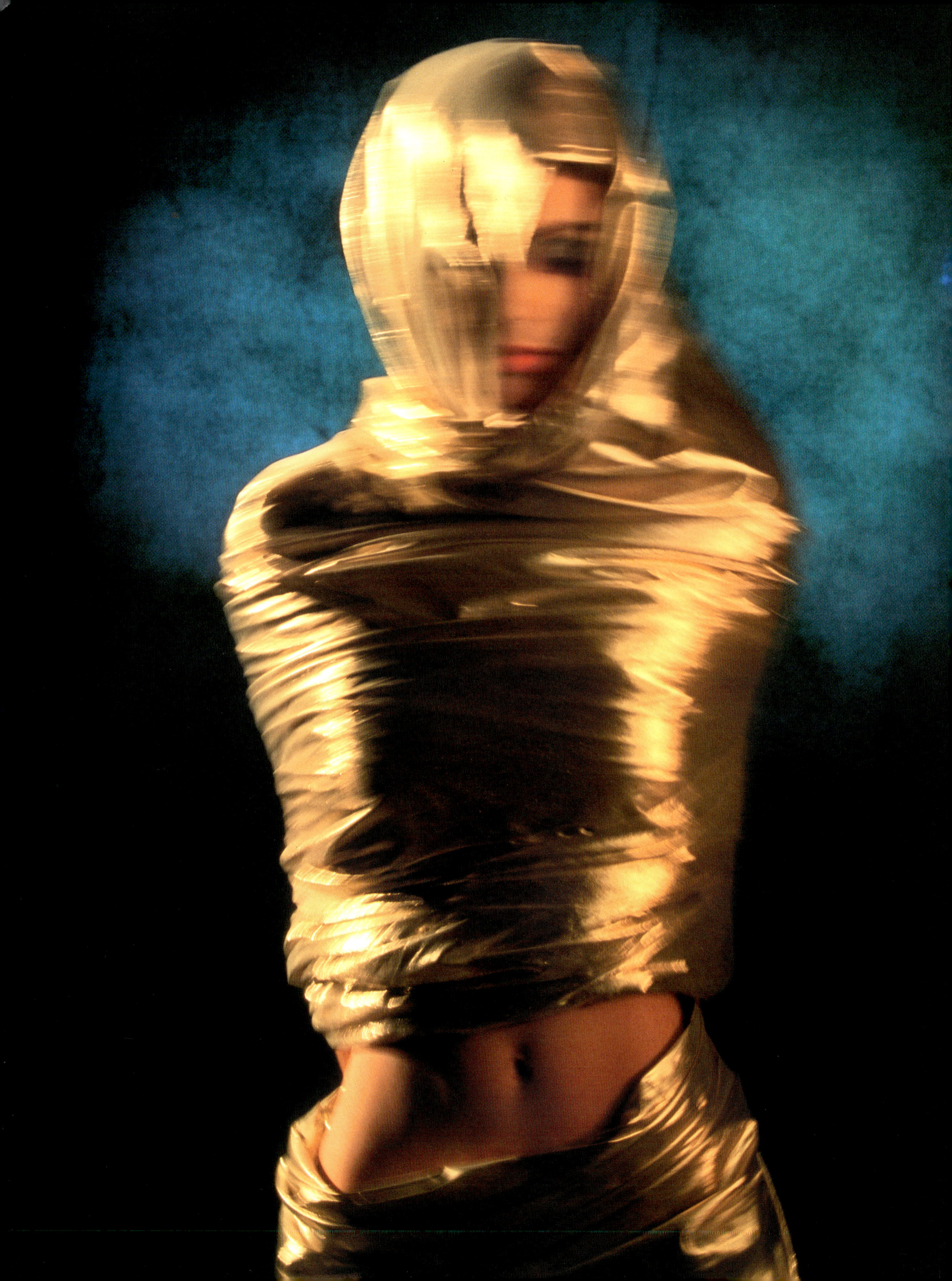

COMMENTARY

KOMMENTAR

COMMENTAIRE

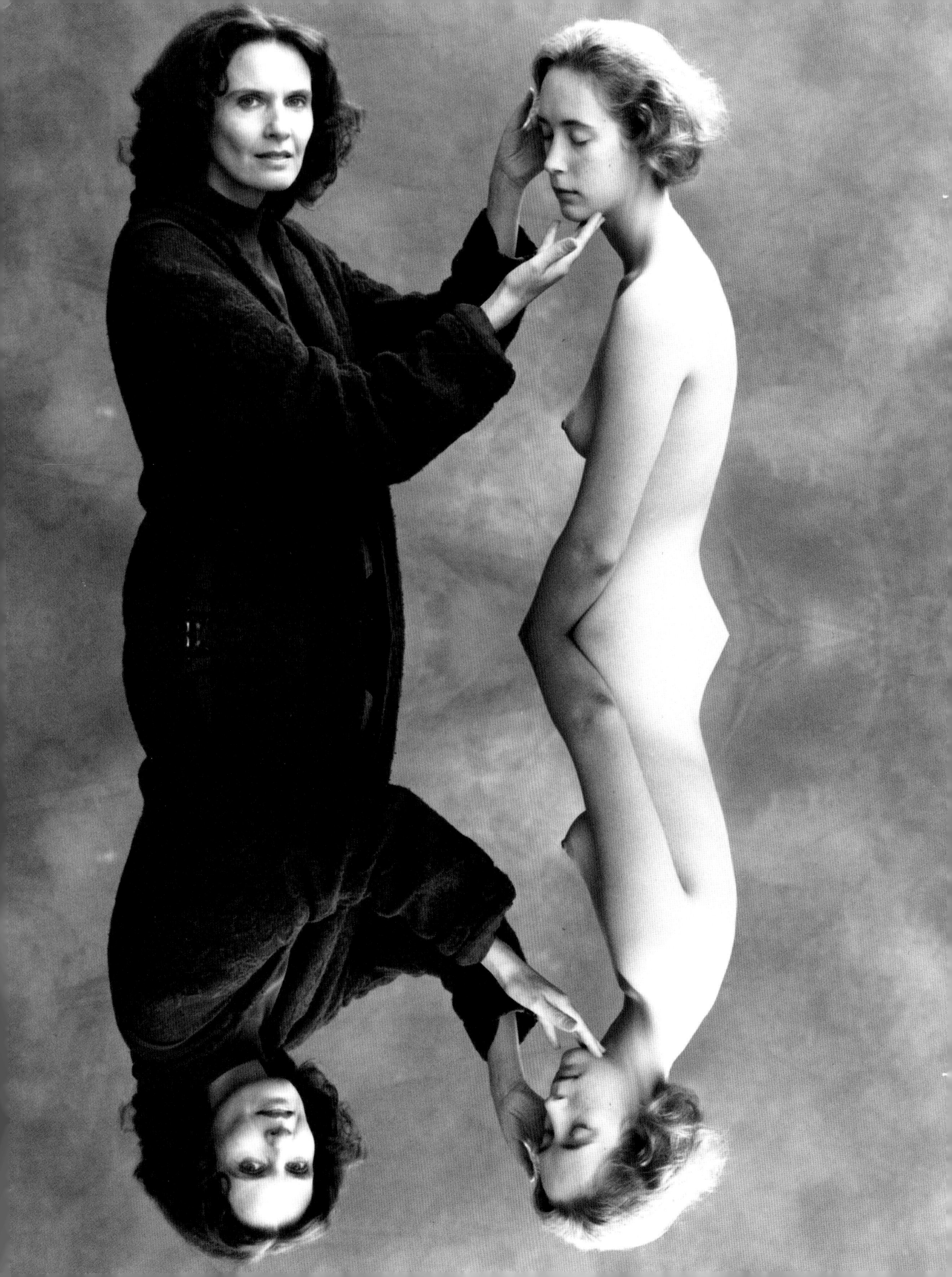

J O Y C E   T E N N E S O N

I don't really understand why I became a photographer. If I examine my early memories, I realize I never dreamed of the kind of life I have now. I never knew any artists or creative people. I was surrounded by people who didn't dare to dream. □ I feel privileged to have somehow, miraculously, leapt over the "no dream" barrier, and to have had the opportunity to explore and develop my artistic talents. All this sounds pretentious on paper, but what I'm trying to say is that I came from a family whose major life goal was to be completely selfless—a "good" person. Unfortunately, although these are worthwhile objectives, for my family they precluded personal growth. I believe it is this suppression of personal aspirations that caused my mother to die of cancer at a young age. Watching this as a child, I decided that I didn't want a similar destiny. □ Somehow, early in my life, I separated from my family. I had a secret kingdom of my own, the world of my imagination. This is where I felt happy. It was also a place where I went when I felt lonely or inspired, or filled with life. □ Perhaps I was lucky not to have had role models, for I created my own visual world with absolutely no self-consciousness. I just trusted that if I were true to my deeper instincts, sooner or later the work would have some value. □ I always enjoyed creating beauty where it never existed. I've had a simultaneous desire to invite others into this world. Photography has been a way for me to communicate with others—to share my visions, my anxieties, my perceptions and my emotions, all at the same time! □ For some photography is a documentary tool, a way of recording exterior reality. For me it is a visual diary, a way of symbolically recreating inner emotional states of being, parts of my life. I've never had to discipline myself to work. On the contrary, I am most happy when I am creating new things. I love to be around beautiful things, but I do not like superficial, unthinking, predictable beauty. That bores and irritates me. What thrills me is pushing out and finding something new, strange and wonderful, even if what I find is disturbing as well. When I work, I try to open myself and then let the unconscious take over, letting go of measured time. I love having images emerge and surprise me when they appear in the camera's lens. Despite the frustrations and hard work, I cannot imagine another life. □ I admire all artists who go within and seek to speak from their own depth. I am grateful that photography has given me the confidence to speak in my own voice. ∎

*I*ch weiss eigentlich nicht, warum ich Photographin wurde. Wenn ich zurückdenke, stelle ich fest, dass ich mir das Leben, das ich jetzt führe, nie habe träumen lassen. Ich kannte überhaupt keine Künstler oder kreative Leute. Um mich herum waren Menschen, die es nicht wagten zu träumen. □ Ich fühle mich privilegiert, dass ich es irgendwie geschafft habe, die «keine-Träume»-Schranke zu überwinden, und dass ich Gelegenheit hatte, meine künstlerischen Talente zu ergründen und zu entwickeln. Das klingt ein bisschen anmassend, wenn man es niederschreibt; ich will damit sagen, dass ich aus einer Familie komme, deren oberstes Gebot es war, vollkommen selbstlos – ein «guter» Mensch – zu sein. Obgleich das ein lobenswertes Ziel war, schloss es bei meiner Familie von vornherein eine persönliche Entwicklung aus. Ich glaube, diese Unterdrückung persönlicher Ziele ist Schuld an der Krebserkrankung und am frühen Tod meiner Mutter. Da ich das als Kind miterlebte, stand für mich fest, dass ich nicht ein ähnliches Schicksal erleiden wollte. □ Irgendwie trennte ich mich schon früh von meiner Familie. Ich lebte in meiner eigenen Welt, in der Welt meiner Phantasie. Hier war ich glücklich. Hierhin zog ich mich zurück, wenn ich mich allein fühlte, aber auch wenn es mir gut ging. □ Vielleicht hatte ich Glück, dass ich keine Vorbilder hatte, so konnte ich mir völlig unbefangen meine eigene visuelle Welt schaffen. Ich vertraute darauf, dass ich früher oder später gute Arbeit leisten würde, wenn ich mich nur auf

JOYCE TENNESON GREW UP IN MASSACHUSETTS AS THE YOUNGEST OF THREE GIRLS. HER PERSONAL WORK HAS BEEN SHOWN IN OVER 100 EXHIBITIONS WORLDWIDE AND IS INCLUDED IN MANY MUSEUM AND PRIVATE COLLECTIONS. SHE IS ALSO A MUCH SOUGHT-AFTER COMMERCIAL PHOTOGRAPHER WITH CLIENTS IN EUROPE, JAPAN AND THE UNITED STATES. HER PHOTOGRAPHS HAVE APPEARED IN MANY MAGAZINES INCLUDING ESQUIRE, THE NEW YORK TIMES MAGAZINE, FRENCH AND ITALIAN VOGUE. SHE IS THE AUTHOR OF THREE BOOKS OF PHOTOGRAPHS AND A NEW ONE, ENTITLED TRANSFORMATION. IN 1989 SHE WON THE INTERNATIONAL CENTER FOR PHOTOGRAPHY'S INFINITY AWARD FOR BEST APPLIED PHOTOGRAPHY, AND IN 1990 SHE WAS NAMED "PHOTOGRAPHER OF THE YEAR" BY THE INTERNATIONAL ORGANIZATION WOMEN IN PHOTOGRAPHY. ∎

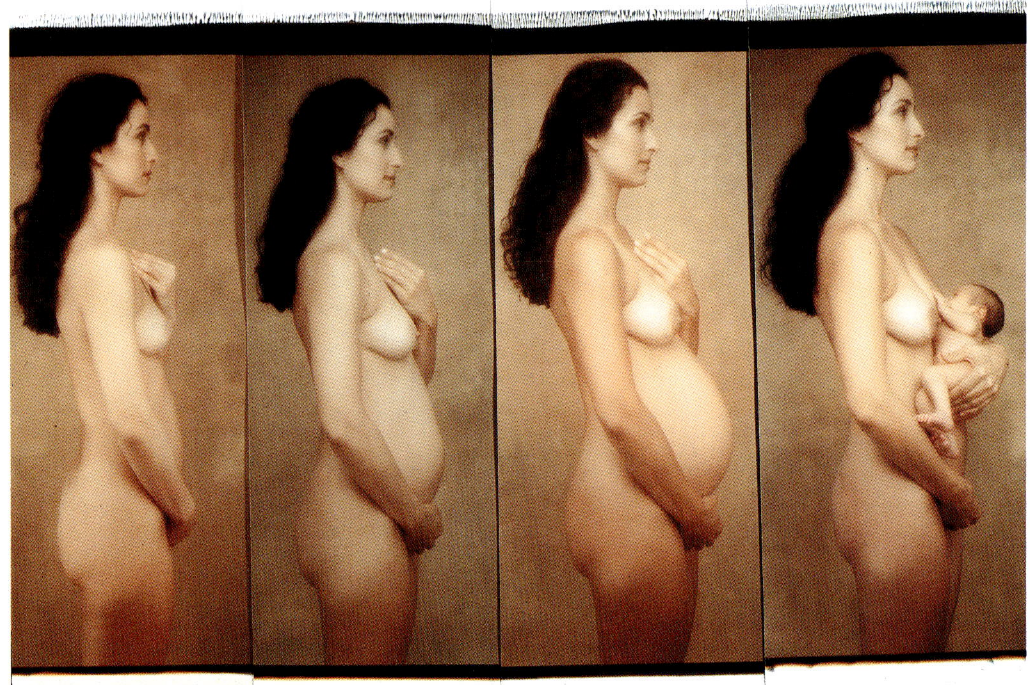

meine innersten Gefühle und meinen Instinkt verliess. □ Schon immer hat es mir Freude gemacht, Schönheit herzustellen, auch dort wo es sie nicht gab. Ich habe dabei das Bedürfnis, andere in diese Welt einzuladen. Photographie ist für mich ein Weg, mit anderen zu kommunizieren – meine Visionen, meine Ängste, meine Wahrnehmungen und meine Gefühle zu teilen, alles zur gleichen Zeit! □ Für einige ist Photographie ein Mittel zur Dokumentation, eine Möglichkeit, die äussere Realität zu registrieren. Für mich ist sie eine Art visuelles Tagebuch, eine Möglichkeit, Gefühlszustände, mein Leben symbolisch darzustellen. Ich musste mich nie zur Arbeit zwingen. □ Gegenteil, ich bin am glücklichsten, wenn ich arbeiten und neue Dinge schaffen kann. Ich habe gern schön Dinge um

mich herum, aber oberflächliche, langweilige, offensichtliche Schönheit sagt mir nichts, sie irritiert mich. Ich will das Verborgene, Unbekannte herausholen, etwas Neues, Seltsames und Wundervolles finden, das manchmal auch etwas Beunruhigendes haben kann. Wenn ich arbeite, versuche ich mich zu öffnen und dann dem Unterbewusstsein freien Lauf zu lassen, alles um mich herum zu vergessen. Ich liebe es, wenn Bilder auftauchen und mich überraschen, wenn ich sie vor der Kamera habe. Trotz all der Frustationen und harten Arbeit kann ich mir kein anderes Leben vorstellen. □ Ich bewundere alle Künstler, die aus sich heraus arbeiten, die sich bemühen, aus sich selbst zu schöpfen. Ich bin dankbar dafür, dass die Photographie mir den Mut gegeben hat, mit meiner eigenen Stimme zu sprechen. ■

A vrai dire, je ne sais pas vraiment pourquoi je suis devenue photographe. Si j'essaie de me remémorer mes premiers souvenirs, je constate que je n'avais jamais imaginé le genre de vie que je mène aujourd'hui. Je ne connaissais pas d'artistes ou de créatifs. J'étais entourée de gens qui n'osaient pas rêver. □ Je me sens privilégiée d'avoir réussi en quelque sorte à franchir cet obstacle que constitue

l'absence de rêves et d'avoir eu l'opportunité d'approfondir et de développer mes propres talents artistiques. Tout cela a l'air plutôt prétentieux quand on l'écrit sur le papier. Ce que j'essaie en fait de dire, c'est que je viens d'une famille dont le principal objectif dans la vie était de supprimer l'ego – où il fallait devenir quelqu'un de bien. Malheureusement, même si cette attitude est tout à fait honorable, pour ma

JOYCE TENNESON WUCHS ALS JÜNGSTE VON DREI TÖCHTERN IN MASSACHUSETTS, USA, AUF. IHRE FREIEN ARBEITEN WURDEN IN ÜBER 100 AUSSTELLUNGEN WELTWEIT GEZEIGT UND SIND VIELEN PRIVATEN UND MUSEUMSSAMMLUNGEN ZU FINDEN. SIE ARBEITET IM KOMMERZIELLEN BEREICH VOR ALLEM FÜR KUNDEN IN EUROPA, JAPAN UND USA. IHRE AUFNAHMEN WURDEN IN ZAHLREICHEN ZEITSCHRIFTEN VERÖFFENTLICHT, U.A. IN ESQUIRE, THE NEW YORK TIMES MAGAZINE, VOGUE PARIS UND VOGUE ITALIA. ES SIND BEREITS VIER PHOTOBÄNDE VON IHR ERSCHIENEN, DER NEUSTE UNTER DEM TITEL TRANSFORMATION. 1989 WURDE SIE VOM INTERNATIONAL CENTER FOR PHOTOGRAPHY MIT DEM «INFINITY AWARD» FÜR DIE BESTE KOMMERZIELLE PHOTOGRAPHIE AUSGEZEICHNET, 1990 ERNANNTE DIE INTERNATIONALE ORGANISATION WOMEN IN PHOTOGRAPHY SIE ZUR «PHOTOGRAPHIN DES JAHRES». ■

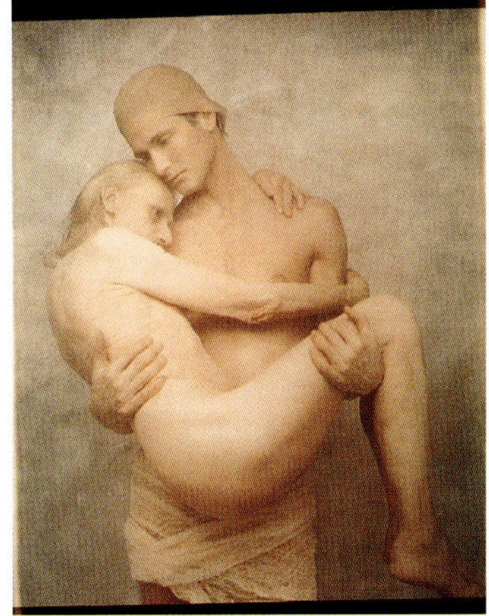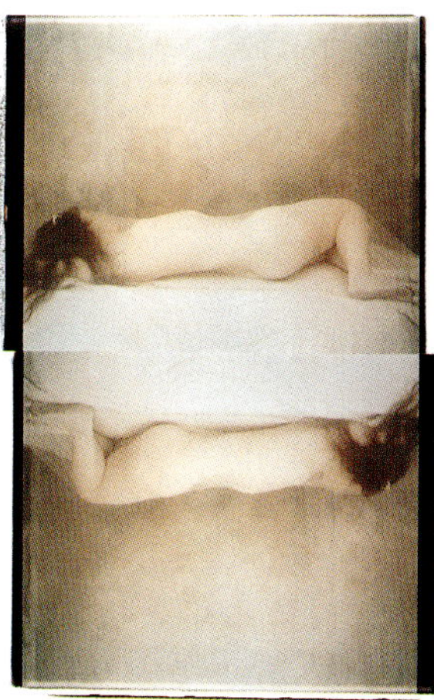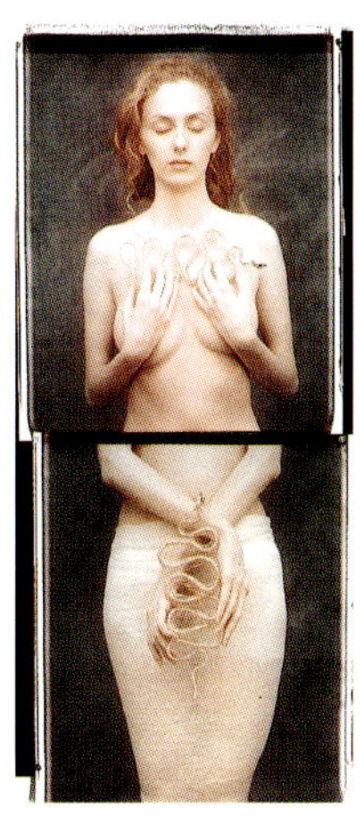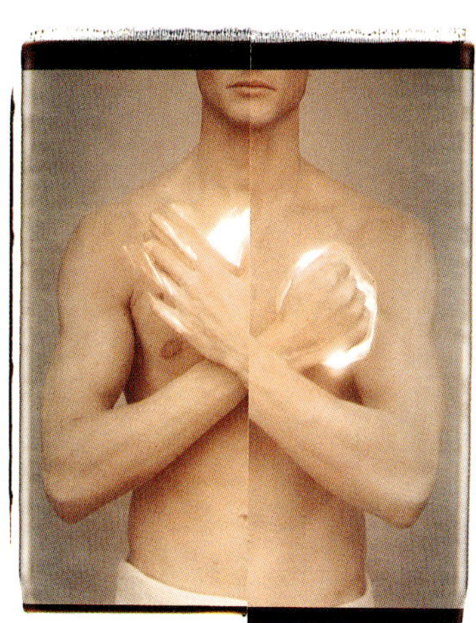

(OPPOSITE PAGE) "PREGNANCY AND BIRTH" 1992. ■ THIS PAGE FIRST IMAGE: "PETER WITH WILLIAM," 1990. SECOND IMAGE "SLEEPING BEAUTY," 1992. THIRD IMAGE "SUZANNE WITH SNAKE SKELETON" 1990. LAST IMAGE "PETER WITH 'LIGHT' IN FIST AND HAND," 1992. THE FIRST, THIRD, AND LAST IMAGES SHOWN ON THIS PAGE WERE ORIGINALLY PUBLISHED IN THE BOOK "JOYCE TENNESON TRANSFORMATIONS," A COMPILATION OF 81 COLOR AND 21 BLACK AND WHITE PHOTOGRAPHS BY TENNESON, PUBLISHED IN 1993 BY BULFINCH PRESS. ■

famille, cela excluait tout développement individuel. Je crois que c'est cette suppression des aspirations personnelles qui a été la cause de la mort prématurée de ma mère, des suites d'un cancer. J'assistais à tout cela alors que je n'étais encore qu'une enfant, et c'est ainsi que je pris la décision d'échapper à une tel destinée. □ Toujours est-il que très tôt, j'ai quitté le milieu familial. J'avais mon royaume secret, le monde de mon imagination. Là, je me sentais heureuse. C'était aussi un endroit où je me réfugiais quand je me sentais trop seule, remplie d'inspiration ou d'énergie. □ Peut-être que cela a été une chance pour moi de ne pas avoir de modèles, car j'ai ainsi pu créer mon propre monde visuel sans aucun complexe. J'étais persuadée que si j'étais fidèle à mes instincts les plus profonds, tôt ou tard, mon travail aurait quelque valeur. □ J'ai toujours aimé créer de la beauté là où elle n'a jamais existé. J'avais en même temps le désir d'inviter les autres à pénétrer dans ce monde. La photographie a été pour moi le moyen de communiquer avec les autres – de partager à la fois mes visions, mes angoisses, mes perceptions et mes émotions. □ Pour certains, la photographie est un instrument de documentation, une manière de rappeler la réalité extérieure. Je la considère comme une sorte de journal visuel, une manière de recréer symboliquement les états d'esprit, les émotions les plus intimes, des fragments de ma vie. Je n'ai jamais eu besoin de me discipliner pour travailler. Au contraire, je suis ravie quand je peux créer quelque chose de nouveau. J'aime être entourée de beaux objets mais je n'aime pas la beauté superficielle, irréfléchie, gratuite. Elle m'ennuie et elle m'irrite. Ce qui me fait vibrer, c'est d'exprimer et de découvrir quelque chose qui soit nouveau, étrange et merveilleux, même s'il arrive que cela soit aussi troublant. Quand je travaille, j'essaie d'être ouverte à tout, puis je laisse mon inconscient prendre le dessus, je m'évade du temps mesuré. J'aime que les images surgissent et me surprennent lorsqu'elles apparaissent au travers de l'objectif de l'appareil. Malgré toutes les frustrations et un travail souvent pénible, je ne peux pas m'imaginer un autre genre de vie. □ J'admire tous les artistes qui vont au fond des choses et qui cherchent à s'exprimer à partir de leur inconscient. La photographie m'a donné la confiance de parler avec ma propre voix, et je lui en suis reconnaissante. ■

JOYCE TENNESON EST LA CADETTE D'UNE FAMILLE DE TROIS ENFANTS, TOUTES DES FILLES. SES TRAVAUX ONT ÉTÉ PRÉSENTÉS DANS PLUS DE 100 EXPOSITIONS DANS LE MONDE ENTIER ET ELLES FIGURENT DANS DE NOMBREUX MUSÉES ET COLLECTIONS PRIVÉES. JOYCE TENNESON TRAVAILLE DANS LE SECTEUR DE LA PRESSE ET DE LA PUBLICITÉ AUSSI BIEN EN EUROPE QU'AU JAPON ET AUX USA. SES PHOTOS ONT ÉTÉ PUBLIÉES DANS DE NOMBREUX MAGAZINES, PARMI LESQUELS ESQUIRE, THE NEW YORK TIMES MAGAZINE, VOGUE PARIS ET VOGUE ITALIA. ELLE A DÉJÀ FAIT PARAITRE QUATRE VOLUMES DE PHOTOGRAPHIES PERSONNELLES; LE PLUS RÉCENT EST INTITULÉ TRANSFORMATION. EN 1989, ELLE A REÇU L'«INFINITY AWARD», QUI RÉCOMPENSE LA MEILLEURE PHOTO COMMERCIALE. EN 1990, L'ORGANISATION INTERNATIONALE WOMEN IN PHOTOGRAPHY L'A ÉLUE «PHOTOGRAPHE DE L'ANNÉE».■

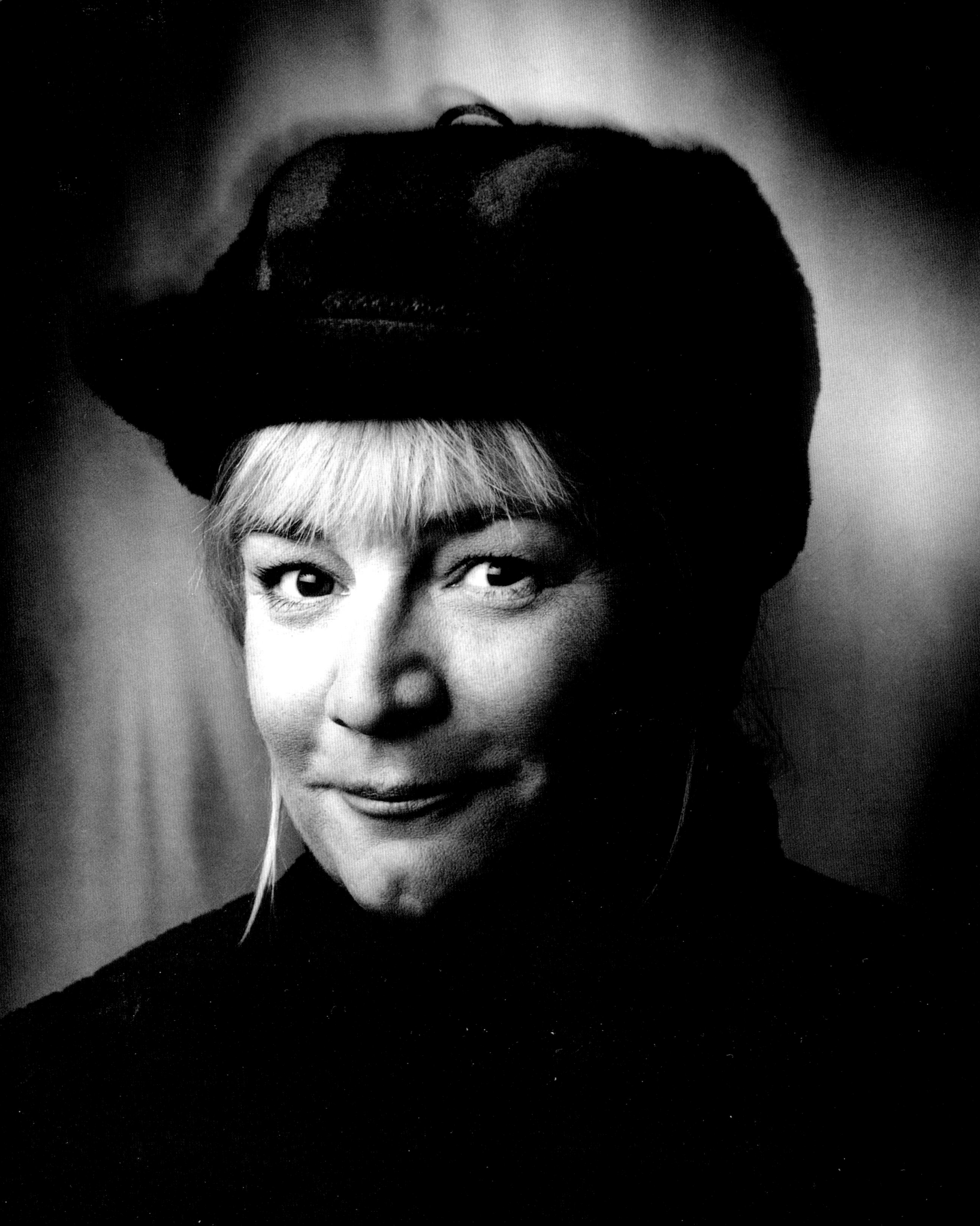

L A U R I E   K R A T O C H V I L

PORTRAIT BY MARK SELIGER

$\mathcal{P}$hotographs have been a part of my consciousness since I was four years old. My parents had a large brown album filled with scallop-edged, black-and-white Brownie photos of my older sister, Vicki. They documented her every move: playing in the surf in front of our house in Newport Beach, sitting with a big smile in her turquoise pedal car on her birthday, standing in our father's workshop wearing his big shirt and tie. Below the pictures were clever captions my father had written. Some of them were in quotation marks, which gave the impression that my sister, magically able to speak from birth, was wryly commenting on her own childhood. □ What fascinated me about the photos was my discovery of something from a time when I did not exist and their ability to transport me to a place where I had not been. Looking at them now, my original reaction is the same, only made richer and deeper over time: I hear the sound of water slapping the shore. I feel the warmth of the California sun. I remember my family and the sense of well-being I had then. □ Still images continue to absorb me; there is so much yet to be learned and imagined. Perhaps this explains why photography is such a big part of my life. □ Although I have held different positions in photography over the last two decades, my eleven years as photo editor of Rolling Stone have been the most rewarding. The broad range of stories and subjects we cover is a constant challenge. From Axl Rose and Chuck Berry to skinheads and gun runners in Afghanistan, it is my responsibility to present stories in a compelling and powerful way. □ It all starts with choosing the right photographer. A lot goes into this: the nature of the story, the feeling I would like the images to convey, past photographers who have covered the subject, the mix of other photographs in the issue, and the time and location restraints imposed on us by everything from the monsoon season to publicists. □ Although I give direction and encouragement to the photographers before they go out, I never impose my vision on the story. I want their thoughts and impressions to be in the photograph. I share Richard Avedon's belief that "a photograher is nothing but a machine unless he editorializes." I believe that photographers have an important voice, and I encourage them to use it. ∎

$\mathcal{M}$eine allererste Begegnung mit Photographien hatte ich im Alter von vier Jahren. Meine Eltern besassen ein grosses, braunes Album voller Schwarzweissphotos mit Büttenrand. Sie zeigen meine ältere Schwester Vicki, dokumentieren quasi jede ihrer Bewegungen: am Strand spielend vor unserem Haus in Newport Beach, an ihrem Geburtstag strahlend in ihrem türkisfarbenen Tretauto sitzend, im Arbeitsraum unseres Vaters in seinem riesigen Hemd und mit seiner Krawatte. Unter den Bildern stehen witzige Bemerkungen, von meinem Vater geschrieben. Einige davon sind in Anführungszeichen gesetzt, so dass der Eindruck entsteht, meine Schwester kommentiere ironisch ihre eigene Kindheit, als habe sie wunderbarerweise schon von Geburt an gesprochen. □ Was mich an diesen Photos fasziniert, ist die Entdeckung von etwas, das zu einer Zeit stattgefunden hat, als es mich noch nicht gab. Auch jetzt noch habe ich beim Anschauen der Bilder das gleiche Gefühl, wenn es mit den Jahren auch komplexer und tiefer geworden ist. Ich höre das Geräusch der sich am Strand brechenden Wellen, fühle die Wärme der kalifornischen Sonne. Ich erinnere meine Familie und das Gefühl des Wohlbefindens, das ich damals hatte. □ Noch immer nehmen Bilder mich gefangen; es gibt noch so viel zu erfahren und zu erträumen. Vielleicht erklärt das, wieso Photographie einen so wichtigen Platz in meinem Leben einnimmt. n Obwohl ich in den vergangenen zwanzig Jahren nicht nur bei Rolling Stone mit Photographie zu tun hatte, sind meine elf Jahre als Photo Editor von Rolling Stone für mich die wichtigsten. Das breite Spektrum von Geschichten und Themen in dieser Zeitschrift sind eine ständige Herausforderung. Meine Aufgabe ist es, jedes Thema, von Axl Rose oder Chuck Berry über Skinheads oder Waffenschieber in Afghanistan, attraktiv und

LAURIE KRATOCHVIL FIRST JOINED ROLLING STONE AS PHOTOGRAPHY EDITOR IN 1978, AFTER WORKING AT THE LOS ANGELES TIMES AND A&M RECORDS. IN 1980, SHE BECAME PHOTOGRAPHY EDITOR OF NEW WEST MAGAZINE, AND RETURNED TO ROLLING STONE IN 1982. UNDER HER DIRECTION, ROLLING STONE HAS BEEN NOMINATED THREE TIMES FOR THE NATIONAL MAGAZINE AWARDS FOR PHOTOGRAPHY, AND IN 1988 THE MAGAZINE WON THIS HONOR. IN ADDITION, HER WORK HAS WON NUMEROUS PRIZES AND CITATIONS FROM: THE SOCIETY OF PUBLICATION DESIGNERS, THE NEW YORK ART DIRECTORS CLUB, AMERICAN PHOTOGRAPHY AND GRAPHIS. IN 1989, ROLLING STONE: THE PHOTOGRAPHS, A TWENTY-YEAR RETROSPECTIVE THAT SHE PRODUCED AND EDITED, APPEARED ON THE NEW YORK TIMES BEST SELLER LIST. THAT YEAR, SHE WAS NAMED DIRECTOR OF PHOTOGRAPHY, THE TITLE SHE CURRENTLY HOLDS. ∎

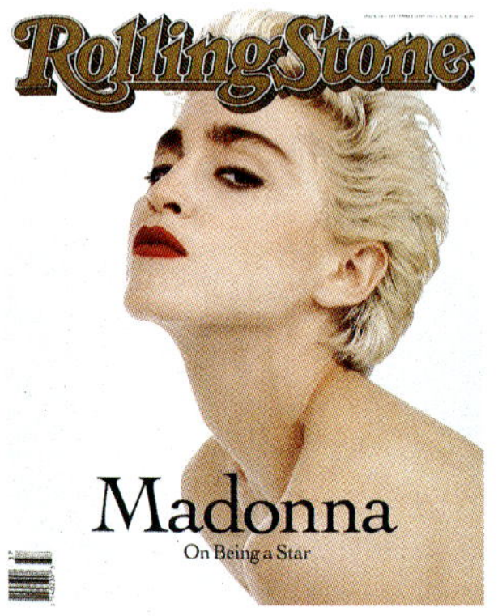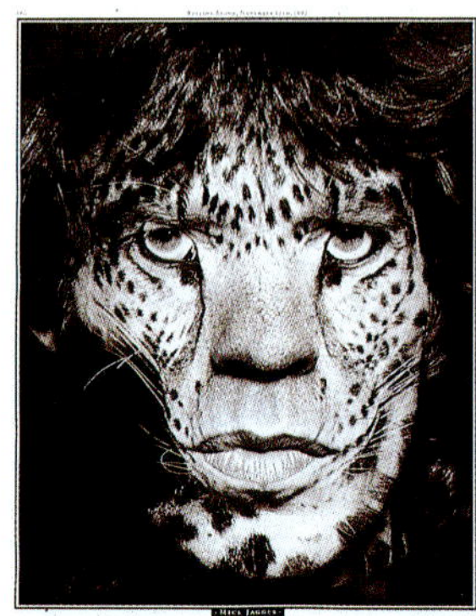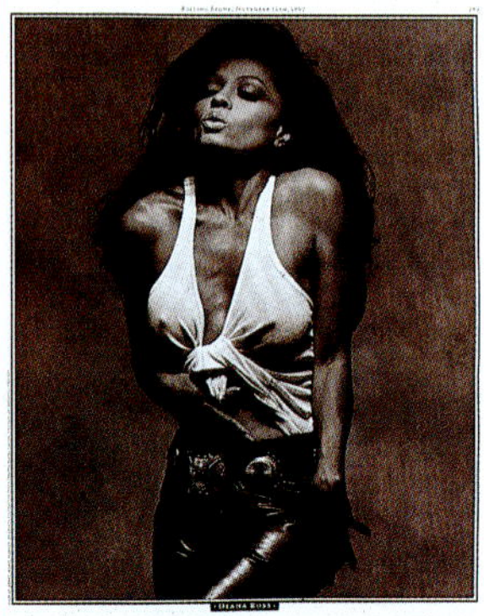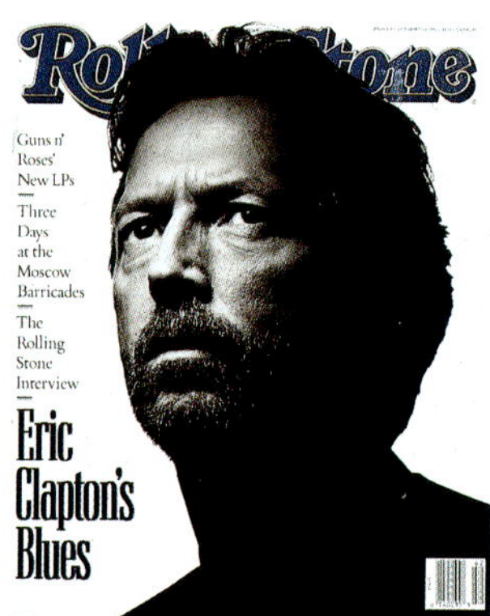

(ABOVE AND FACING) IMAGES FROM ROLLING STONE MAGAZINE (LEFT) SEPTEMBER 10, 1987; PHOTO: HERB RITTS. COVER WITH CONTROVERSIAL AMERICAN ROCK SINGER MADONNA DISPLAYING YET ANOTHER NEW IMAGE, IN THE ACCOMPANYING ARTICLE, SHE DISCUSSED WHAT BEING A STAR MEANT TO HER. (MIDDLE) NOVEMBER 12, 1992, PHOTO: ALBERT WATSON. SPREAD TAKEN FROM THE 25TH ANNIVERSARY ISSUE: A PHOTOGRAPHIC TRIBUTE TO THE ICONS OF ROCK AND ROLL. ON THE LEFT IS PERENNIAL ROCK SUPERSTAR MICK JAGGER, ON THE RIGHT IS R&B/CONTEMPORARY MUSIC DIVA DIANA ROSS. (RIGHT) OCTOBER 17, 1991, PHOTO: ALBERT WATSON. THIS DRAMATIC PORTRAIT OF LEGENDARY ROCK AND ROLL GREAT ERIC CLAPTON WAS TAKEN SIX MONTHS AFTER THE TRAGIC DEATH OF HIS FOUR YEAR OLD SON CONOR. THIS HAS BEEN CONSIDERED THE STRONGEST COVER EVER PUBLISHED BY ROLLING STONE MAGAZINE. ∎

interessant zu präsentieren. ☐ Alles beginnt mit der Wahl des richtigen Photographen. Dabei ist viel zu beachten: die Art der Geschichte, die von mir gewünschte Wirkung der Photos, schon existierende Aufnahmen zum Thema, die Mischung der anderen Bilder in der betreffenden Ausgabe, und schliesslich Termine und Location, wobei wir von allen möglichen Dingen abhängig sind, von der Monsunzeit bis hin zu Publizisten. ☐ Obwohl ich die Photographen informiere und ermutige, bevor sie sich an die Arbeit machen, versuche ich nie, meine eigene Vorstellung durchzusetzen. Ich will, dass ihre Gedanken und Eindrücke in der Aufnahme zum Ausdruck kommen. Ich teile Richard Avedons Überzeugung, dass «ein Photograph nichts als eine Maschine ist, wenn er sich nicht einbringen kann». Ich glaube, dass Photographen etwas zu sagen haben, und ich ermutige sie dazu. ∎

𝜋a première rencontre avec la photographie a eu lieu à l'âge de quatre ans. Mes parents possédaient un grand album brun, rempli de photos noir et blanc aux bords dentelés de ma sœur aînée Vicki. Ils documentaient chacun de ses mouvements: Vicki faisant du surf en face de notre maison de Newport Beach, Vicki rayonnante dans sa petite voiture à pédales bleu turquoise le jour de son anniversaire, Vicki debout dans le bureau de notre père, arborant son immense chemise et sa cravate. Au-dessous des images étaient inscrits des petits commentaires spirituels que mon père avait rédigés. Quelques-uns étaient entre guillemets, ce qui donnait l'impression que ma sœur, capable comme par enchantement de parler dès sa naissance, commentait avec ironie sa propre enfance. ☐ Ce qui me fascinait dans ces photos, c'était de découvrir quelque chose qui s'était déroulé alors que je n'étais pas encore née. Quand je les regarde aujourd'hui, elles me font toujours la même impression; cette expérience est toutefois plus enrichissante et

LAURIE KRATOCHVIL KAM 1978 ALS PHOTO EDITOR ZU ROLLING STONE, NACHDEM SIE FÜR DIE LOS ANGELES TIMES UND A&M RECORDS GEARBEITET HATTE. 1980 WURDE SIE PHOTOREDAKTEURIN BEI DER ZEITSCHRIFT NEW WEST, 1982 KEHRTE SIE ZU ROLLING STONE ZURÜCK. UNTER IHRER LEITUNG WURDE ROLLING STONE DREI MAL FÜR DEN NATIONAL MAGAZINE AWARD (NATIONALER ZEITSCHRIFTENPREIS) FÜR PHOTOGRAPHIE NOMINIERT, UND 1988 WURDE DIE ZEITSCHRIFT MIT DEM PREIS AUSGEZEICHNET. DARÜBER HINAUS WURDE IHRE ARBEIT VIELE MALE MIT PREISEN AUSGEZEICHNET BZW. LOBEND ERWÄHNT: VON DER SOCIETY OF PUBLICATION DESIGNERS, VOM NEW YORK ART DIRECTORS CLUB, VON AMERICAN PHOTOGRAPHY UND GRAPHIS. 1989 ERSCHIEN DAS BUCH ROLLING STONE: THE PHOTOGRAPHS, EINE VON IHR HERAUSGEGEBENE UND PRODUZIERTE RETROSPEKTIVE ÜBER 20 JAHRE, AUF DER BESTSELLERLISTE DER NEW YORK TIMES. IM GLEICHEN JAHR WURDE SIE ZUM DIRECTOR OF PHOTOGRAPHY BEI ROLLING STONE ERNANNT. ∎

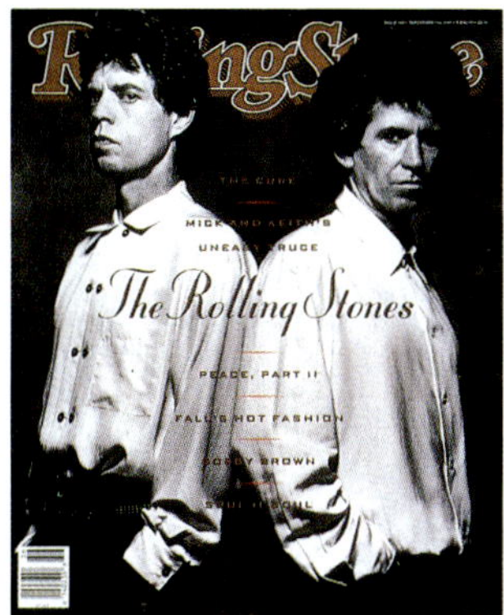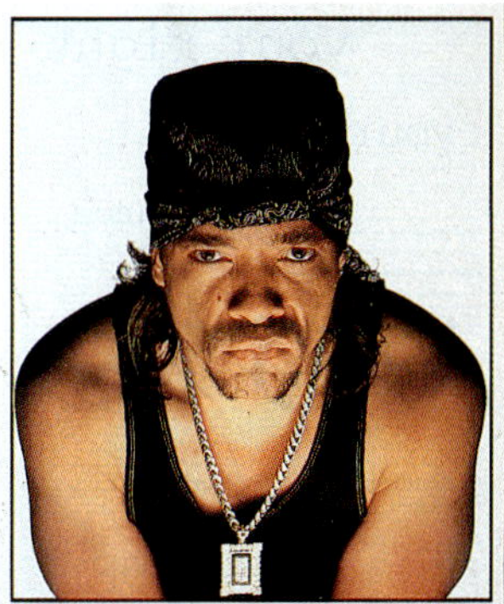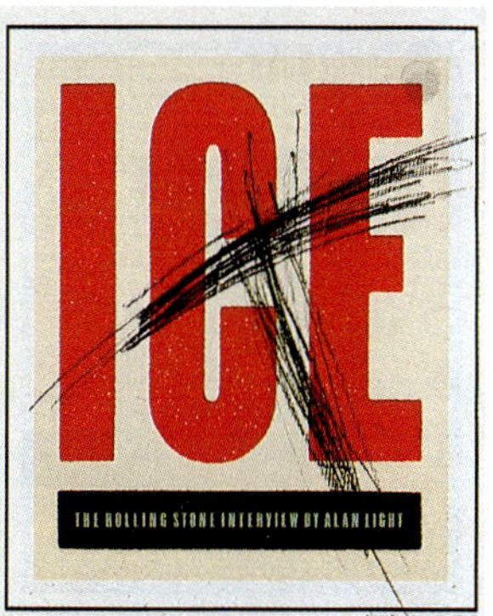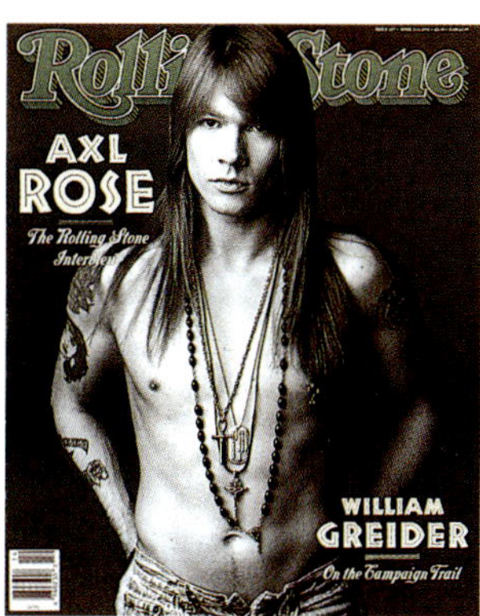

(LEFT) SEPTEMBER 7, 1989, PHOTO: ALBERT WATSON. WITH THE IMPENDING REUNION CONCERT OF THE CLASSIC ROCK GROUP THE ROLLING STONES LOOMING IN THE FUTURE, A TENUOUS PEACE BETWEEN THE DISSENTING MICK JAGGER (LEFT) AND KEITH RICHARDS (RIGHT) WAS REACHED. AS THIS PICTURE SHOWS, HOWEVER, TENSIONS WERE STILL EVIDENT. (MIDDLE) AUGUST 20, 1992, PHOTO: MARK SELIGER. THIS SPREAD IS FROM AN INTERVIEW WITH RAP ARTIST ICE-T. CAPITALIZING ON HIS HIGHLY CONTROVERSIAL SONG "COP KILLER," THE COVER OF THIS ISSUE FEATURED A PICTURE OF HIM WEARING A POLICE OFFICER'S UNIFORM. (RIGHT) APRIL 2, 1992, PHOTO: HERB RITTS. AXL ROSE, LEAD SINGER OF THE HEAVY METAL GROUP GUNS 'N' ROSES IS THE PERSONALITY FEATURED ON THIS COVER. THE ACCOMPANYING ARTICLE WAS A VERY INTIMATE INTERVIEW IN WHICH HE DETAILED SEVERAL VERY DELICATE INCIDENTS FROM HIS PAST. ■

plus profonde avec le temps. J'entends le bruit des vagues qui viennent se briser contre le rivage. Je sens encore la chaleur du soleil californien. Je me souviens de ma famille et de la sensation de bien-être qui m'habitait. □ Les images exercent toujours sur moi la même fascination. Il y a tellement de choses à apprendre et à inventer. Peut-être que cela explique pourquoi la photographie occupe une place aussi grande dans ma vie. ▯ Bien que j'ai occupé différents postes dans ce secteur au cours des deux dernières décennies, les onze années que j'ai passées comme responsable de la photographie chez *Rolling Stone* ont sans doute été les plus gratifiantes. L'énorme quantité d'histoires et de sujets traités représente un défi perpétuel. Qu'il s'agisse d'Axl Rose et de Chuck Berry, des skinheads ou des trafiquants d'armes en Afghanistan, ma tâche consiste à présenter les articles d'une manière attrayante et intéressante. ▯ Tout d'abord, il me faut choisir le bon photographe. Il faut pour cela tenir compte de nombreux paramètres: le contenu de l'histoire, le sentiment que je souhaite transmettre dans ces images, les photographies qui ont déjà été faites sur le même sujet, le mélange des diverses photos dans le numéro, enfin, les délais et les locations qui nous sont imposées par une foule de choses, que ce soit la saison de la mousson ou les publicistes. □ Bien que je donne des instructions aux photographes et que je les encourage avant qu'ils se mettent au travail, je n'impose jamais ma propre vision. Je veux qu'ils transmettent leurs idées et leurs impressions dans leurs photos. Je partage l'opinion de Richard Avedon qui dit qu'«un photographe n'est rien de plus qu'une machine s'il ne met rien de lui-même dedans». Je crois que les photographes ont quelque chose à dire et j'aimerais les y encourager. ■

LAURIE KRATOCHVIL EST ENTRÉE COMME PHOTO EDITOR CHEZ *ROLLING STONE* EN 1978 APRES AVOIR TRAVAILLÉ POUR LE *LOS ANGELES TIMES* ET A&M RECORDS. EN 1980, ELLE DEVIENT RESPONSABLE DE LA PHOTO AU MAGAZINE *NEW WEST*; ELLE RETOURNERA CHEZ *ROLLING STONE* EN 1982. SOUS SA DIRECTION, *ROLLING STONE* A ÉTÉ CITÉ TROIS FOIS POUR LE NATIONAL MAGAZINE AWARD DE LA PHOTOGRAPHIE ET EN 1988, LE MAGAZINE A ENFIN REÇU CET HONNEUR. EN OUTRE, SES TRAVAUX ONT ÉTÉ FRÉQUEMMENT PRIMÉS, NOTAMMENT PAR LA SOCIETY OF PUBLICATION DESIGNERS, LE NEW YORK ART DIRECTORS CLUB, *AMERICAN PHOTOGRAPHY* ET *GRAPHIS*. EN 1989, LE LIVRE *ROLLING STONE: THE PHOTOGRAPHS*, RÉPERTORIANT LES PHOTOS PARUES CES VINGT DERNIERES ANNÉES, QU'ELLE A PUBLIÉ ET ÉDITÉ, FIGURAIT SUR LA LISTE DES BEST-SELLERS DU *NEW YORK TIMES*. LA MEME ANNÉE, ELLE A ÉTÉ NOMMÉE À SON POSTE ACTUEL DE DIRECTRICE DE LA PHOTOGRAPHIE CHEZ *ROLLING STONE*. ■

C H R I S T I A N   V O N   F A B E R - C A S T E L L

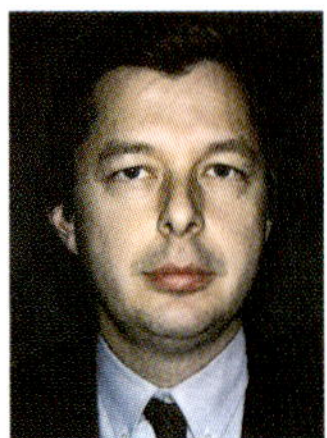

*T*he invention and subsequent introduction of photography for practical use in the mid-19th century caused an immediate revolution in the art world. In retrospect, however, the far-reaching scope of that discovery has rarely been properly acknowledged. Due to the new, unerringly objective competition posed by photography, the art of painting saw itself robbed of one of its ancient goals: the reproduction of reality in the most natural, precise and truthful manner. Simultaneously, it was freed from the constraints to which it had previously been bound. Artists could feel free to leave the dutiful reproduction of esoteric reality to the more ideally-suited medium of photography. This contributed greatly to the genesis of those new approaches to perception and painting commonly referred to collectively as Modernism. Starting with the Barbizon movement of the 19th century, through the schools of Impressionism and Expressionism which were direct descendants, to the abstract and constructivist painting of this century photography redefined the nature of art. □ Perhaps it was precisely this midwifery of new stylistic avenues for art—coupled with the conspicuous, technique-oriented nature of photography—that kept photography from being considered an art form of its own for so long. After all, photography did require over 100 years before being admited to the arena of pure art, to museums and to related collections. Although a number of far-sighted artists and experts never even asked themselves whether photography could be art, the broader acceptance of photography as an art form is a relatively recent development. The natural process towards a multifaceted, creative dissection of this medium by experimentally-inclined artists also had a late beginning. □ Dyed-in-the-wool, l'art pour l'art purists might grieve that this long-overdue emancipation of the art of photography, has been encouraged by the involvement of innovative commercial galleries, as well as by the multinational auction houses Sotheby's and Christies, all of whom tend to be ever-watchful for new, biddable material. That influence is, needless to say, reflected in the astoundingly high prices that have been fetched at auction in recent years. □ Viewed soberly and without moralistic prejudice, the convergence of photography and the art market harbors indisputable advantages including a refreshing, liberating effect on the previously much-too-eletist and isolated art-photography scene. Among the most important is the sensible positioning of photography from within the multidimensional unviverse of art. □ In the search for generic relatives of artistic photography, one unavoidably encounters the broad market sector of graphic art, where the technical similarities between the two, such as the inherent quality of reproducibility, by no means play a major role. Much more important to understanding the special position of photography within the realm of art are the commonalities of content. Just as the forms of graphic art range from ordinary, prosaic commerical art all the way through to artistic, graphic masterpieces, so do the dimensions of photography. It too spans the extremes between the masterly craftmanship of the professional photographer: fulfilling his assignment on the one hand, and on the other, the pure, freely-formed work of art in which photography acts solely as the means of acheiving an artistic end, while relegating

CHRISTIAN VON FABER-CASTELL, ZURICH, BORN 1950, IS ART MARKET COMMENTATOR FOR THE SWISS BUSINESS JOURNAL *FINANZ UND WIRTSCHAFT*, AS WELL AS ART MARKET CORRESPONDANT FOR MUNICH'S *WELTKUNST*, DUSSELDORF'S *HANDELSBLATT*, AND NEW YORK'S *ART NEWSLETTER*. ∎

the technical facets to the background. The fact that photography also creates art outside of the aforementioned pure, freely-formed art photography is demonstrated in this annual, in which, above and beyond the actual theme of "Fine Art," many artistically impressive and valuable examples of applied, purpose-oriented photography are represented.□ Within these extremes—which are intentionally used here in place of a necessarily unsatisfactory attempt at defining the term "art"—one finds a whole series of analogous characteristics: Graphics and photography share their reciprocal fertilization of art and commerce, of applied and free-form art, of technique and expression, to an extent hardly found elsewhere. In the same way that the world of graphic art encompasses both advertising graphics and classical-historical landscape portrayals of book illustration, in photography one also finds the mostly independent disciplines of the traditional, historical (and long since collectible) landscape and travel photography, advertising photography and illustrative photography. □

These expandable examples and parallels do not serve as a mere theoretic classification of photography within the market for art. Rather, they are meant to present the quite practical, concrete value of photography, an art that is all too easily dismissed—even by photographers themselves—as a utilitarian, throw-away medium within today's cultural world. □ Processing the wealth of photographic art that stemmed from its first 150 years, along with the critically challenging dissection of today's photographic works, provides art historians, museums and ardent collectors with a breadth of activity that can hardly be gauged at this point. Photographers themselves should participate in this process by playing a responsible leading role in all of these areas. This starts with such banal chores as creating all-inclusive documentation of their professional and, in particular, their free-form work—this wholly aside from the requisite archival processing involved and careful storage—and is far from being finished with the submitting of their own works to books, exhibitions and events relative to the topic. ■

*D*ie Erfindung und praktische Einführung der Photographie um die Mitte des 19. Jh. bedeutete für die bildende Kunst jener Zeit eine Revolution, deren Tragweite im Rückblick nur selten richtig gewürdigt wird: Durch die neue, unbestechlich objektive Konkurrenz der Lichtbildnerei sah sich die Malerei plötzlich eines ihrer jahrhunderte-, ja jahrtausende alten Ziele, nämlich der möglichst naturalistischen, genauen und wahrhaftigen Wiedergabe der Realität, beraubt - und zugleich von bisherigen einengenden Fesseln befreit. Der Umstand, dass der Künstler die pflichtgetreue Wiedergabe äusserlicher Realität fortan getrost der dafür besser geeigneten Photographie überlassen konnte, hat auf jeden Fall wesentlich zur Entstehung jener neuen Seh- und Malweisen beigetragen, die man üblicherweise unter dem Begriff der Moderne zusammenfasst, beginnend mit dem Barbizonismus des 19. Jh. über den sich daraus entwickelnden Impressionismus und den Expressionismus bis hin zur abstrakten und konstruktiven Malerei dieses Jahrhunderts. n Möglicherweise war es andererseits gerade diese Geburtshelferrolle für neue Kunststilrichtungen - gepaart natürlich mit ihrem unübersehbar technisch-anwendungsorientierten Wesen - , die der Photographie so lange die allgemeine Anerkennung als eigenständige Kunstform vorenthielt. Immerhin brauchte die Photographie ihrerseits ja über 100 Jahre, um selbst in der Arena der reinen Kunst, in den Museen und in verwandten Sammlungen, Einzug zu halten. Einigen weitblickenden

Künstlern und Kennern hat sich die Frage, ob Photographie Kunst sein kann, zwar gar nie gestellt. Die breitere Anerkennung der Lichtbildnerei als künstlerische Ausdrucksform ist aber noch vergleichsweise jung - und dementsprechend spät setzte naturgemäss auch die vielfältige schöpferische Auseinandersetzung experimentierwilliger Künstler mit diesem Medium ein. □ Eingefleischte L'Art pour l'Art-Puristen mögen sich vielleicht darüber grämen, dass an dieser überfälligen Emanzipation der photographischen Kunst neben einer Reihe initiativer kommerzieller Galerien auch die stets nach neuem versteigerungstauglichem Material suchenden multinationalen Kunstauktionskonzerne Sotheby's und Christie's eine entscheidende Rolle gespielt haben, was sich nicht zuletzt in den zuweilen erstaunlich hohen - und weiter steigenden - Versteigerungspreisen der letzten Jahre spiegelt. □ Nüchtern und ohne moralisierende Vorurteile betrachtet, birgt die gegenseitige Annäherung von Kunstmarkt und Photographie indes unleugbare Vorteile. Zu deren wichtigsten gehören neben der erfrischenden, befreienden Wirkung auf die früher allzu elitär abgeschottete Kunstphotographie-Szene auch eine Reihe hilfreicher Ansatzpunkte für die sinnvolle Situierung der Kunstform Photographie innerhalb des ganzen vielschichtigen Universums der Kunst. □ Auf der Suche nach Wesensverwandten der künstlerischen Photographie stösst man dabei unwillkürlich auf das weite Kunstmarktgebiet der

Graphik, wobei vordergründige technische Ähnlichkeiten wie etwa das der Photographie ebenso wie der Graphik innewohnende Prinzip der Vervielfältigbarkeit durchaus nicht die Hauptrolle spielen. Für das Verständnis der besonderen Stellung der Photographie innerhalb der Kunst viel wichtiger sind nämlich inhaltliche Verwandschaften: So wie beispielsweise die Ausprägungen der Graphik von der alltäglichen prosaischen Gebrauchsgraphik bis zur künstlerischen Meistergraphik reichen, so findet ja auch die Kunst in der Photographie zwischen zwei Extremen statt, nämlich zwischen der (kunst-)handwerklichen Meisterschaft des auftragserfüllenden Berufsphotographen und dem reinen, ohne jede Zweckbestimmung geschaffenen Kunstwerk, bei dem die Photographie ganz im Dienst des künstlerischen Ziels steht und als Technik weitgehend in den Hintergrund tritt. Dass die Photographie auch ausserhalb dieser letzterwähnten puren, zweckfreien Kunstphotographie Kunst schafft, zeigt übrigens nicht zuletzt dieses Jahrbuch, in dem ja auch ausserhalb der eigentlichen Rubrik «Kunst» oder «Fine Art» zahlreiche künstlerisch überzeugende, wertvolle Beispiele angewandter, zweckorientierter Photographie verteten sind. ▫ Und zwischen diesen Extremen - die hier ganz bewusst an Stelle eines zwangsläufig unbefriedigenden Definitionsversuches des Begriffes «Kunst» gegeben seien - findet man seinerseits eine ganze Reihe analoger Merkmale: Sowohl der Graphik als auch der Photographie eigen ist beispielsweise die gegenseitige Befruchtung von Kunst und Kommerz, von angewandter und zweckfreier Kunst, von Technik und Ausdruck, wie sie in diesem Ausmass in kaum einem anderen Gebiet anzutreffen ist. Und so, wie es in der

Graphik etwa die Werbegraphik, die klassisch-historischen Landschaftsdarstellungen oder die Buchillustrationsgraphik als ganz unterschiedliche, eigenständige Bereiche gibt, so findet man ja auch in der Photographie die weitgehend unabhängigen Disziplinen der traditionellen, historischen (und heute längst gesammelten) Landschafts- und Reisephotographie, die Werbephotographie und die Illustrationsphotographie... ▫ Diese beliebig vermehrbaren Beispiele und Vergleiche dienen hier natürlich nicht bloss einer theoretischen Klassifizierung der Photographie innerhalb des Kunstmarktes. Vielmehr sollen sie den ganz praktischen, konkreten Stellenwert der Photographie, die ja noch immer allzu leichtfertig - und zwar nicht zuletzt von den Photographen selbst - als blosses Wegwerf- und Gebrauchsmedium behandelt wird, innerhalb unserer heutigen Kulturlandschaft darlegen. ▫ Die Aufarbeitung des bisherigen Fundus an photographischer Kunst aus den ersten 150 Jahren, aber auch die kritisch-fördernde Auseinandersetzung mit der heutigen Kunst der Photographie bieten Kunstwissenschaftlern, Museen und engagierten Sammlern jedenfalls ein Tätigkeitsfeld von derzeit noch kaum erahnbarem Umfang. Die Photographen selbst sind dabei als Hauptakteure an erster Stelle zu verantwortungsvoller Mitarbeit in allen Bereichen aufgerufen. Dies beginnt mit so banalen Selbstverständlichkeiten wie der lückenlosen Dokumentation ihrer beruflichen und insbesondere ihrer freien Arbeiten - ganz abgesehen natürlich von deren archivsicherer Verarbeitung und sorgfältigen Aufbewahrung - und hört mit eigenen Beiträgen zu entsprechenden Büchern, Ausstellungen und verwandten Anlässen noch längst nicht auf! ■

. . . .

*L*a découverte de la photographie et son application pratique, vers le milieu du 19ᵉ siècle, correspondait à une révolution dans le domaine des arts plastiques de l'époque dont, rétrospectivement, on a rarement mesuré la portée. Gräce à cette nouvelle concurrence absolument objective de la photographie, la peinture se voyait d'un seul coup dépouillée de ce qui avait été l'une de ses fonctions pendant des centaines, voire des milliers d'années: rendre la réalité de la manière la plus réaliste, la plus précise et la plus véridique possible. Elle était en même temps libérée des contraintes auxquelles elle avait été jusqu'alors soumise. Le fait que l'artiste puisse désormais abandonner en toute tranquillité à la photographie, qui s'y prêtait mieux, le soin de reproduire fidèlement la réalité

extérieure, a en tout cas largement contribué à l'apparition de cette nouvelle manière de voir et de peindre que l'on résume généralement par le terme d'Art moderne – à commencer par l'Ecole de Barbizon au 19ᵉ, puis l'Impressionnisme qui en est issu et l'Expressionnisme, pour arriver à la peinture abstraite et constructiviste du 20ᵉ siècle. n Peut-être ce rôle d'accoucheur de nouveaux styles artistiques – qui allait naturellement de pair avec son caractère technique, orienté sur la pratique – a-t-il justement empêché si longtemps la photographie d'être reconnue comme un art à part entière. Toujours est-il qu'il lui a fallu plus de cent ans pour faire son entrée dans les sanctuaires de l'Art, musées et collections publiques. Pour quelques artistes et connaisseurs clairvoyants, la question de savoir si la photogra-

. . . .

CHRISTIAN VON FABER-CASTELL, ZÜRICH, JAHRGANG 1950, IST KUNSTMARKTBERICHTERSTATTER DER SCHWEIZER WIRTSCHAFTSZEITUNG FINANZ UND WIRTSCHAFT SOWIE KUNSTMARKTKORRESPONDENT DER MÜNCHNER WELTKUNST, DES DÜSSELDORFER HANDELSBLATTES UND DES NEW YORKER ARTNEWSLETTER. ■

phie était de l'art ou pas ne s'est toutefois jamais posée. La reconnaissance plus large de la photographie comme forme d'expression artistique est cependant, en comparaison, encore assez récente – et c'est par conséquent tardivement que les artistes désireux d'expérimenter ont commencé à se tourner vers les possibilités créatives variées de cette nouvelle technique. □ Les puristes, partisans endurcis de l'art pour l'art, s'affligent peut-être de voir qu'à côté de toute une série de galeries qui ont pris l'initiative, les grandes maisons de ventes d'art internationales telles que Sotheby's et Christie's, toujours en quête de nouveaux objets pouvant être mis aux enchères, ont joué un rôle déterminant dans cette émancipation tardive de l'art photographique. Ceci s'est notamment traduit par des prix astronomiques – et continuellement en hausse – au cours des dernières années. □ Considéré d'un point de vue objectif et sans aucun préjugé moralisateur, ce rapprochement du marché de l'art et de la photographie comporte pourtant des avantages indéniables. Parmi les plus importants, outre l'effet rafraîchissant, libérateur, que cela aura eu sur le milieu par trop élitaire, très fermé, de la photographie d'art, on peut établir toute une série de points de départ qui permettent de situer judicieusement la photographie au sein de l'univers de l'art. □ Si l'on recherche des phénomènes apparentés à la photographie artistique, on se heurte inévitablement à l'immense marché de l'art graphique, bien que les ressemblances techniques qui sautent aux yeux, comme par exemple le principe de la reproduction en série, inhérent à la photographie ainsi qu'à l'art graphique, ne jouent certainement pas le rôle principal. Les analogies de contenu sont en effet beaucoup plus importantes si l'on veut comprendre la position particulière de la photographie dans l'art. Par exemple, tout comme le graphisme recouvre aussi bien le dessin publicitaire quotidien le plus prosaïque que l'art graphique proprement dit, l'art photographique se situe également entre deux extrêmes, c'est-à-dire entre le savoir-faire du photographe professionnel qui exécute une commande et la production de l'œuvre d'art, créée sans aucune finalité, la photographie étant ici complètement au service de l'objectif artistique, la technique étant largement reléguée à l'arrière-plan. Mais la photographie peut aussi être un art en dehors de cette dernière catégorie que nous venons d'évoquer, la photo d'art proprement dite, absolument désintéressée: nous en avons du reste la démonstration dans cet annuaire de la pho-

tographie où, en dehors des rubriques «Art» ou «Fine Art», figurent également de nombreux exemples de valeur, convaincants au niveau artistique, de photographie appliquée. □ Et entre ces extrêmes – qui sont ici présentés à la place d'une tentative de définition, forcément insatisfaisante, de la notion d'«art» –, on dénote par ailleurs toute une série de caractères analogues. Ce qui est par exemple spécifique à l'art graphique comme à la photographie, c'est l'apport réciproque de l'art et du commerce, de l'art appliqué et de l'art désintéressé, de la technique et de l'expression, un phénomène que l'on ne rencontre à un tel degré dans pratiquement aucun autre secteur. Ainsi, tout comme il y a dans l'art graphique différents domaines indépendants, à savoir la publicité, la représentation de paysages classiques historiques ou l'illustration de livres, dans la photographie, on trouve également des disciplines largement autonomes, telles que la traditionnelle photographie de paysage et de voyage, qui a déjà une valeur historique (elle est depuis longtemps collectionnée), la photo de publicité et la photo d'illustration… □ Bien entendu, ces exemples et ces comparaisons, que l'on pourrait multiplier à volonté, ne servent pas seulement ici à une classification théorique de la photographie à l'intérieur du marché de l'art. Leur rôle est plutôt de montrer la valeur tout à fait pratique, concrète, de la photographie dans le cadre du paysage artistique actuel, elle qui est encore trop souvent considérée avec désinvolture – et qui plus est par les photographes eux-mêmes – comme un simple objet de consommation, à jeter après usage. □ Répertorier le fonds de créations photographiques qui s'est accumulé depuis 150 ans, mais aussi procéder à une critique constructive de l'art de la photographie contemporaine: voilà que s'offre aux historiens d'art, aux musées et aux collectionneurs engagés un champ d'action d'une ampleur encore insoupçonnée. Les photographes eux-mêmes, en tant que protagonistes, sont invités en tout premier lieu à collaborer de manière responsable dans tous les domaines. Cela commence par des choses aussi banales et évidentes qu'une documentation complète de leurs travaux professionnels et surtout, de leurs œuvres personnelles – sans parler naturellement de leur archivage et de leur conservation soigneuse –, la rédaction d'articles personnels au sujet des livres qu'ils publient, des expositions et autres manifestations du même genre, et encore, la liste n'est pas exhaustive! ■

CHRISTIAN VON FABER-CASTELL, ZURICH, NÉ À KONSTANZ EN 1950, EST REPORTER SPÉCIAL-ISÉ DANS LE MARCHÉ DE L'ART AUPRES DU JOURNAL ÉCONOMIQUE SUISSE *FINANZ UND WIRTSCHAFT*, ET CORRESPONDANT, TOUJOURS DANS LE MEME MARCHÉ DE L'ART, AUPRES DU MAGAZINE *WELTKUNST* À MUNICH, DE LA *HANDELSBLATT* À DÜSSELDORF ET DE *ARTNEWSLETTER* À NEW YORK. ■

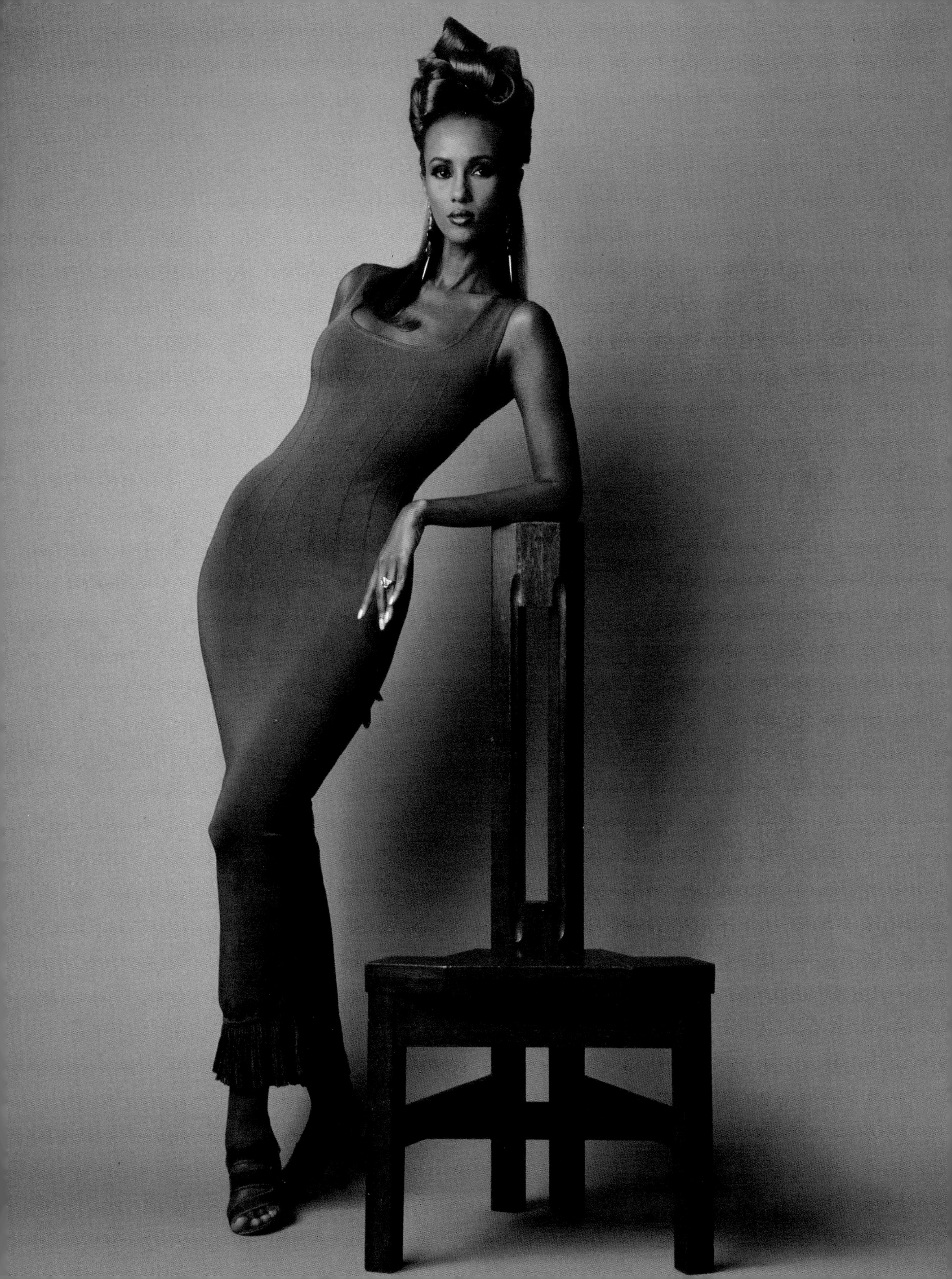

FASHION

MODE

MODE

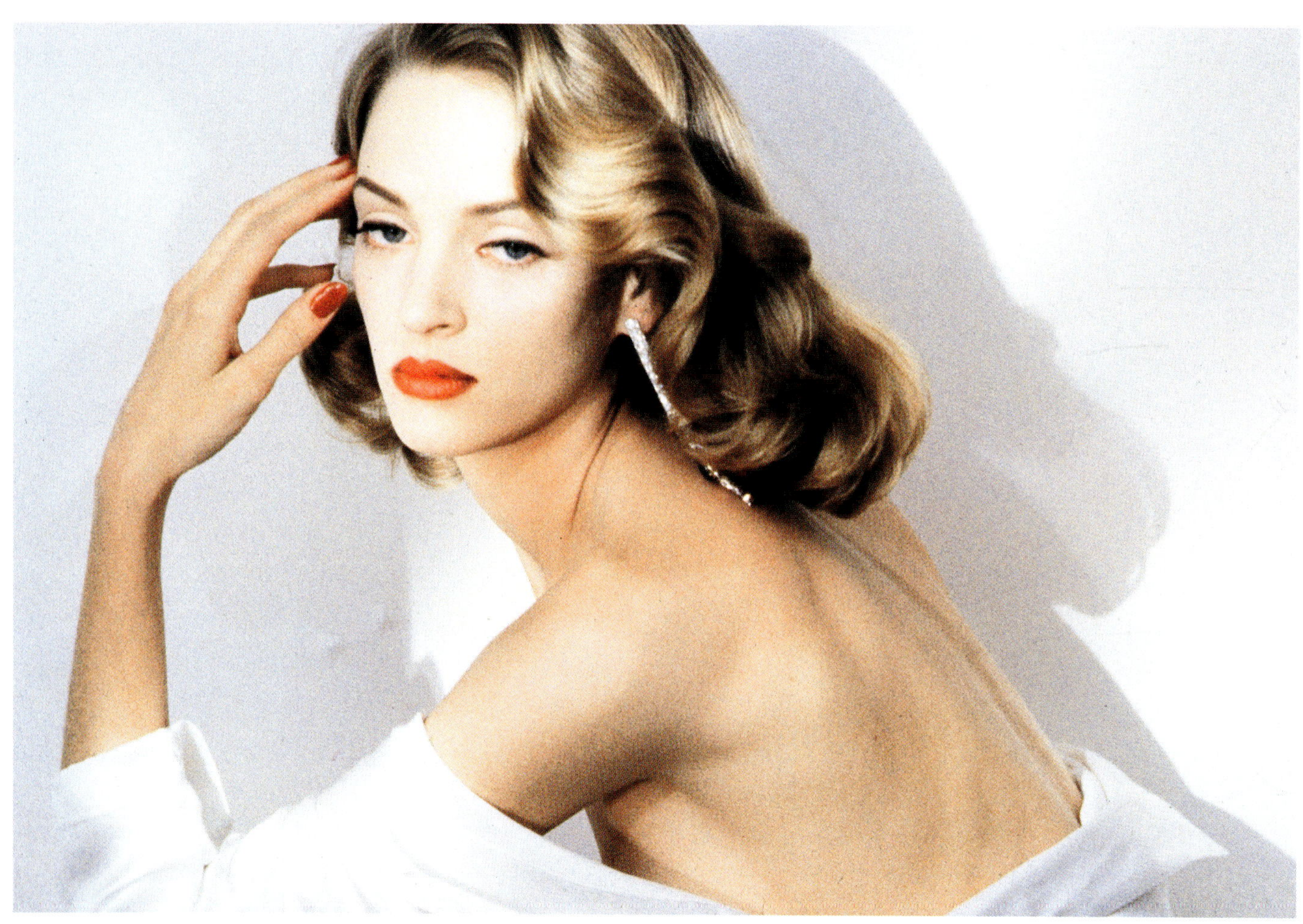

Preceeding Spread: Andrew Eccles | Above: Sheila Metzner

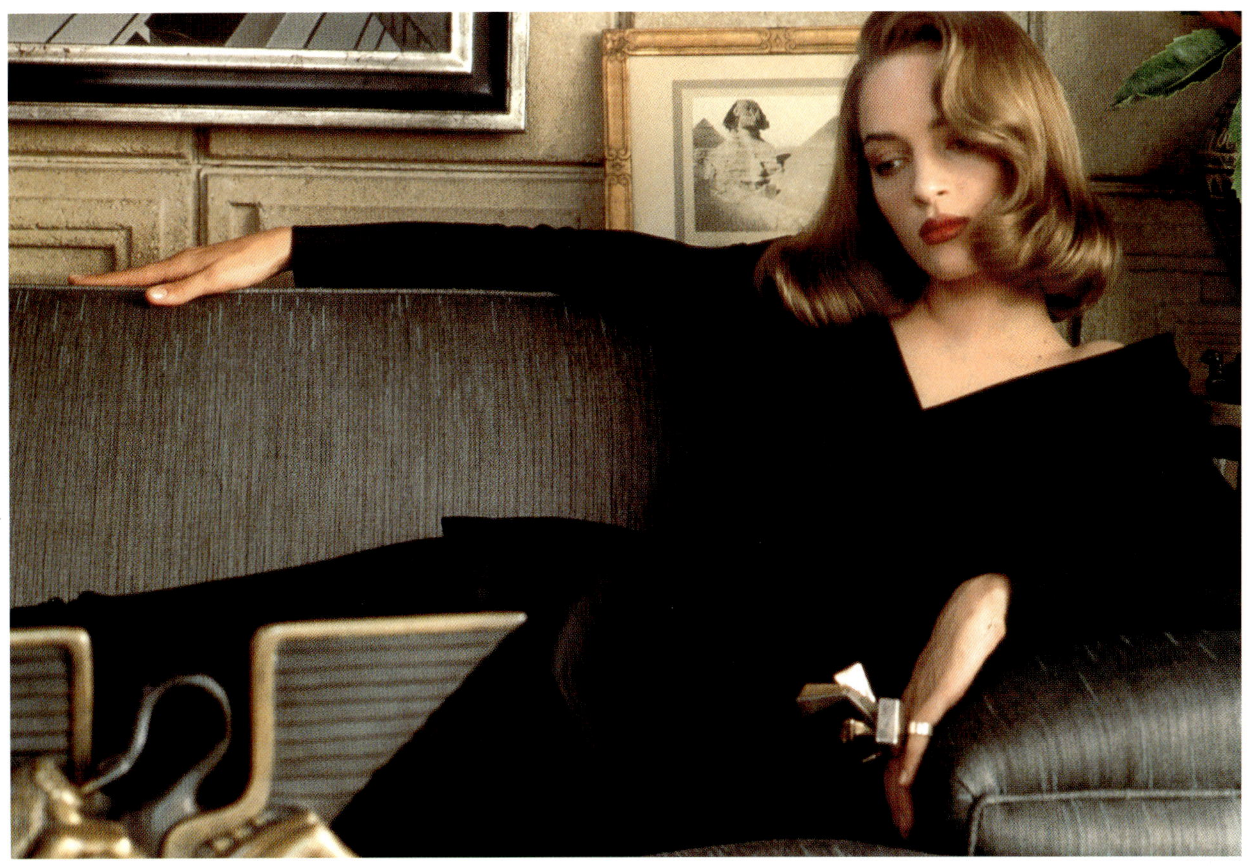

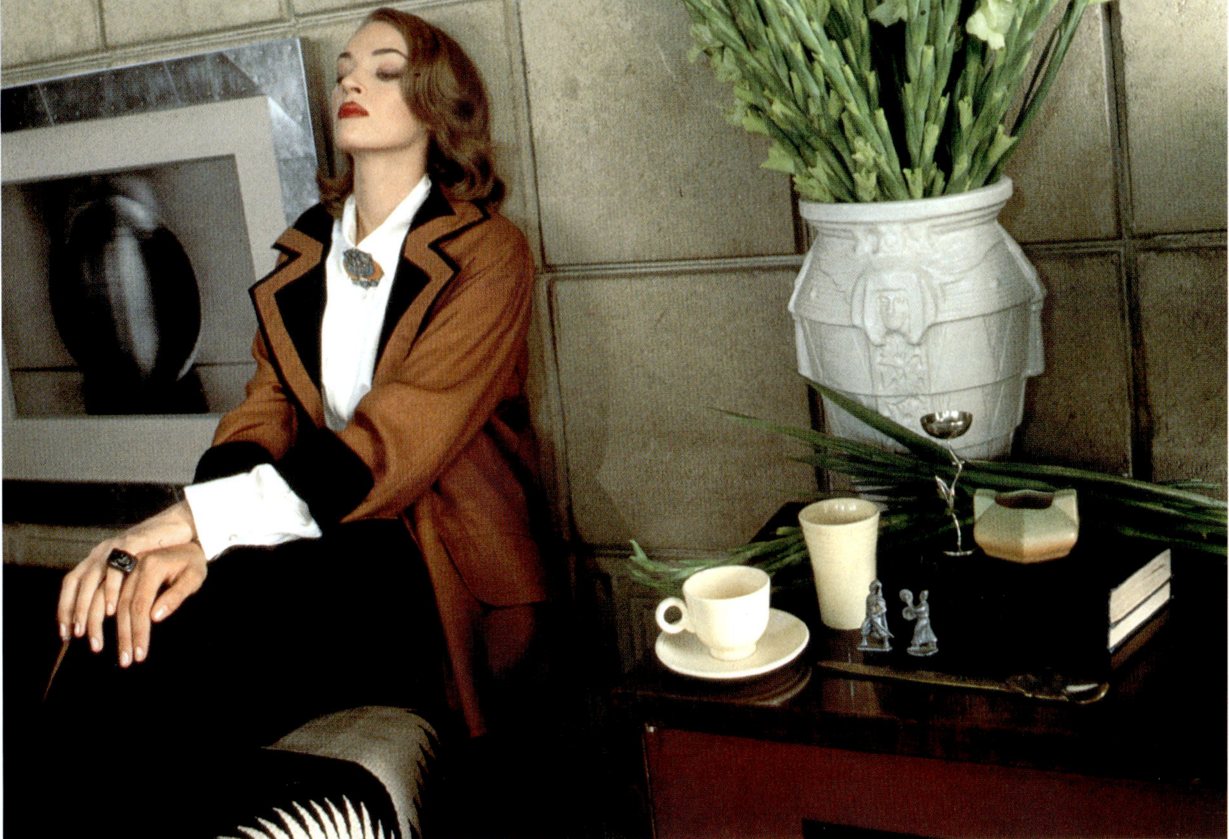

Sheila Metzner

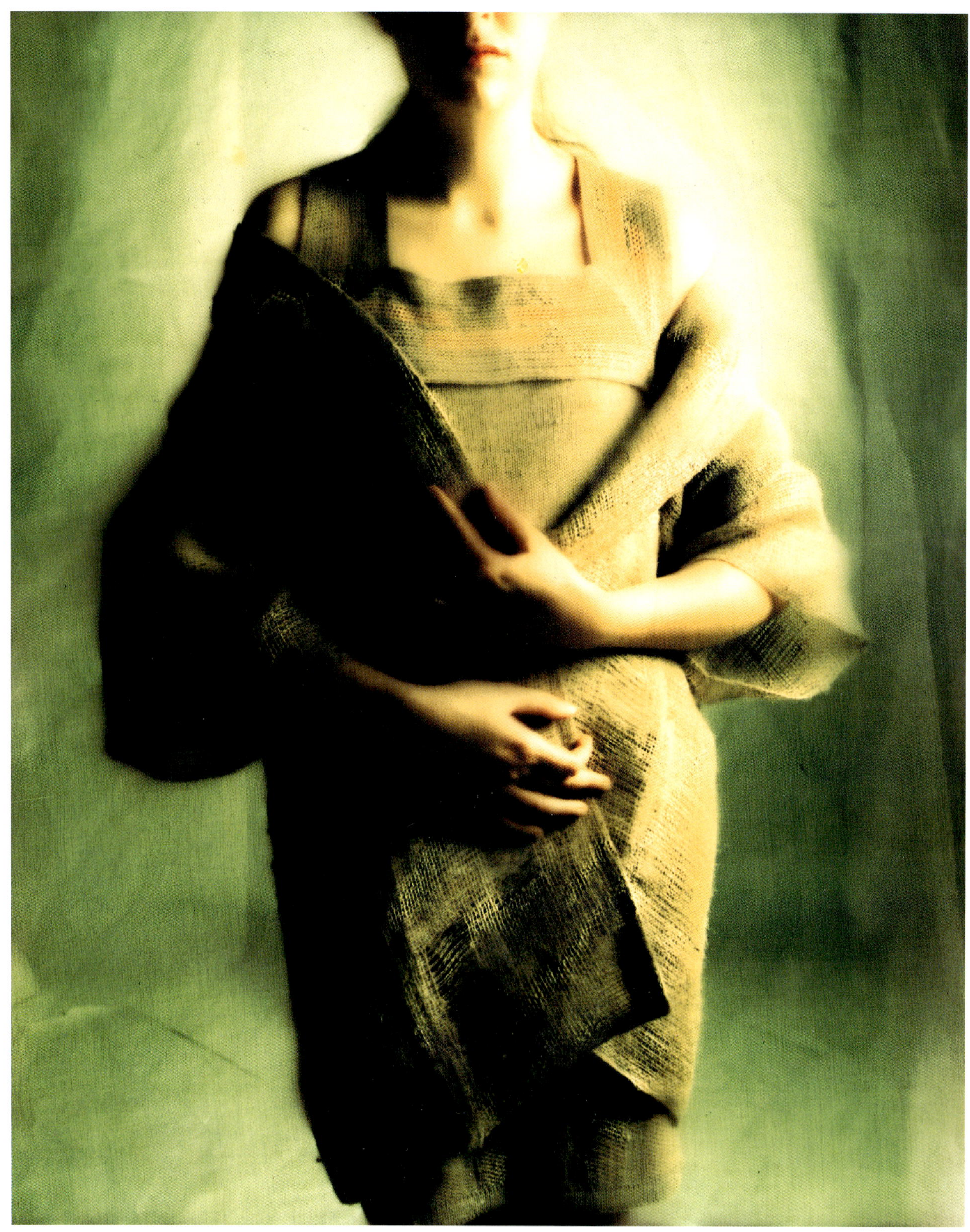

Hans-Georg Merkel

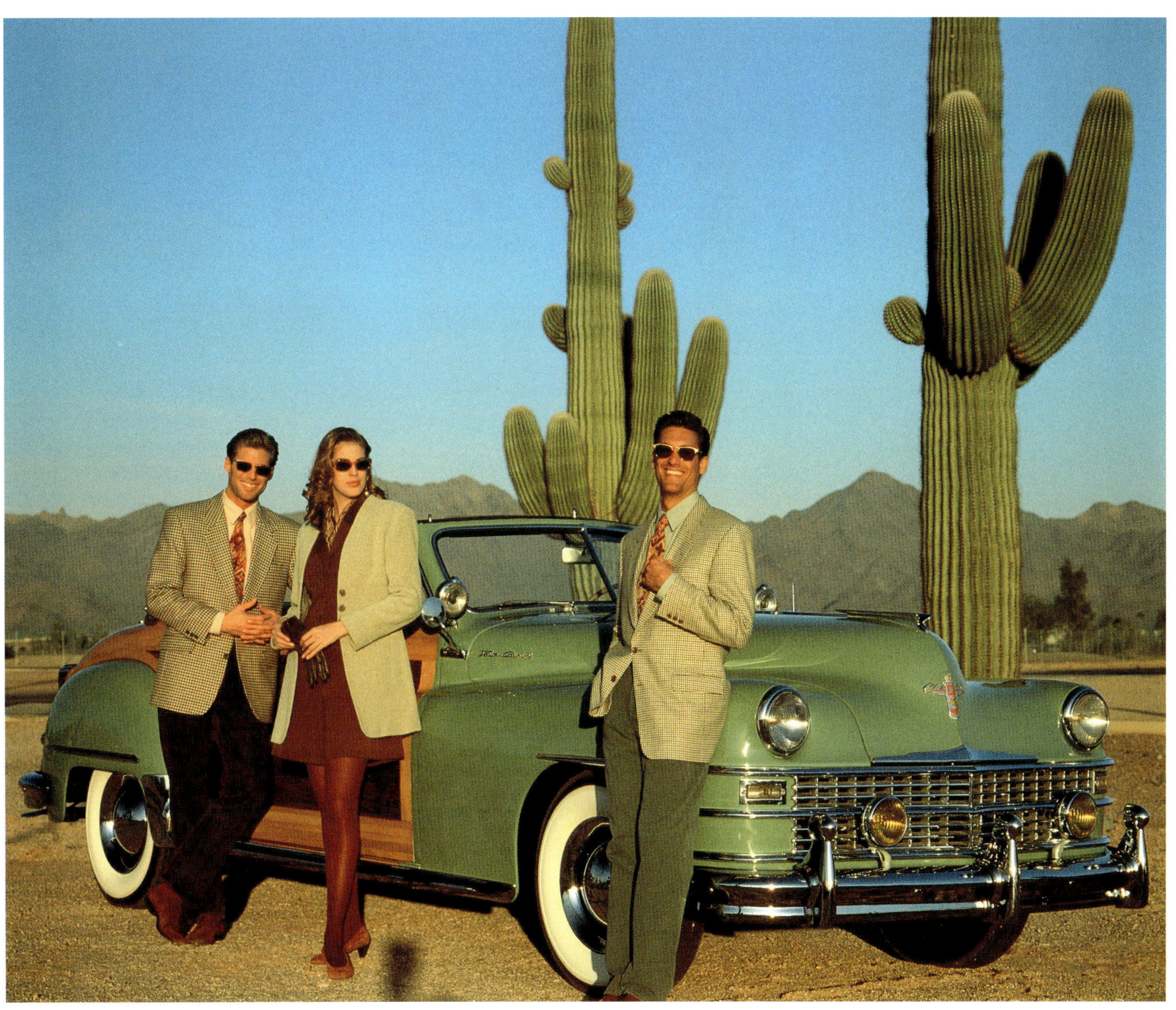

Klaus Kampert

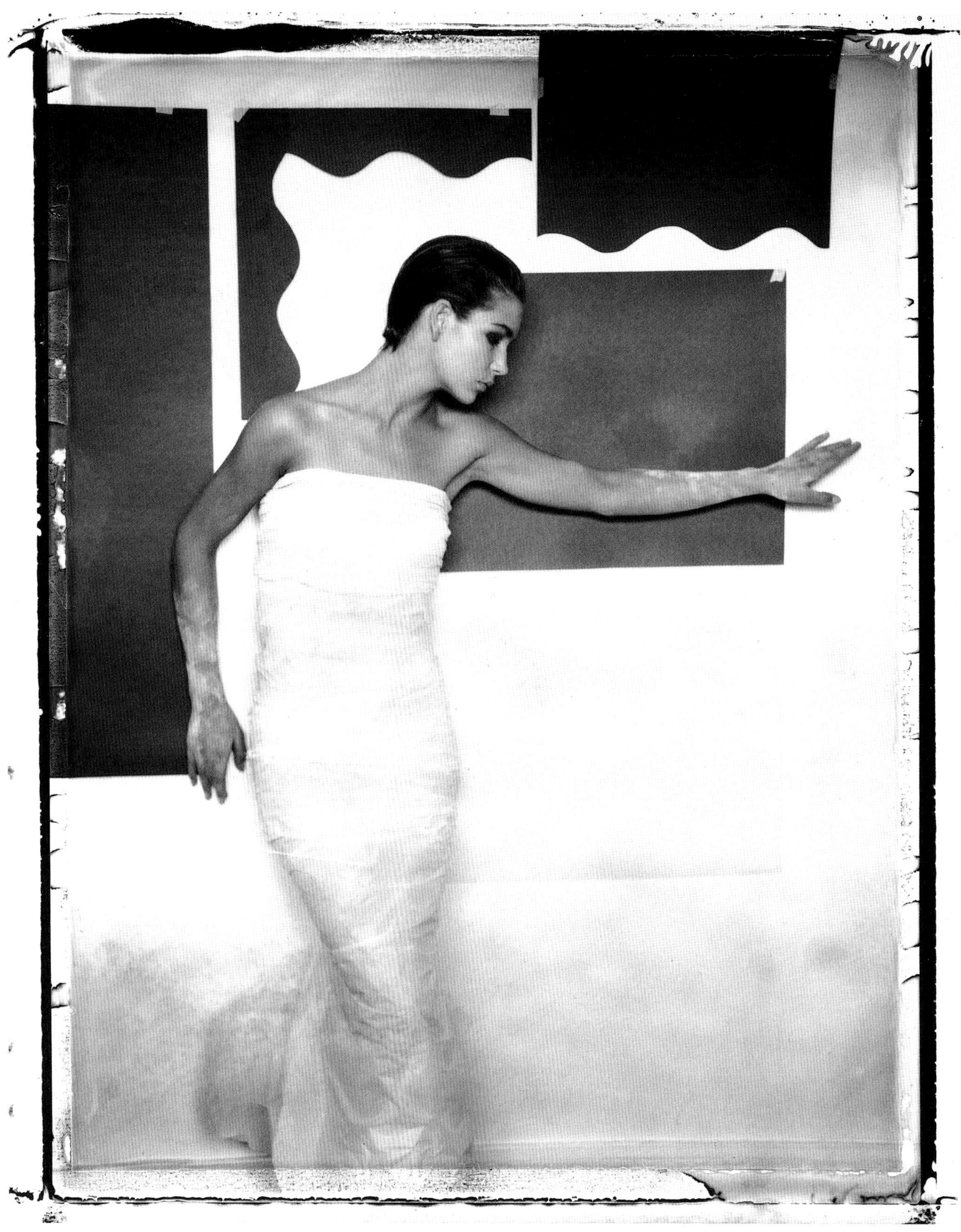

Frédéric Marsal

Tiko Lajczyk

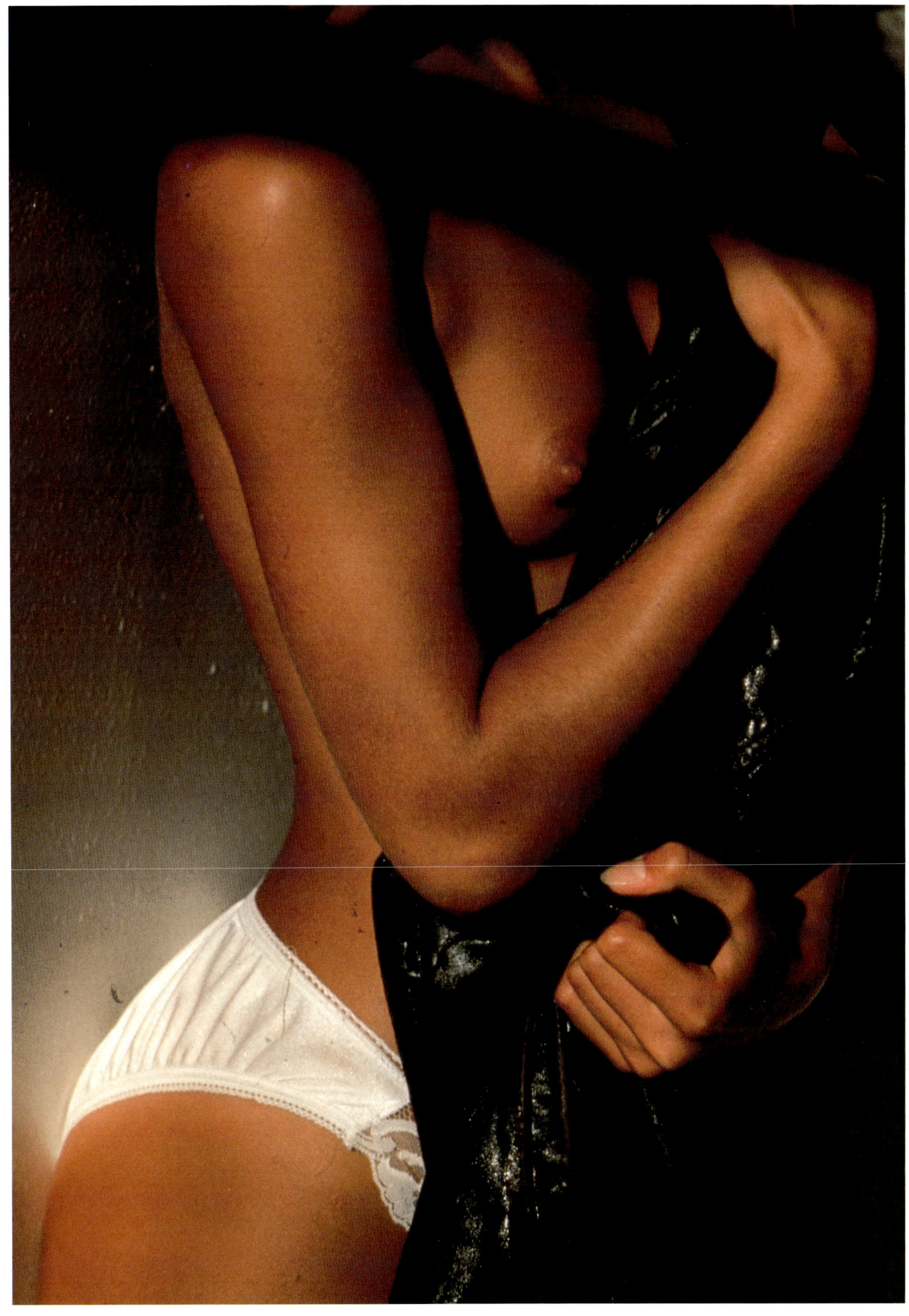

Tiko Lajczyk

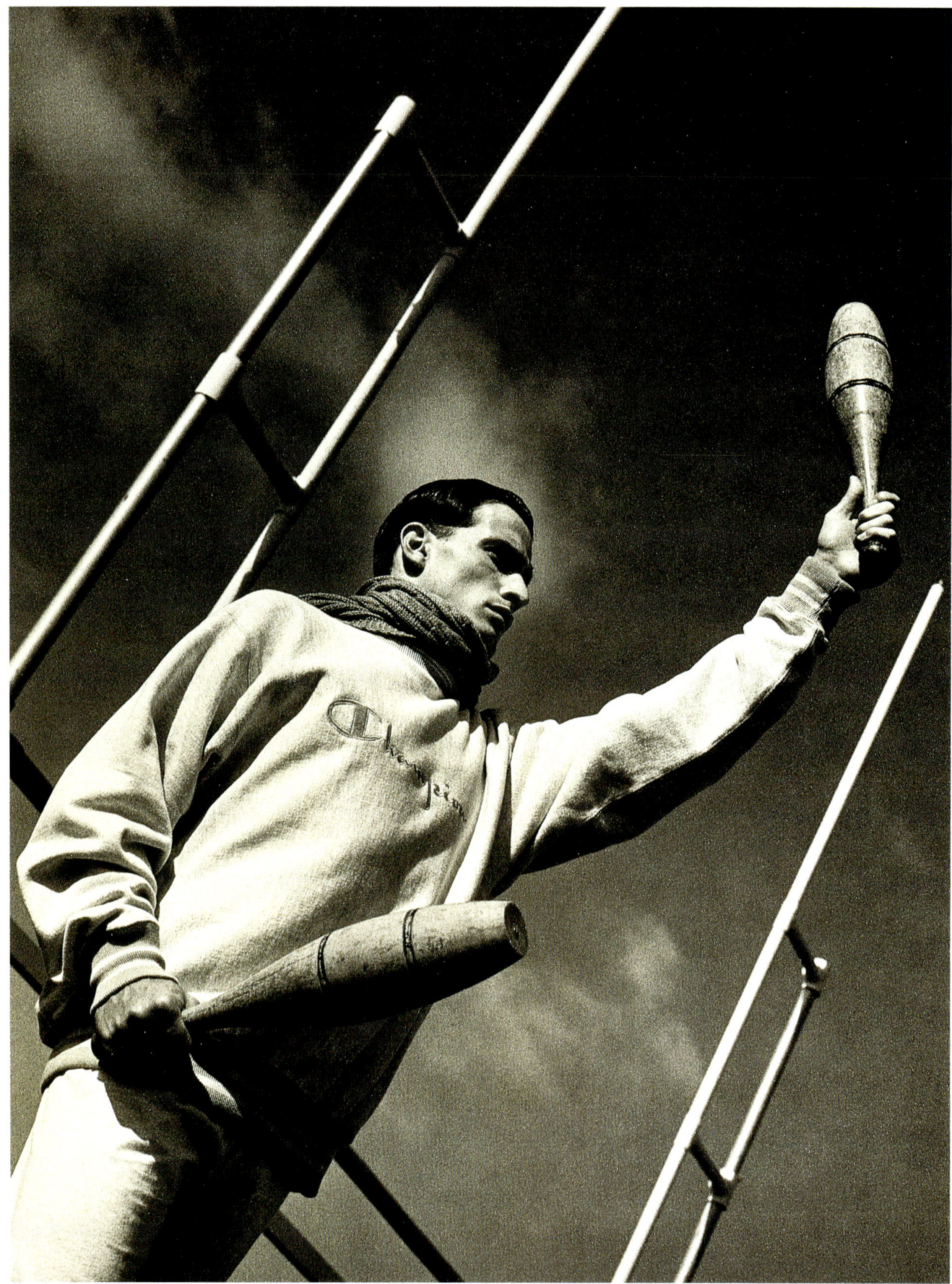

Hornick/Rivlin Studio

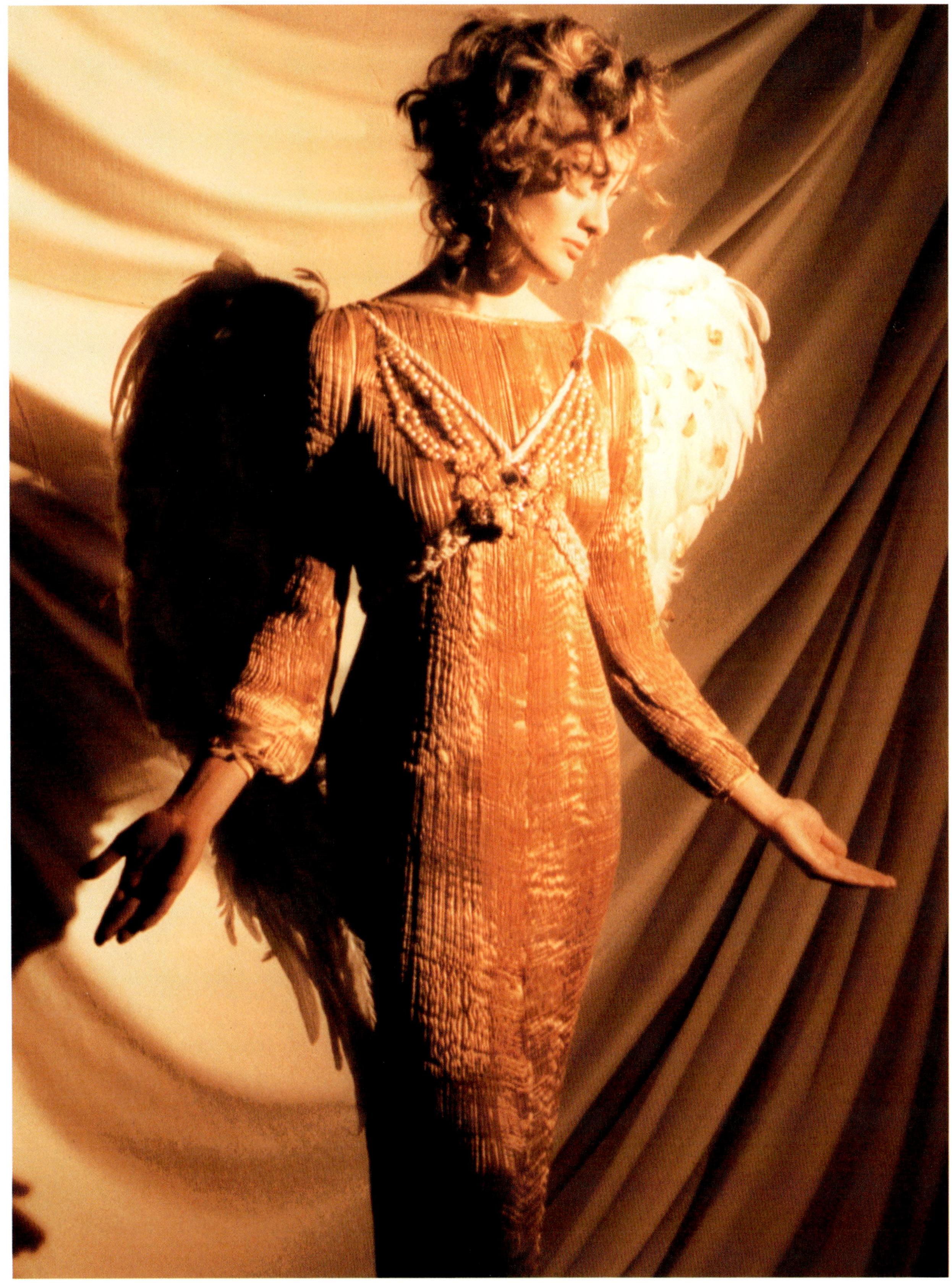

Ranjit Grewal

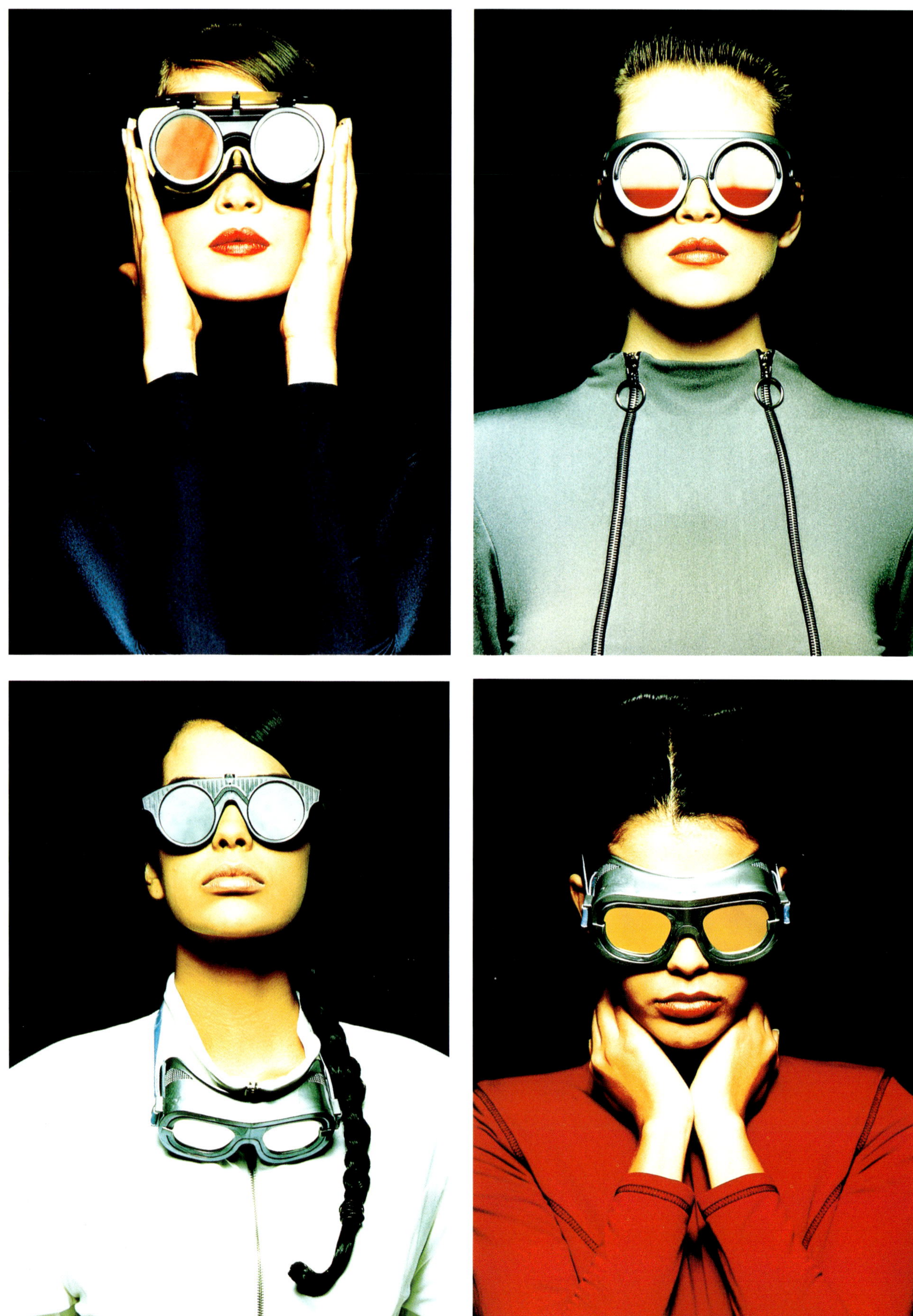

Stefan Schütz

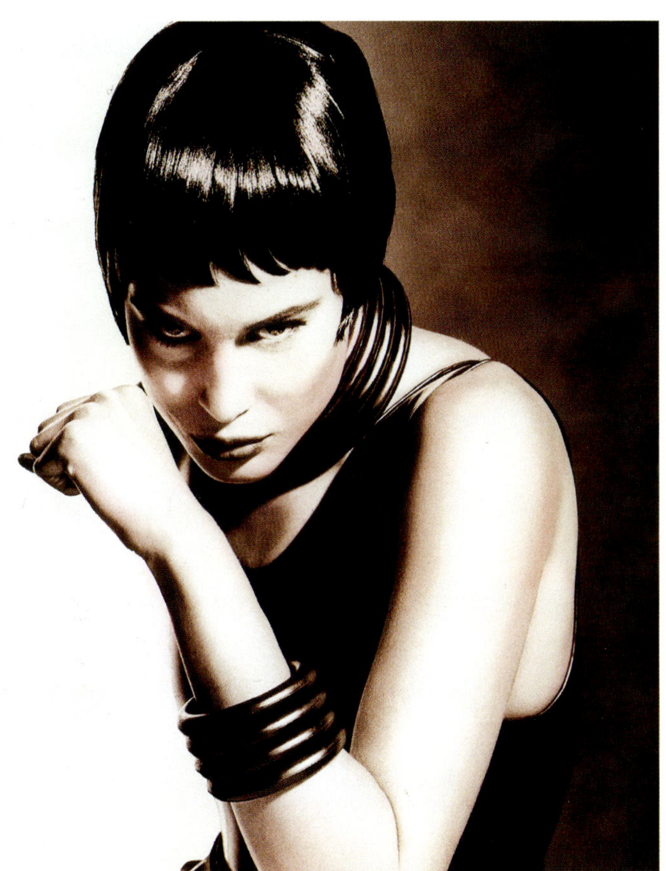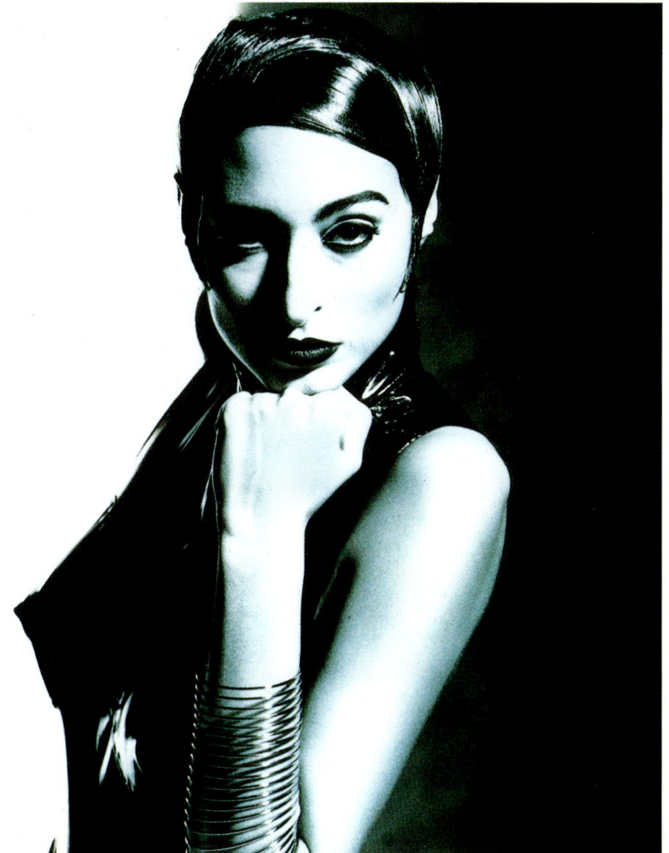

Leif Schmodde

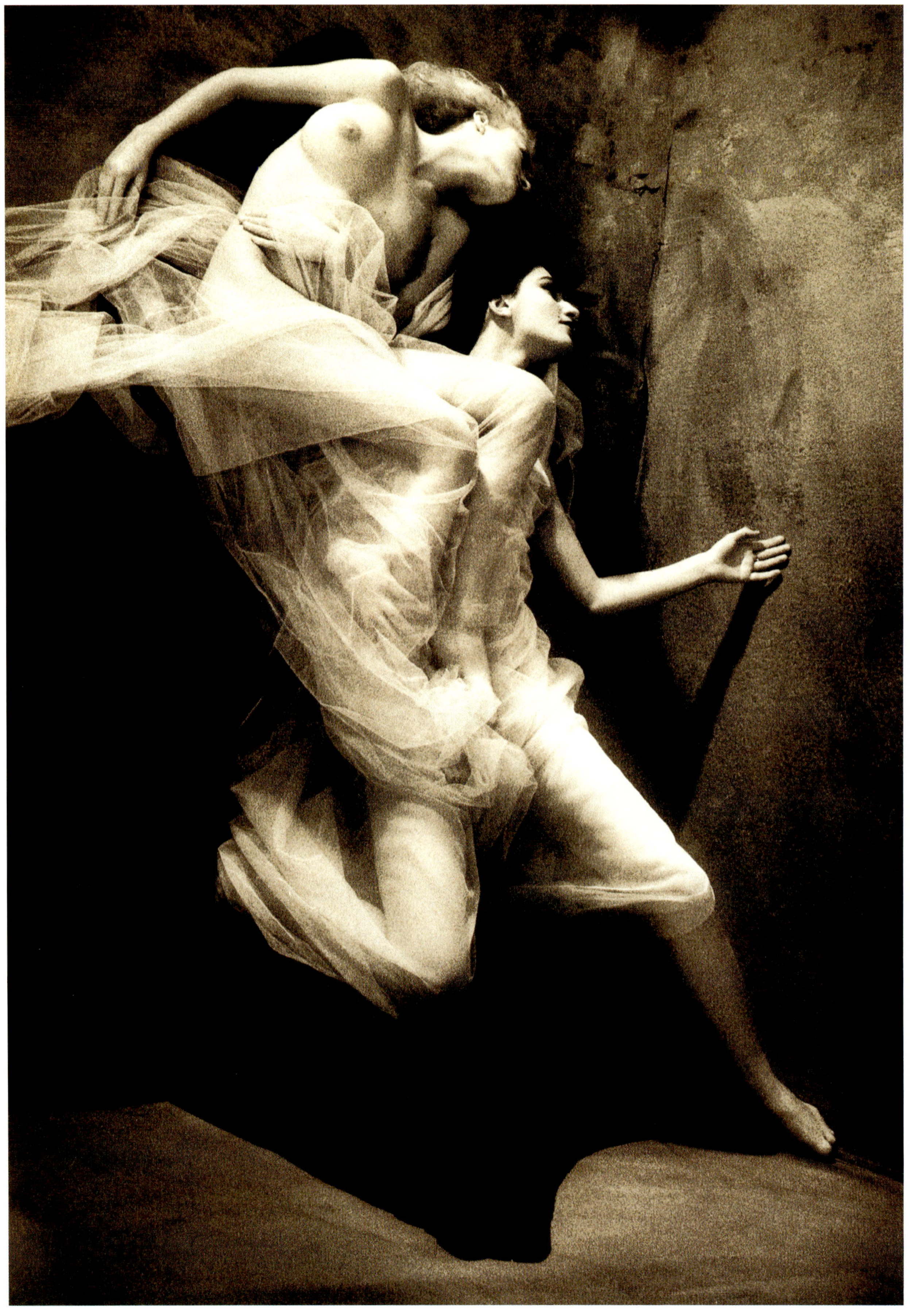

Barbara Jakse / Stane Jersic

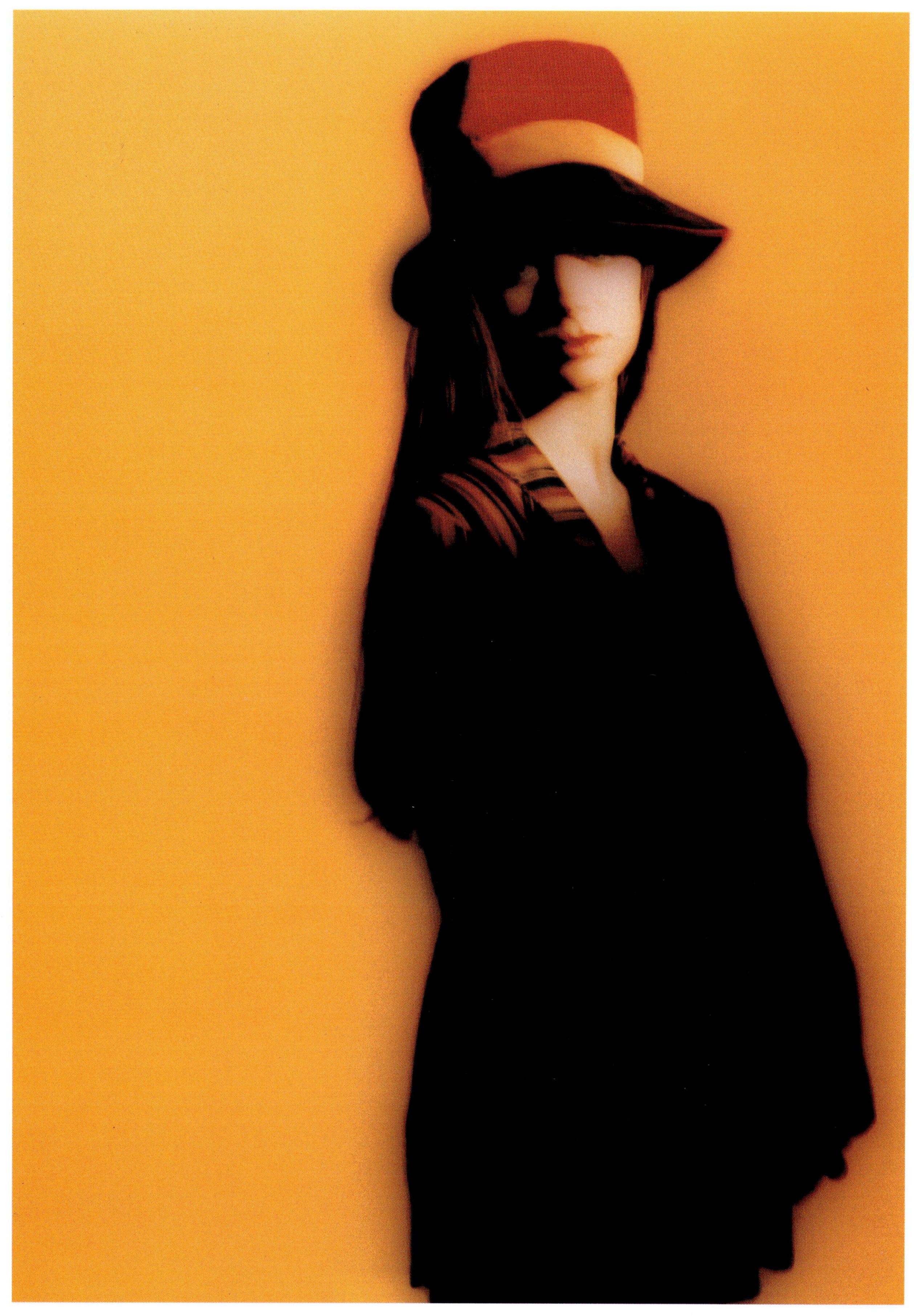

ANDY THOMPSON

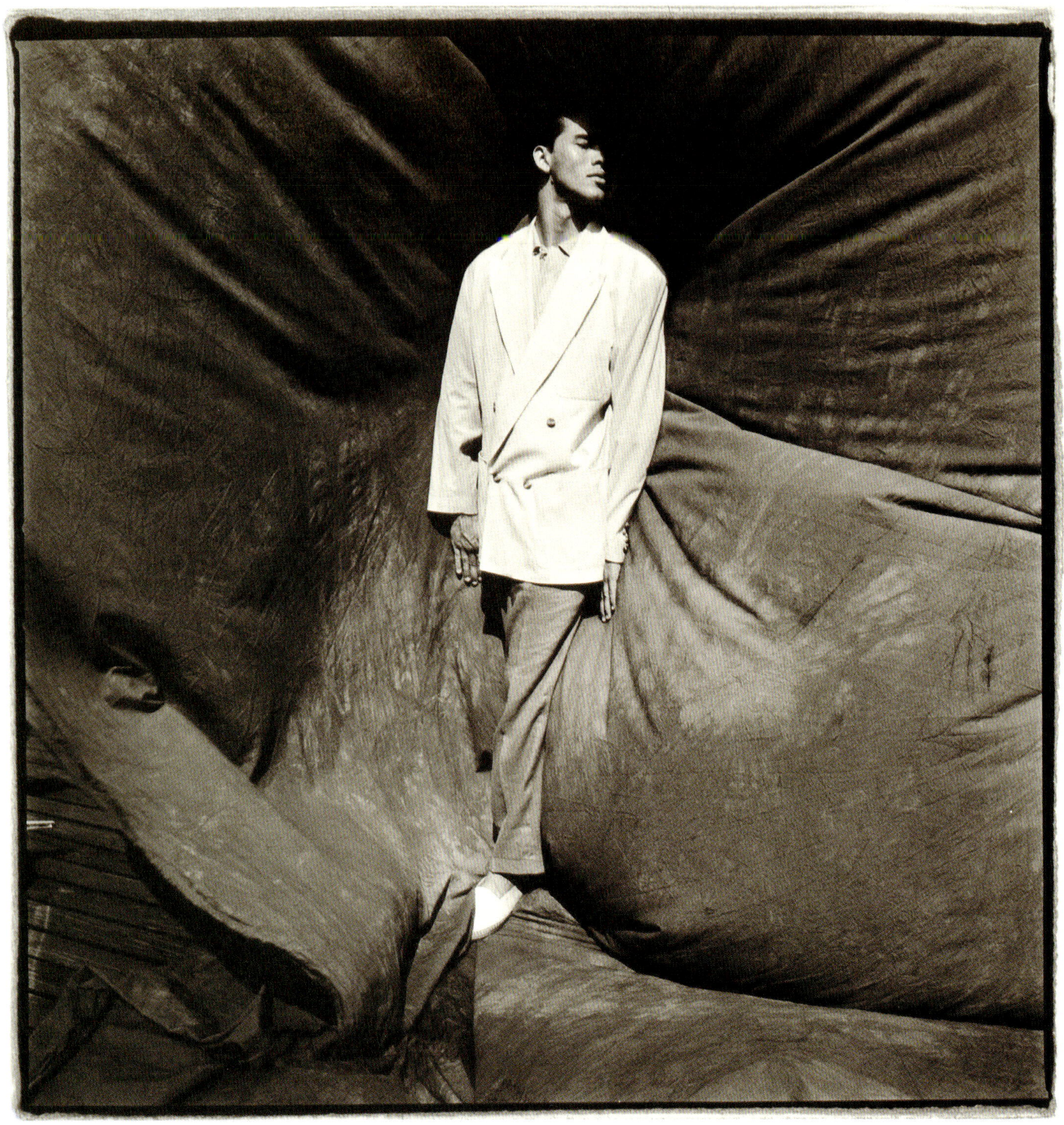

Michael Biondo

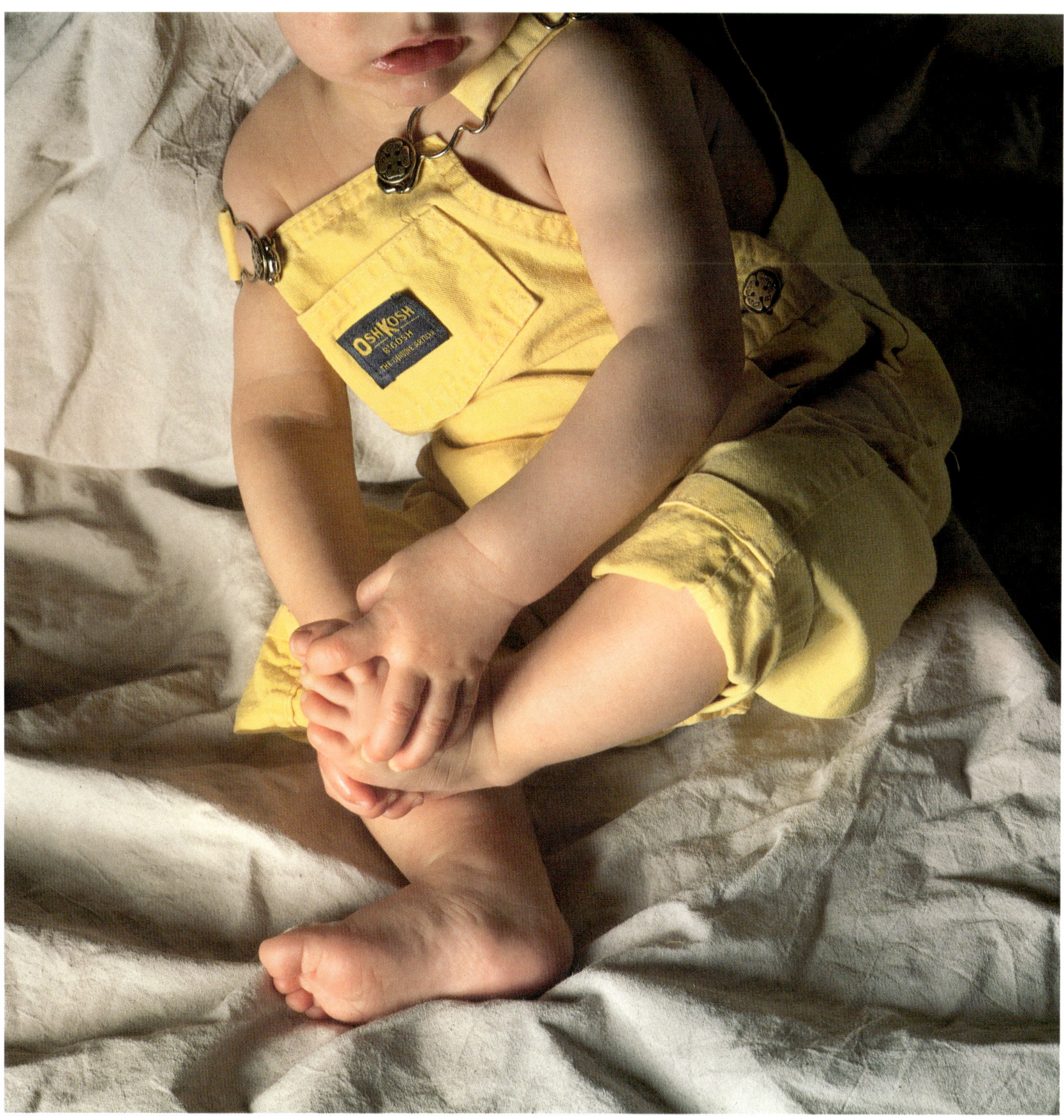

Linda Bohm

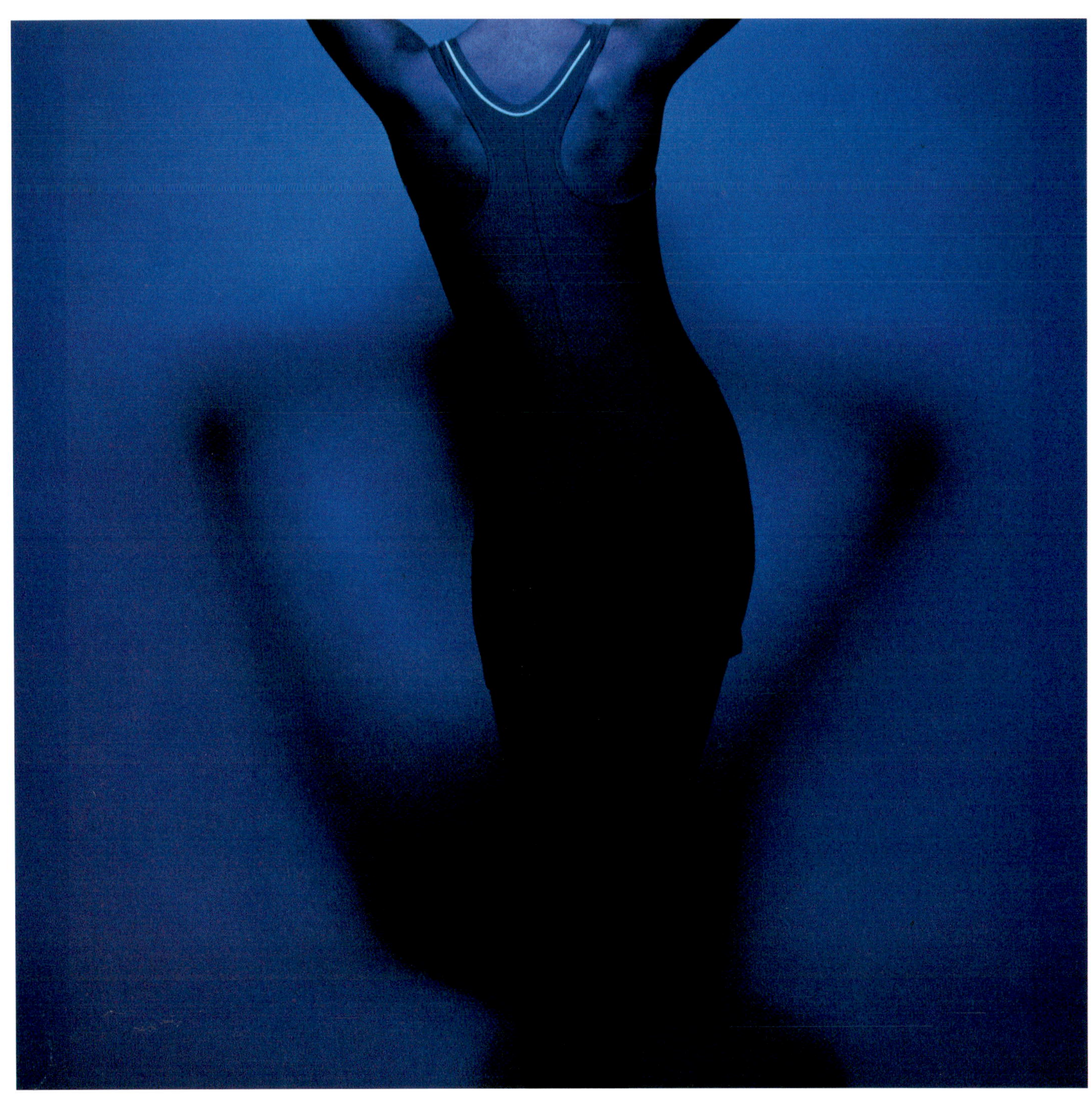

Robert Quick

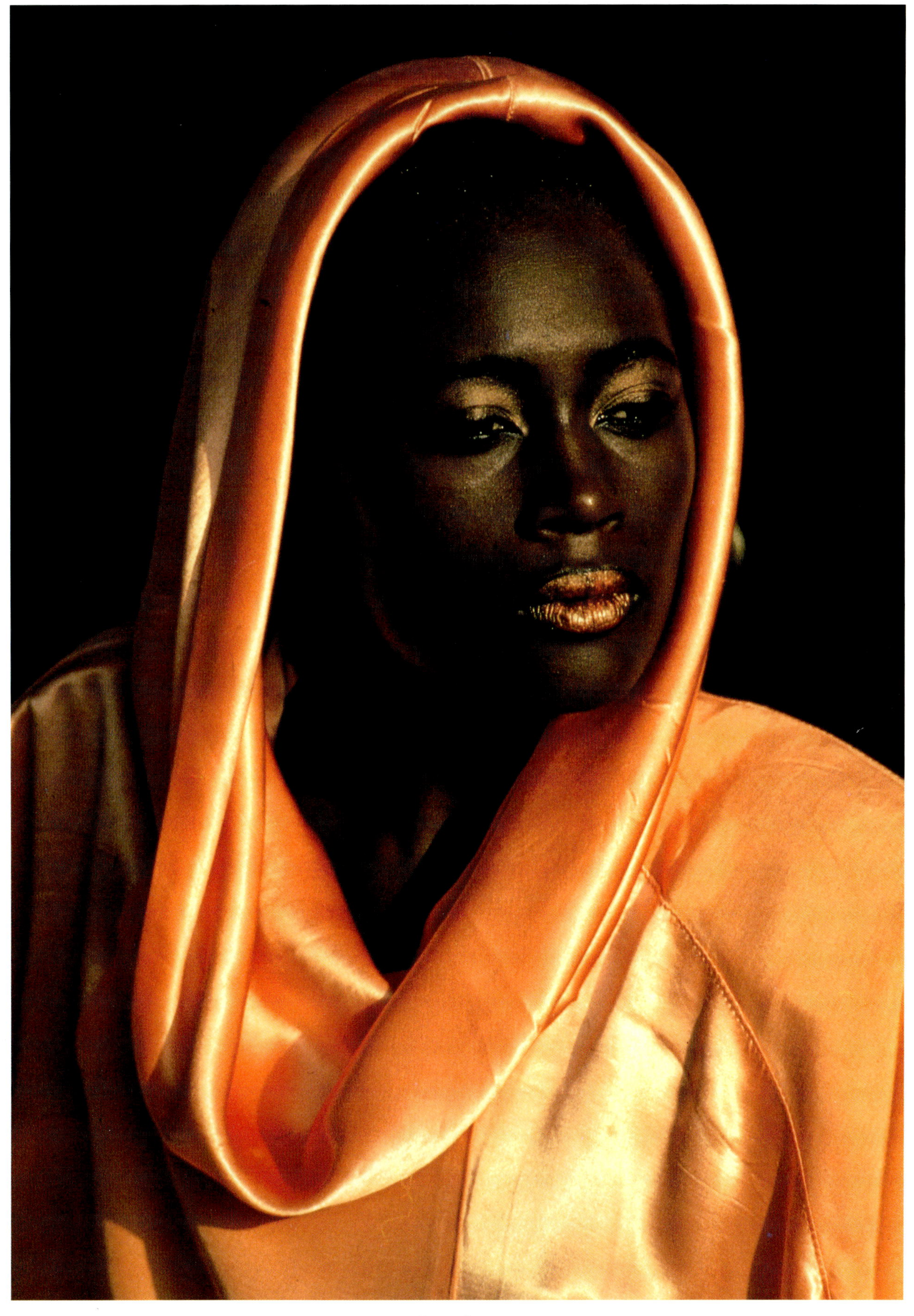

Miko Lajczyk

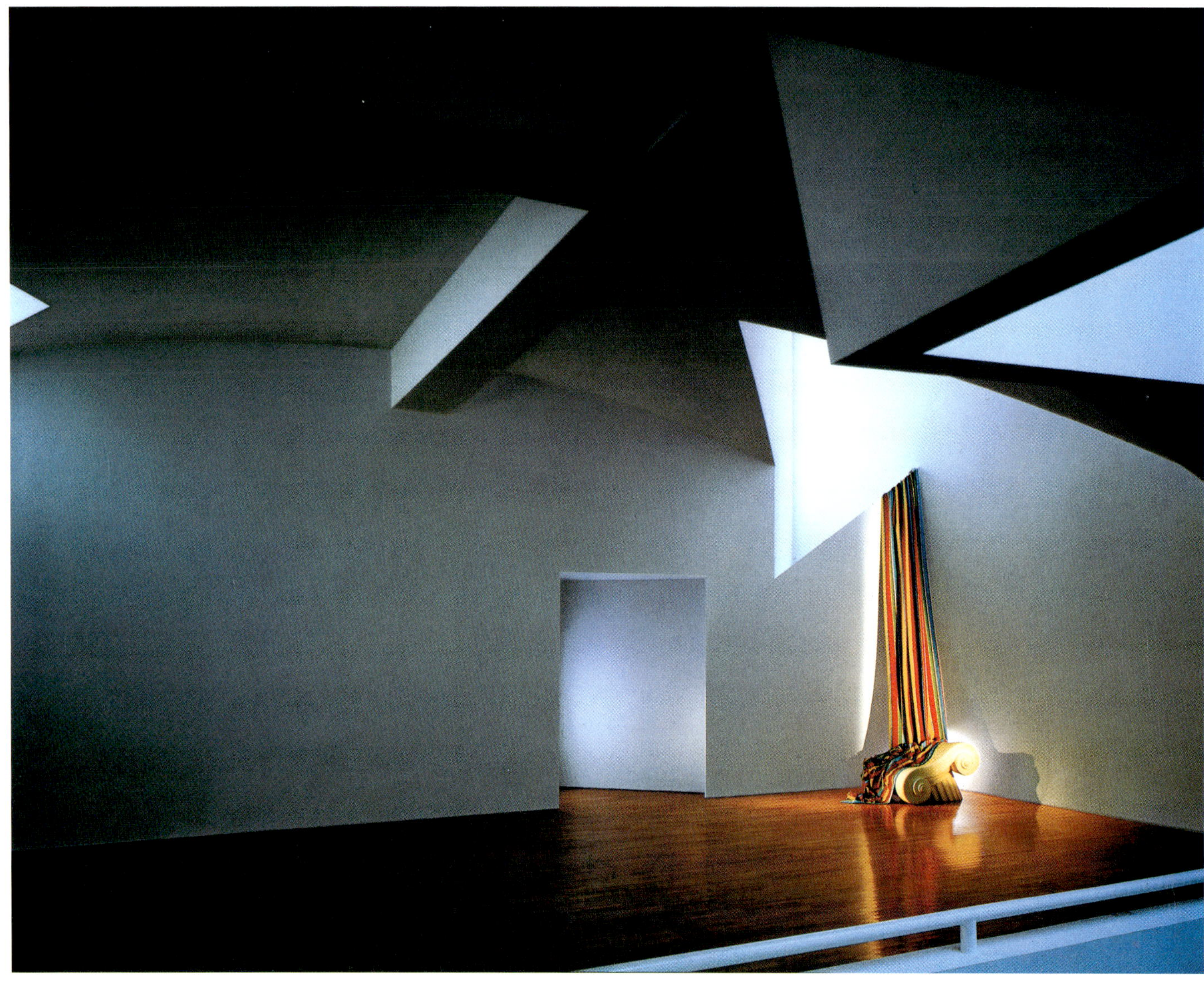

Günter Pfannmüller

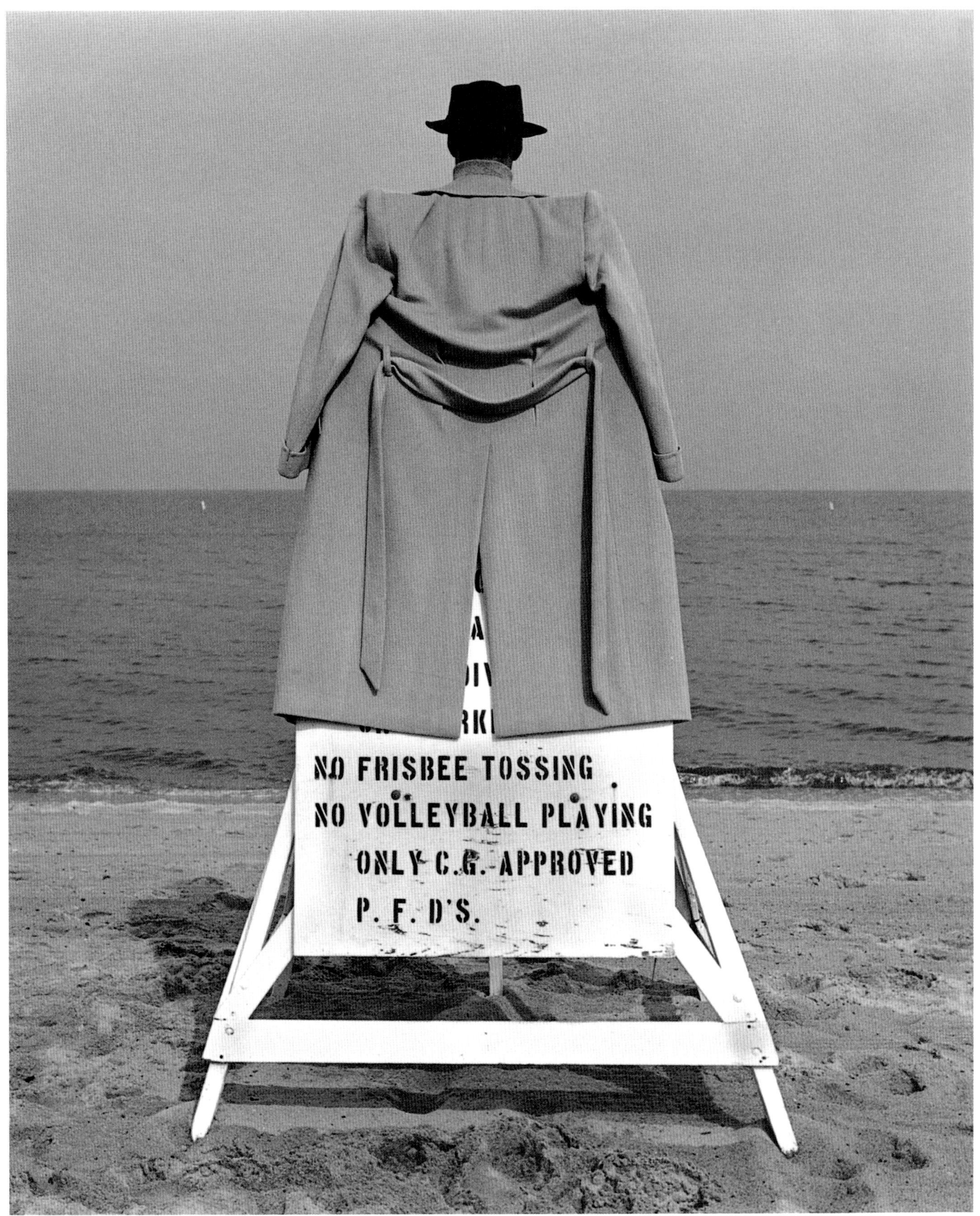

Rodney Smith

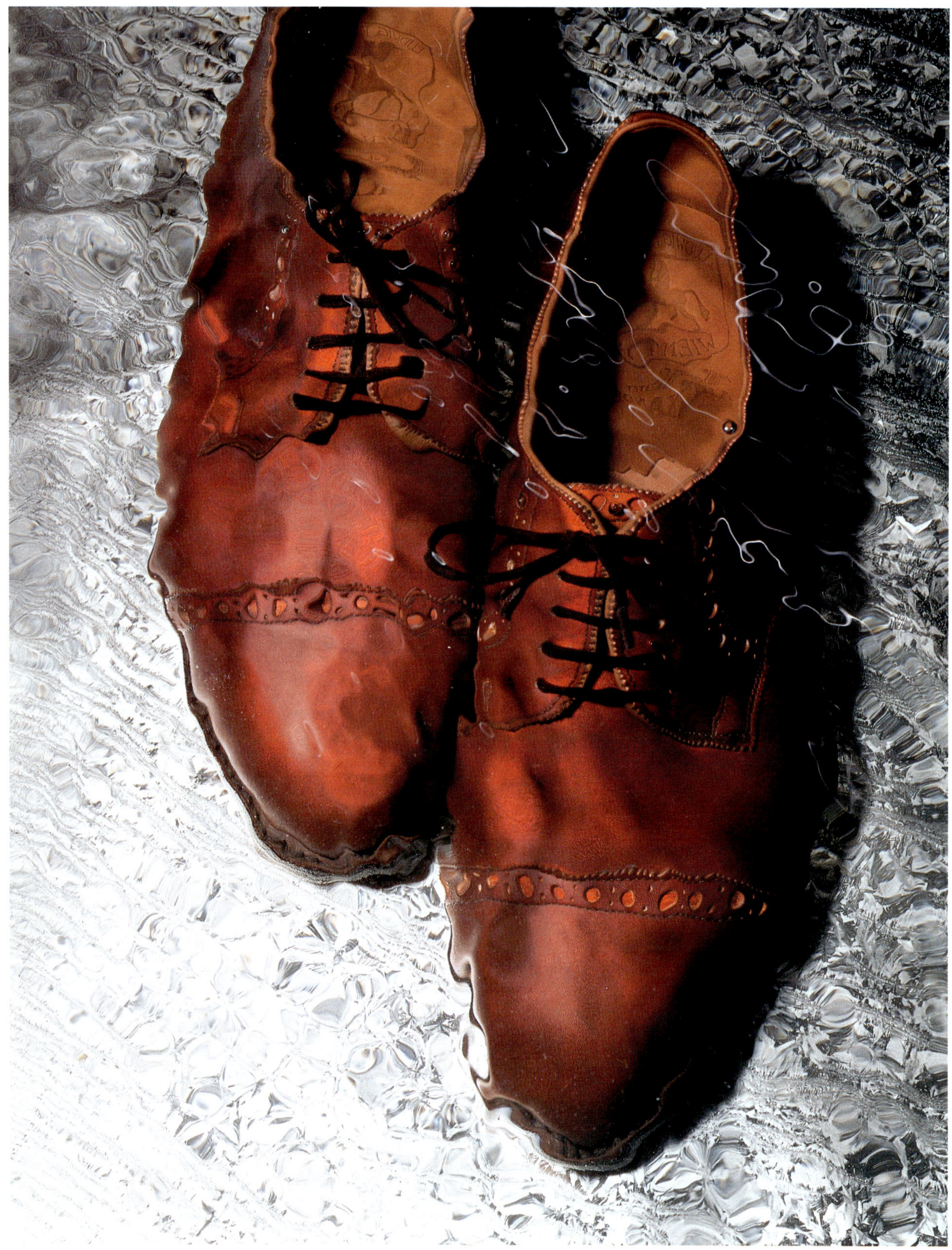

Bernhard Angerer

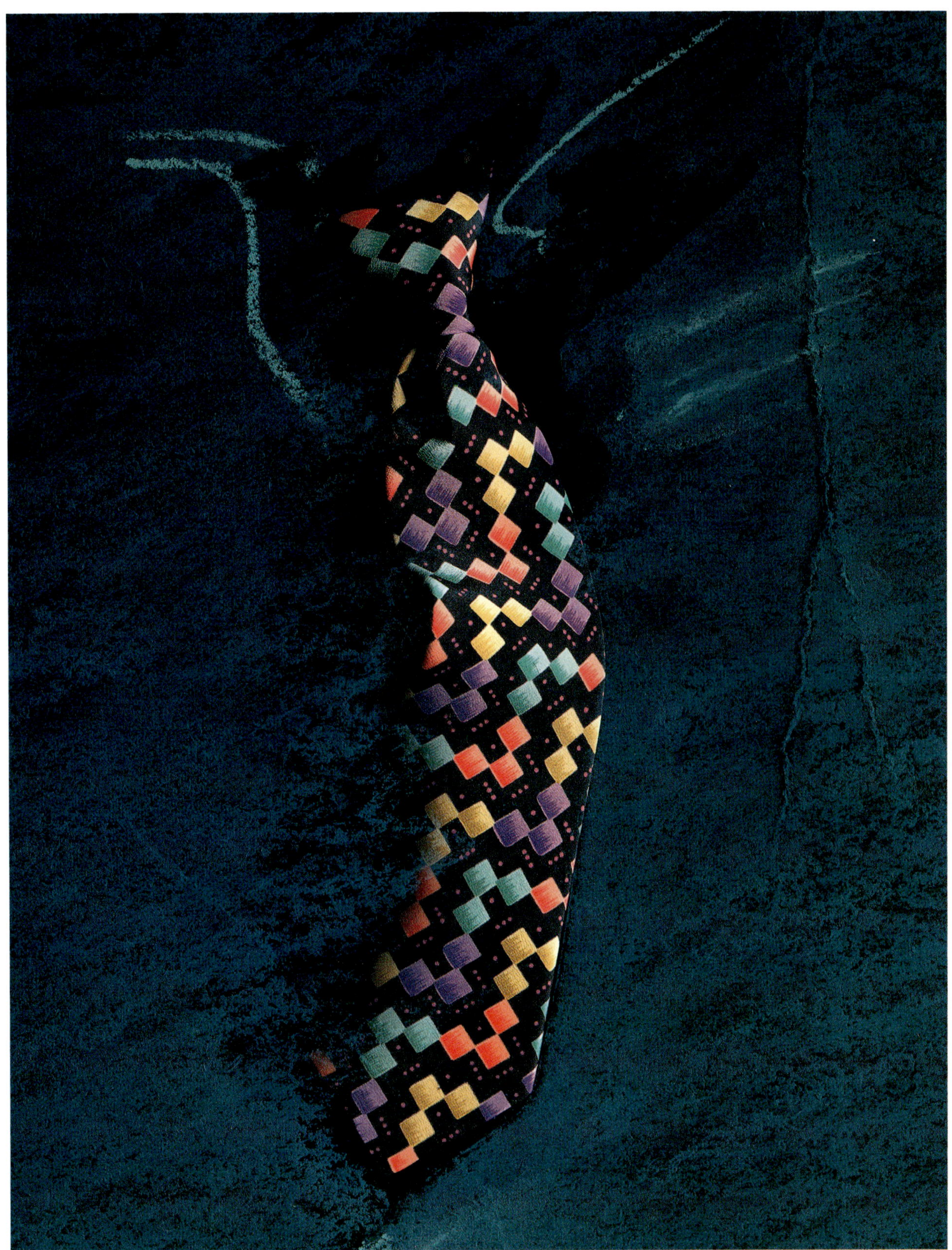

Chris Meier

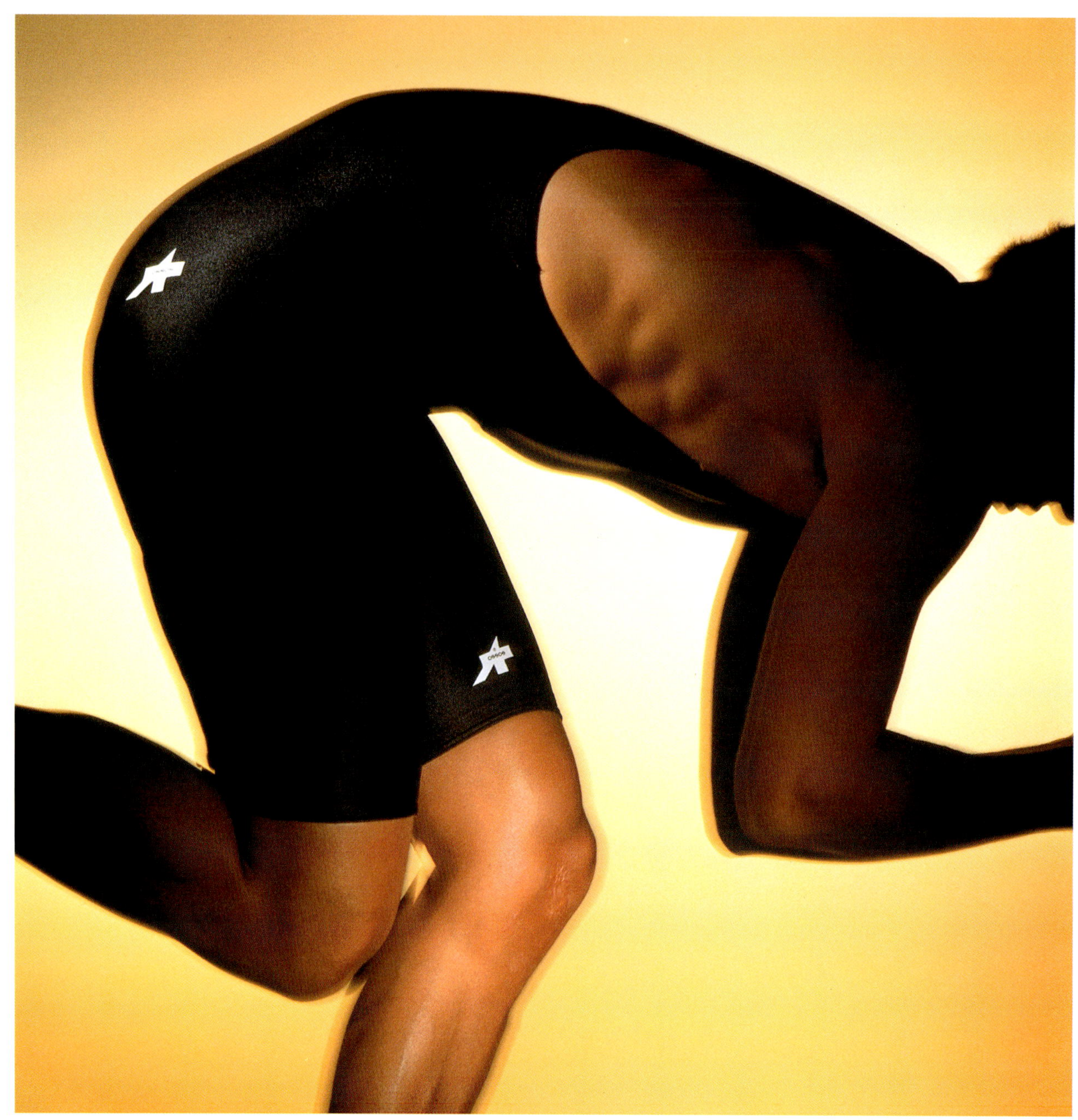

Daniel Wreszin

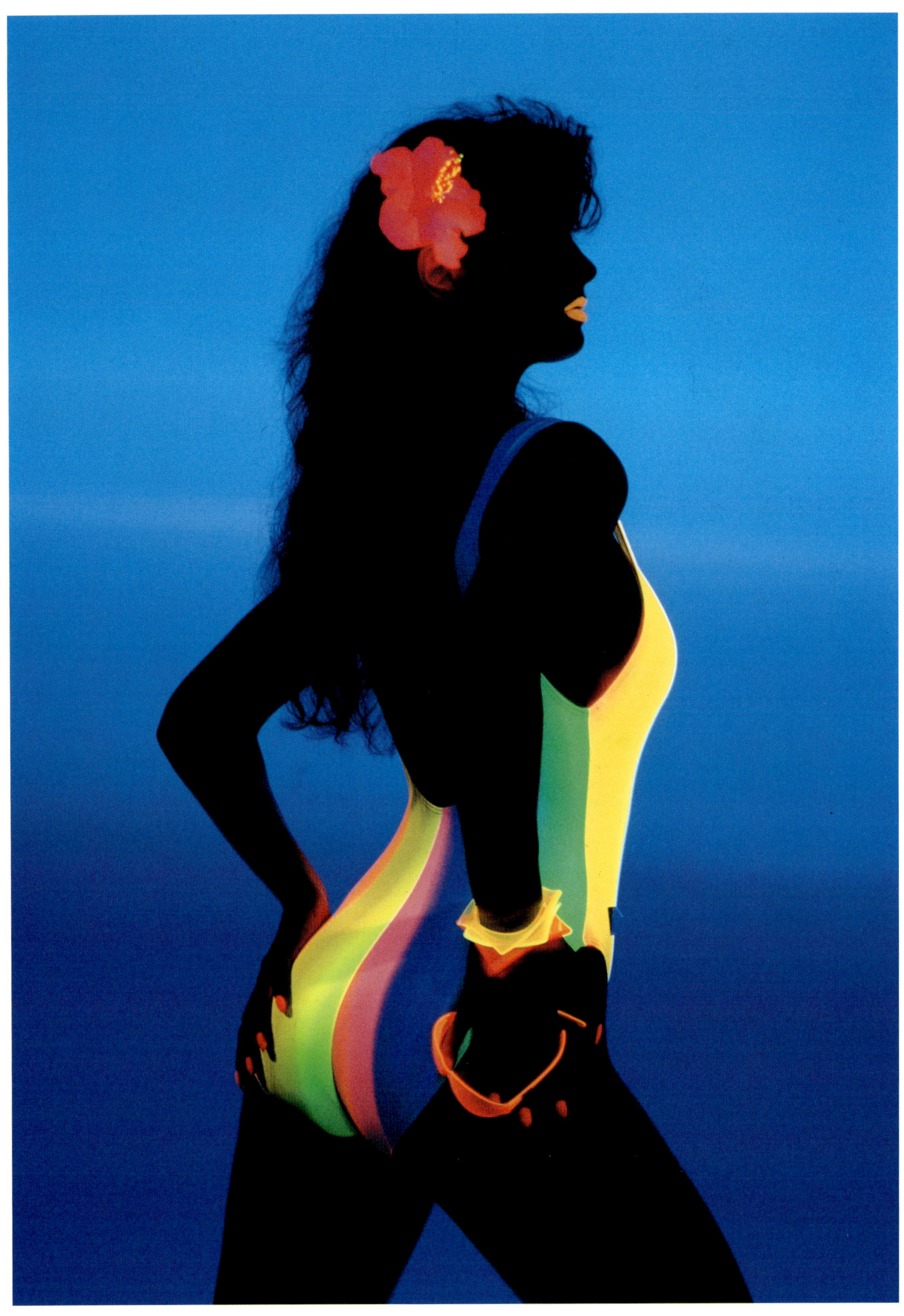

Tak Kojima

Jost Wildbolz

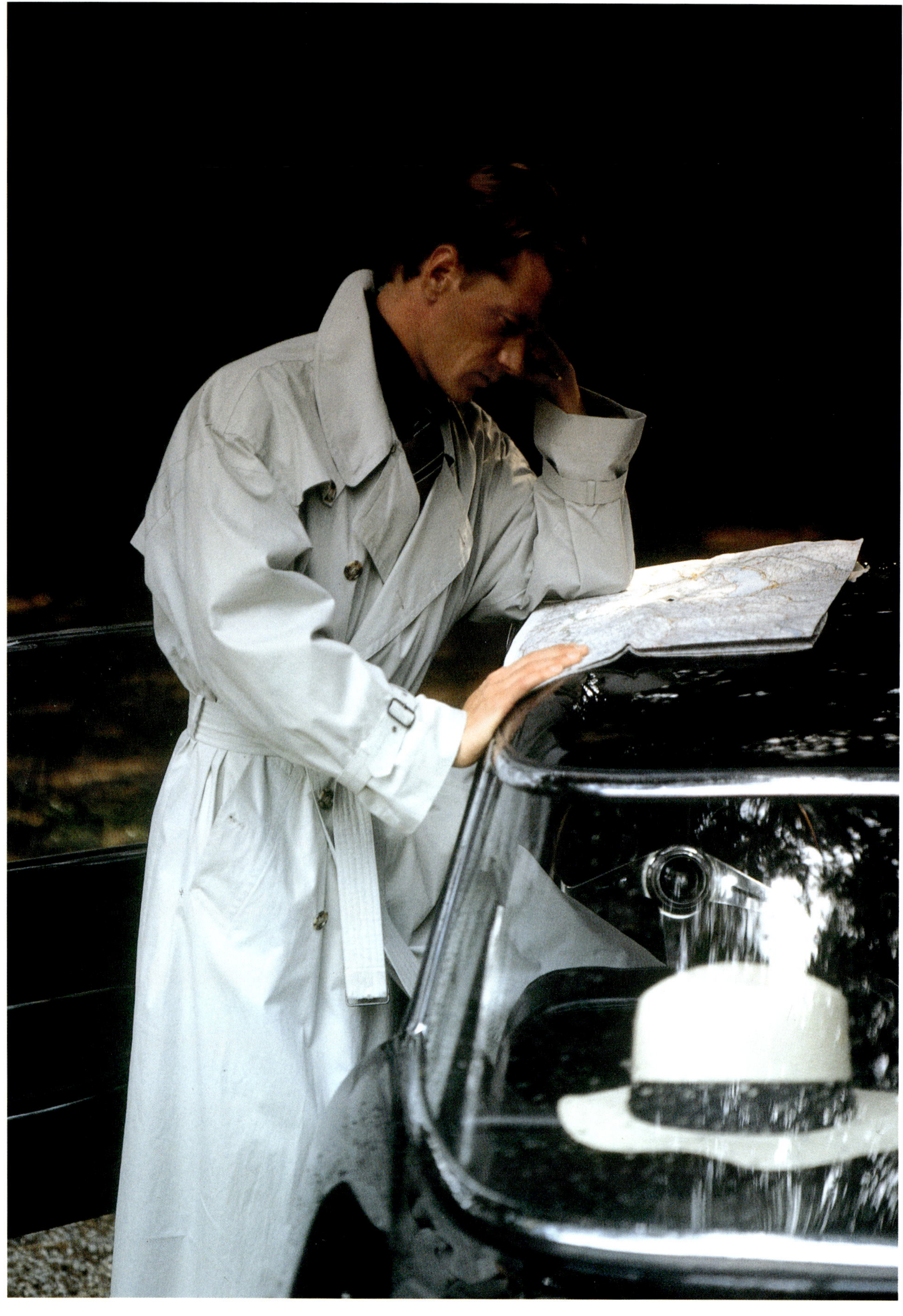

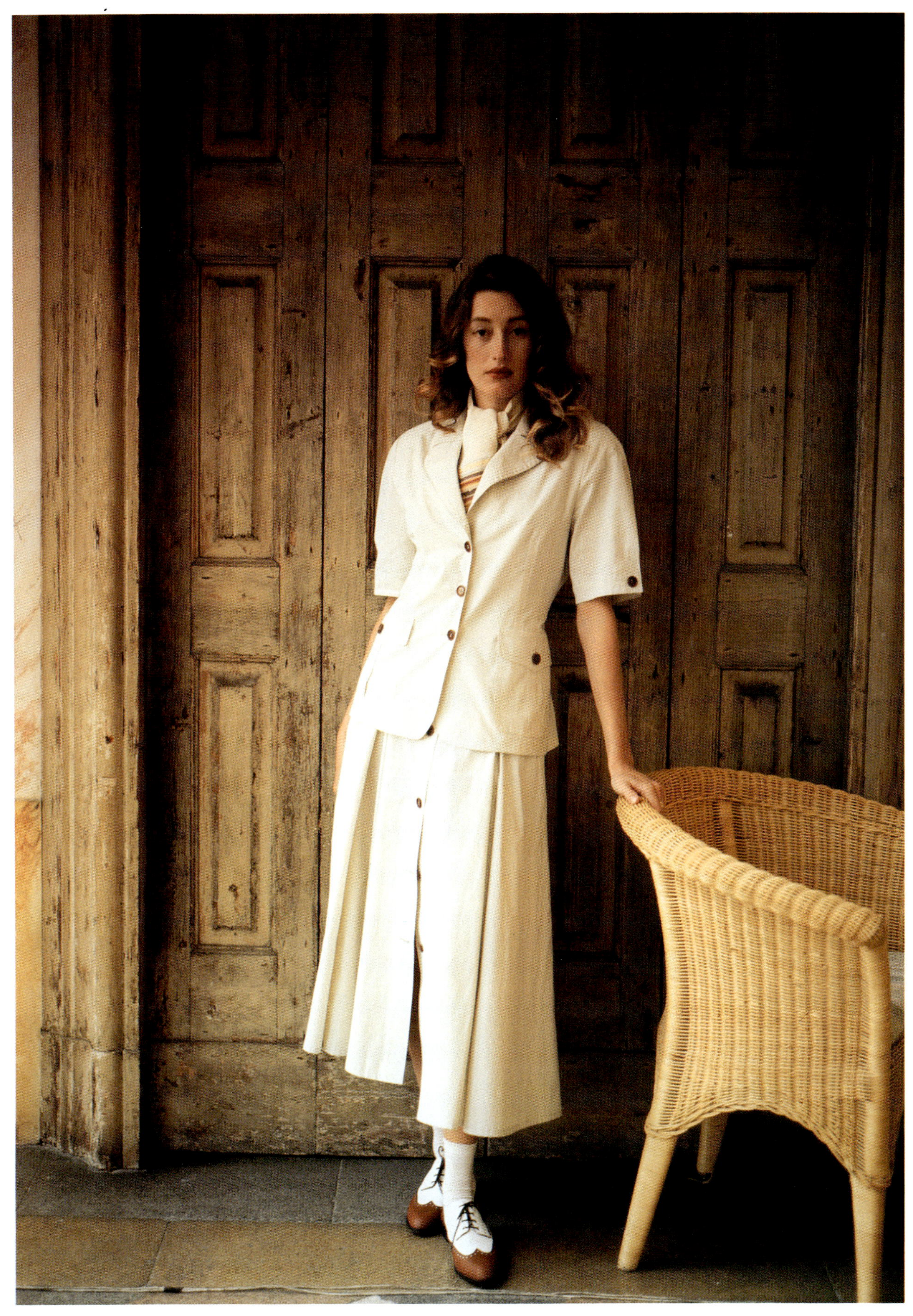

Jost Wildbolz

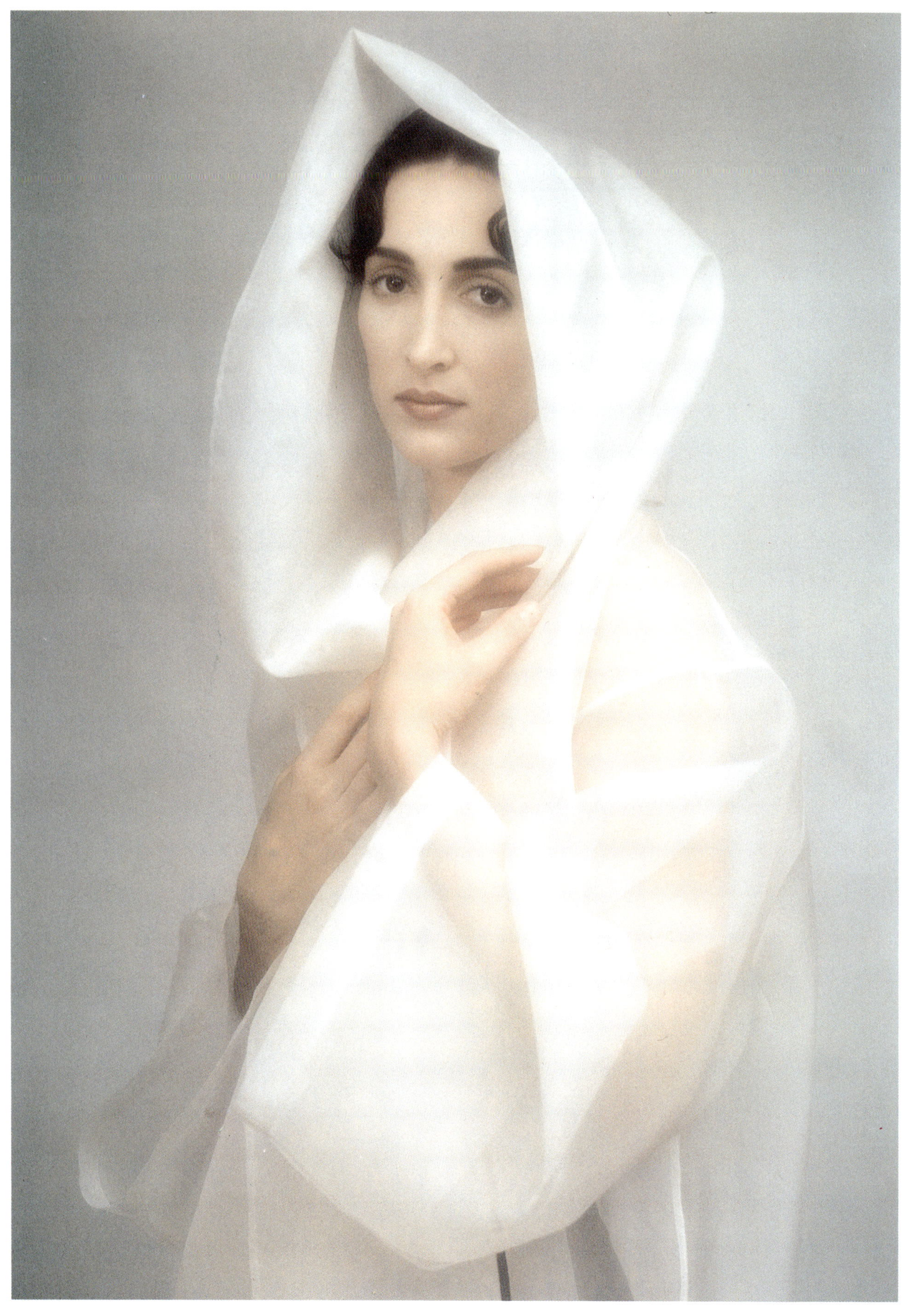

Joyce Tenneson

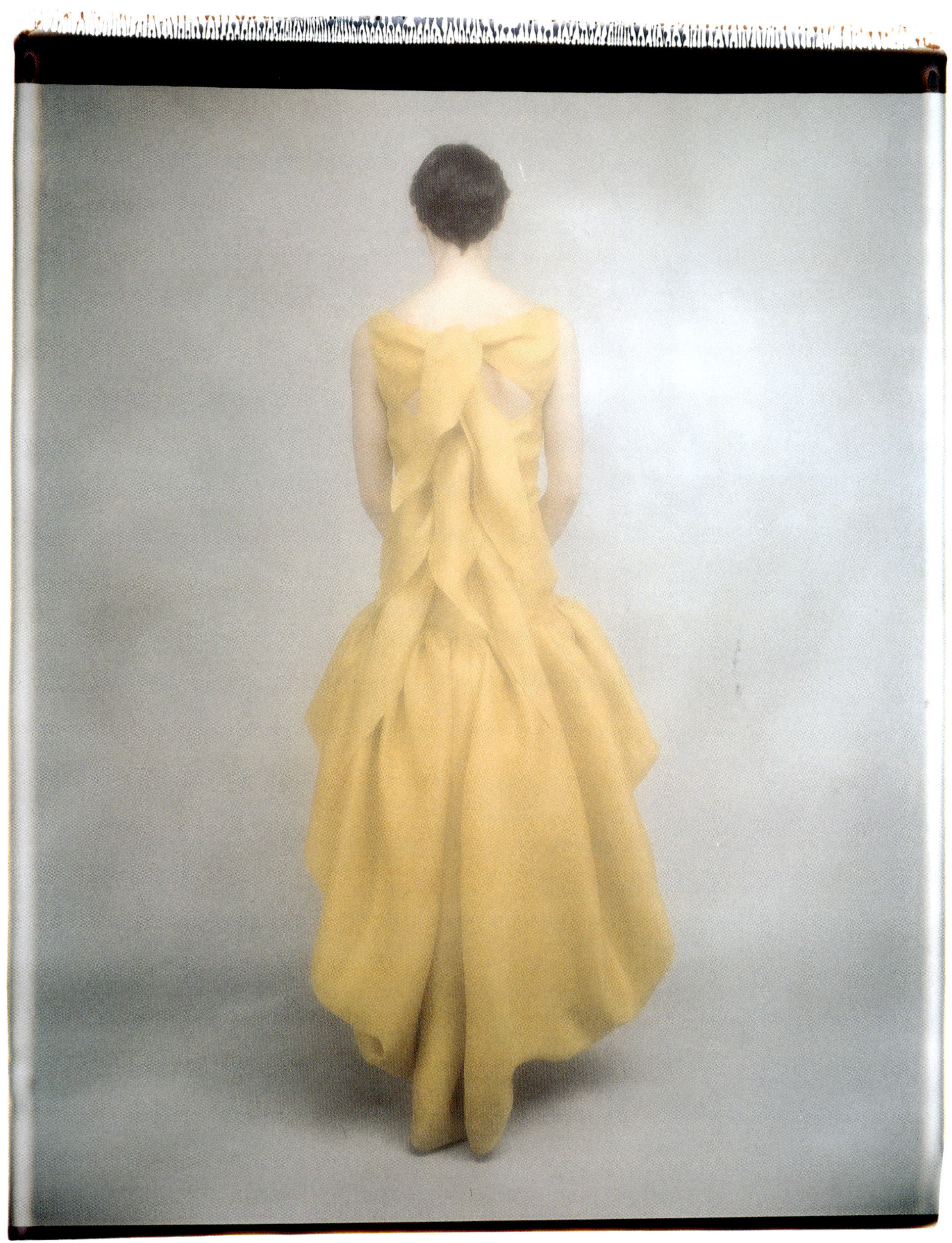

Joyce Tenneson

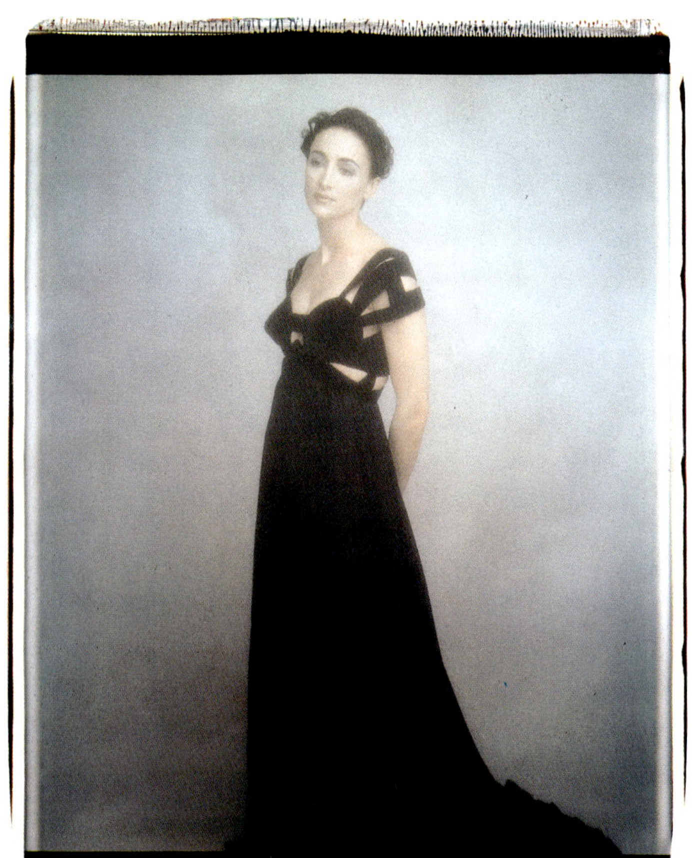 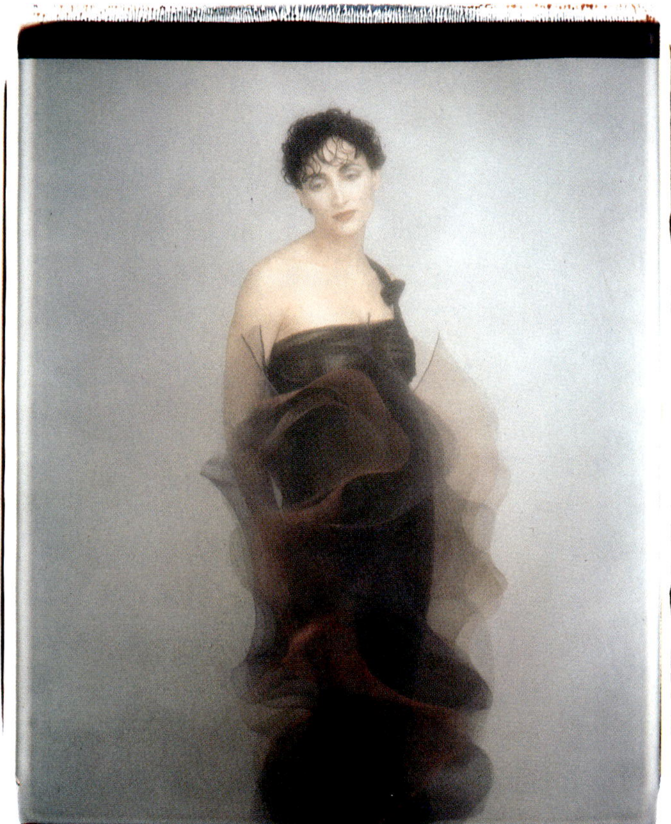

Joyce Tenneson

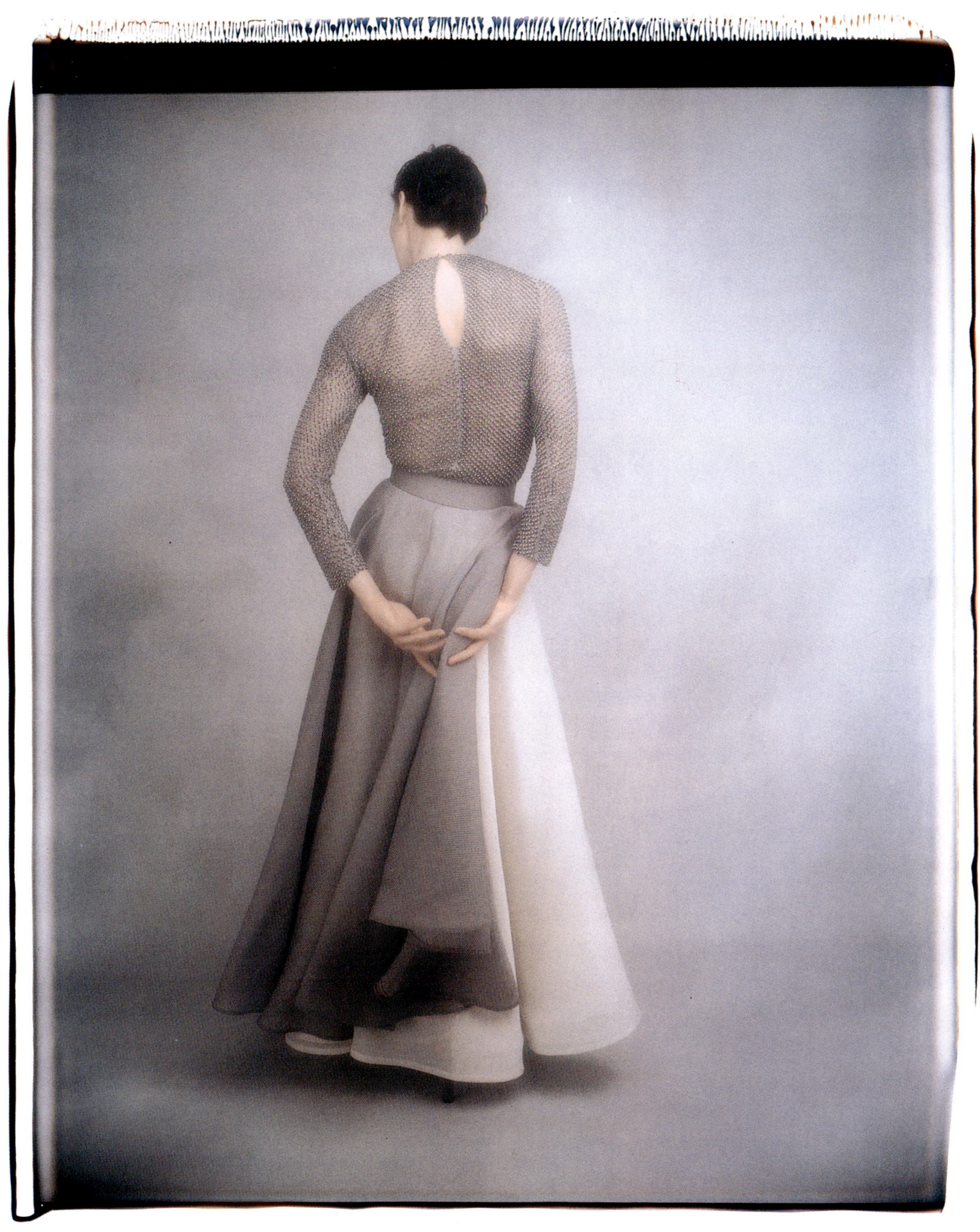

Joyce Tenneson

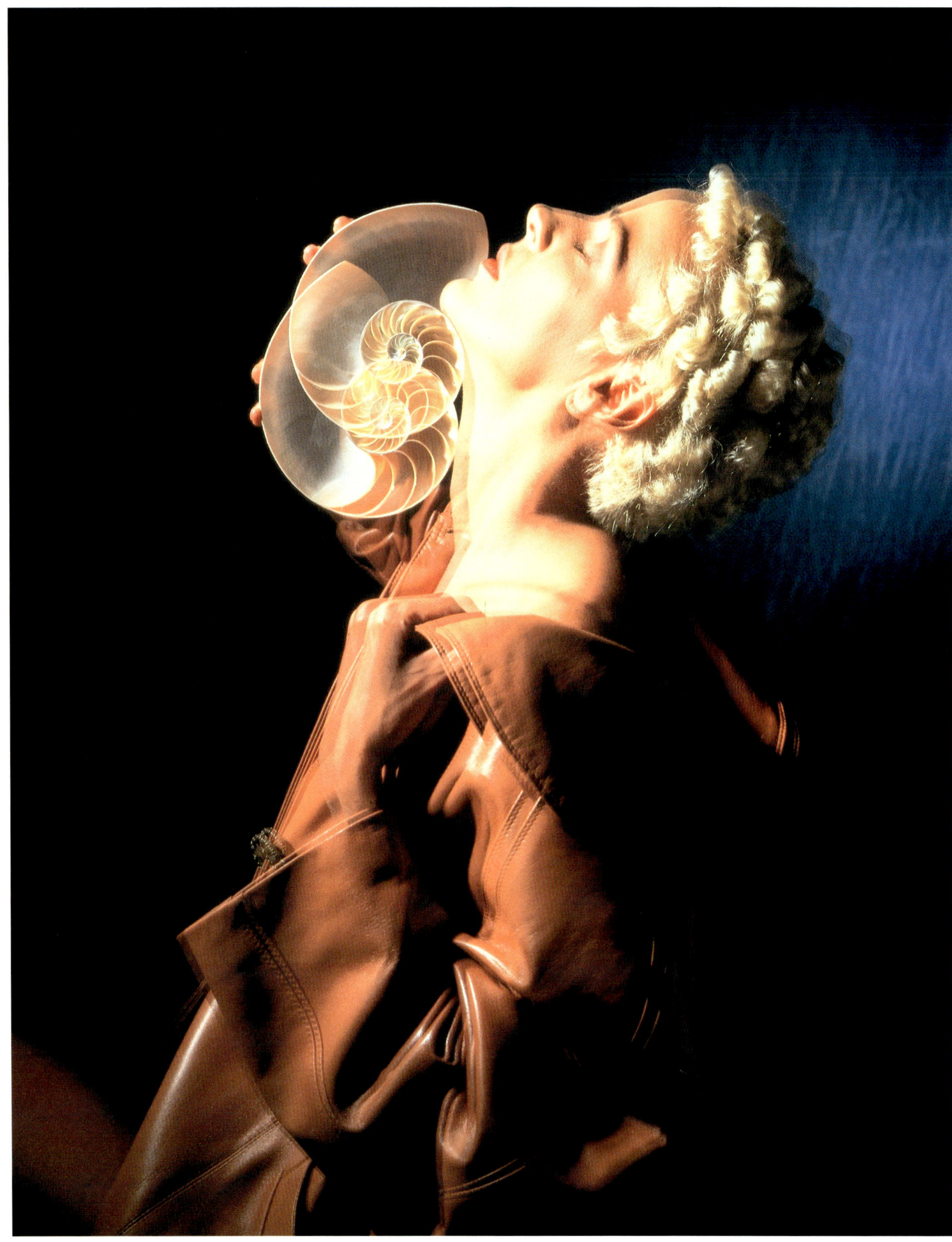

Monica Rosello

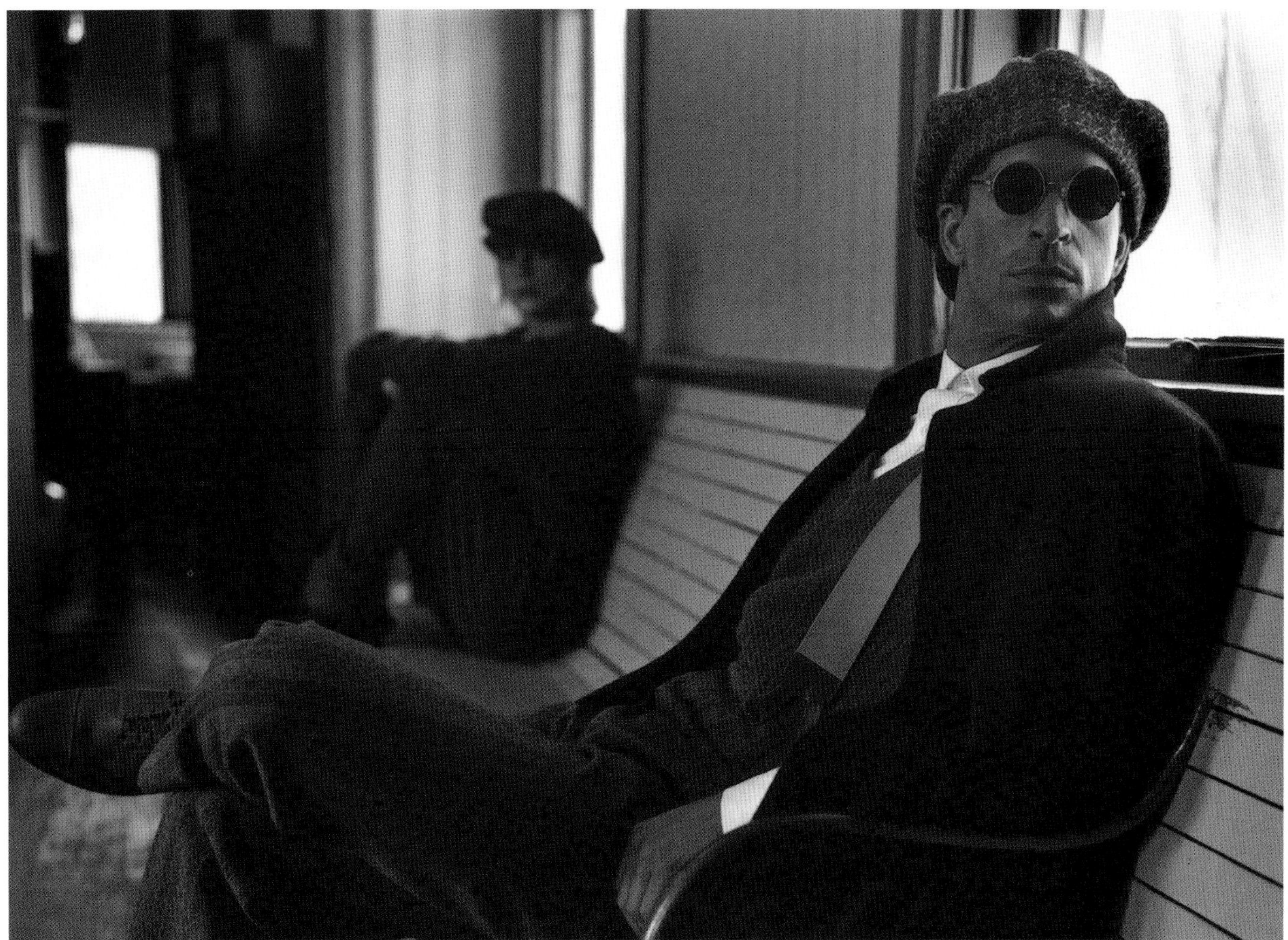

John Huet

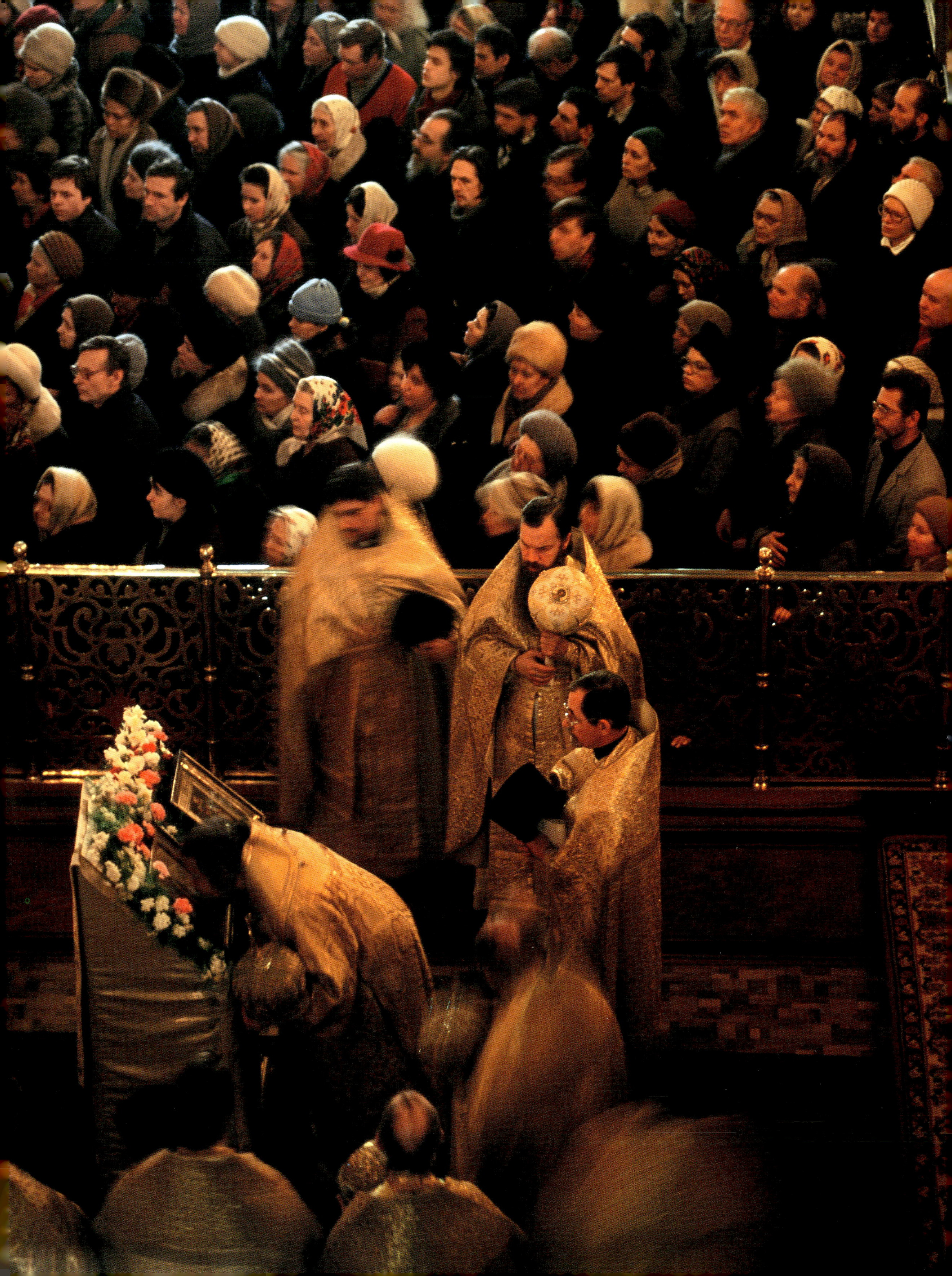

JOURNALISM

JOURNALISMUS

JOURNALISME

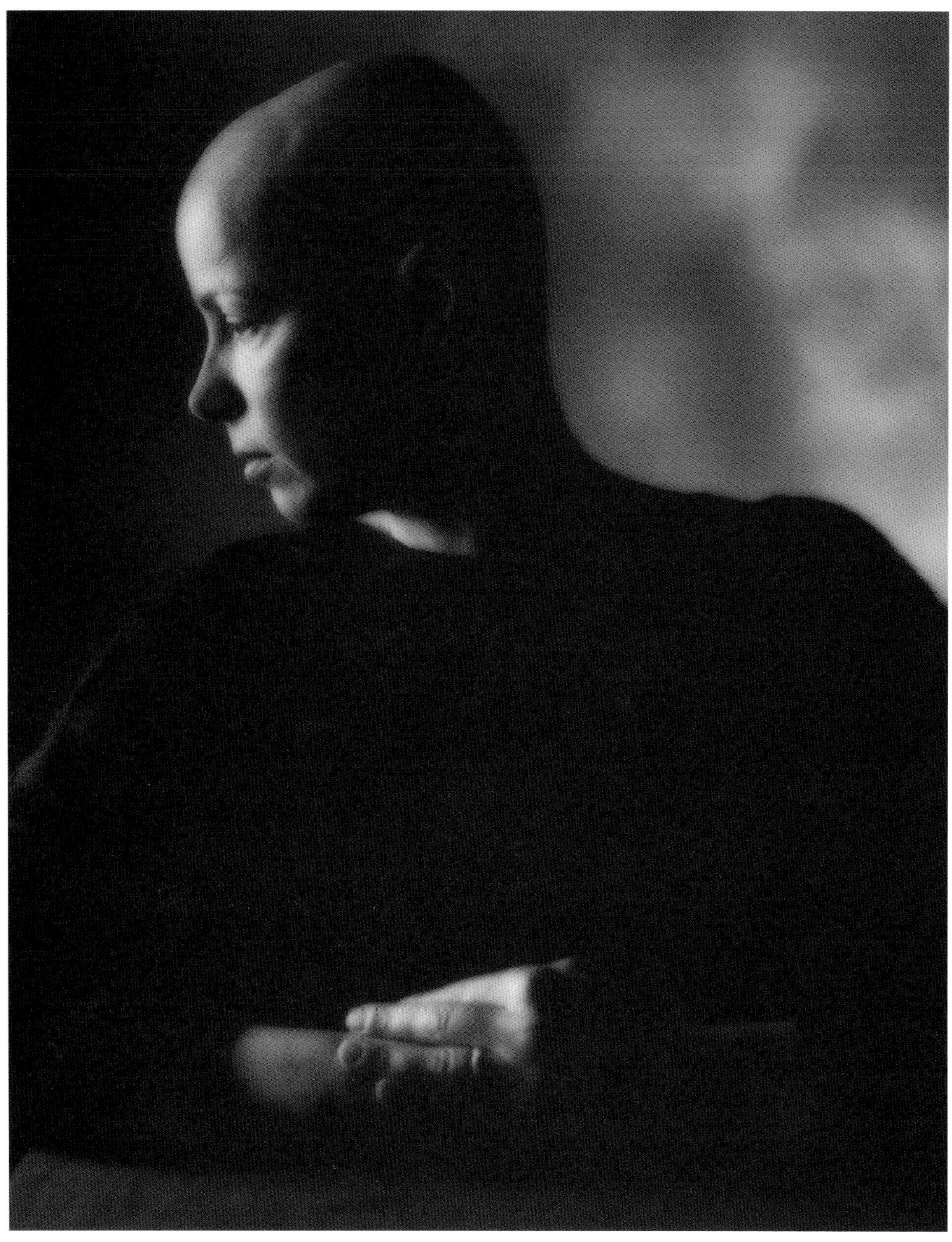

Preceeding Spread: Jeffrey Aaronson Above: David Powers

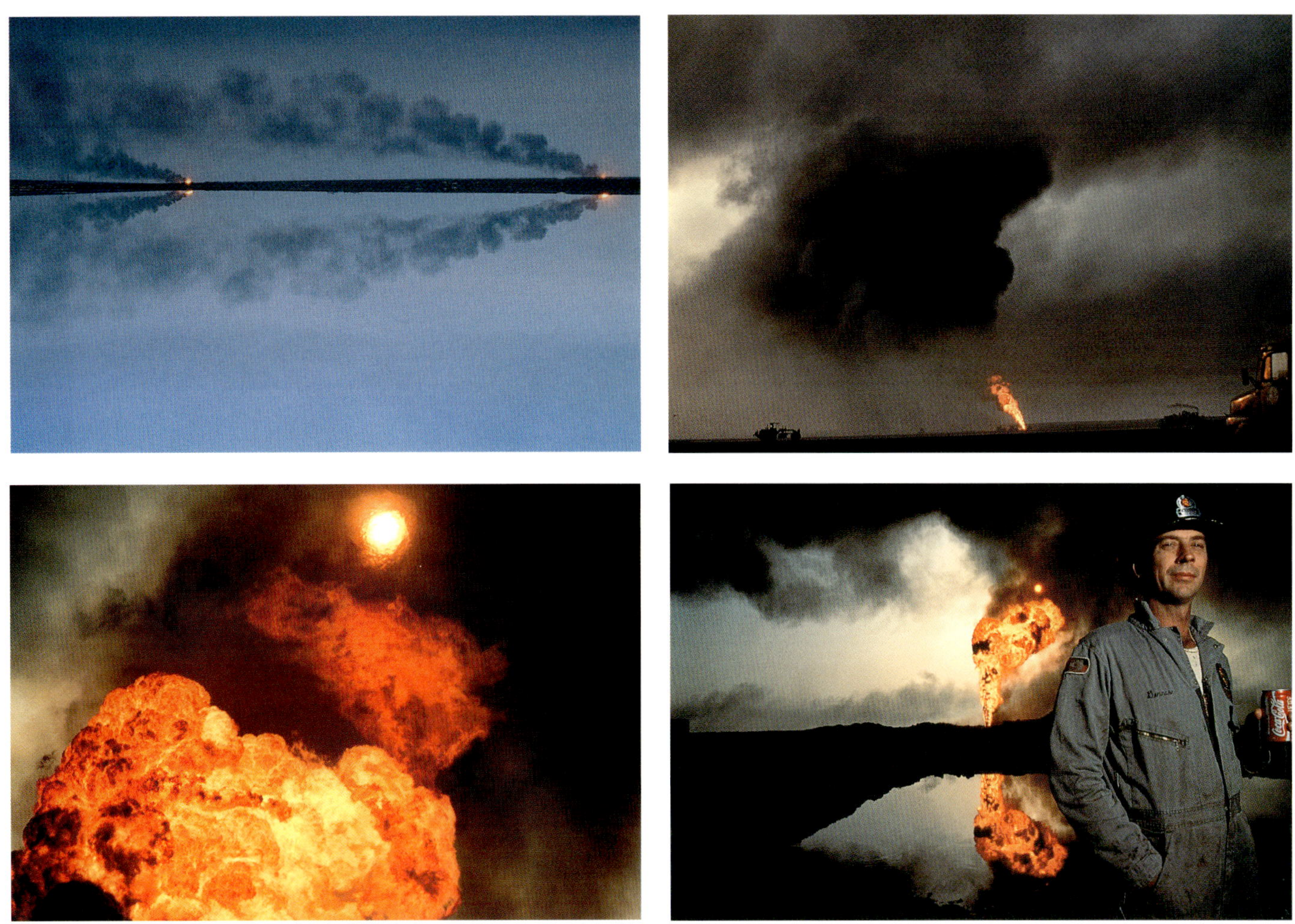

Arthur Meyerson

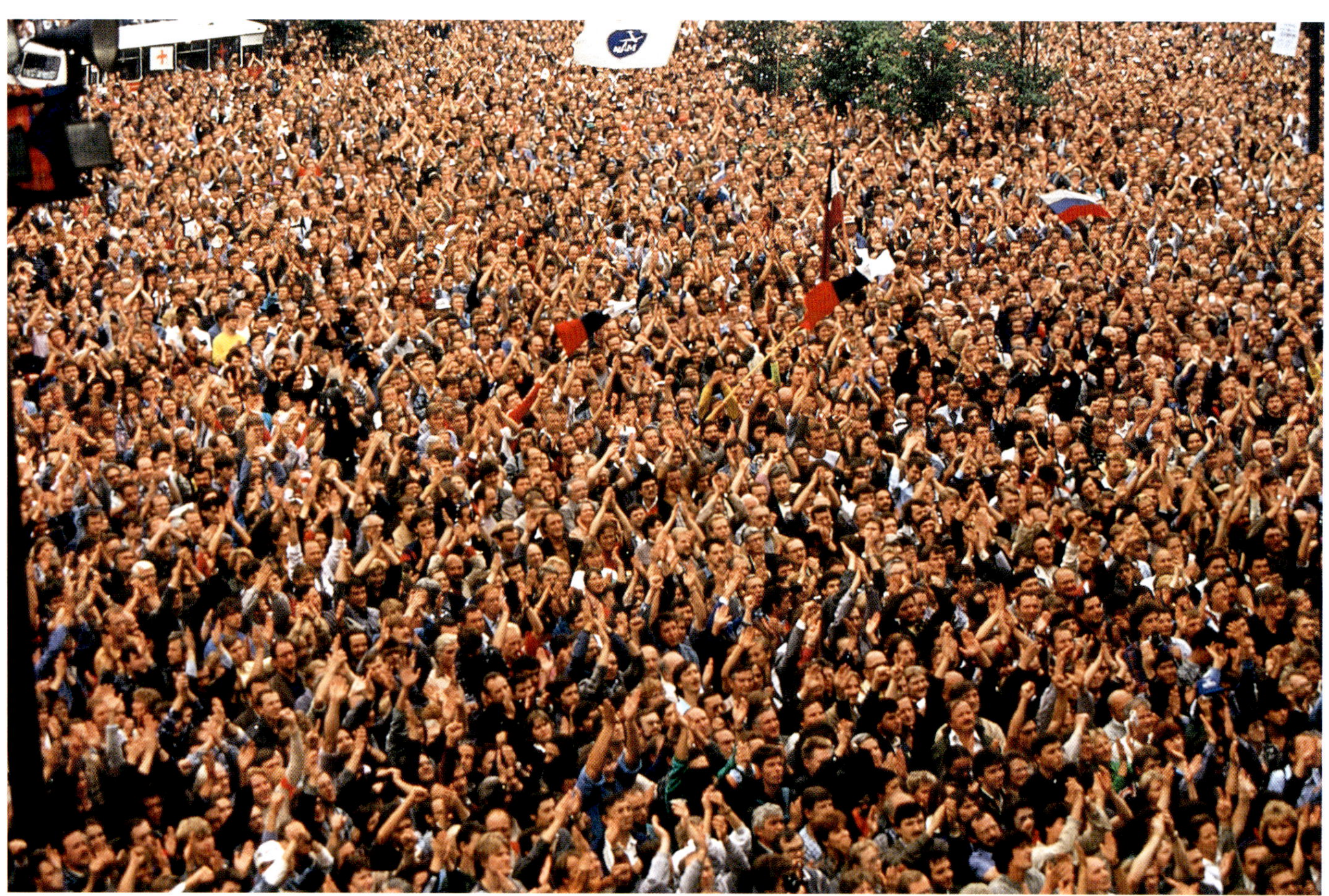

Andy Hernandez

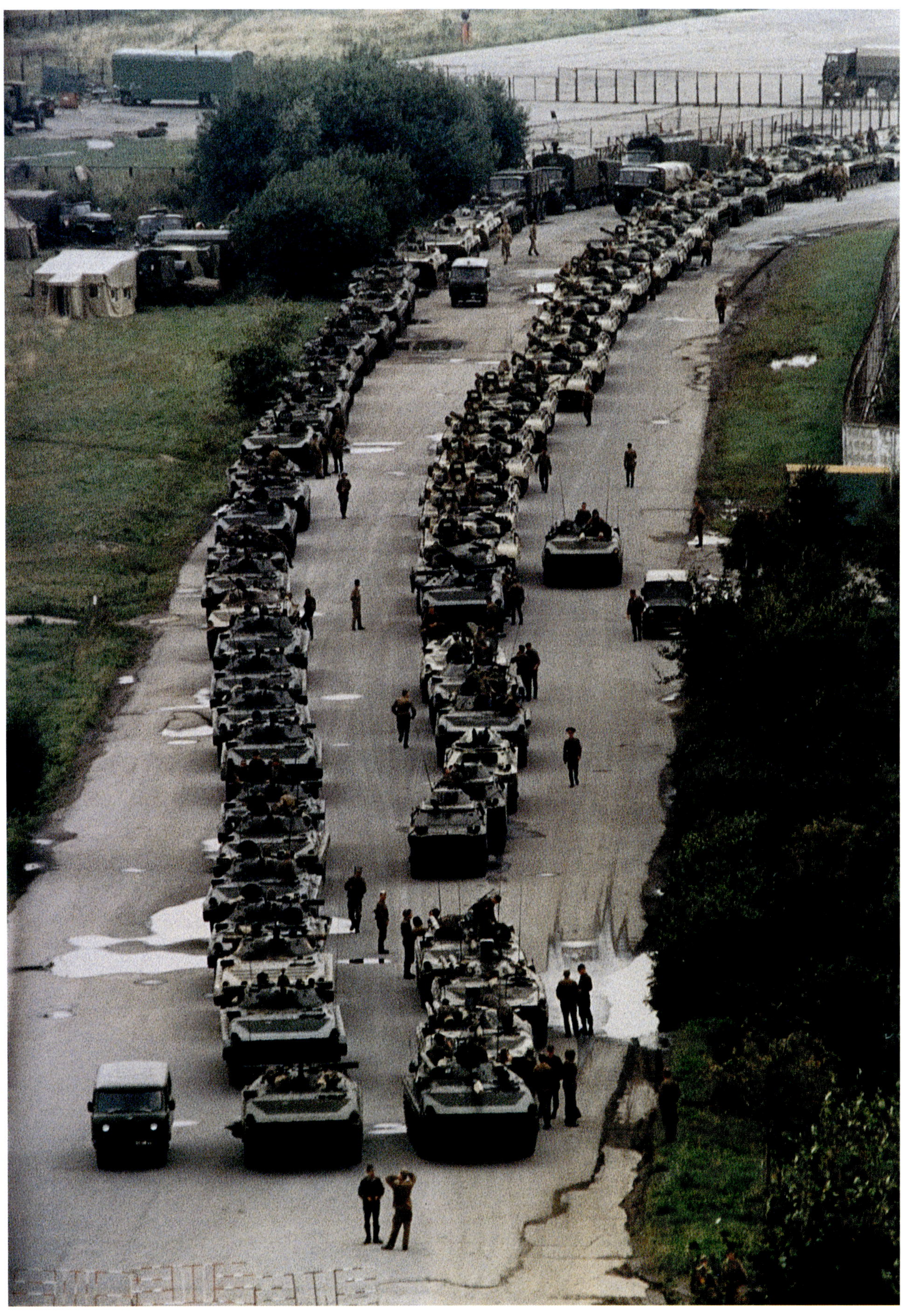

Boris Yurchenko

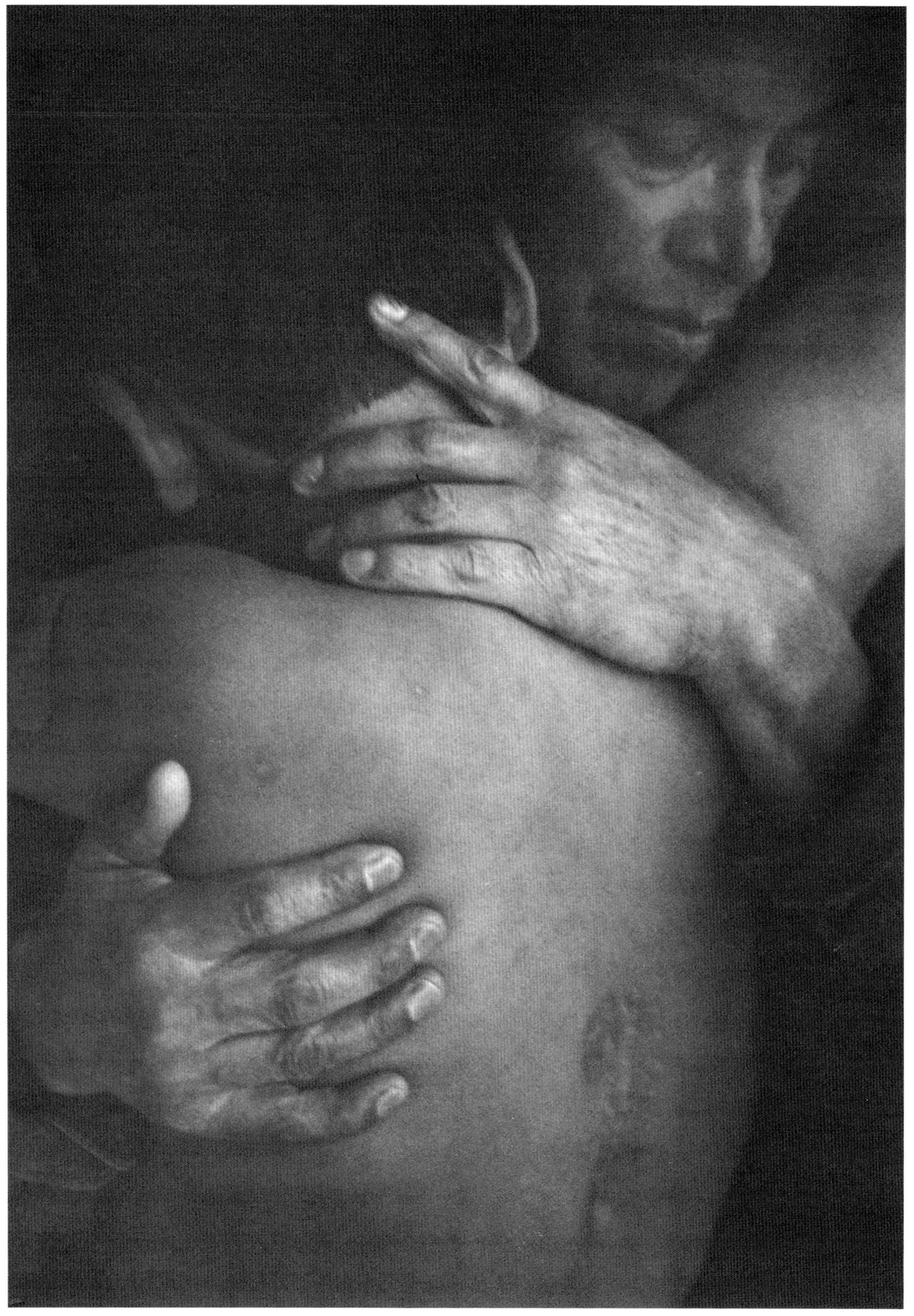

Raymond Meeks

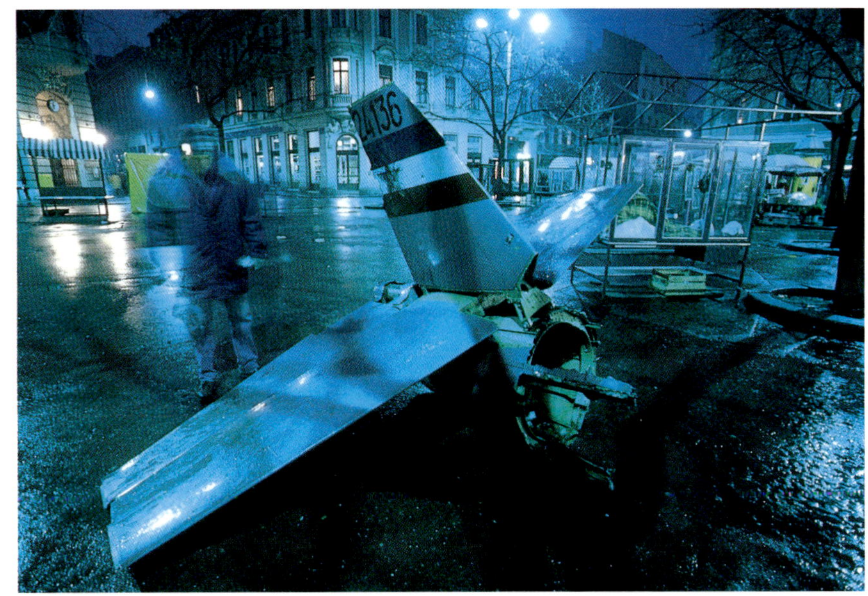

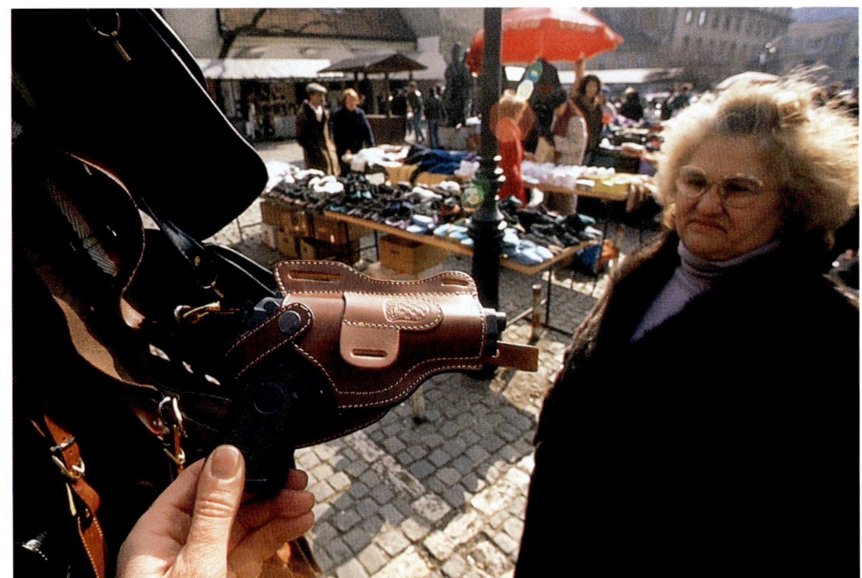

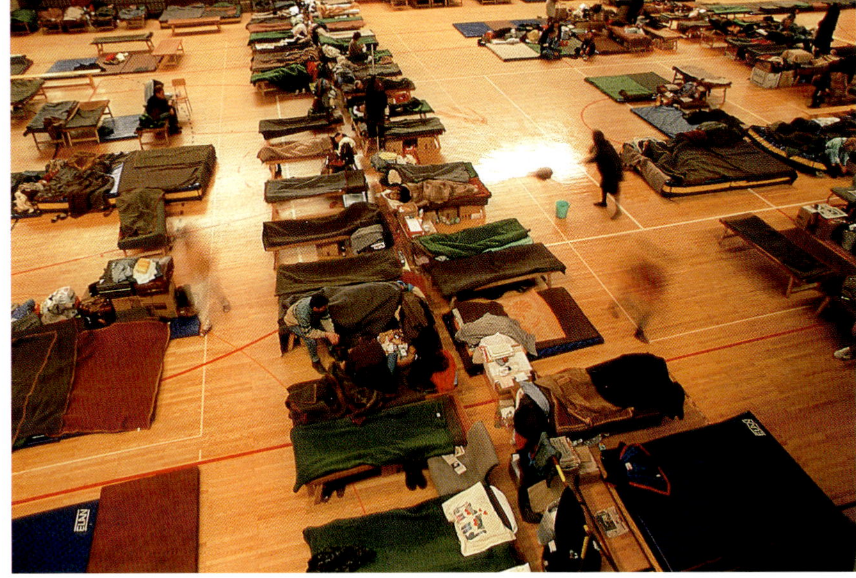

Wilfried Bauer

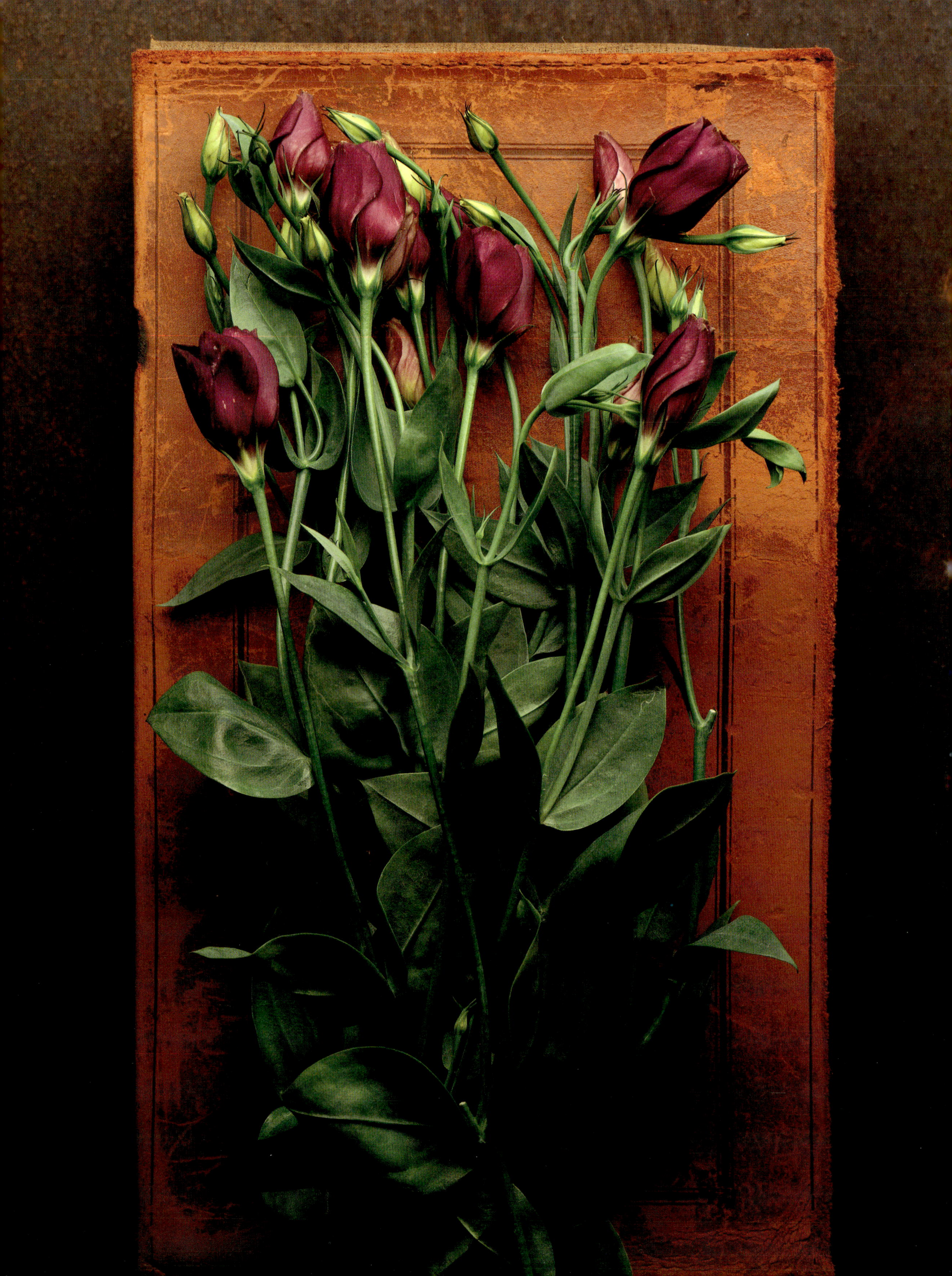

STILL LIFE

STILLEBEN

NATURE MORTE

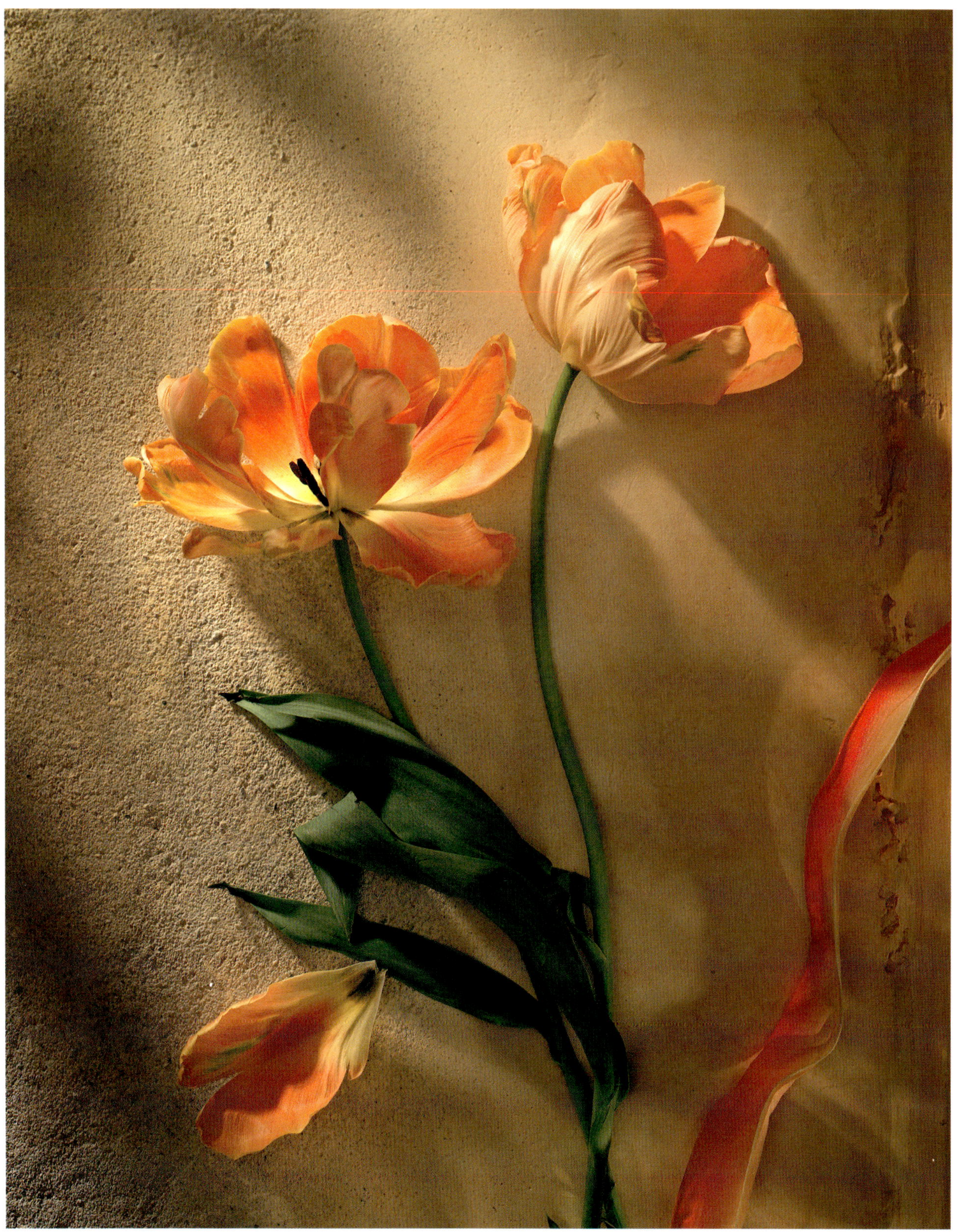

Preceeding Spread: John Payne / Above: Mike Ryan

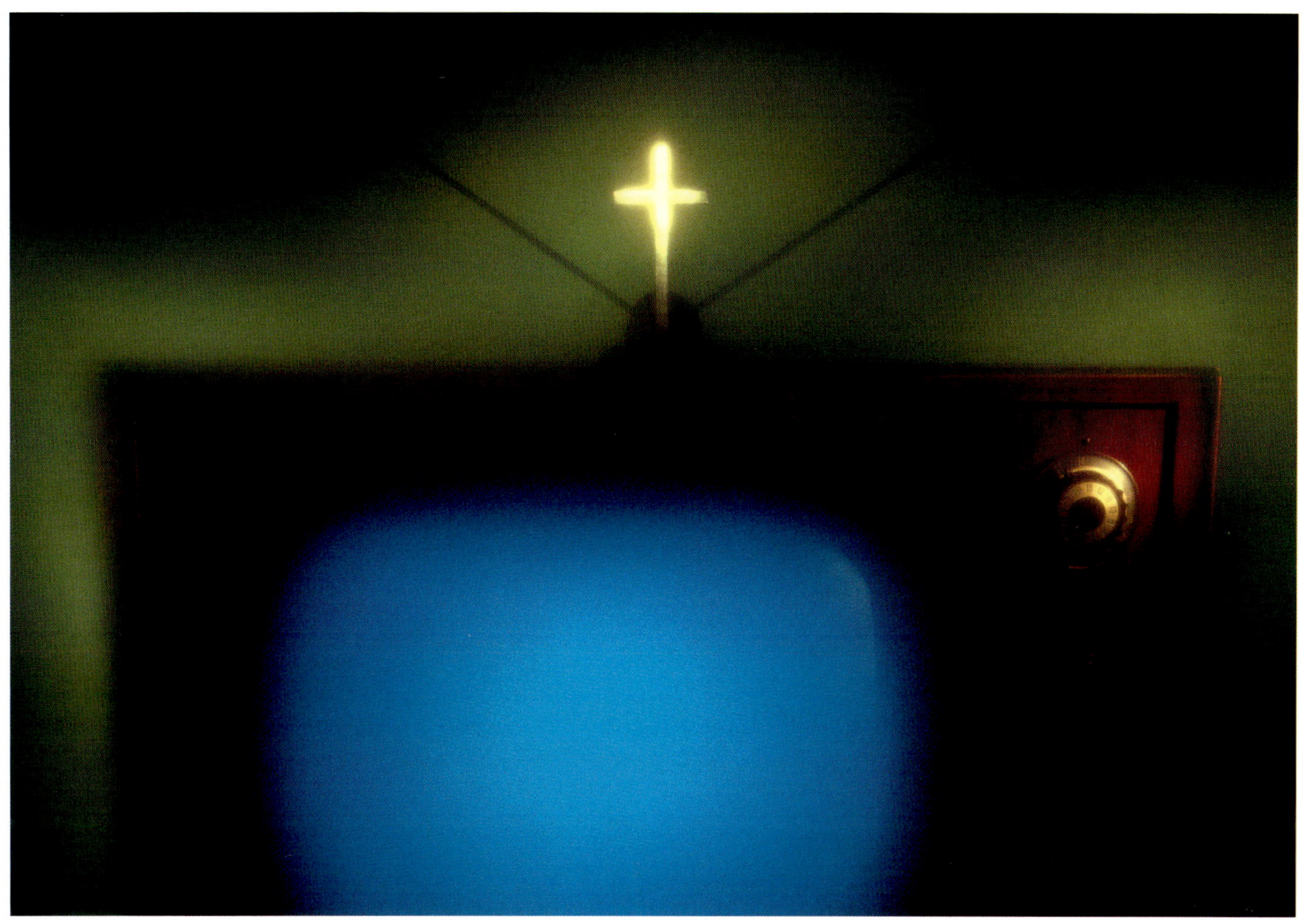

Mark Wiens

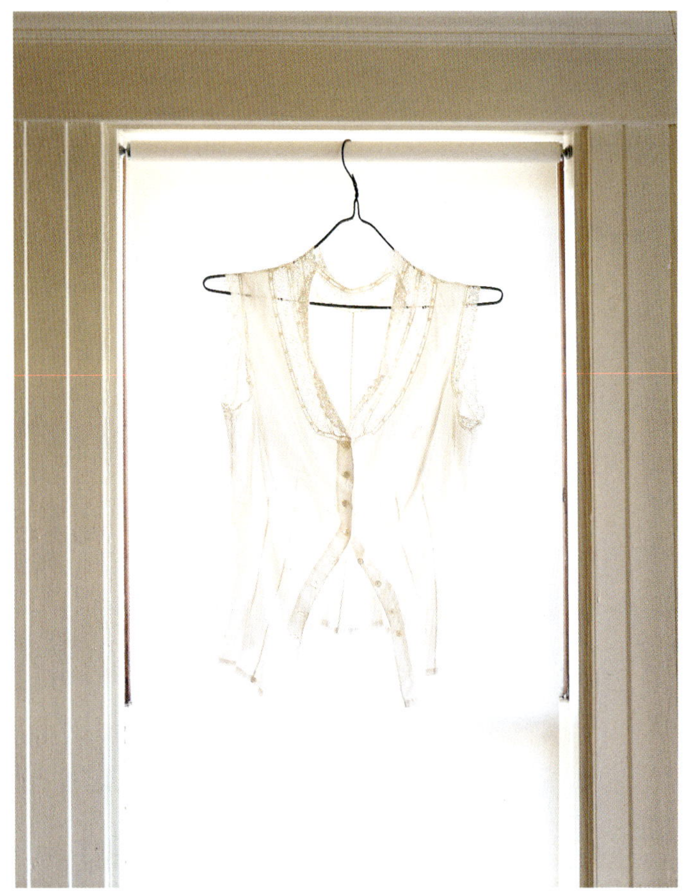

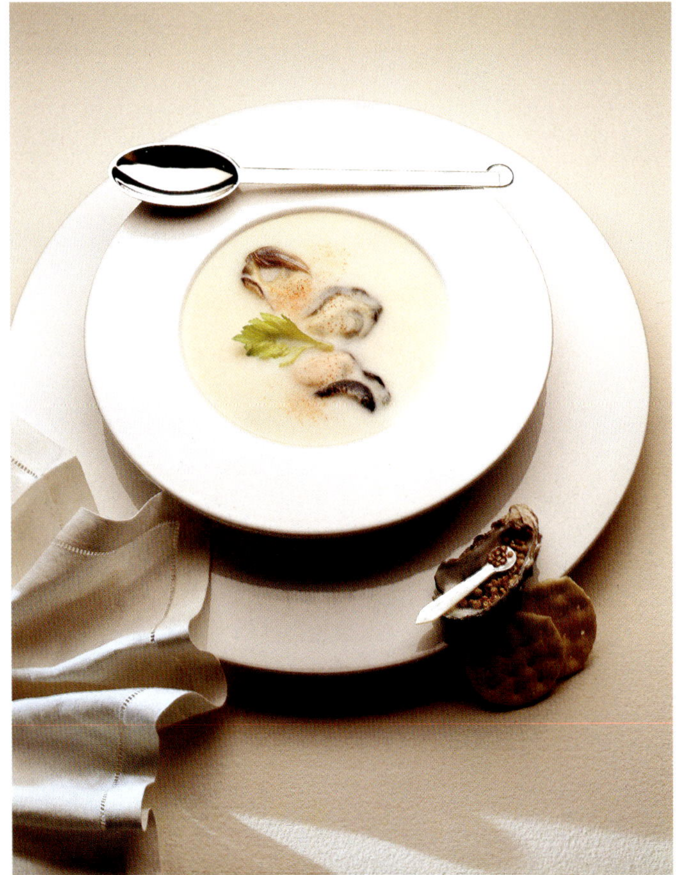

HOLLY STEWART

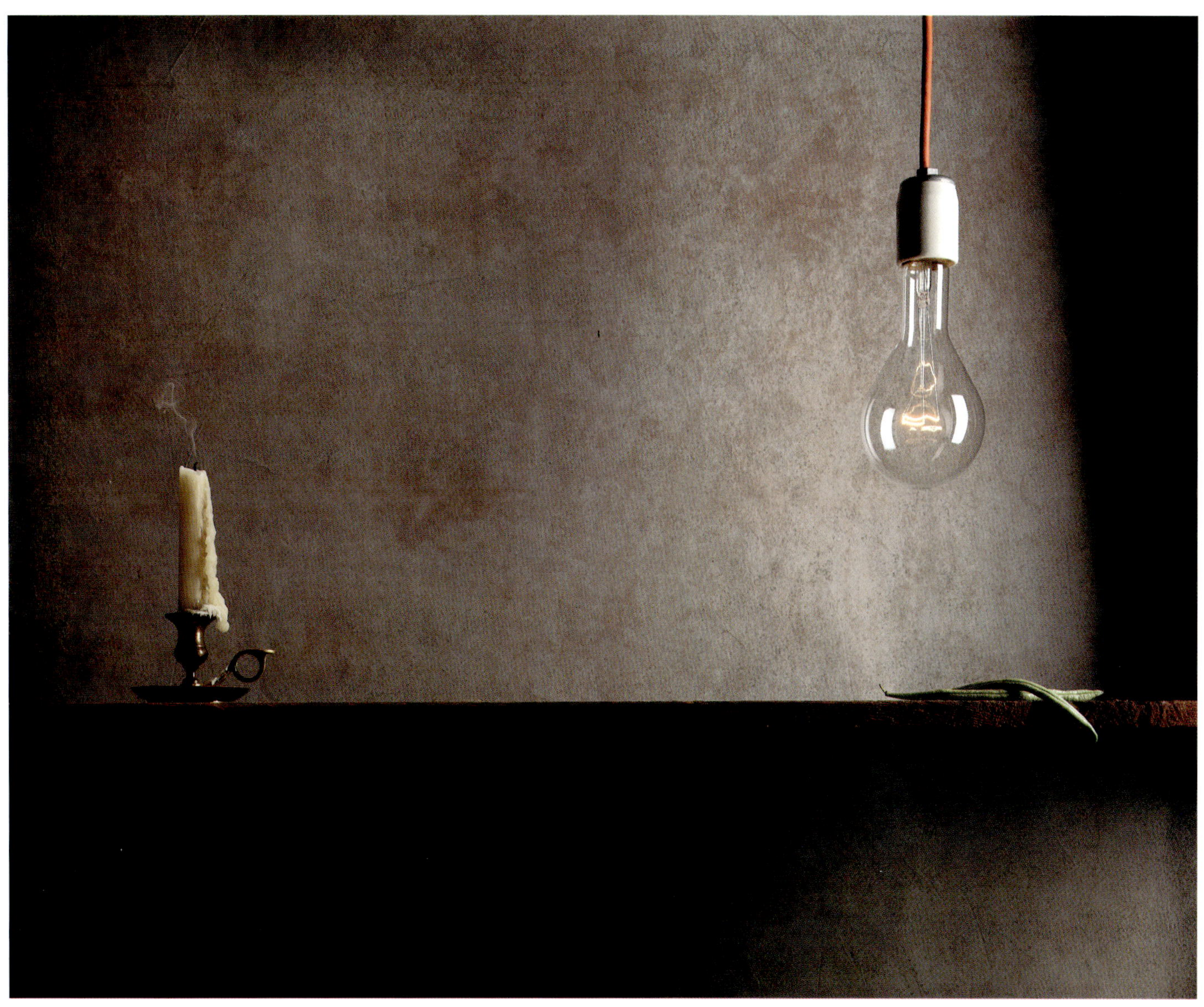

Terry Heffernan

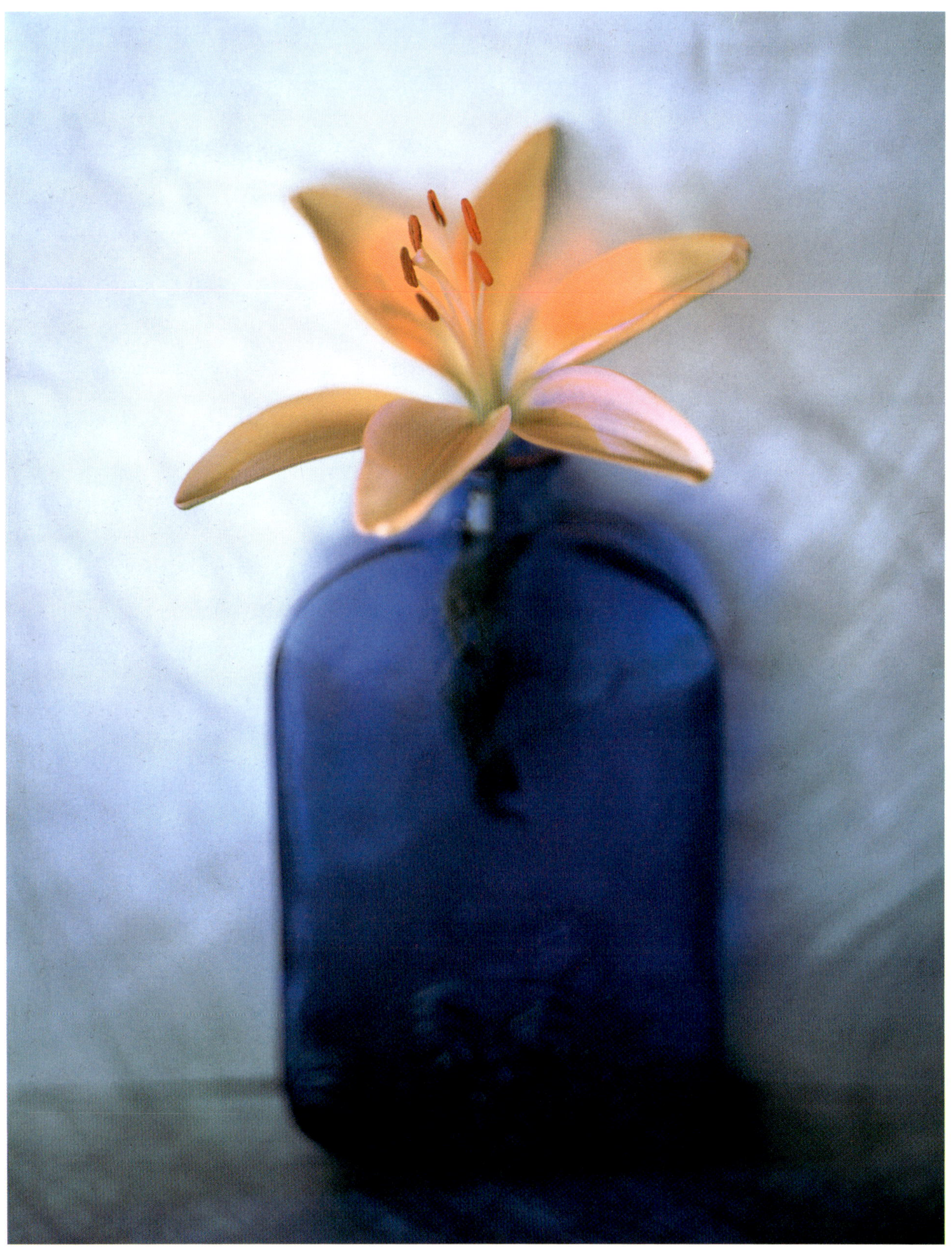

Andy Livesey

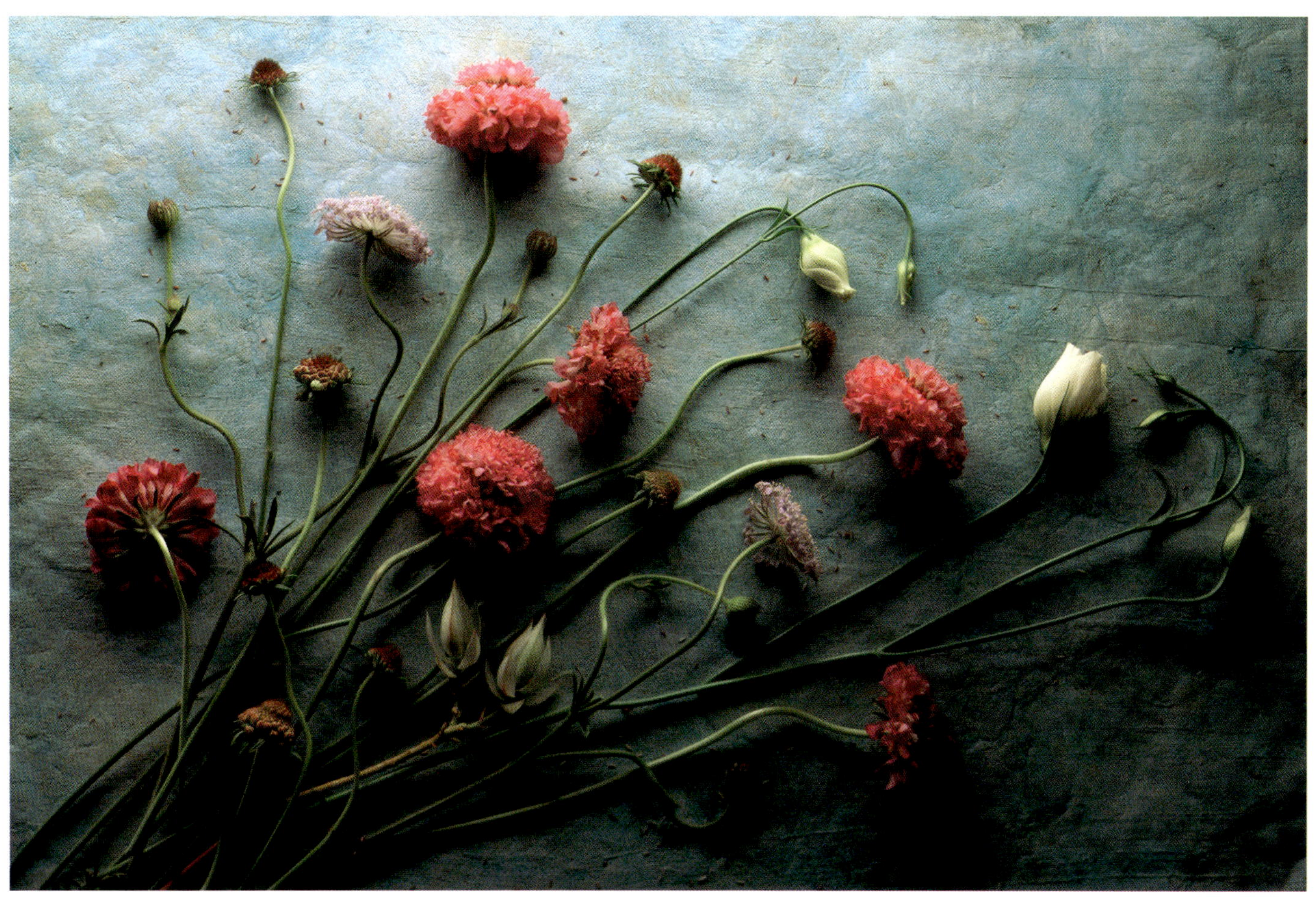

Parish Kohanim

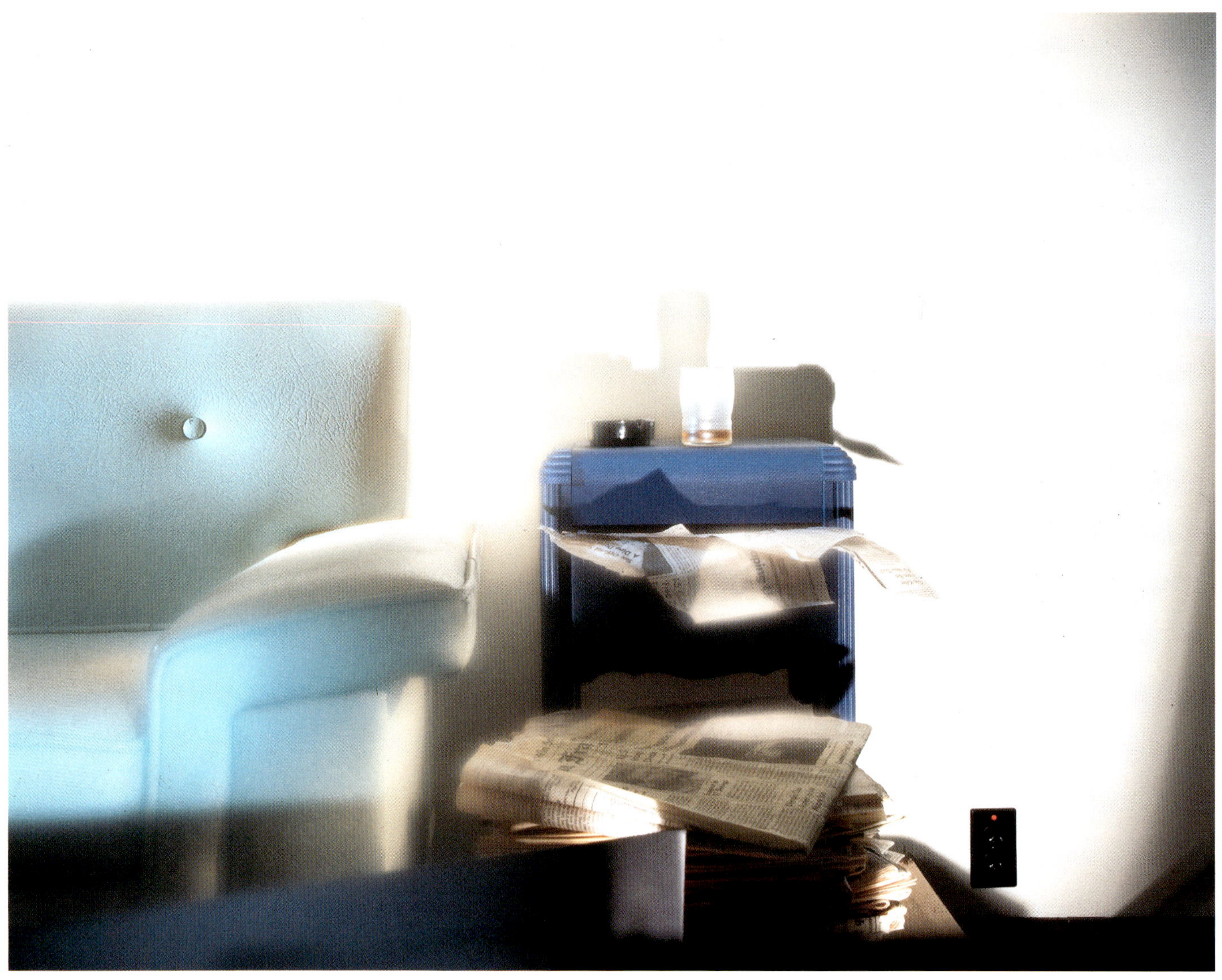

Dale E. McNeely Jr.

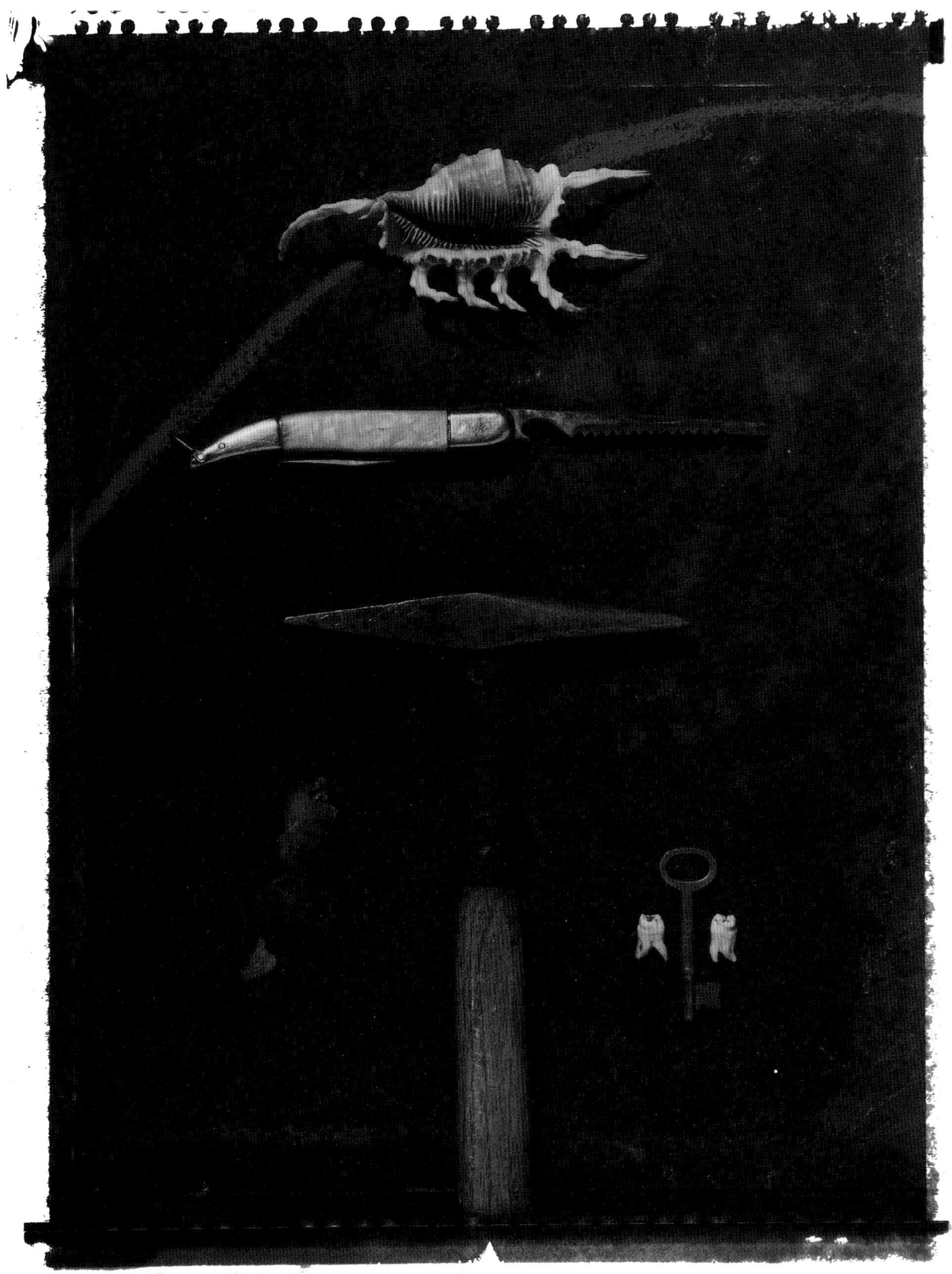

Ron Baxter Smith

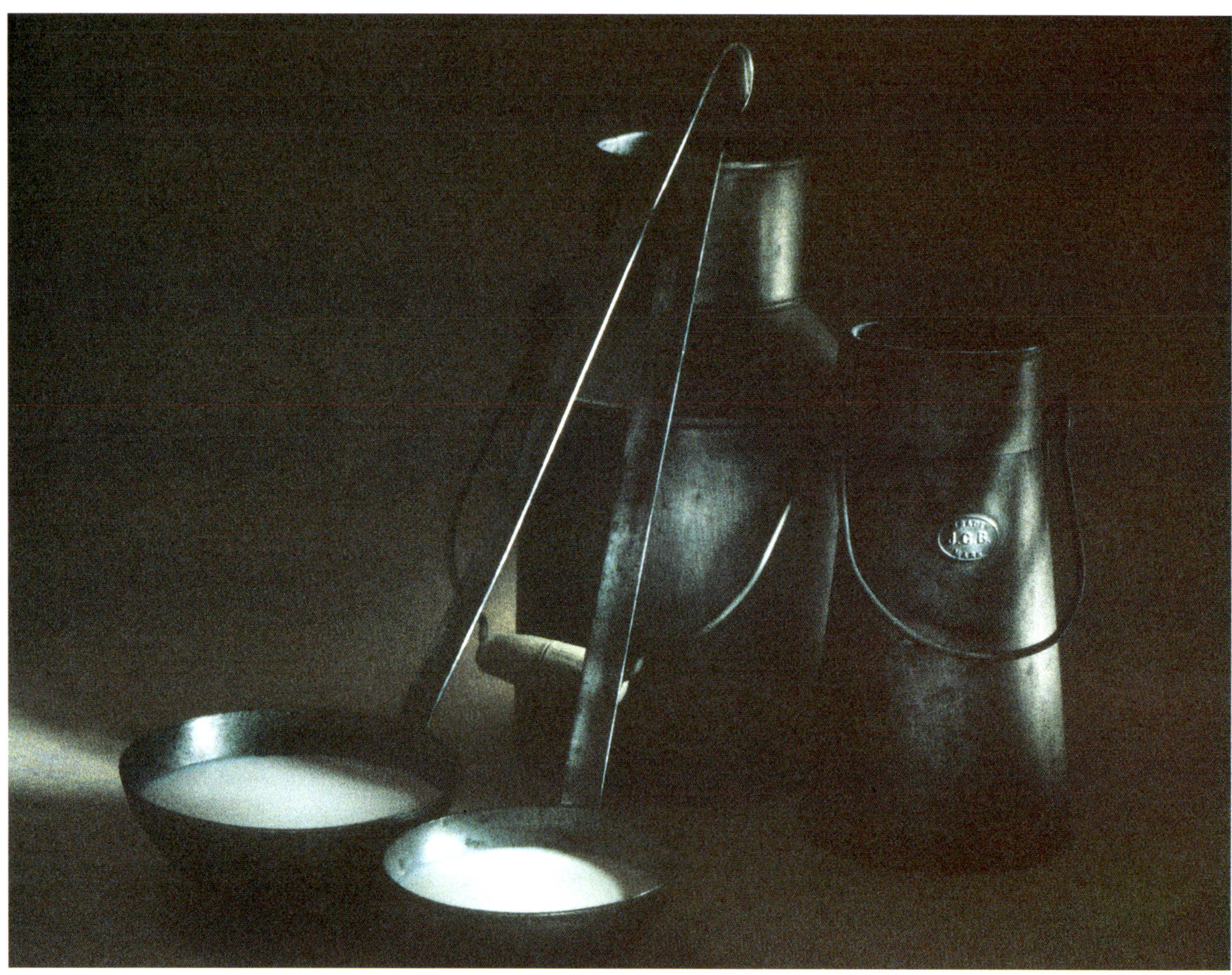

Gerrit Buntrock

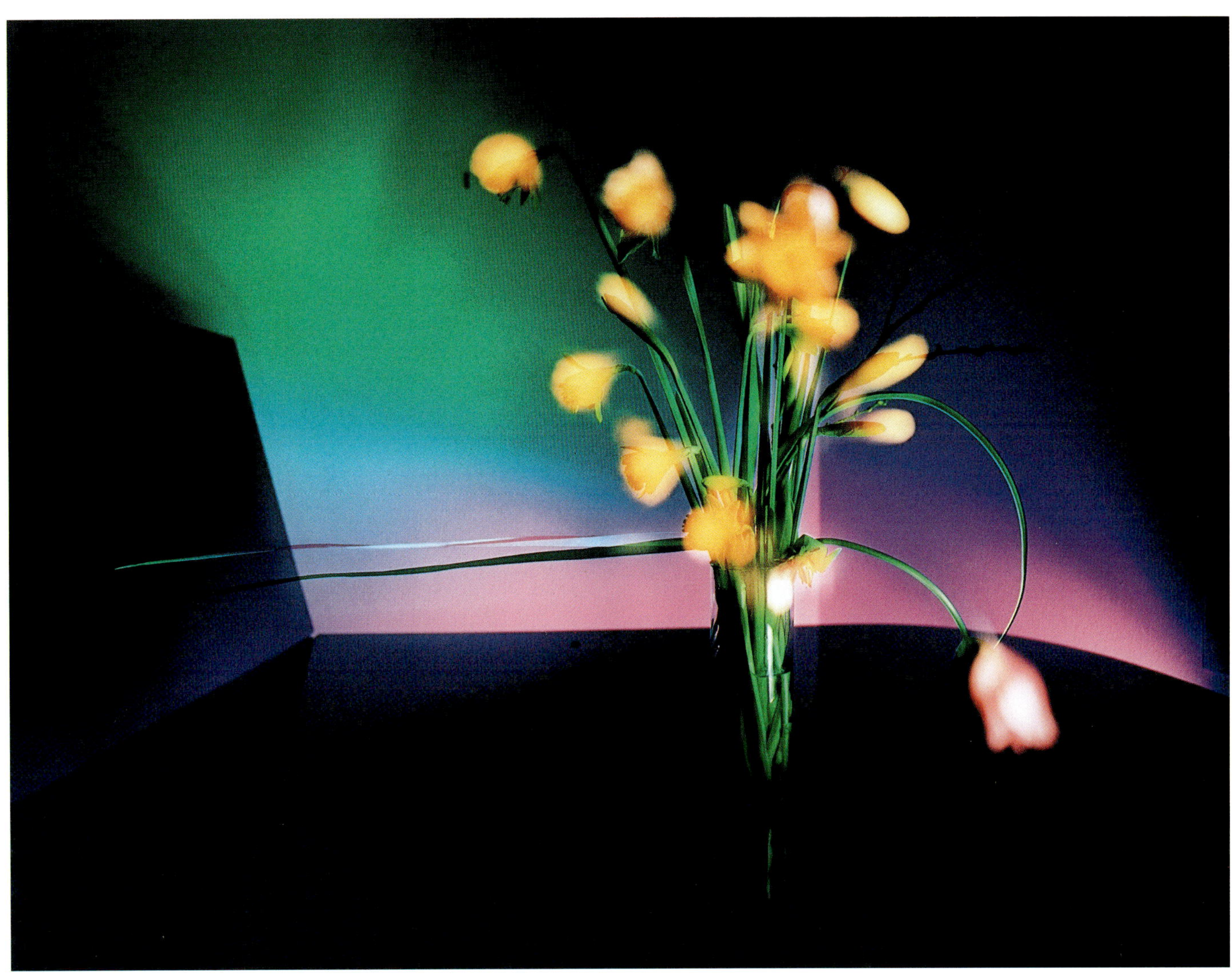

Michael Northrup

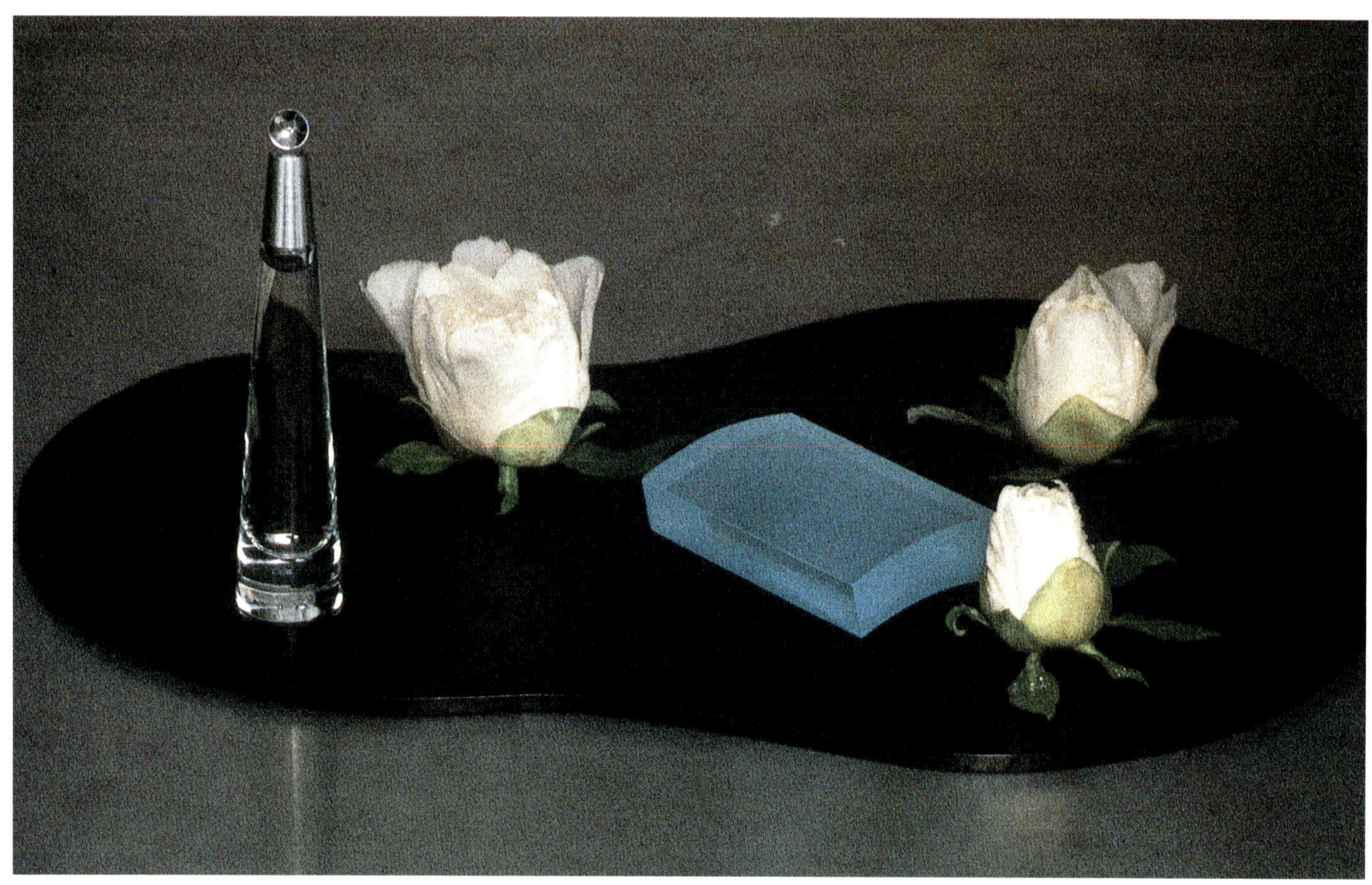

Sheila Metzner

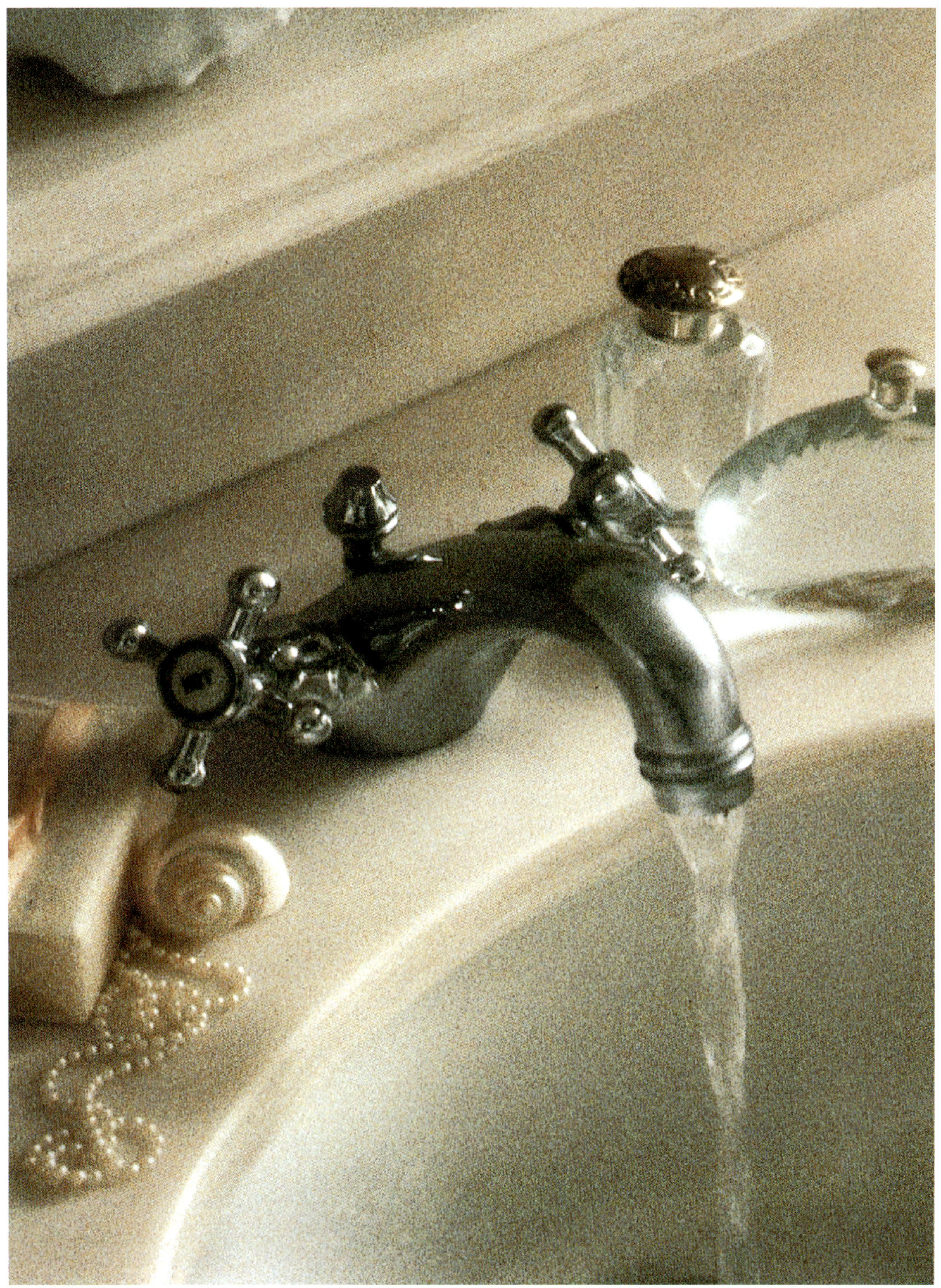

Jennifer Baumann

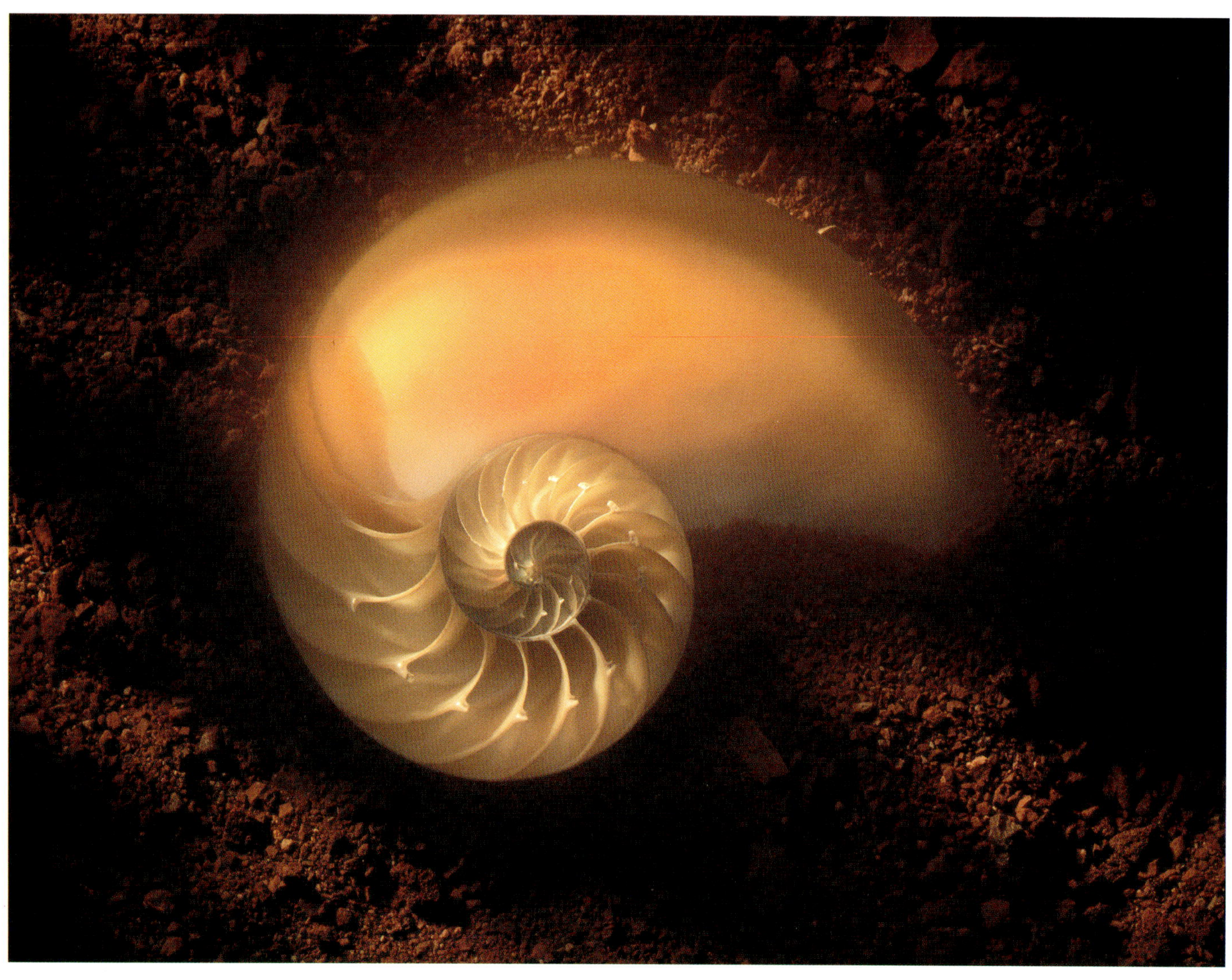

Jim DiVitale

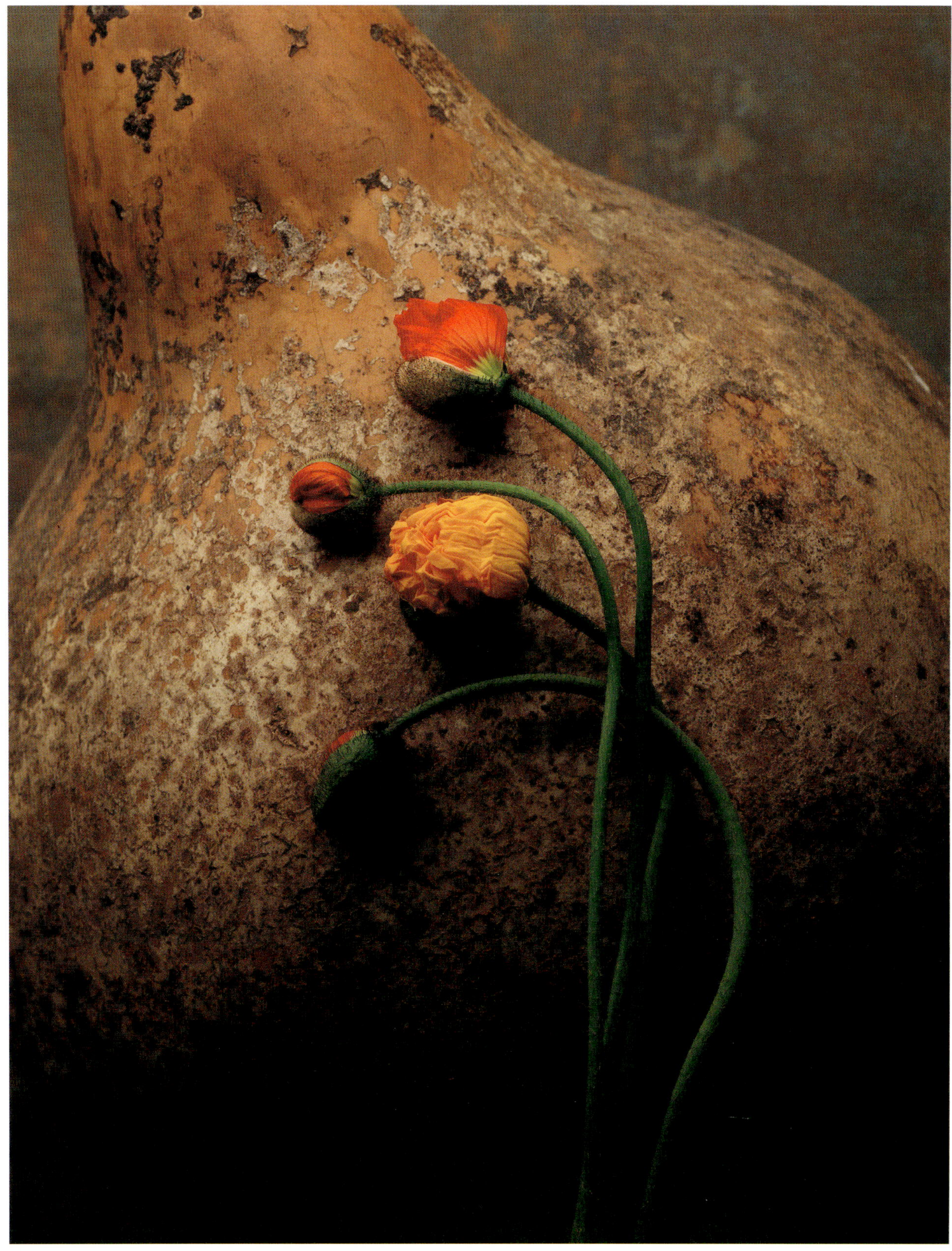

John Payne

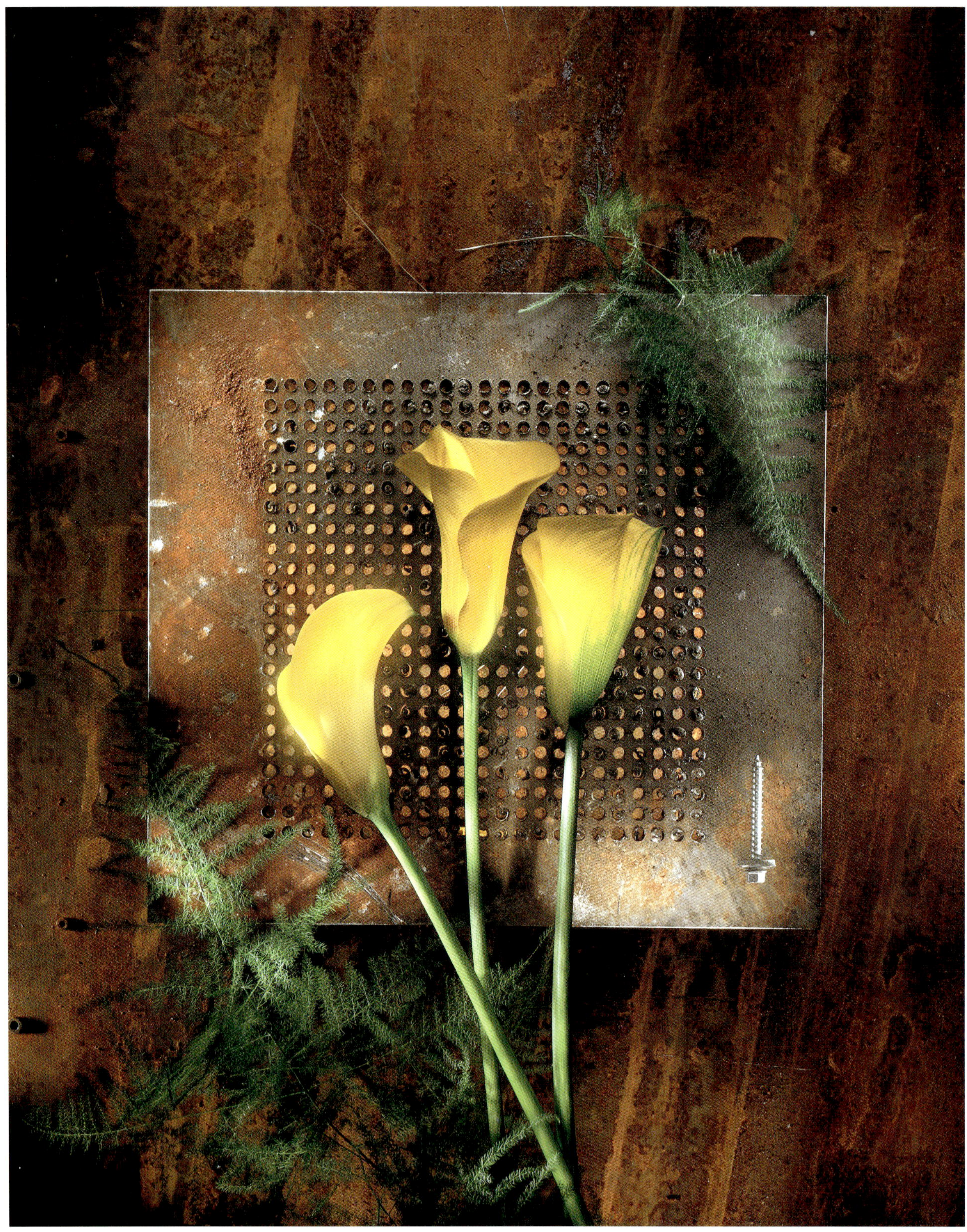

Alexander Bayer

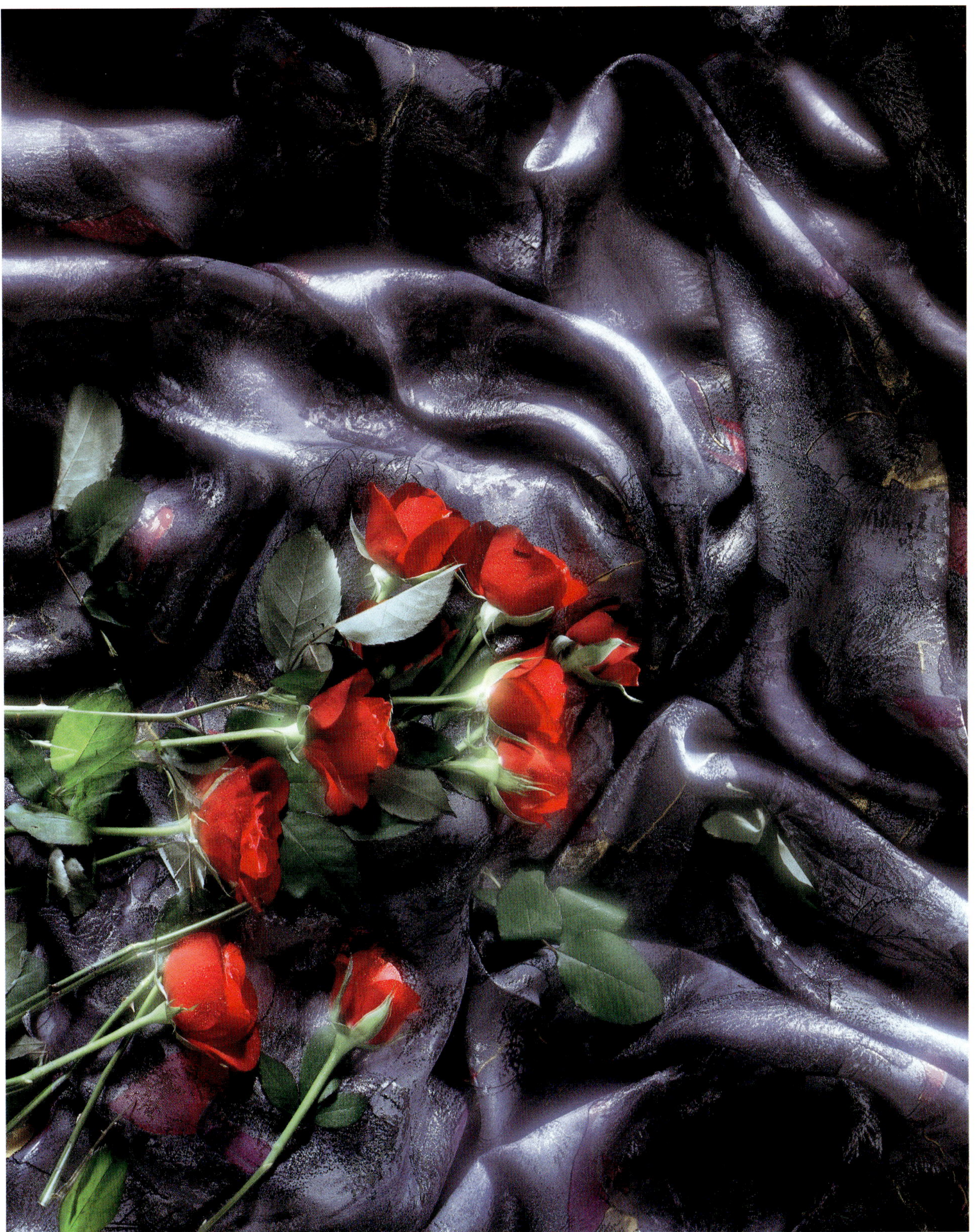

Alexander Bayer

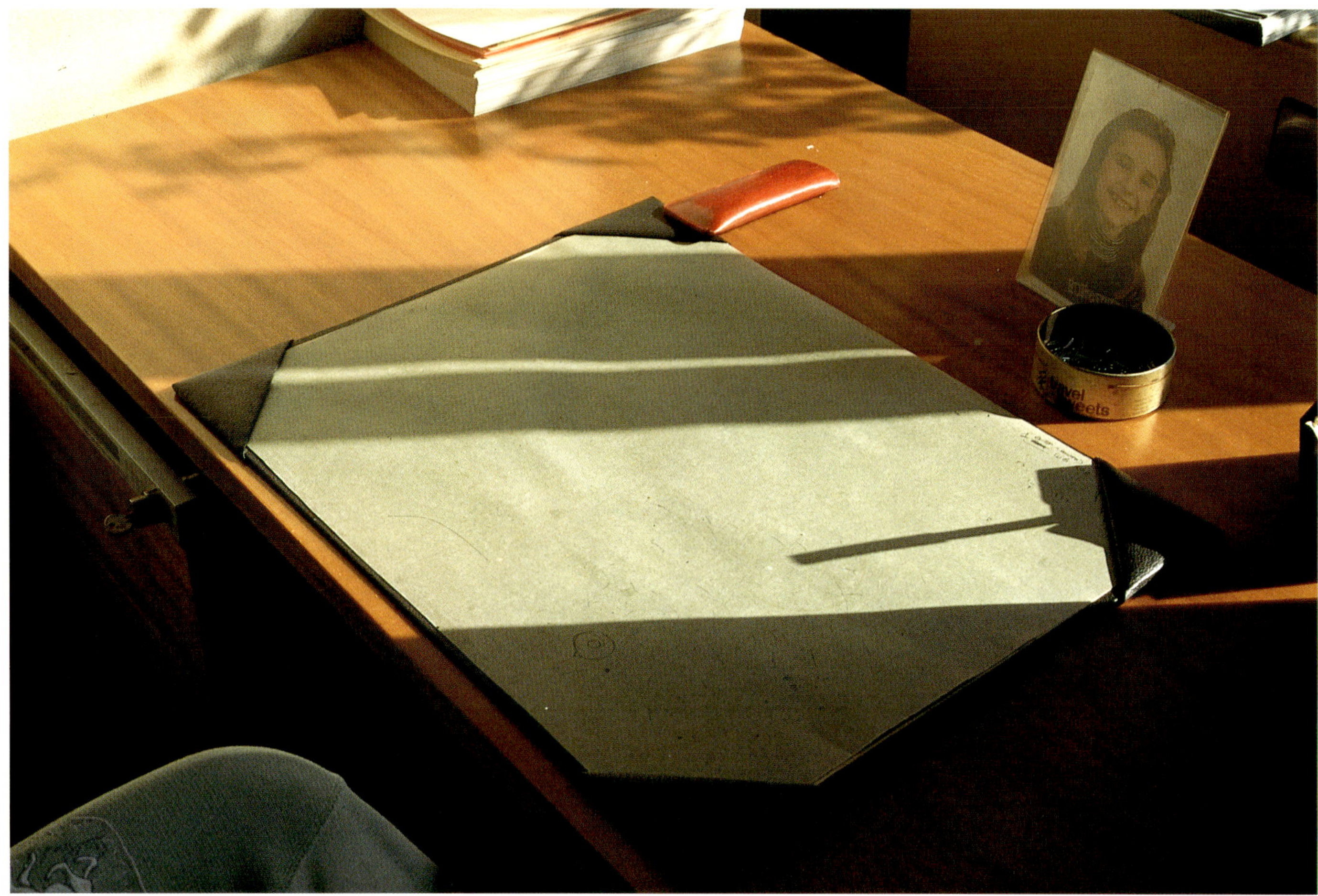

Christian Vogt

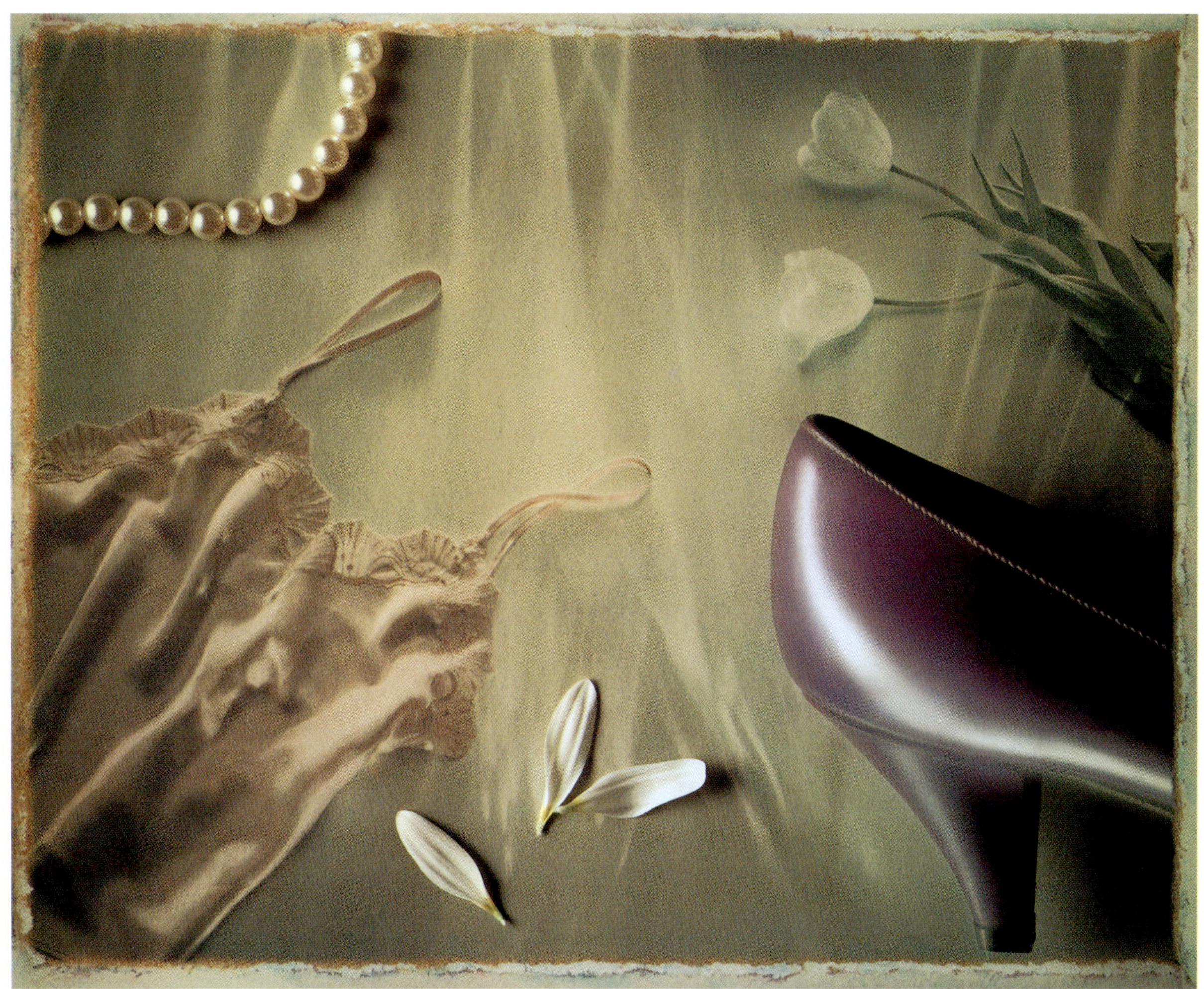

Craig Van Der Lende

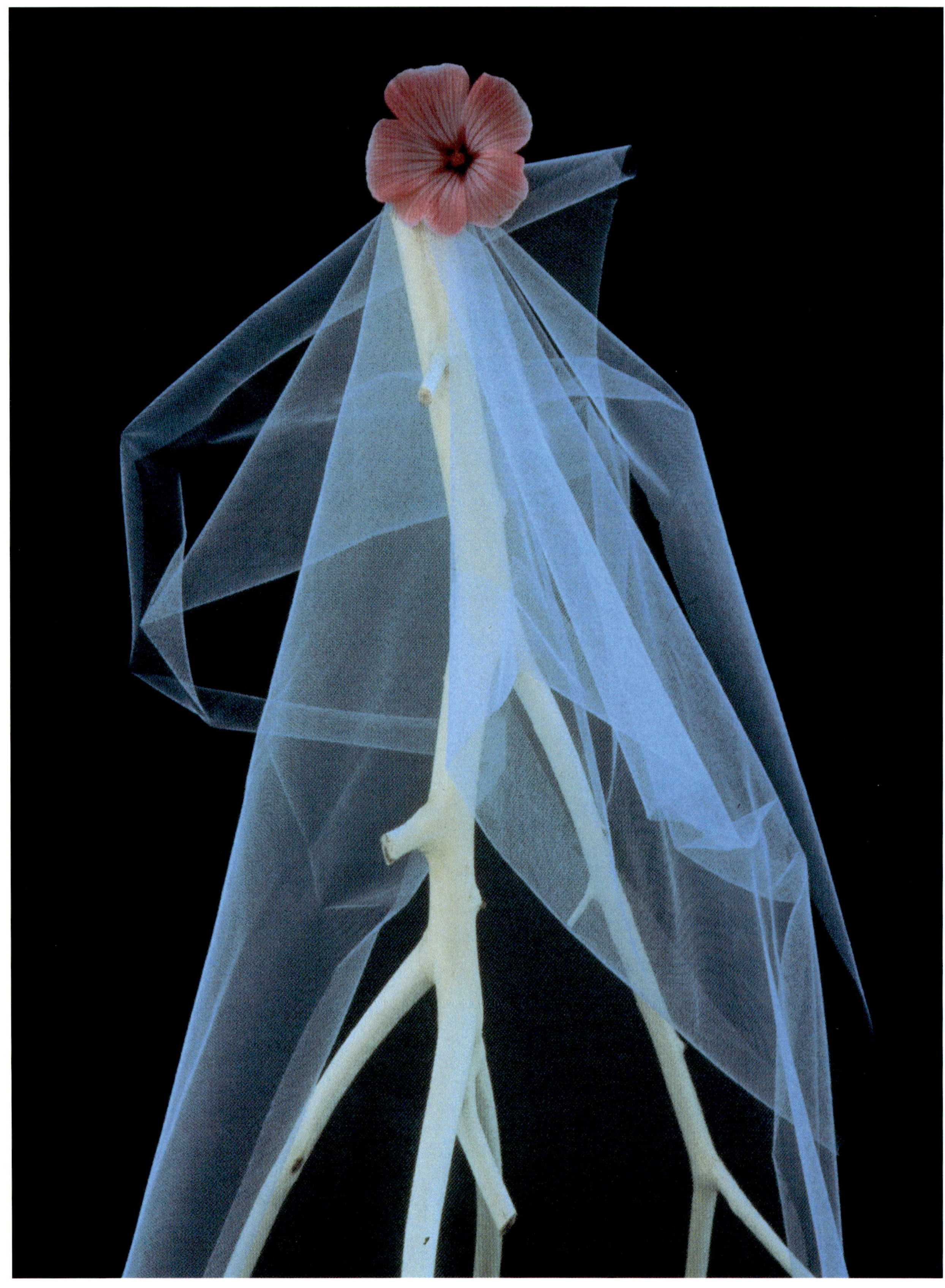

Alfons Iseli

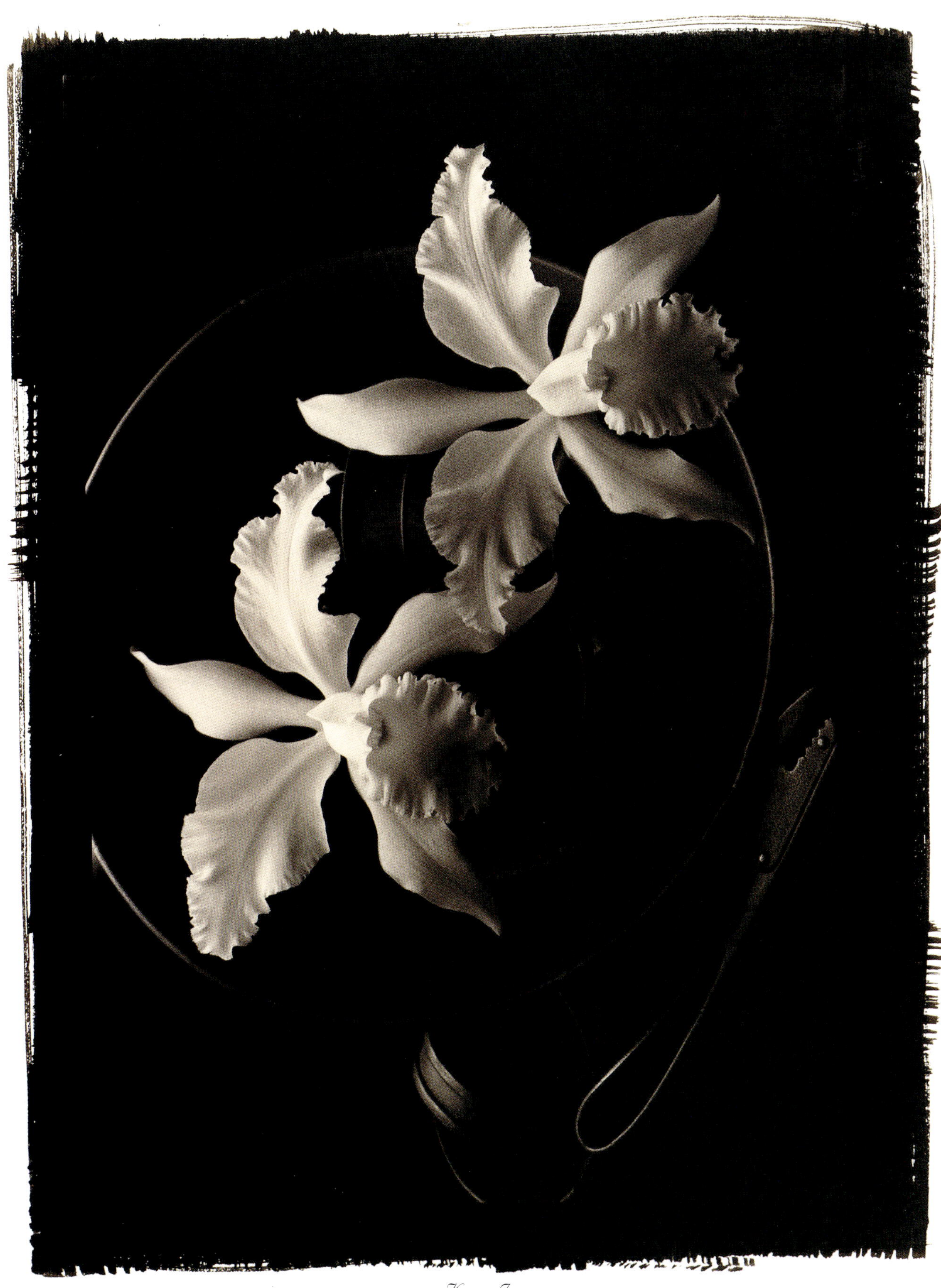

Kenro Izu

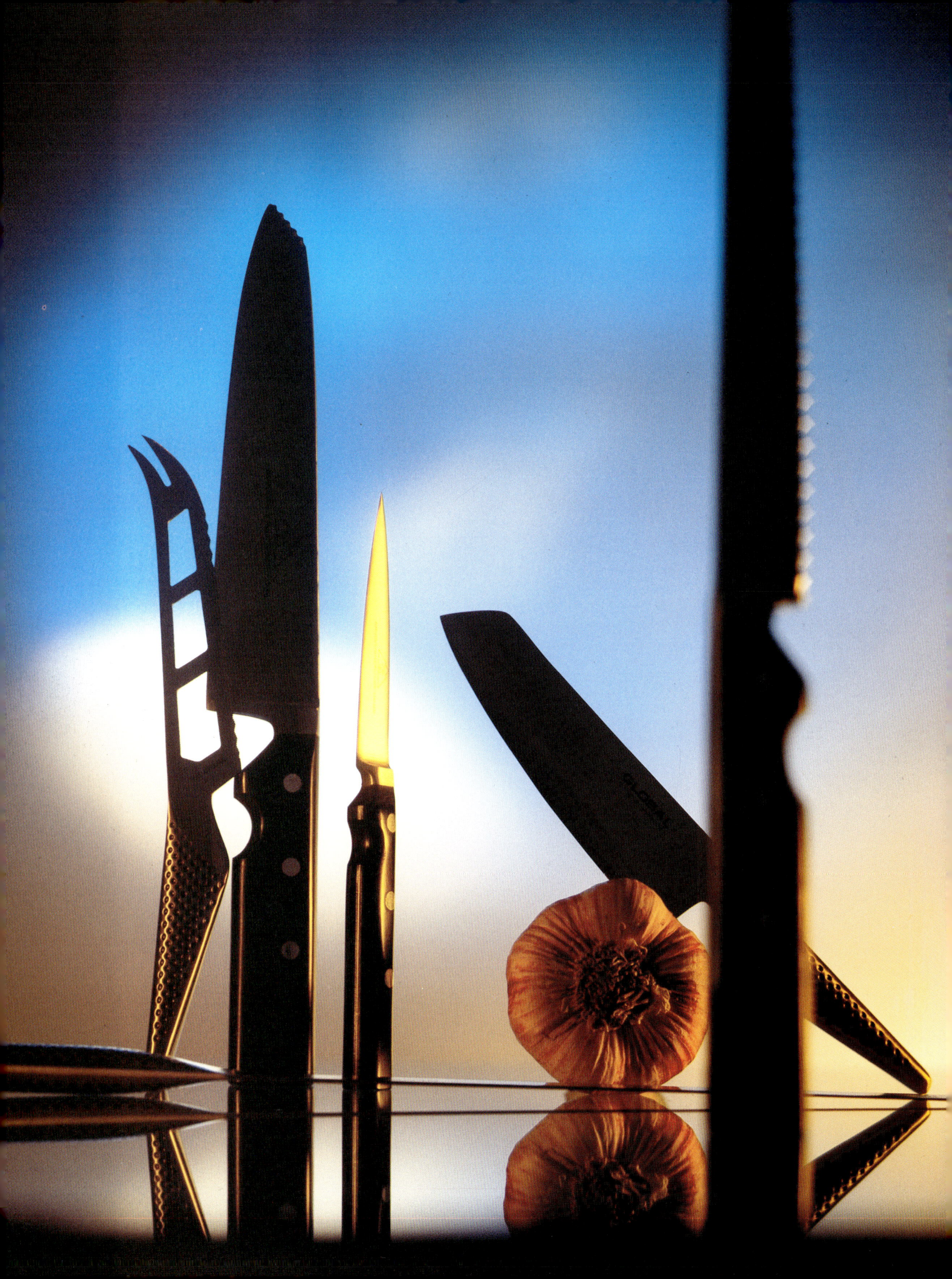

FOOD

LEBENSMITTEL

CUISINE

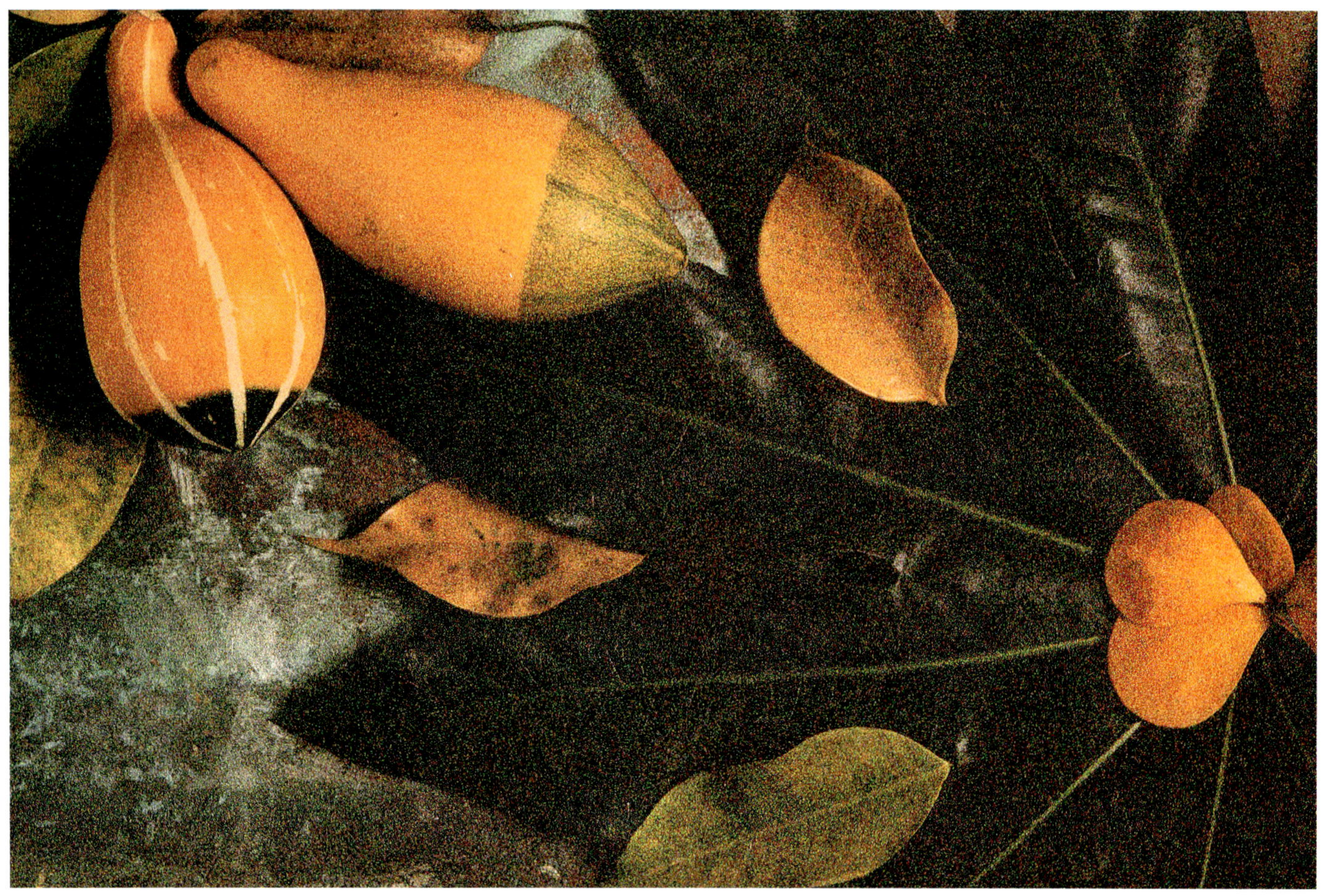

Preceeding Spread: Luzia Ellert / Above: Christiane Marek

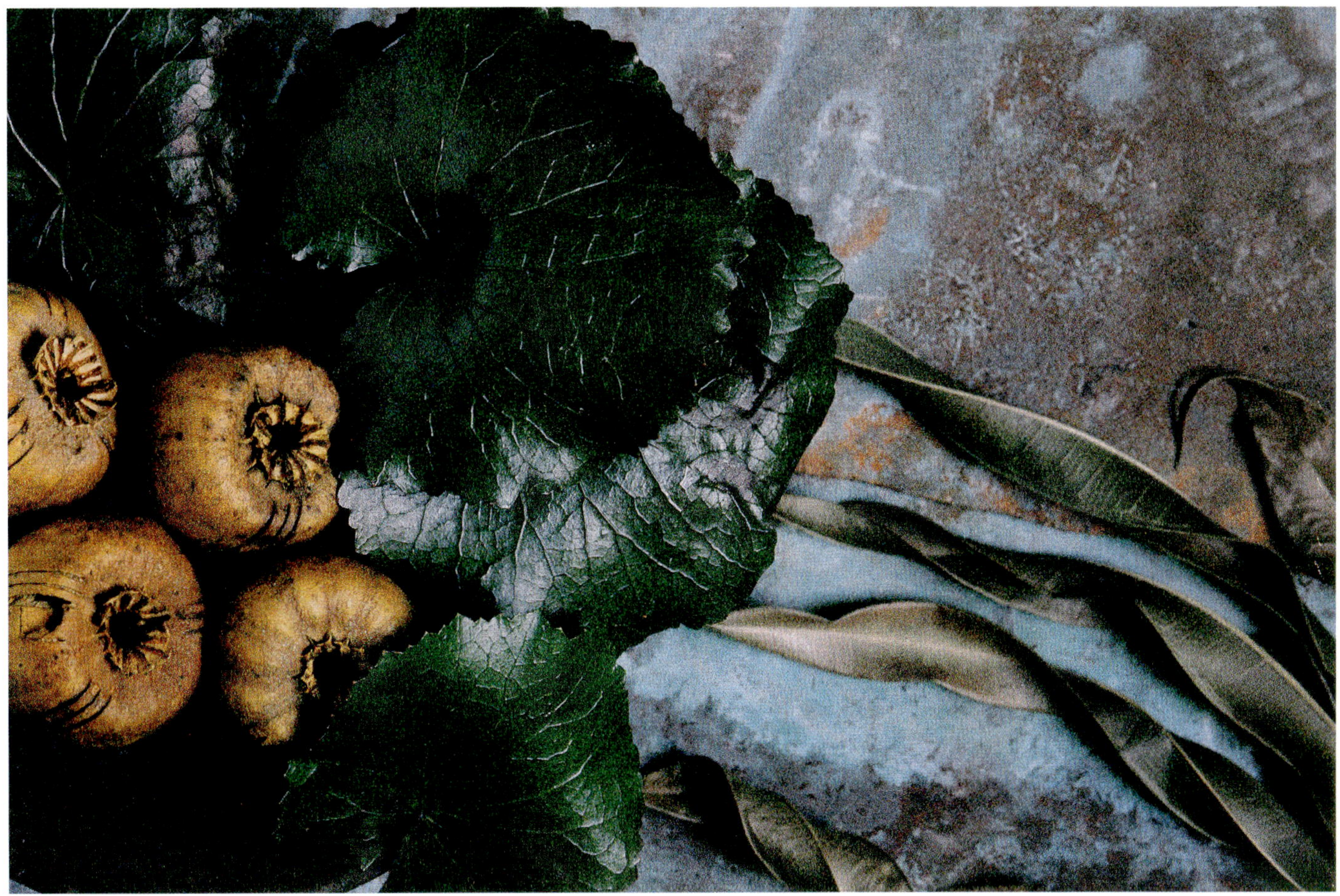

Christiane Marek

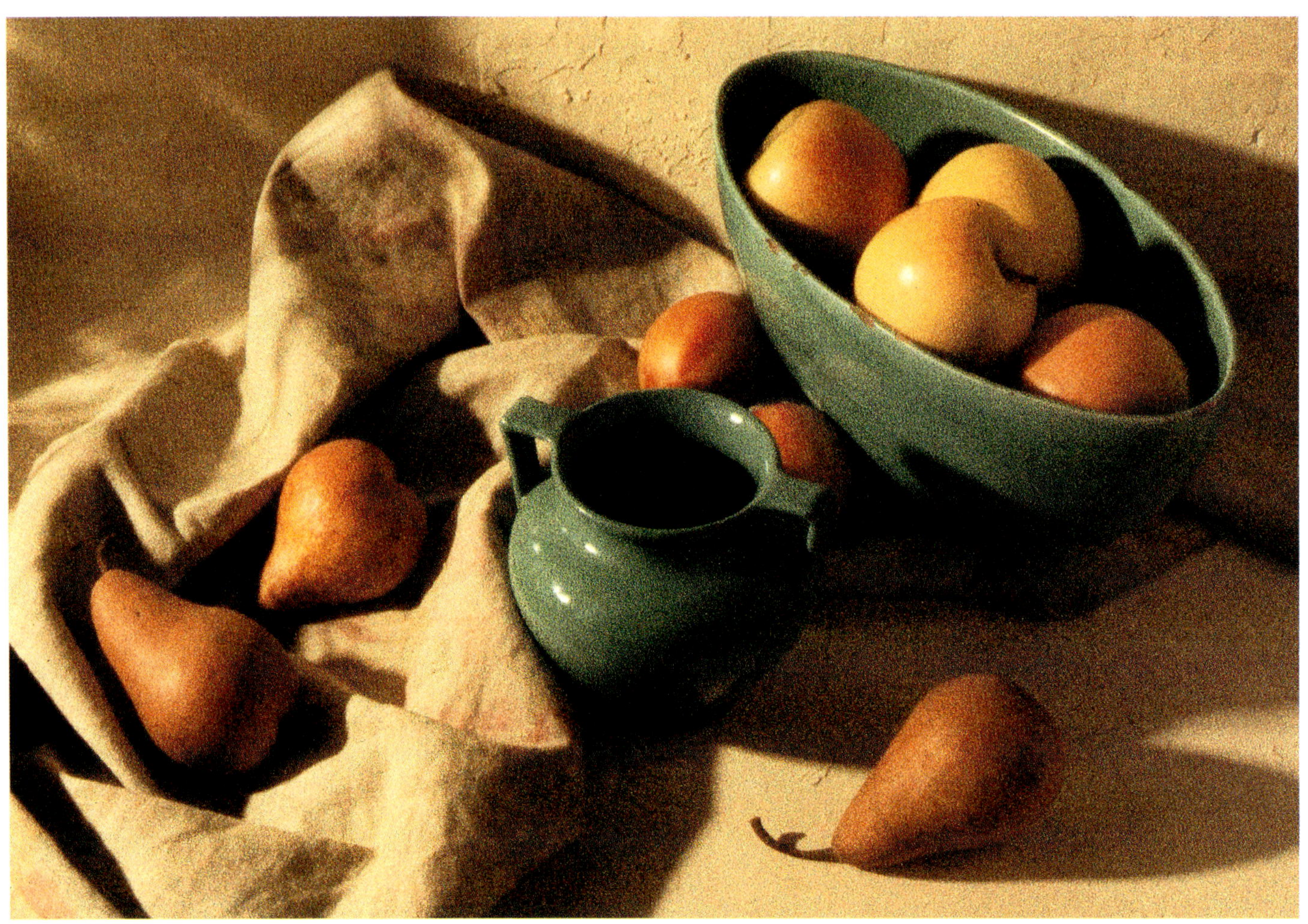

Carol Kaplan

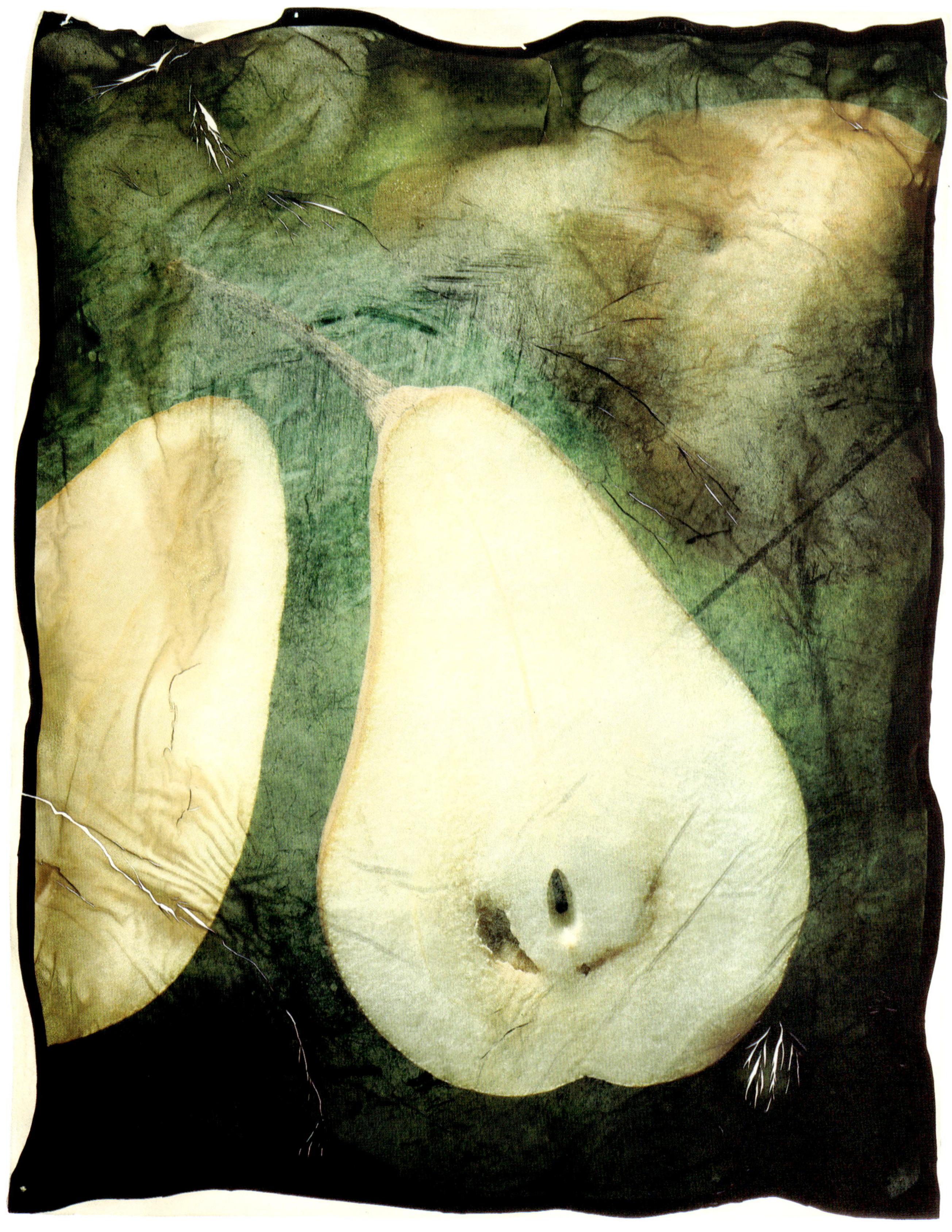

Rahmesh Amruth

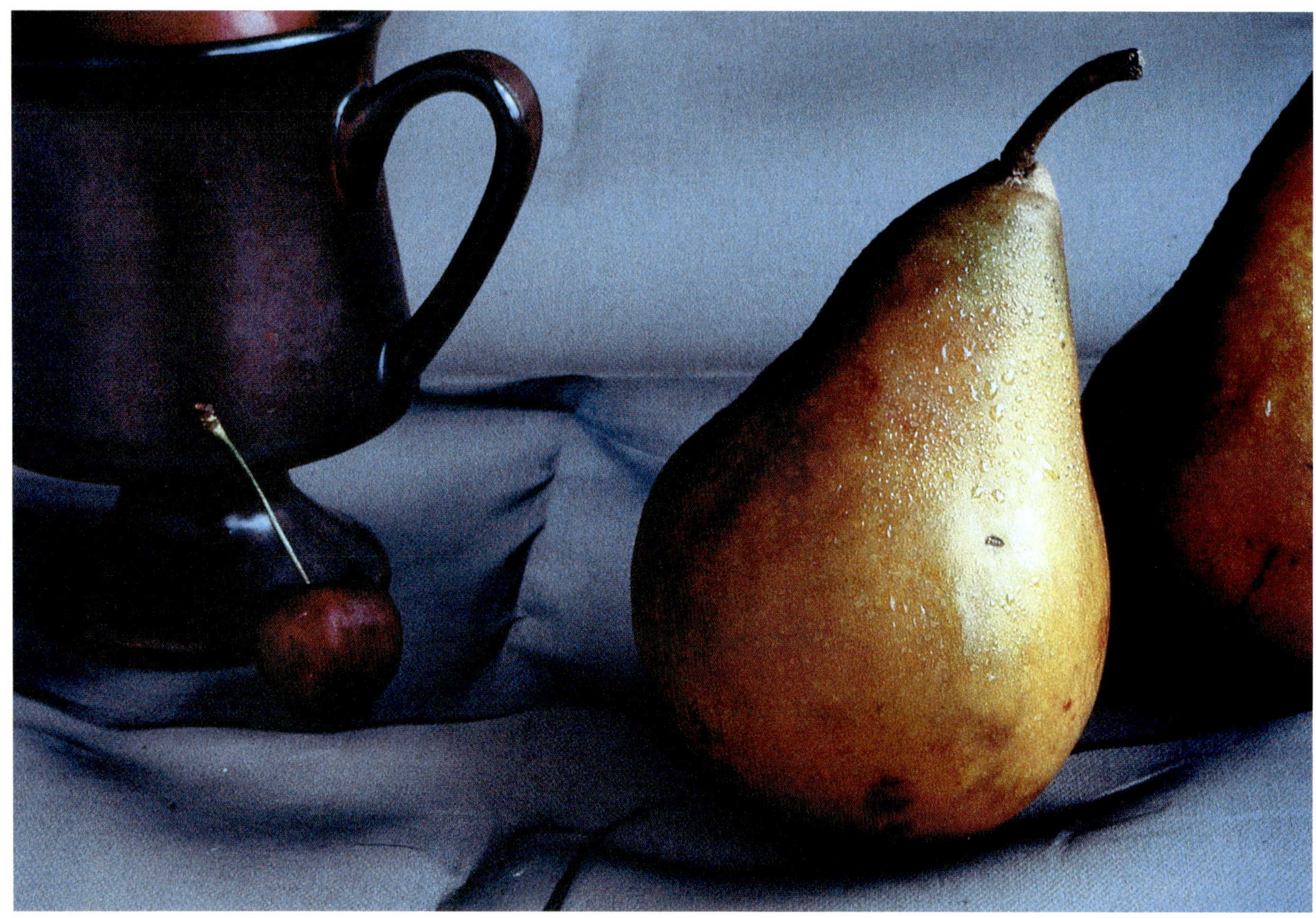

André Baranowski

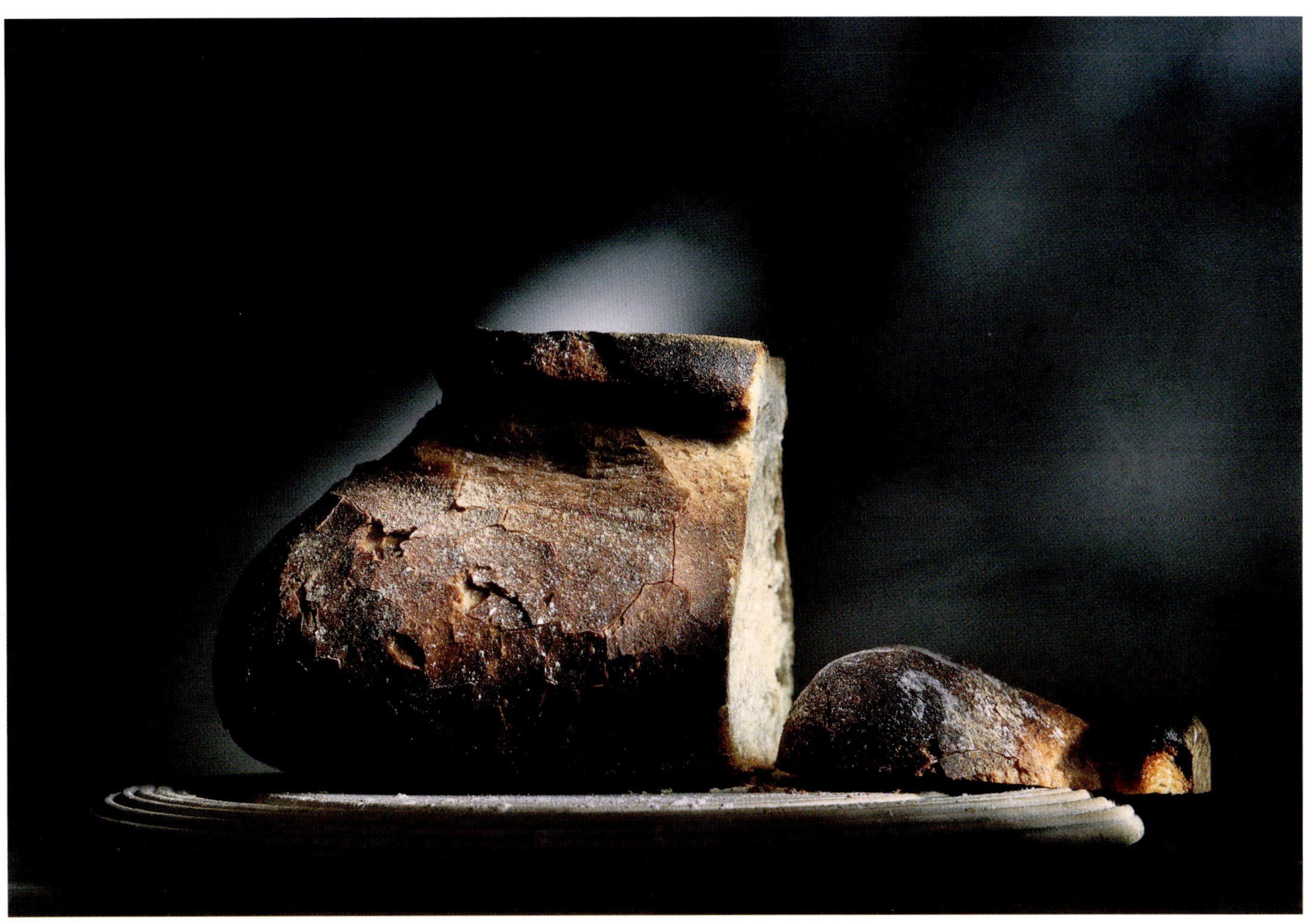

Gerrit Buntrock

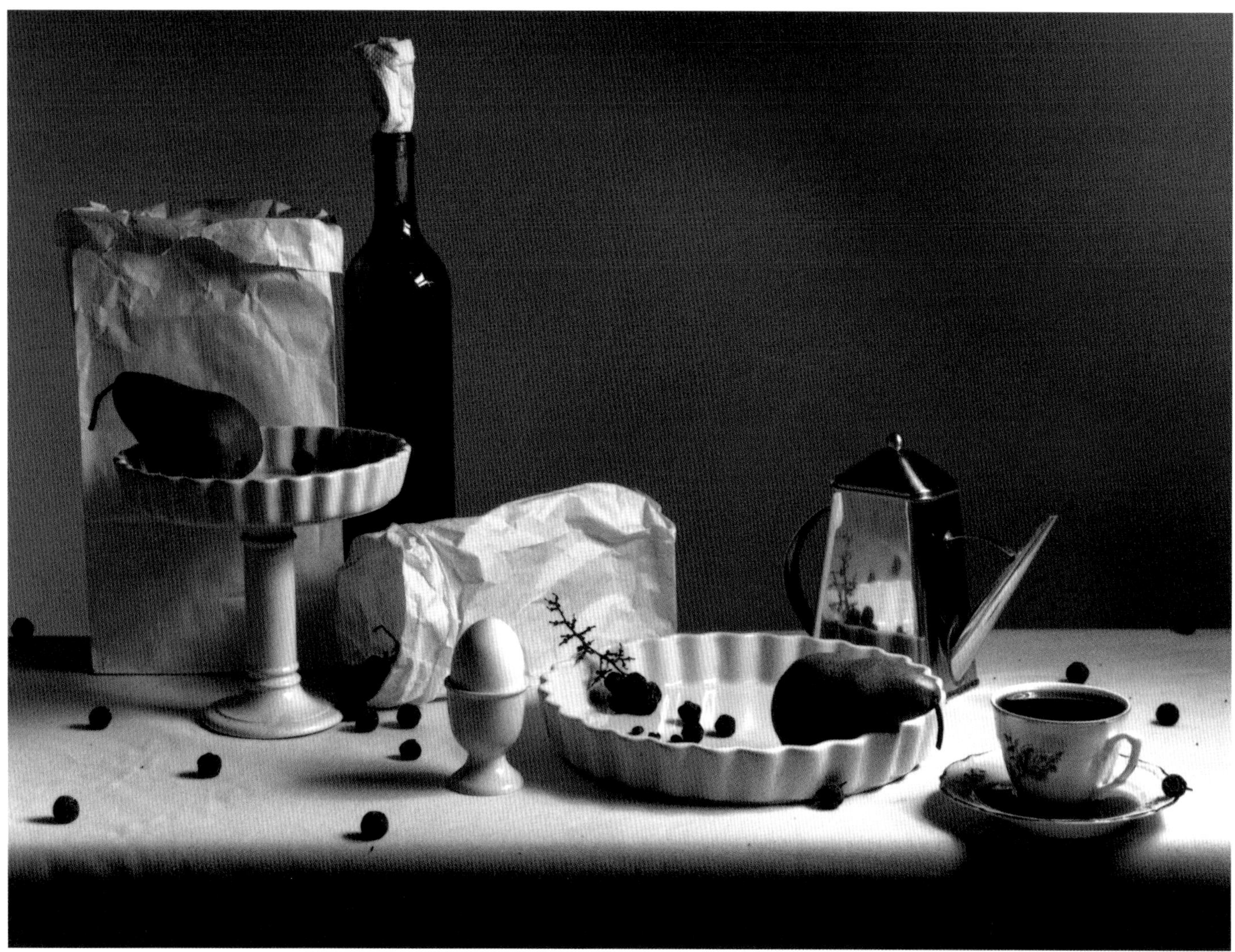

André Baranowski

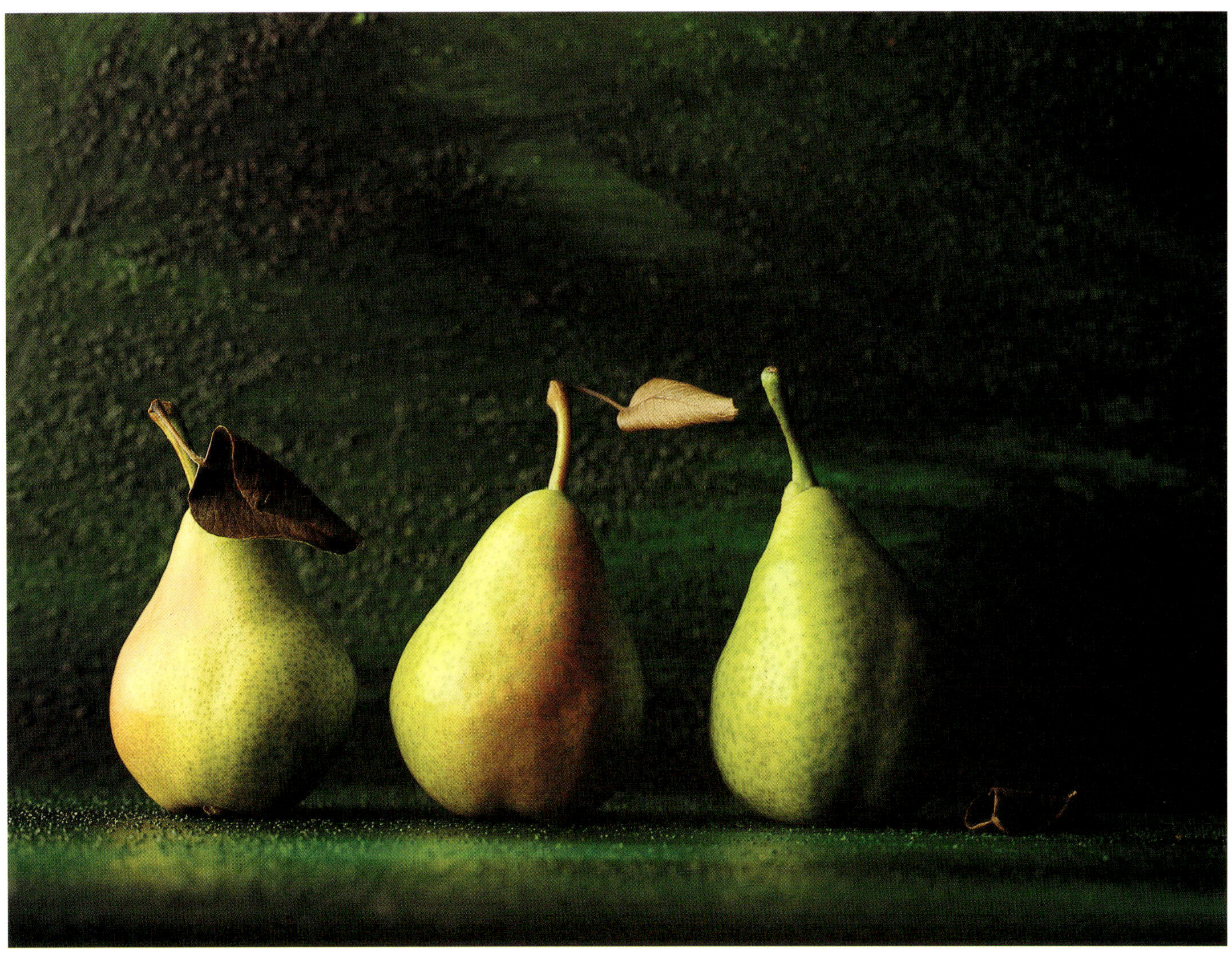

Michael Vissing

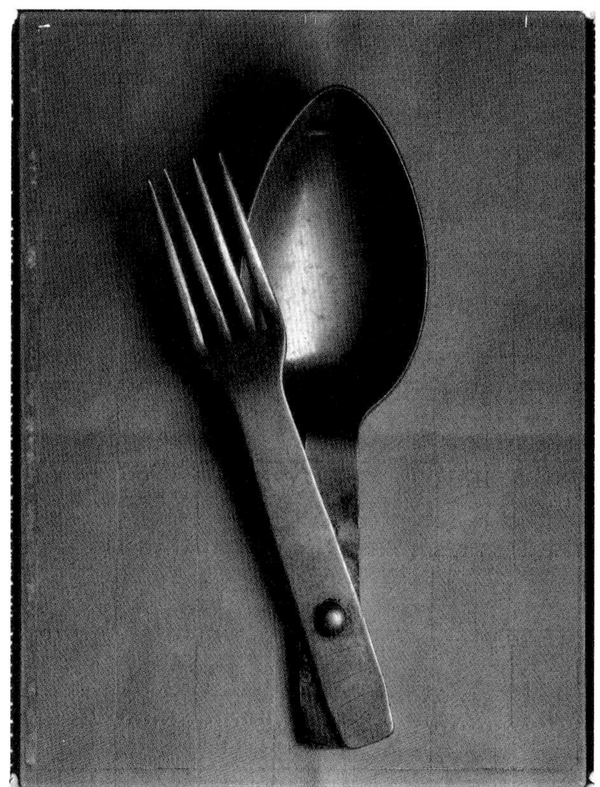

Christian Von Alvensleben

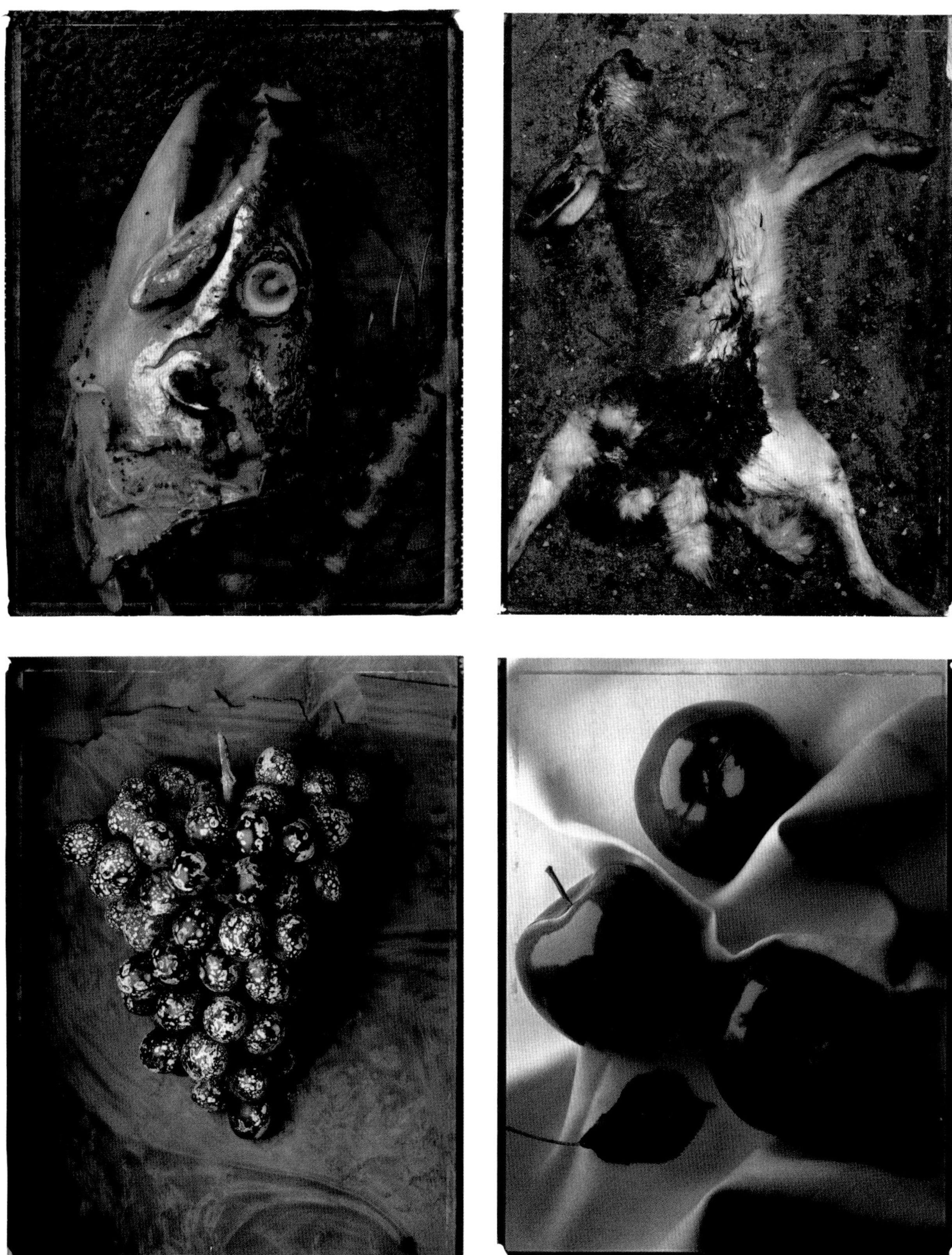

Christian Von Alvensleben

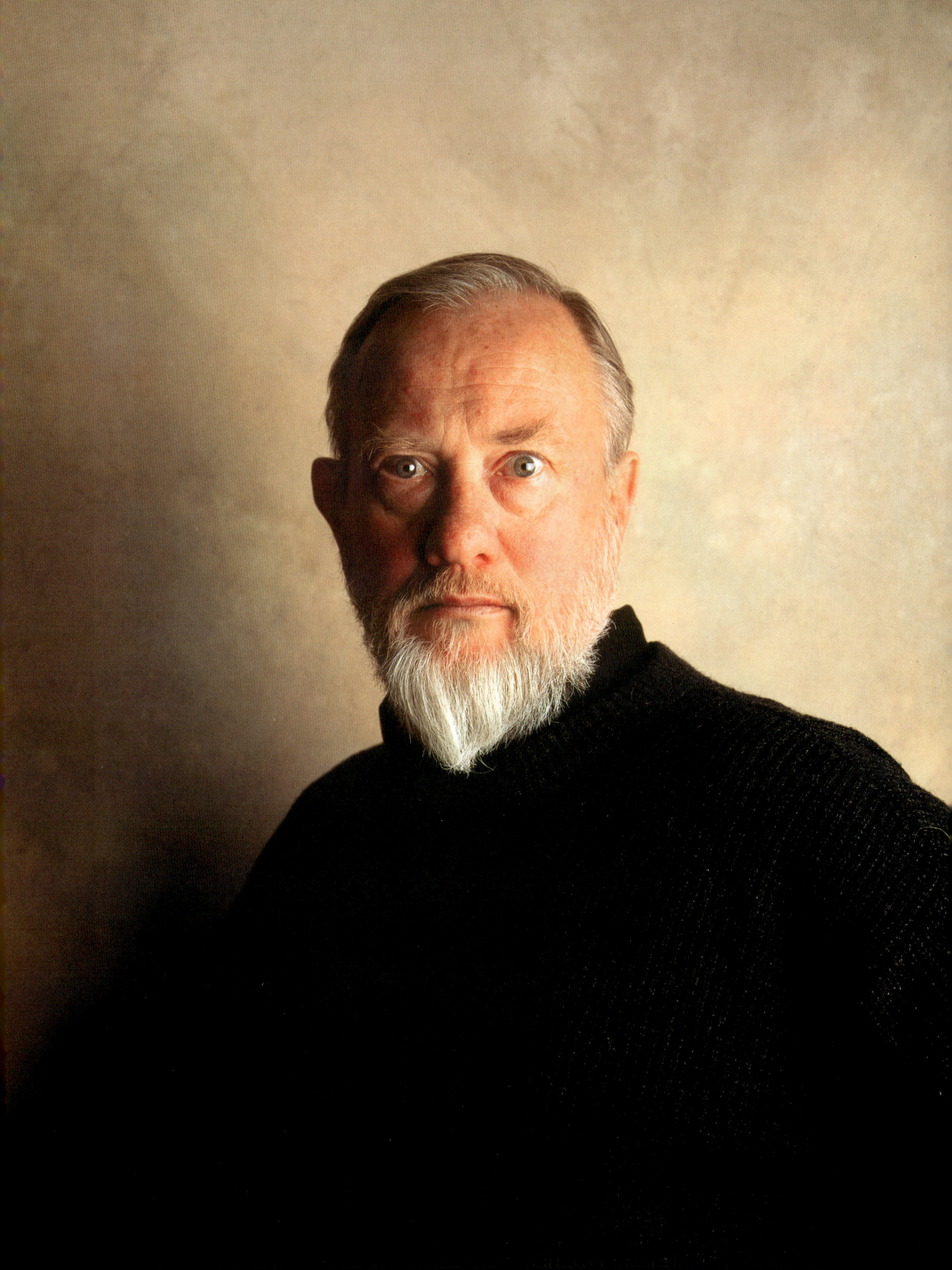

PEOPLE

MENSCHEN

PERSONNES

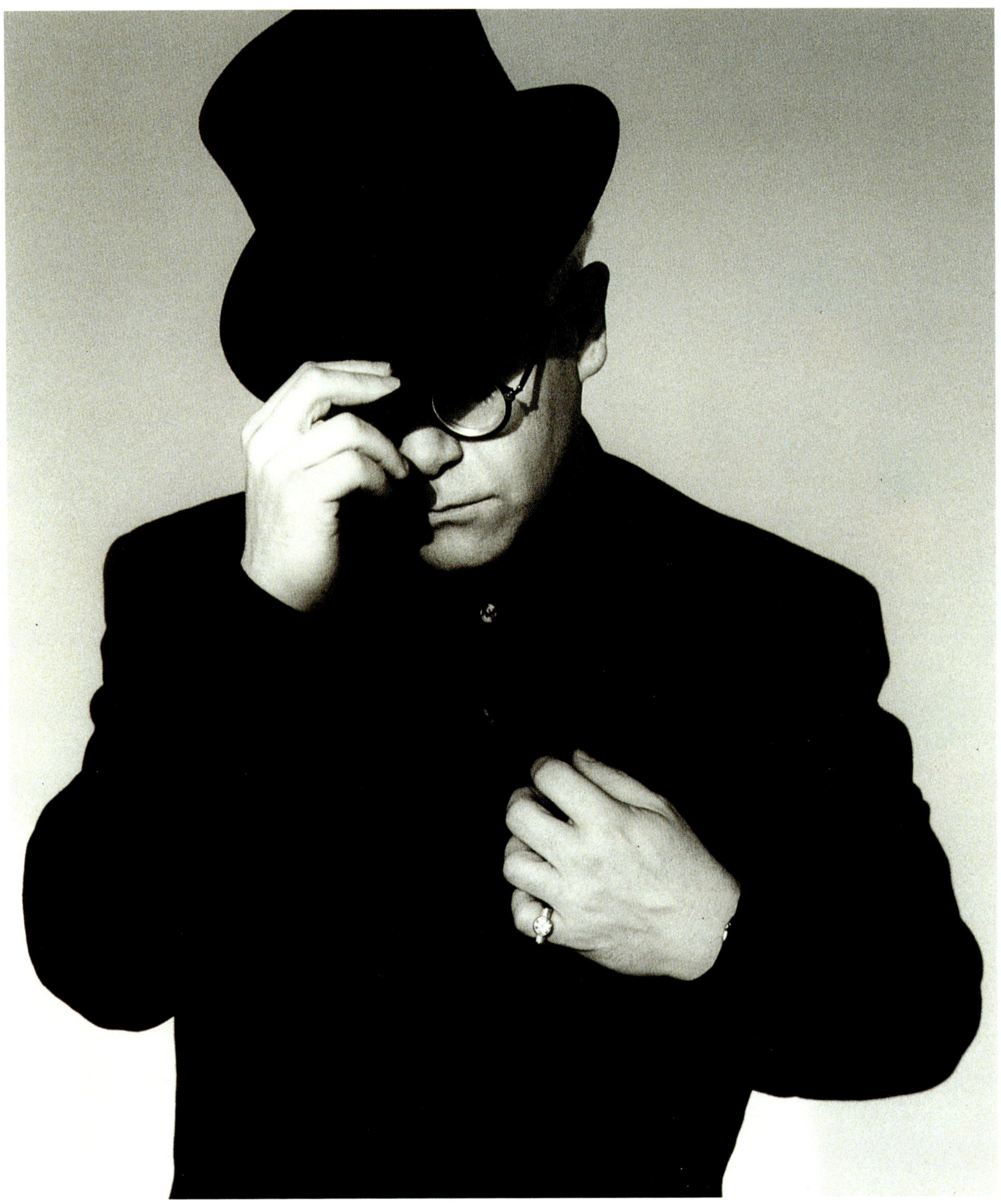

Preceeding Spread: Michael O'Brien | Above: Herb Ritts

Herb Ritts

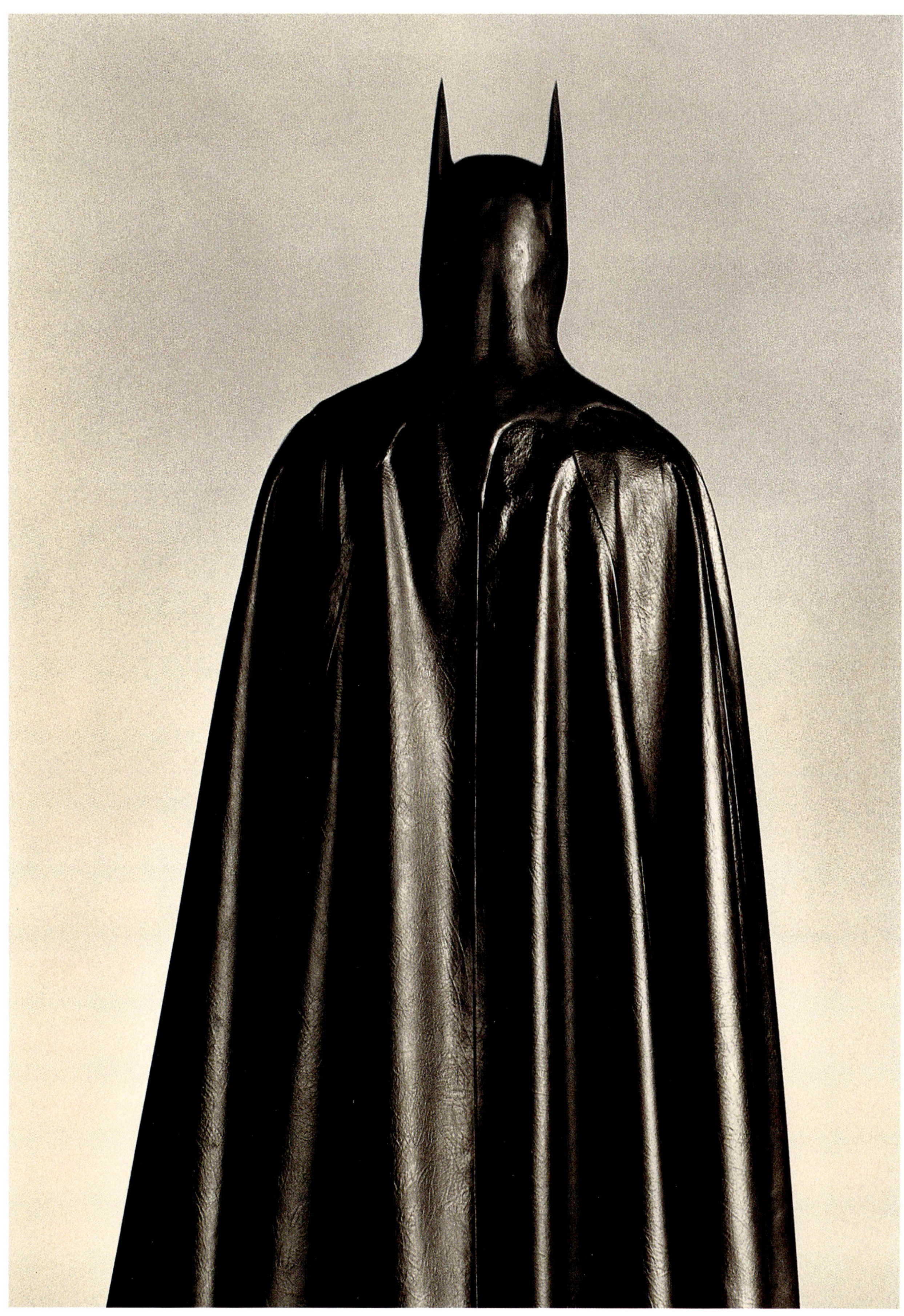

Herb Ritts

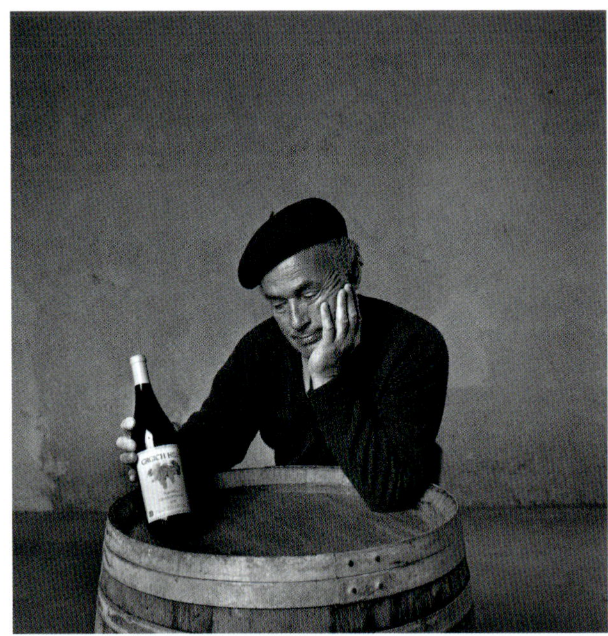

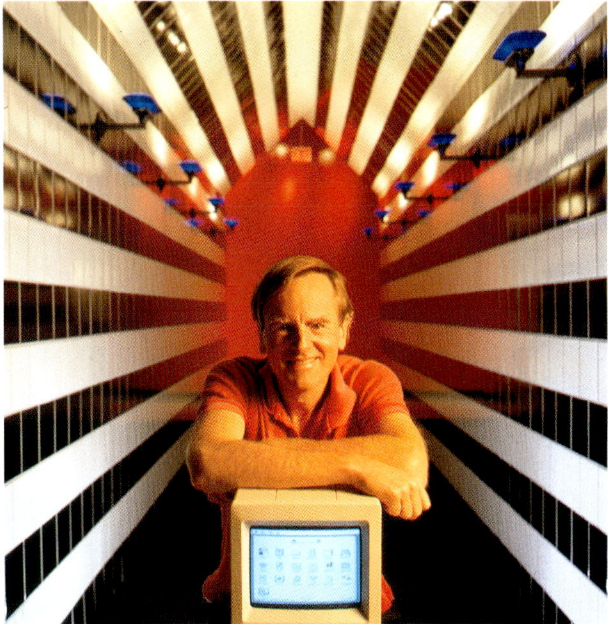

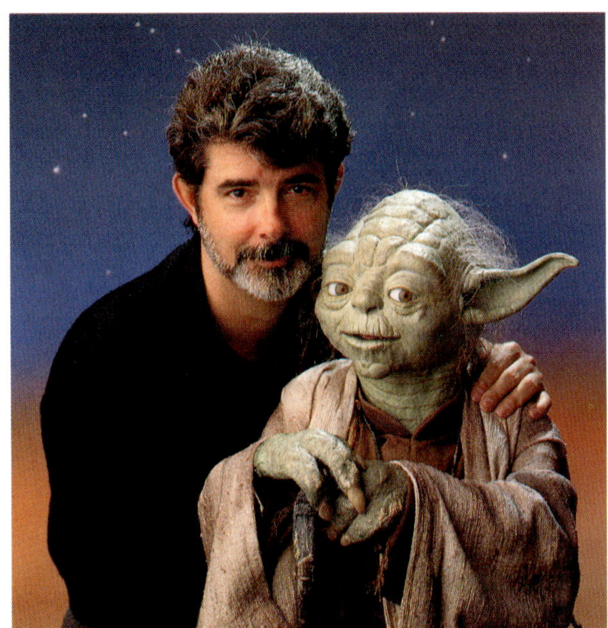

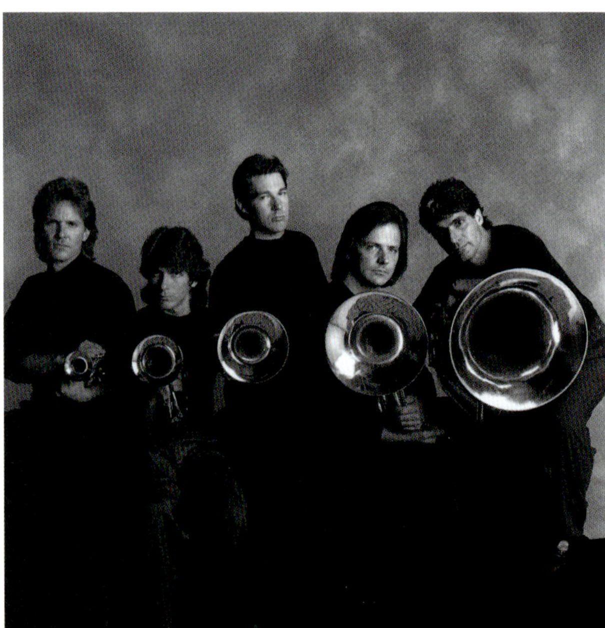

Tom Zimberoff

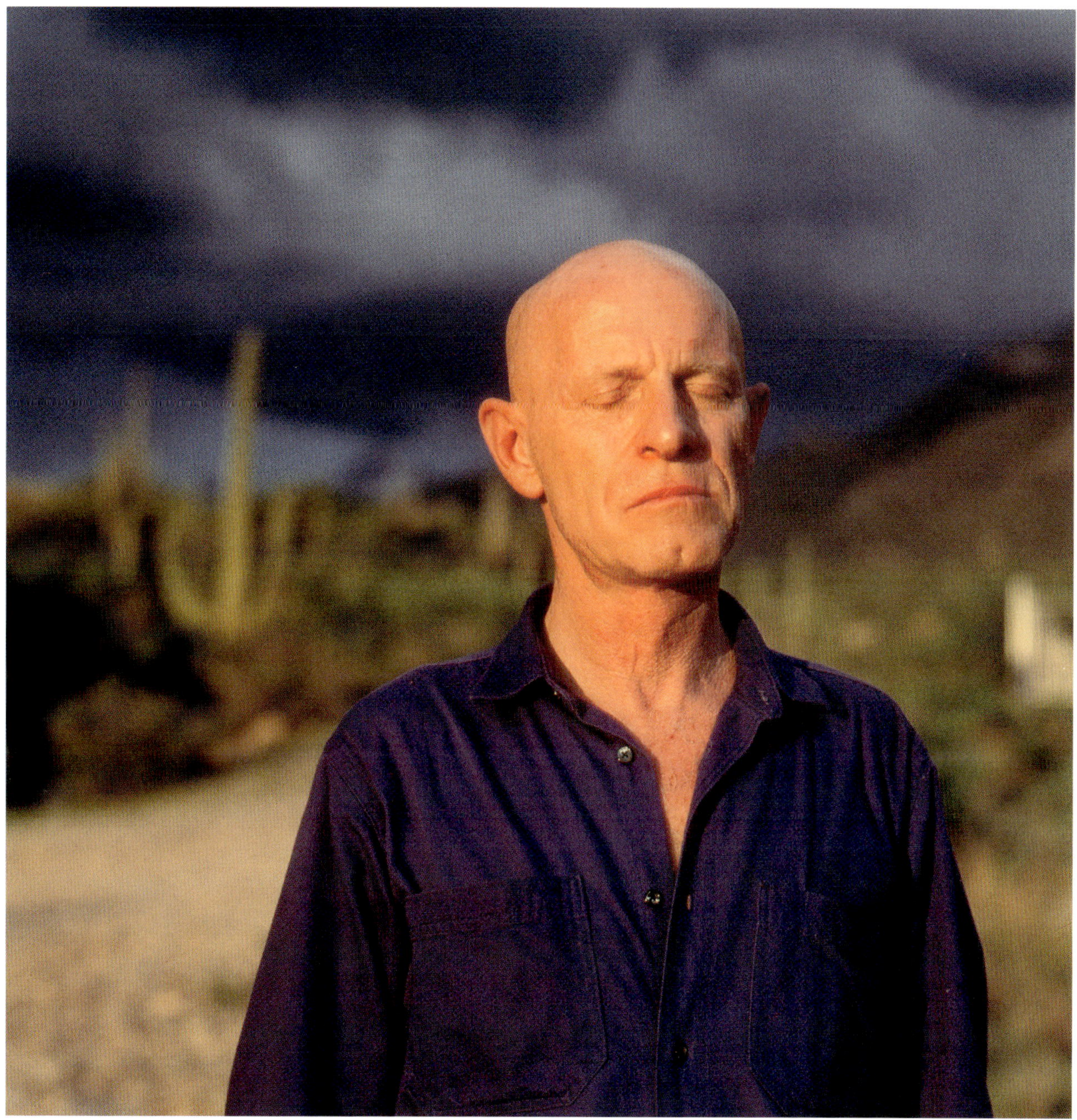

Tom Zimberoff

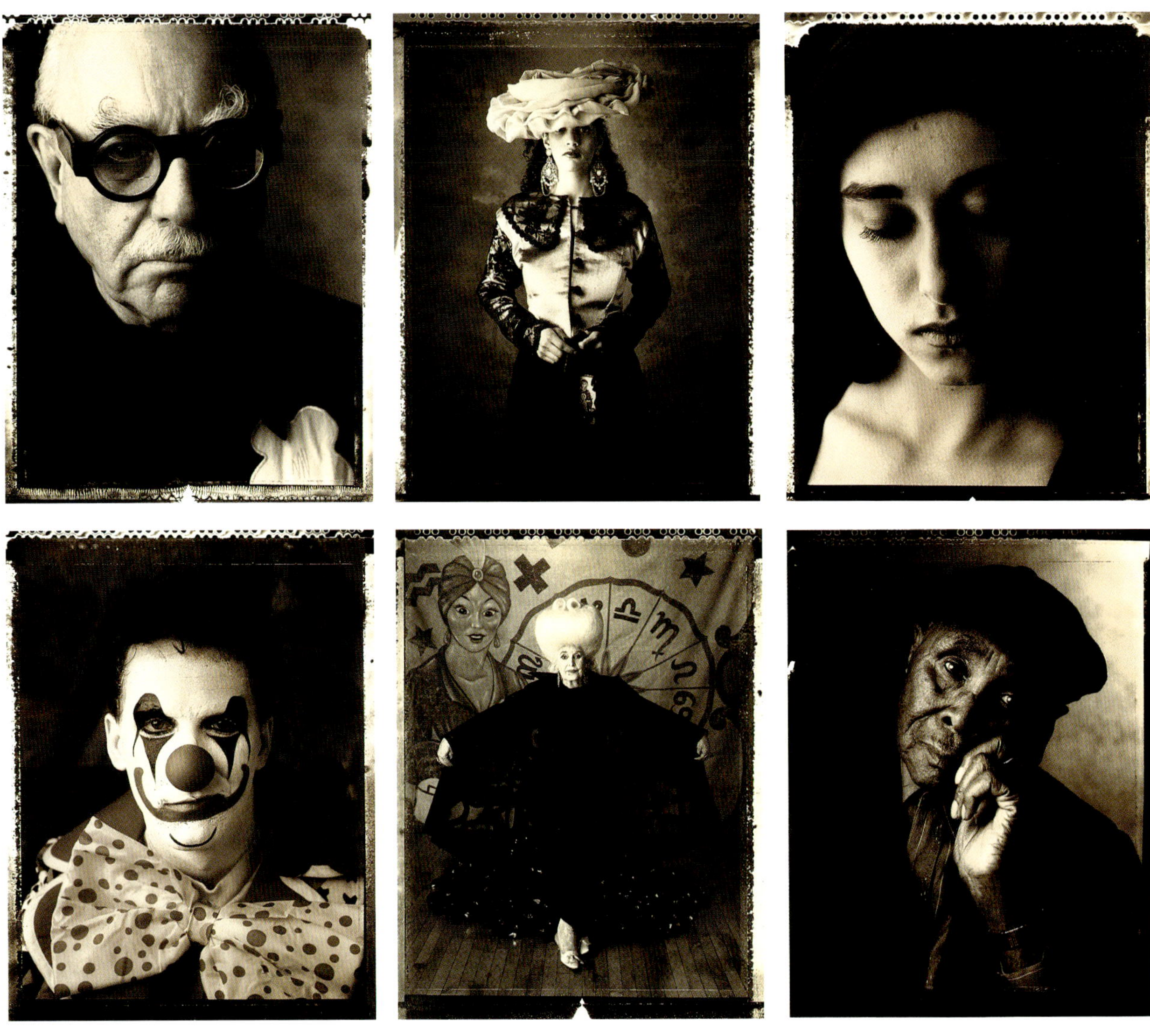

Marc Hauser

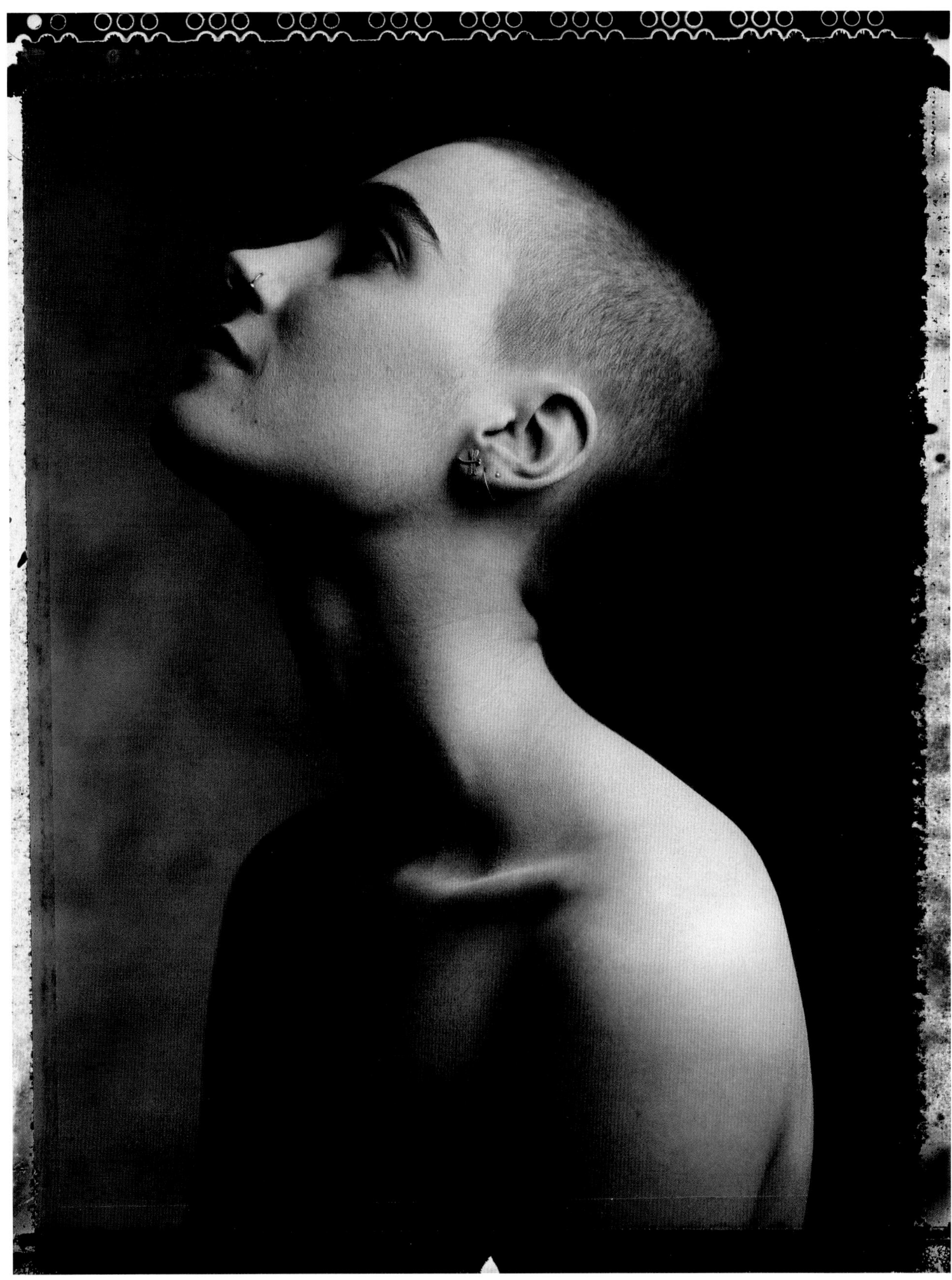

Marc Hauser

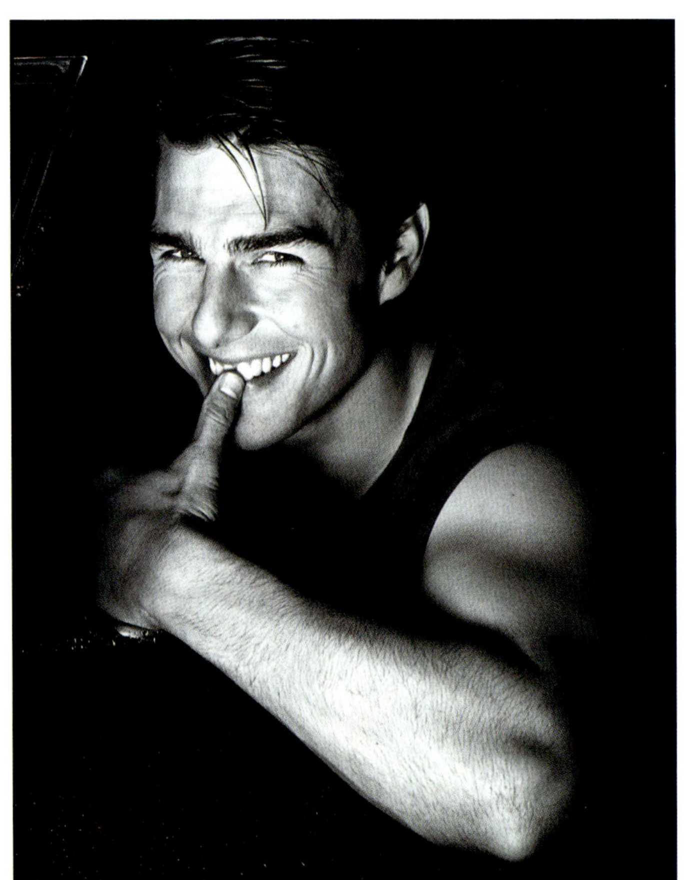
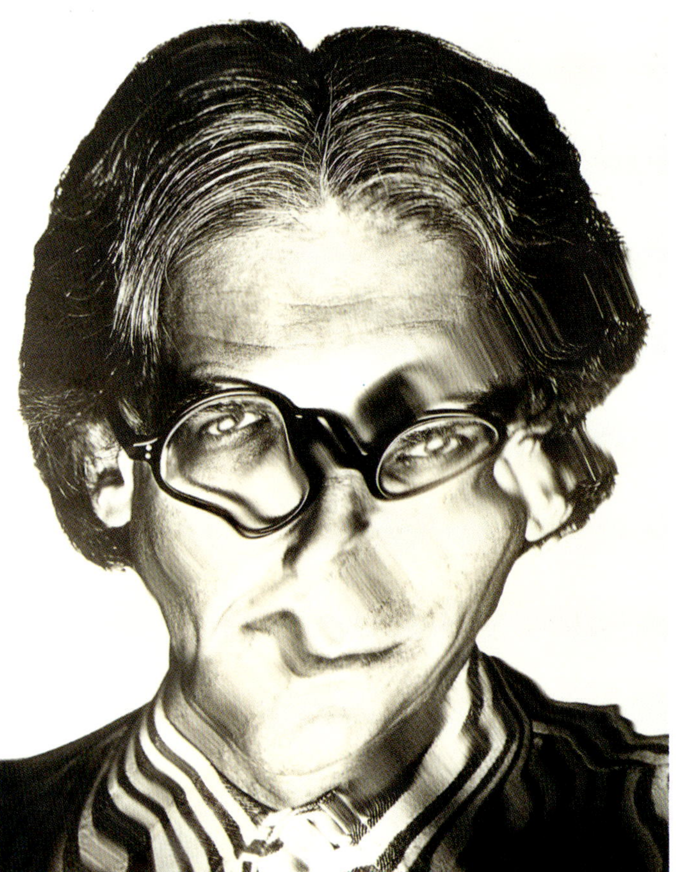

Above and Opposite: Albert Watson

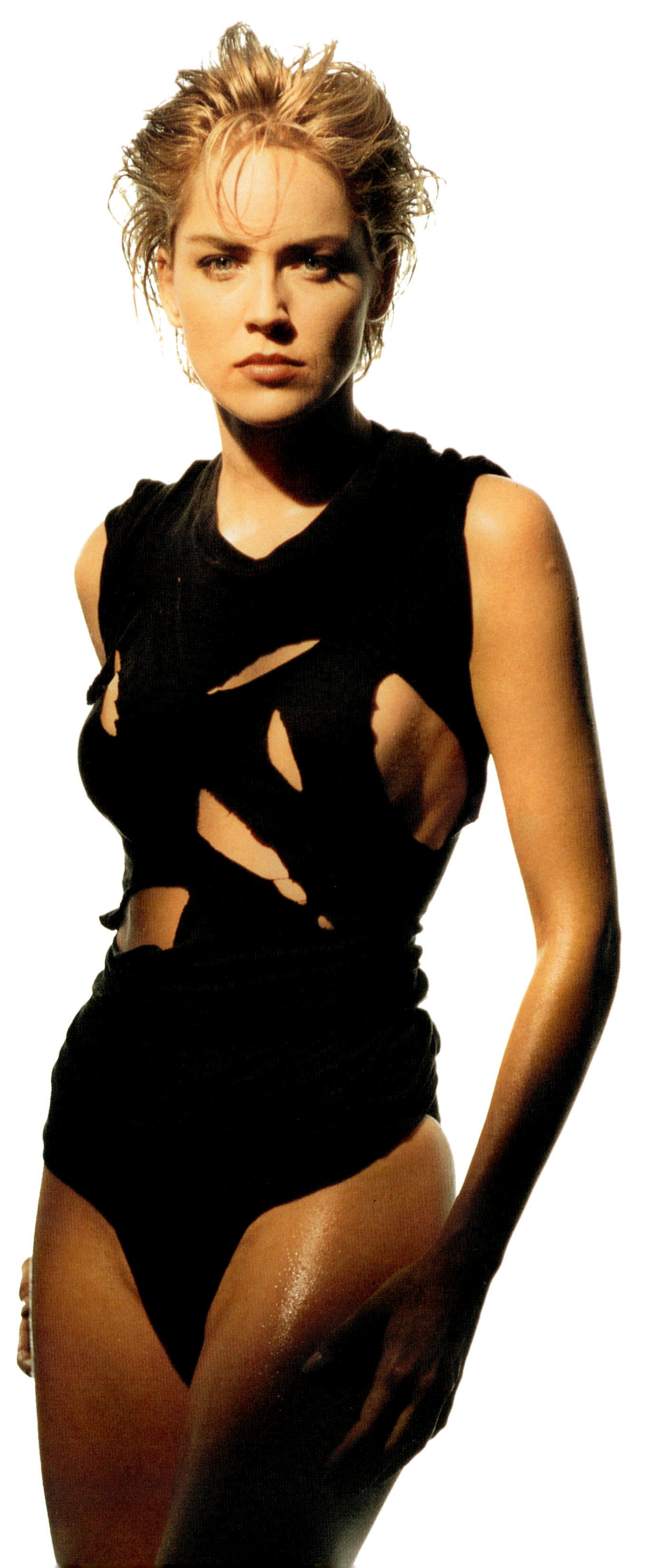

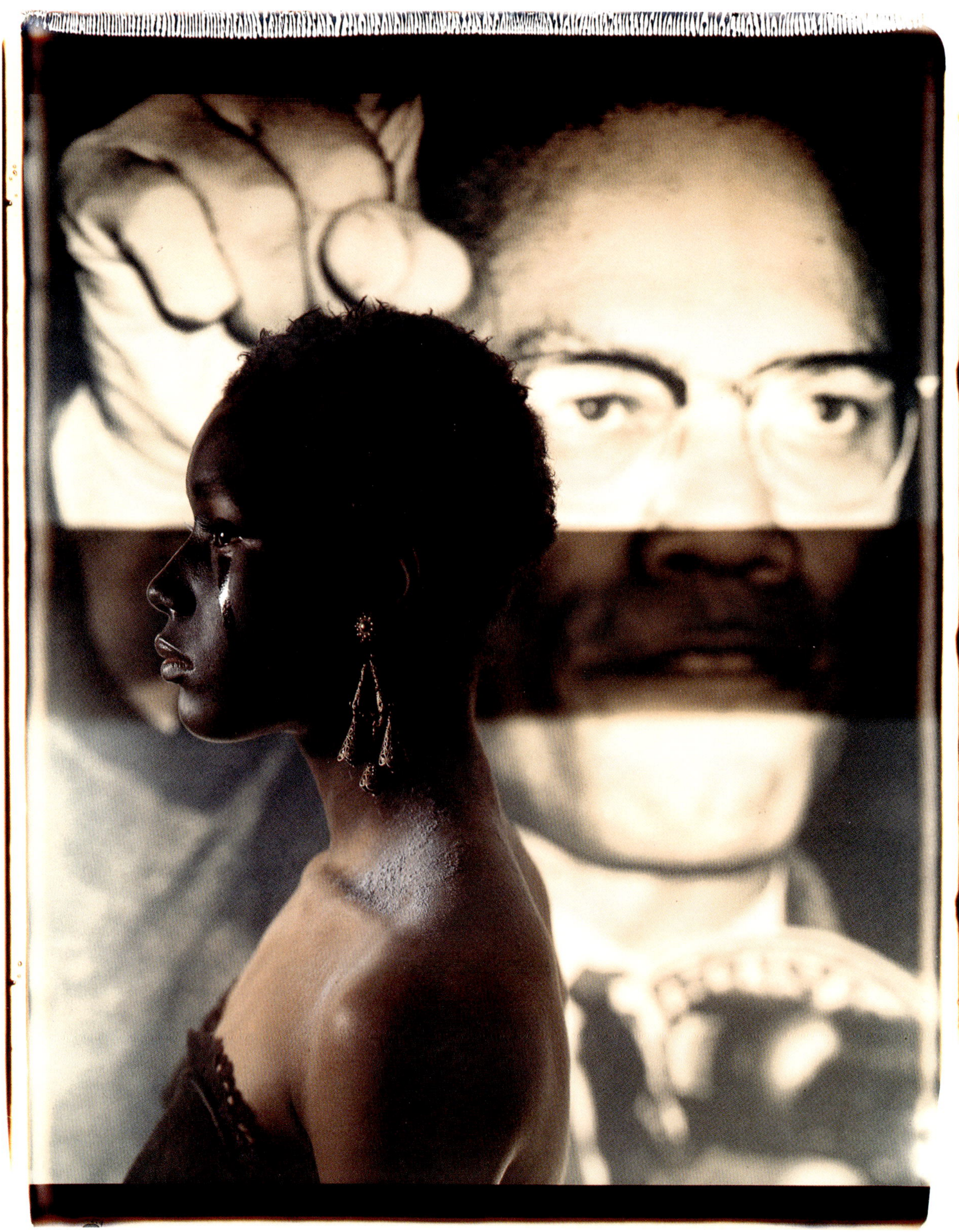

Ron Baxter Smith

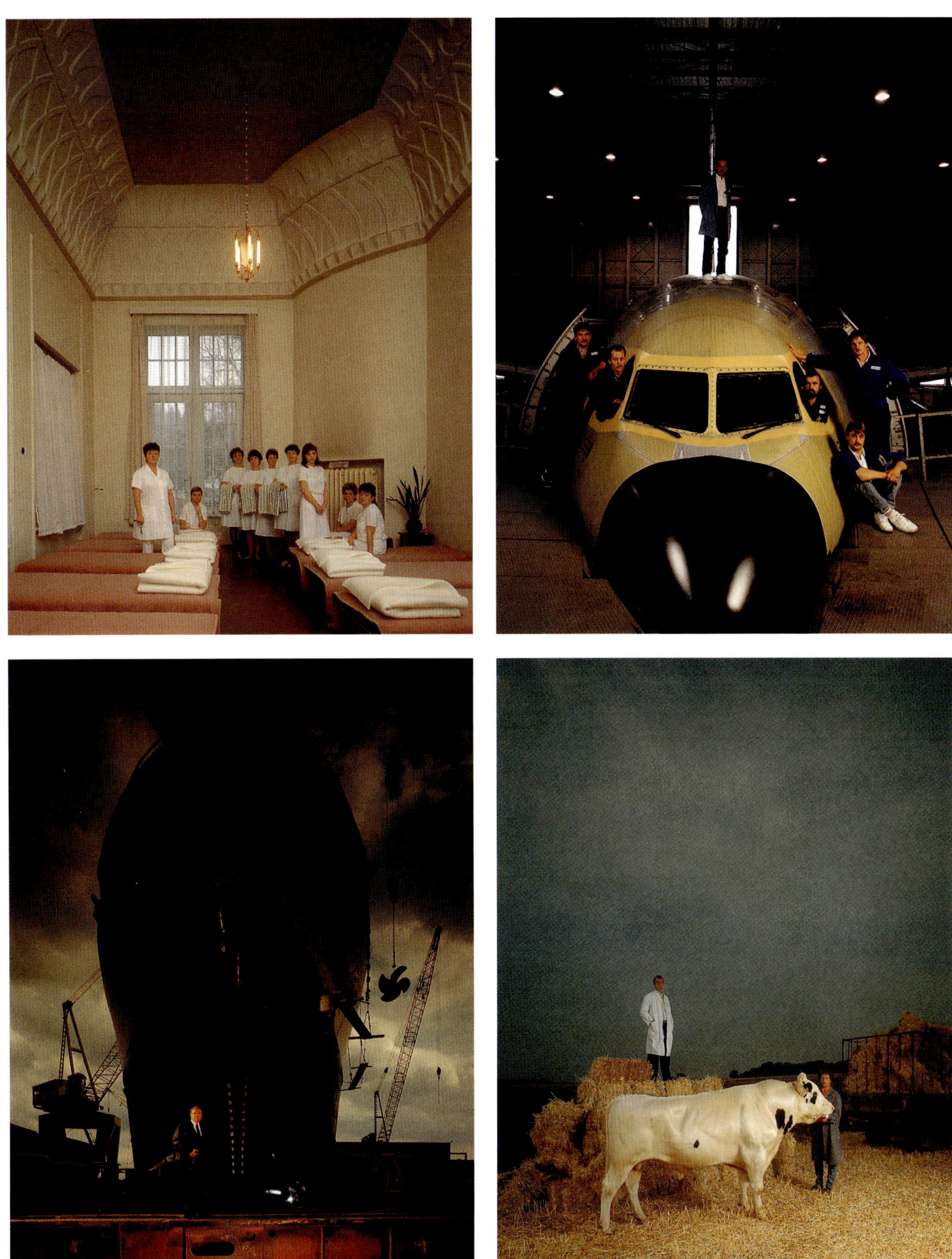

Aernout Overbeeke

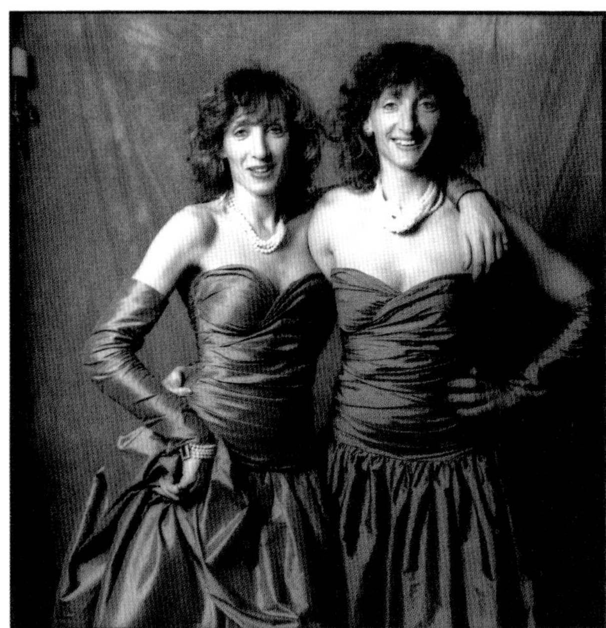

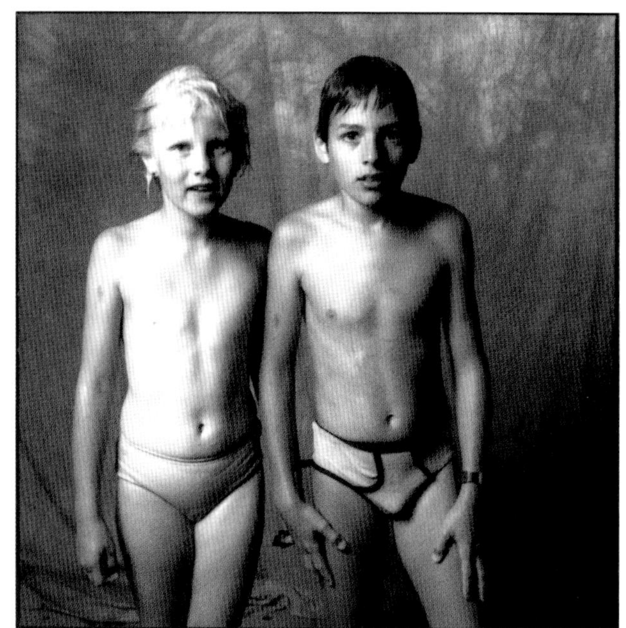

Wulf-Eike

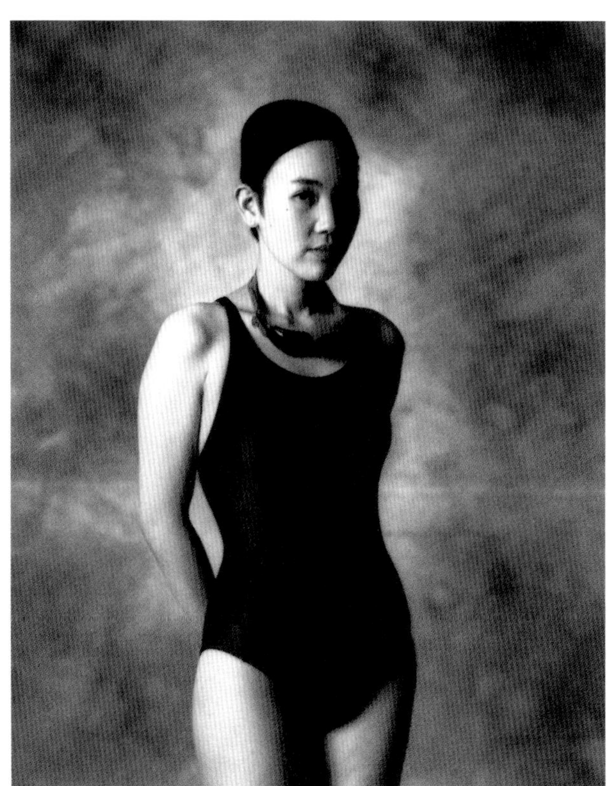

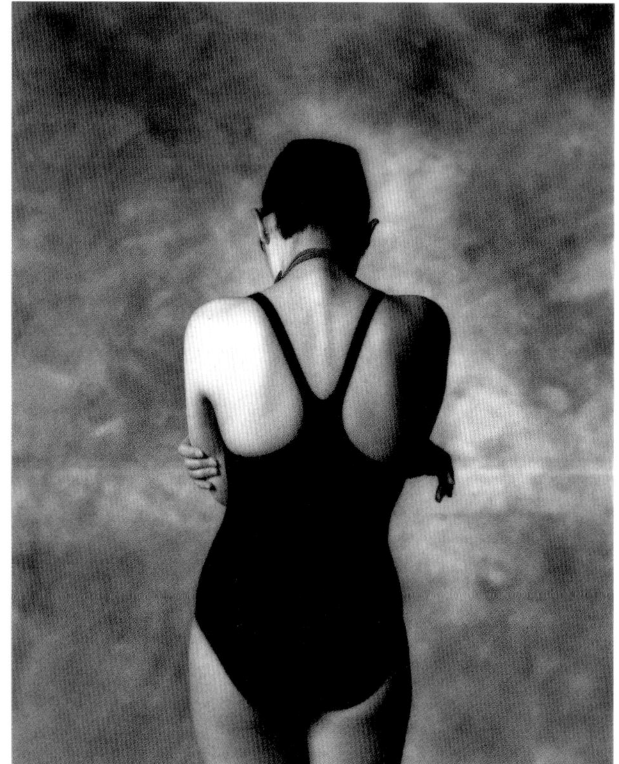

Junji Futashima

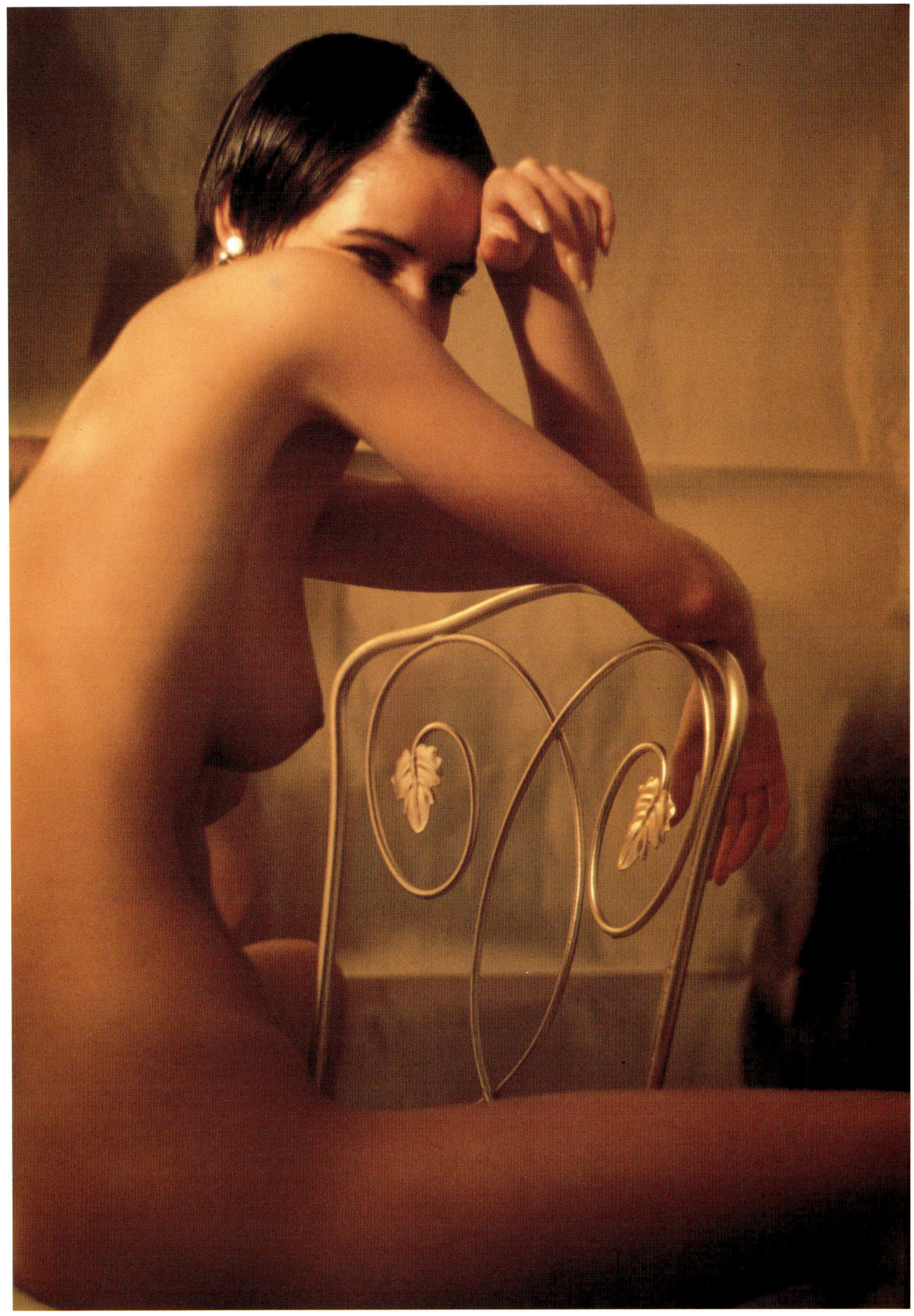

Philip Alan Poe

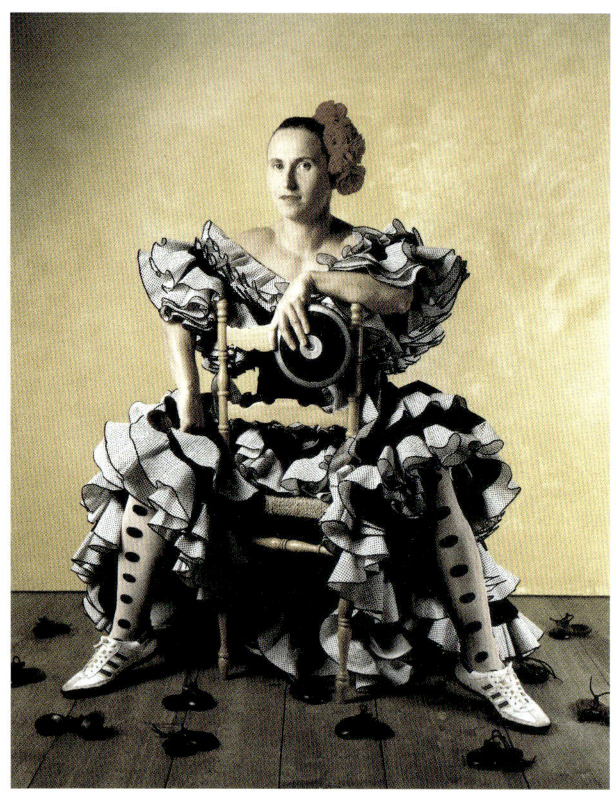

Claudio Alessandri

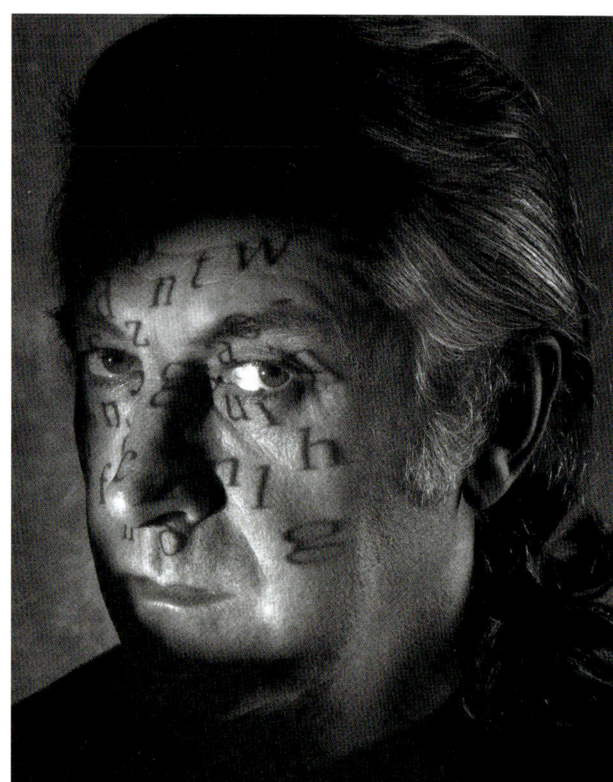

Steve Marsel

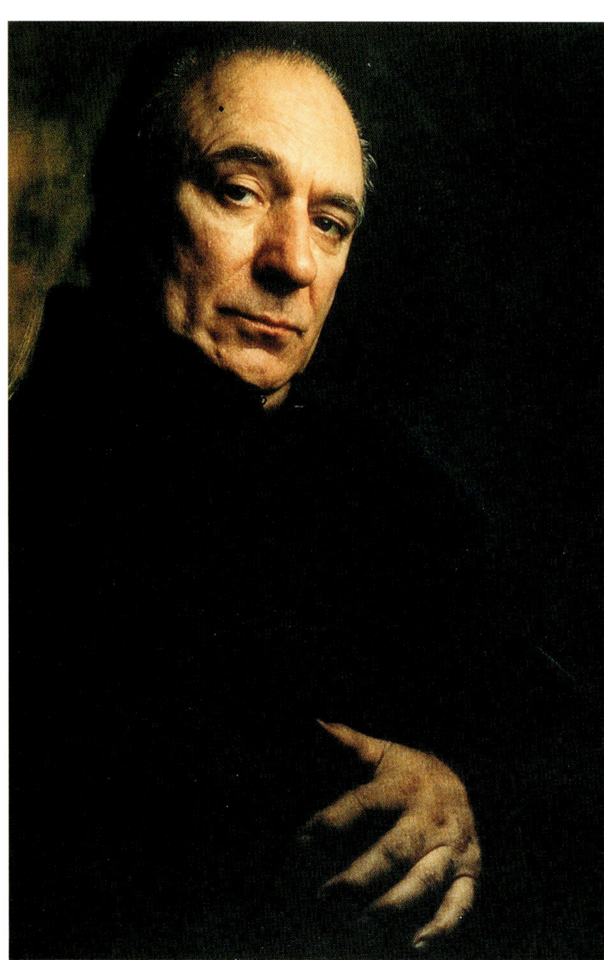

Peter Liepke

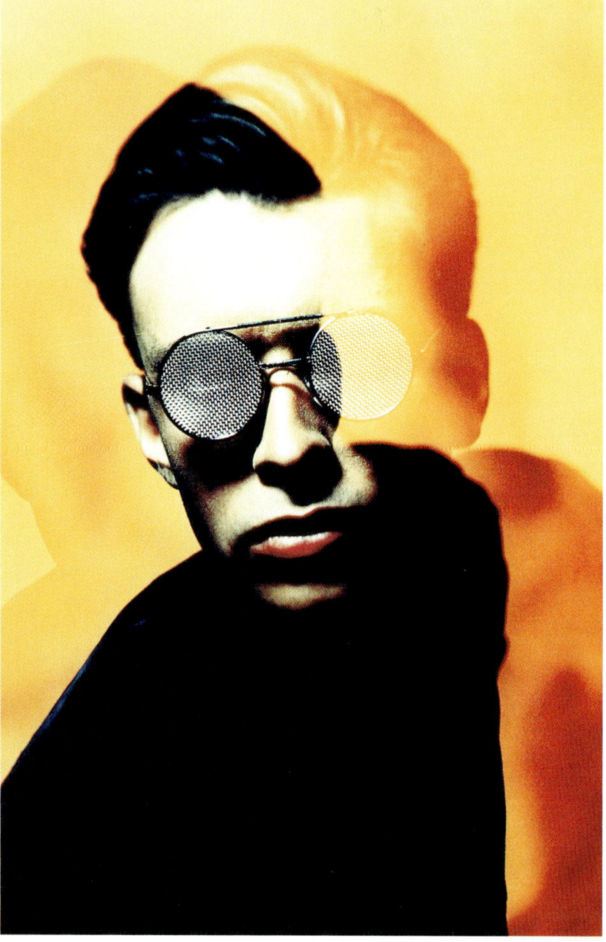

Christiane Marek

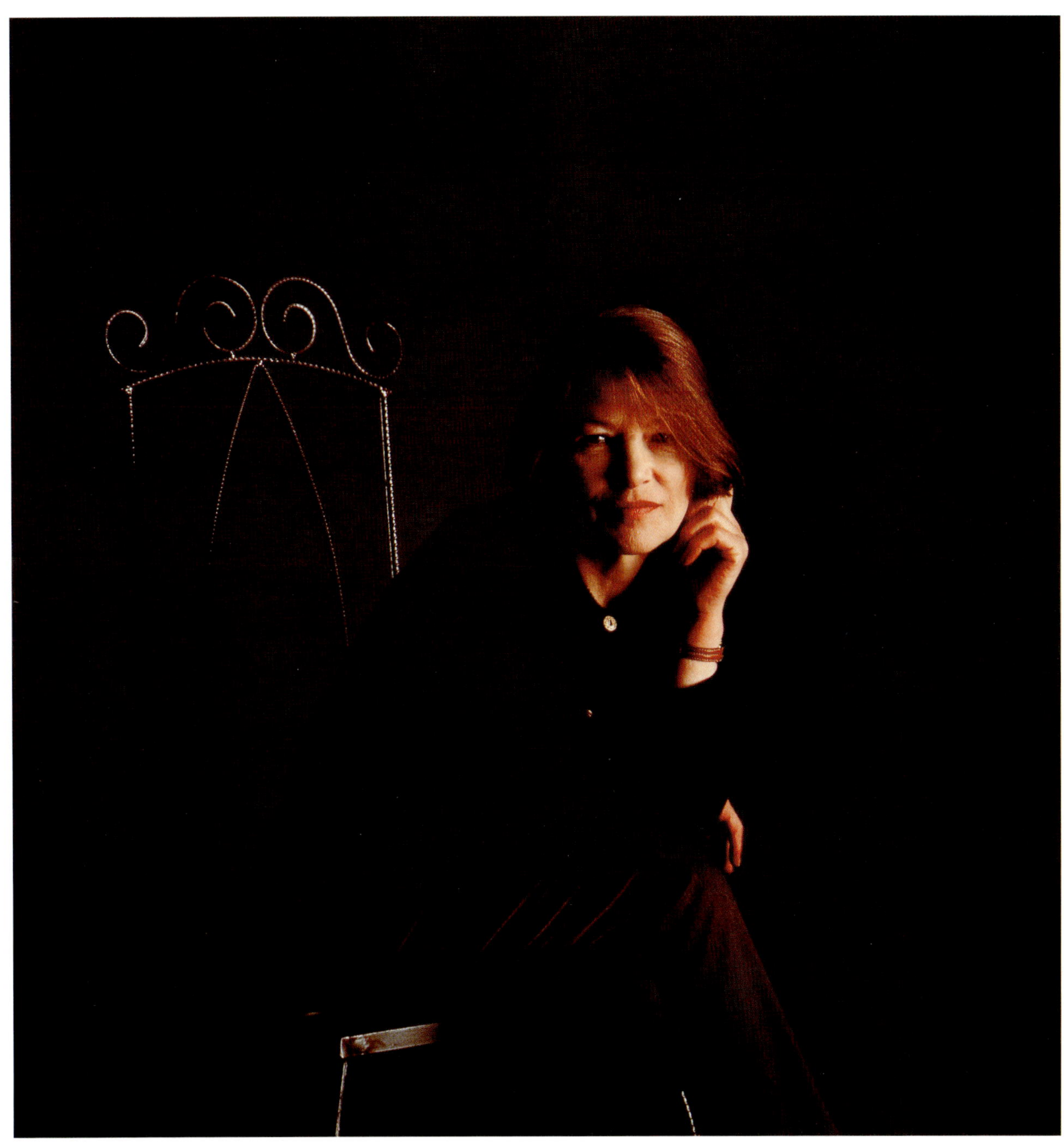

F. McGHEE

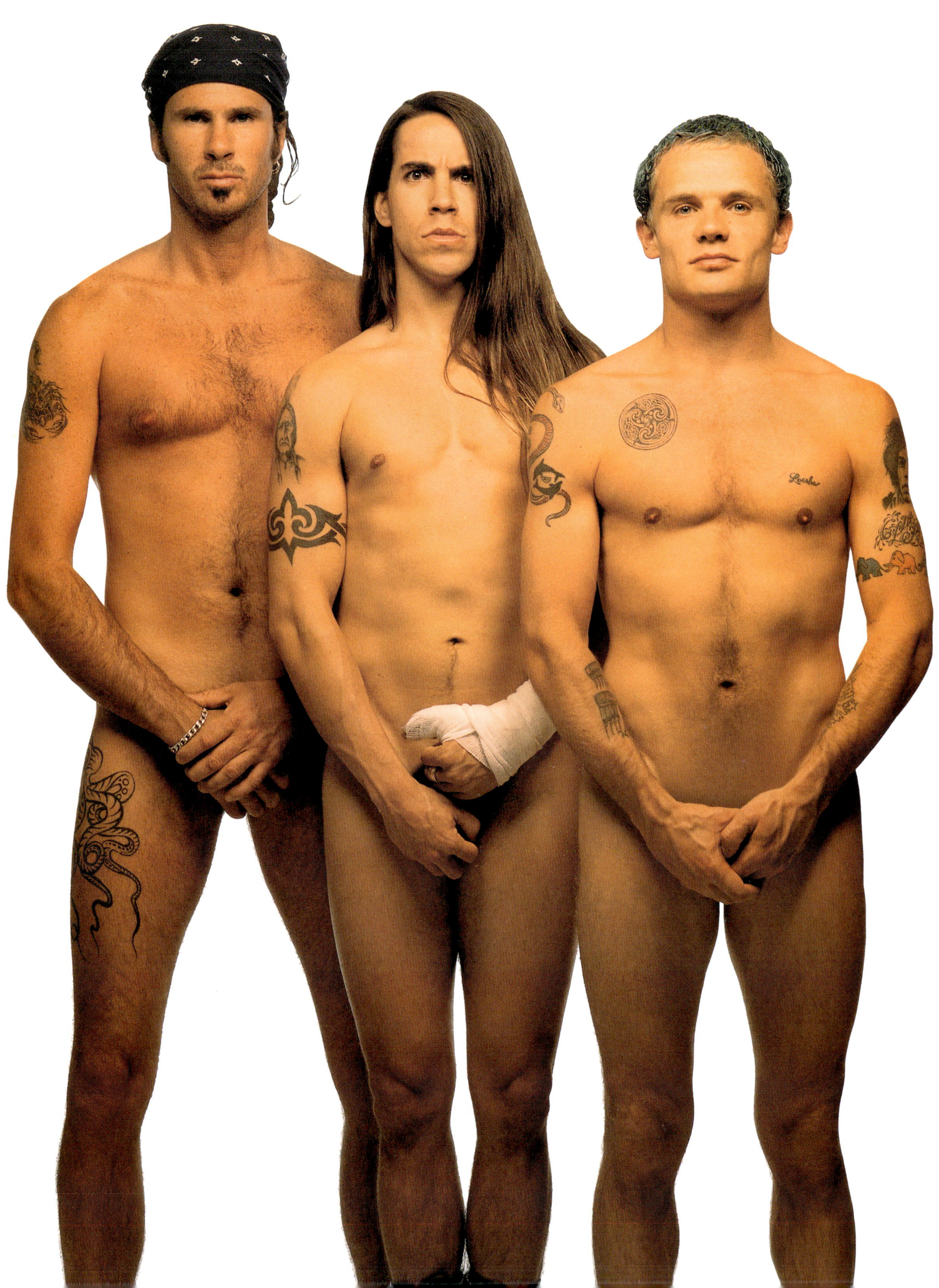

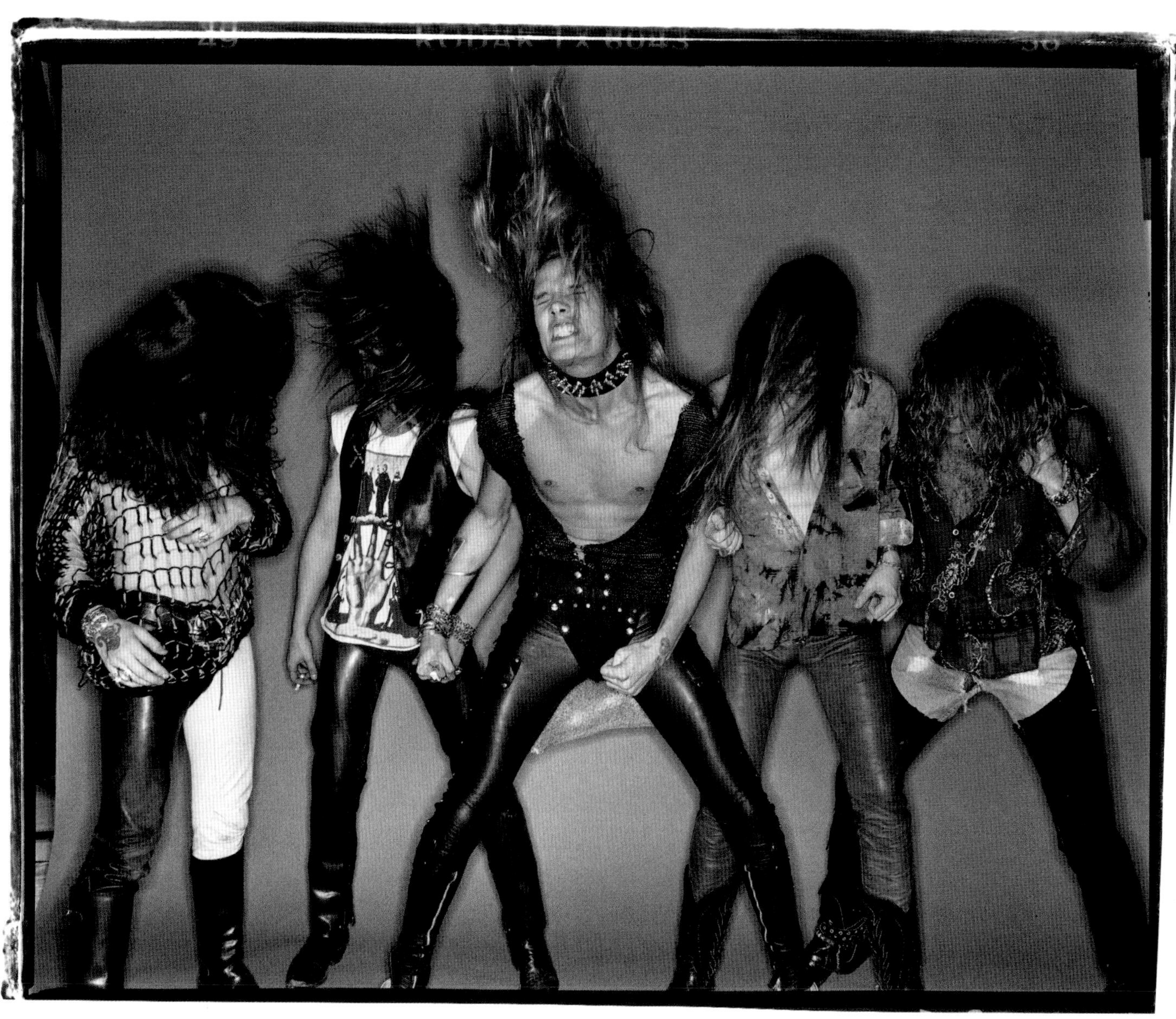

Opposite and Above: Mark Seliger

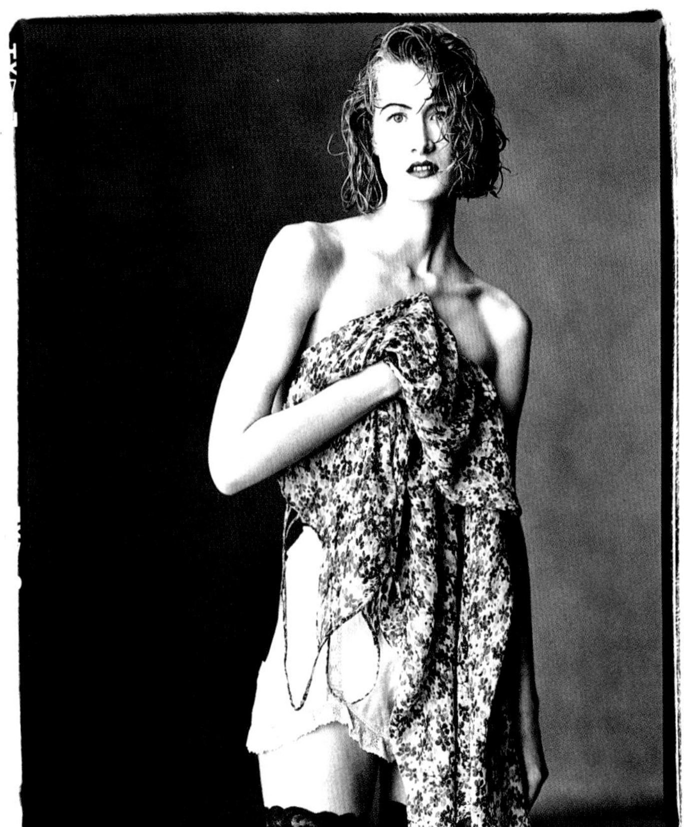 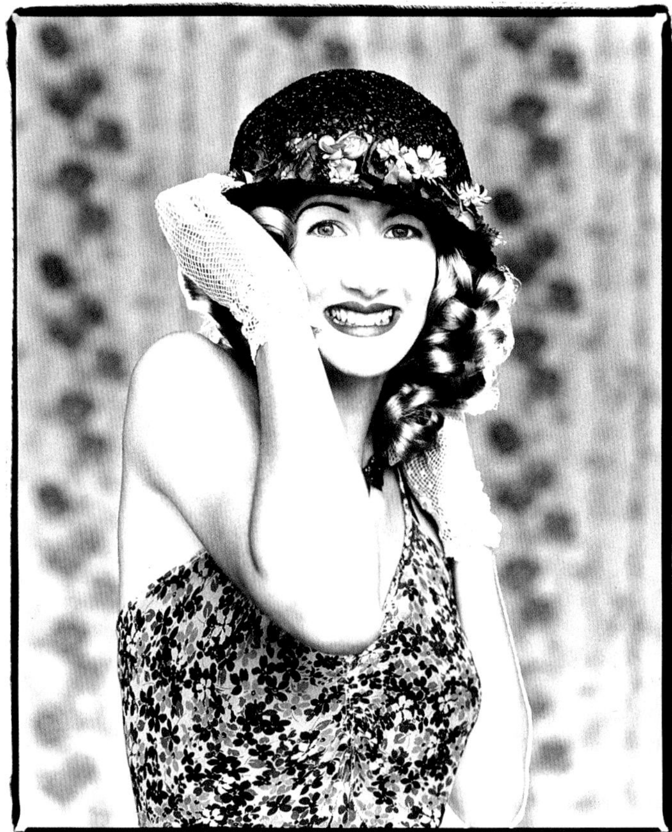

Matthew Rolston

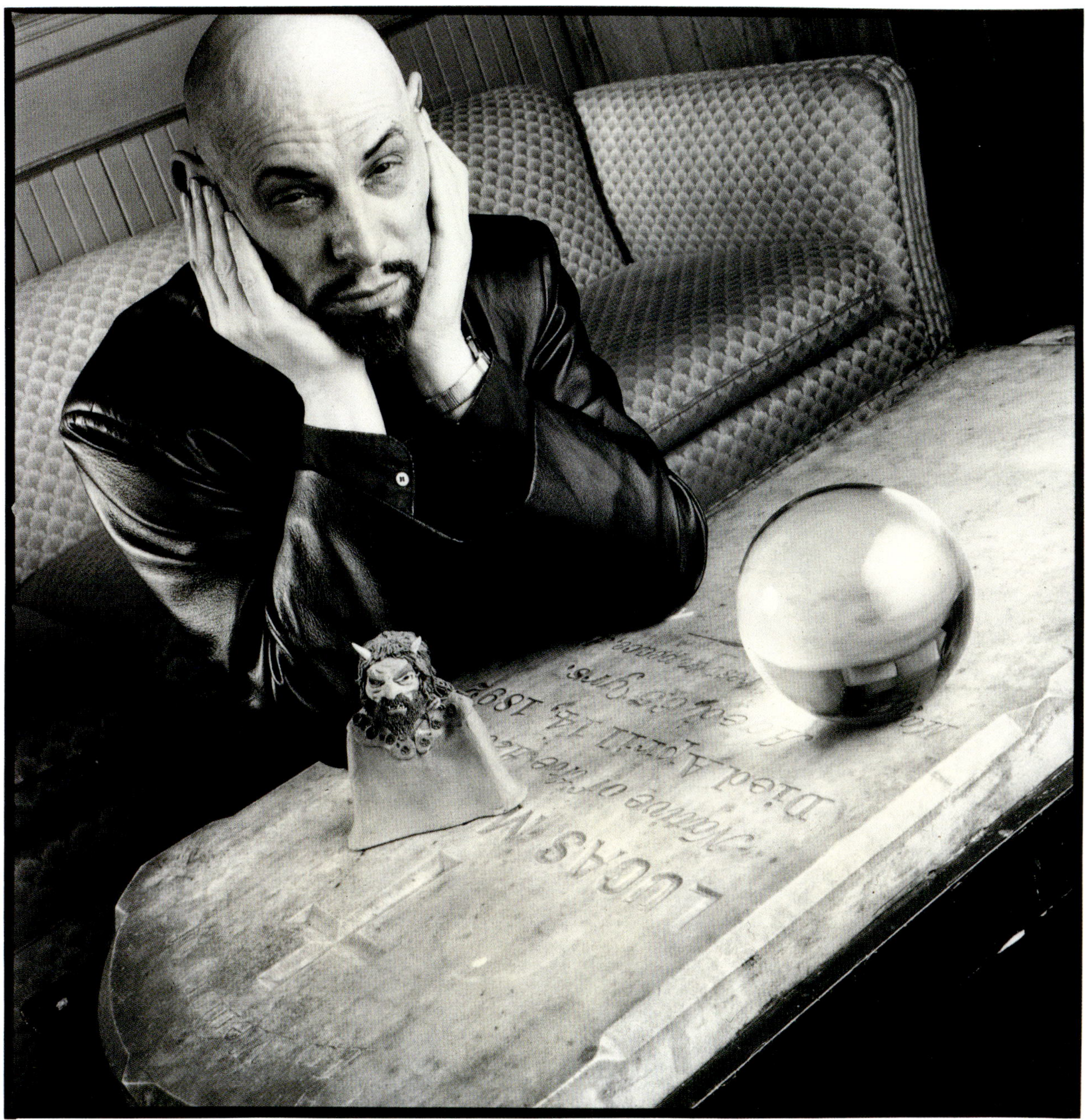

Mary Ellen Mark

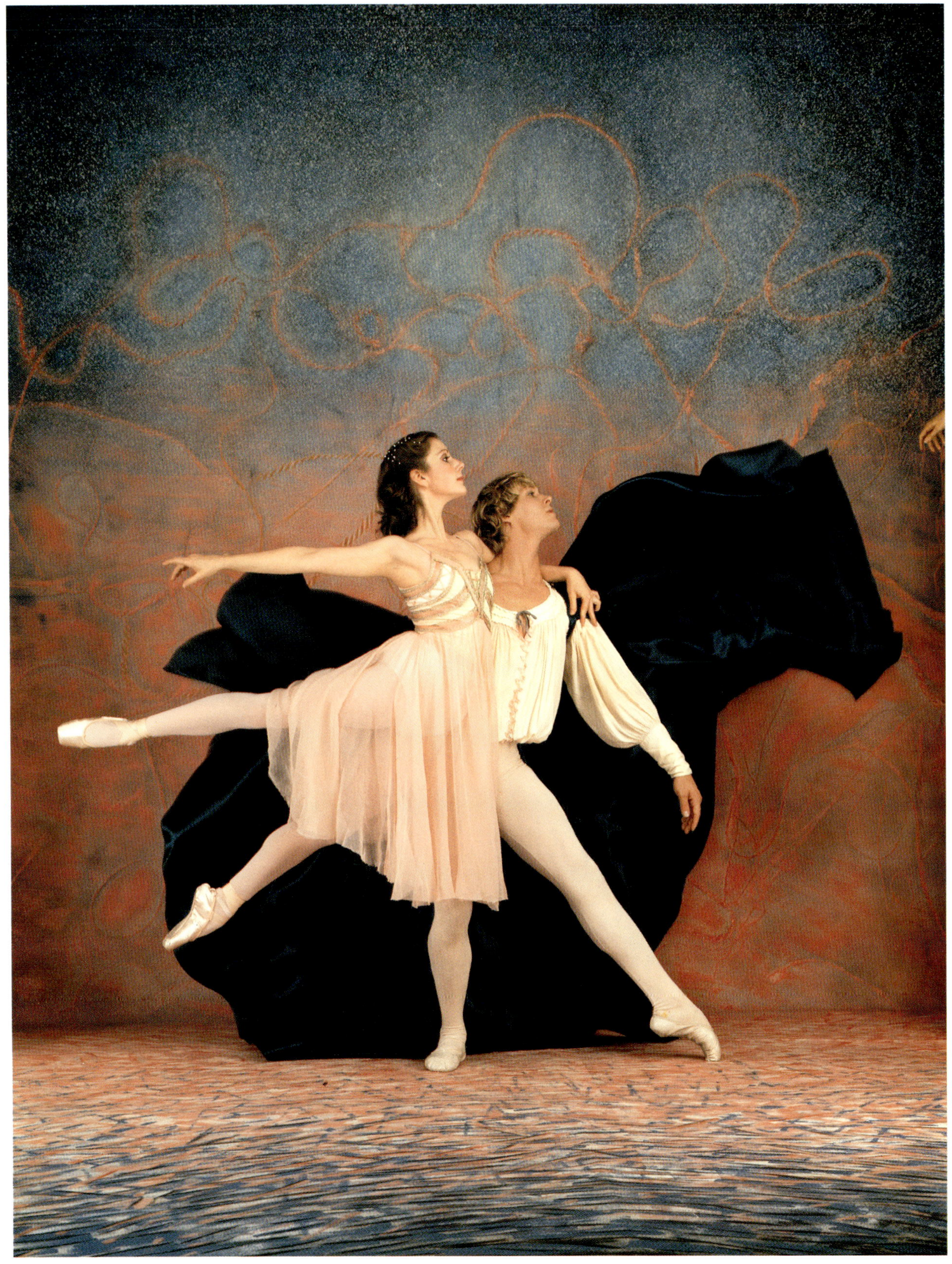

Gilles Larrain

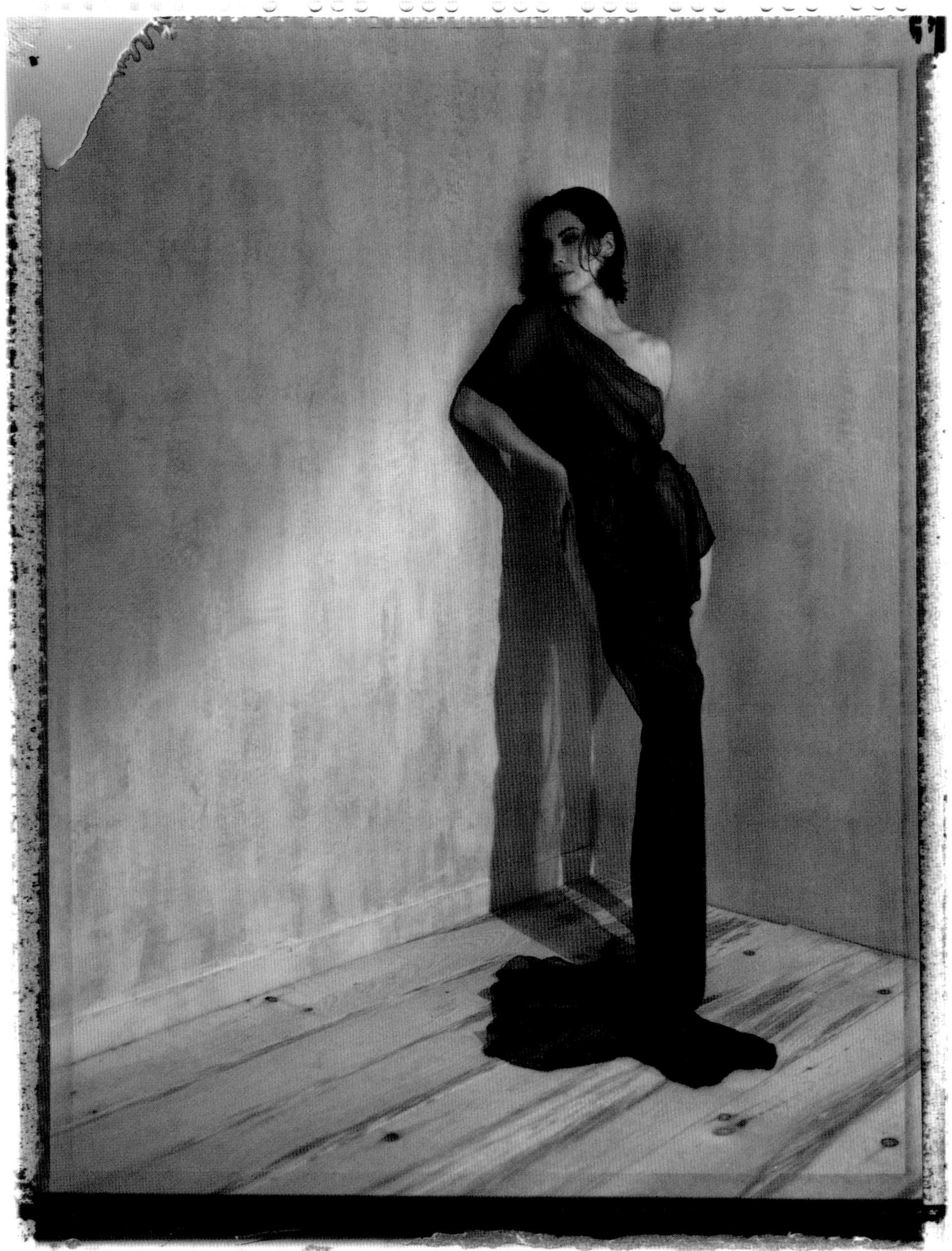

Ron Baxter Smith

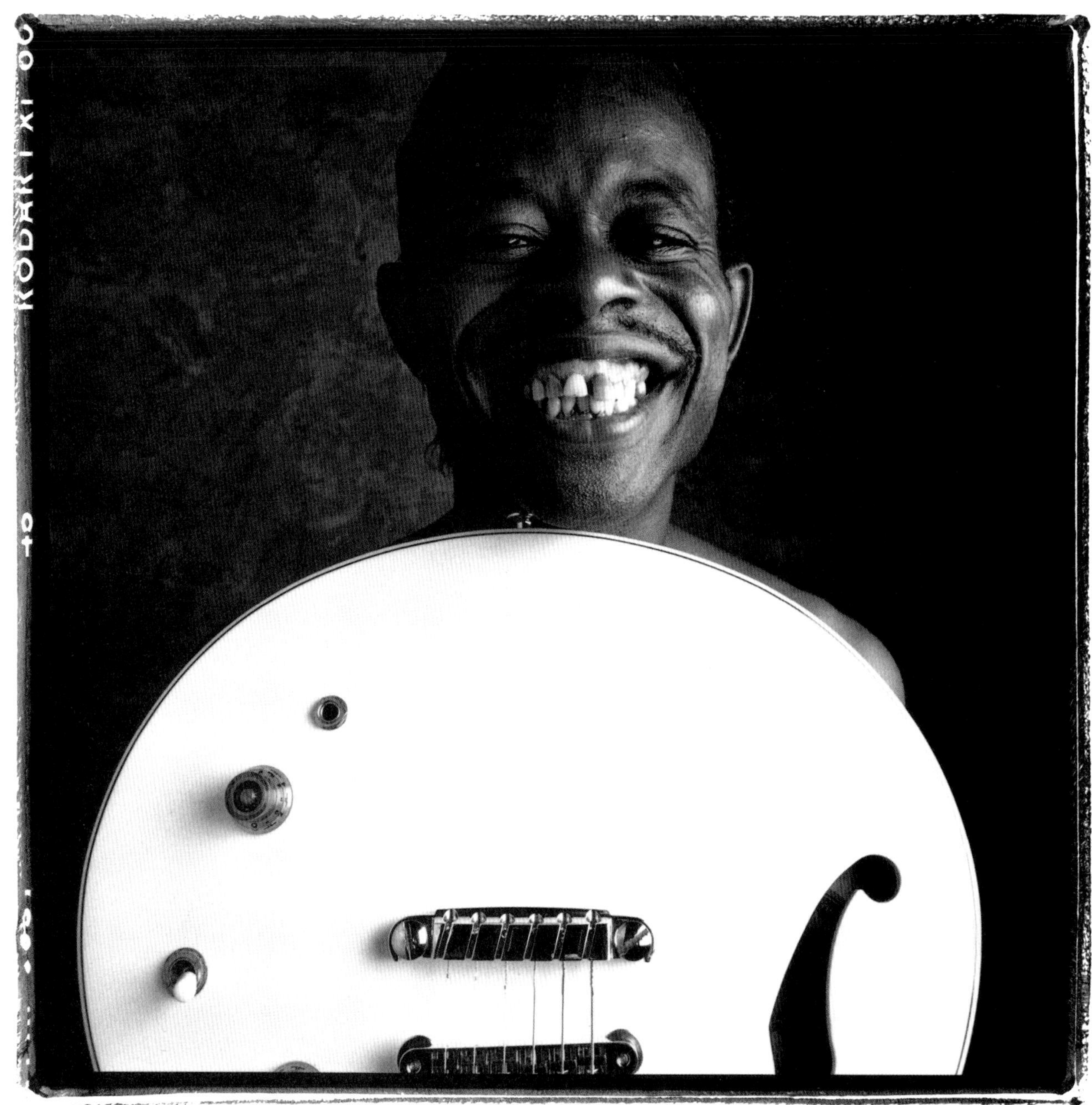

Marc Norberg

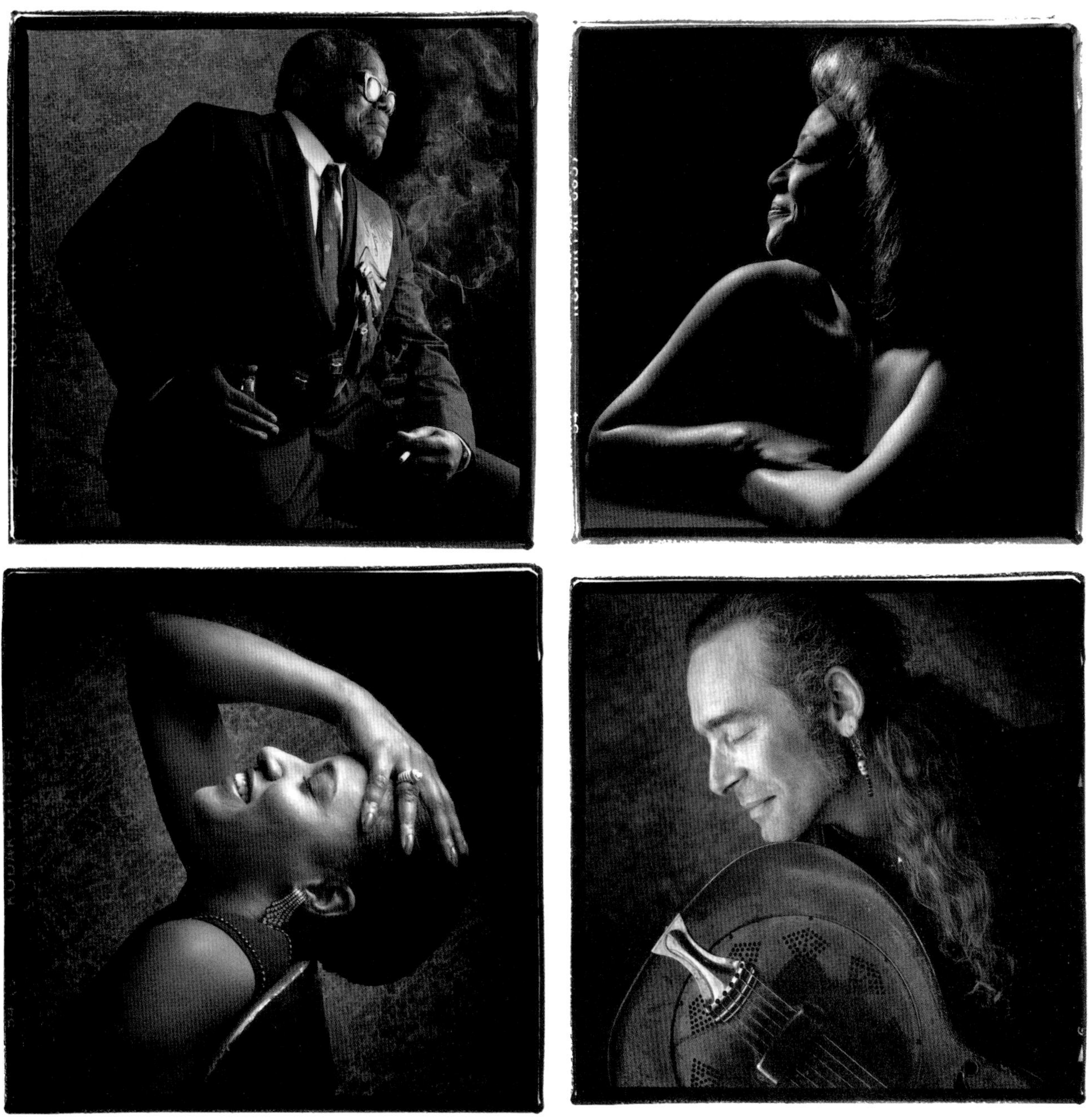

Marc Norberg

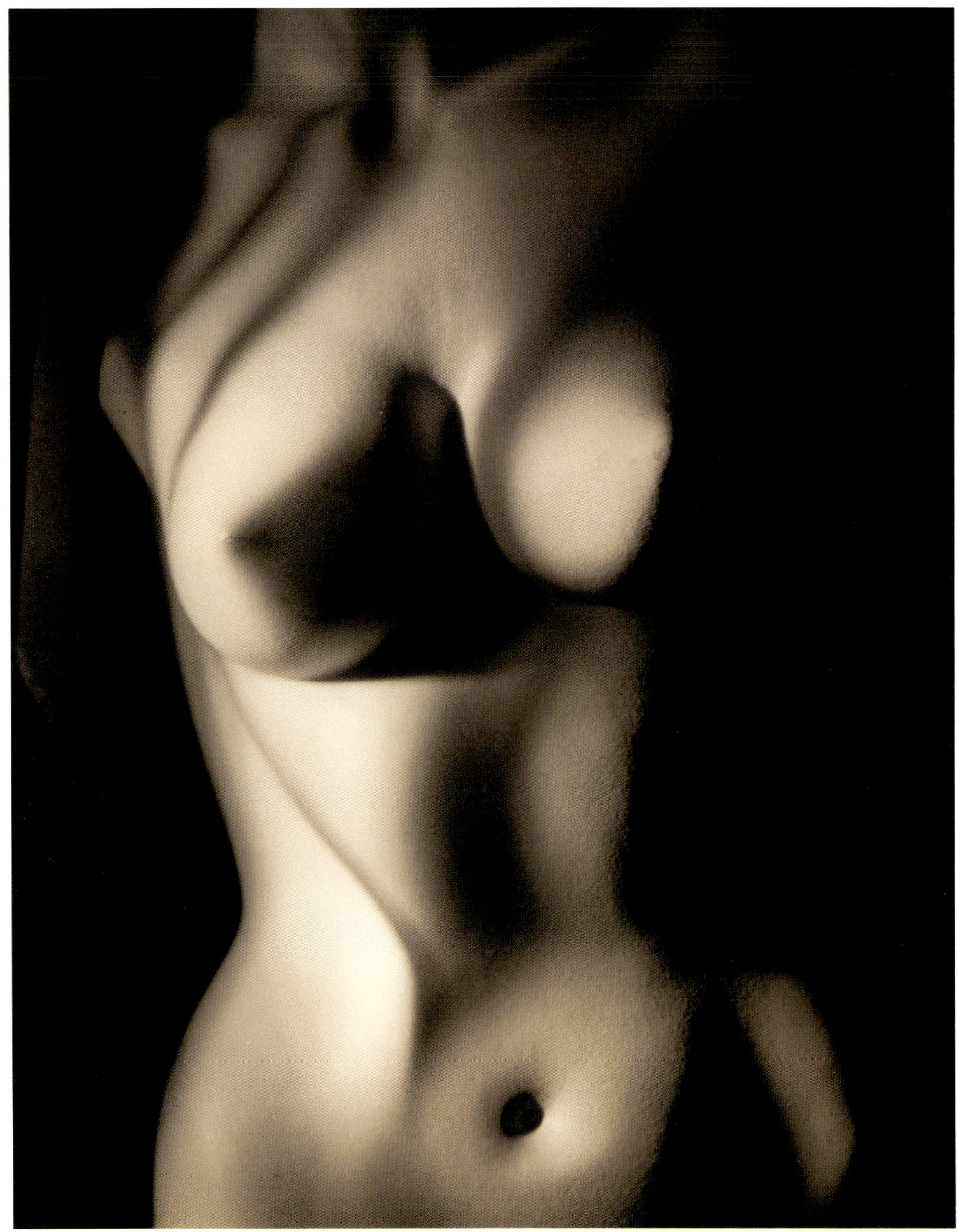

Ringo Tang

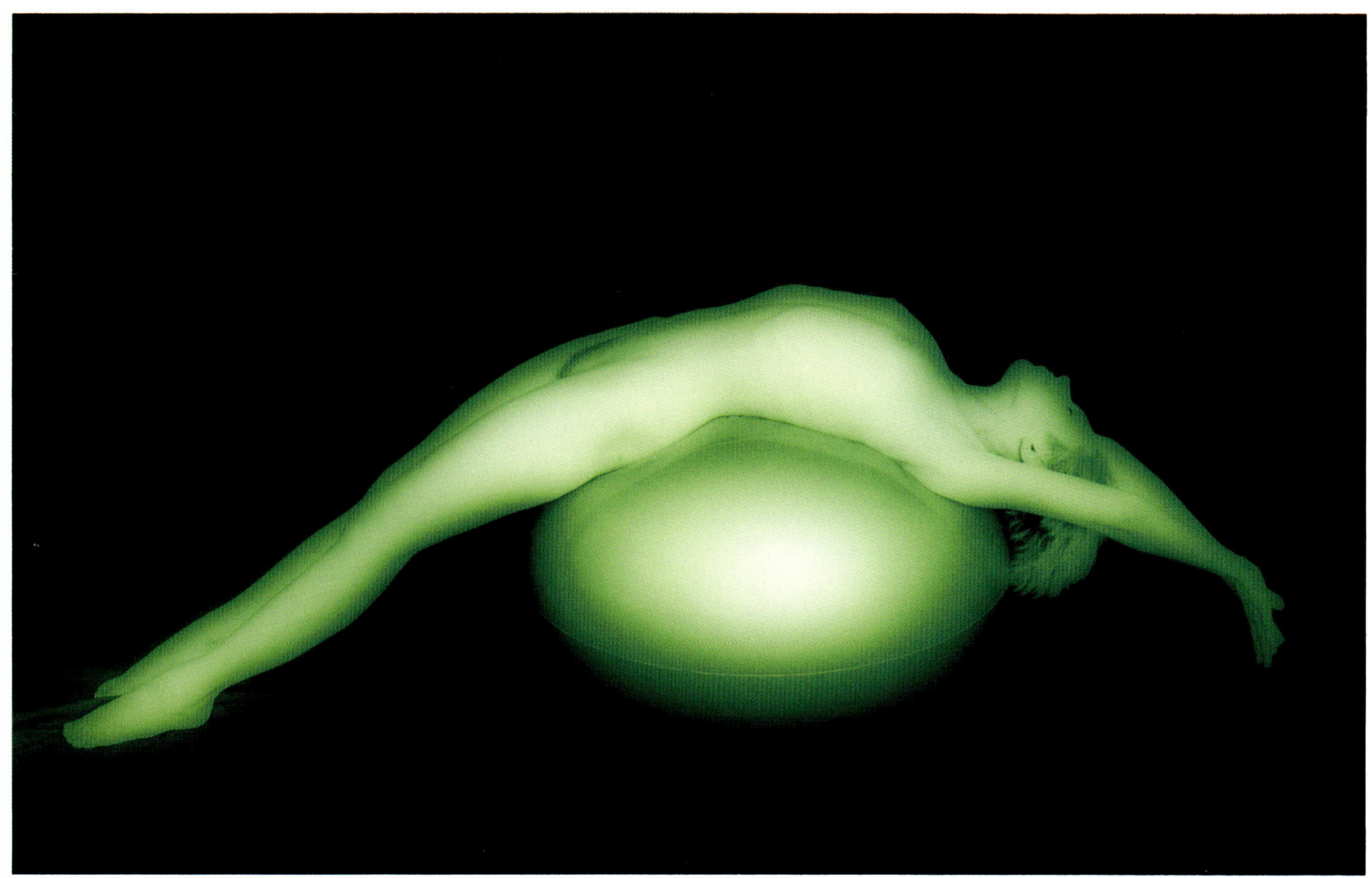

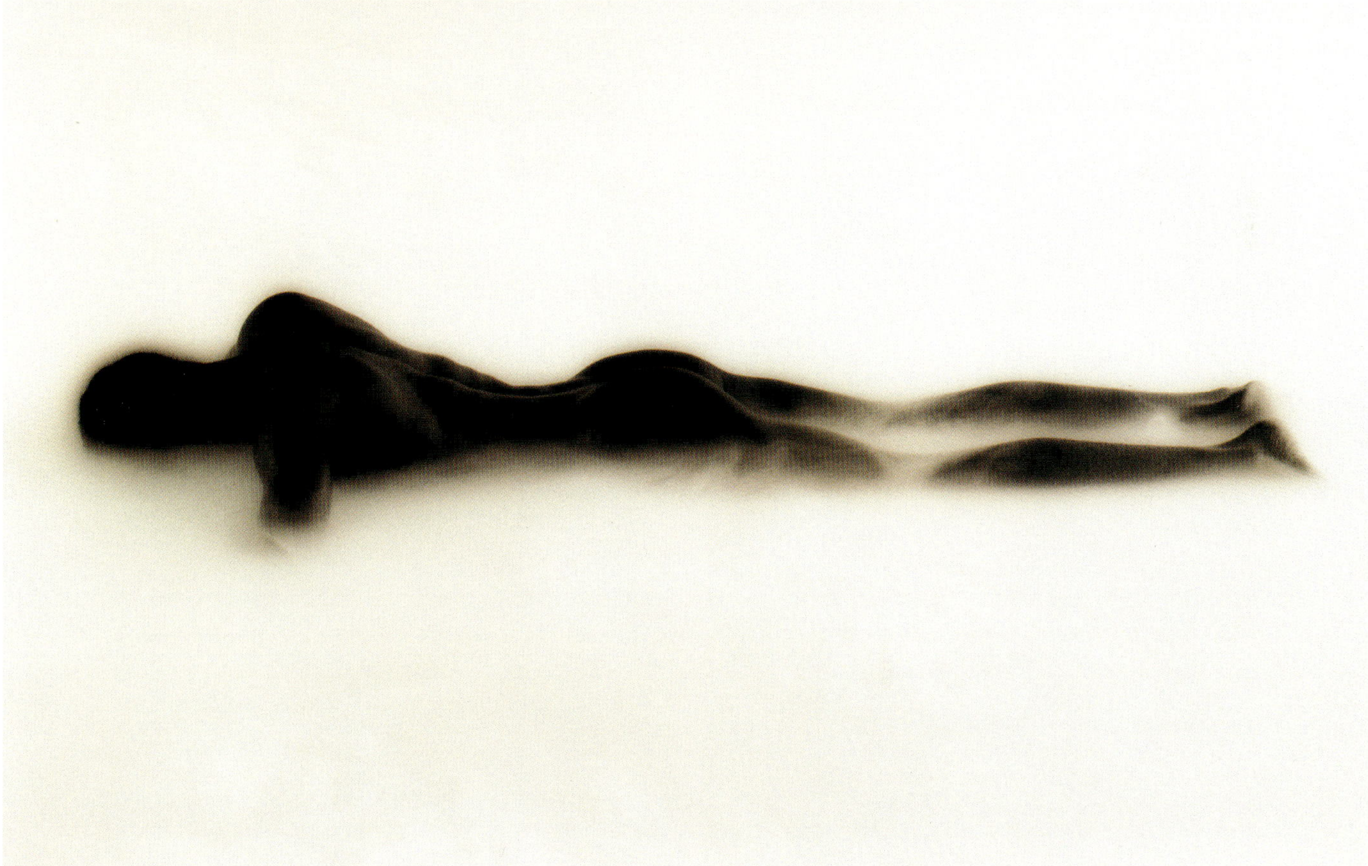

Toshiaki Takeuchi

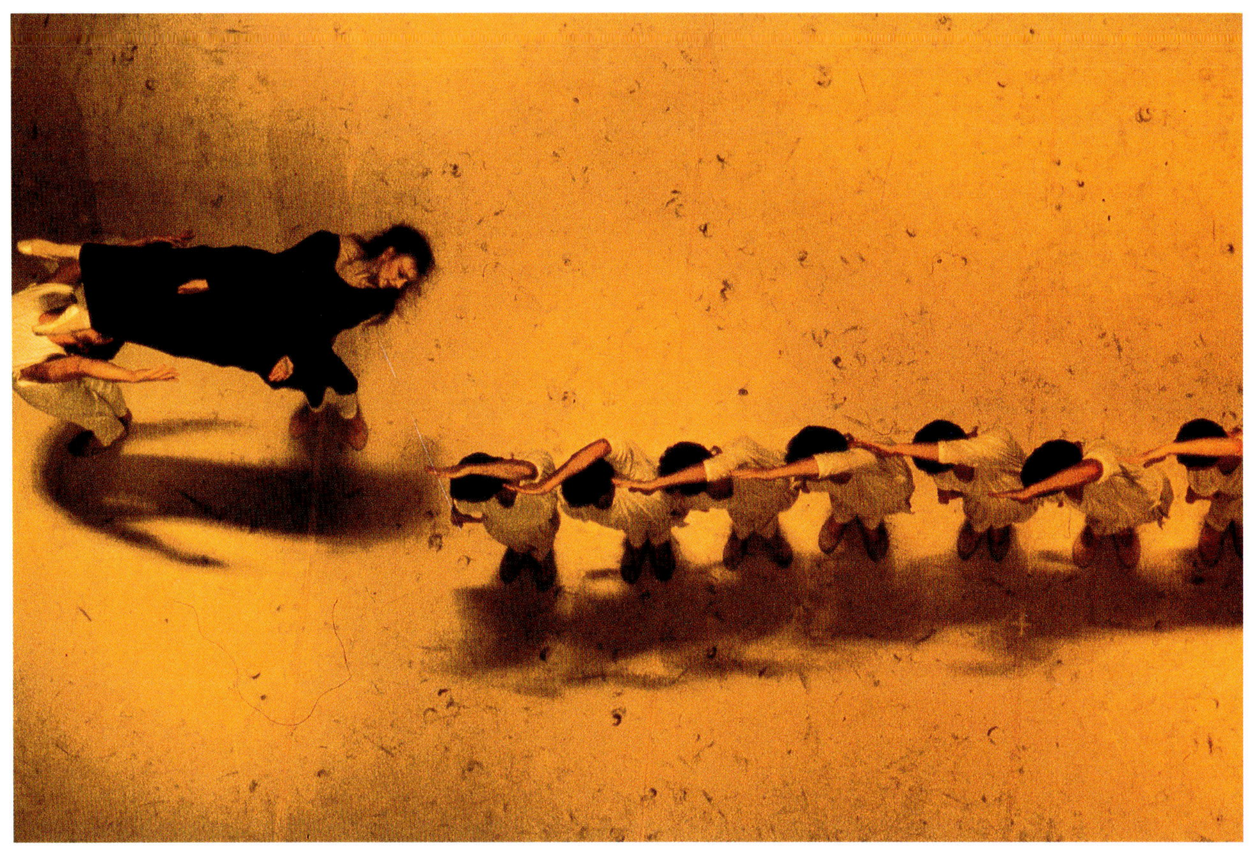

Dieter Blum

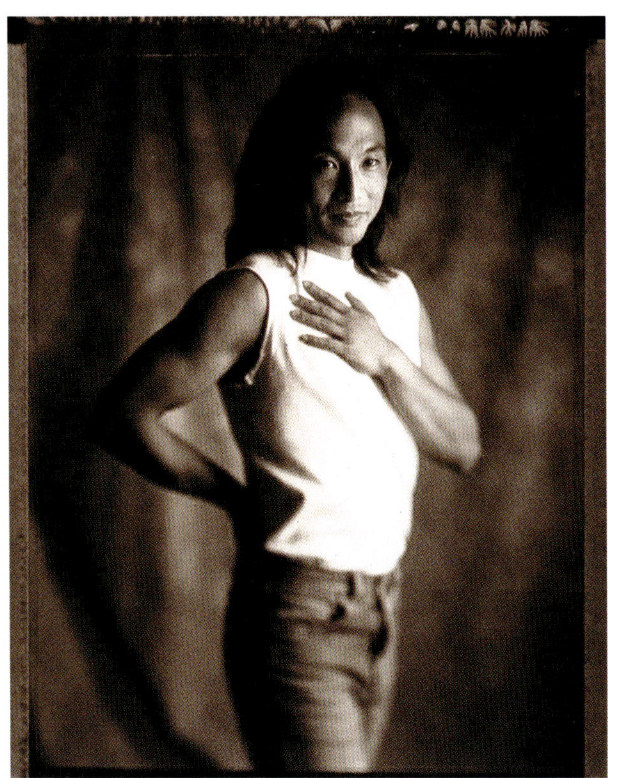

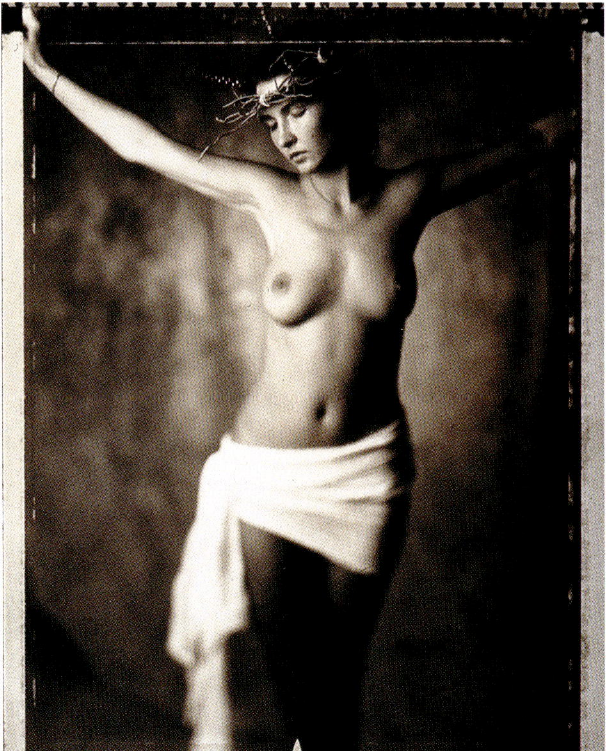

Roseanne Olson

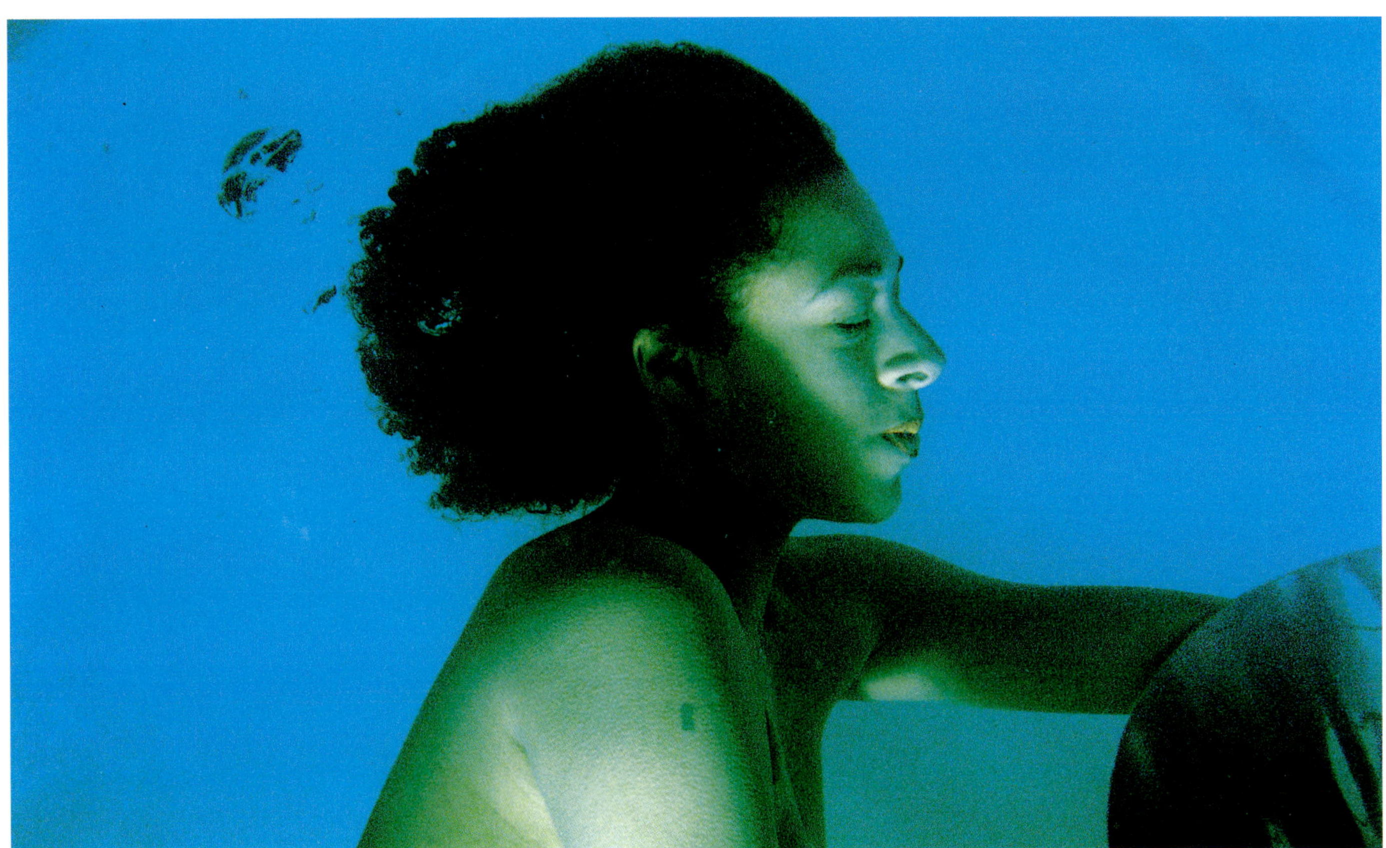

Walter Fogel

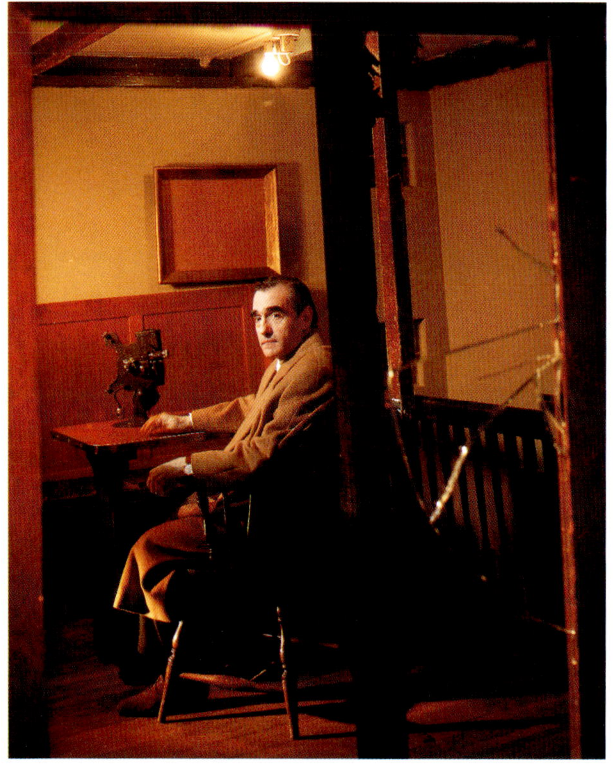

Max Aguilera-Hellweg

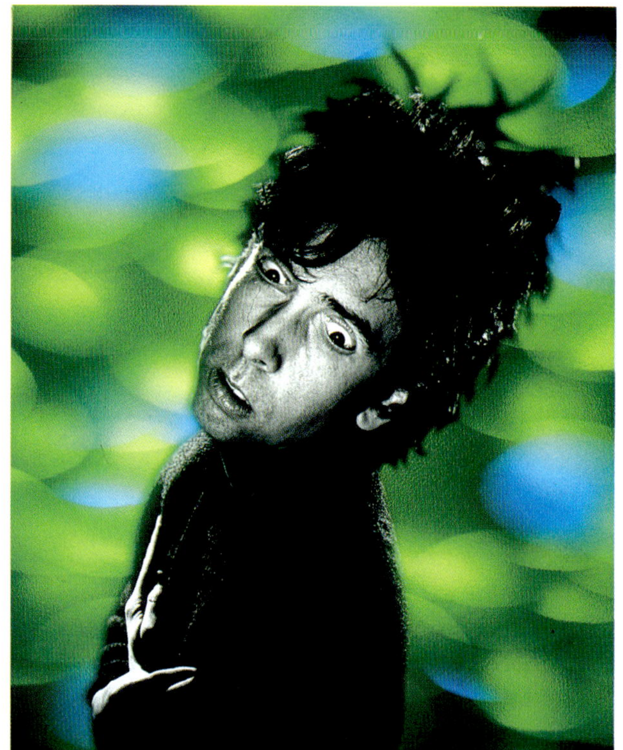

Michael Llewellyn

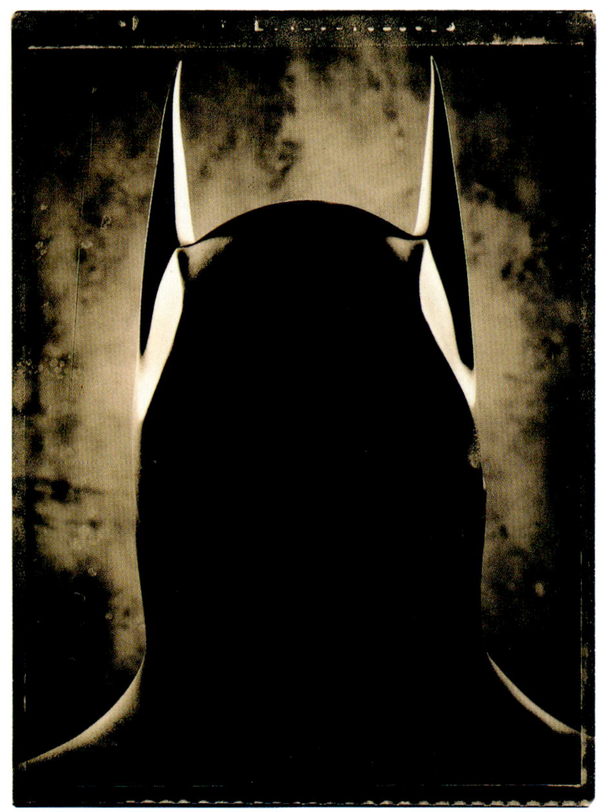

Mark Hanauer

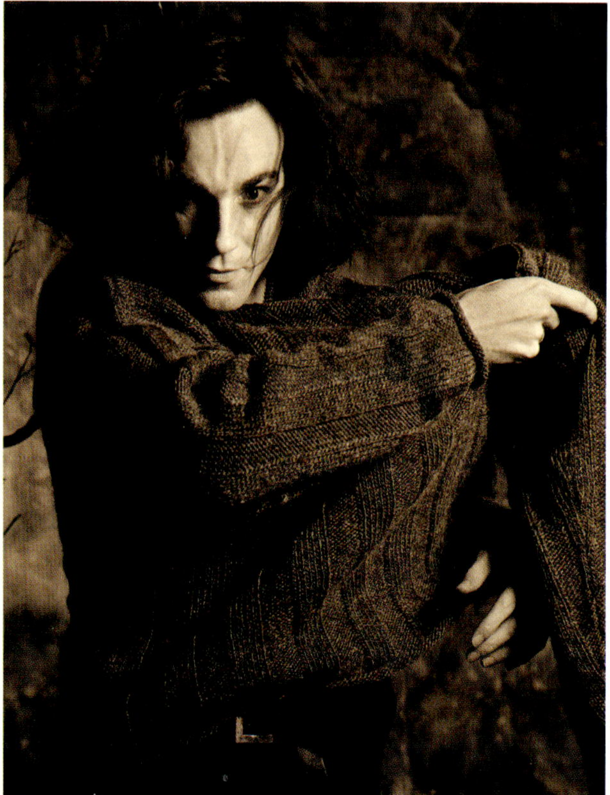

Michele Clement

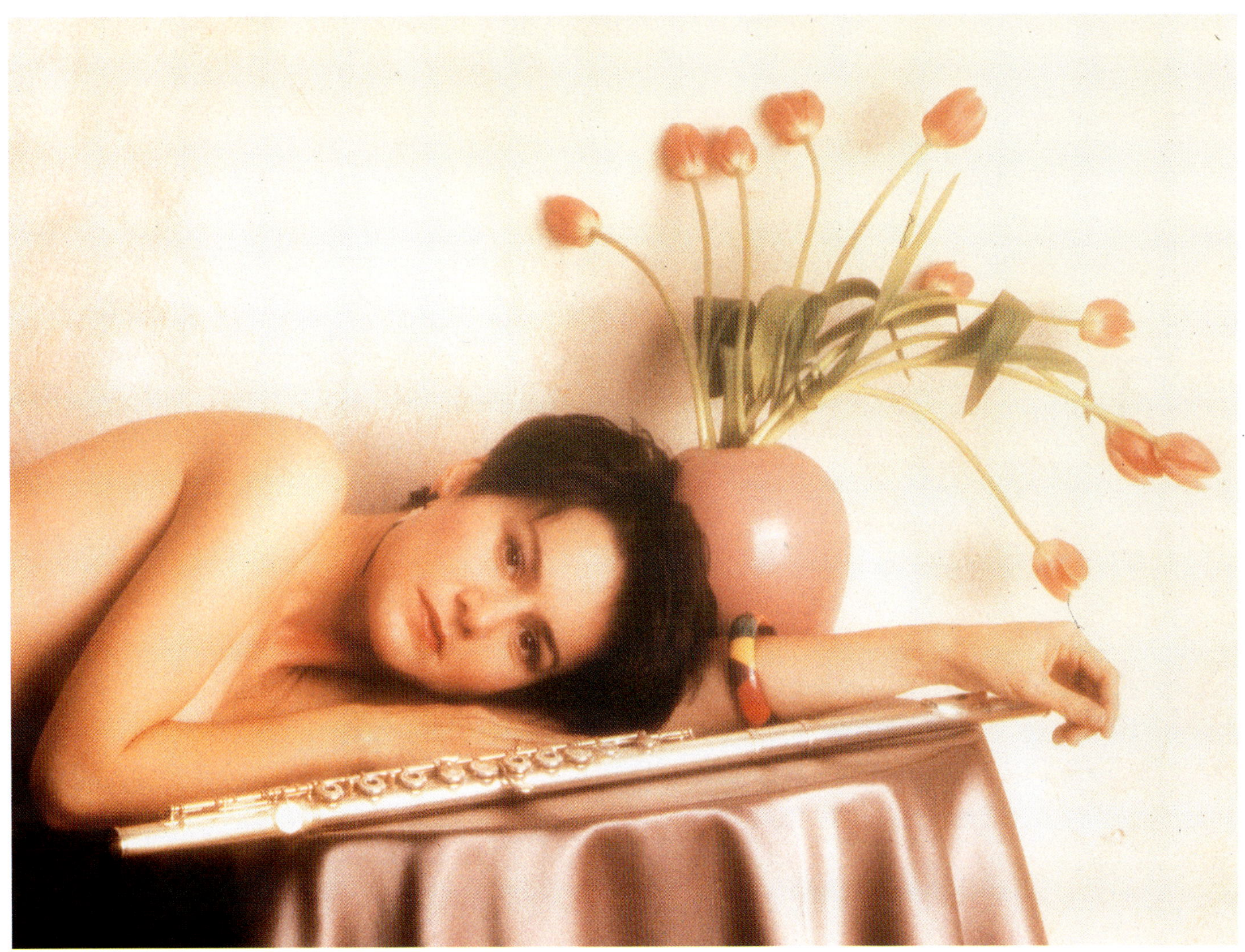

Sandra Eisner

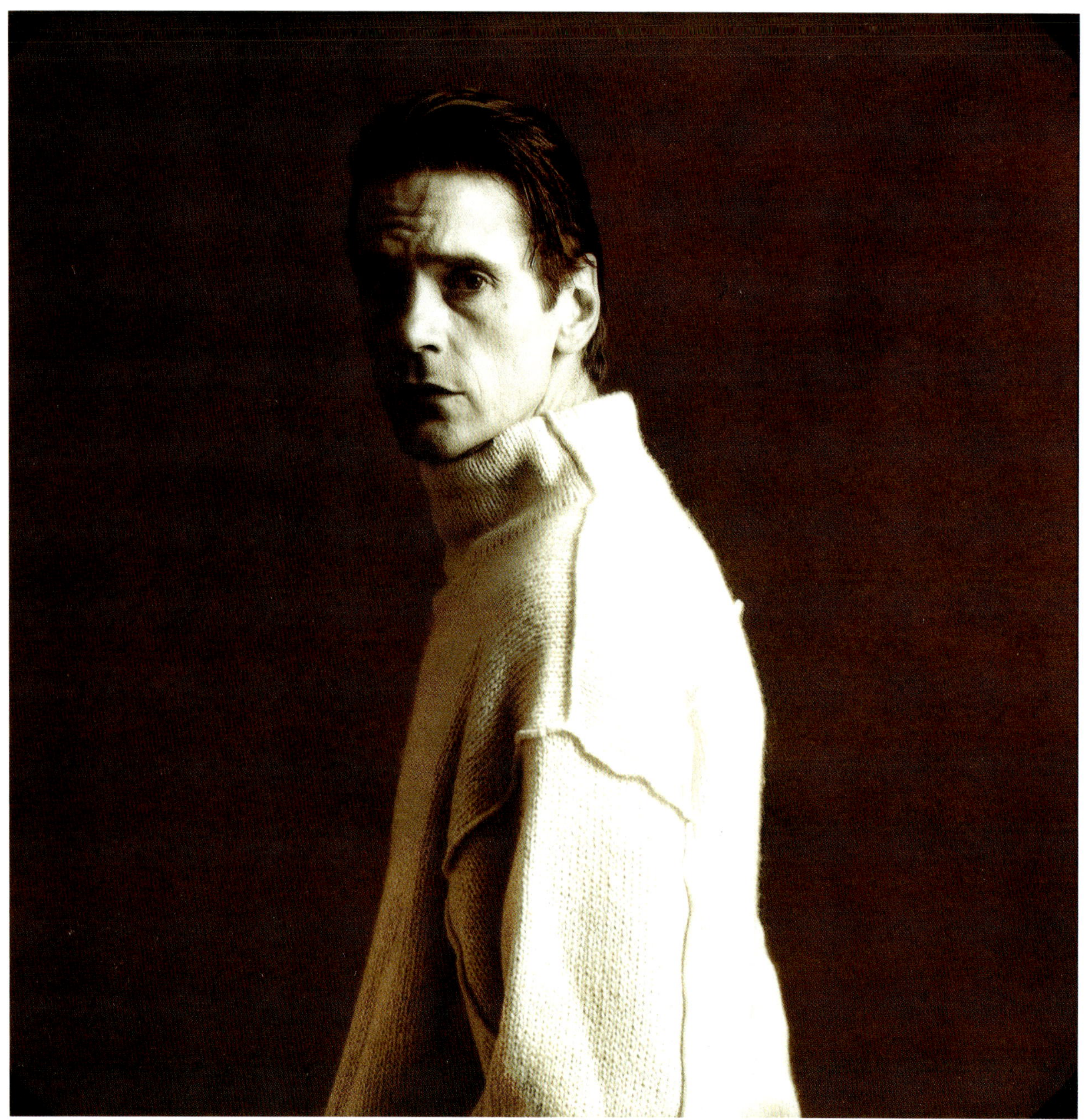

Timothy White

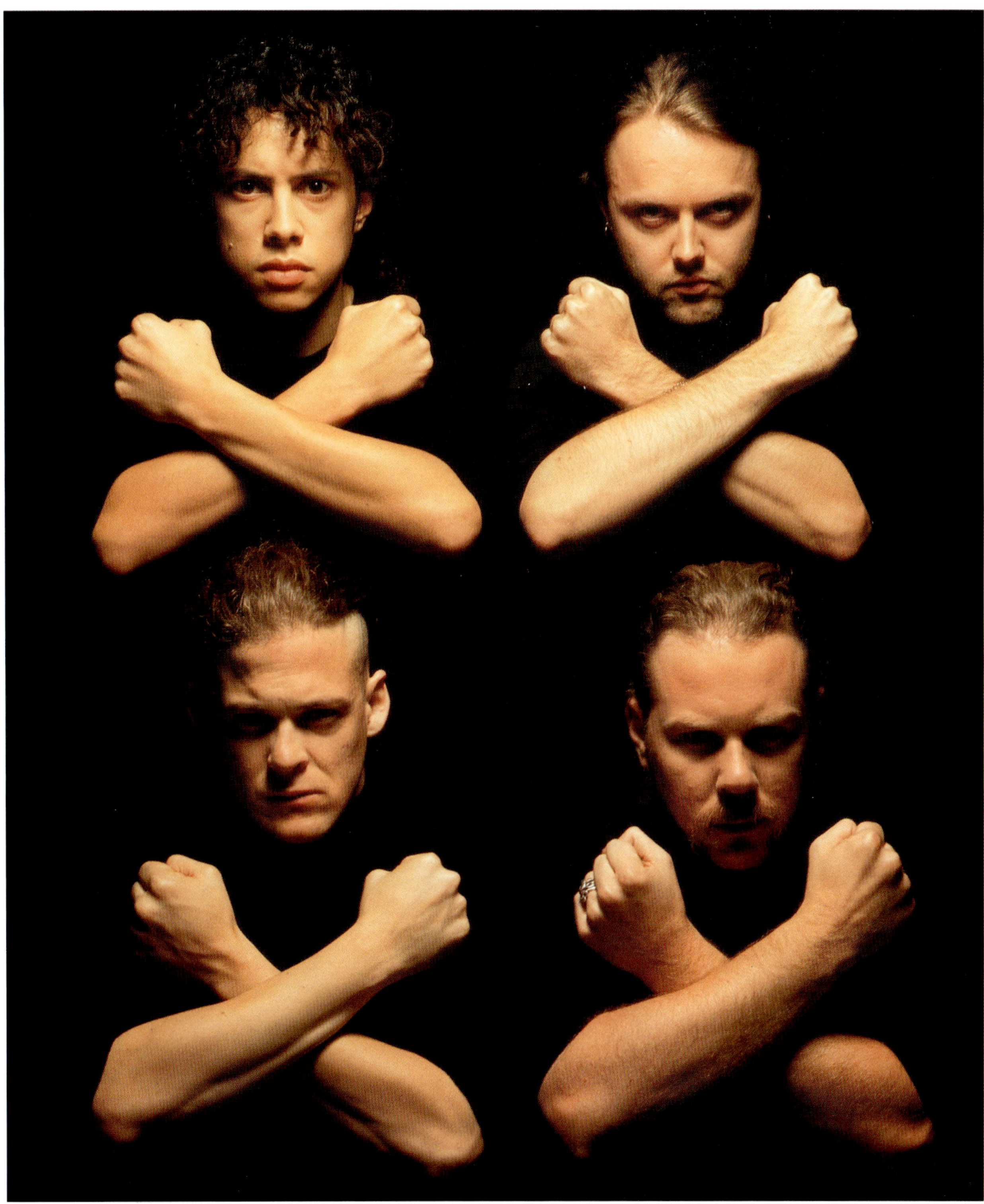

Mark Seliger

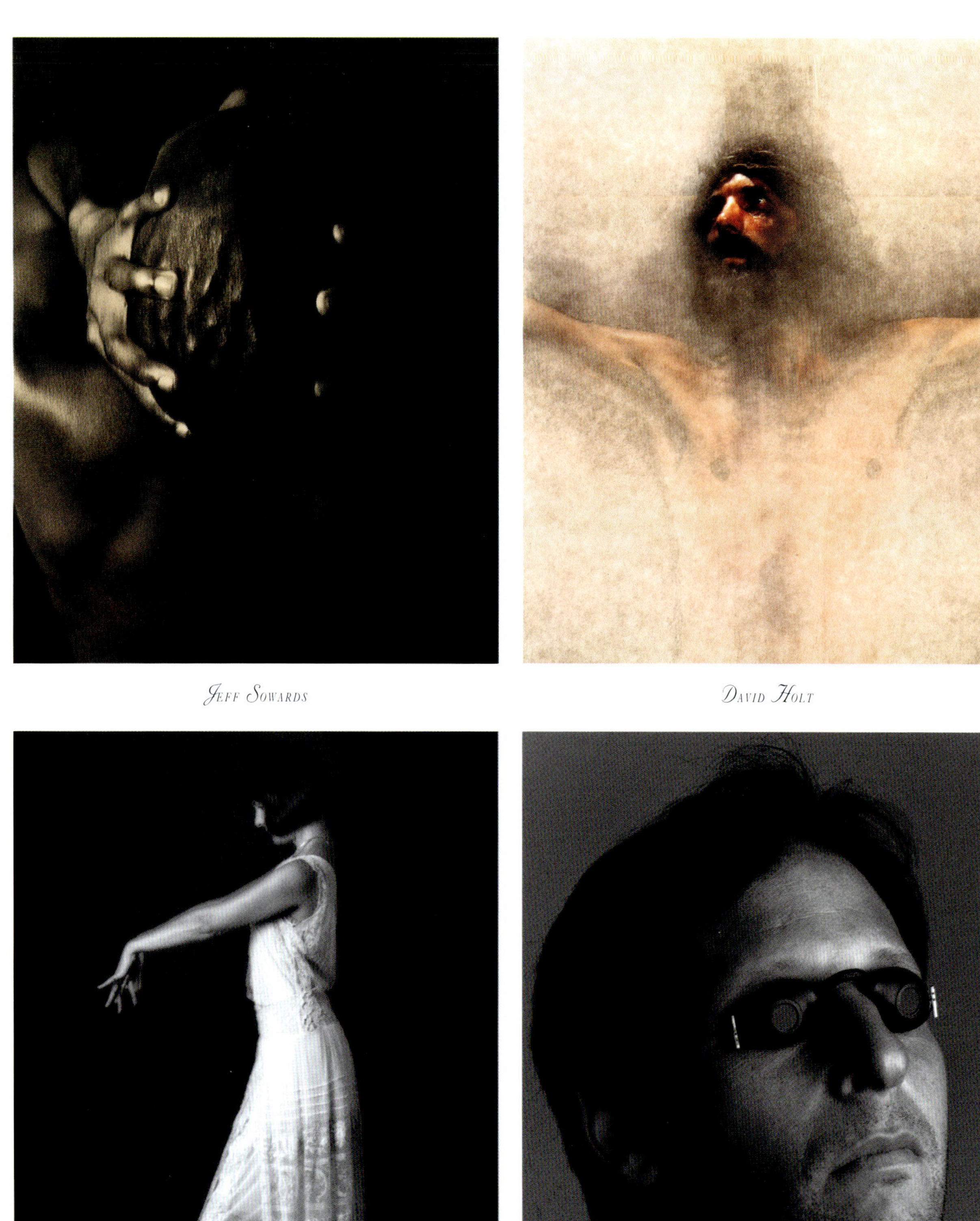

Jeff Sowards

David Holt

Howard Schatz

Steve Marsel

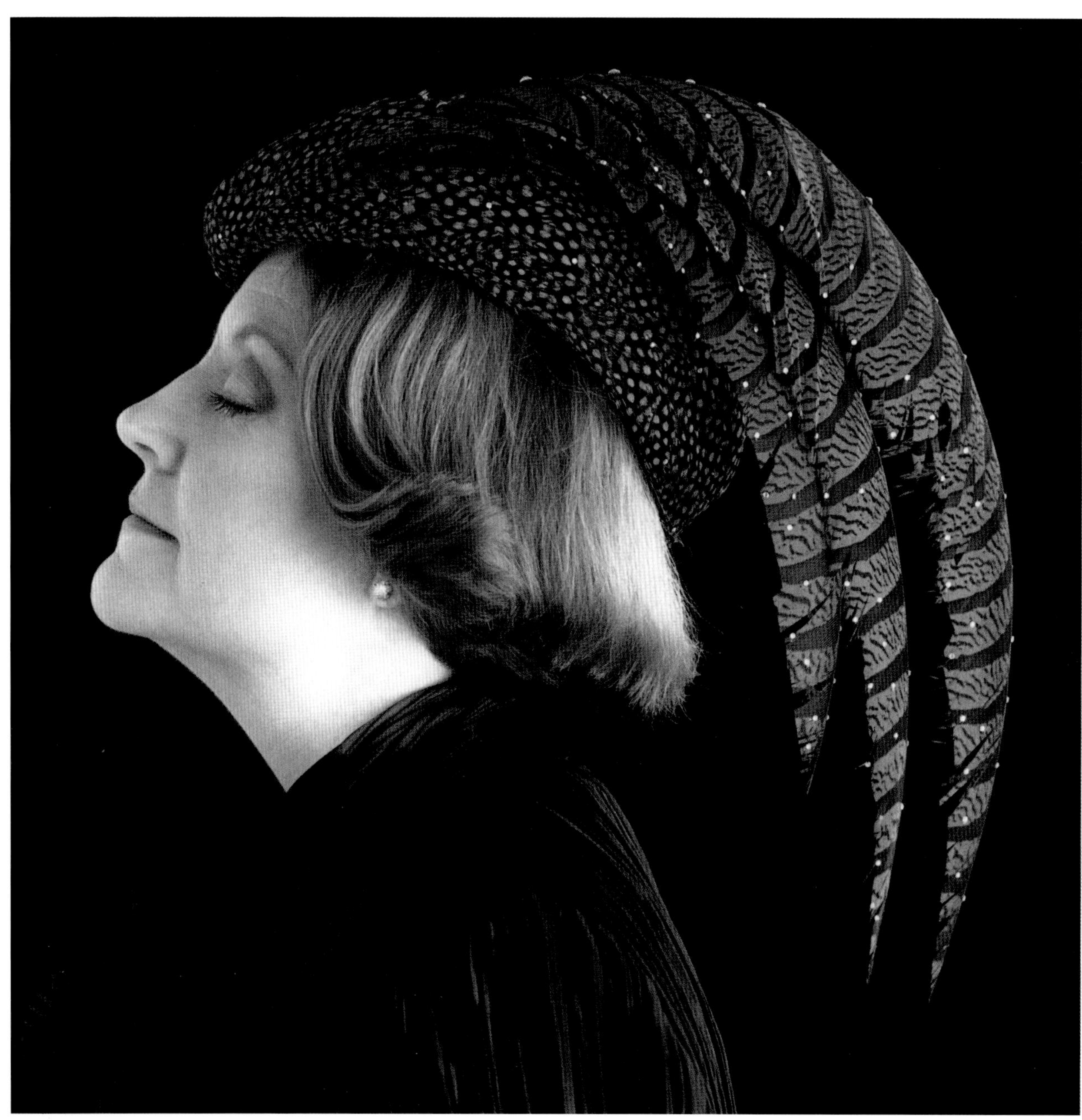

Howard Schatz

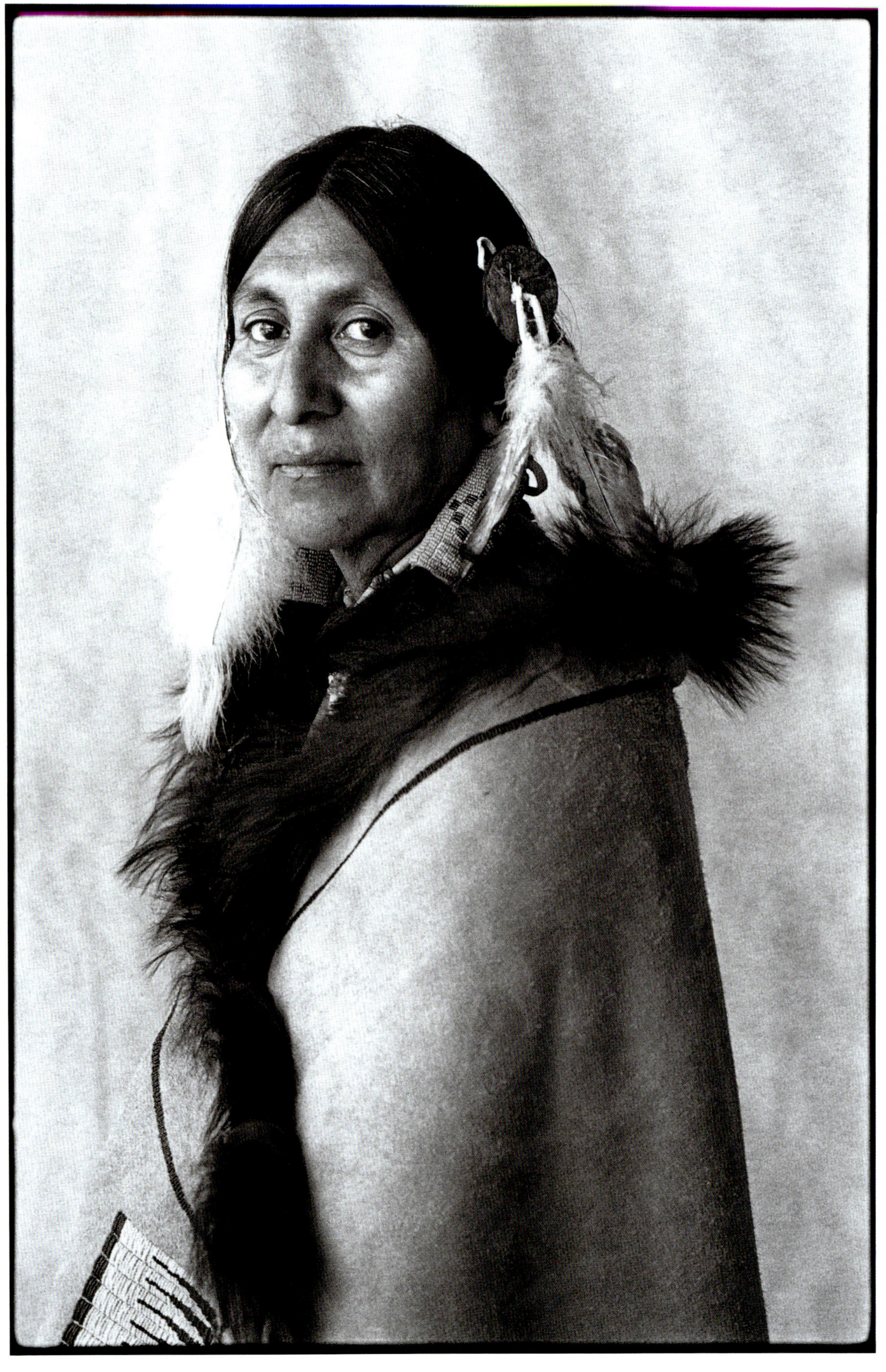

Sue Bennett

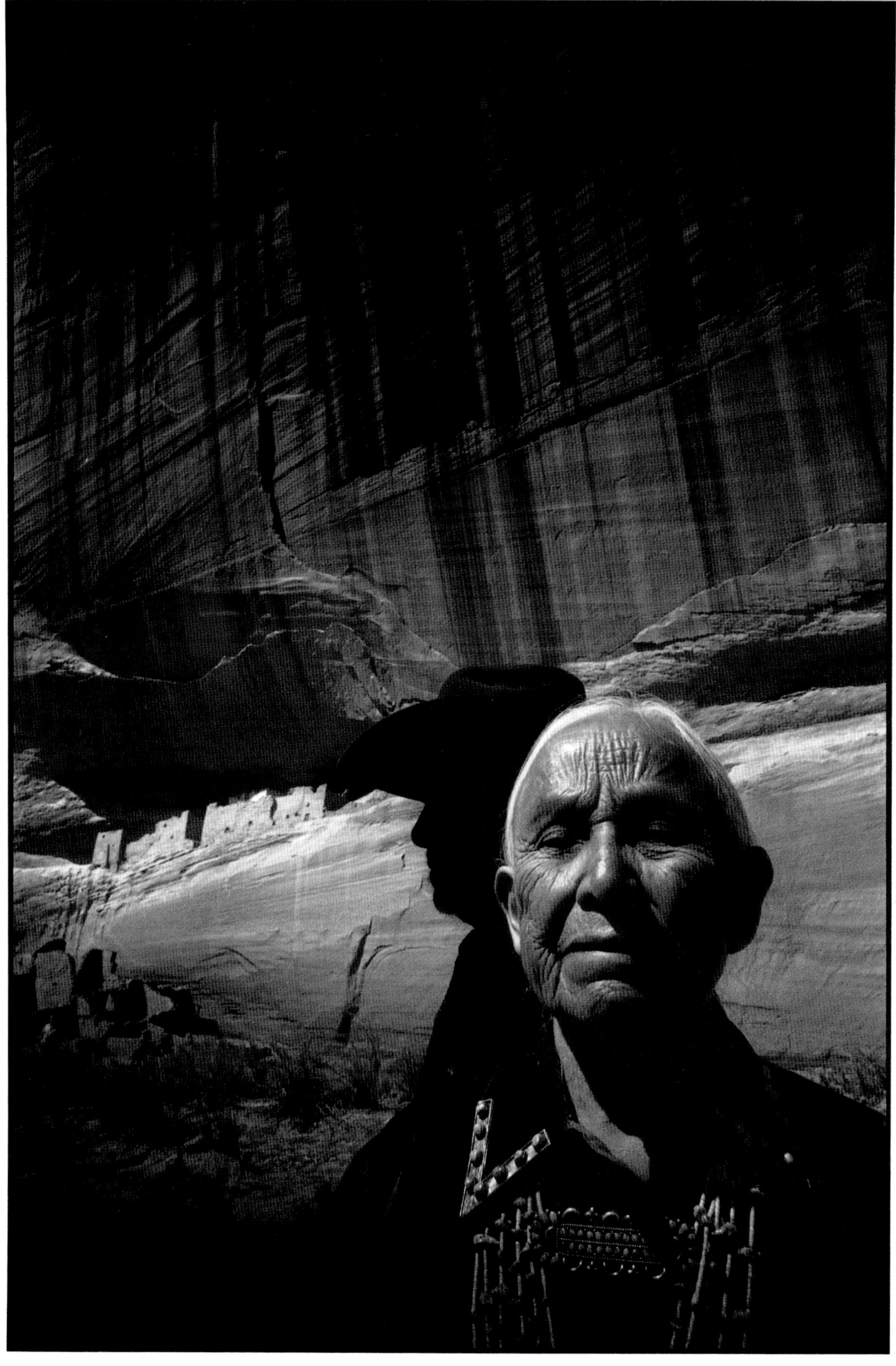

Greg Booth

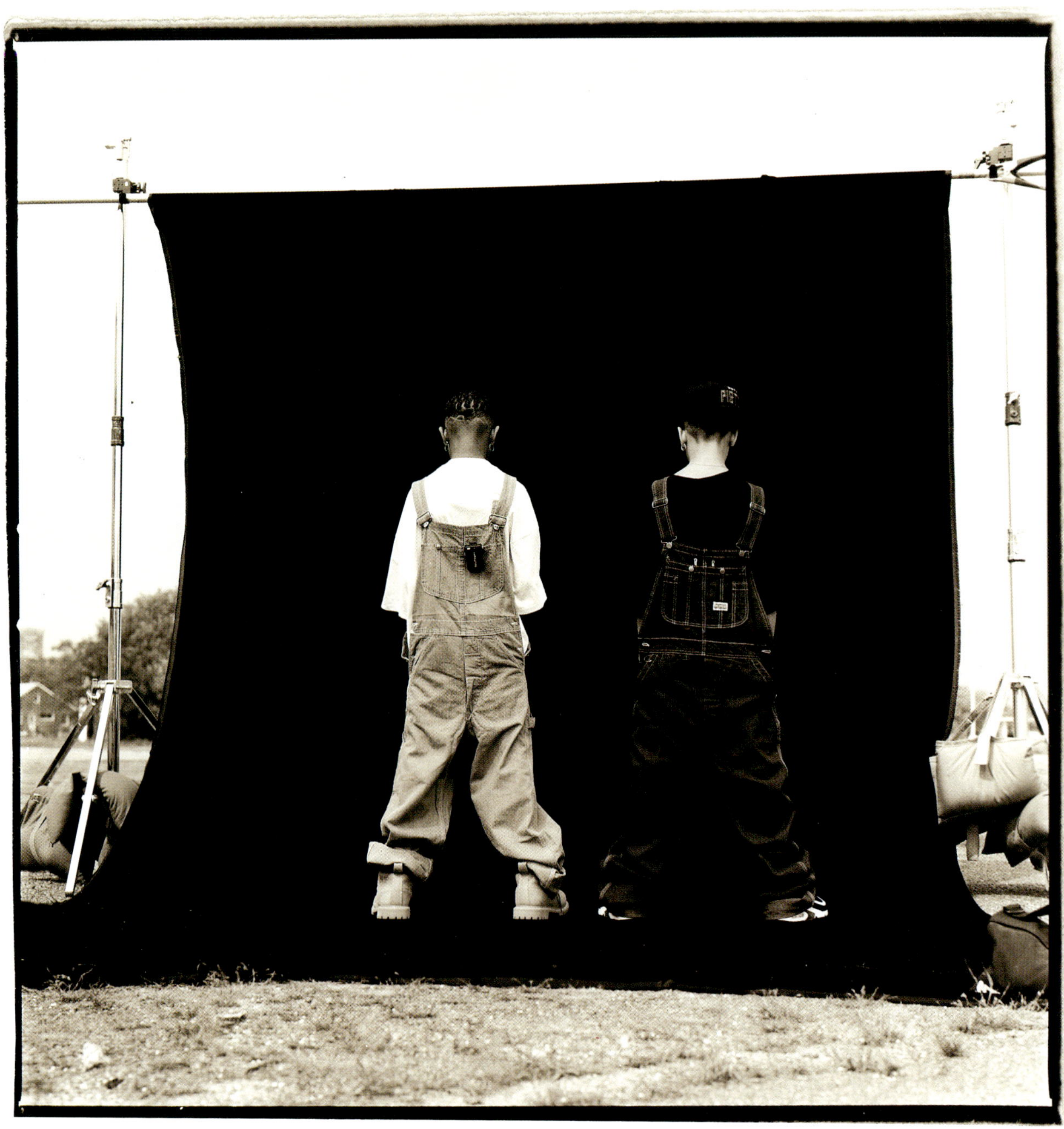

Michael Biondo

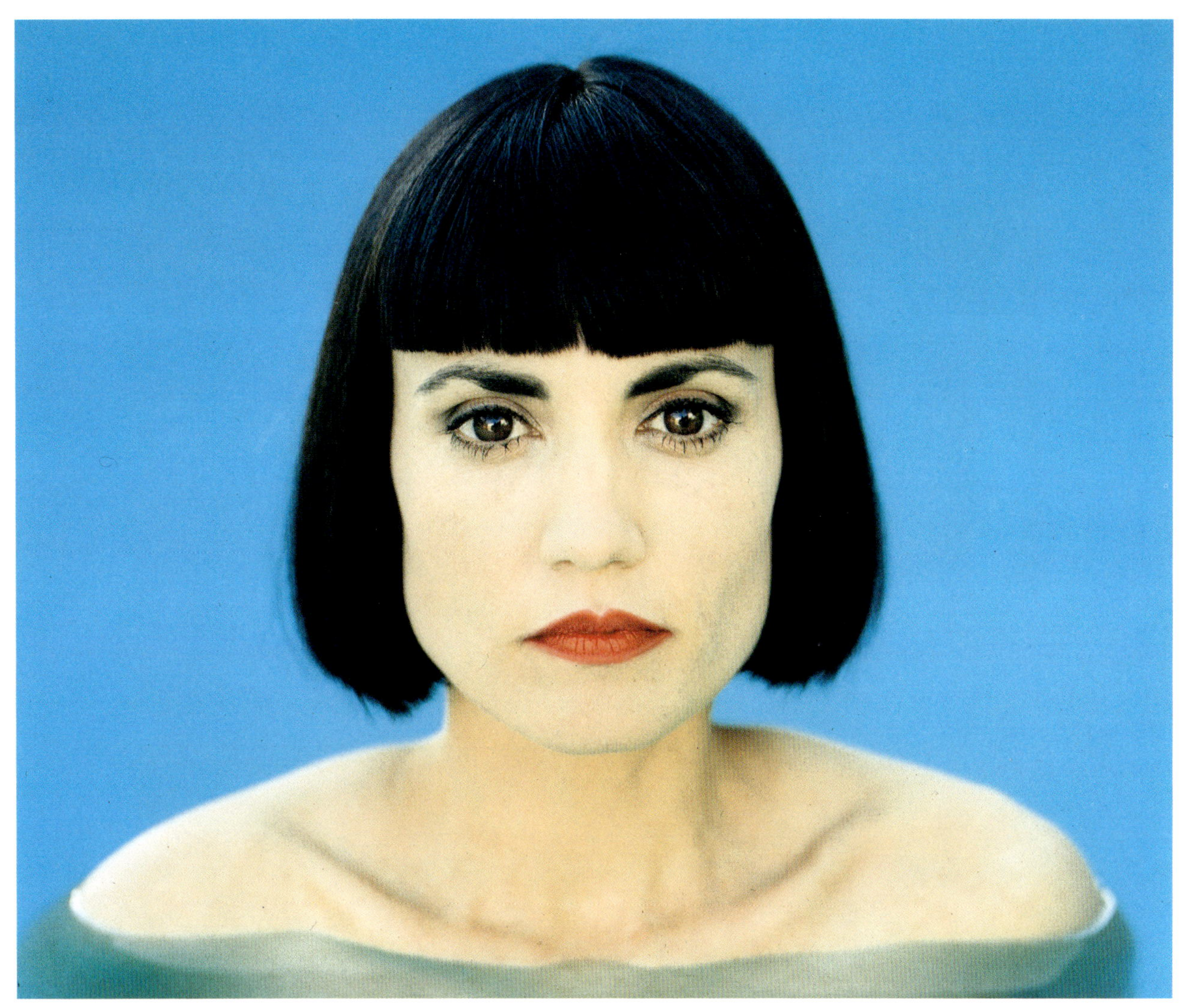

Roland Fischer

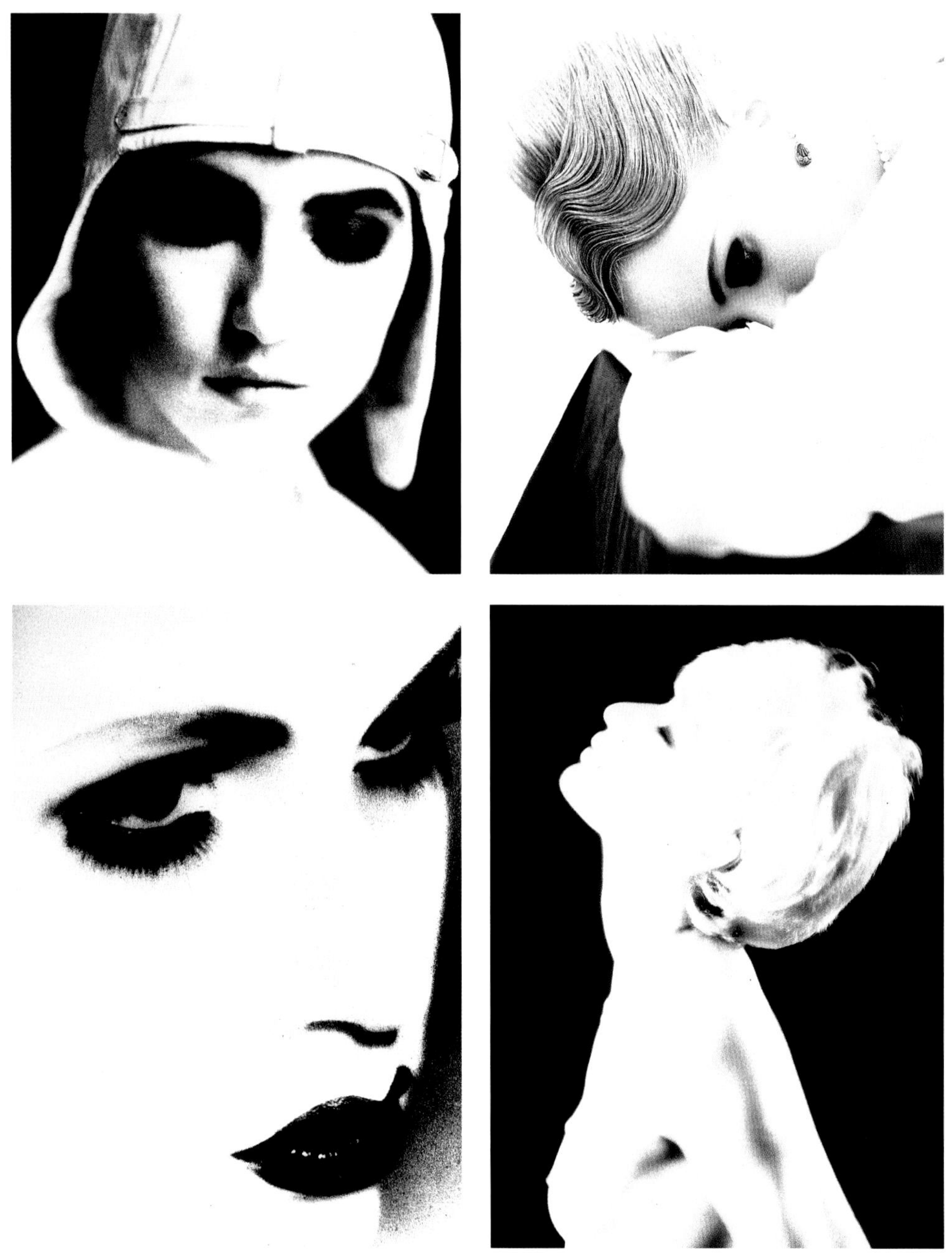

Michel Dubois

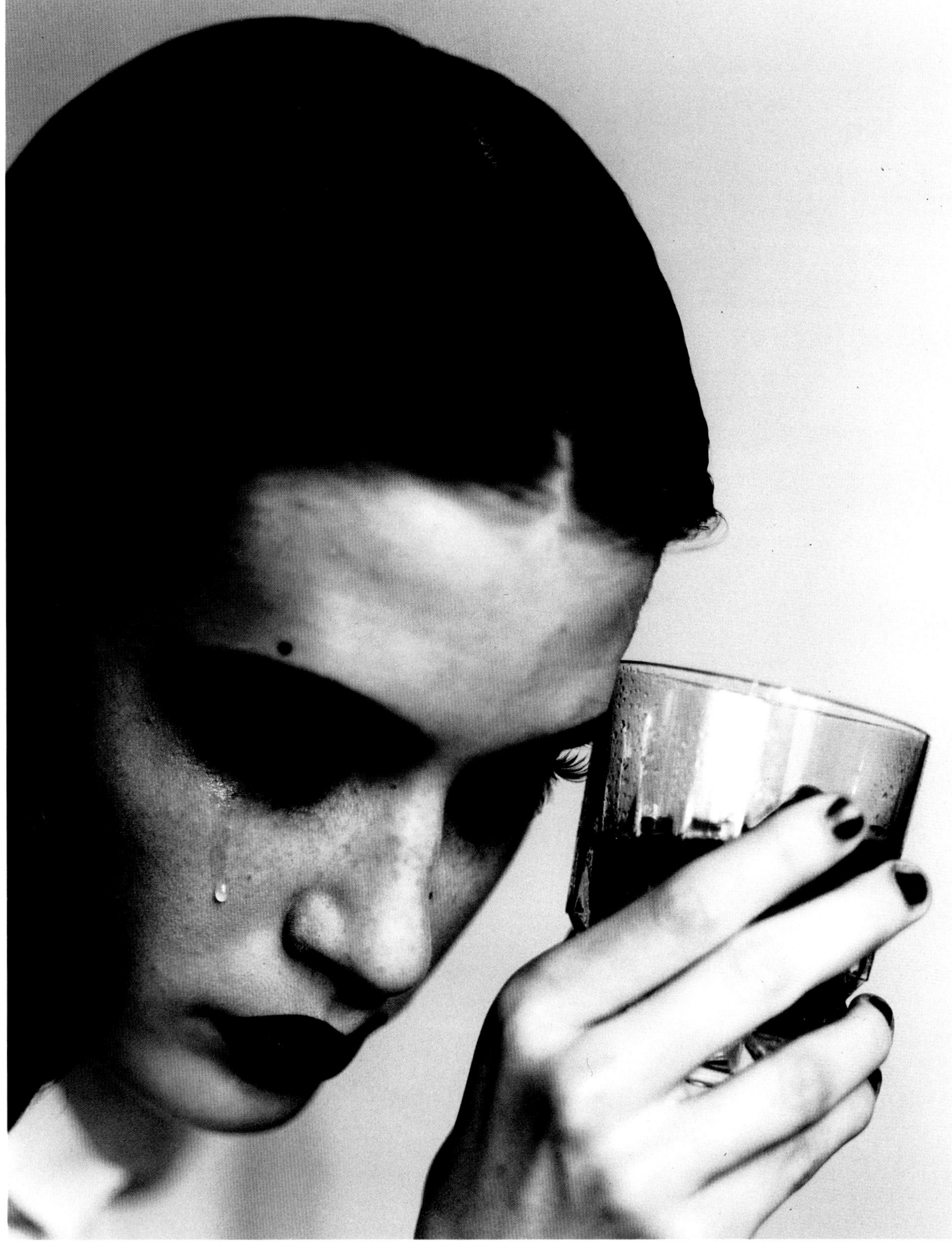

Michel Dubois

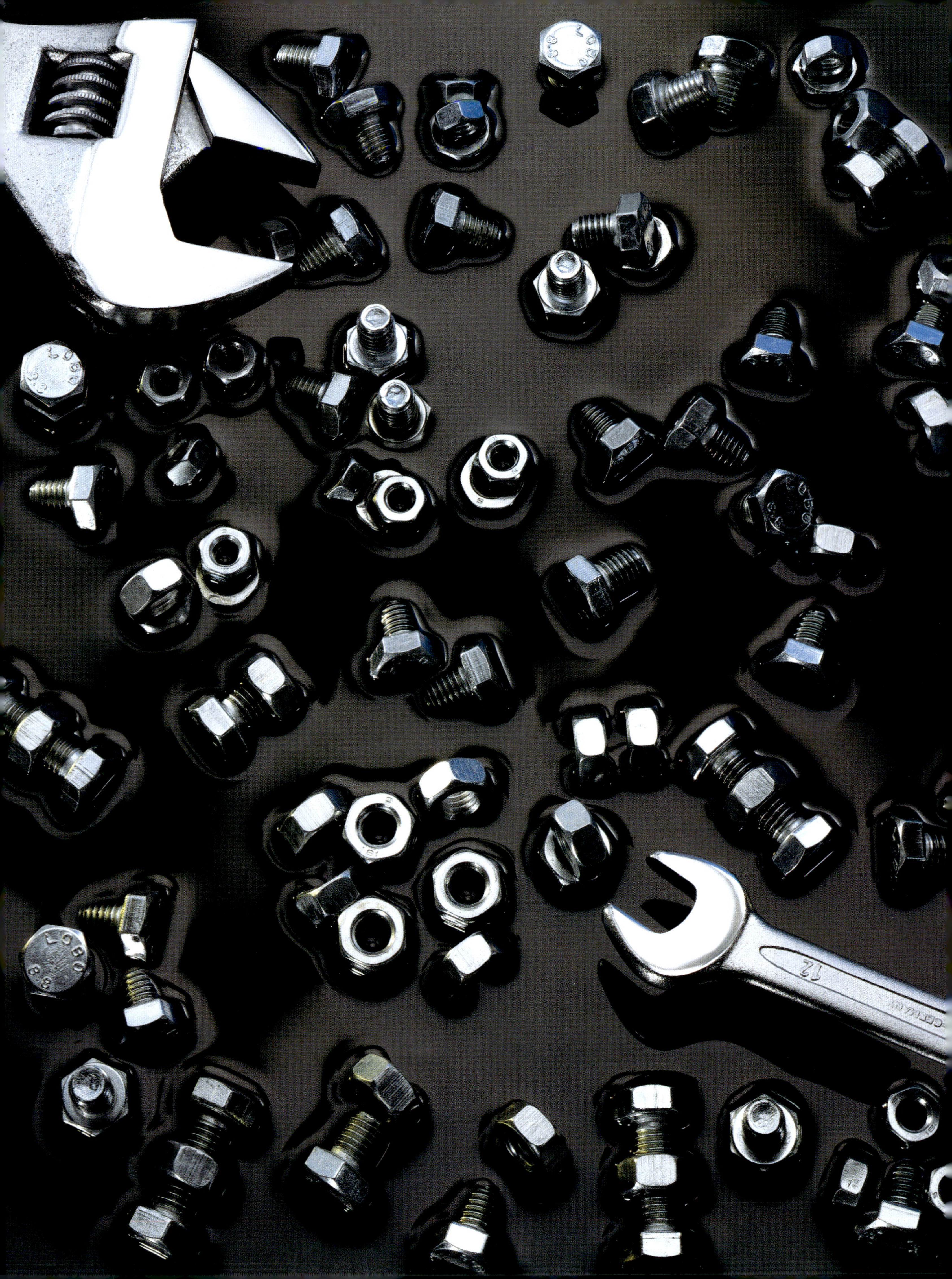

PRODUCTS

SACHAUFNAHMEN

PRODUITS

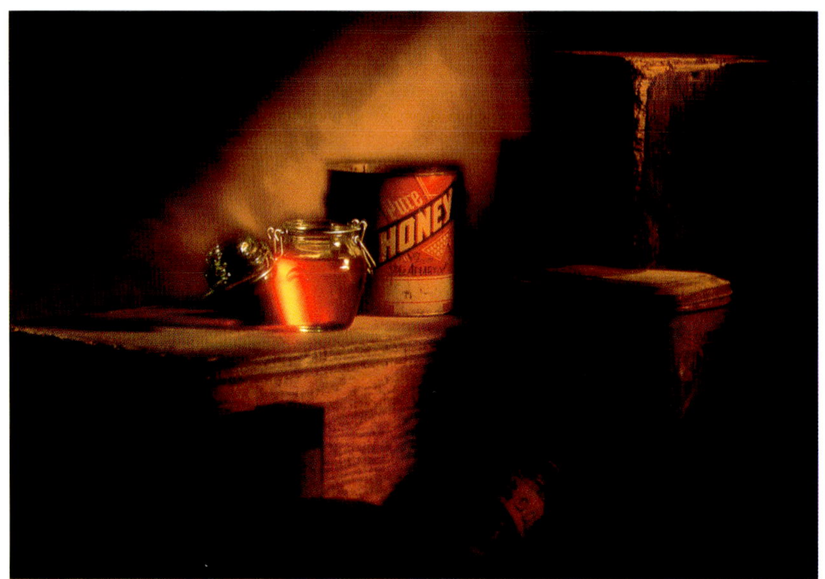

Preceeding Spread: Michael Hogrefe / Above: Ron Fehling

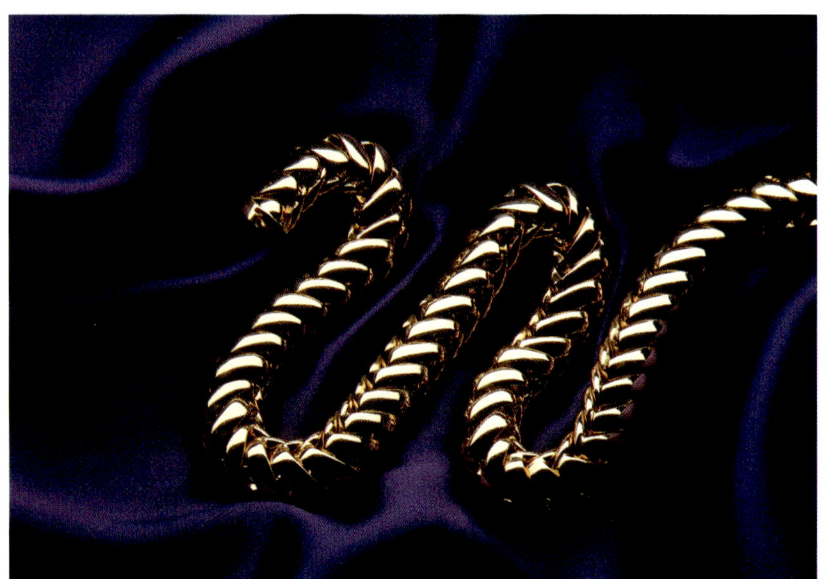

Terry Heffernan

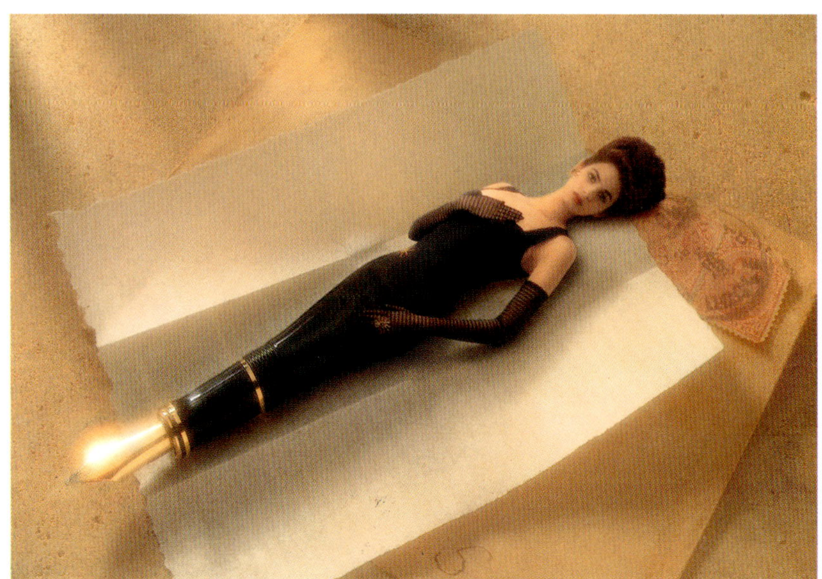

Laurie Rubin

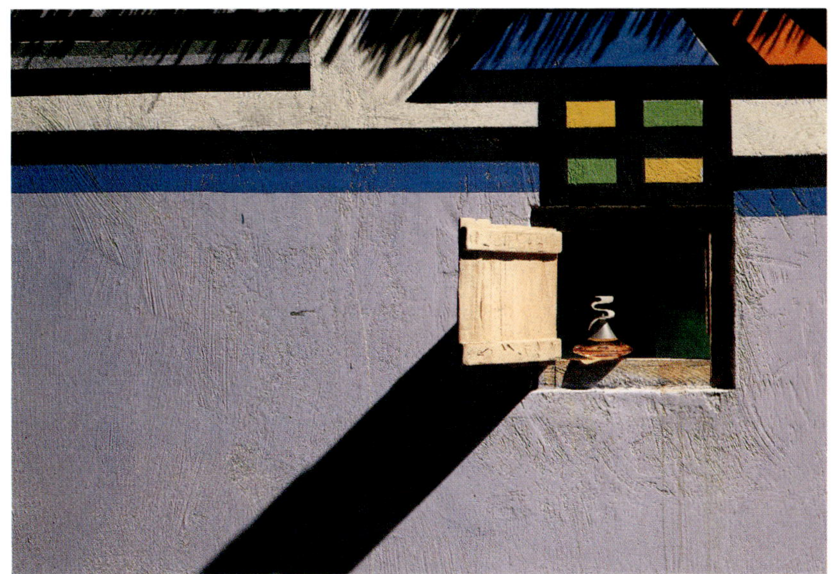

Stefan Kirchner

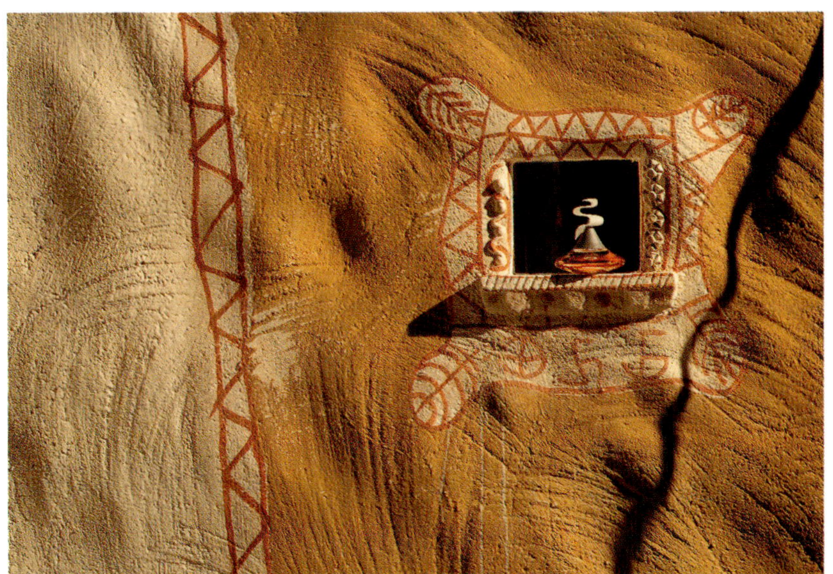

Stefan Kirchner

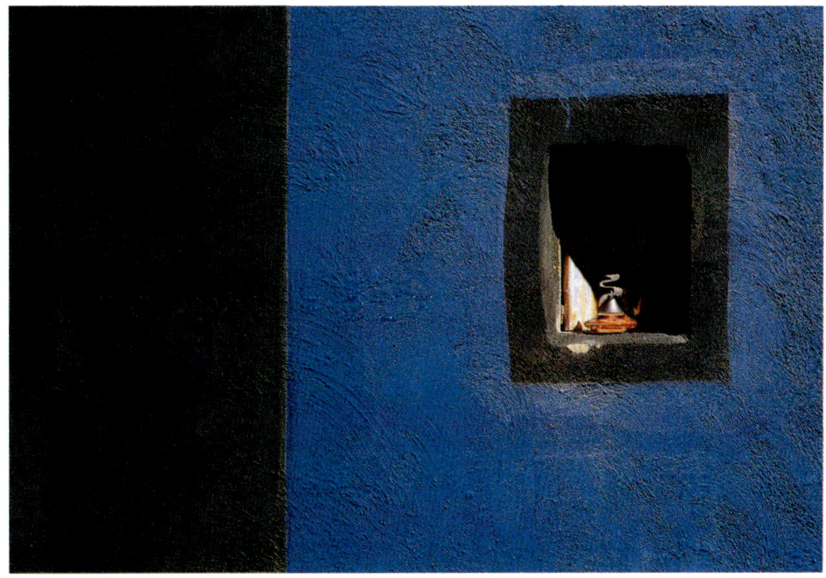

Stefan Kirchner

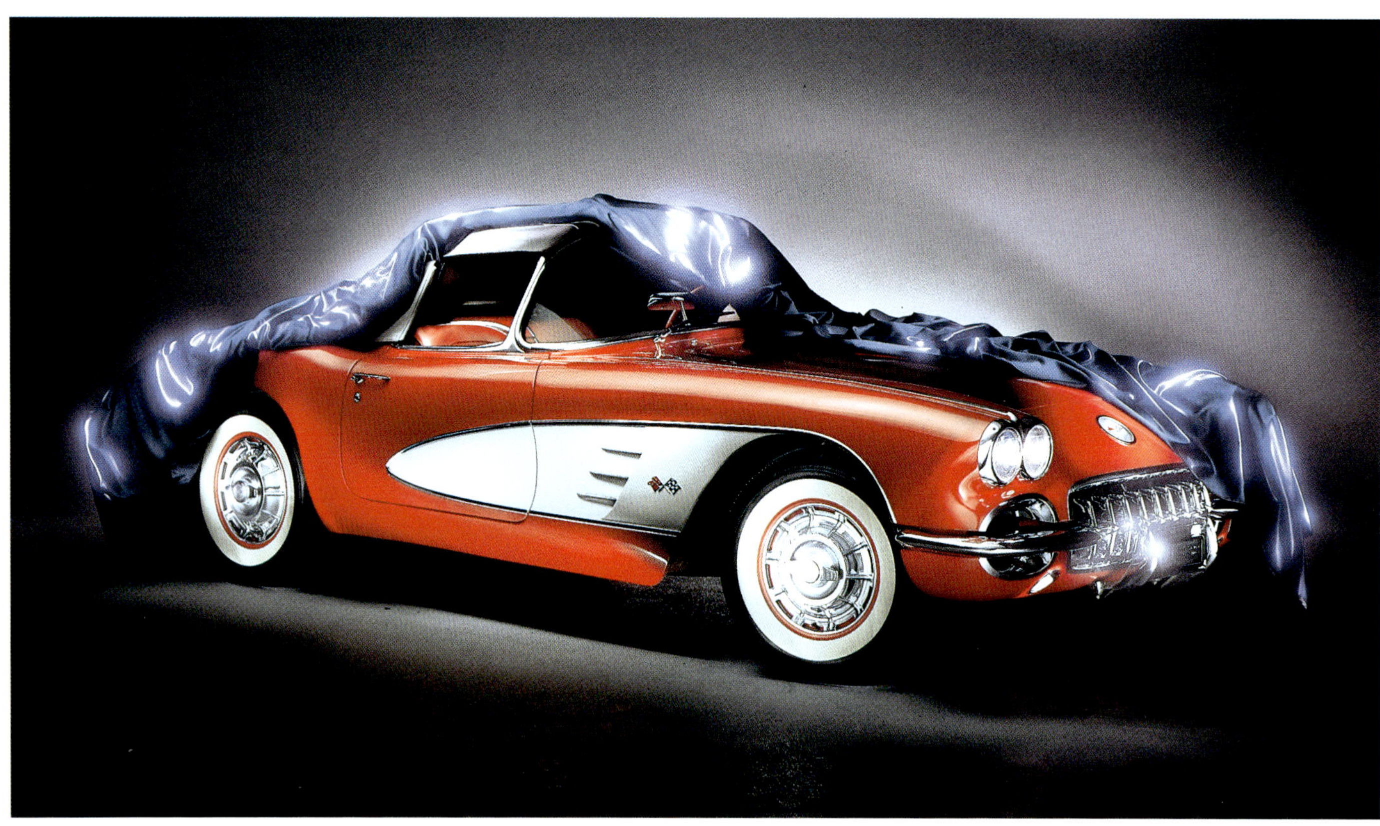

Alexander Bayer

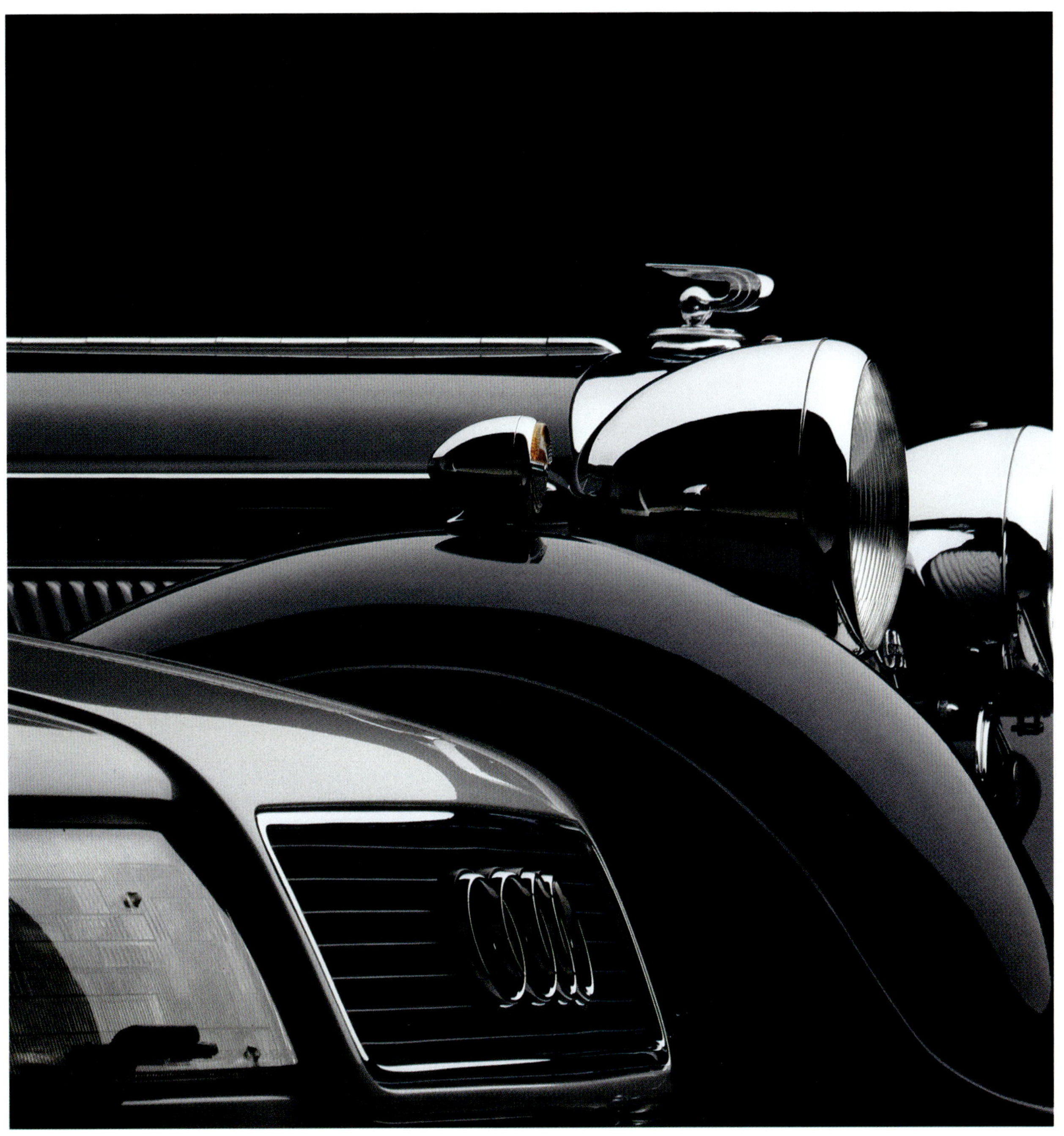

Rodney Rascona

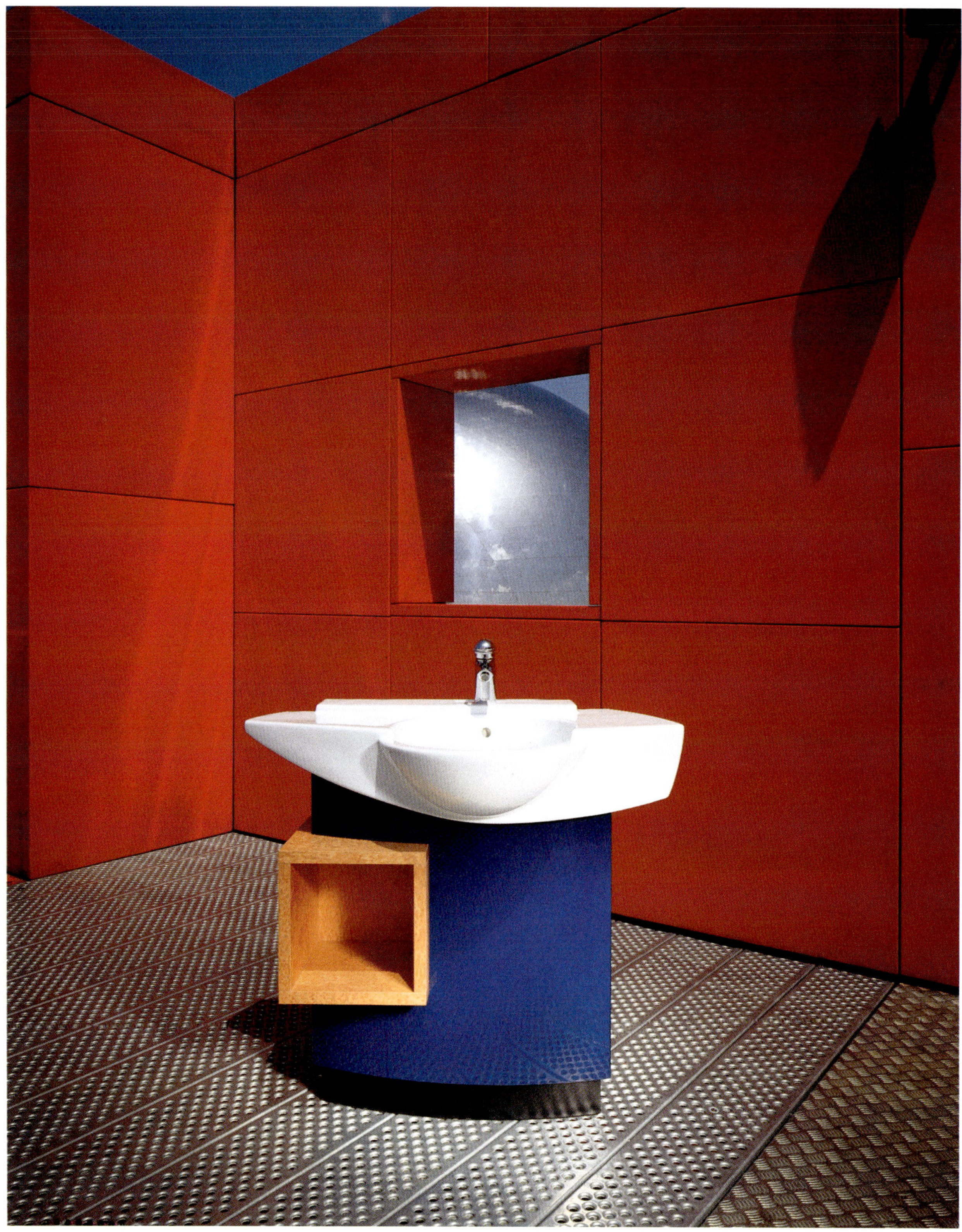

Daniel M. Hartz

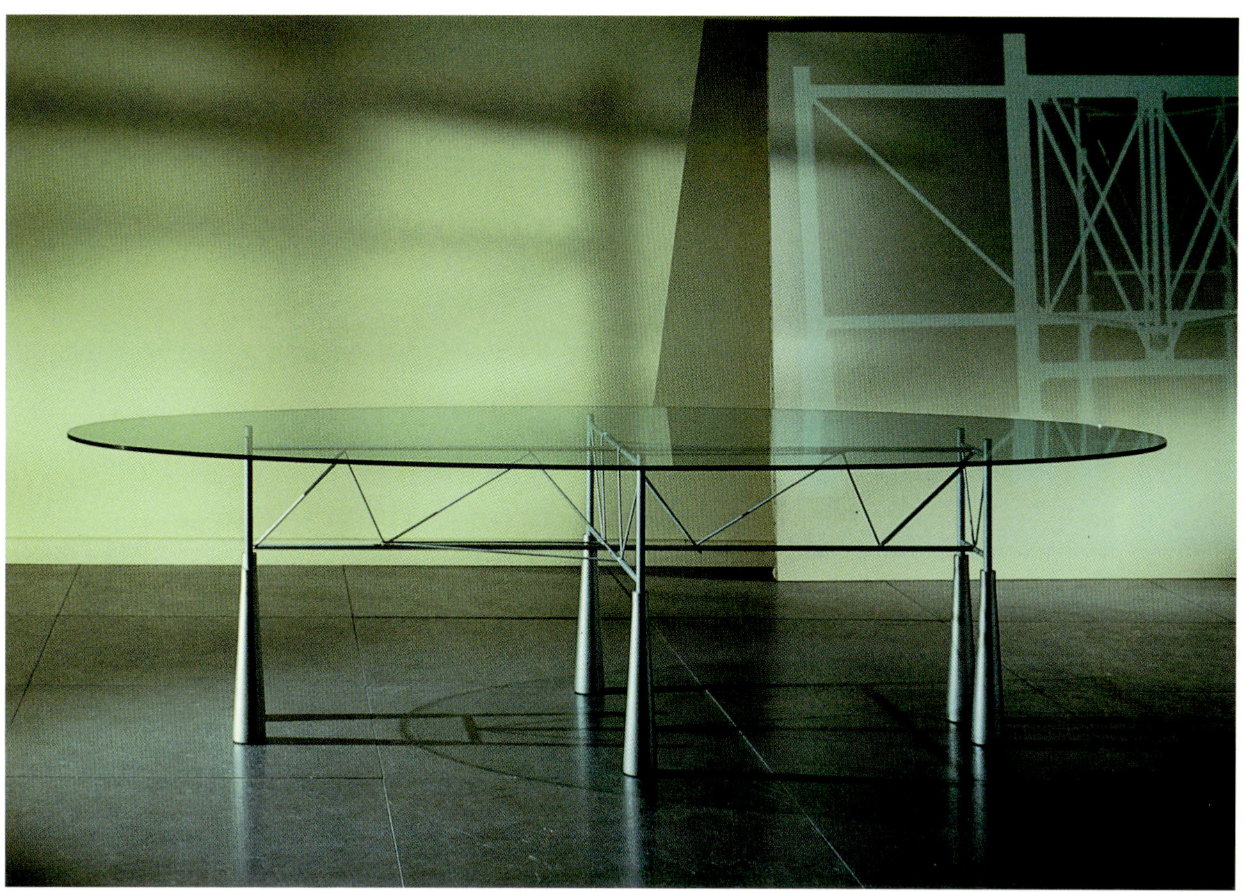

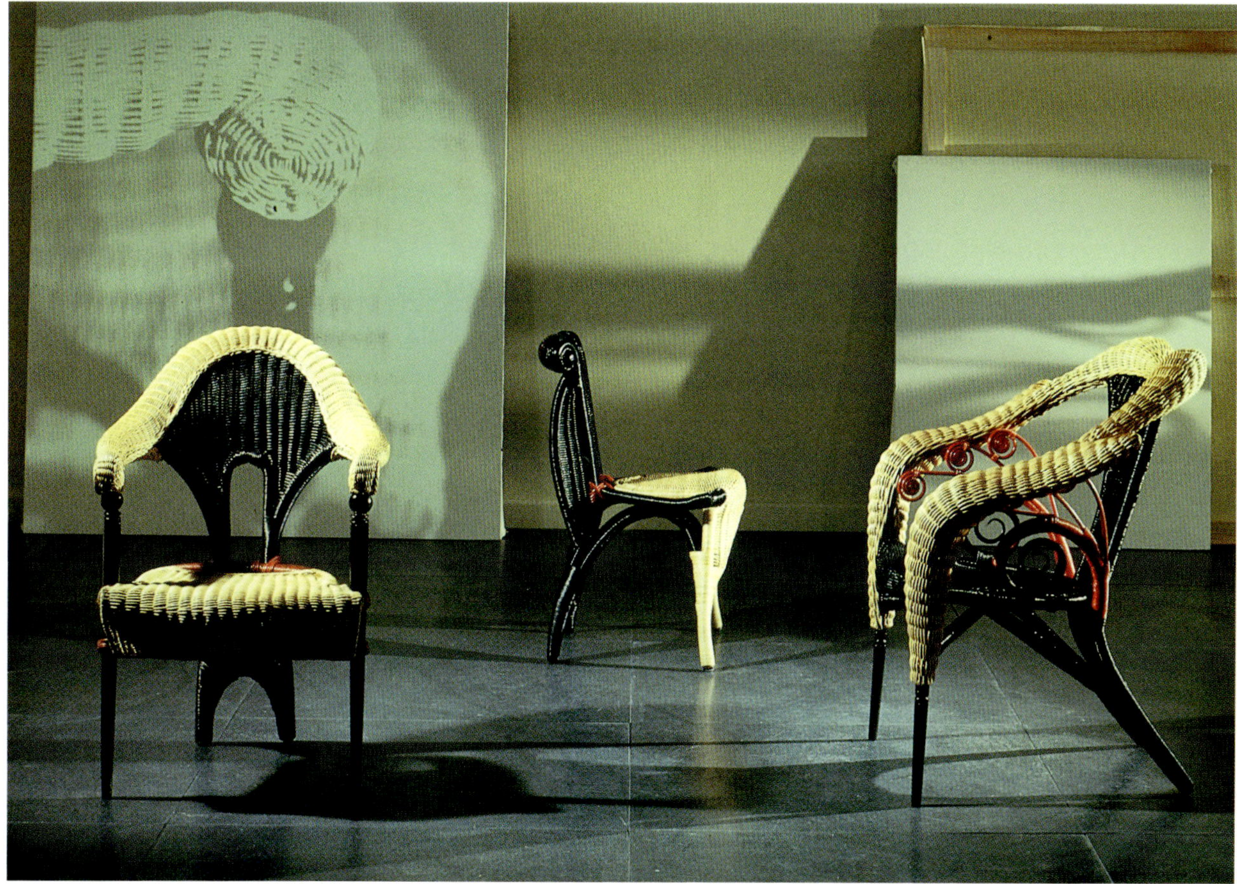

Emilio Tremolada

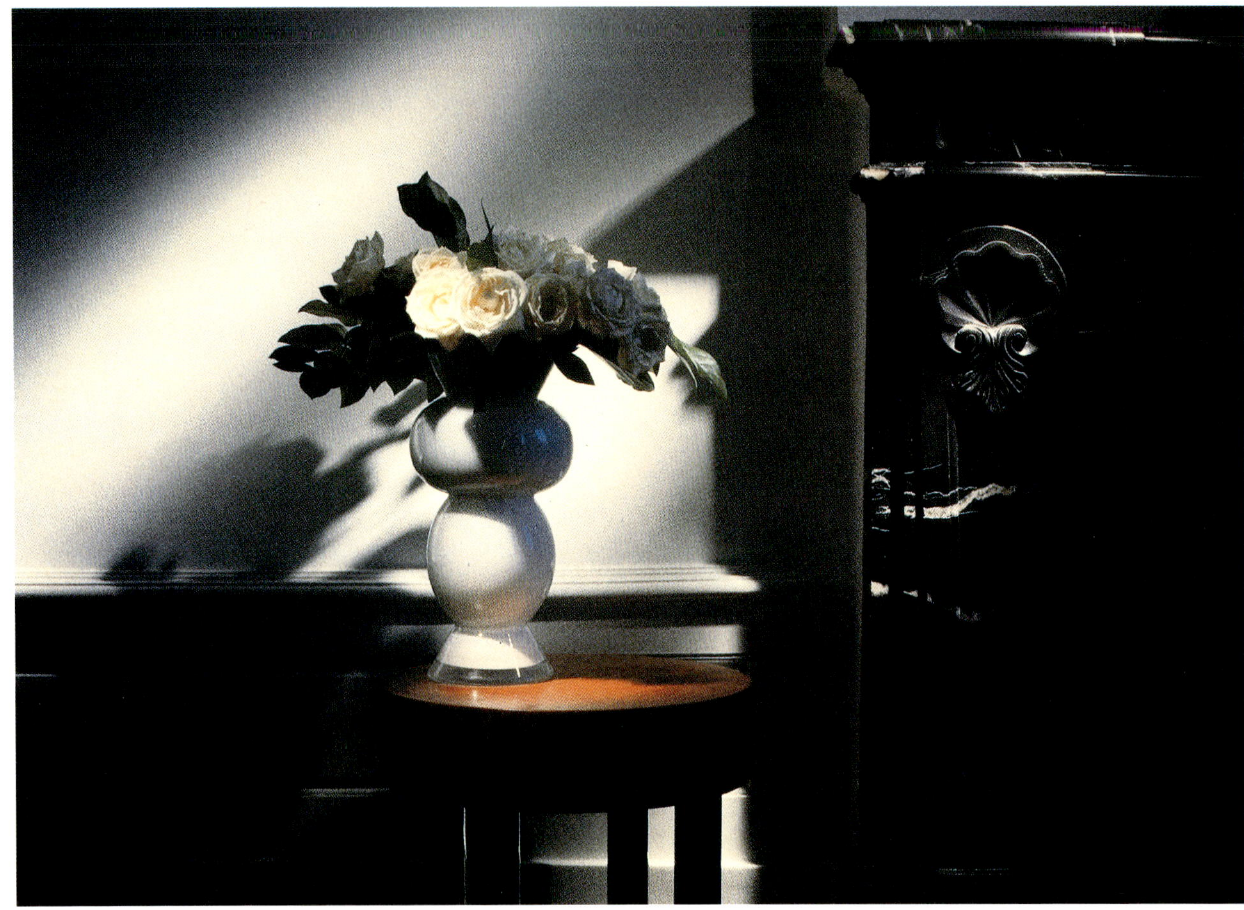

Michael Sieger

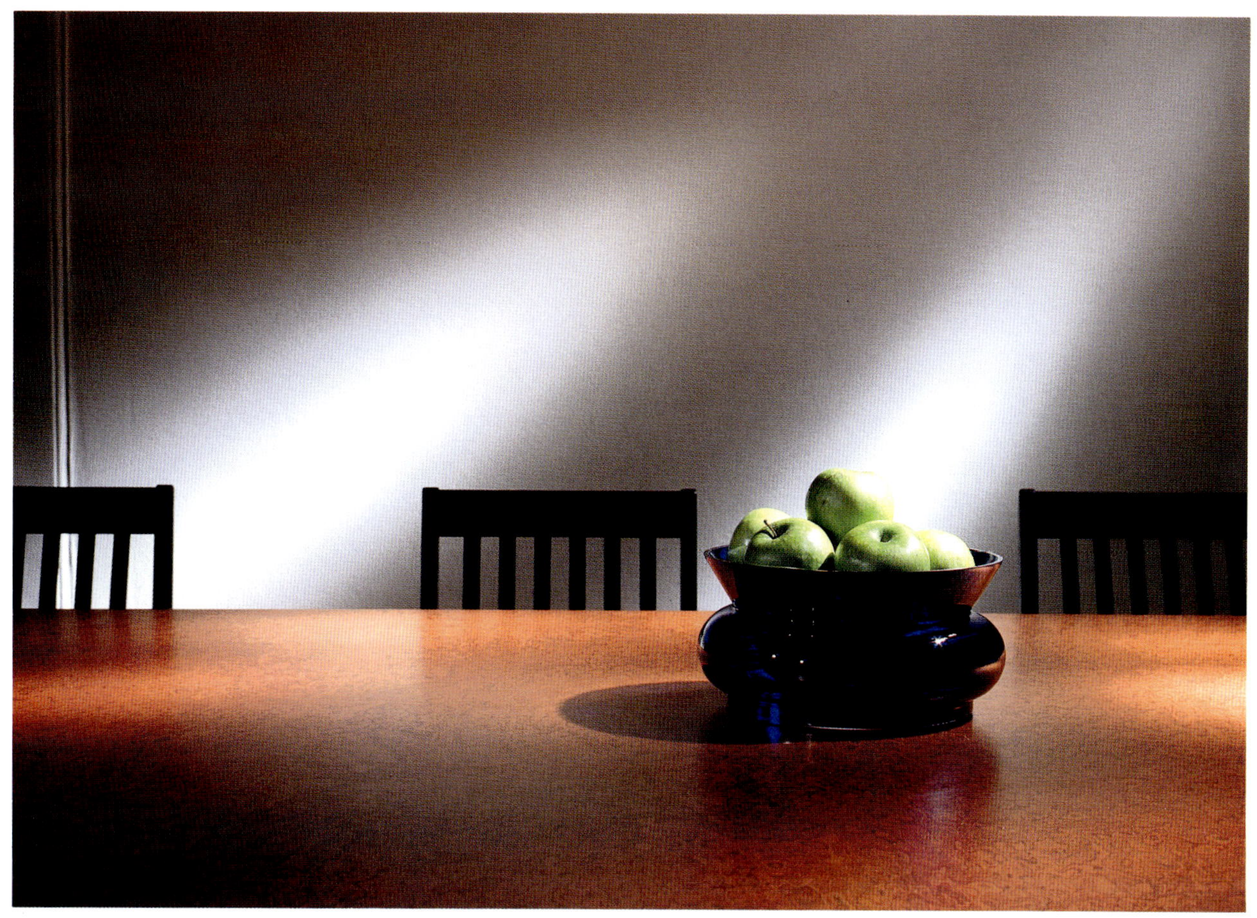

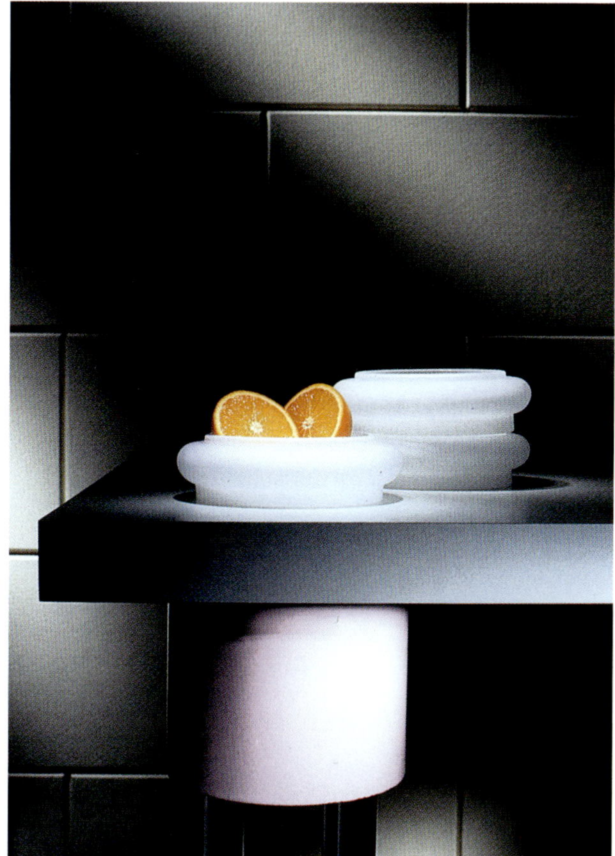

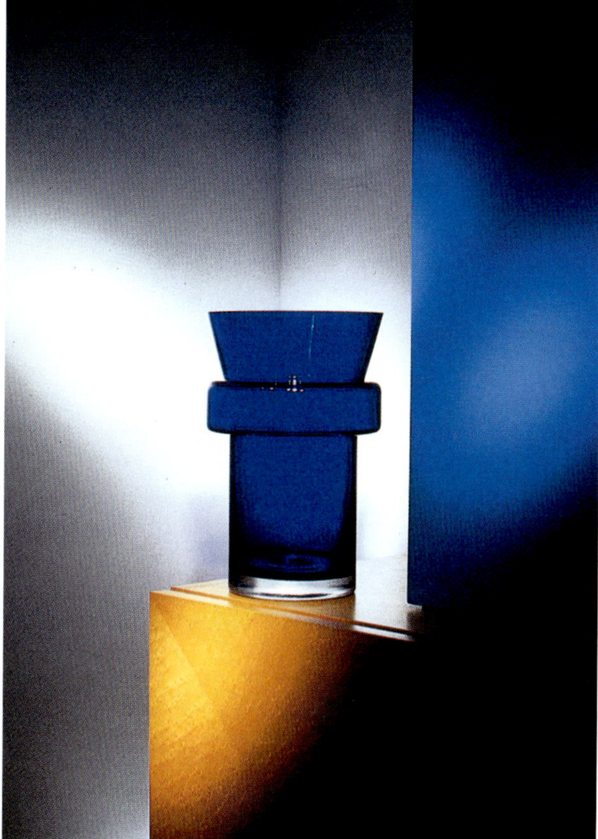

Michael Sieger

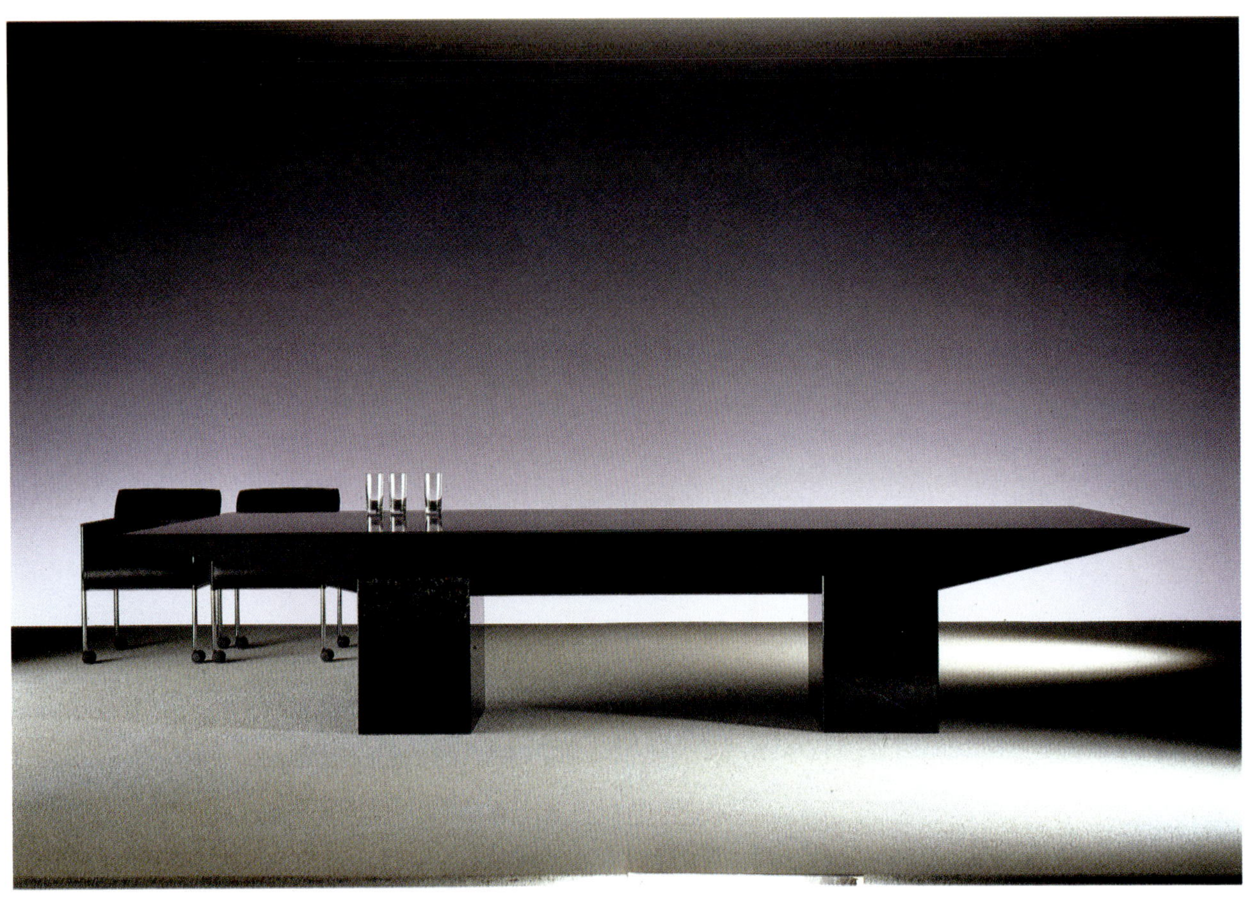

AK Werbefotografie

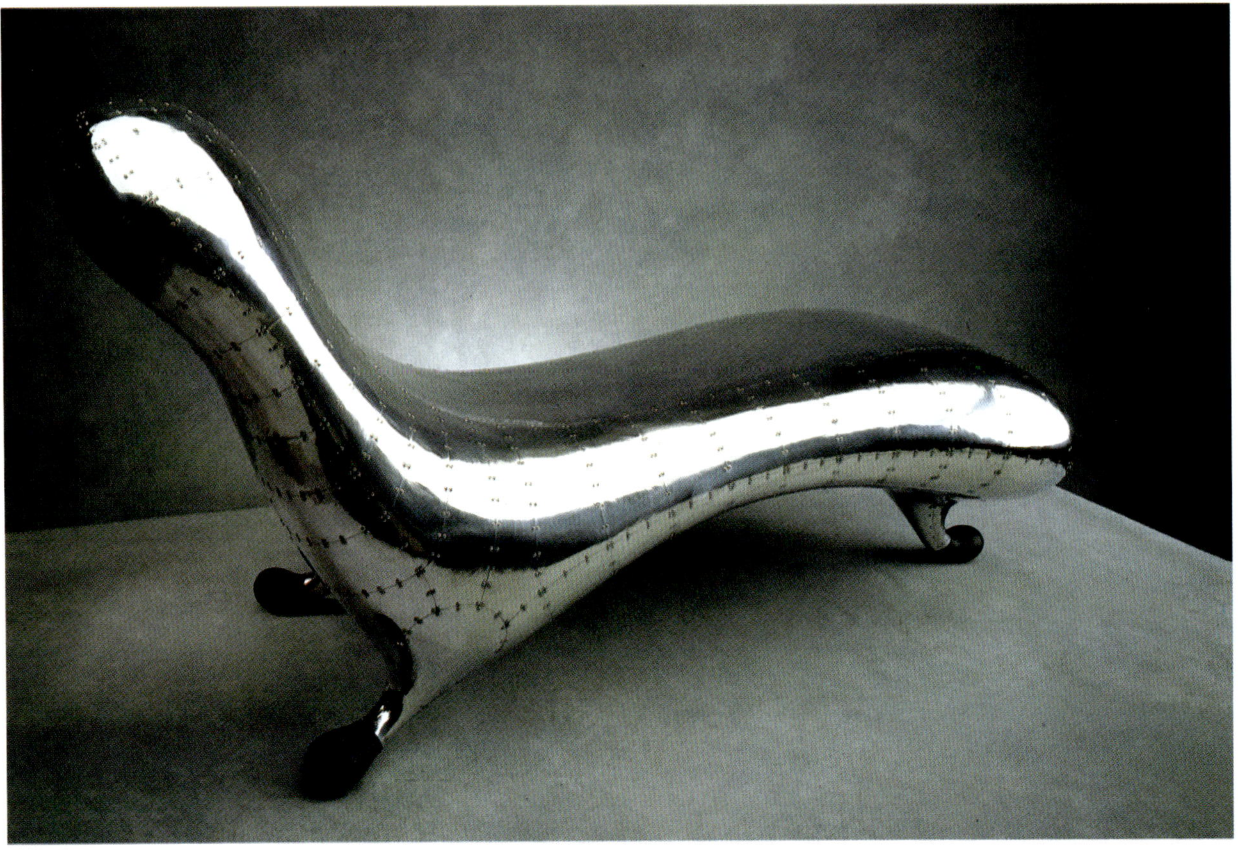

Sue Stafford

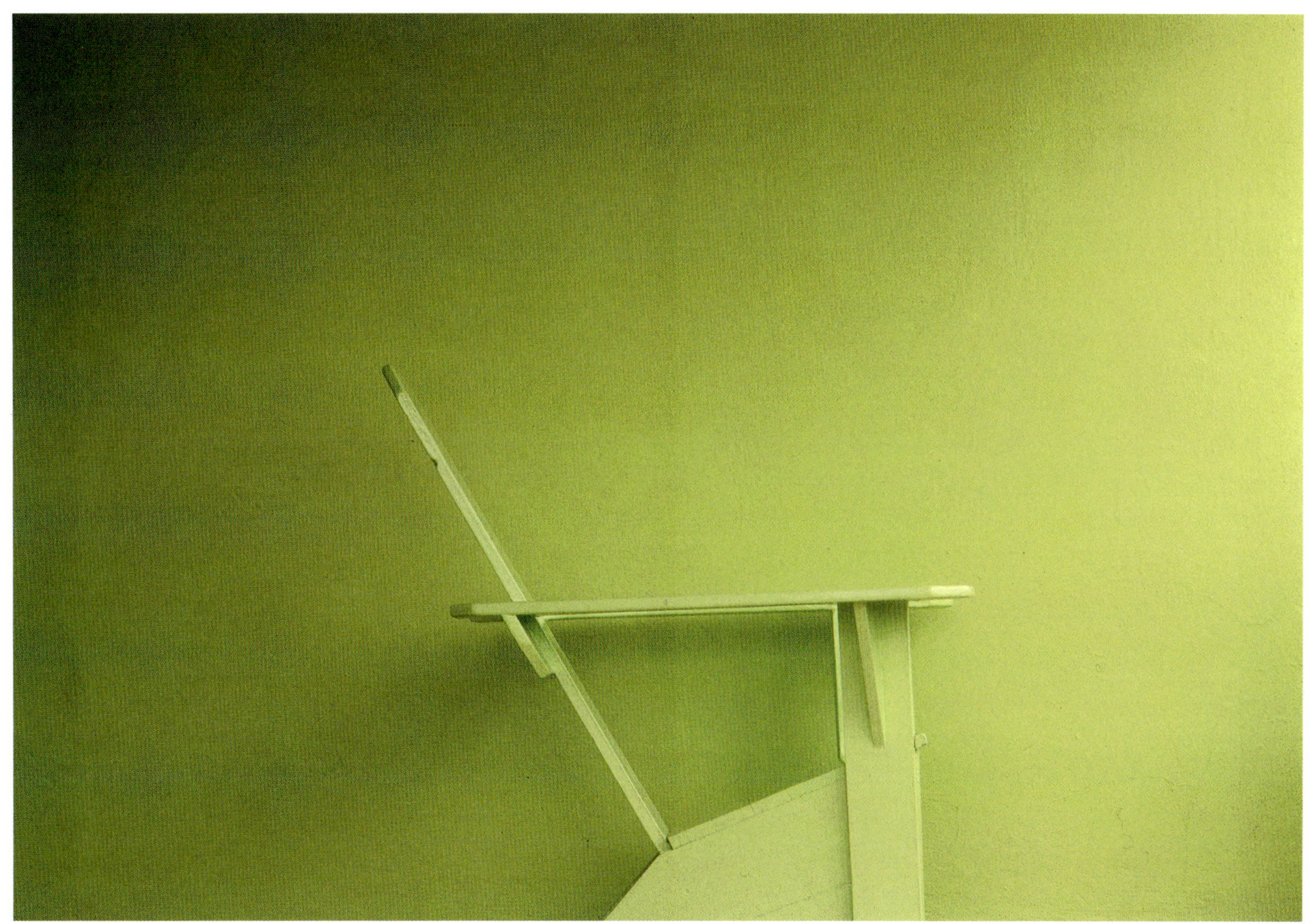

Kris Rodammer

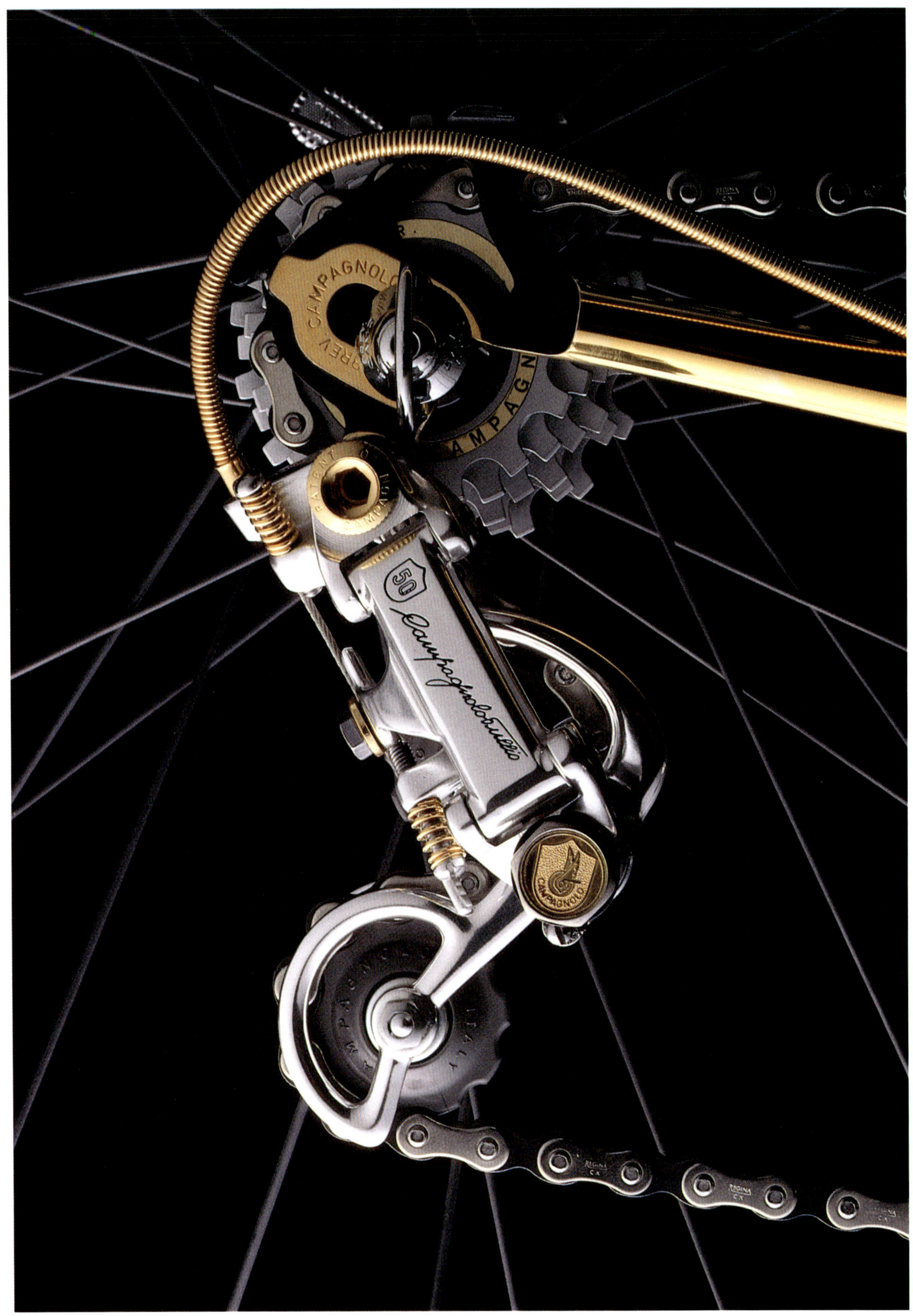

Michael Furman

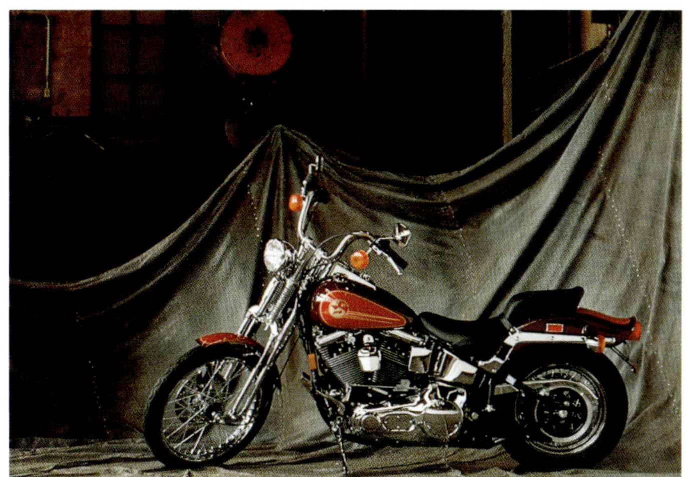
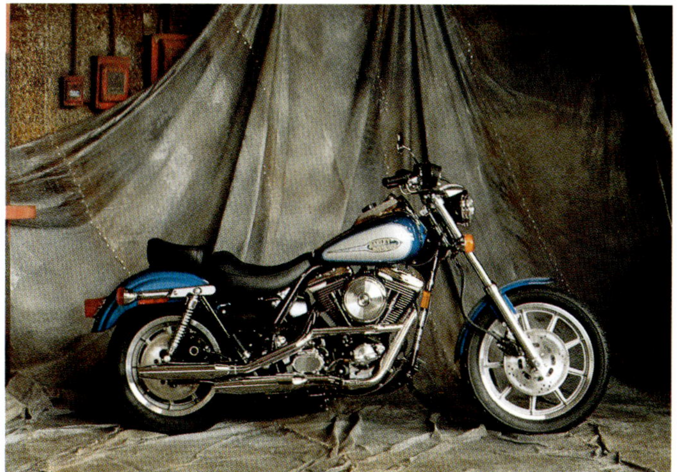
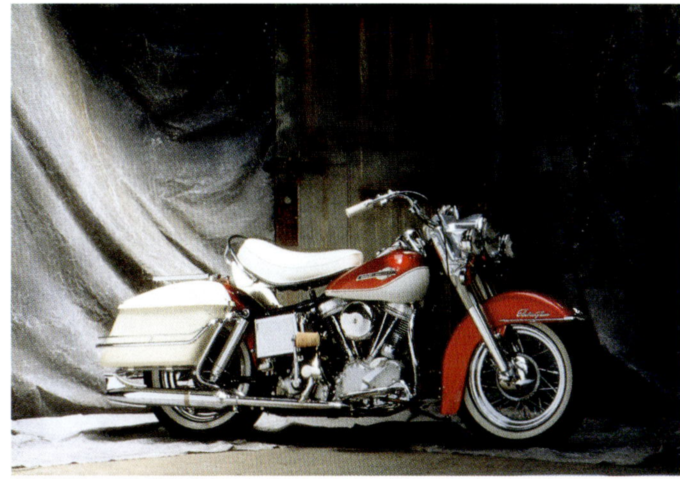
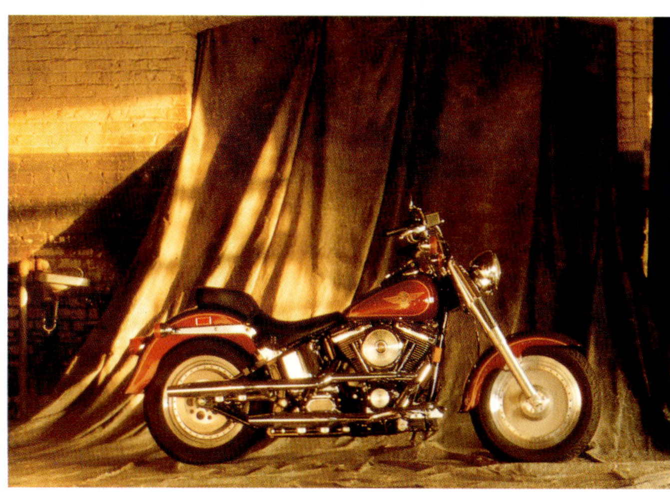
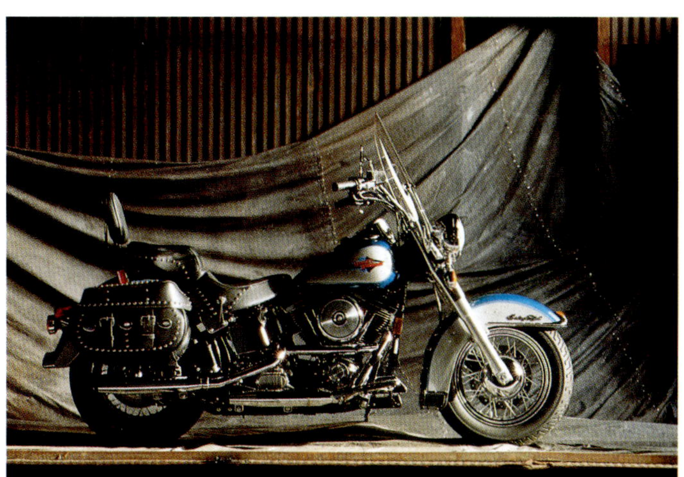
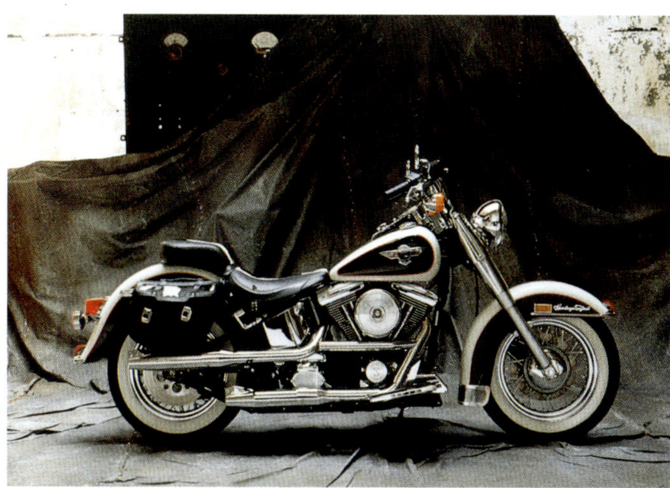

Clint Clemens

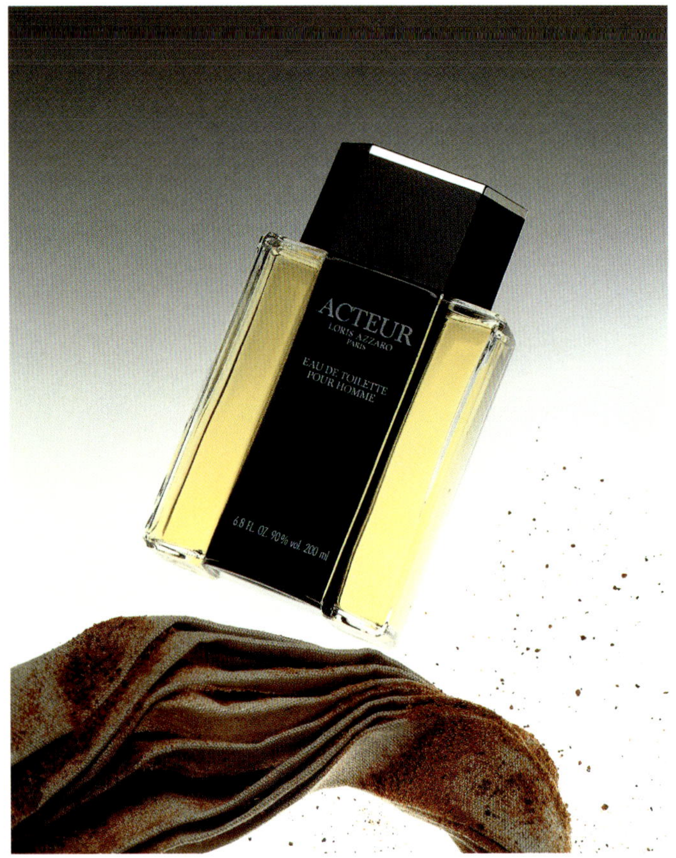

Claudio Lazi

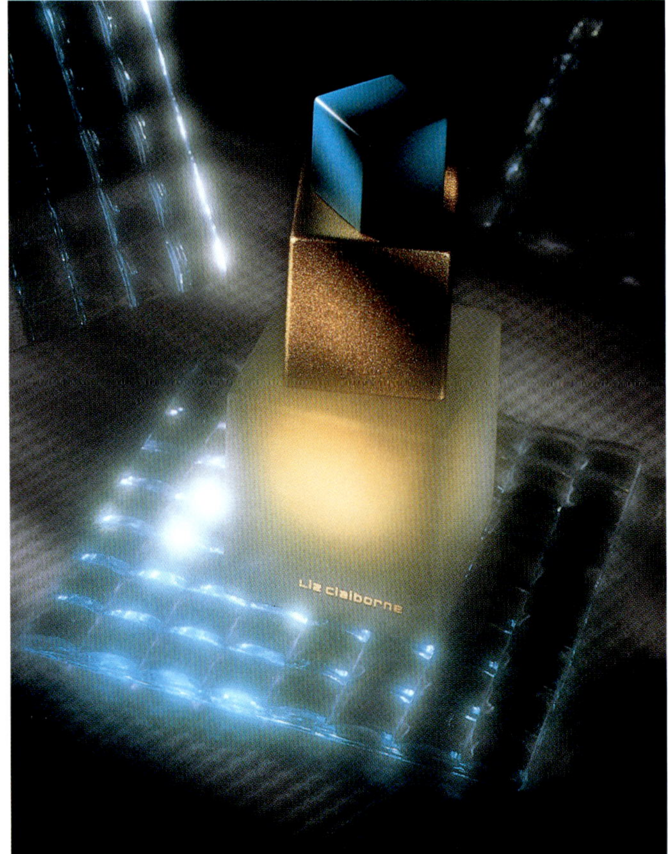

Jim DiVitale

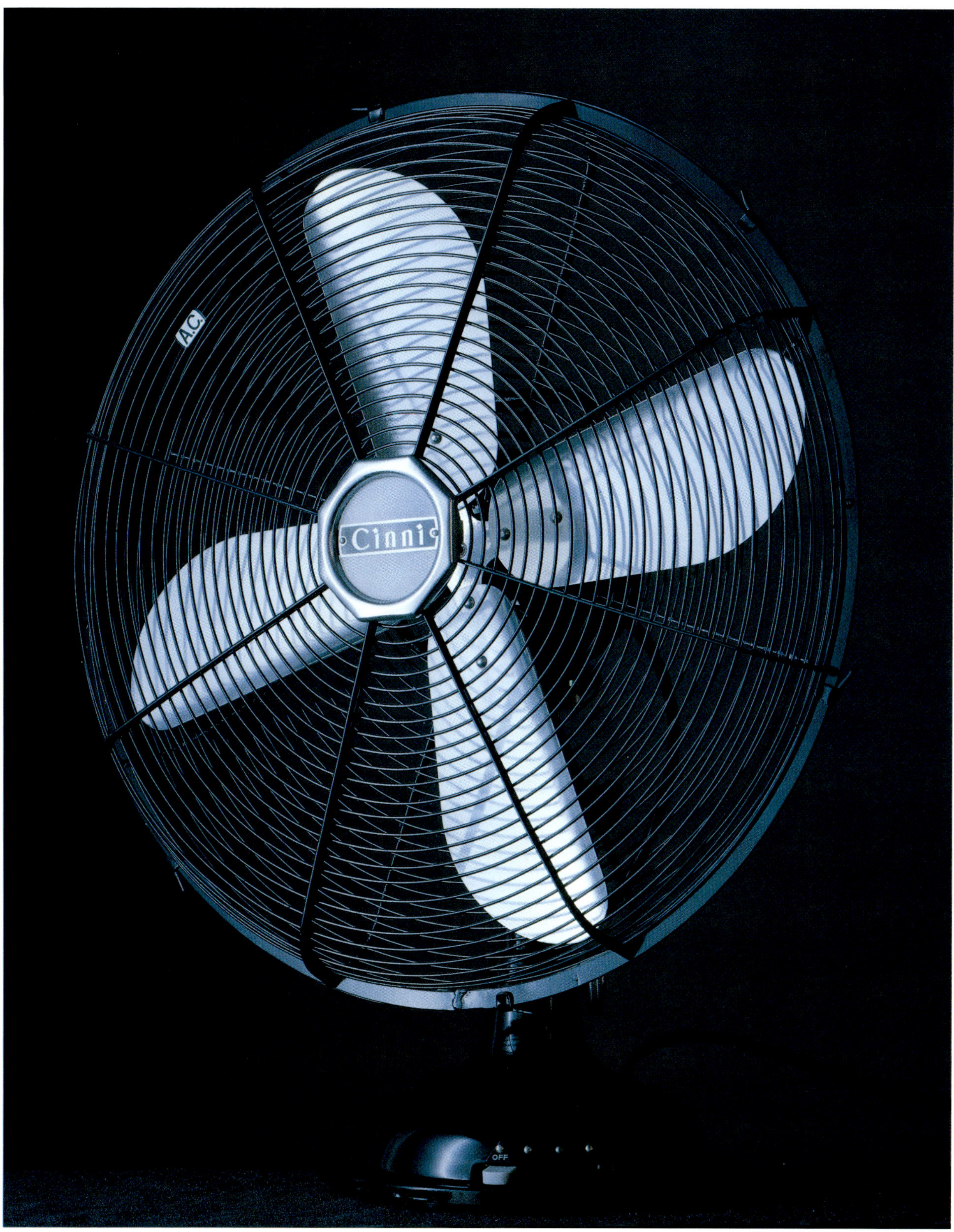

Detlef Odenhausen

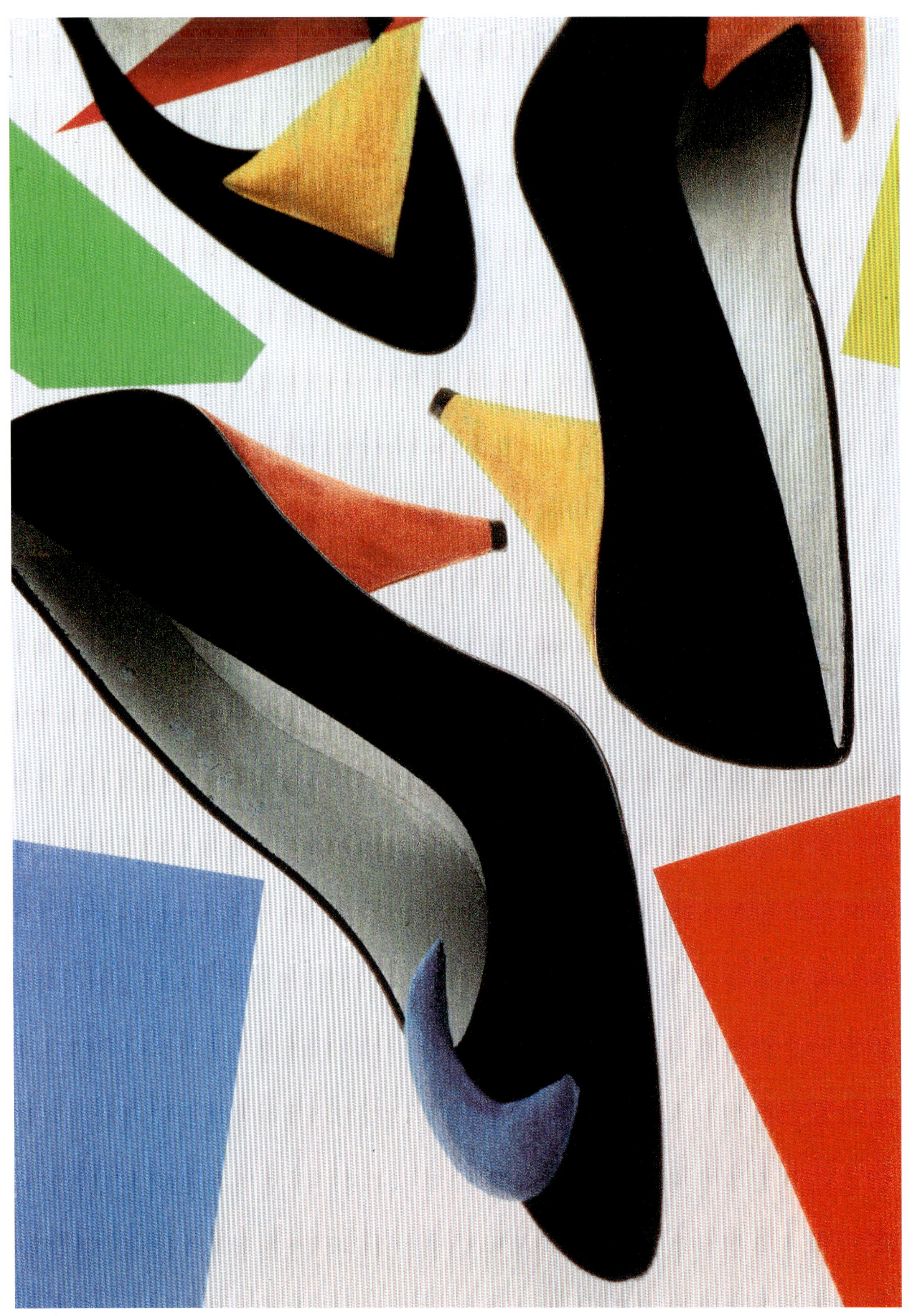

Paulo Greuel

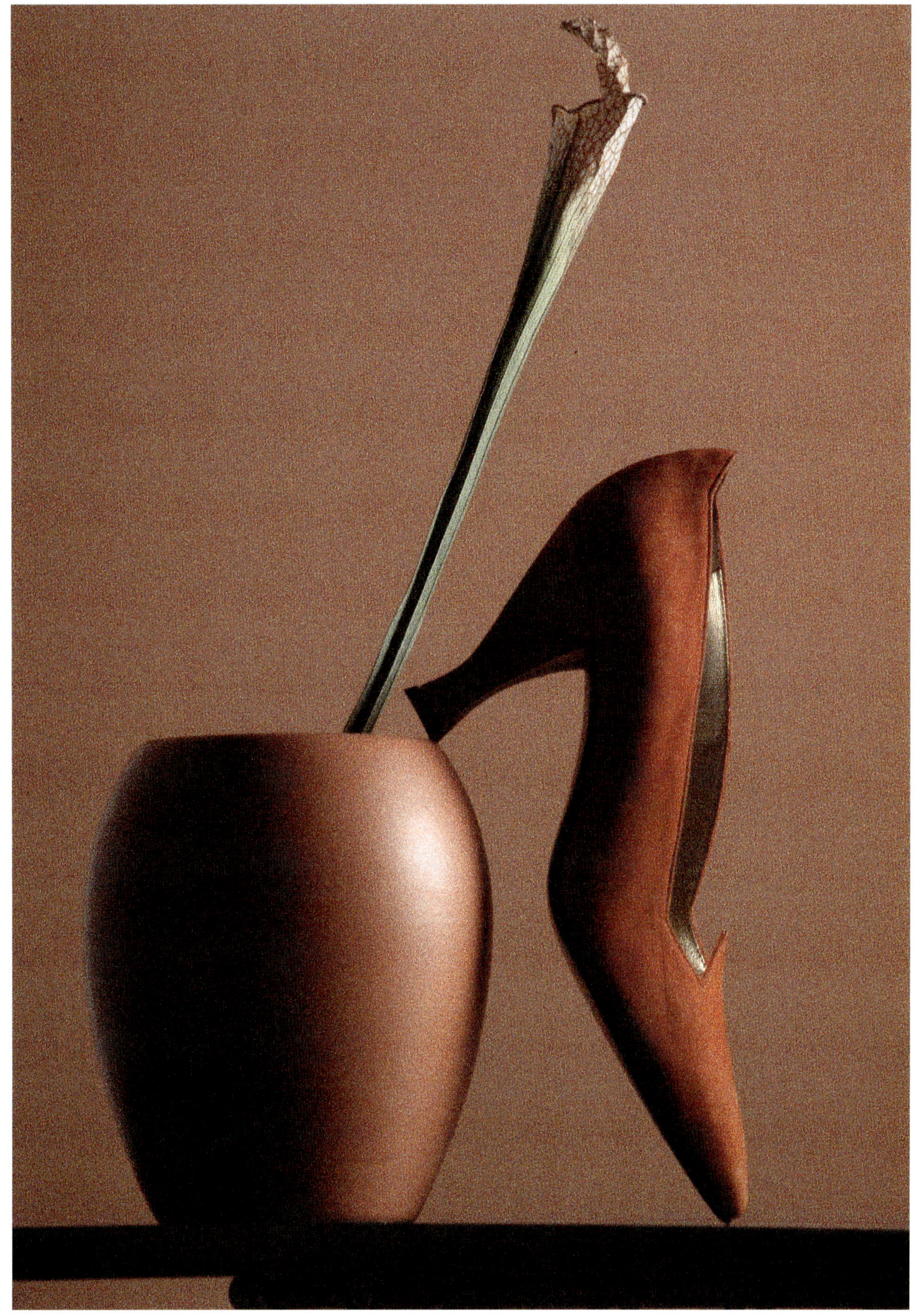

Victoria Huber

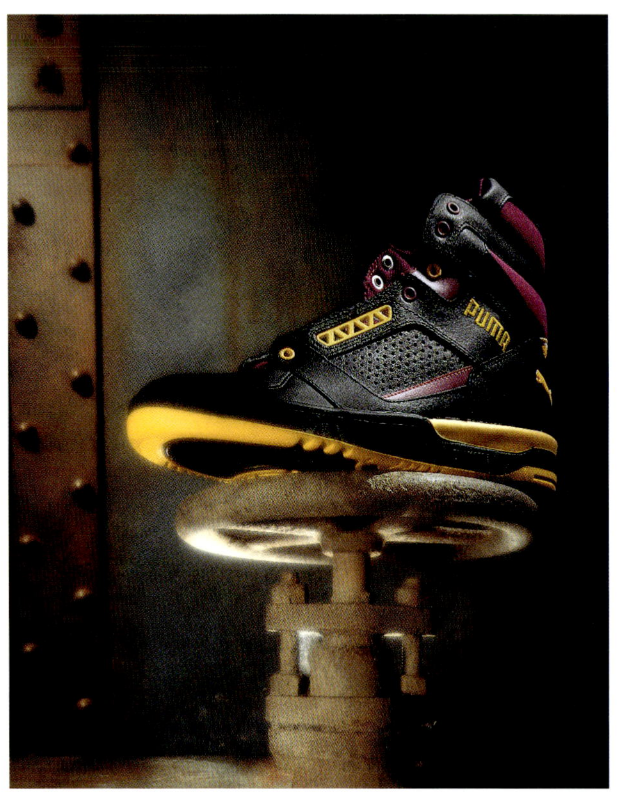

Axel Döhler

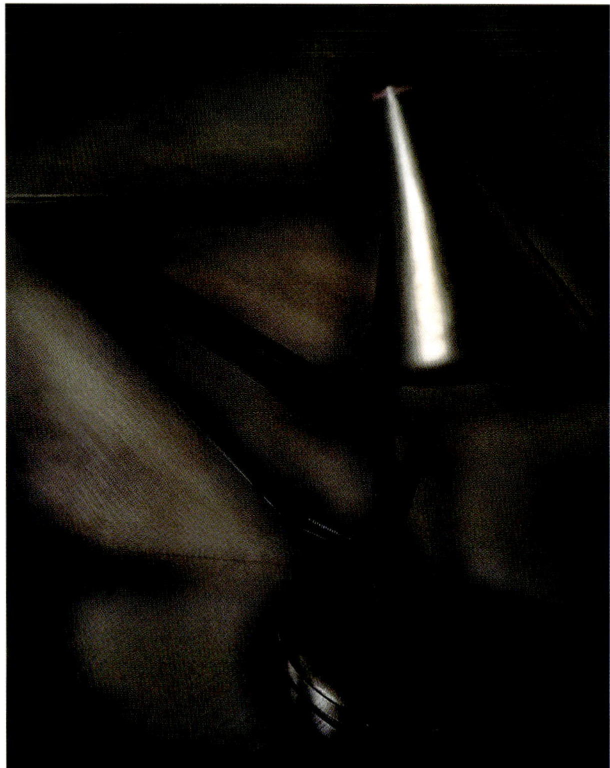

Chris Airey

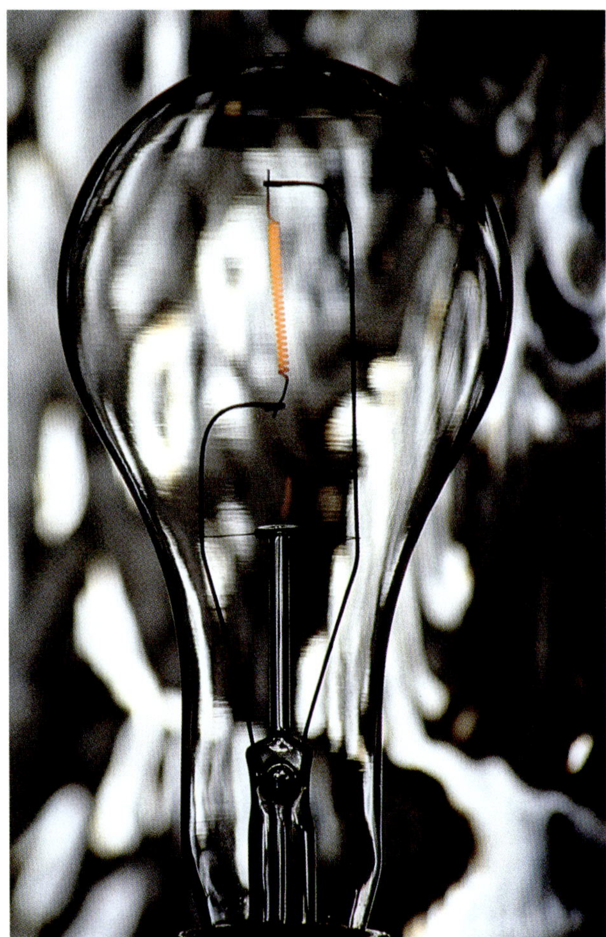

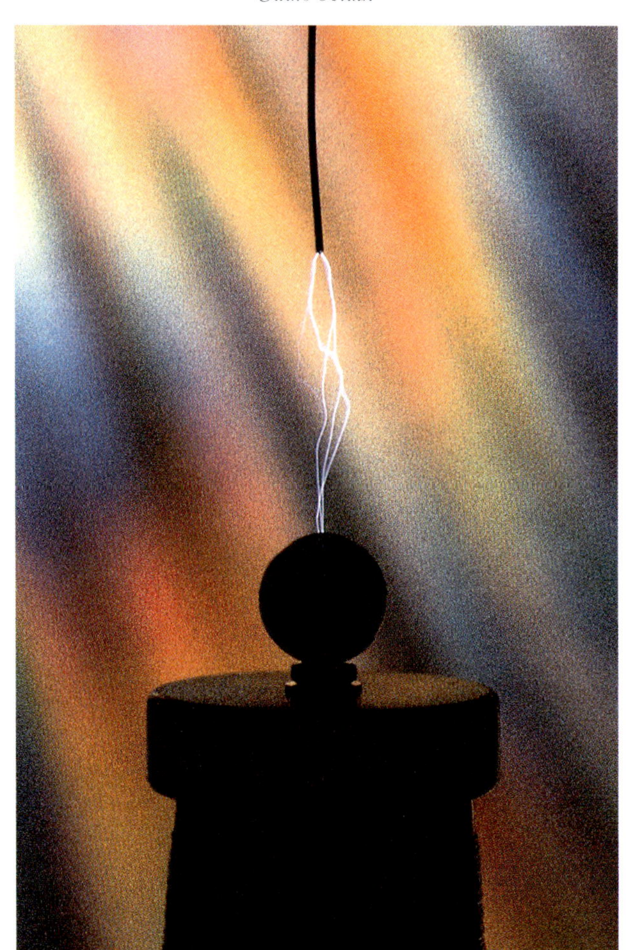

Jody Döle

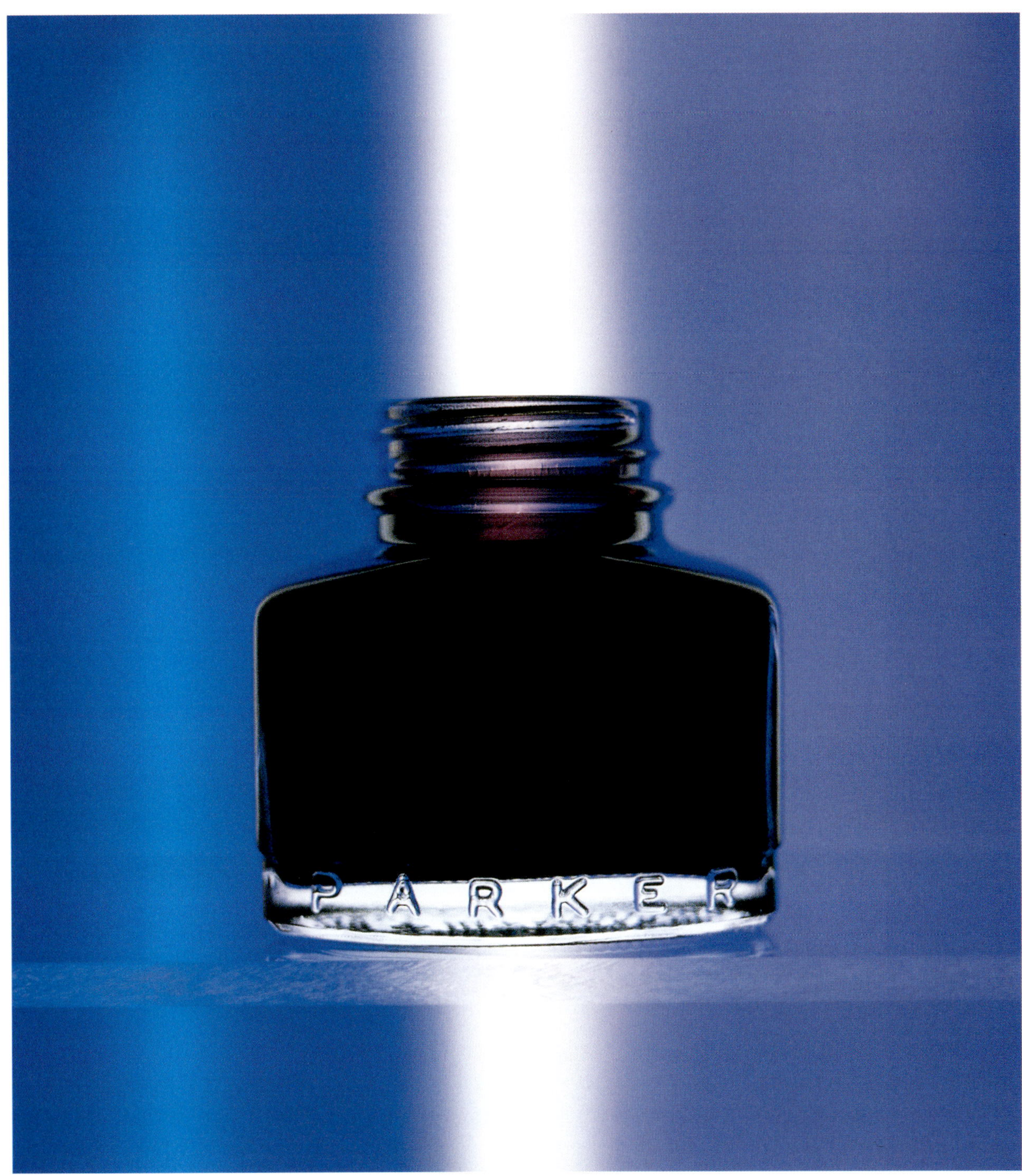

Zafer & Barbara Baran

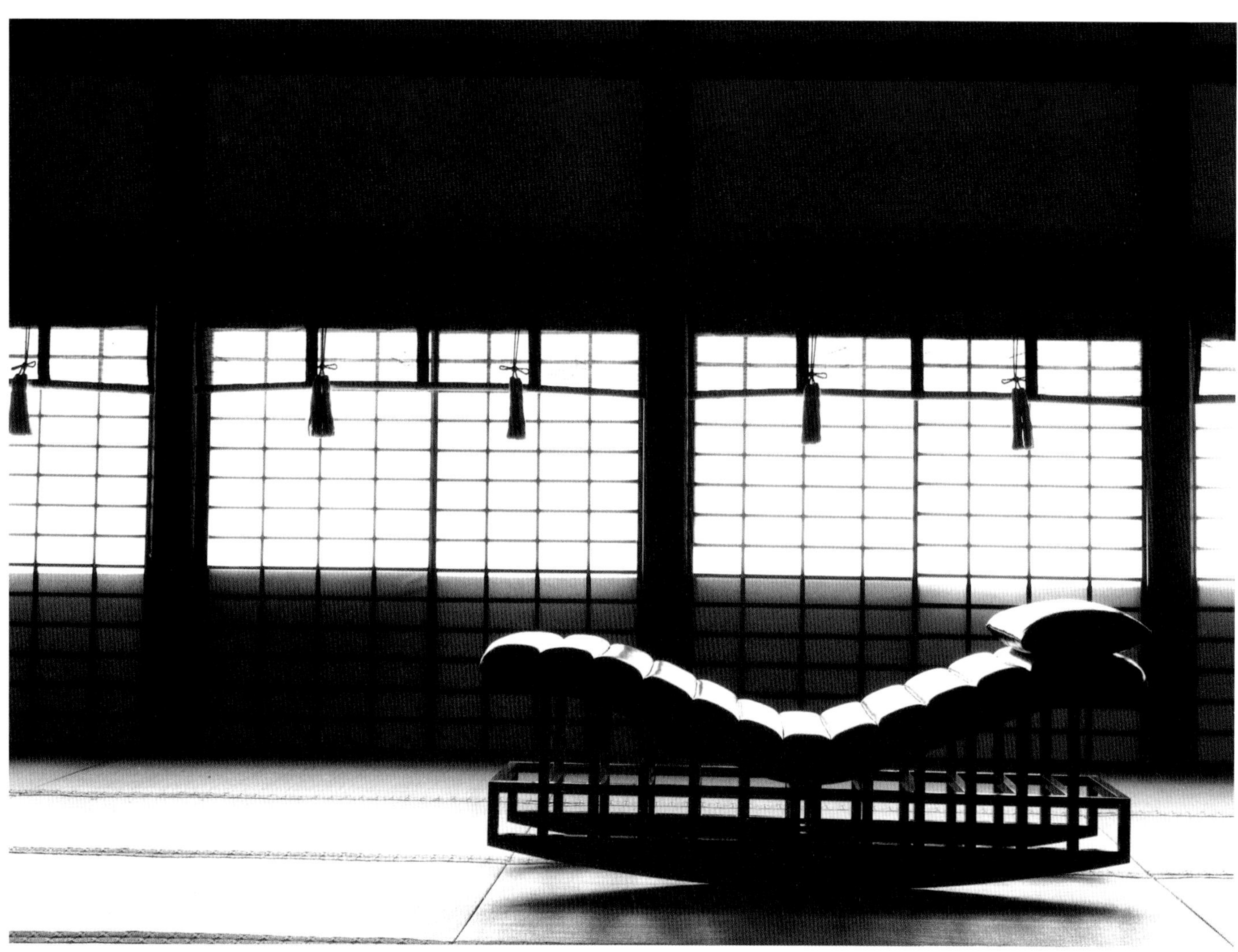

Nob Fukuda

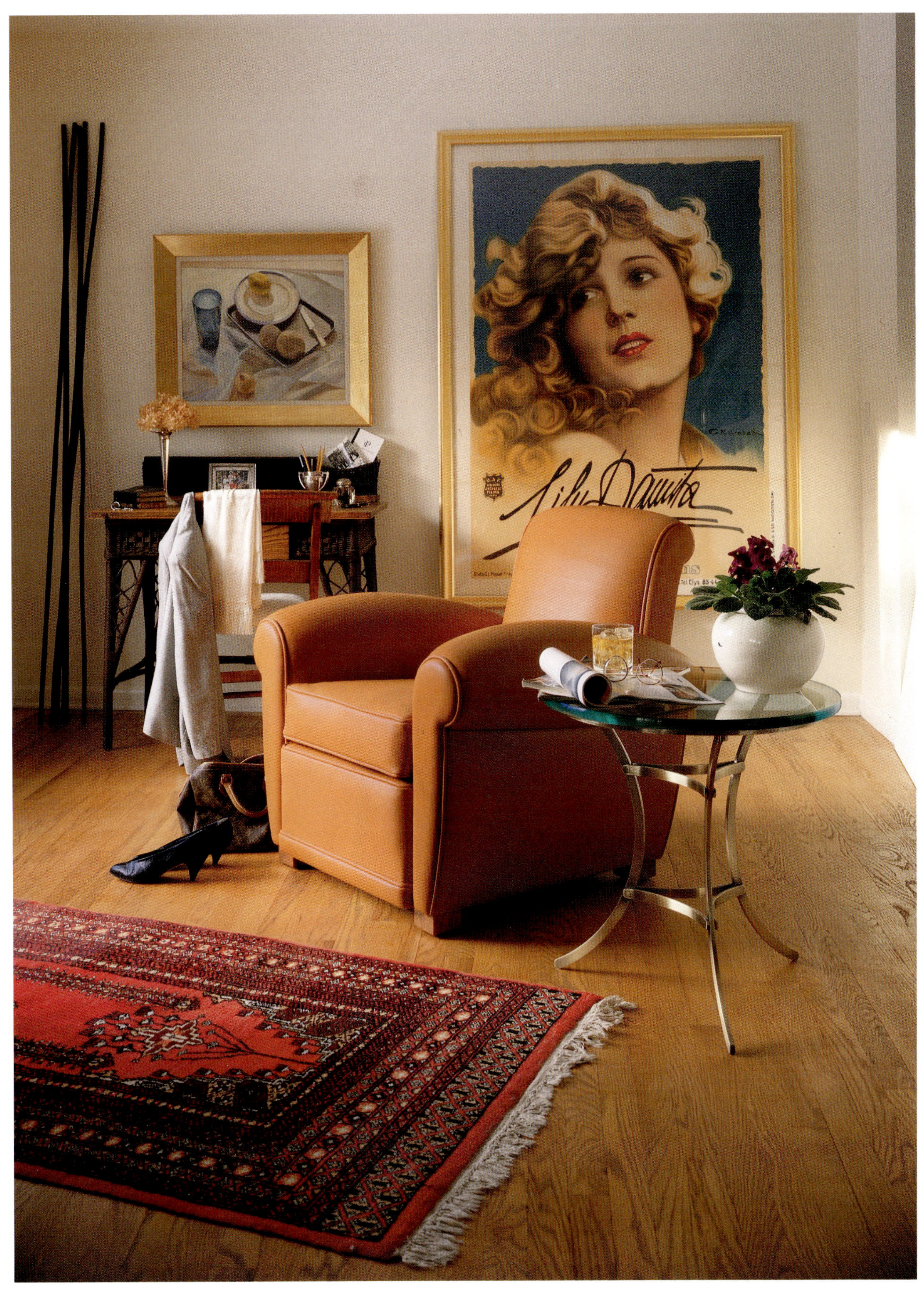

William Sharpe

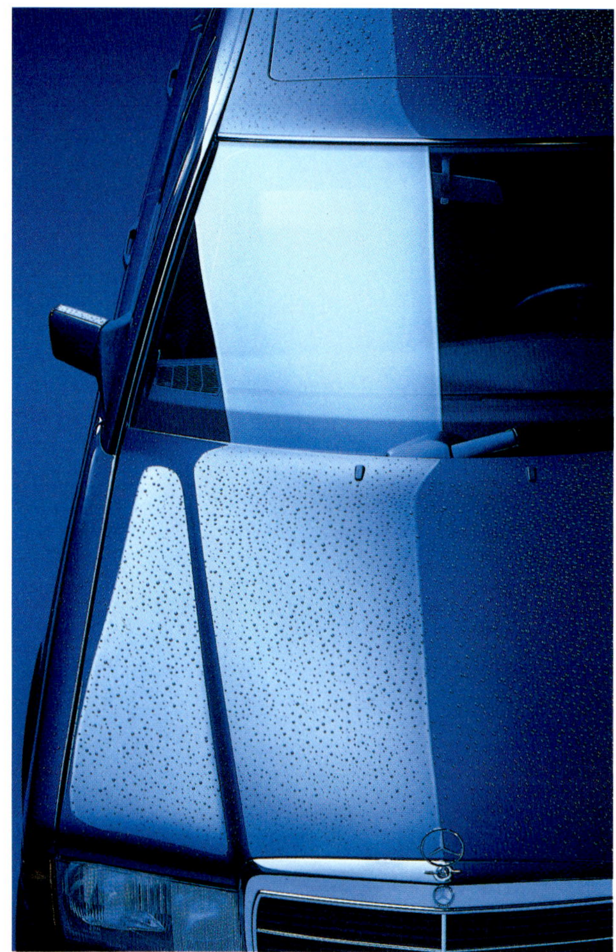

Andreas Marx

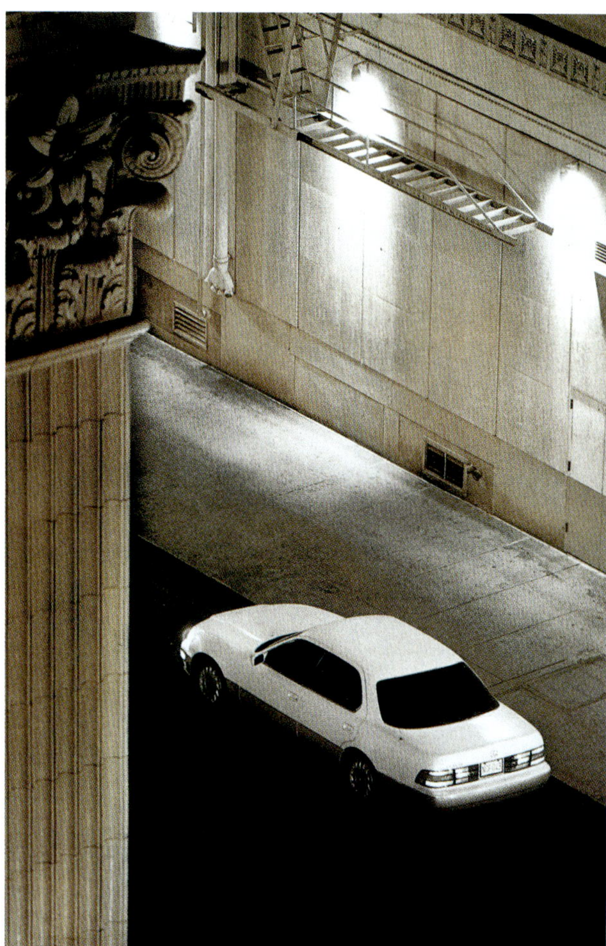

Doug Taub

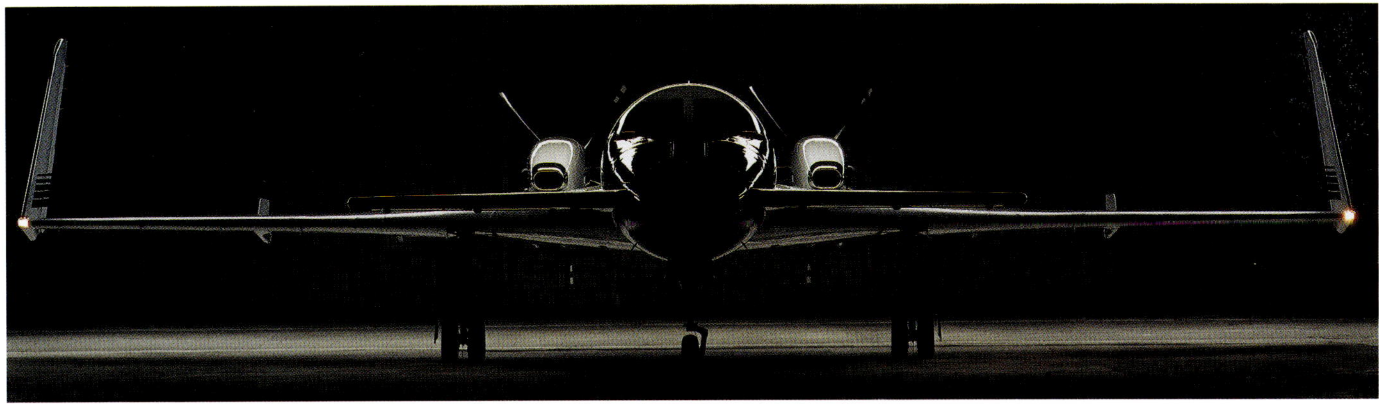

Rick Rusing

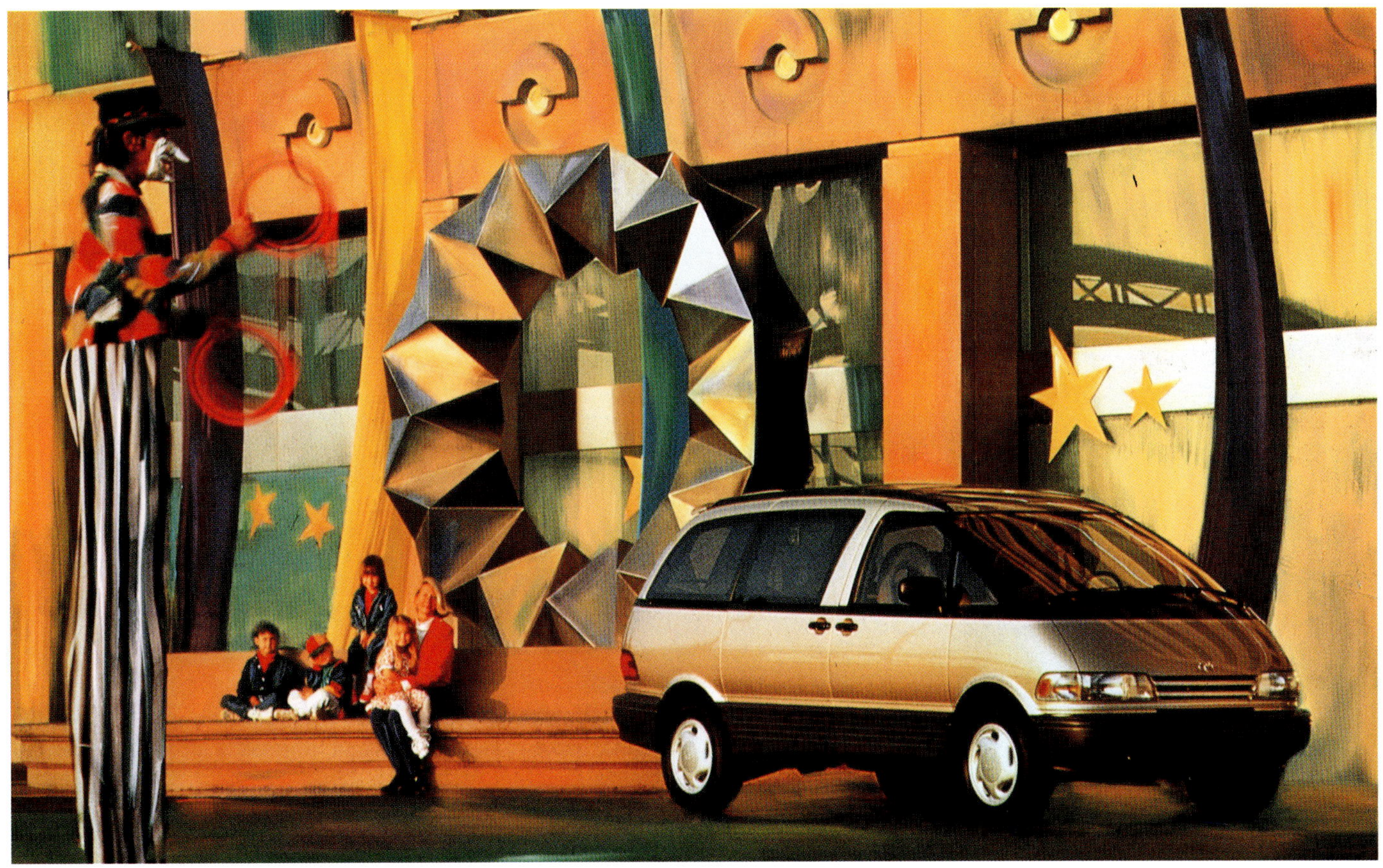

Deborah Roundtree

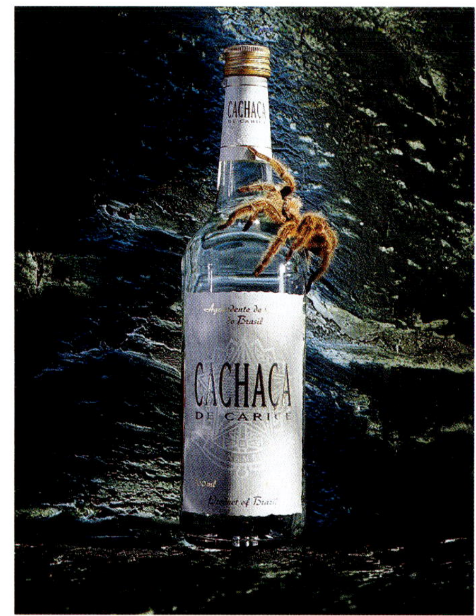
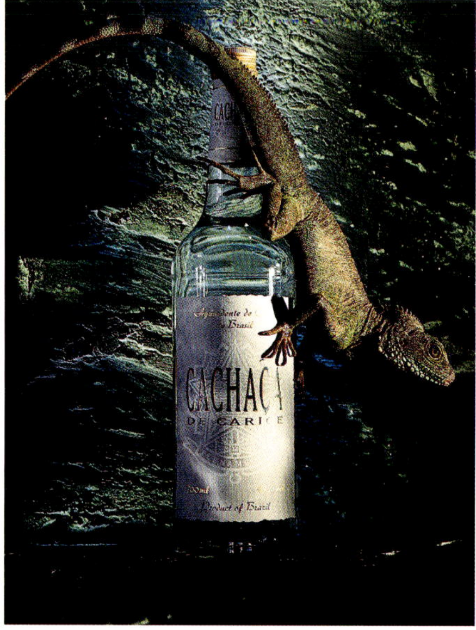
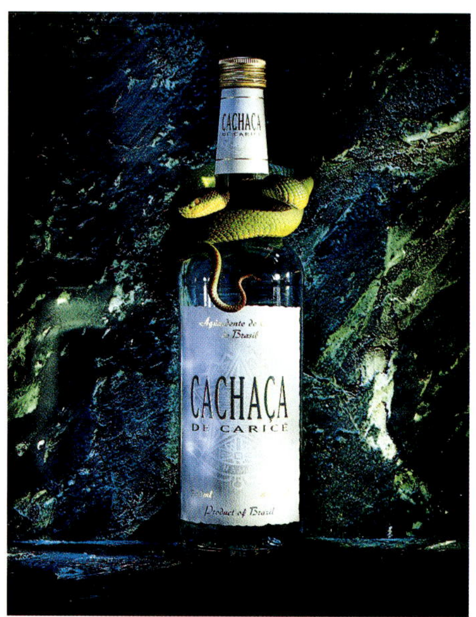

Christopher Thomas

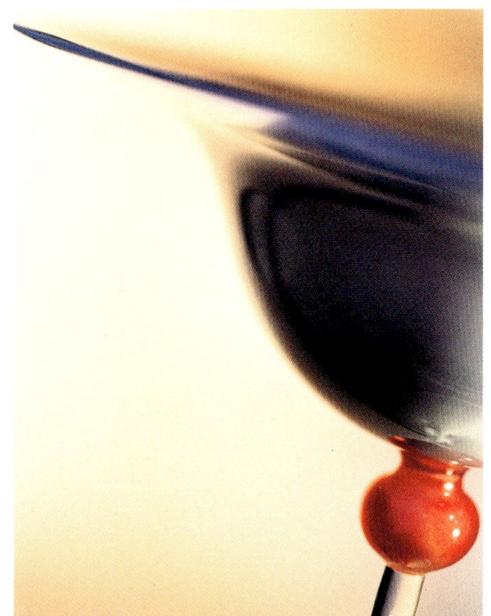
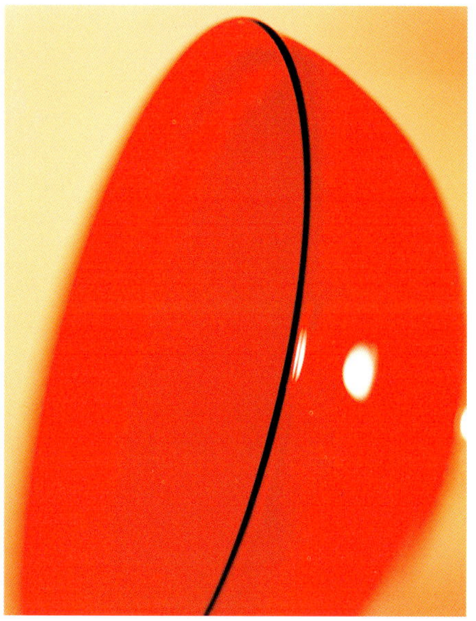
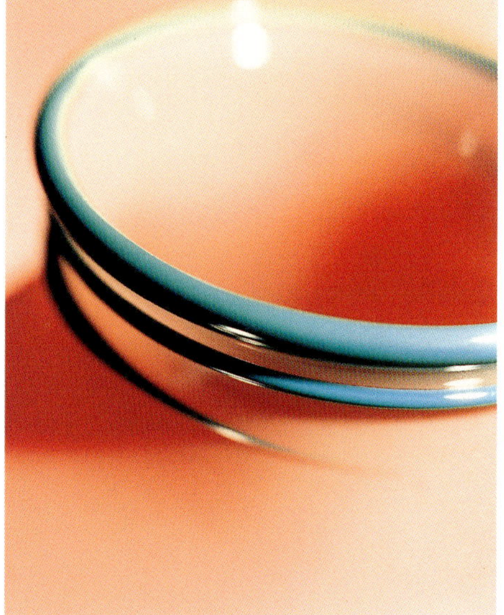

Craig Cutler

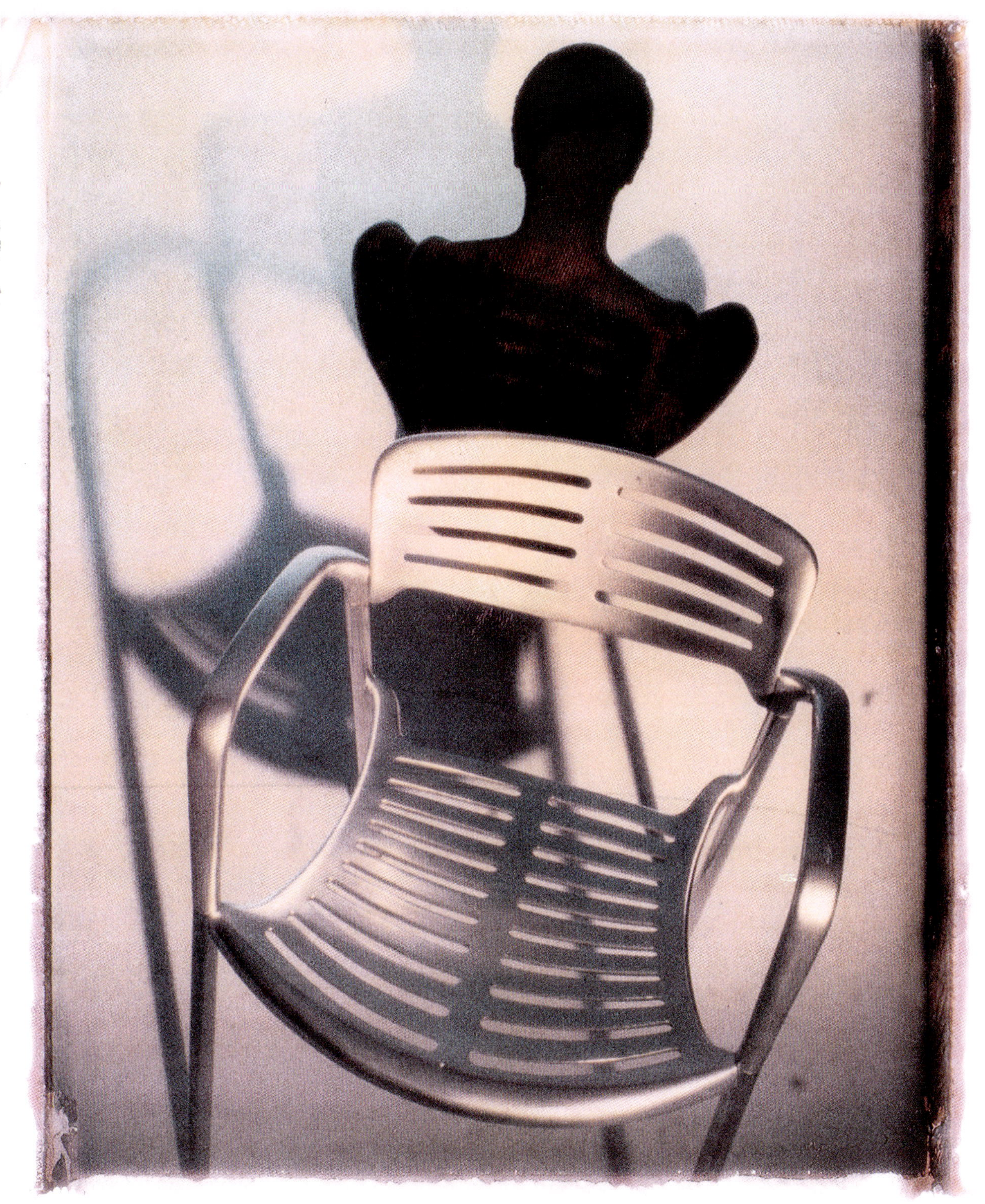

Conny J. Winter

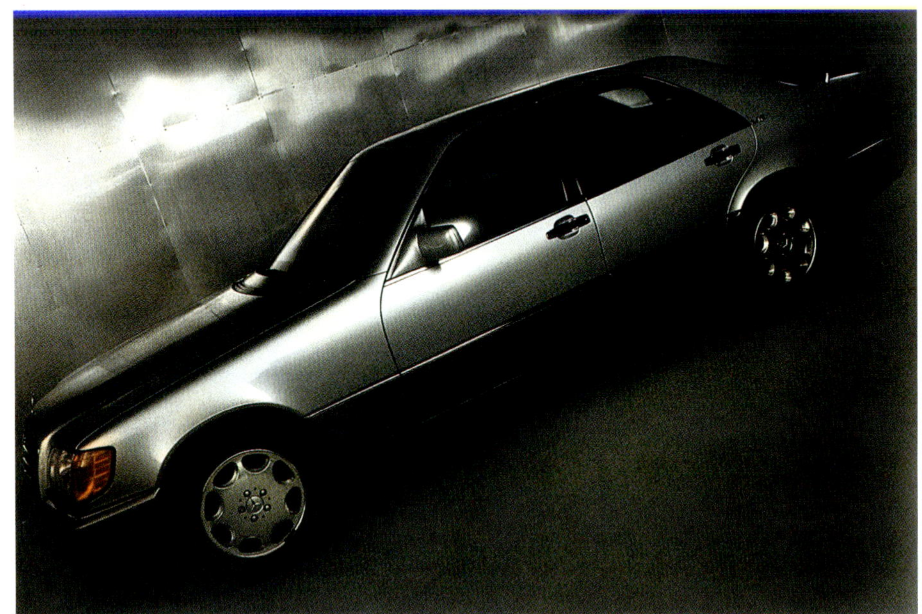

Sheila Metzner

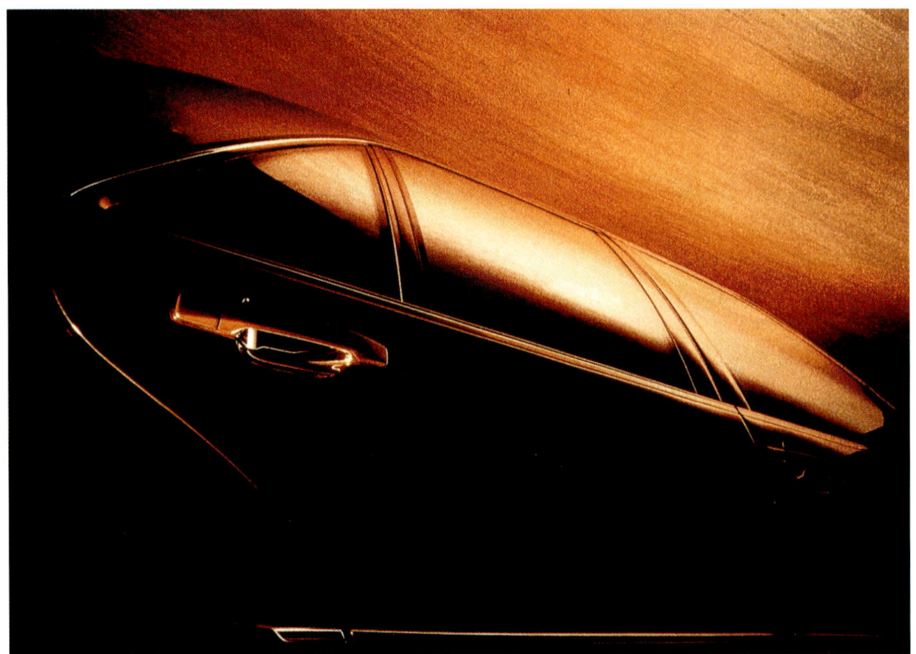

Keiichi Tahara

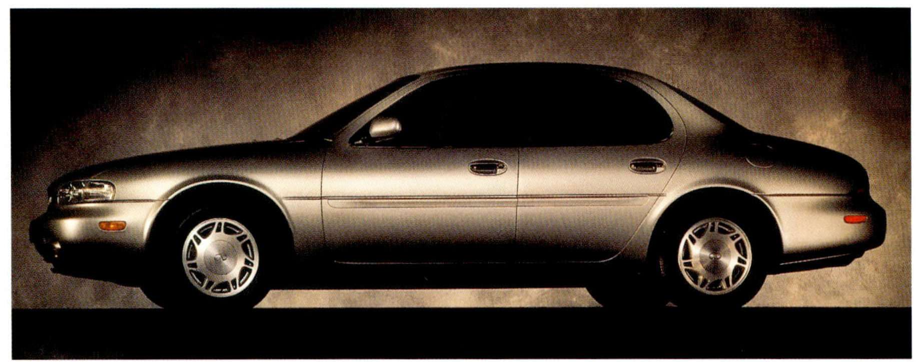

Rick Rusing

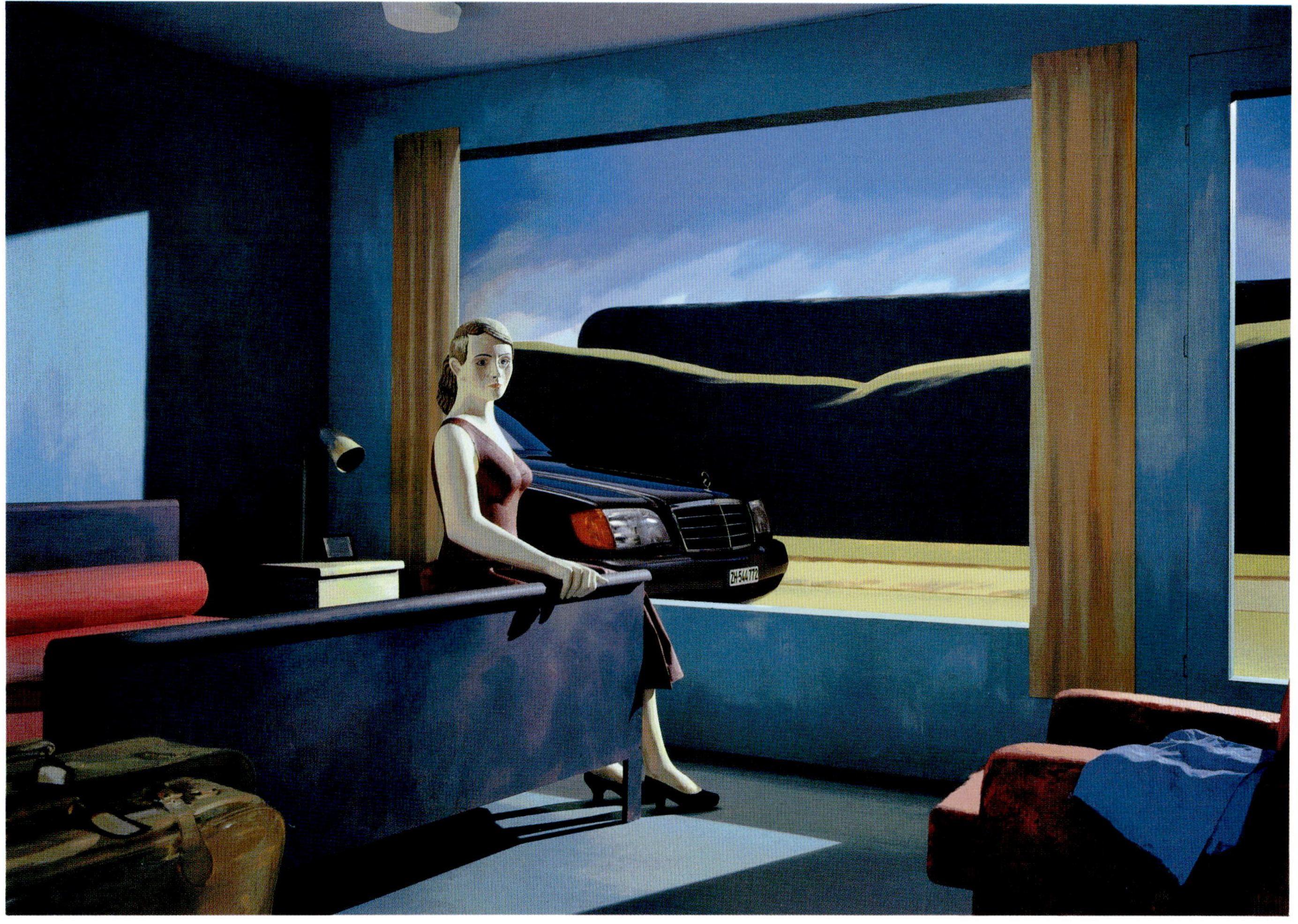

Dietmar Henneka

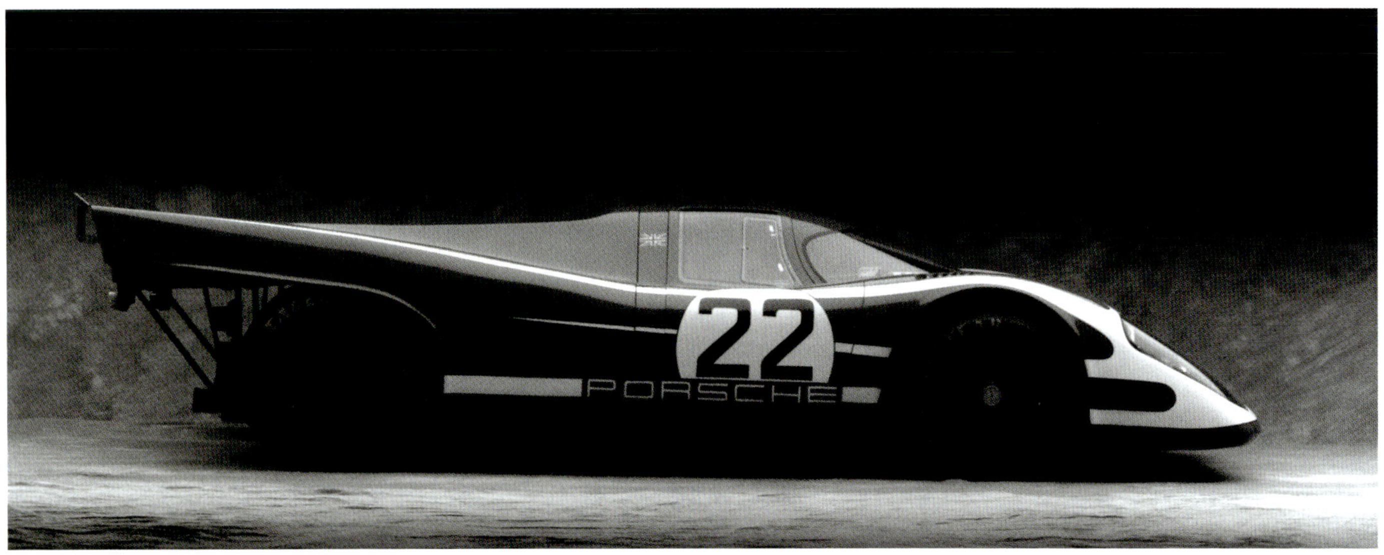

Michael Furman

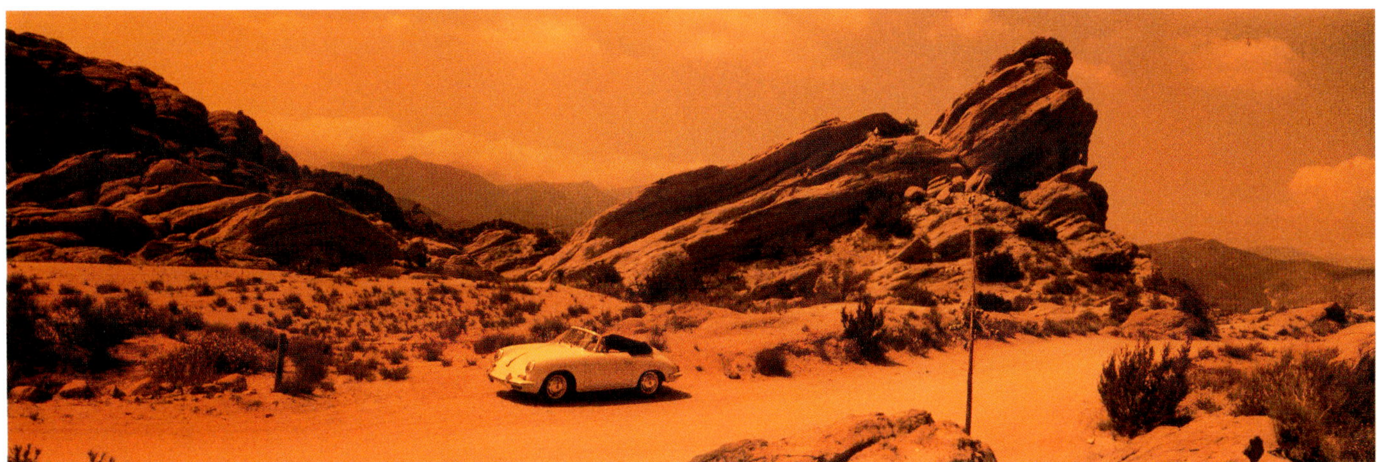

Ron Baxter Smith

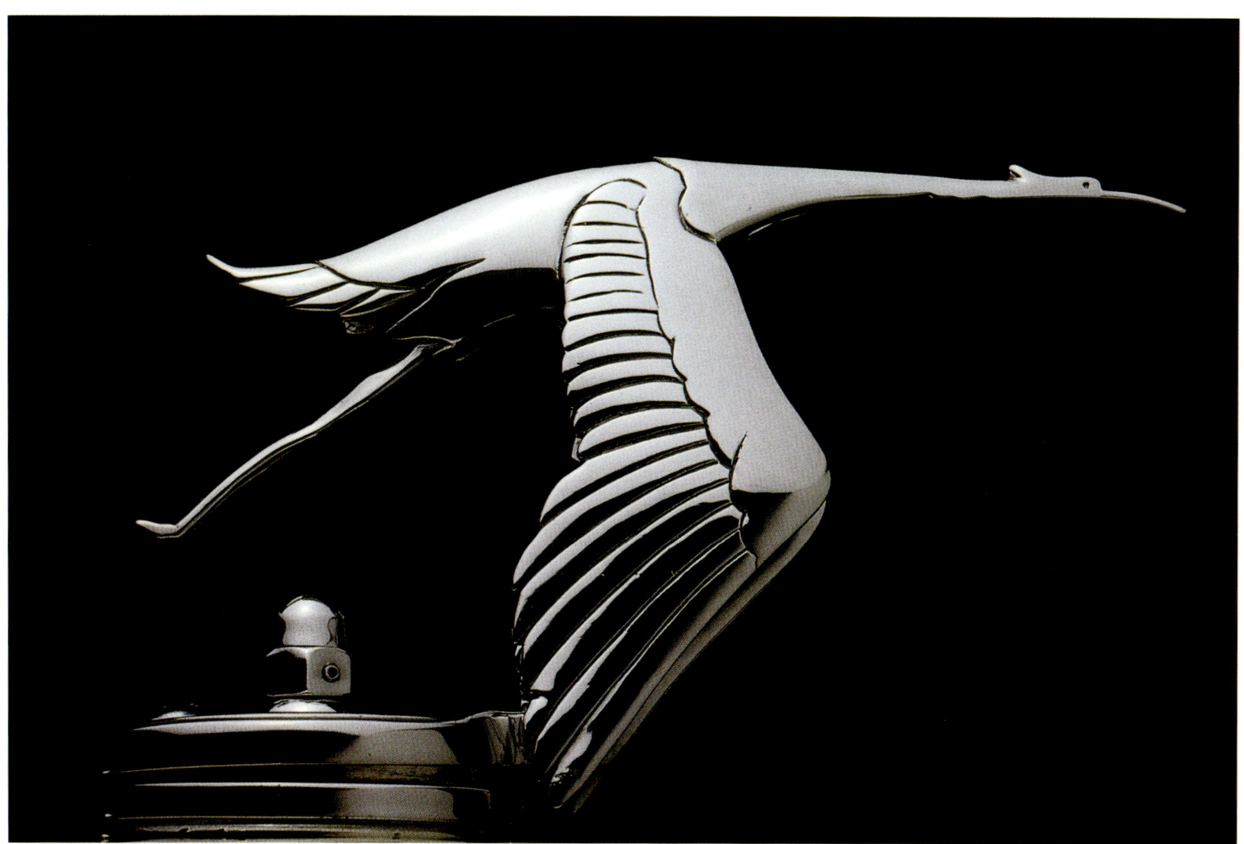

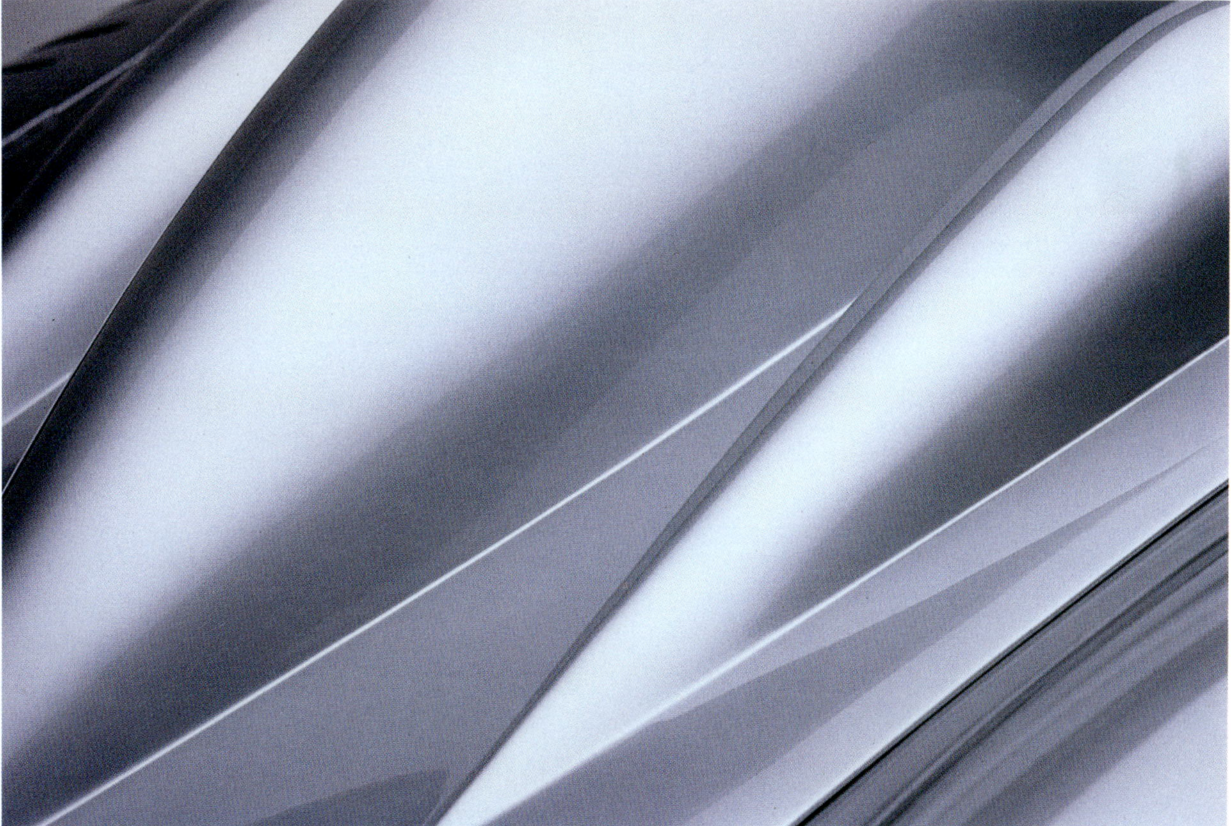

Michael Furman

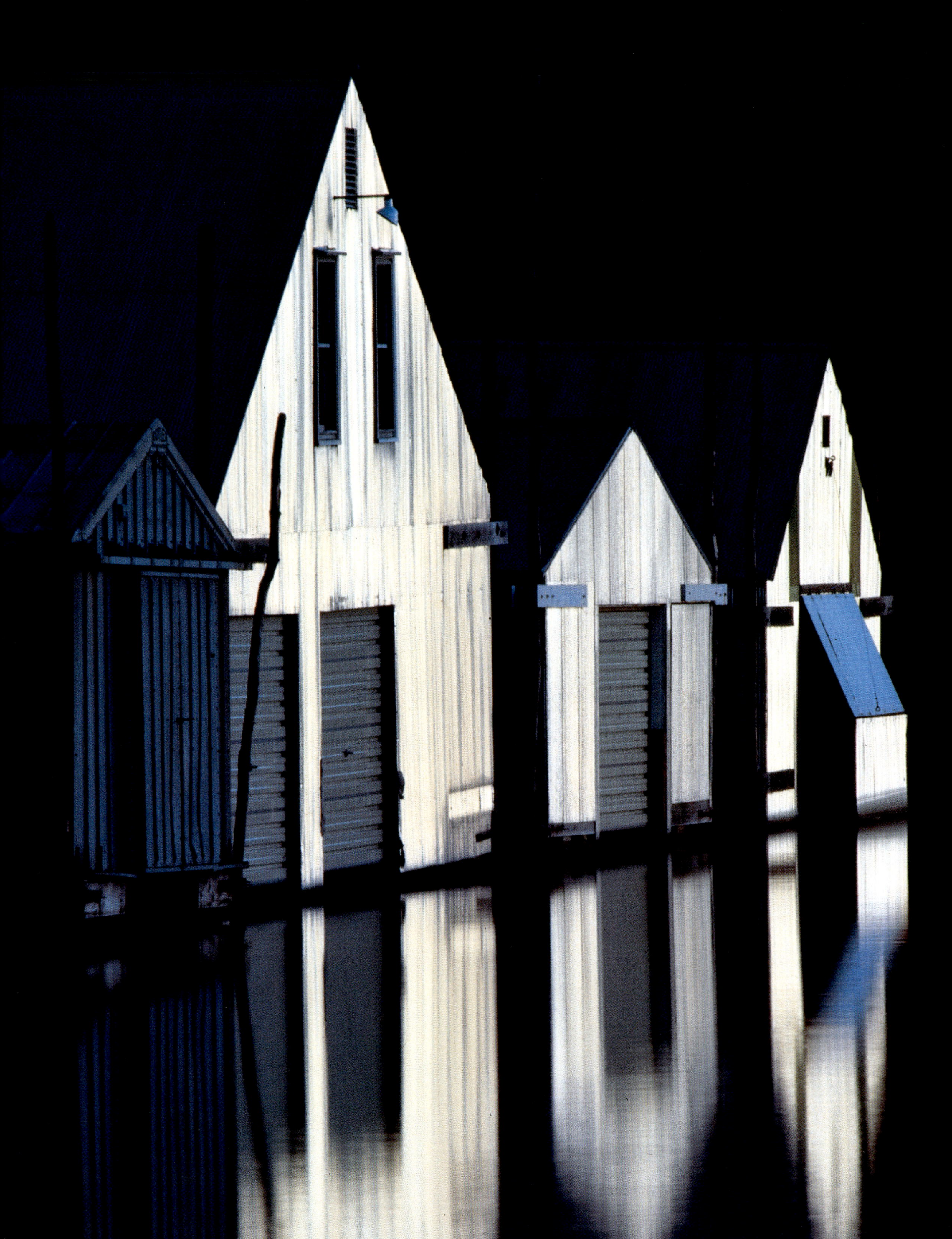

LANDSCAPES

LANDSCHAFTEN

PAYSAGES

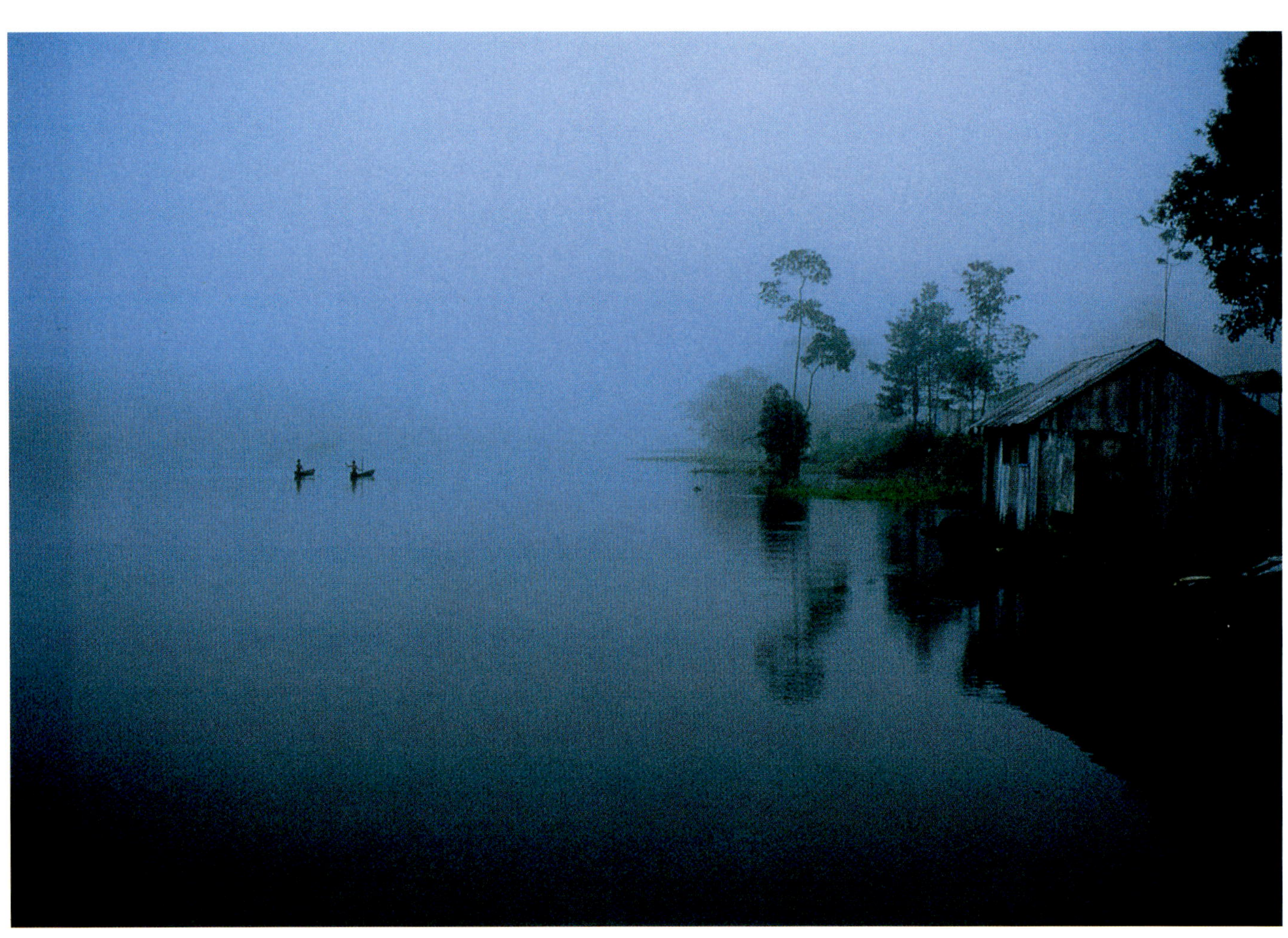

Preceeding Spread: Richard Hamilton Smith / Above: Arthur Meyerson

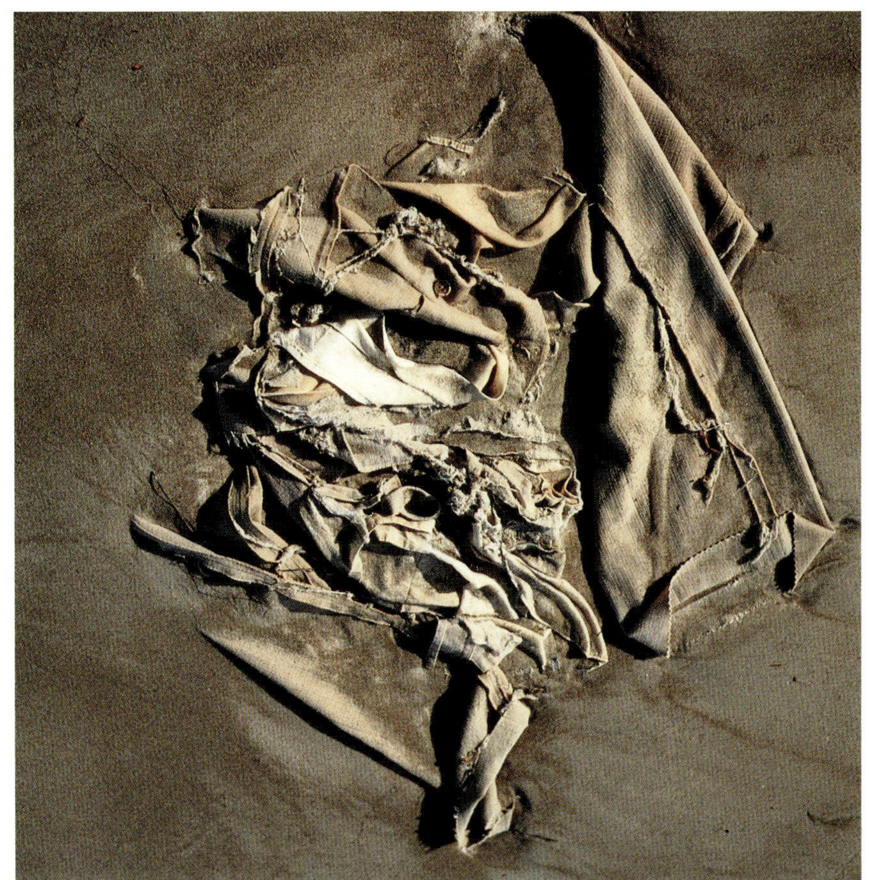

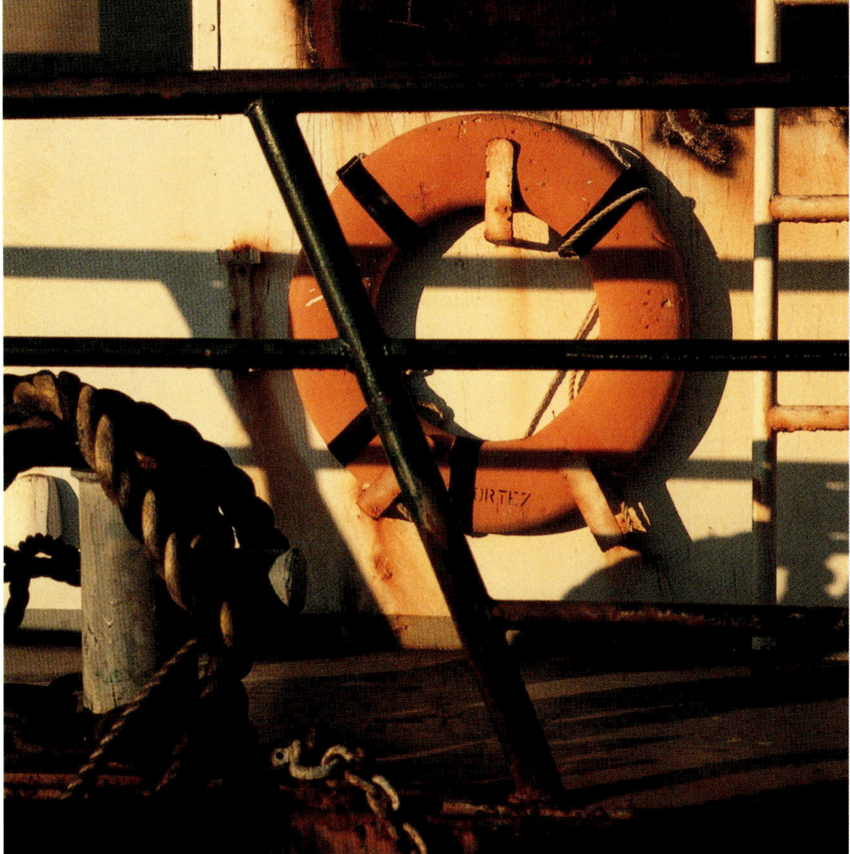

MERCIER/WIMBERG

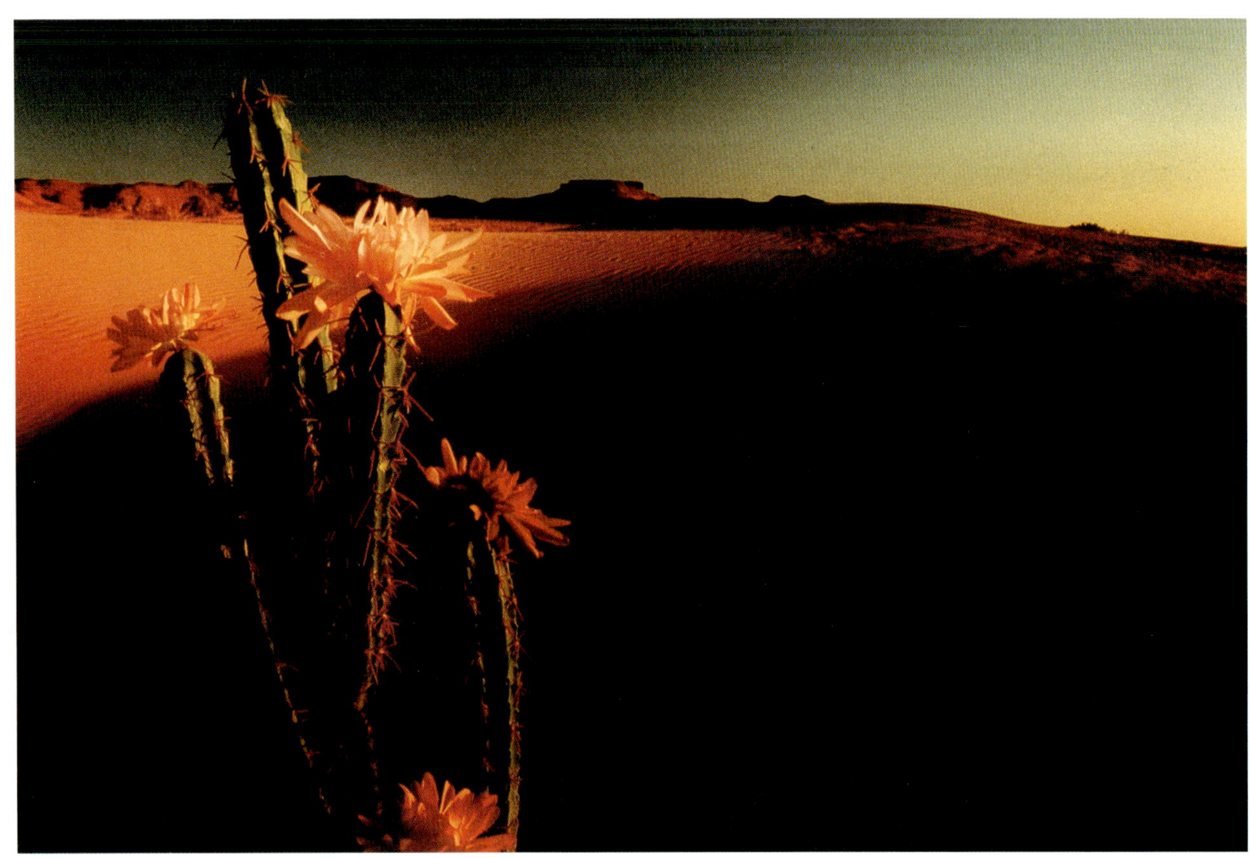

Hai Tui

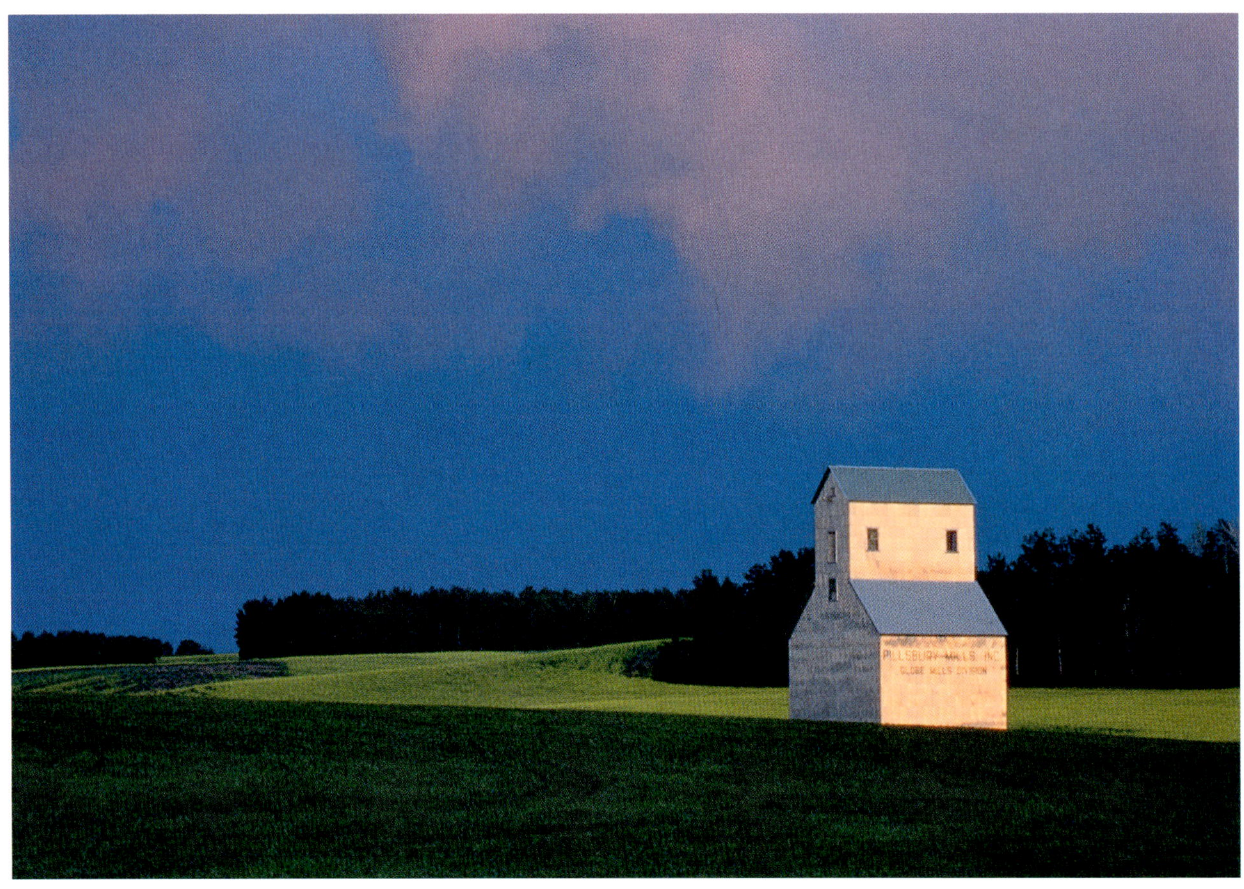

Jamey Stillings

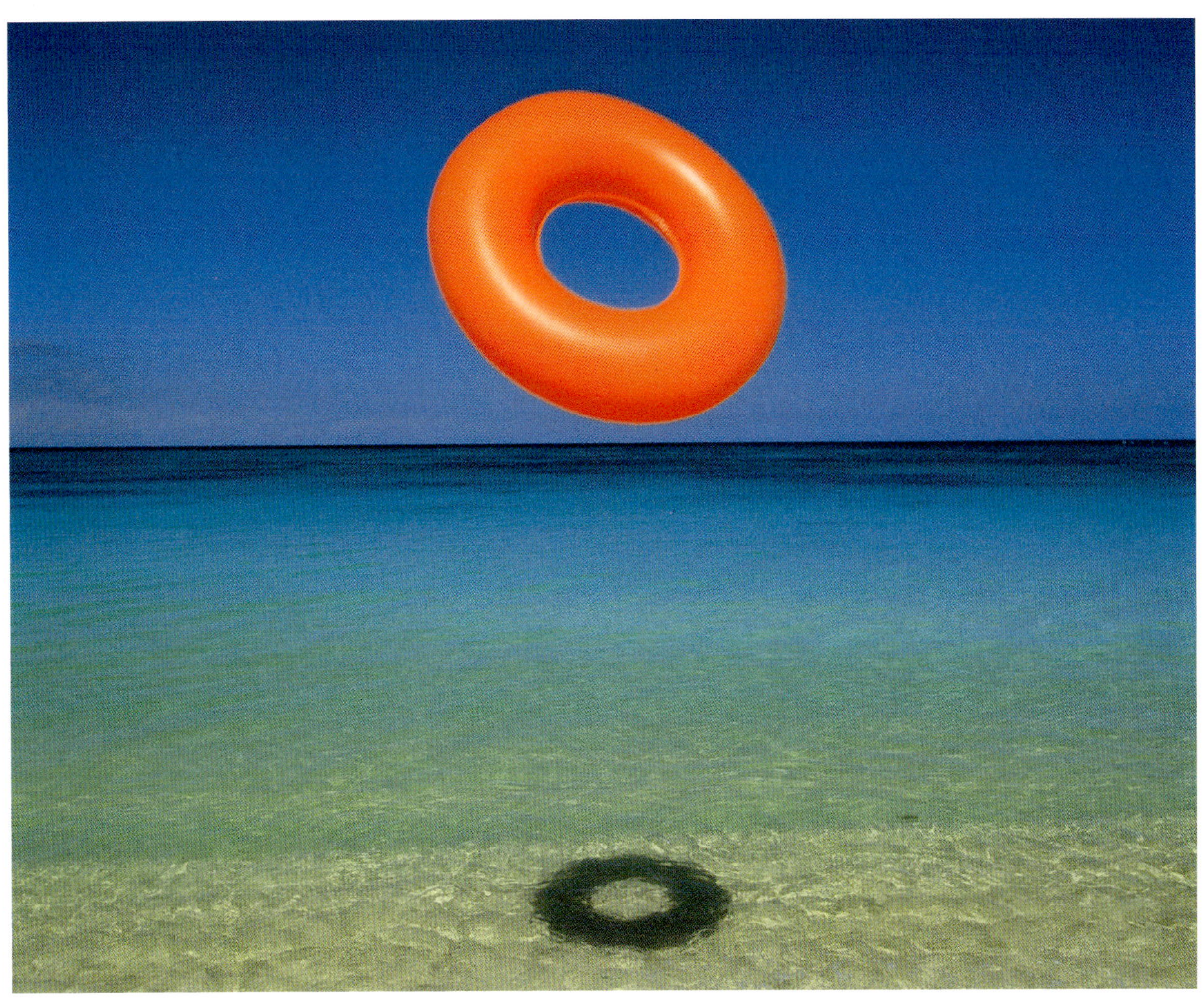

Stuart Dee

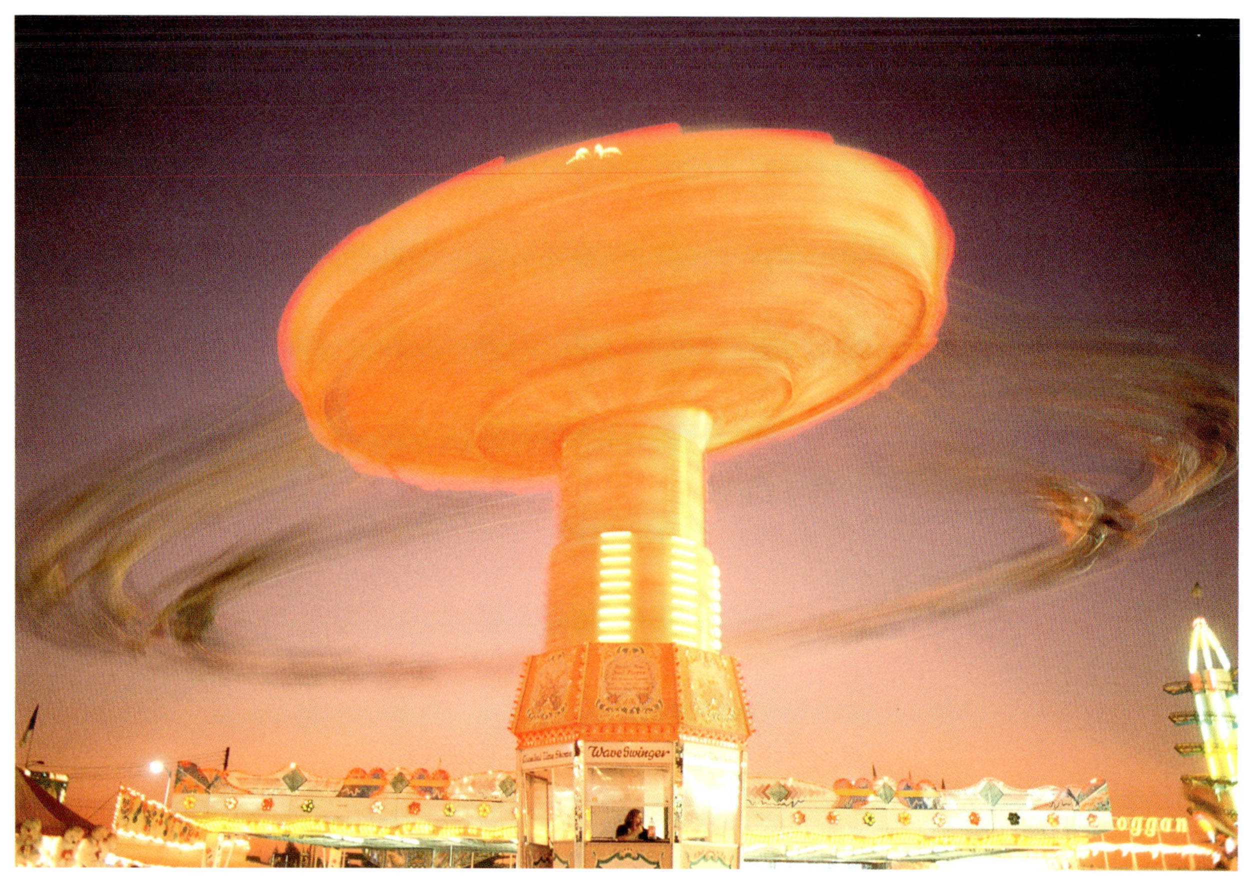

Terry Husebye

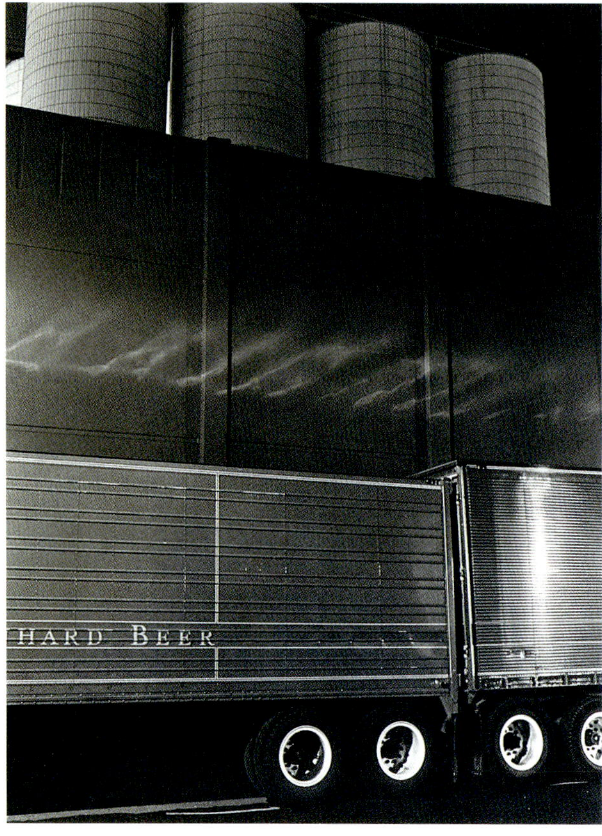
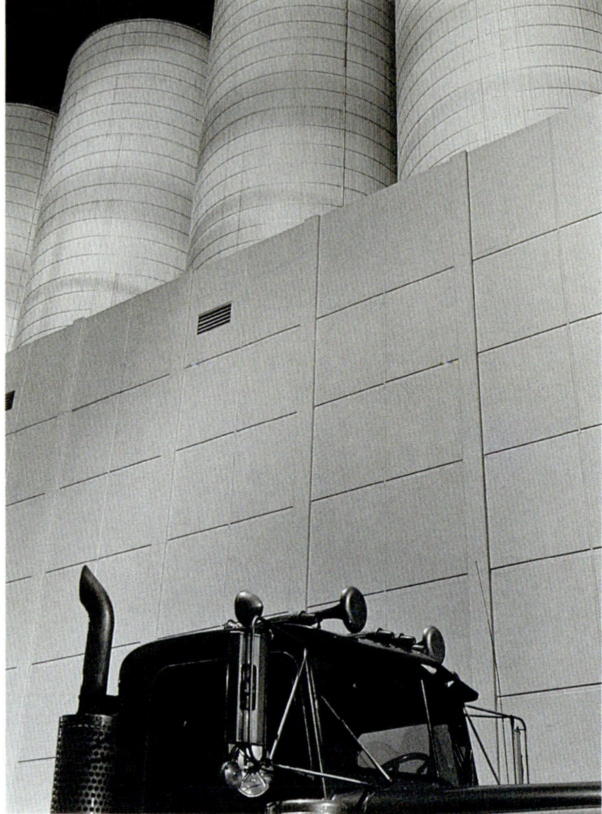

Pete Eckert

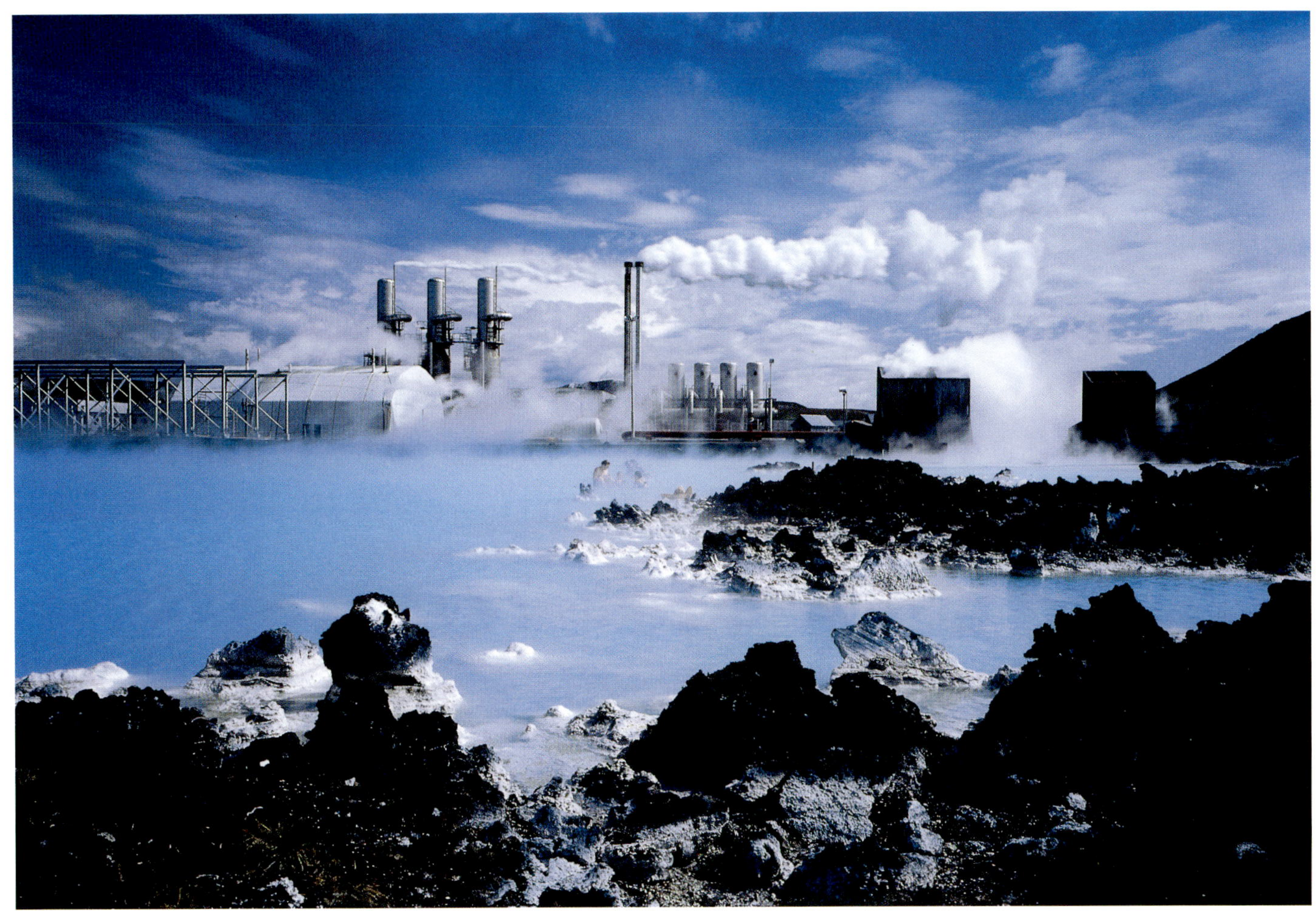

Ron Bambridge

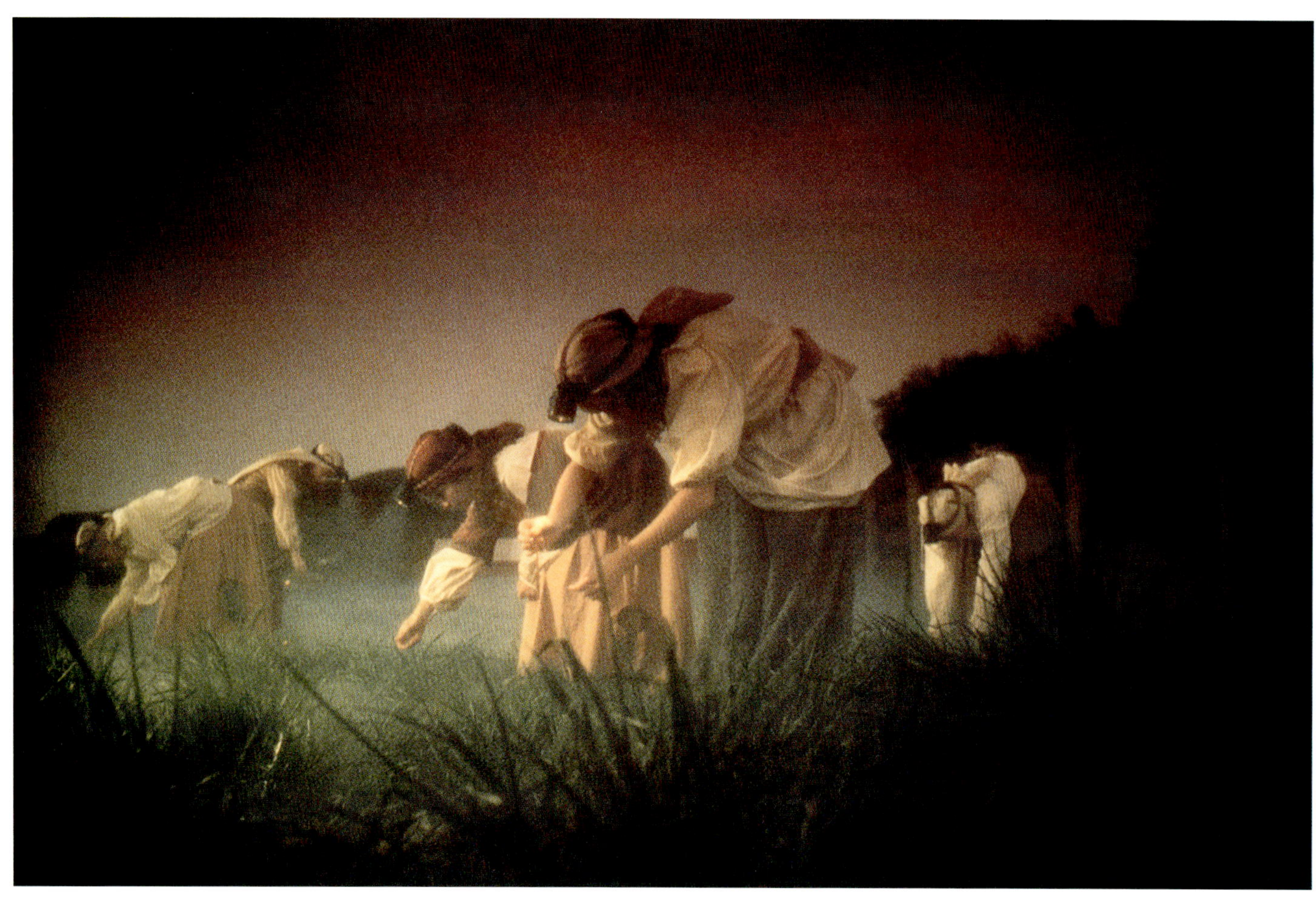

George Simhoni

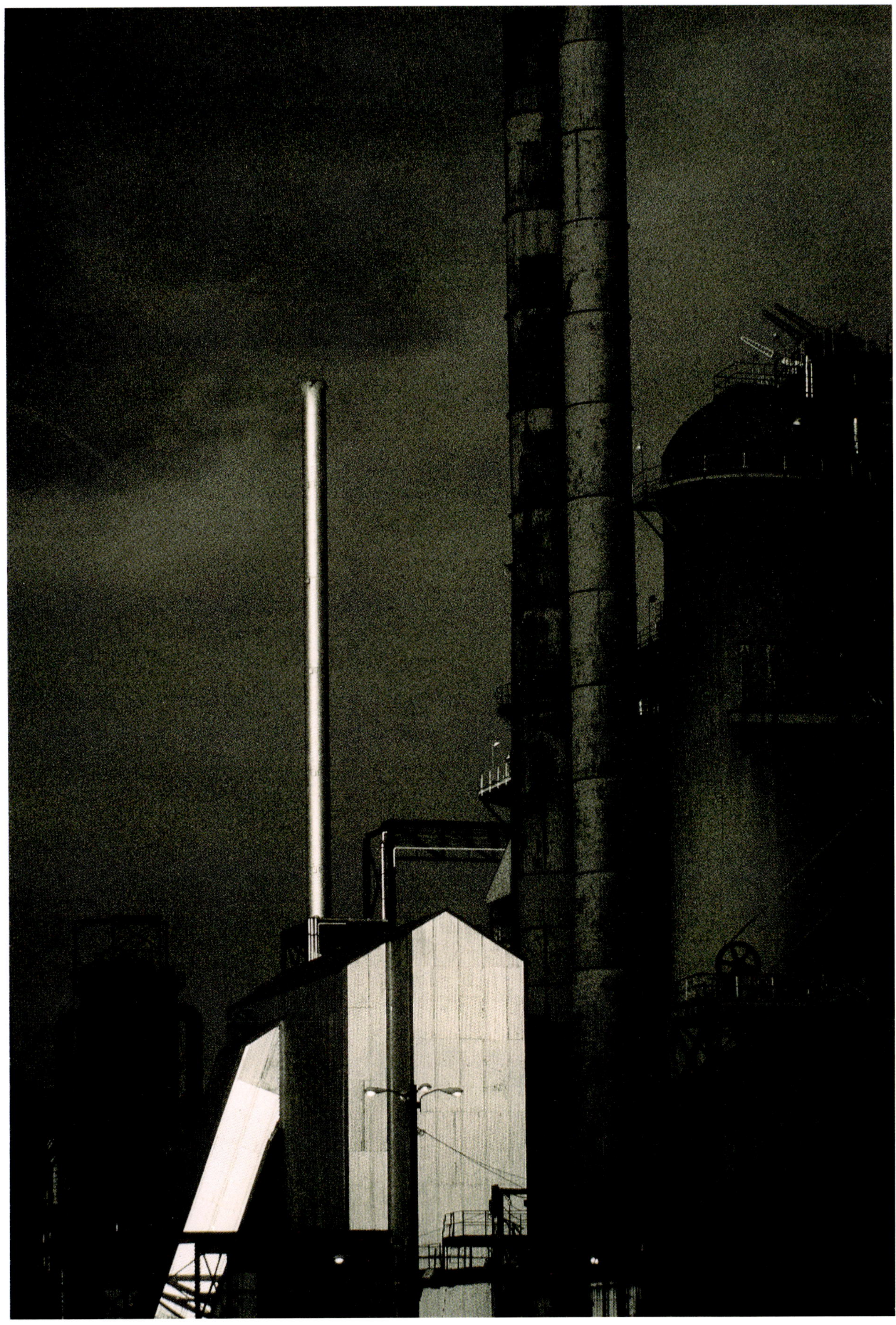

Nicolay Zurek

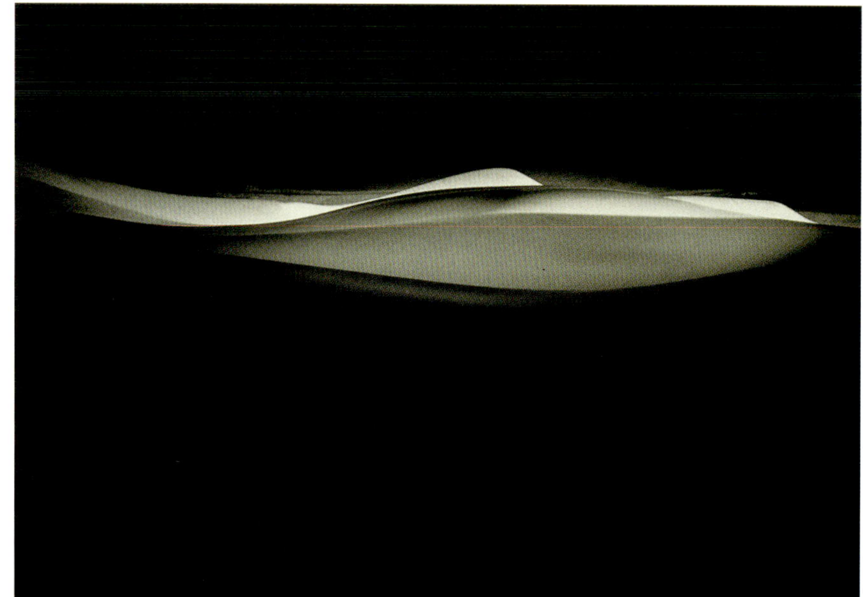

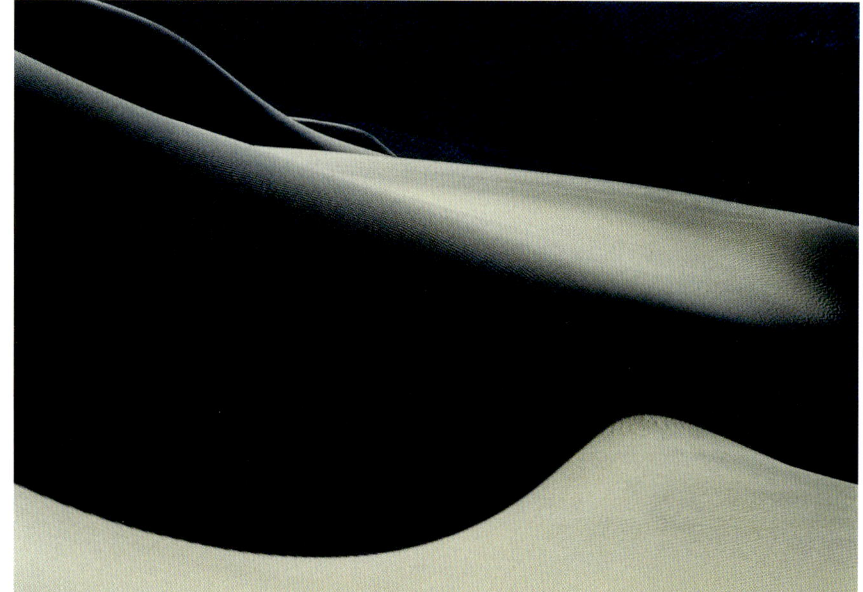

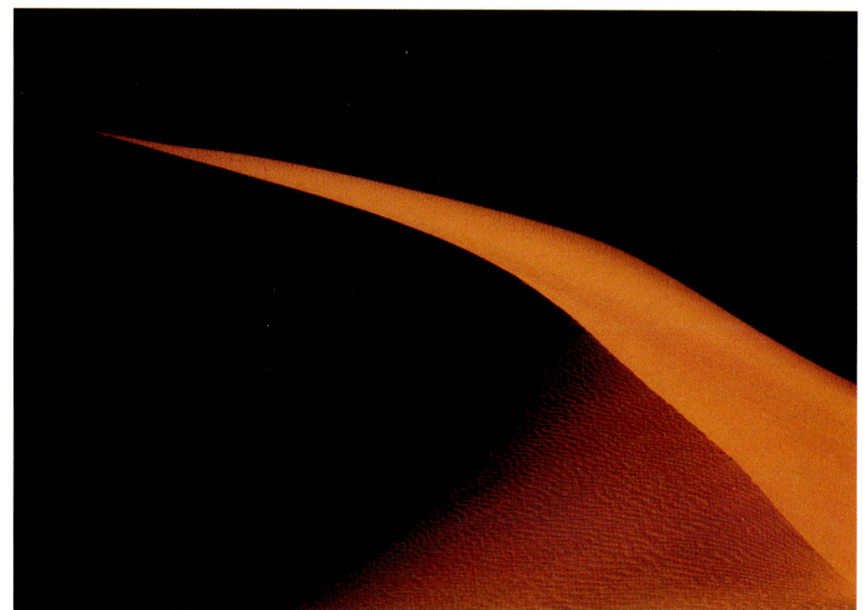

Intae Kim

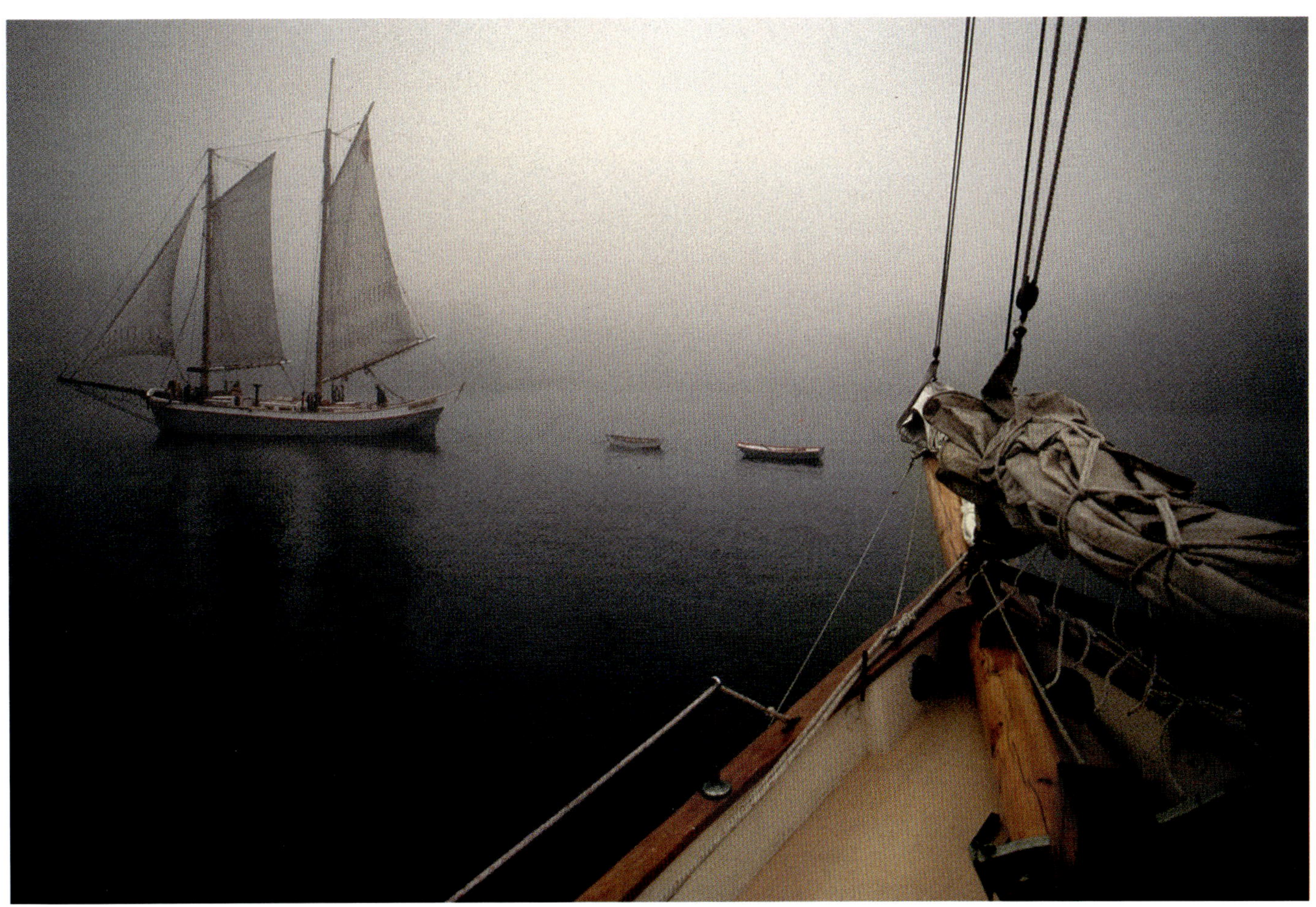

Lou Jones

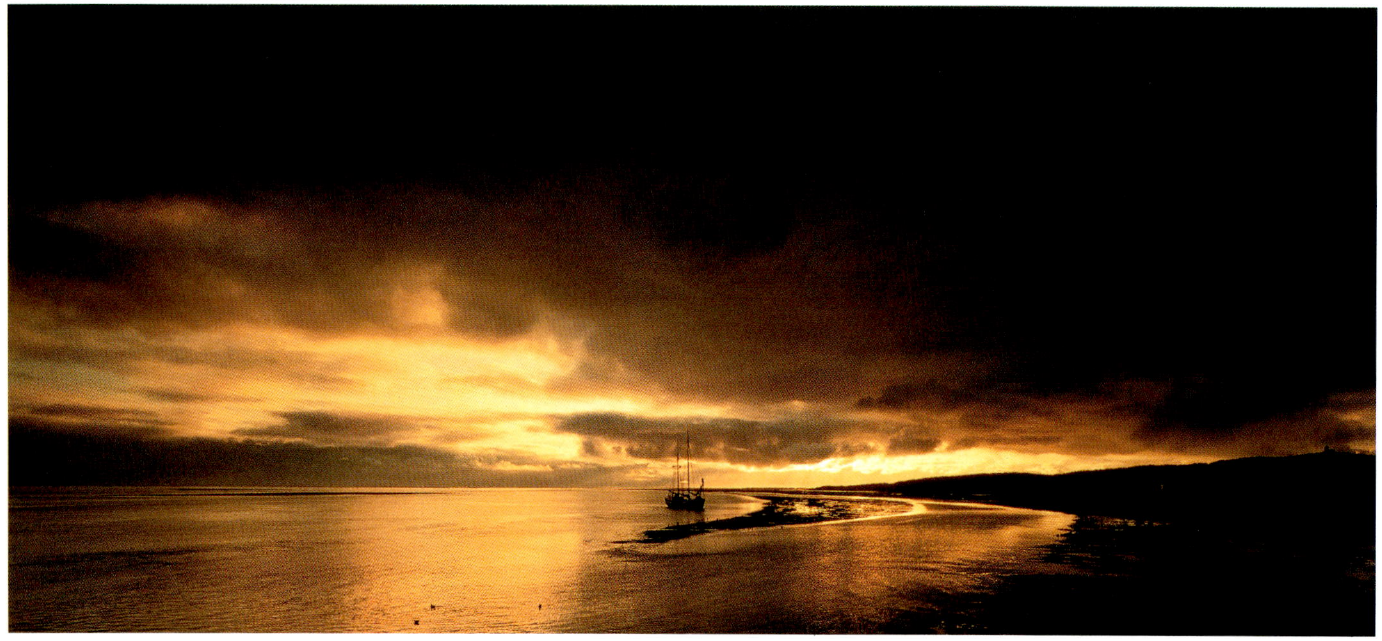

Harry De Zitter | Opposite: Nadav Kander

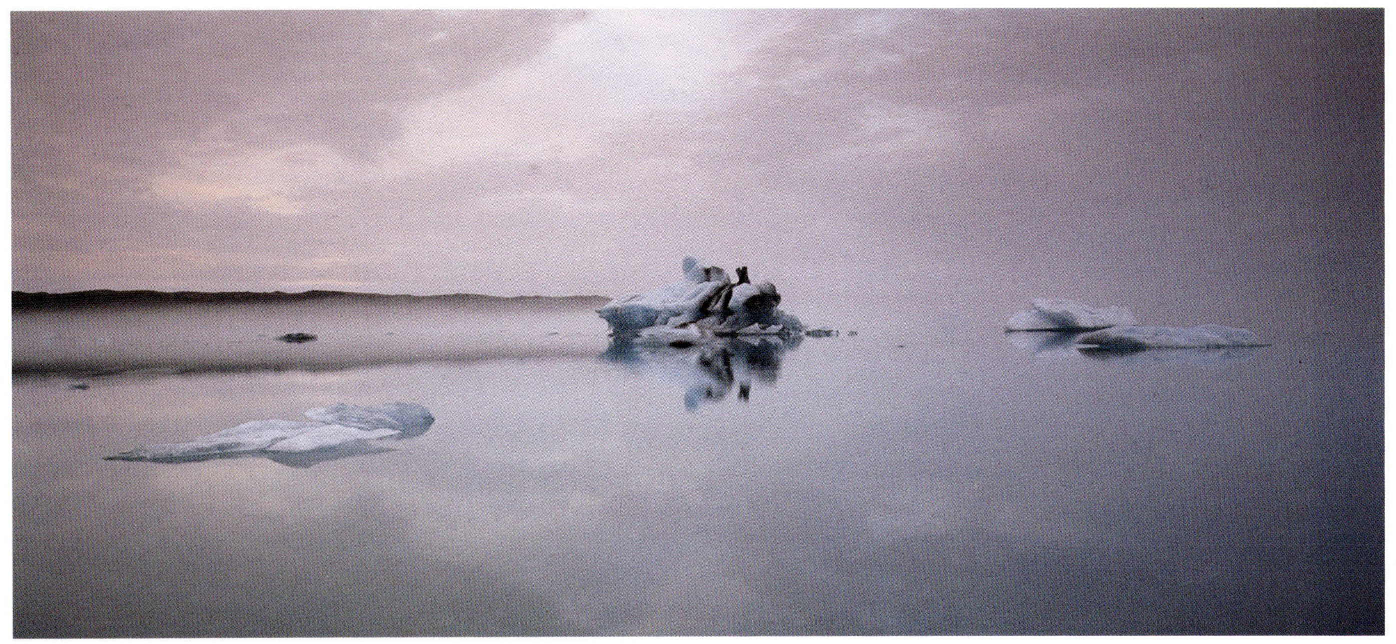

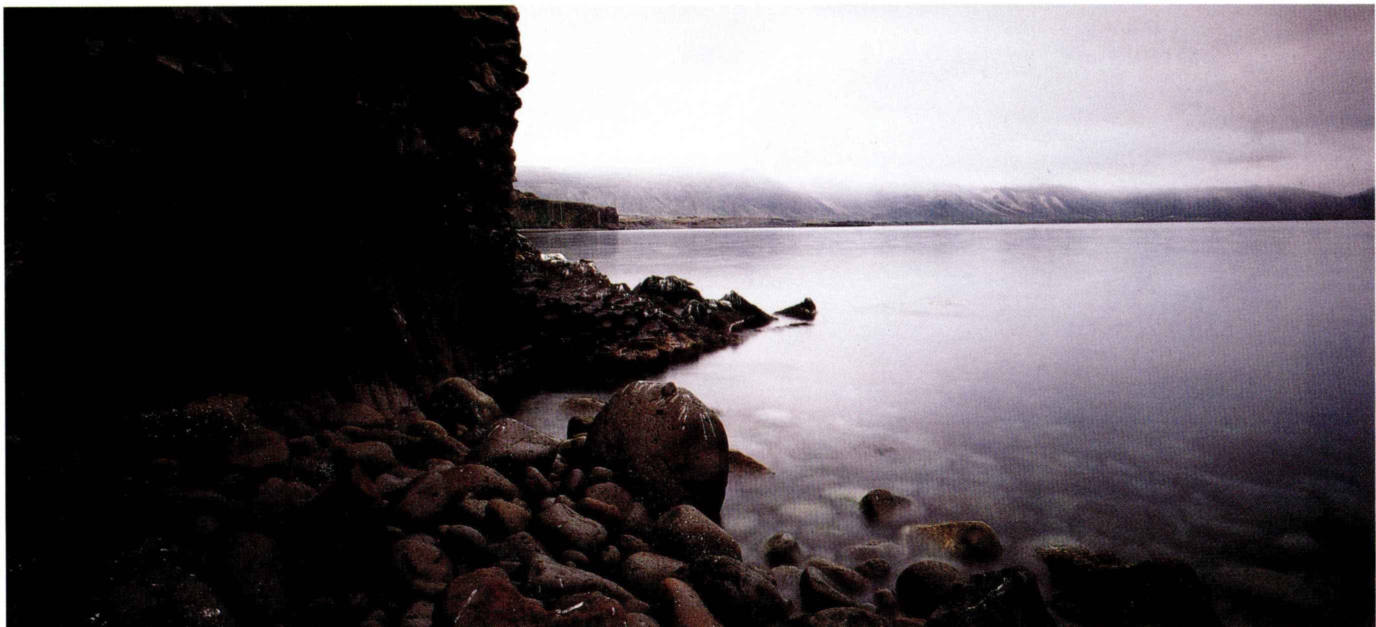

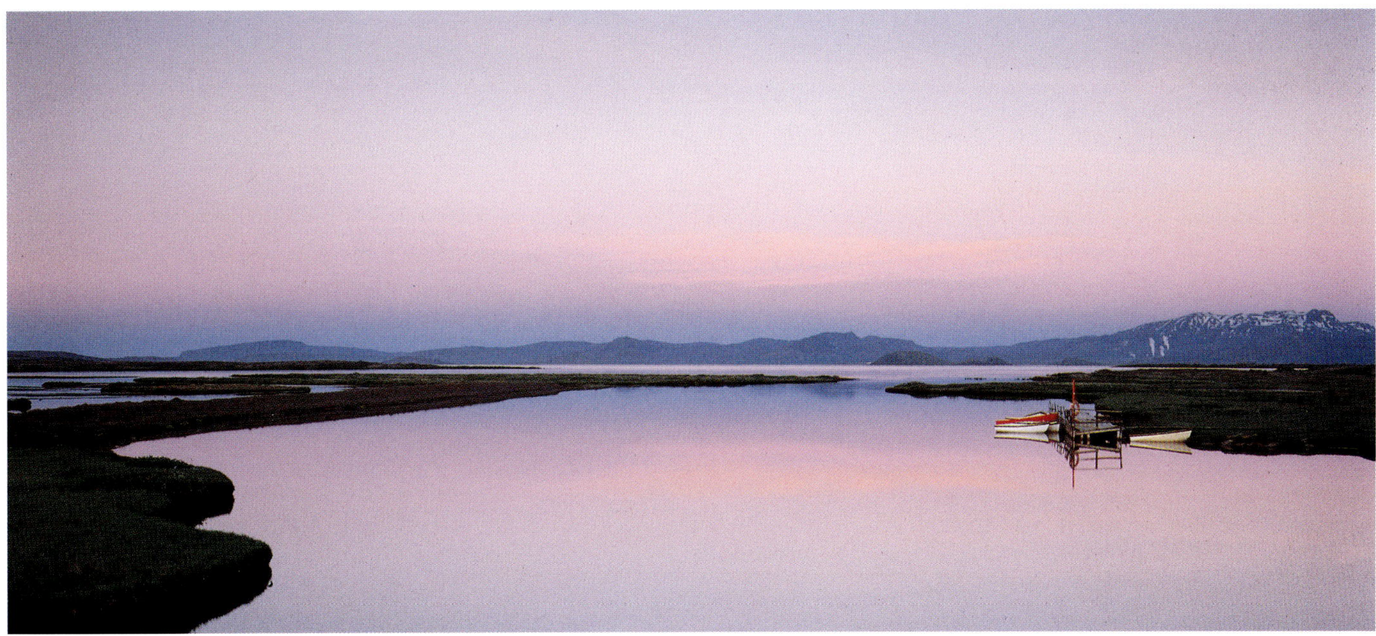

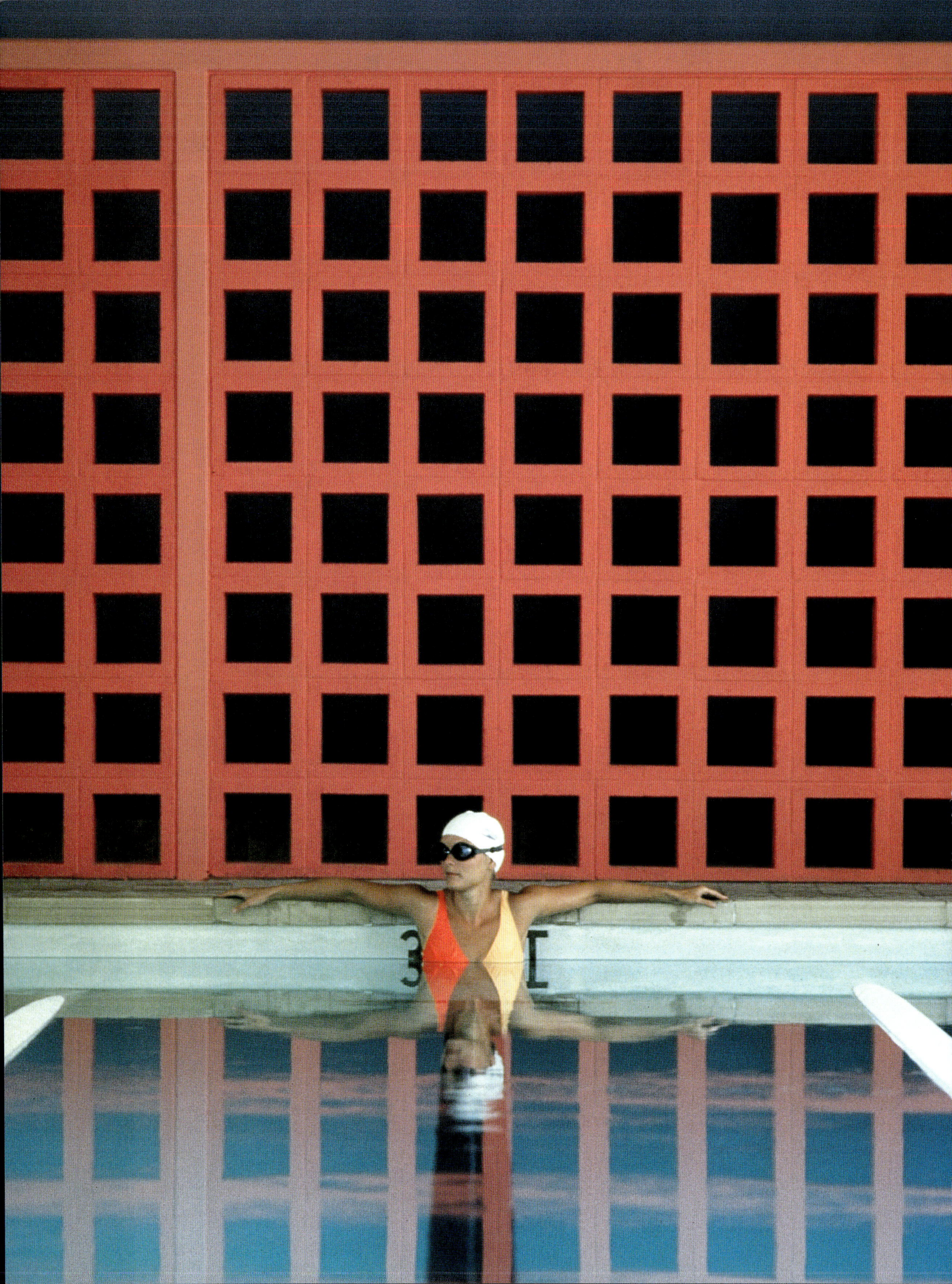

ARCHITECTURE

ARCHITEKTUR

ARCHITECTURE

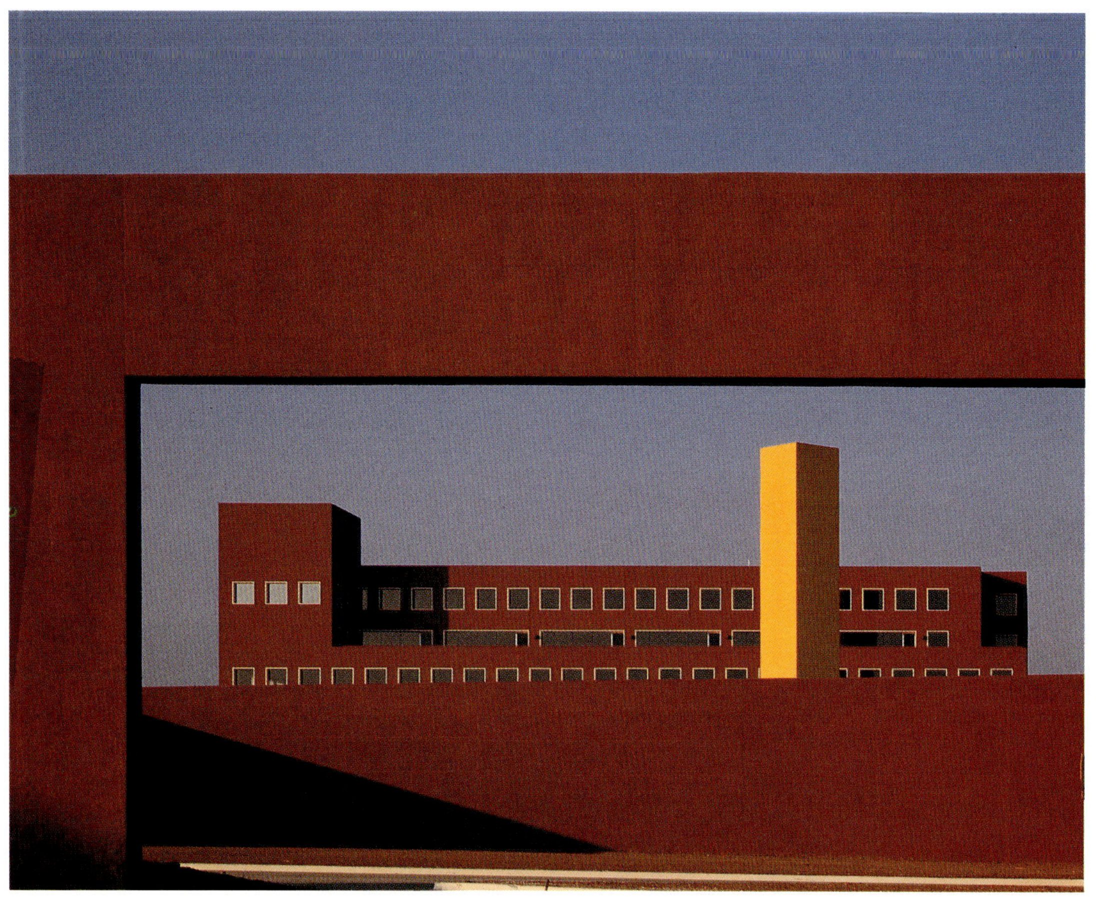

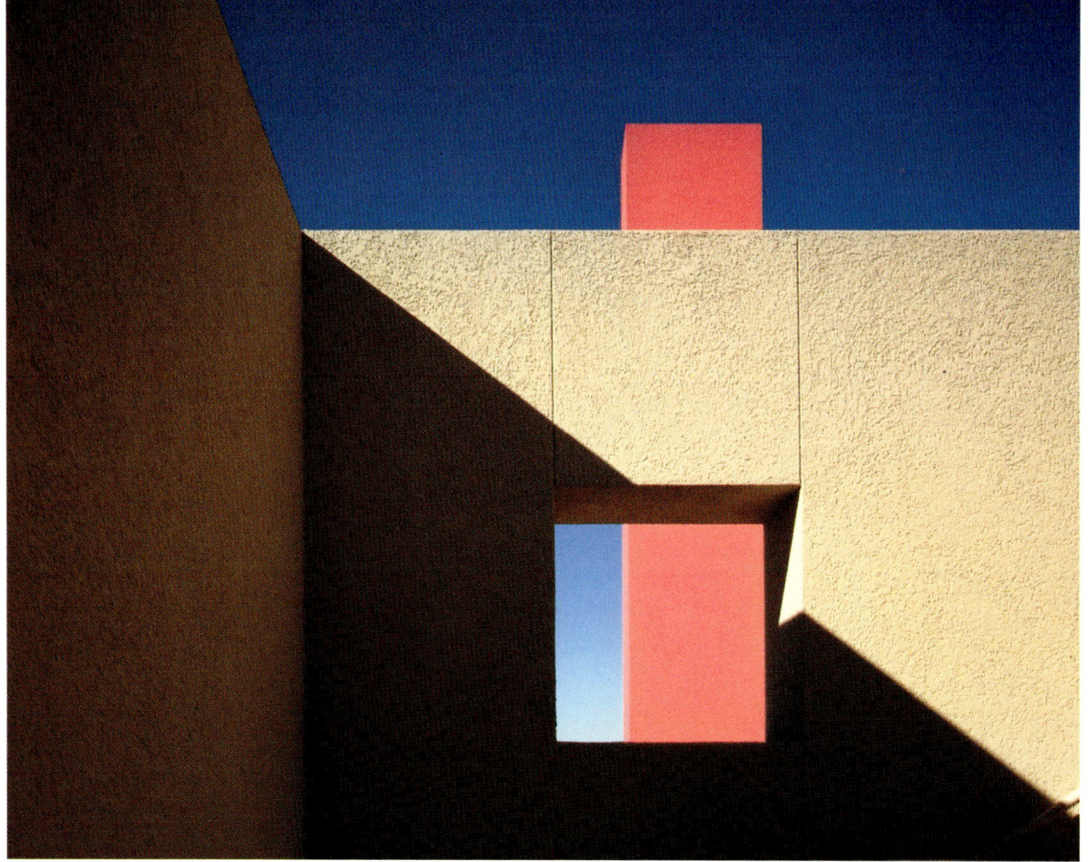

Preceeding Spread: Terry Vine | Above: Jim Hedrich

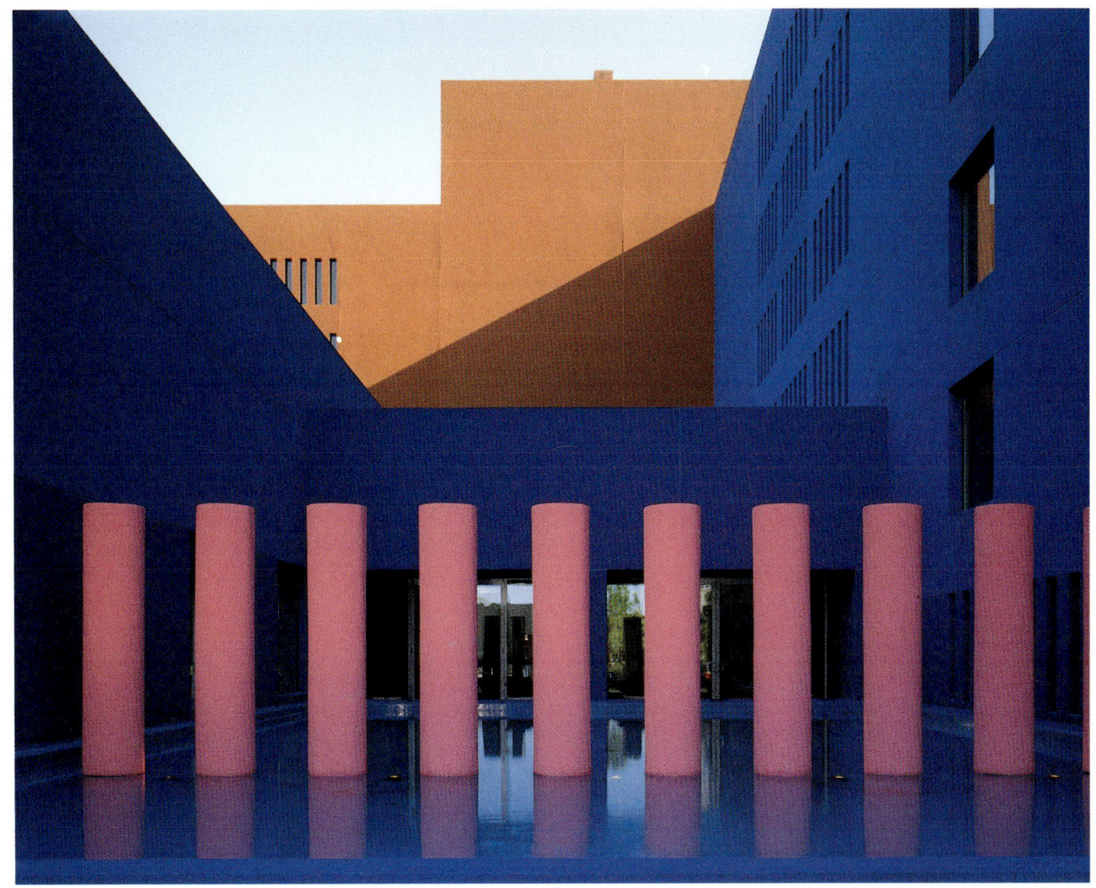

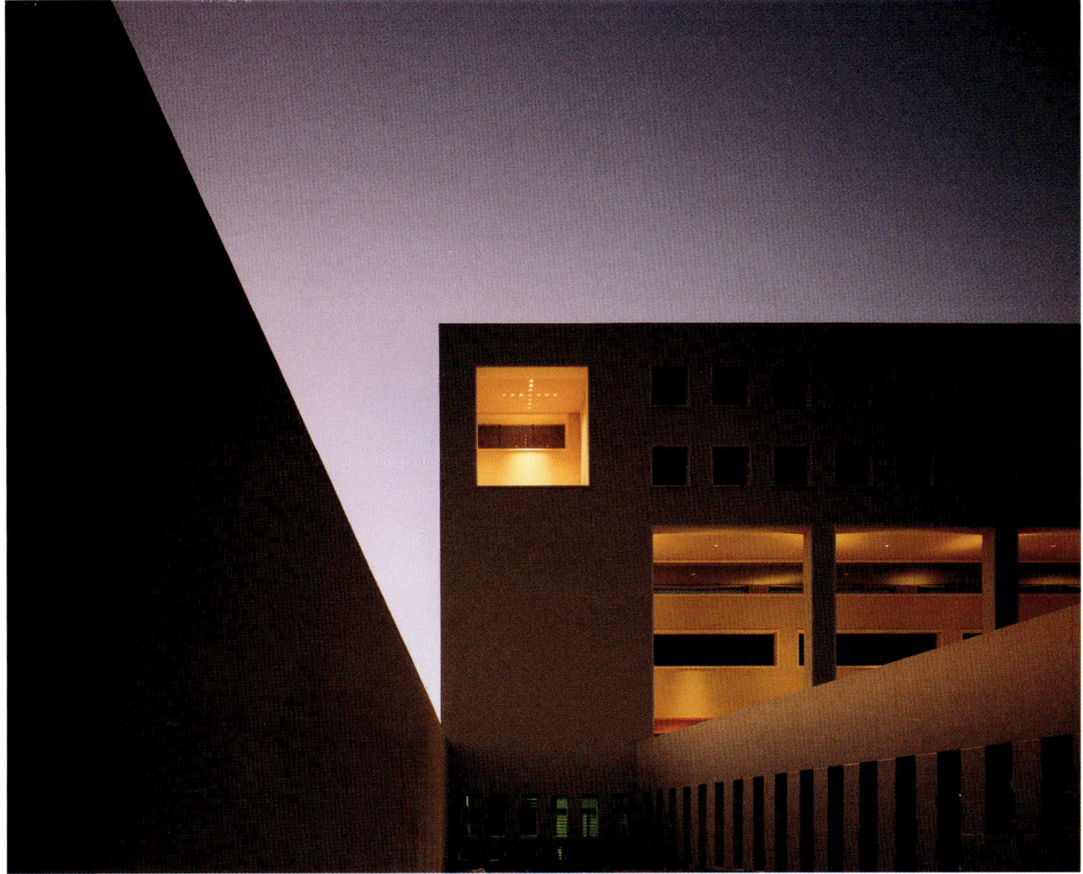

Jim Hedrich

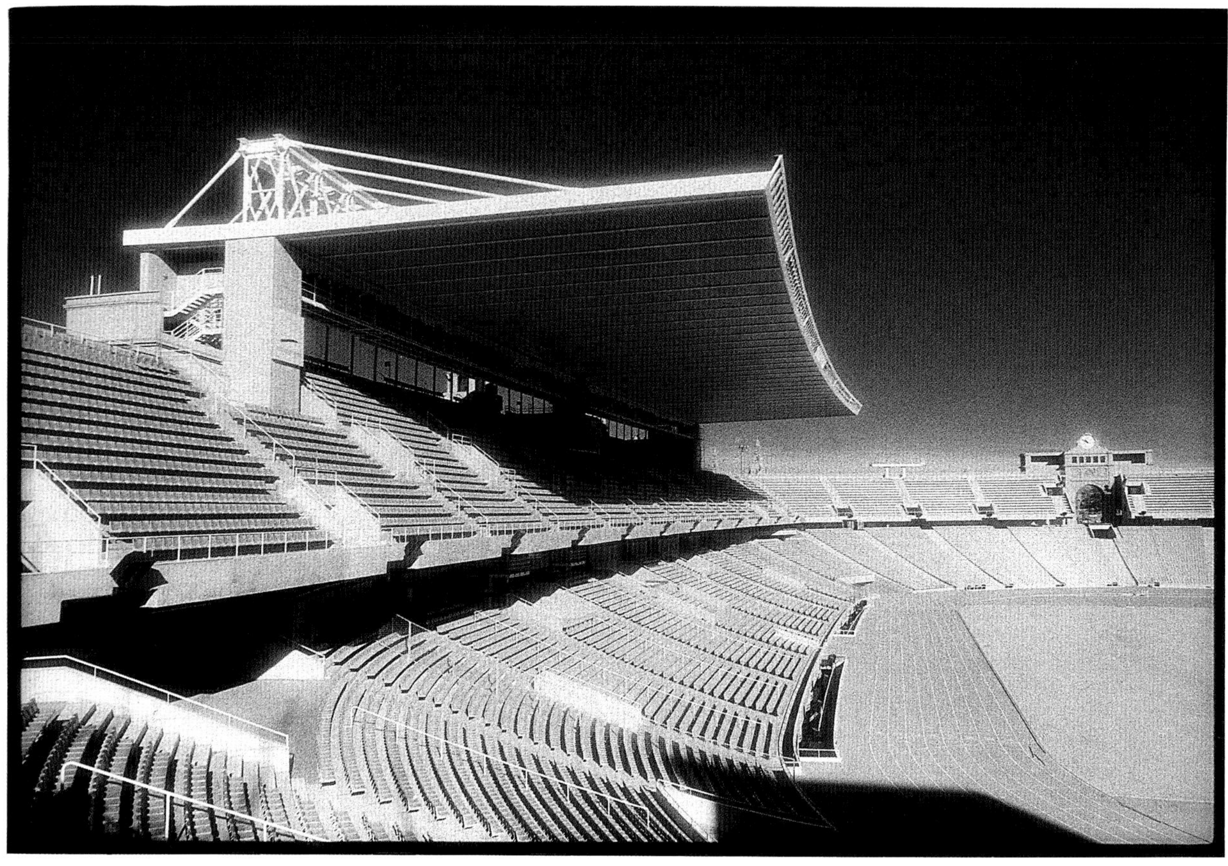

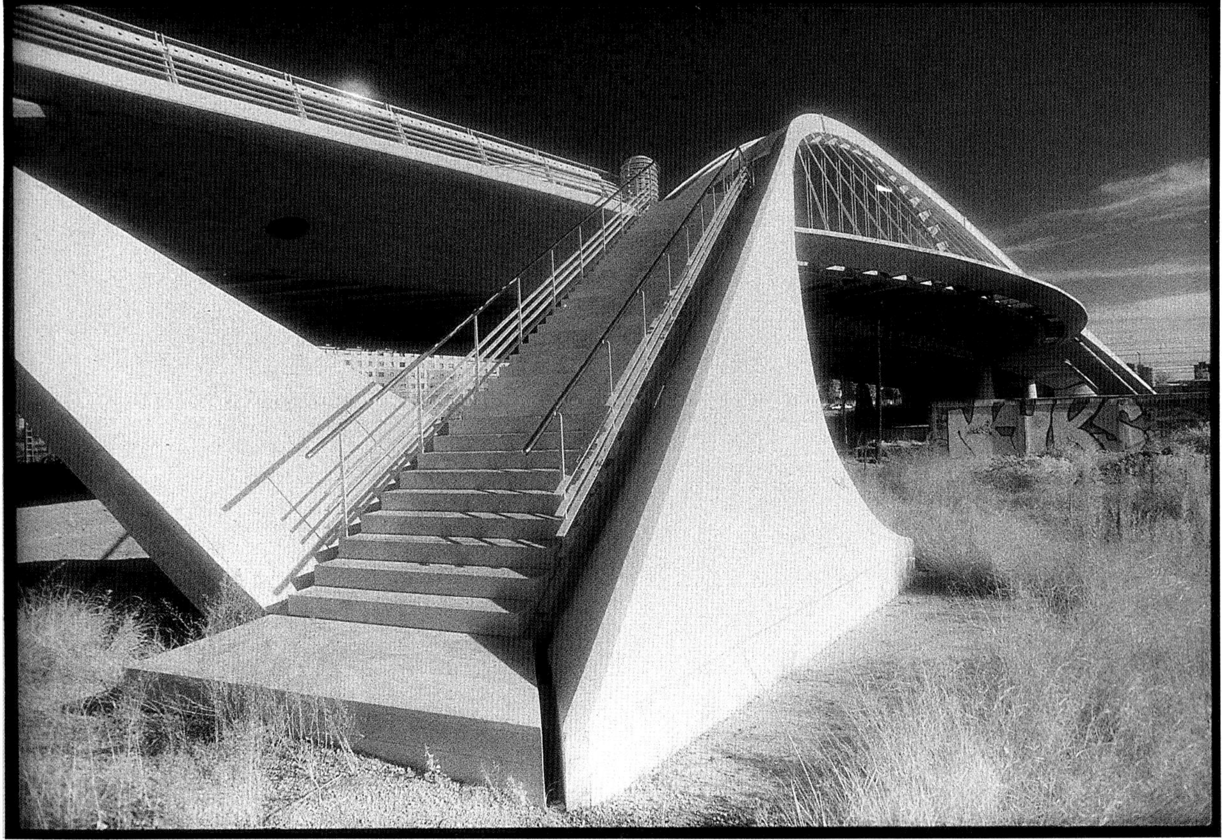

Miquel Gonzales

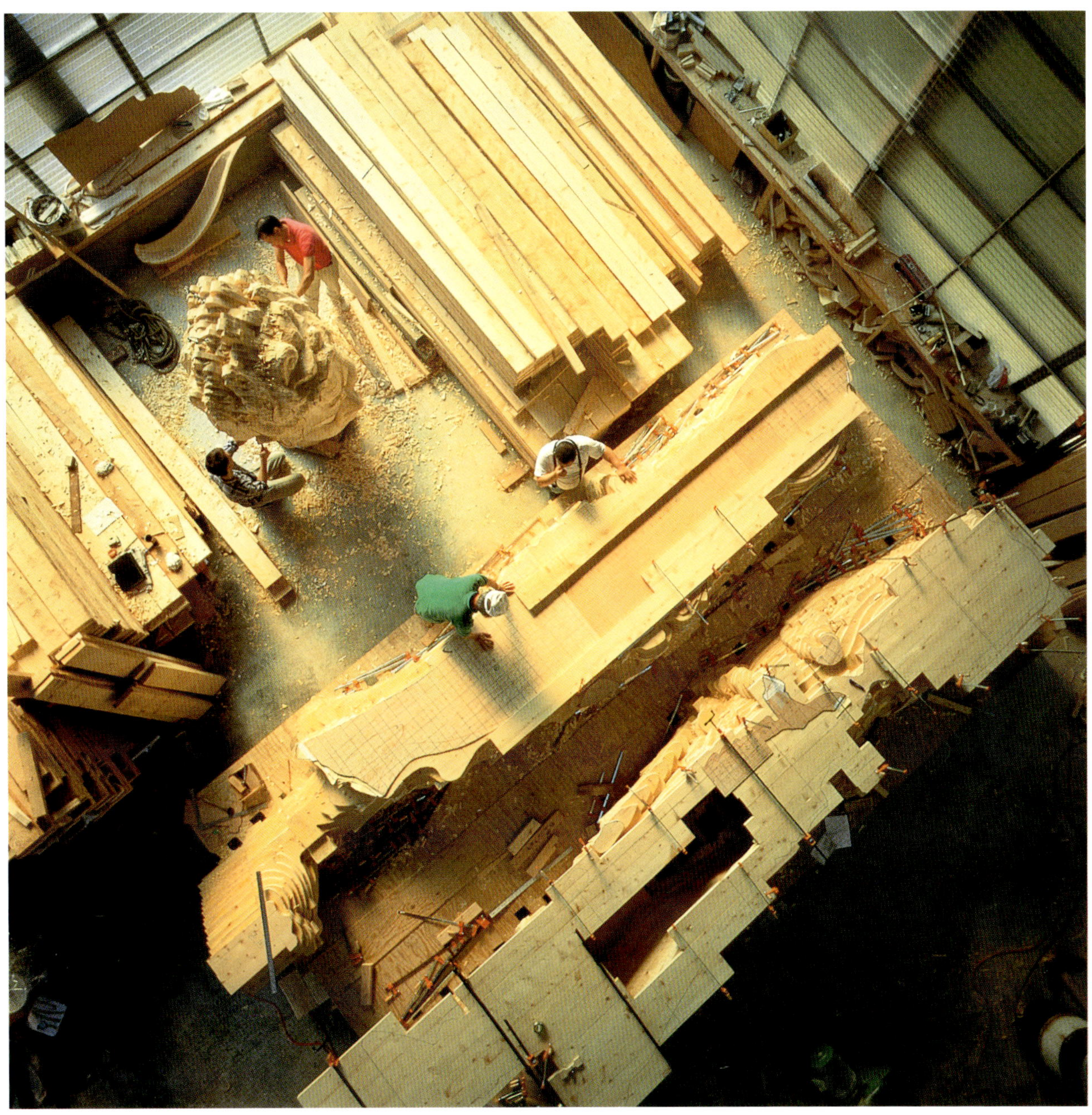

Greg Pease

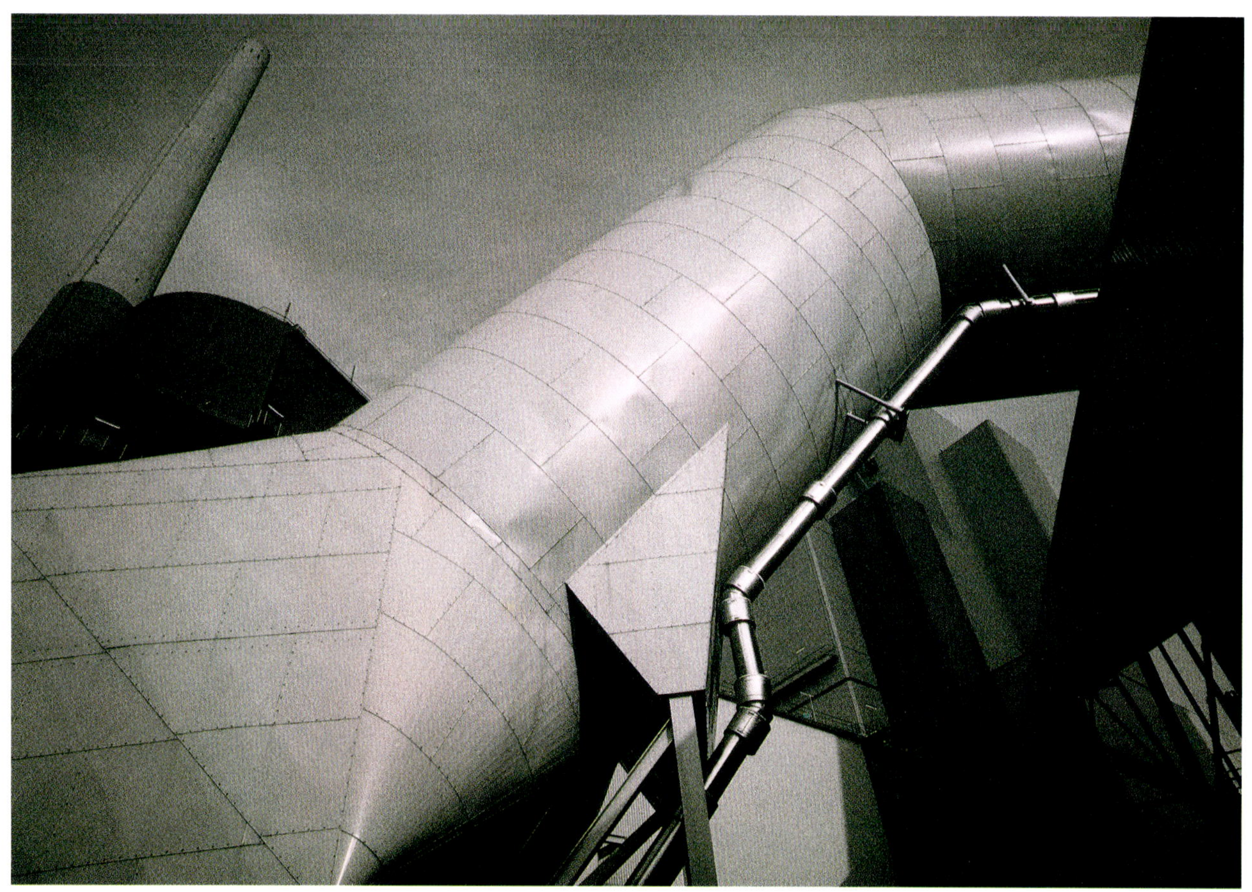

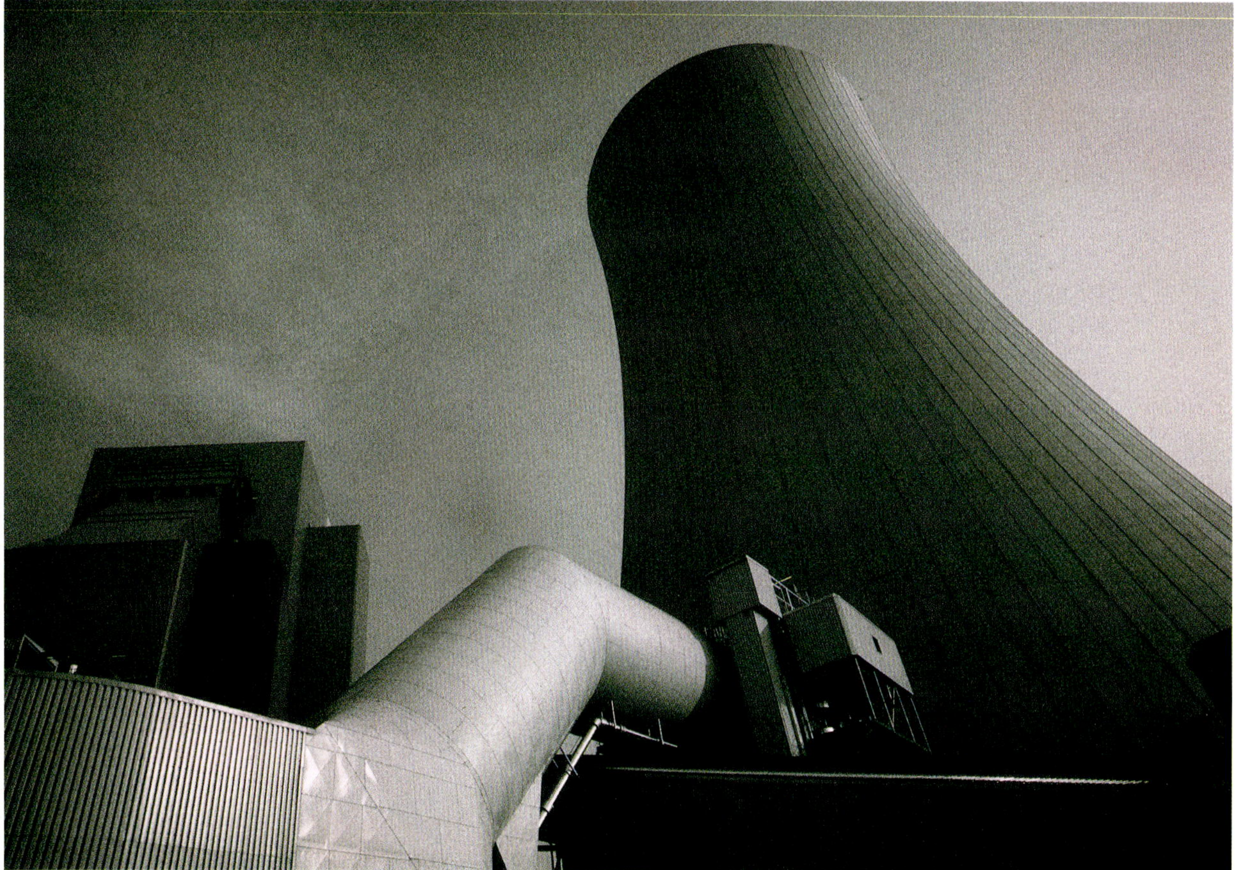

Christoph Seeberger

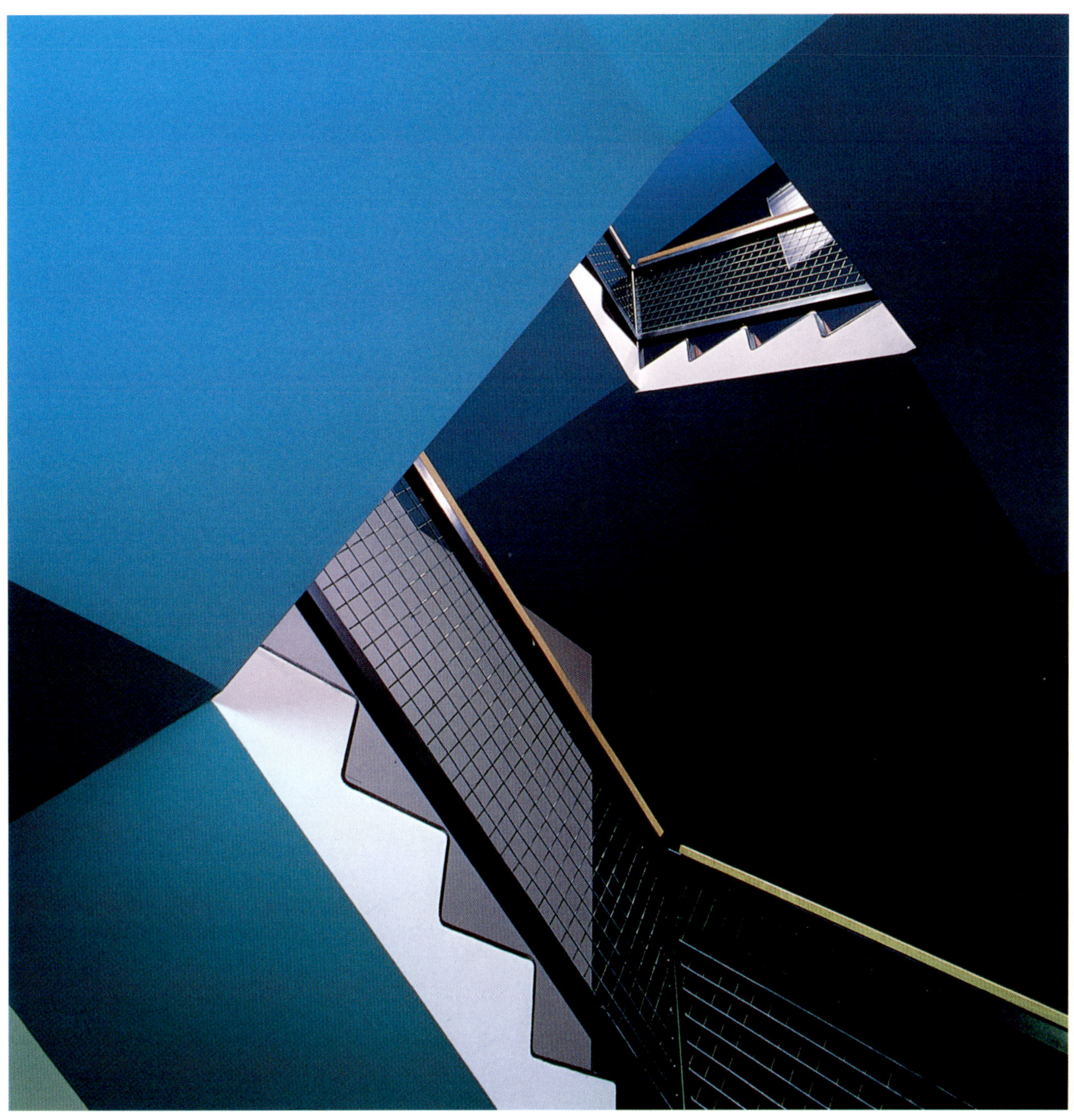

Richard Eastwood

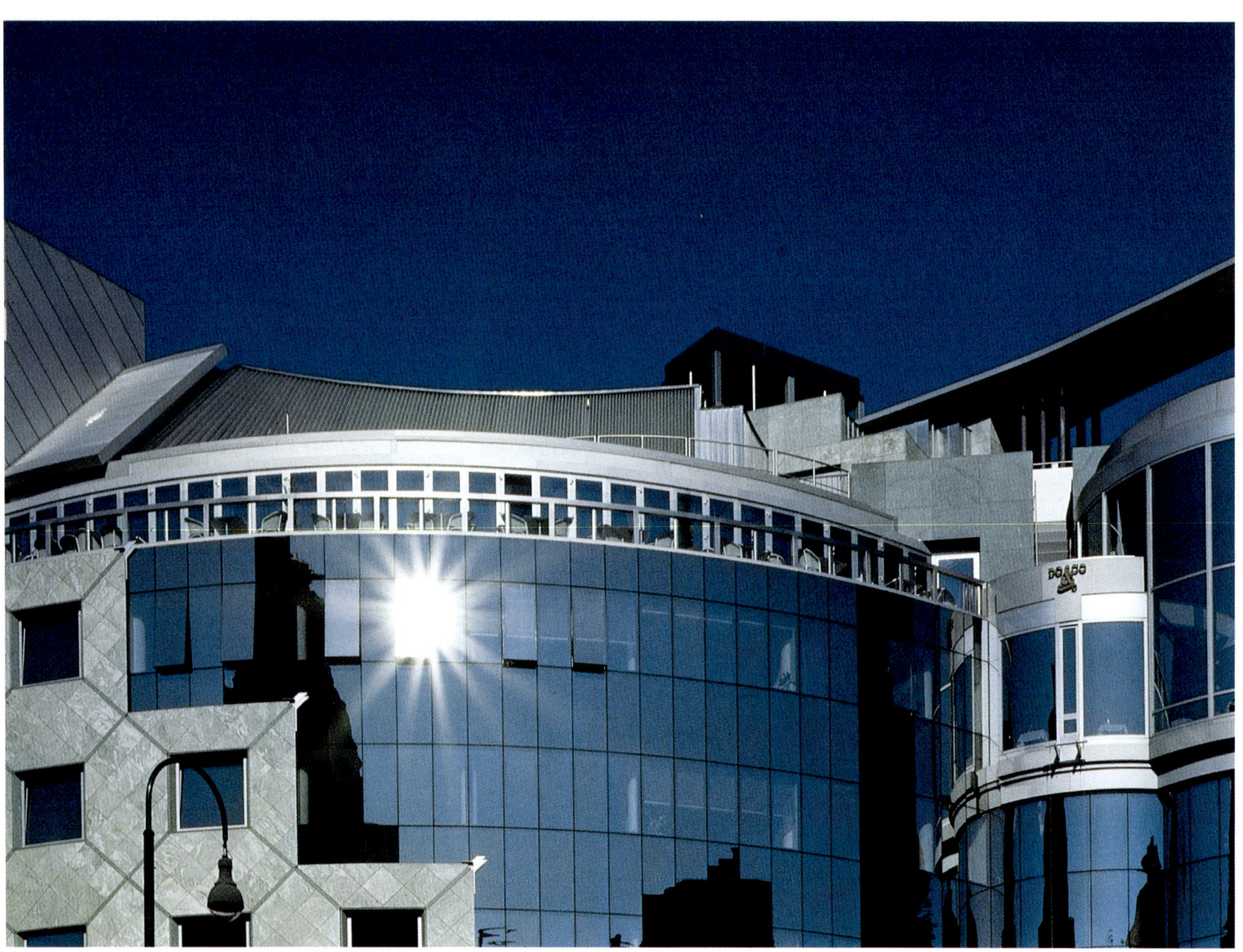

Meinrad Faultner

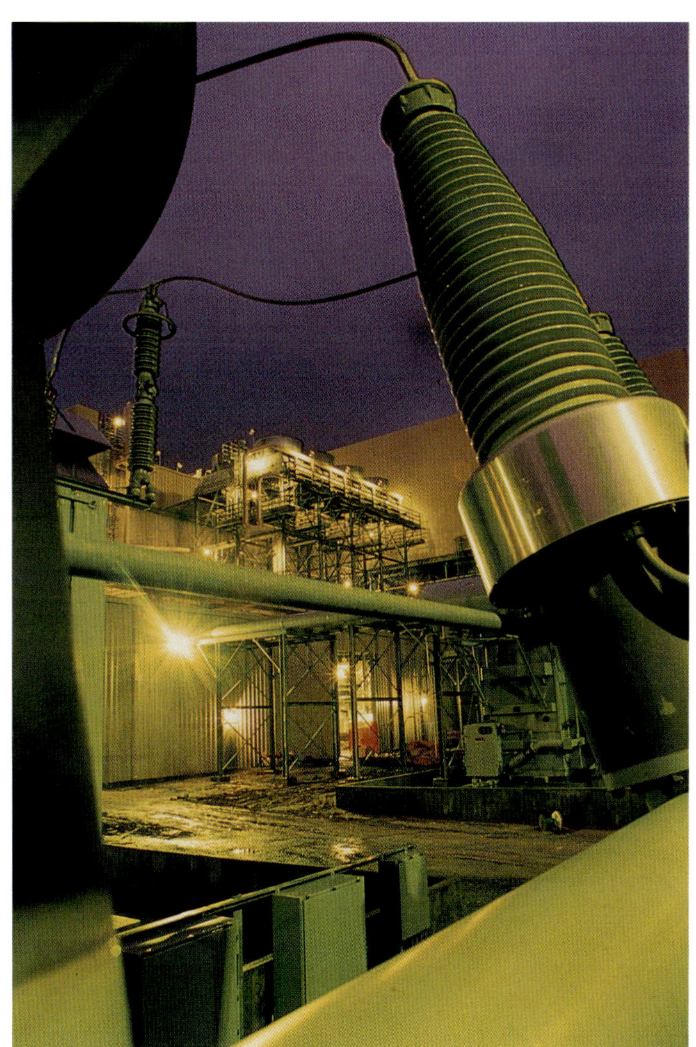
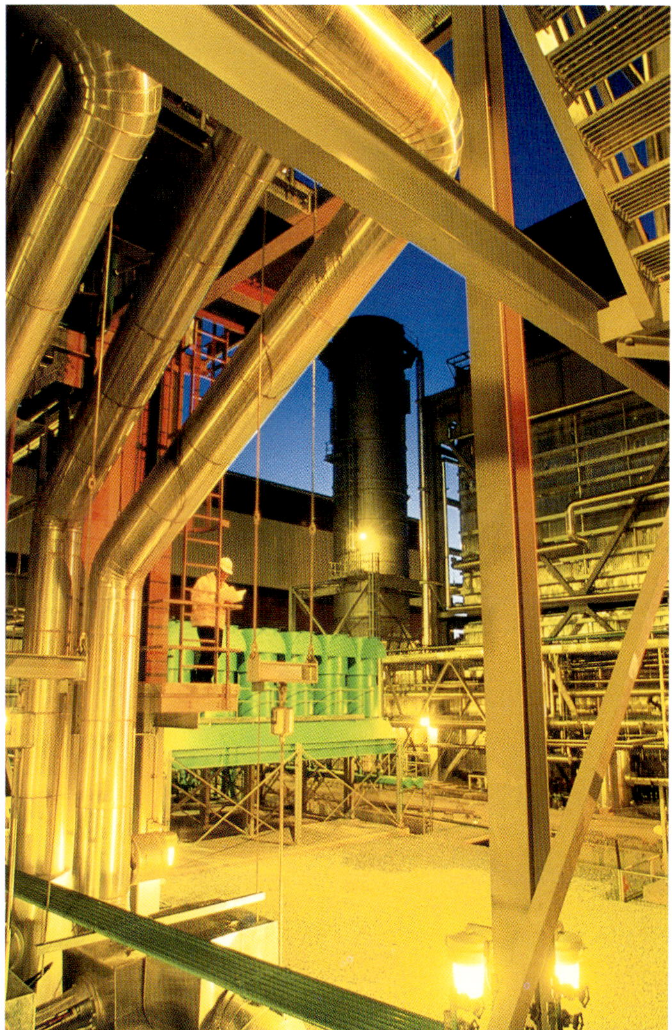

Lonnie Duka

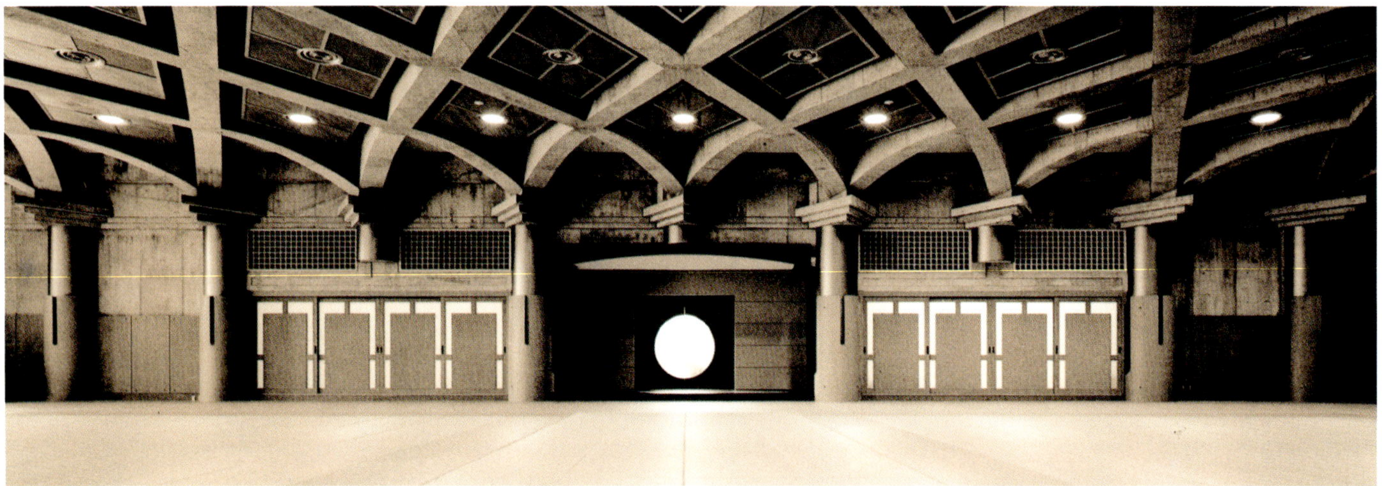

Tim Griffith

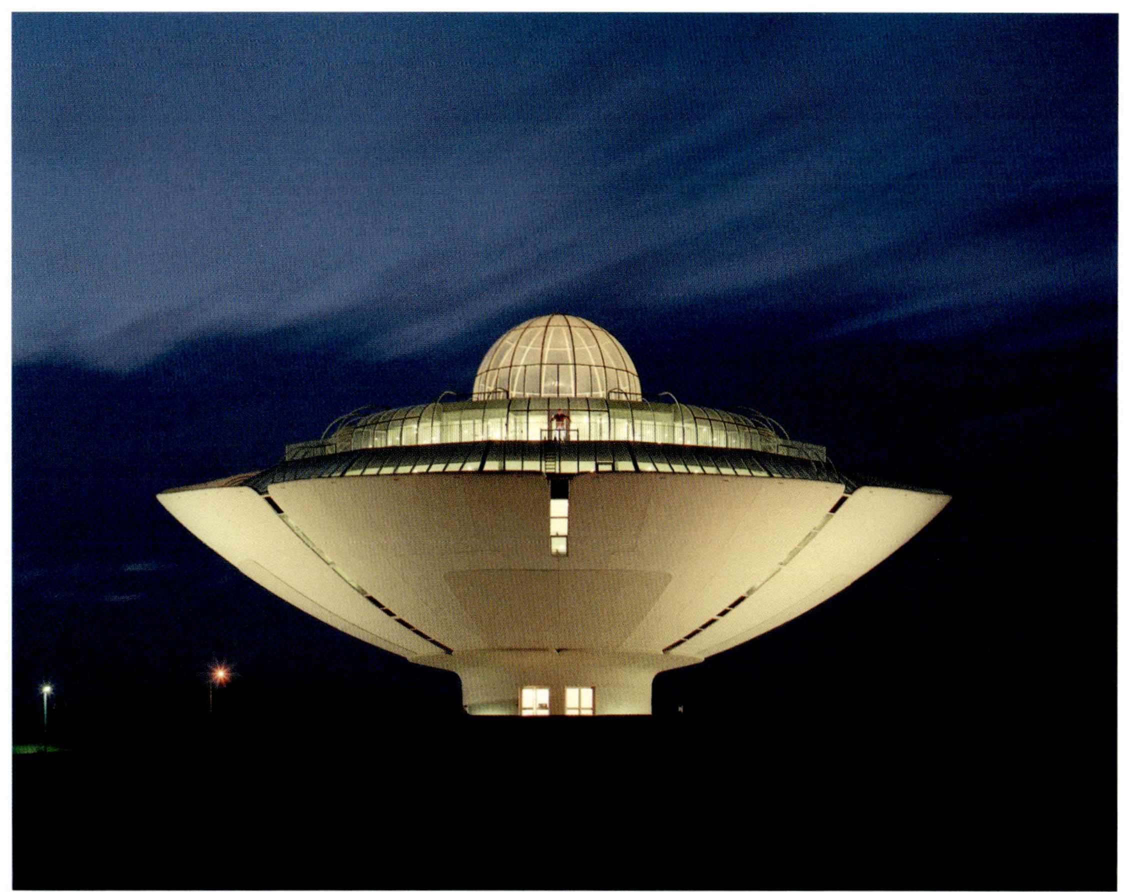

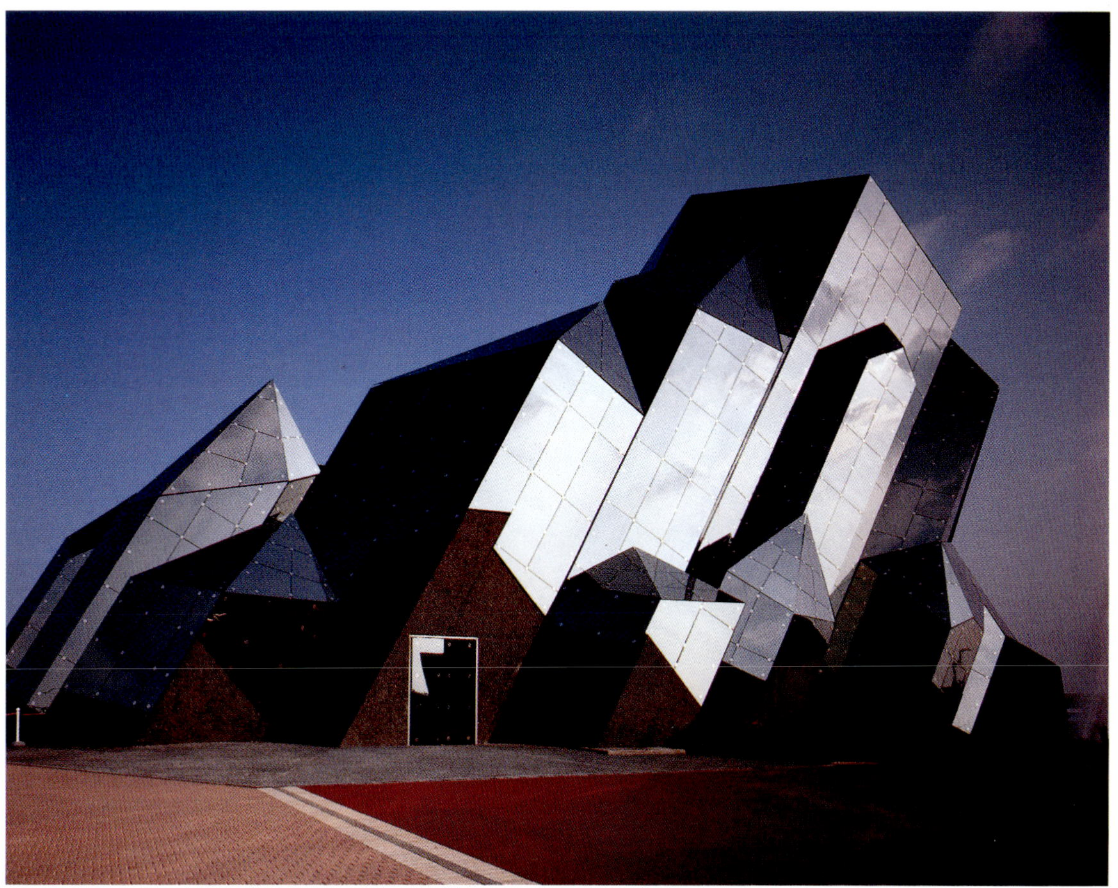

Richard Fischer

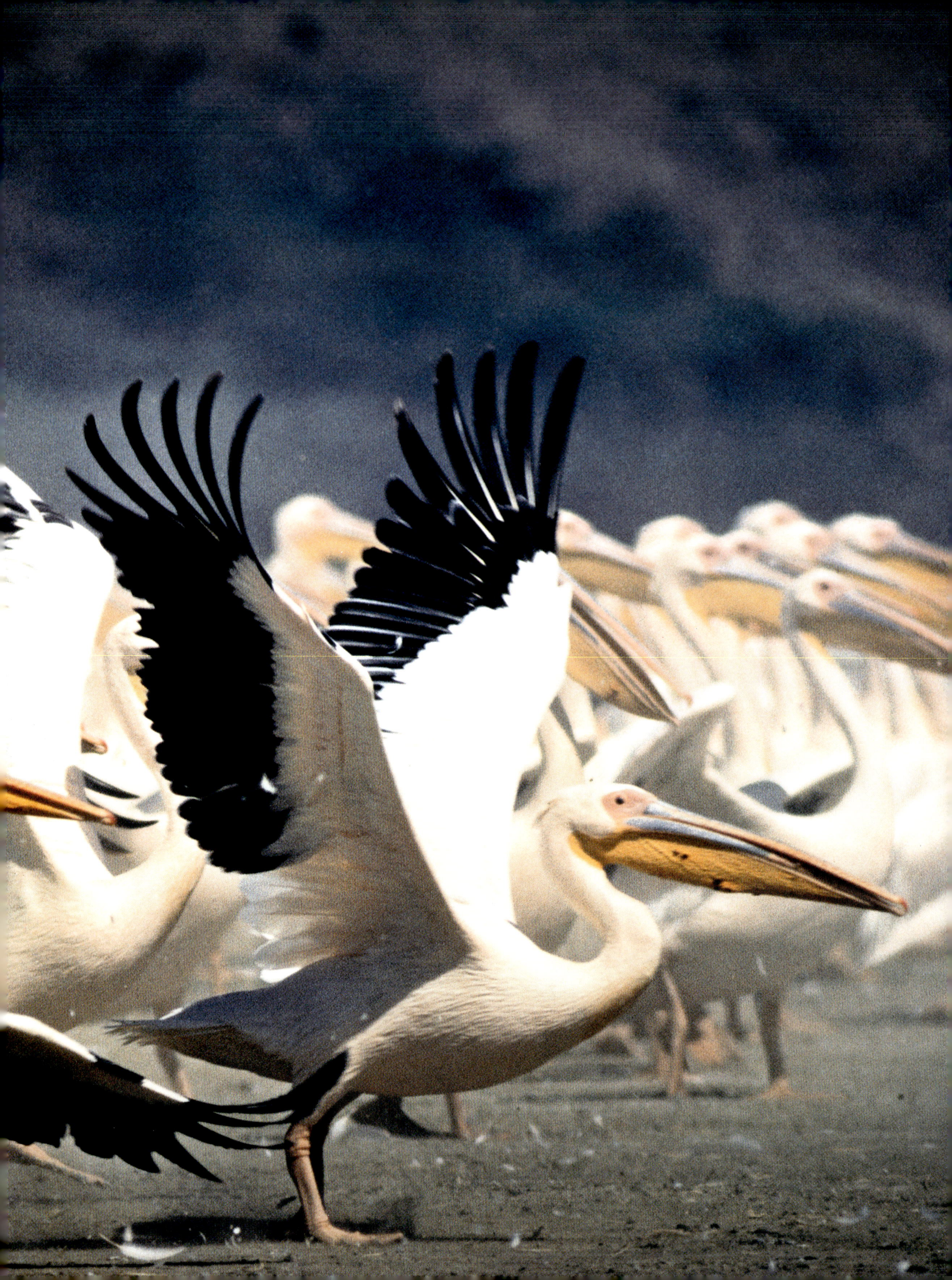

WILDLIFE

YIERE

ANIMAUX

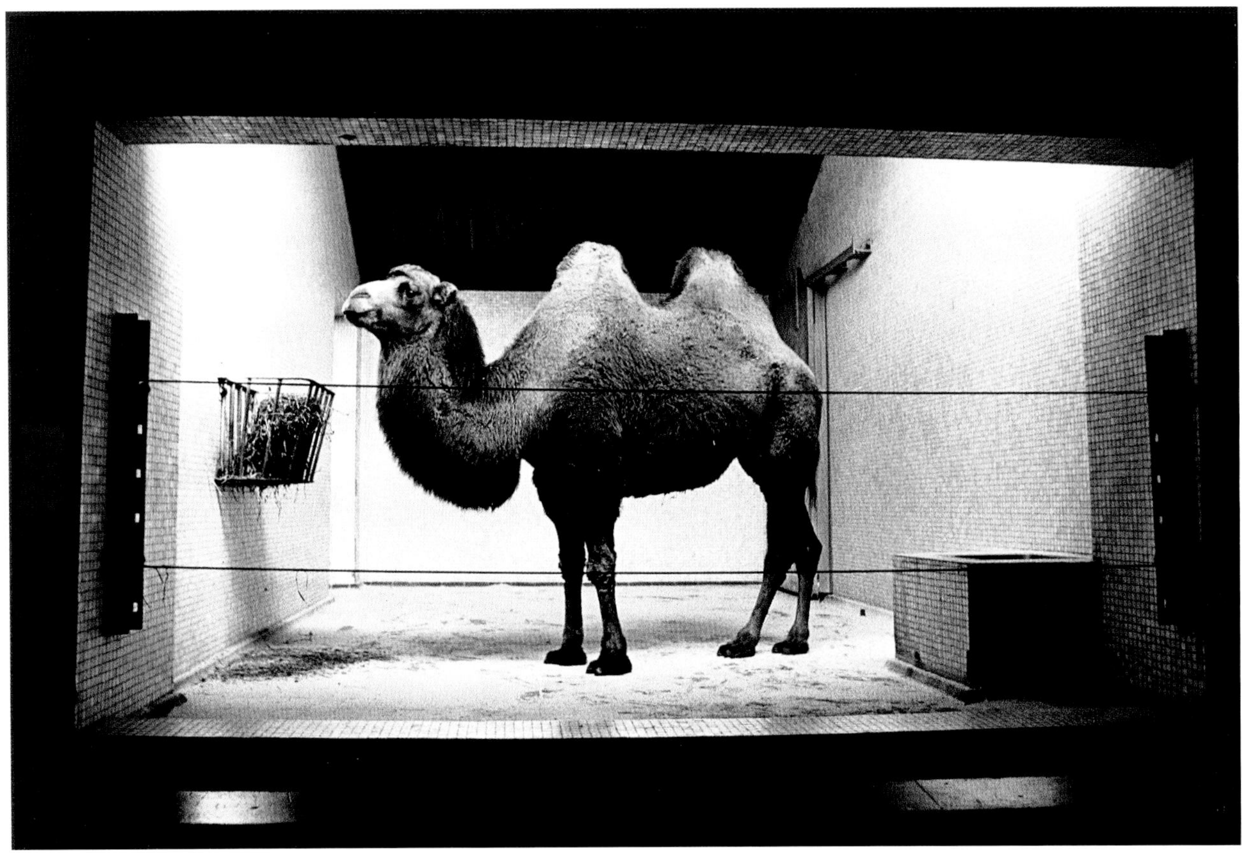

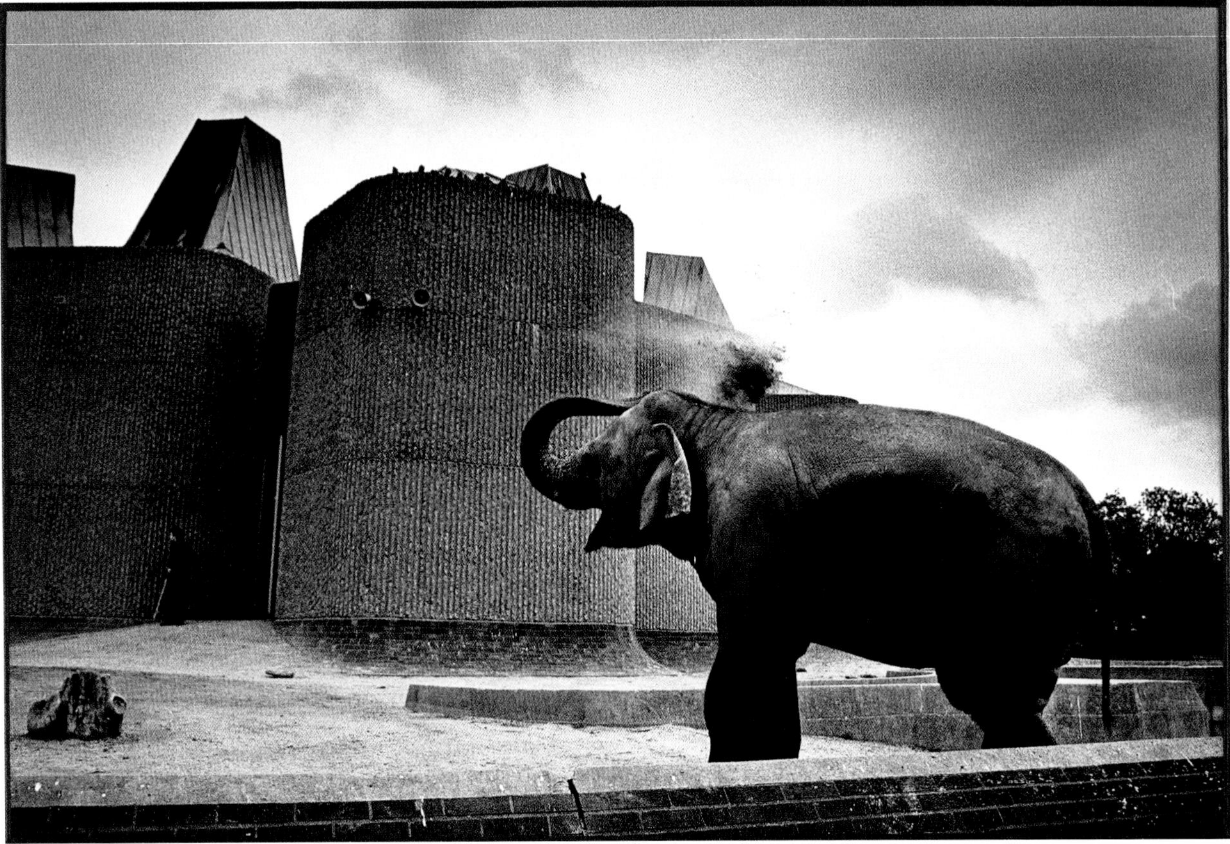

Preceeding Spread: Hara | Above: Britta Jaschinski

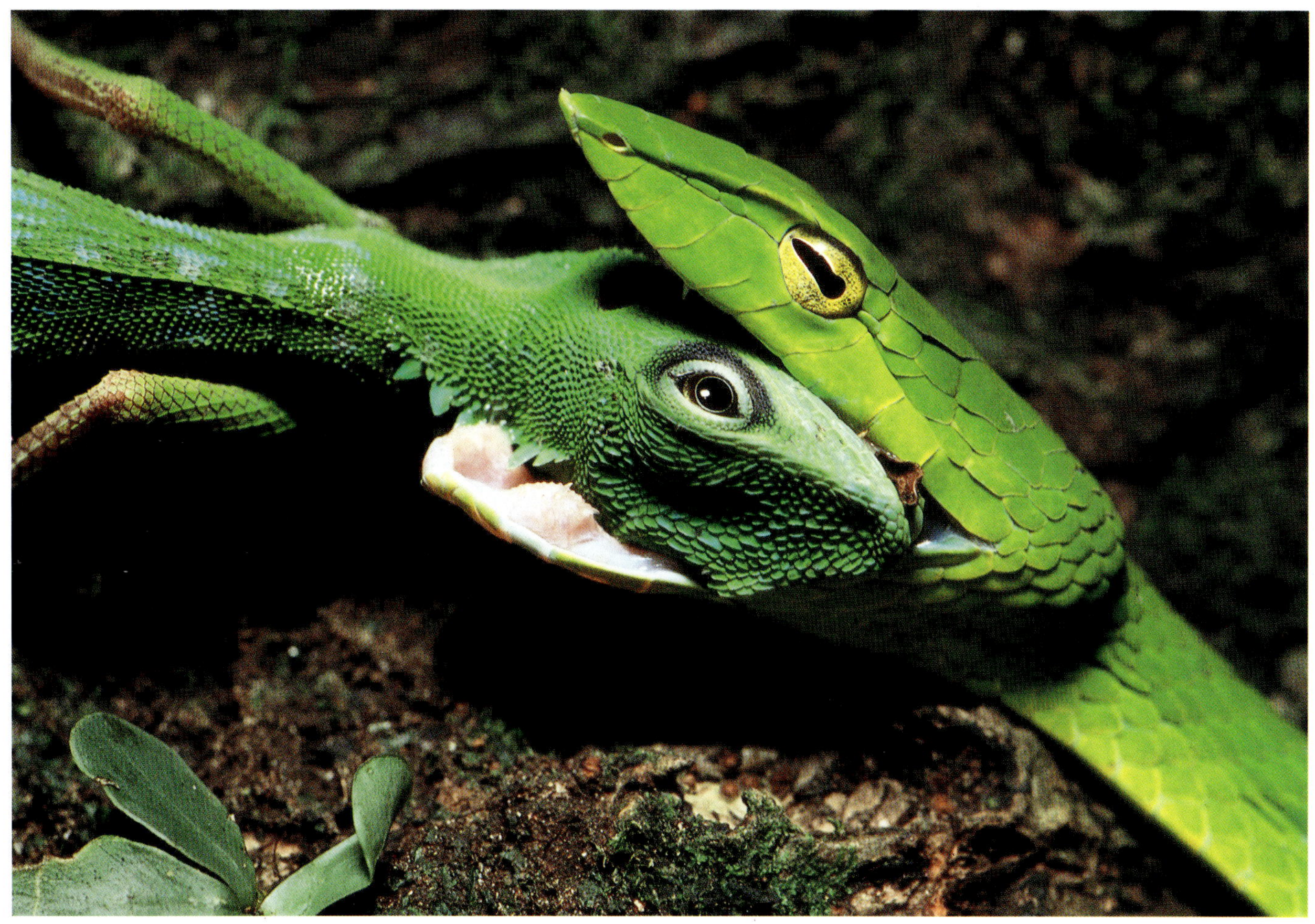

Satish Sreedharan

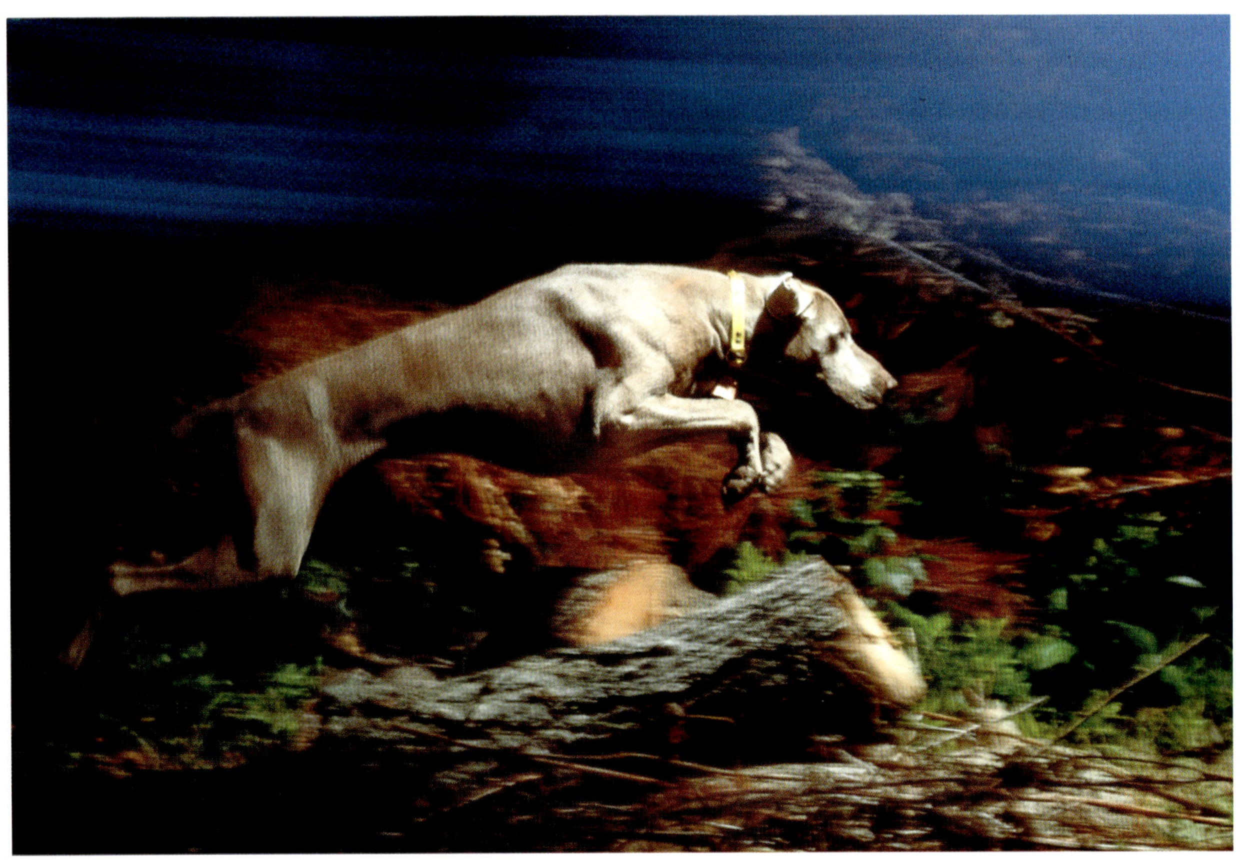

Clint Clemens

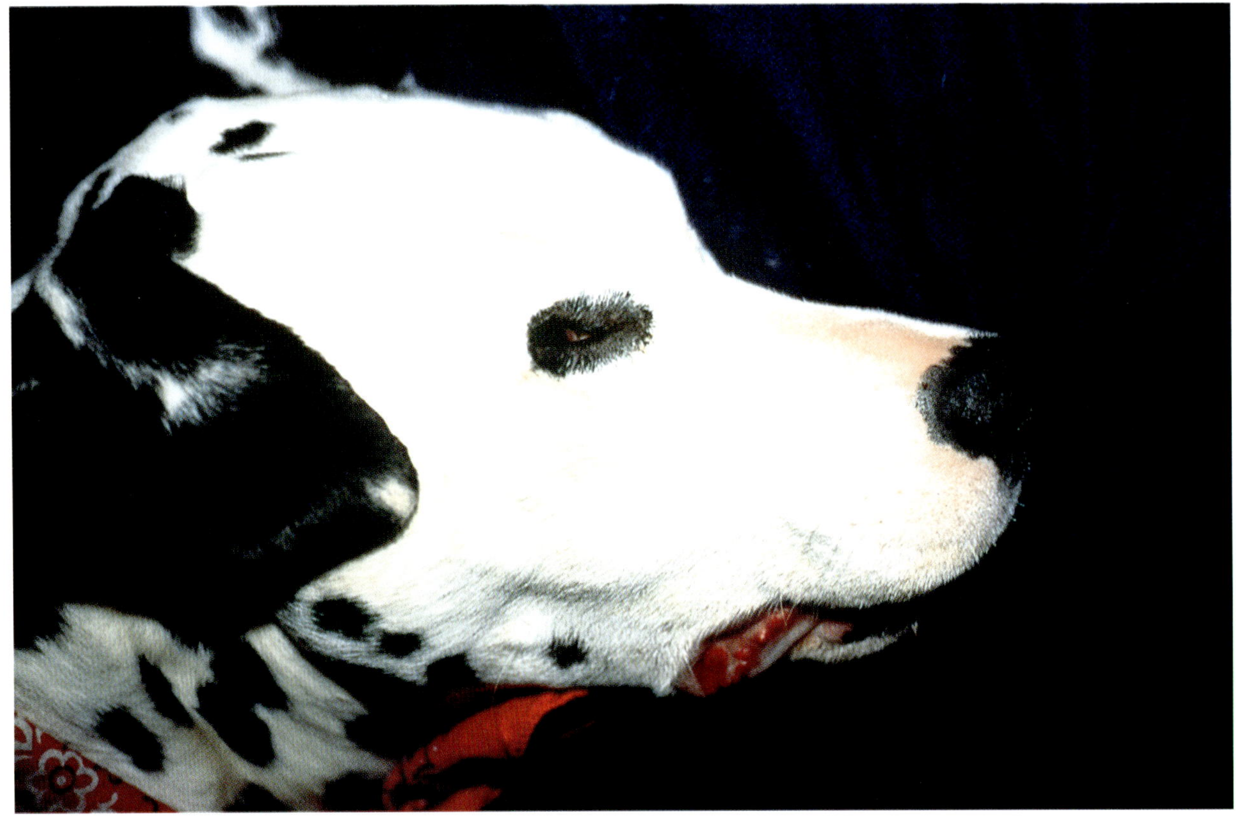

Elke Ritschel

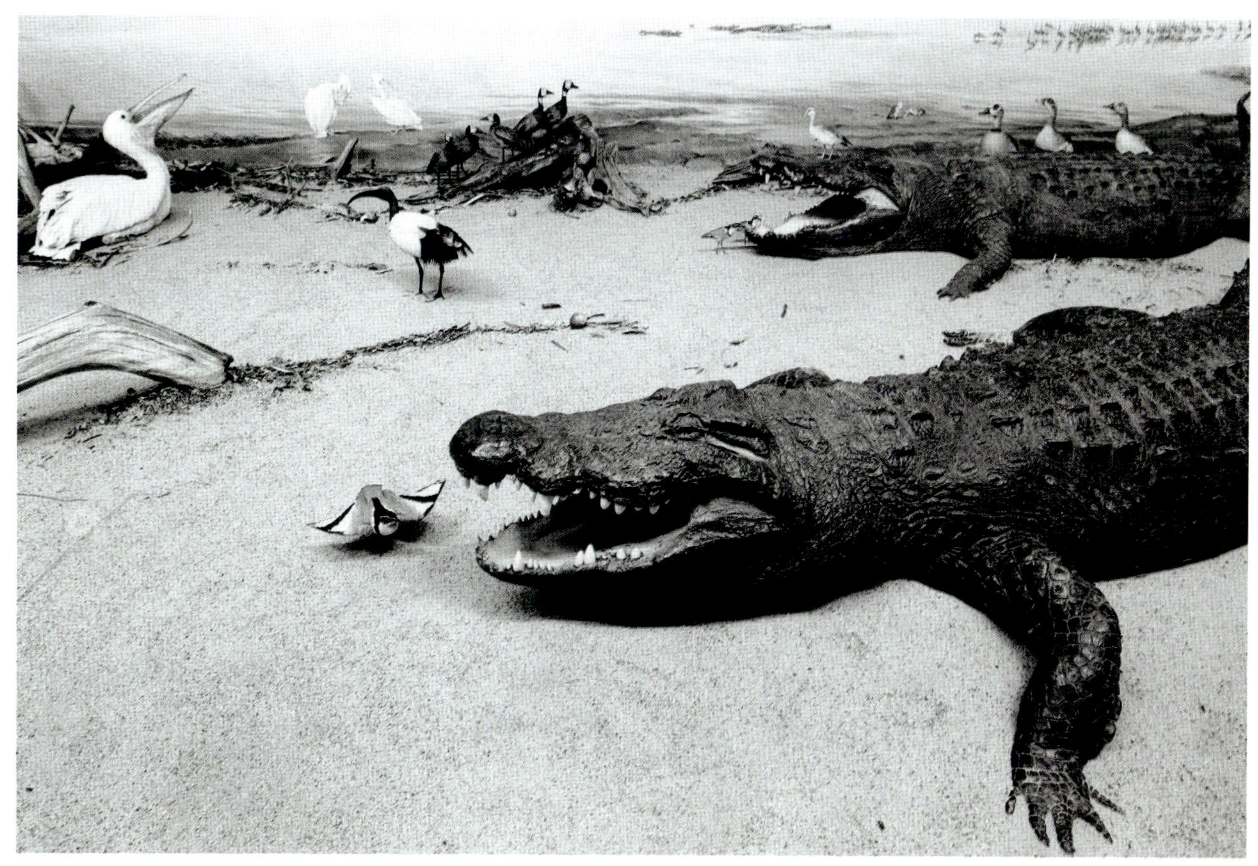

Fiedrich K. Rumpf

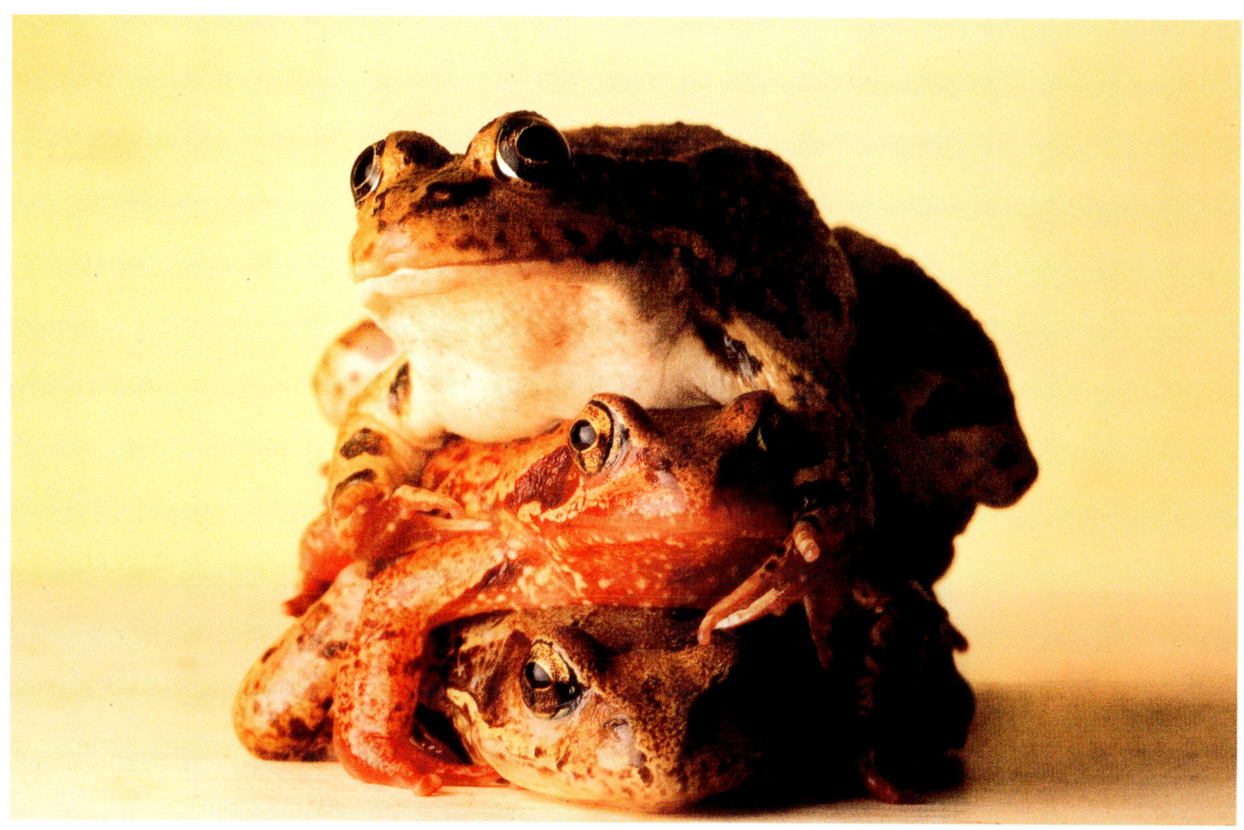

Adrian Burke

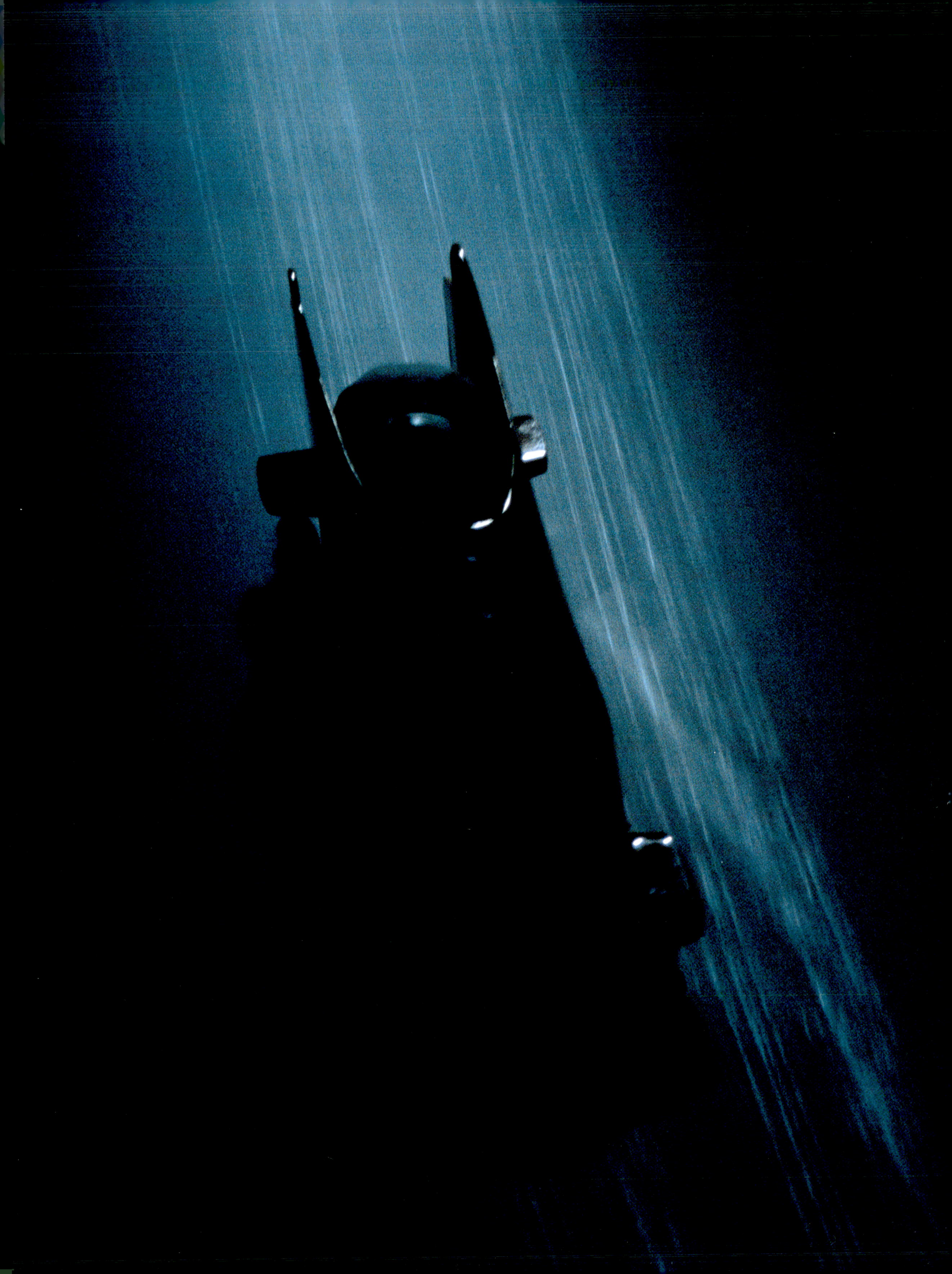

SPORTS

SPORT

SPORT

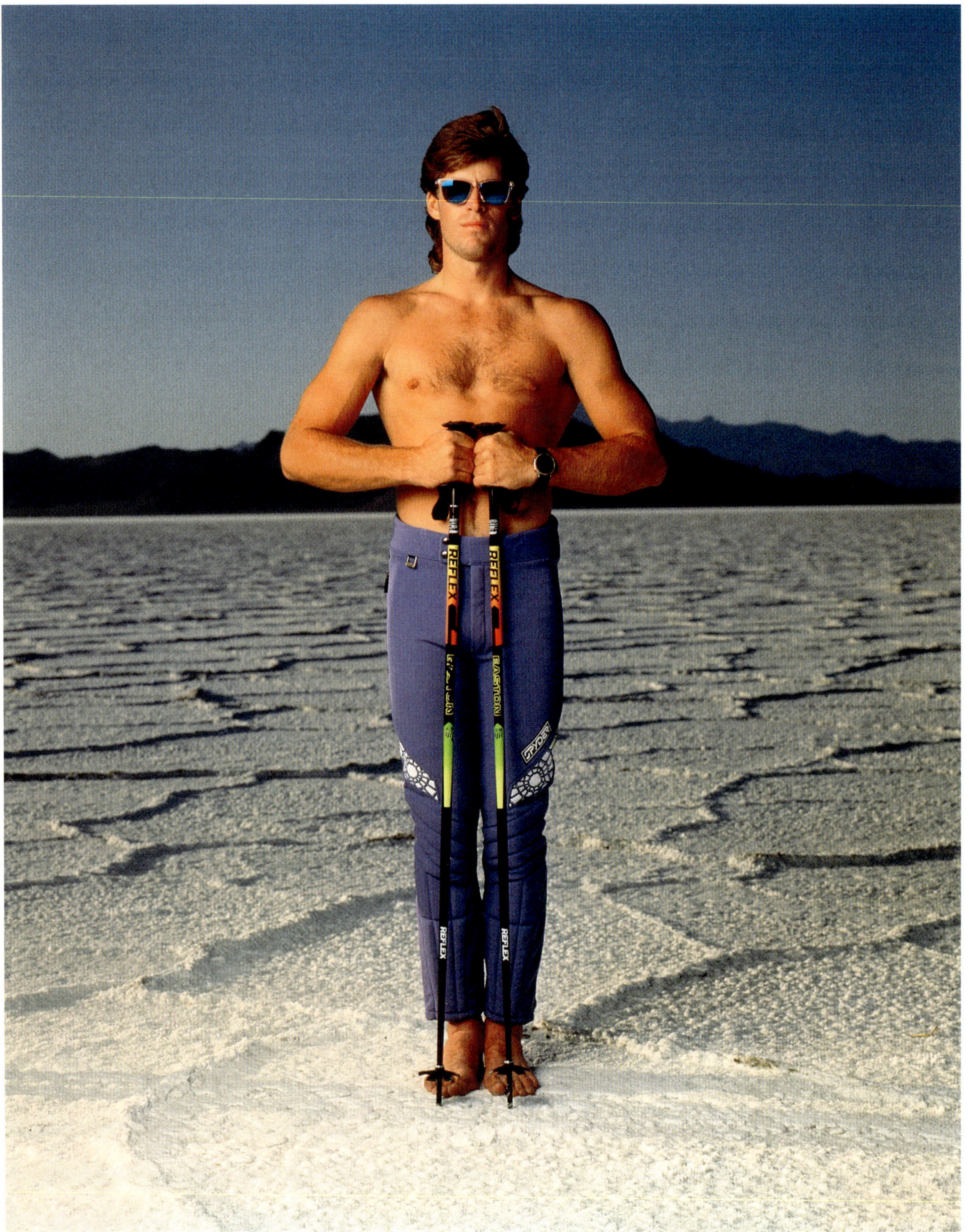

Preceeding Spread: Stefan Warter | Above: Andrew Eccles

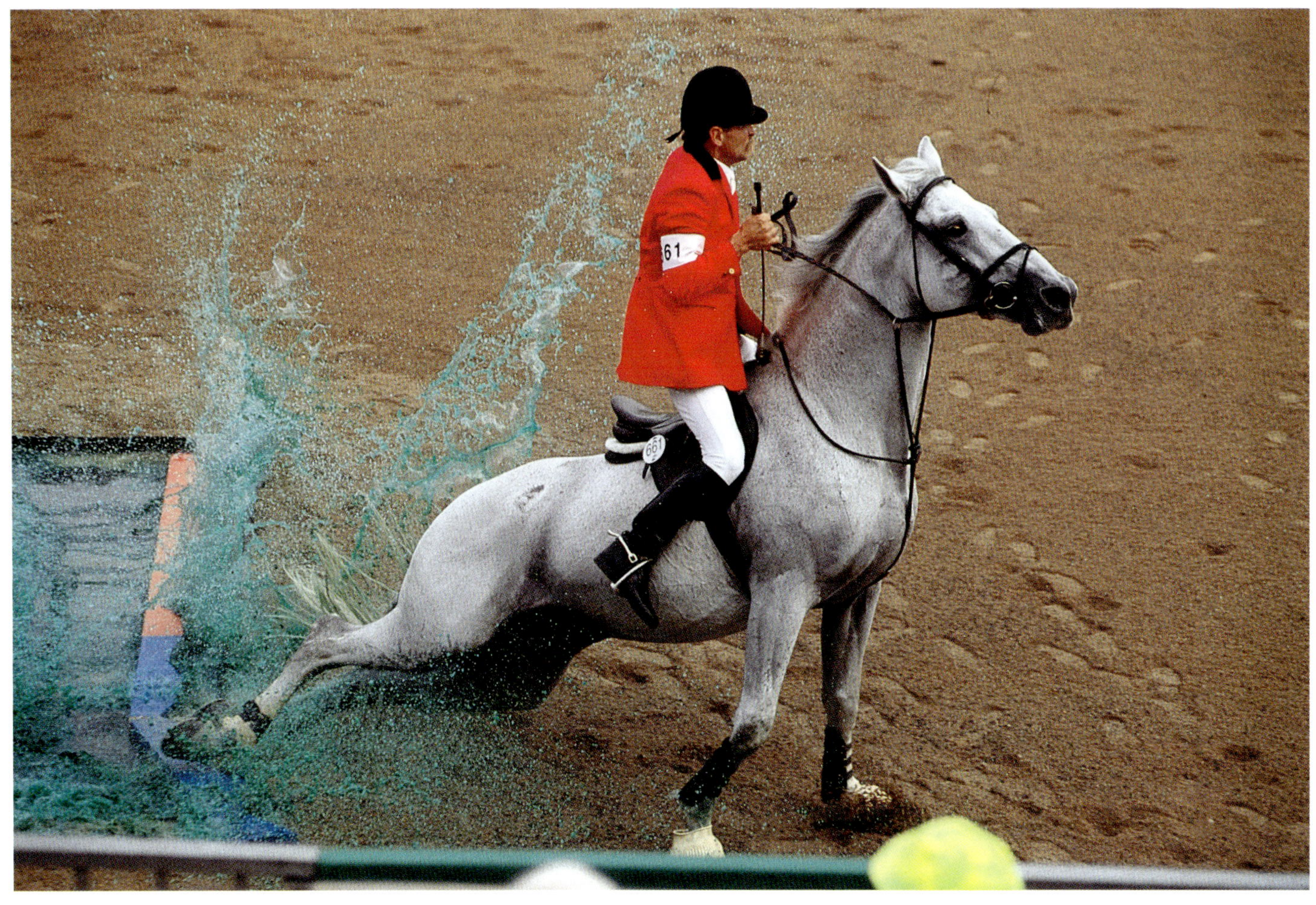

Oliver Reck

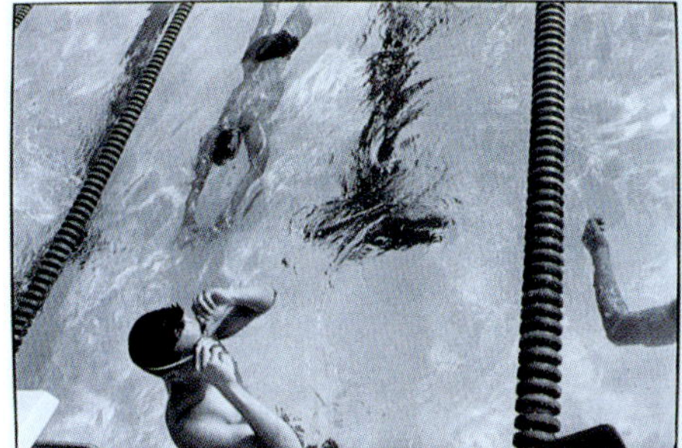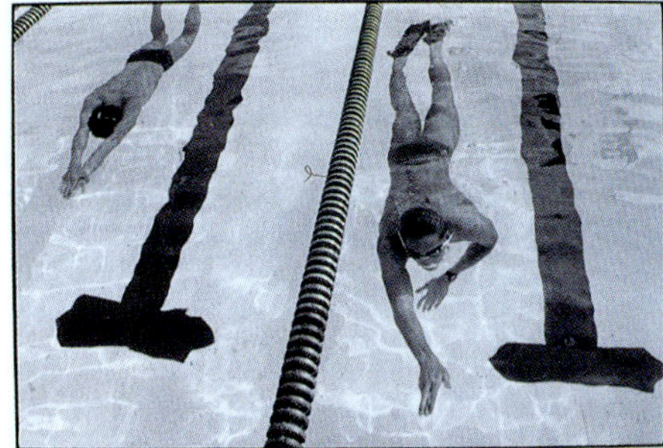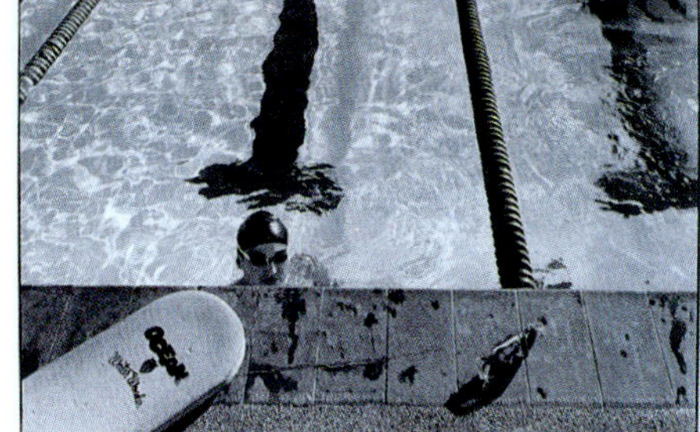

Susan Alinsangan

John Huet

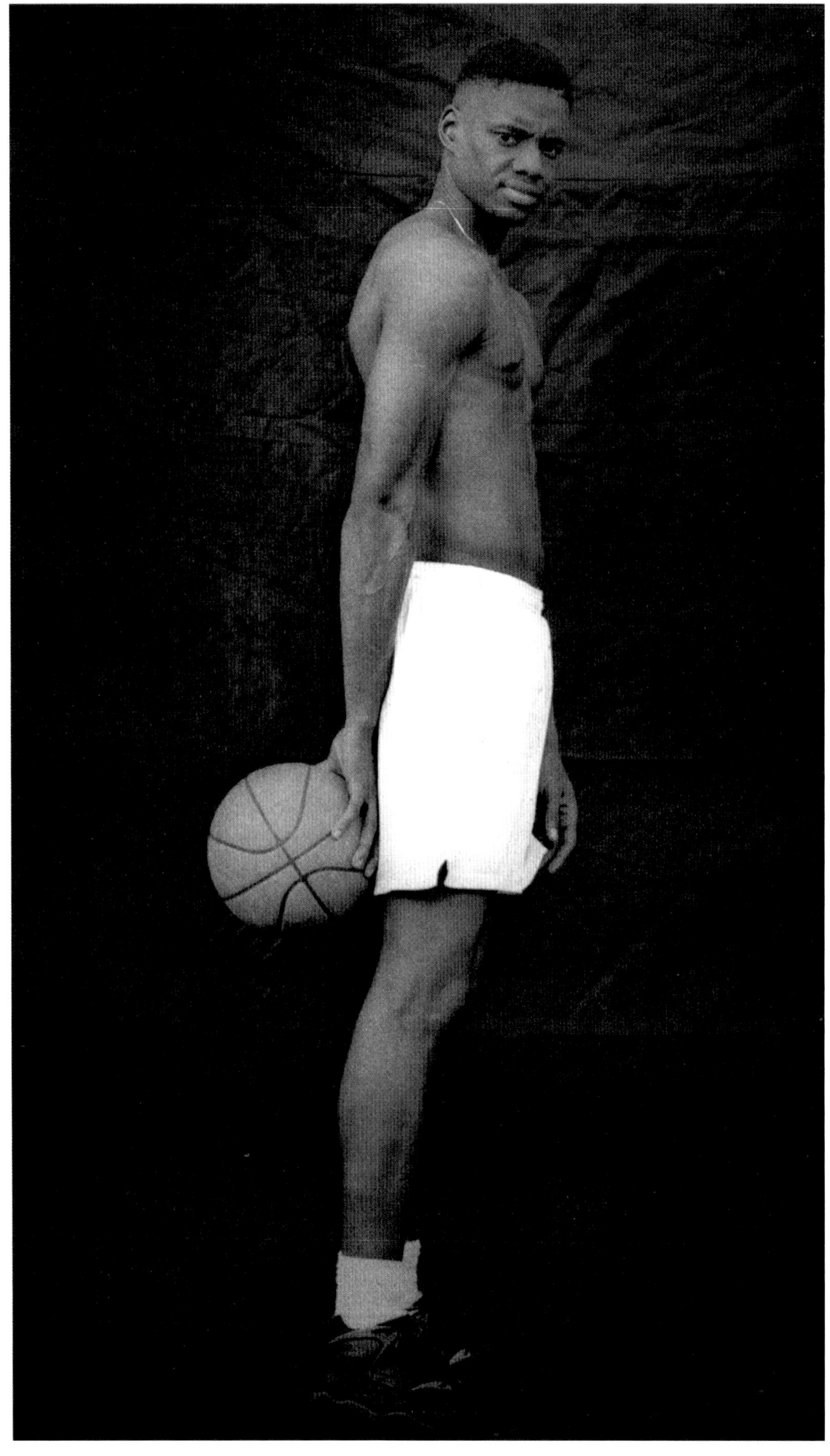

John Huet

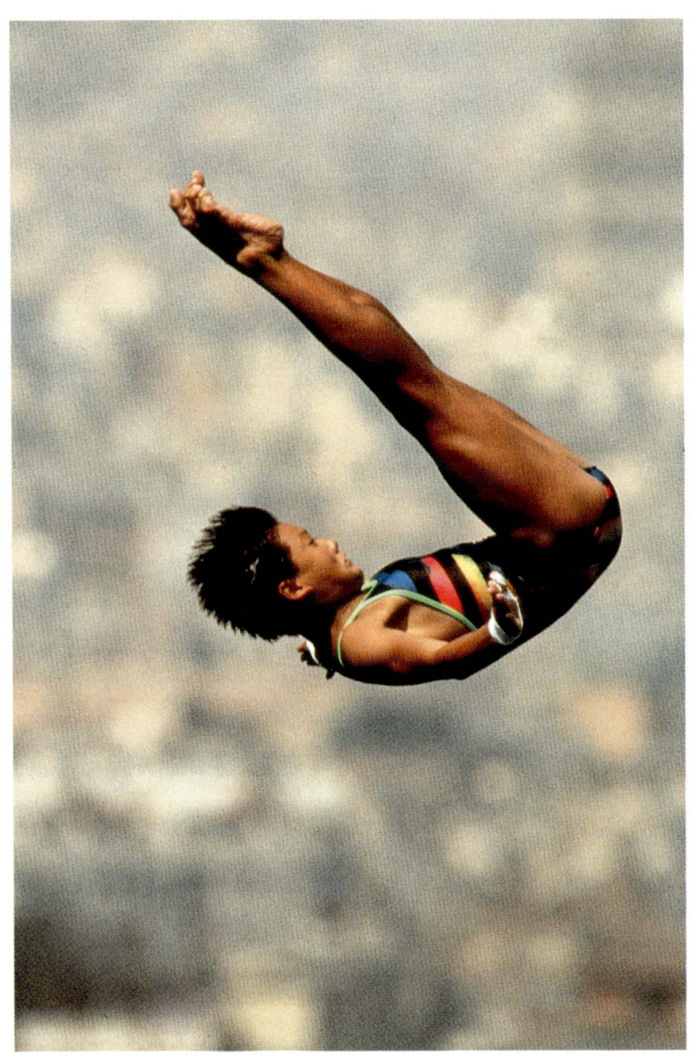

Neil Leifer

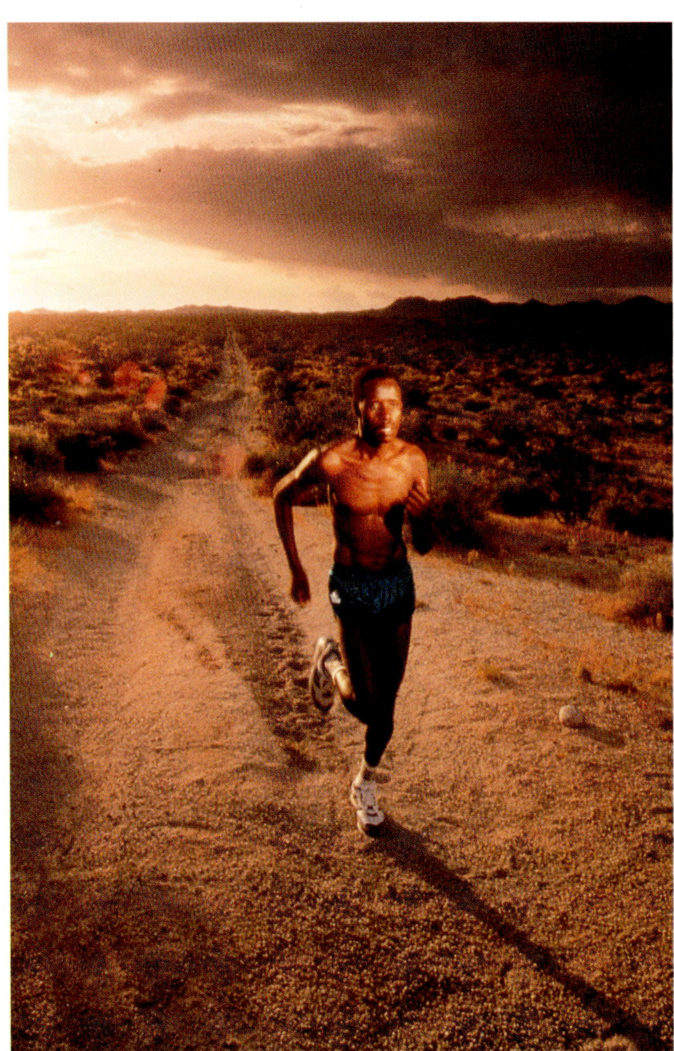

Gregory Heisler

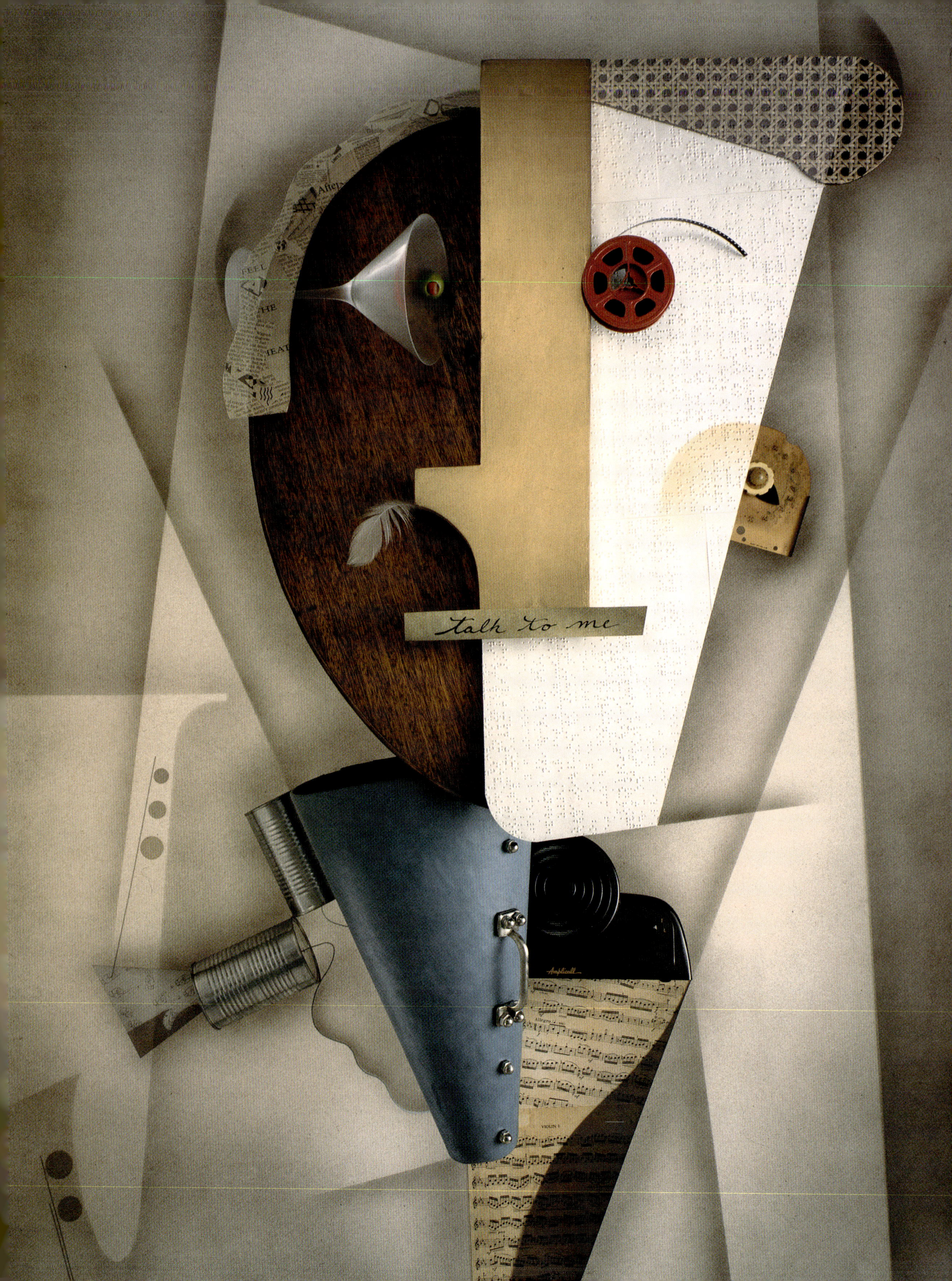
Talk to me

FINE ART

KUNST

ART

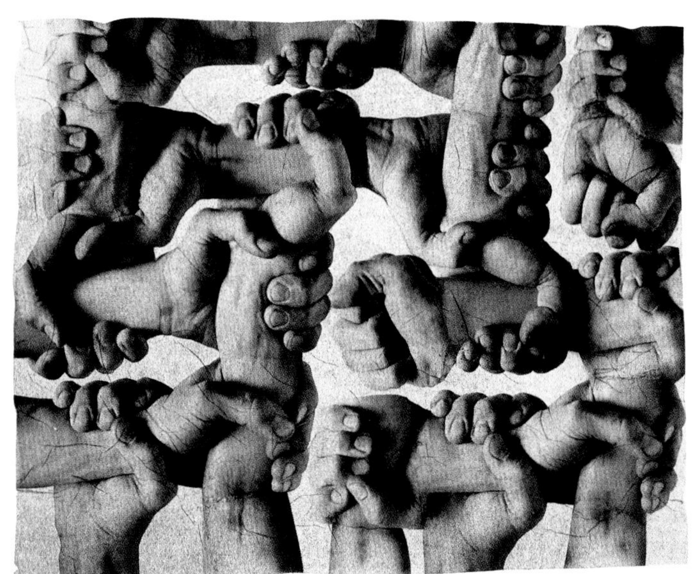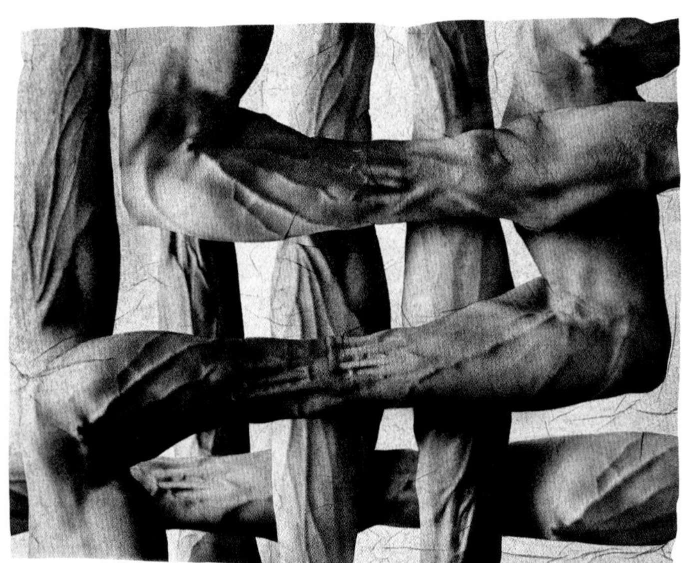

Preceeding Spread: Hugh Kretschmer | Above: Michal Macku | Opposite: Fulton Davenport

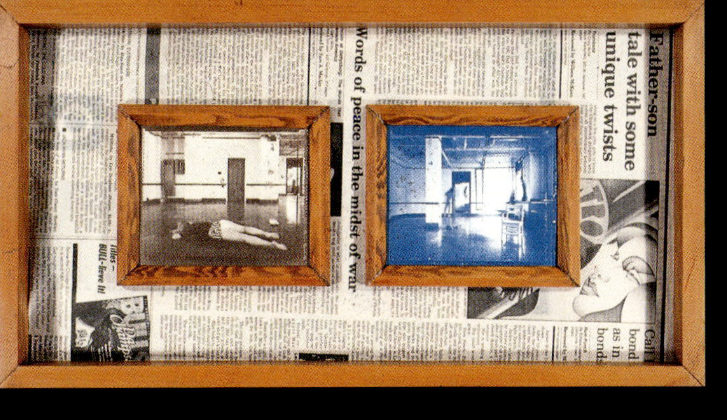
Father-son
tale with some
unique twists
Words of peace in the midst of war
BULL-ieve it!
Call b
bond
as in b
bonds

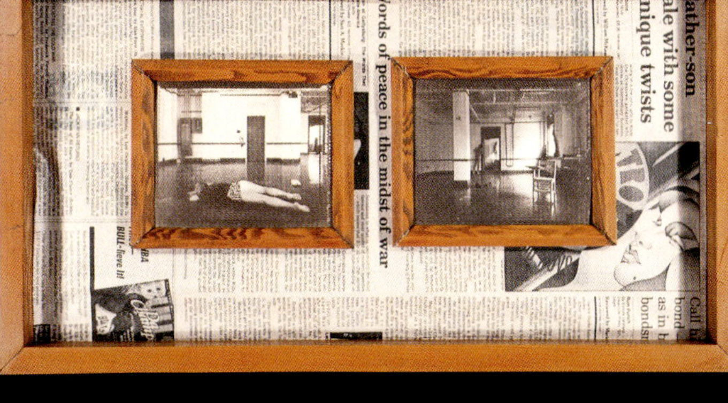
Father-son
tale with some
unique twists
Words of peace in the midst of war
BULL-ieve it!
Call b
bond
as in b
bonds

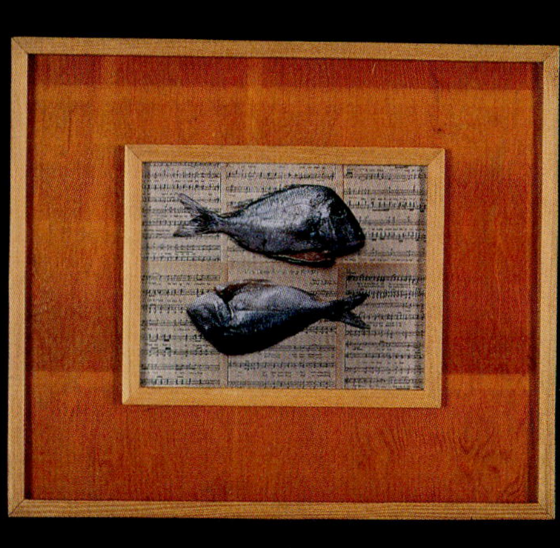

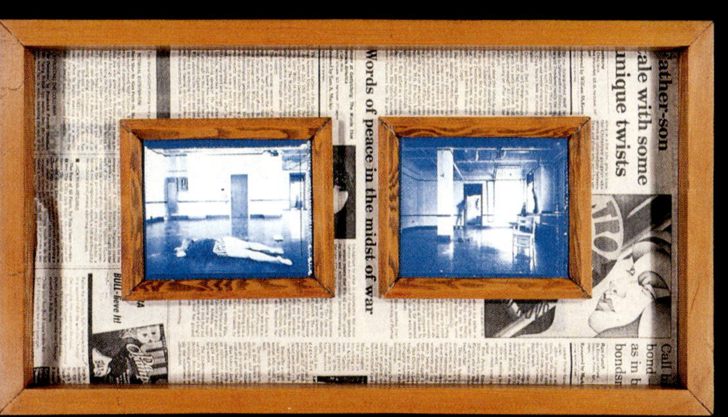
Father-son
tale with some
unique twists
Words of peace in the midst of war
BULL-ieve it!
Call b
bond
as in b
bonds

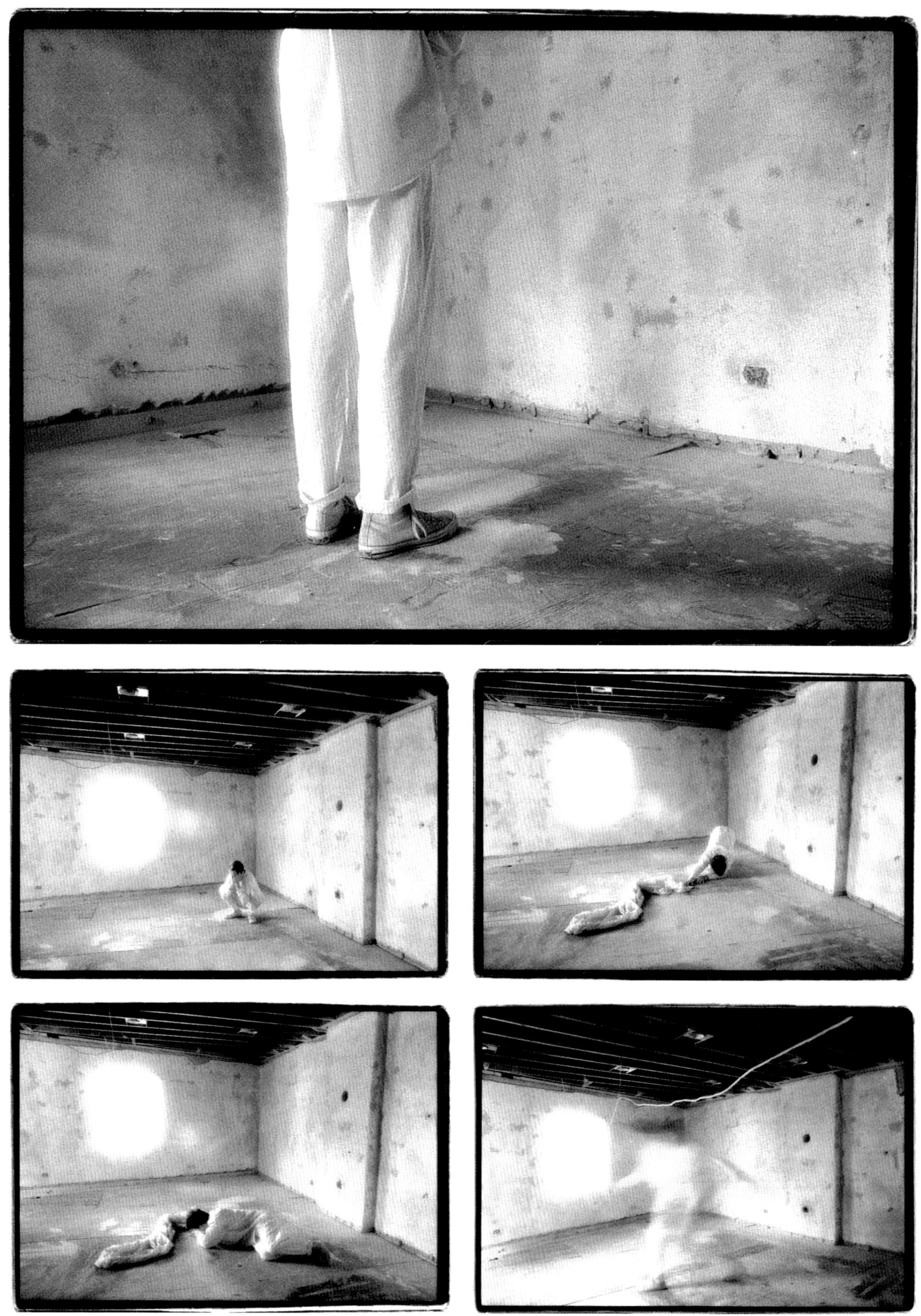

Nancy R. Cohen / Opposite: Hans Xeleman

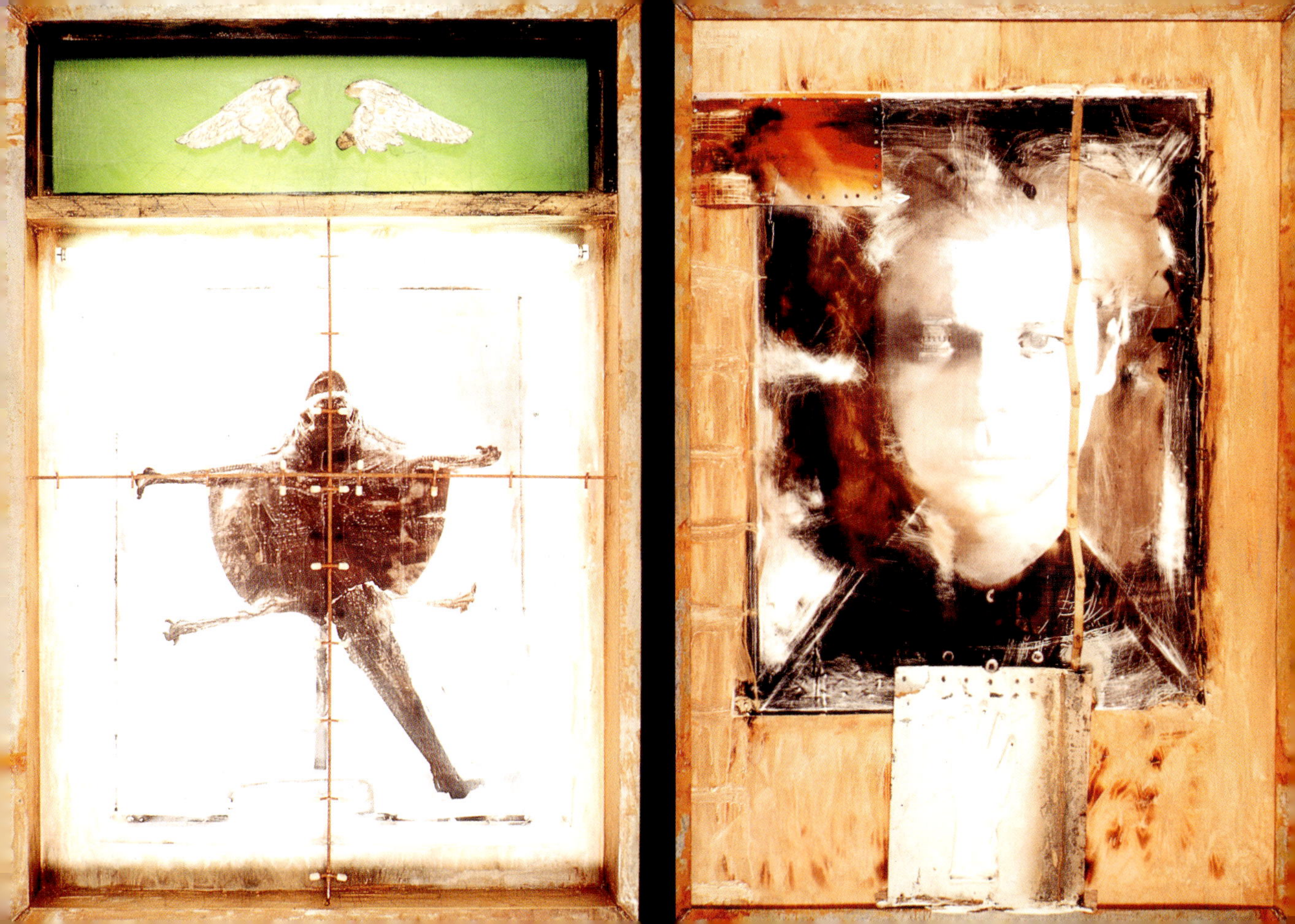

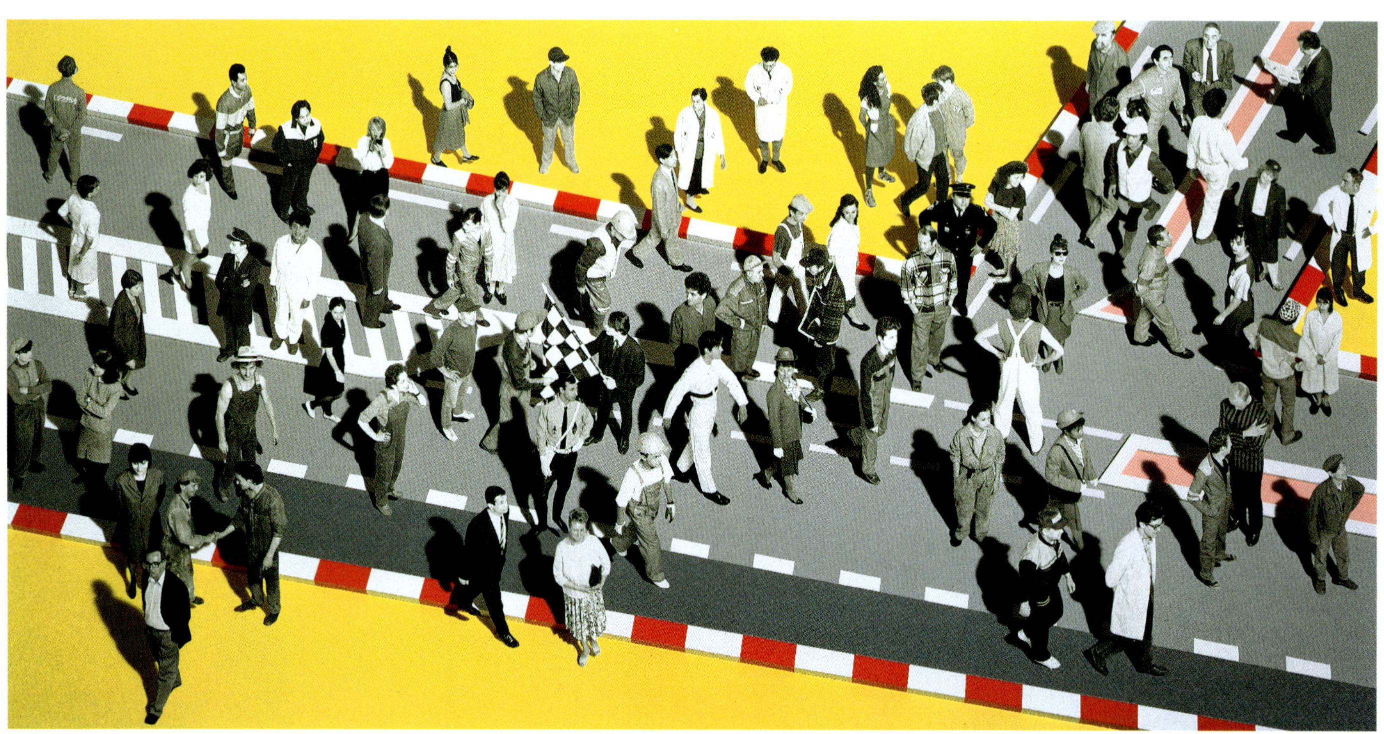

Jean-Louis Leibovitch

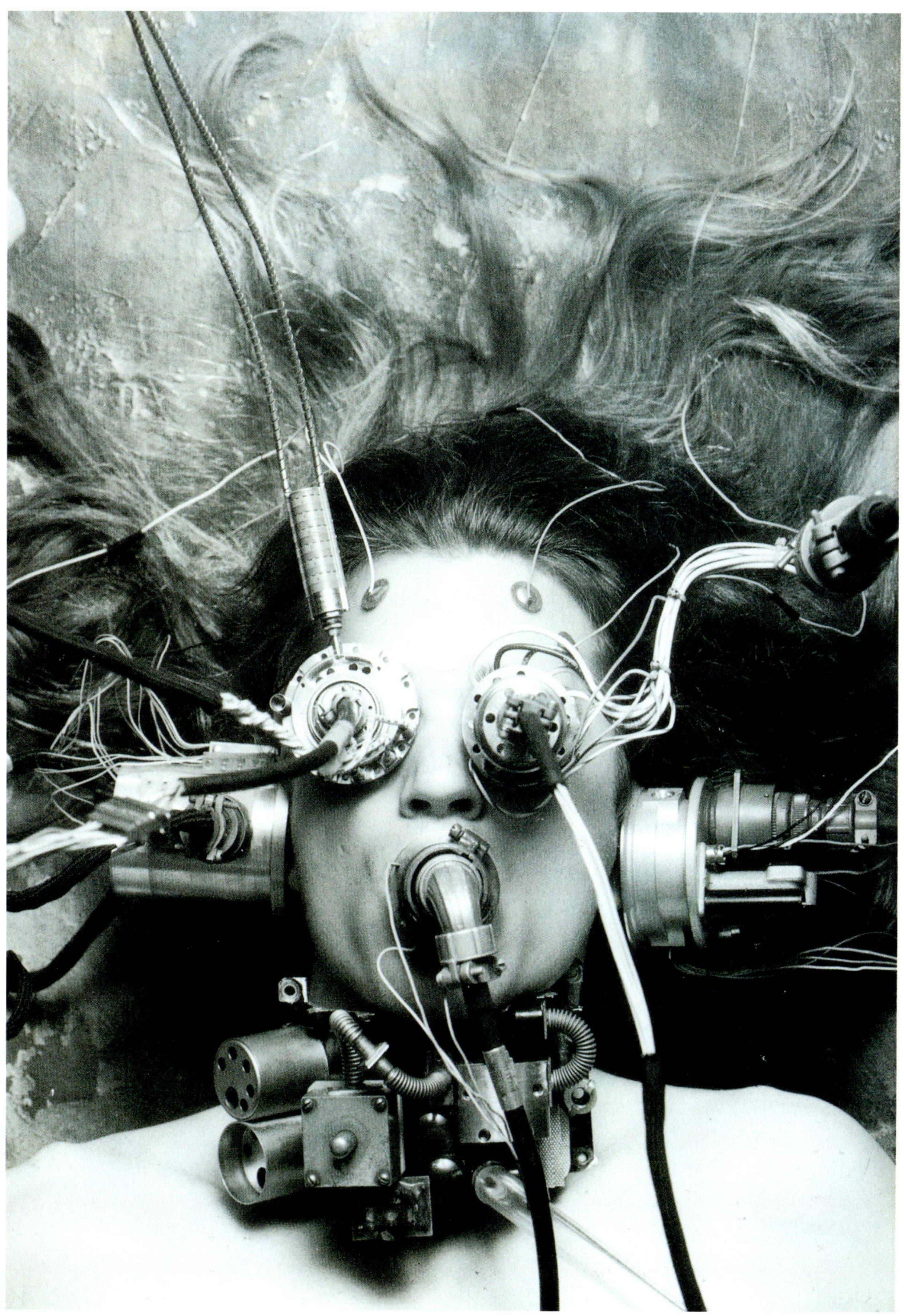

Michele Clement

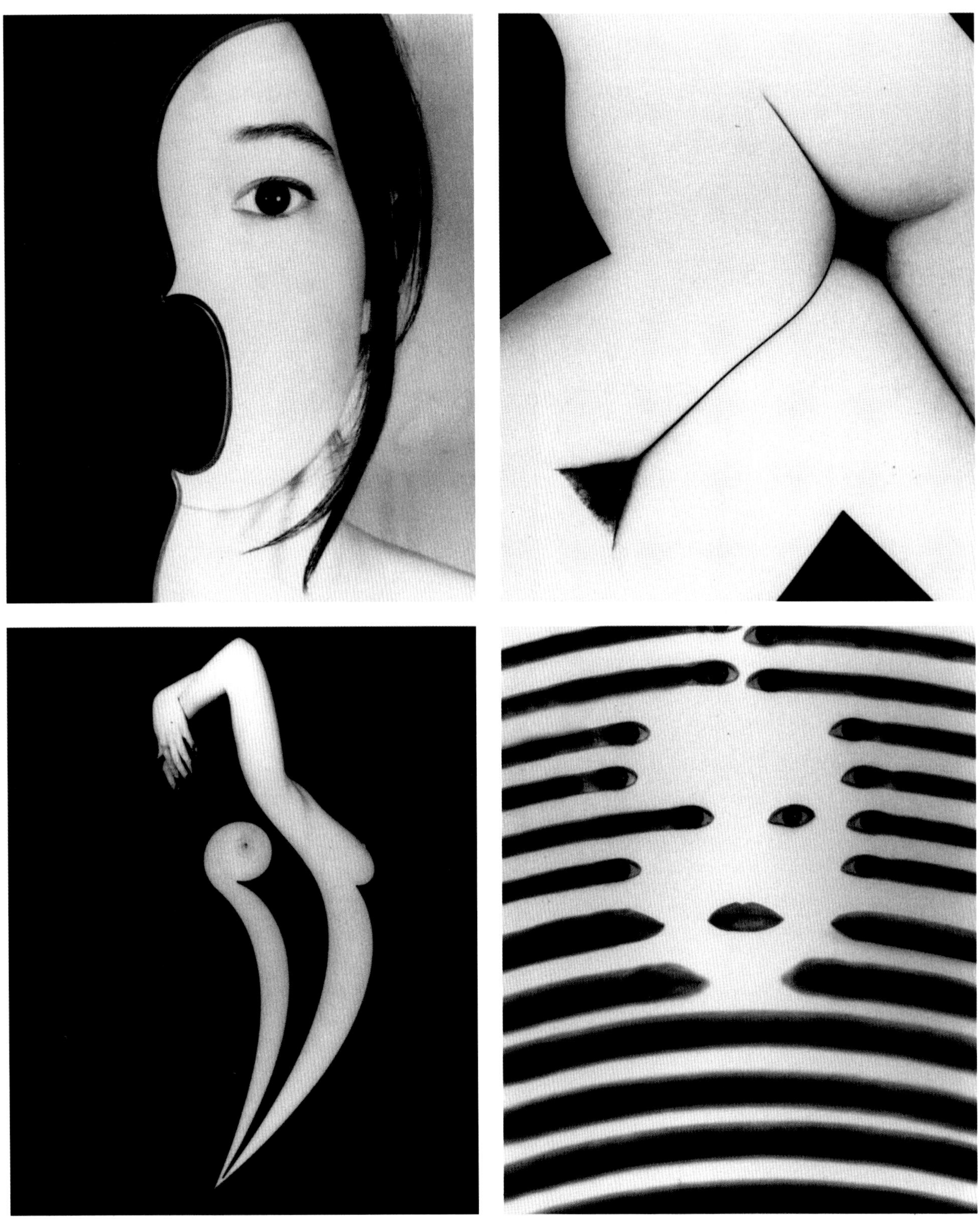

Marcel Ritschel

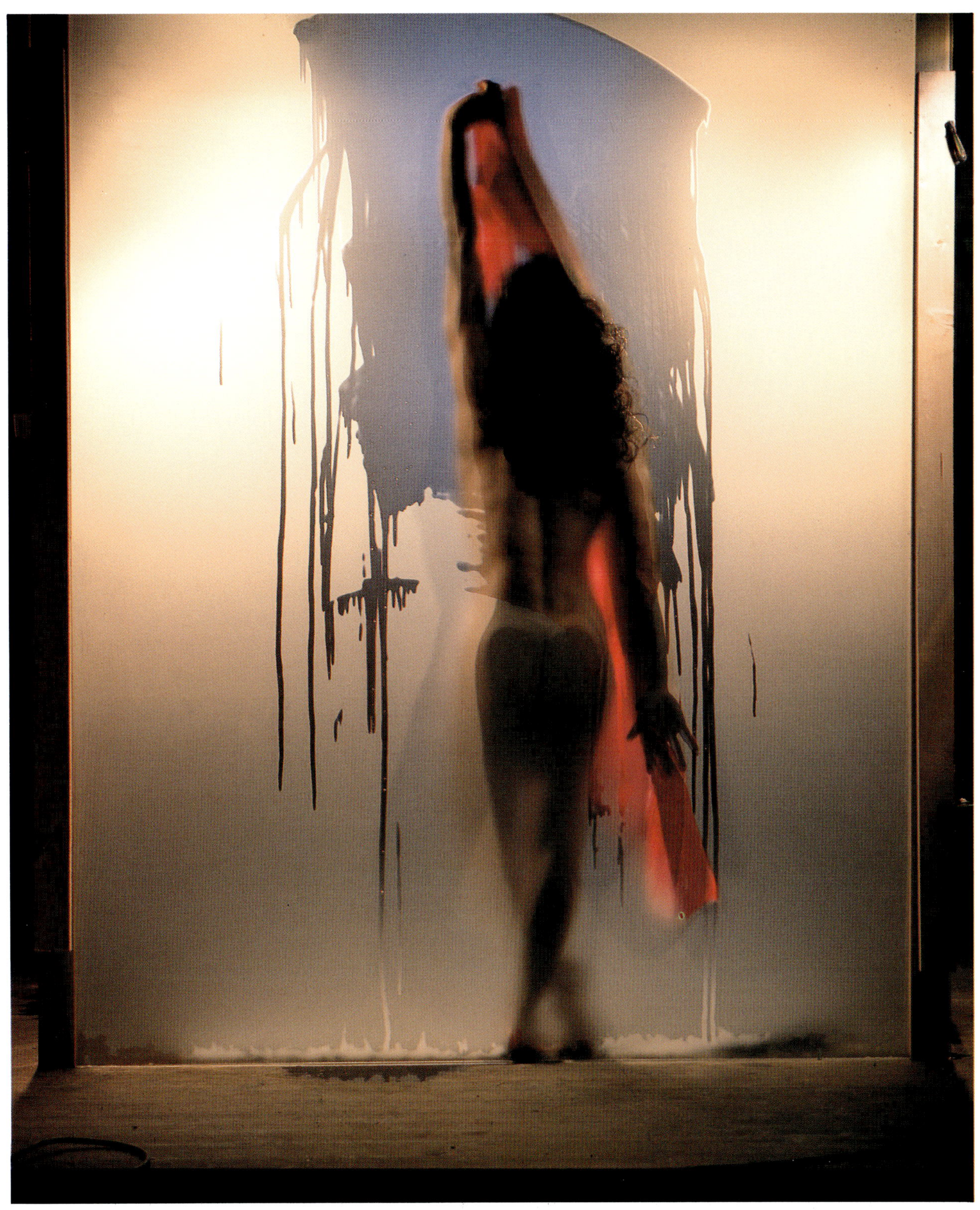

Poby

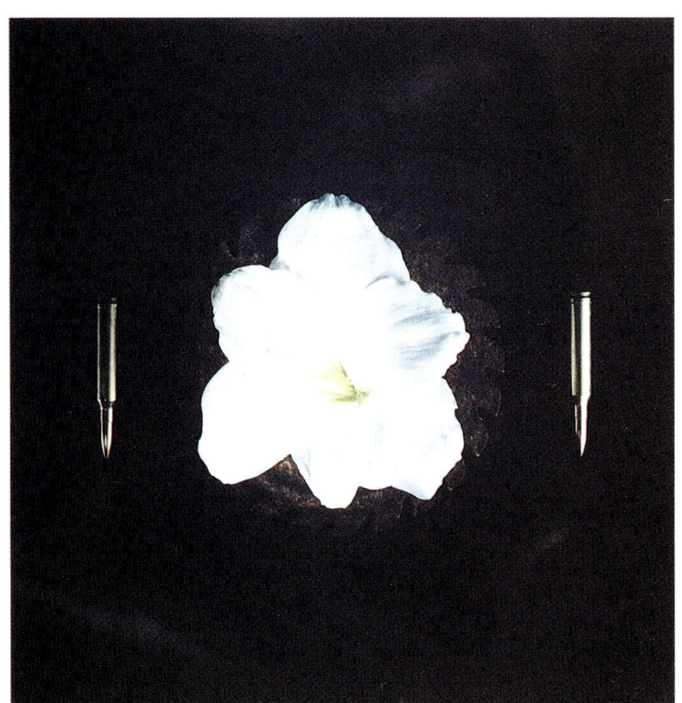 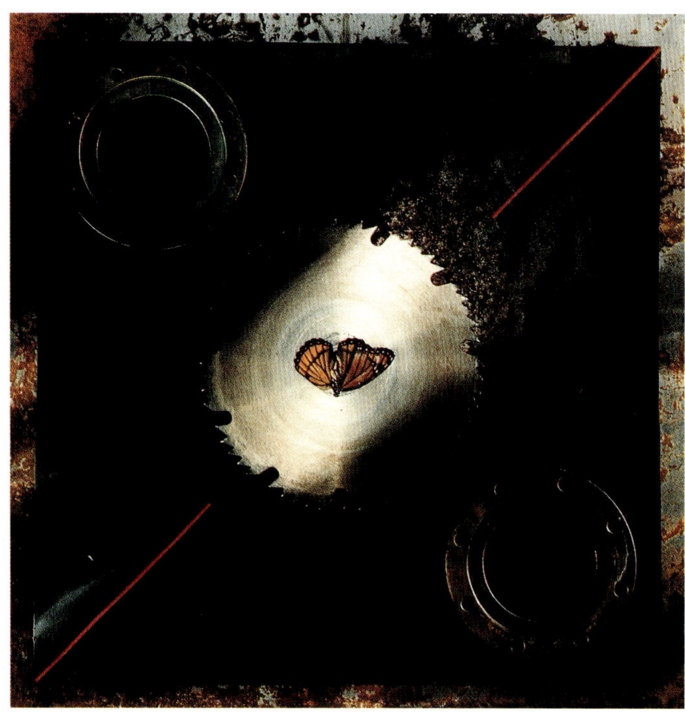

Dean Burton

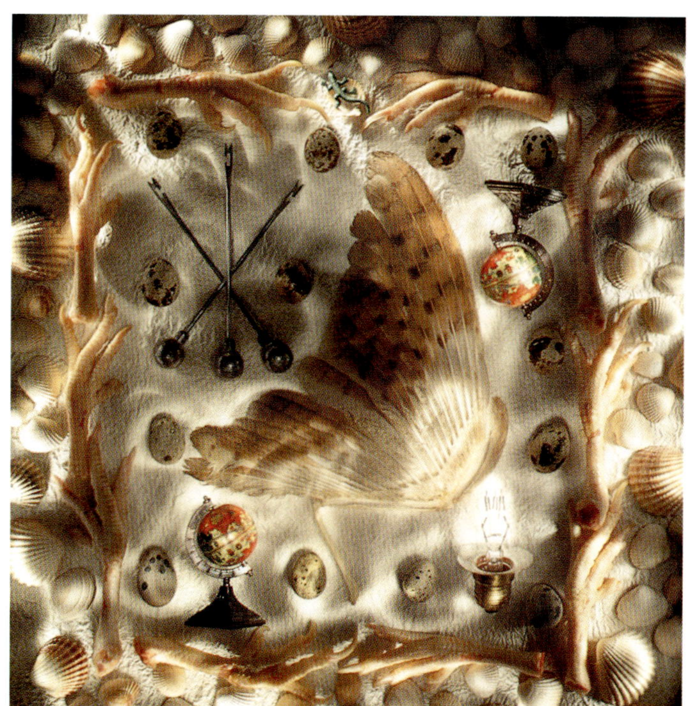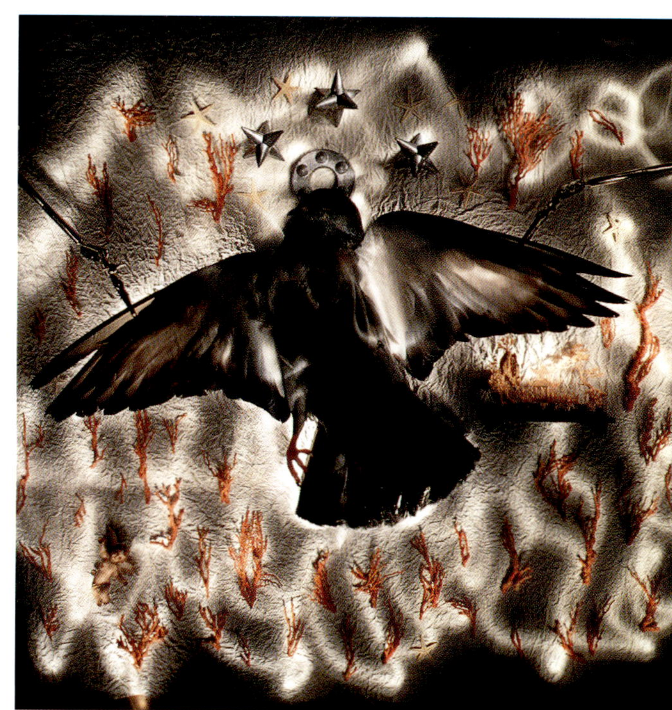

Elie Bernager

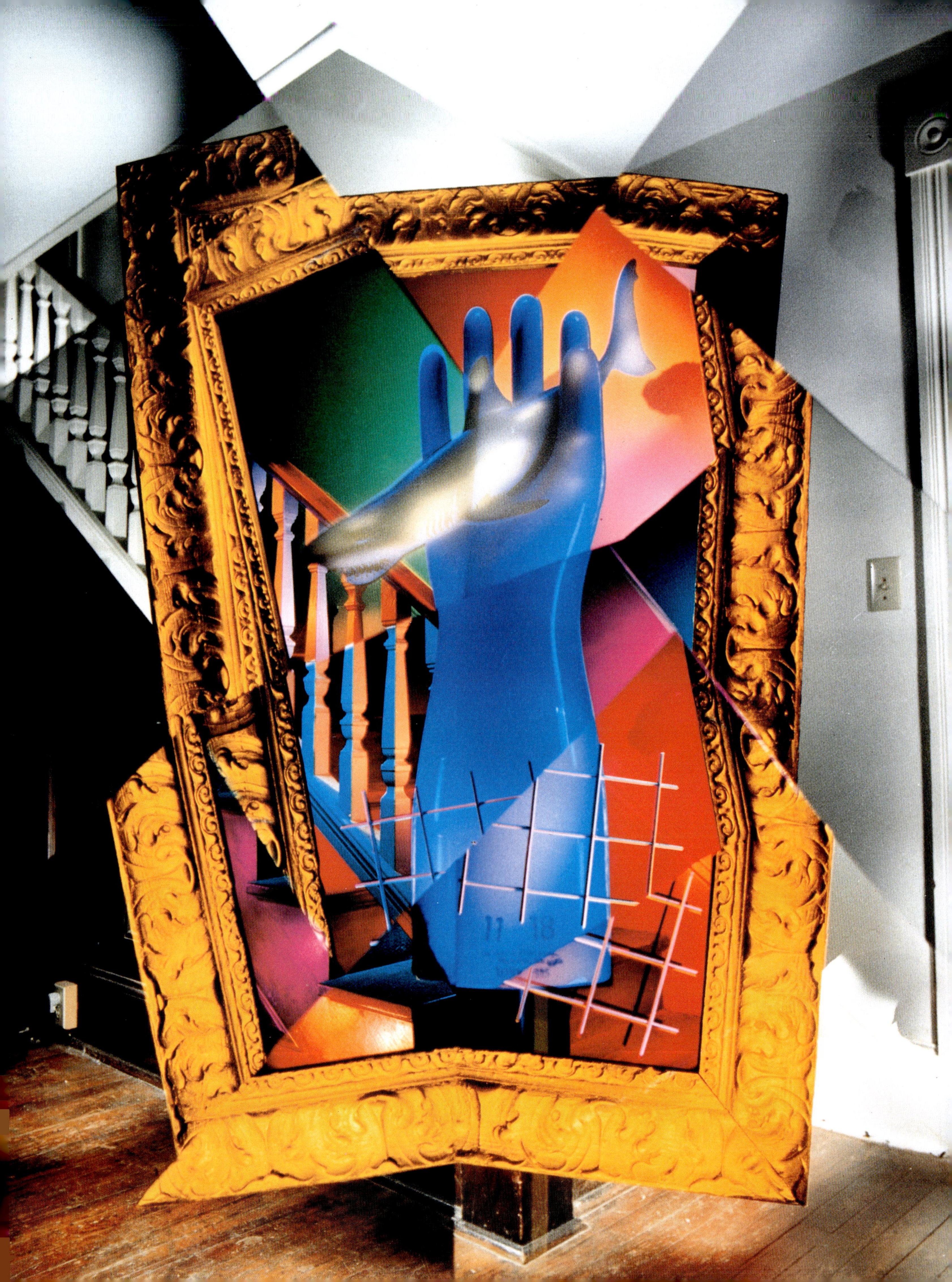

COVER Photographer: SHEILA METZNER Client: SHISEIDO Art Director: IKUO AMANO Designer: YOSHIKATSU OKAMOTO Stylist: FREDDIE LEIBA Model: UMA THURMAN Hair: SAM MCKNIGHT Make-up: MARY GREENWELL Agency: CAN B.

PAGE 2 Photographer: JOHN PAYNE Representative: KELLY CLEVELAND Client: CARL EMIL Camera: HORSEMAN 8"x10" Film: KODAK EKTACHROME EPP 6105 Country: NORWAY ■ This still life was used in a promotional campaign for a Norwegian paper mill. ● Stilleben als Werbung für einen norwegischen Papierhersteller. ▲ Cette nature morte a été utilisée pour la publicité d'un fabricant de papier norvégien.

PAGE 6 Photographer: RICK RUSING Camera: CANON EOS-1 Film: FUJI CHROME RTP64 Art Director: STEVE DITKO Agency: CAMPBELL, FISHER, DITKO DESIGN Country: USA ■ In order to create a surreal image, the photographer first shot his model on 35mm film, then transferred the image to 8x10" Polaroid. ● Die surrealistische Wirkung erreichte der Photograph mit Hilfe technischer Tricks. Zuerst photographierte er das Modell mit 35mm Film und transferierte das Bild dann auf 8x10" Polaroid-Material. ▲ Le photographe a réussi à conférer un aspect surréaliste au moyen d'effets spéciaux. Il a tout d'abord photographié le modèle avec une pellicule 35mm, puis il a procédé à un transfert d'image sur du matériel Polaroïd 8x10".

PAGE 20 Photographer: ANDREW ECCLES Representative: OUTLINE Publisher: *ELLE DECOR* Camera: MAMIYA RZ 67 Film: KODAK EPR 64 Photo Editor: CAROLINE BOWYER Art Director: CAROLINE BOWYER Designer: JO HAY Country: USA ■ "Prominent People with their Favorite Chairs" was the assignment for *Elle Decor* magazine. When David Bowie gave Iman this chair, she remarked, "It's brown and long necked; remind you of anybody?" ● «Prominente mit ihrem Lieblingsstuhl» war das Thema einer Photoreihe in *Elle Decor*. Über diesen Stuhl, ein Geschenk von David Bowie, sagte Iman: «Er ist braun und hat einen langen Hals, erinnert Sie das an jemanden?» ▲ Des personnalités célèbres et leur chaise préférée, tel était le sujet d'une série de photos réalisées pour *Elle Decor*. La splendide Iman, dont la renommée n'est plus à faire, s'exclama devant cette chaise, un cadeau de David Bowie: «Elle est brune et elle a un long cou, cela ne te rappelle personne?»

PAGE 22 Photographer: SHEILA METZNER Publisher: *VOGUE DEUTSCHLAND* Art Director: DONALD SCHNEIDER Stylist: FREDDIE LEIBA Country: GERMANY ■ In this picture of Uma Thurman for a fashion feature in *Vogue*, the photographer wanted to show her as the modern, beautiful and successful woman she is. ● Sheila Metzner photographierte die Schauspielerin Uma Thurman für *Vogue*. ▲ Sheila Metzner a réalisé ce portrait de Uma Thurman pour un article paru dans *Vogue*. La photographie devait refléter la personnalité de cette actrice de talent,.

PAGE 23 Photographer: SHEILA METZNER Client: SHISEIDO Art Director: IKUO AMANO Designer: YOSHIKATSU OKAMOTO Stylist: FREDDIE LEIBA Model: UMA THURMAN Hair: SAM MCKNIGHT Make-up: MARY GREENWELL Agency: CAN B. INC. Country: JAPAN ■ Featuring Uma Thurman as a model, a unique female image was invented for the Japanese cosmetics company Shiseido: that of a radiant woman, both active and mysterious. ● Die Photographin erfand für den japanischen Kosmetikkonzern Shiseido einen ganz speziellen Frauentyp mit starker Ausstrahlung. ▲ Pour une publicité des produits cosmétiques Shiseido, la photographe a voulu créer l'image d'une femme active, rayonnante, et dont il émane cependant un charme mystérieux.

PAGE 24 Photographer: HANS-GEORG MERKEL Client: FACHHOCHSCHULE FÜR MODE-DESIGN TRIER Camera: SINAR NORMA 4x5" Film: KODAK EPN Stylist: URSULA RIEDER Country: GERMANY ■ Making linen and knitted fabrics elements of high fashion with new patterns, structures and surfaces. To handle the coarse, "colorless" material, the photographer used a colored filter, developed the slide film as negative film, and then softened the image during enlargement. ● Mode in Leinen und Strick mit neuen Mustern, Strukturen und Oberflächen. Um dem rauhen, «farblosen» Material zu begegnen, benutzte der Photograph Farbfilter und entwickelte den Diafilm als Negativfilm, der beim Vergrössern weichgezeichnet wurde. ▲ La veste kimono et la robe en lin et tricot, présentant des dessins, des structures et une texture nouvelles. Afin de rendre le caractère «brut», grossier de l'étoffe, le photographe a utilisé des filtres couleurs et développé le film diapo comme un film négatif, en adoucissant les agrandissements.

PAGE 25 Photographer: KLAUS KAMPERT Client: ROY ROBSON GMBH & Co. Camera: HASSELBLAD Film: AGFACHROME 100 Art Director: DIETER MEHLER Stylist: ELKE HAGEMEIER Agency: MPC-COPLAN GMBH Country: GERMANY ■ To create a striking impression and enhance the harmony of the collection, location and car, this photograph was taken in Arizona at sunset. ● Die Harmonie von Kollektion, Location und Auto gehörte zum Konzept. Photographiert wurde in Arizona im Licht der untergehenden Sonne, um eine plakative Wirkung zu erzielen. ▲ Créer une harmonie colorée – tel était ici le propos du photographe. Les couleurs du décor sont en accord avec le ton dominant des vêtements présentés. Les photos ont été prises en Arizona, à la lumière du soleil couchant. Cette image a été utilisée pour un dépliant et pour des annonces.

PAGE 26 Photographer: FRÉDÉRIC MARSAL Representative: ELISABETH LECOCQ Client: AGENCE FAM Camera: POLAROID LAND 195 Film: POLAROID 665 PN Designer: BENITA RAPHAN Country: FRANCE ■ When given carte blanche to create images for a French modeling agency's catalog, this photo resulted. ● Das Bild wurde in einem Katalog der französischen Modellagentur FAM verwendet. ▲ Cette image a été reproduite dans un catalogue de l'agence de modèles FAM.

PAGE 27 Photographer: MIKO LAJCZYK Camera: NIKON FE2 Film: FUJI VELVIA Country: FRANCE ■ The photographer's fascination with contrast is apparent in his use of black and white, heaven and hell, life and death. ● Der Photograph ist fasziniert von Kontrasten: Schwarz und Weiss, Himmel und Hölle, Leben und Tod. ▲ Le photographe est fasciné par les effets de contraste: du blanc et du noir, du ciel et de l'enfer, de la vie et de la mort.

PAGE 28 Photographer: HORNICK/RIVLIN STUDIO Client: BON MARCHÉ Camera: NIKON F3 Film: KODAK TRI-X Art Directors: KEVIN GARDINER, DAVID EKIZIAN Designer: JOHN CLARK Stylist: LOUISE ROCHE Agency: BON MARCHÉ IN-HOUSE Country: USA ■ "Return to Elegance" was the theme of this newspaper advertisement for the Seattle department store Bon Marché. Prepared for the store's anniversary celebration, the theme was conveyed by using a model in comtemporary clothing with 1930s and 1940s elegance suggested by the style as well as the setting. ● «Zurück zur Eleganz» war das Thema einer Kampagne für ein Kaufhaus. Gemeint ist die Eleganz der dreissiger, vierziger Jahre, die hier durch das Umfeld, die Art der Darstellung und den jungen Mann, in moderner Sportkleidung, demonstriert wird. ▲ «Retour à l'élégance», tel était le sujet d'une campagne dans les journaux pour le grand magasin Bon Marché de Seattle. Le vêtement de sport évoque précisément l'élégance décontractée du sportswear des années 30/40.

PAGE 29 Photographer: RANJIT GREWAL Camera: CANON T-90 Film: KODAK VPS 160 Designer: CHARLES LESTER Stylist: VICTOR HUTCHINGS Country: USA ■ The frescos and paintings of Michelangelo and Raphael inspired this angel. The photographer worked with tungsten lights and Kodak VPS 160 daylight film to achieve the warm glow. ● Die Fresken und Bilder von Michelangelo und Raphael inspirierten den Photographen. Er arbeitete mit Kunstlicht und Kodak VPS 160 Tageslichtfilm, um den warmen Ton zu erreichen. ▲ Pour cette image le photographe s'est inspiré des fresques de Michel-Ange et de Raphaël. Il a travaillé avec des lampes tungstène et un film lumière naturelle Kodak VPS 160, afin d'obtenir un ton chaud.

PAGE 30 (all images) Photographer: STEFAN SCHÜTZ Client: LASERVISION Camera: PENTAX 6x7 Film: KODAK EPP Country: GERMANY ■ The high-tech look of models in futuristic clothing wearing laser protective glasses was accented by the special effects achieved by manipulation during development. ● Laserschutzbrillen im High-Tech-Look, mit Modellen in futuristischer Kleidung in Szene gesetzt. Die Effekte erreichte der Photograph durch Manipulation im Entwicklungsprozess. ▲ Look «high tech» pour la présentation d'une collection de lunettes de protection contre les rayons laser. Le photographe a obtenu certains effets spéciaux au cours du développement.

PAGES 31 Photographer: LEIF SCHMODDE Client: PIRELLI Camera: HASSELBLAD Film: KODAK PLUS-X PAN Art Director: JOACHIM HAUSER Stylist: CLEMENTINE SCHMODDE Agency: SAATCHI & SAATCHI ADVERTISING Country: GERMANY ■ Dynamic, sporty, energetic, erotic women were used in advertising for Pirelli tires. ● Dynamische, sportliche, kraftvolle, erotische Frauen – mit diesen Porträts wurde für Pirelli-Reifen geworben. ▲ Des femmes sexy, dynamiques, énergiques, sportives. Ces photos ont été utilisées pour la publicité des pneus Pirelli.

PAGE 32 Photographers: BARBARA JAKSE, STANE JERSIC Publisher: *MINOLTA MIRROR* Camera: MINOLTA Art Director: FRED O. BECHLEN Country: JAPAN ■ The images which Barbara Jakse and Stane Jersic from Slovenia produce deal with life and death, reality and dream, pain and love. ● In den gemeinschaftlichen Bildern der Photographin Barbara Jakse und ihres Kollegen Stane Jersic aus Slowenien geht es um Leben und Tod, Realität und Traum, Schmerz und Liebe. ▲ Les images que la photographe Barbara Jakse produit en collaboration avec Stane Jersic parlent de la vie et de la mort, de la réalité et du rêve, de la douleur et de l'amour.

PAGE 33 Photographer: ANDY THOMPSON Representative: NATASHA FOX Camera: MAMIYA RB 6x7" Film: KODAK EPP Country: GREAT BRITAIN ■ The photographer, a graduate student in professional photography at Blackpool College, prefers a minimalistic style. In this photo he attempted to express nonchalance through the pose, expression, distribution of light and predominance of yellow. ● Der Photograph machte diese Aufnahme als Student der Abschlussklasse für Berufsphotographen am Blackpool College. Er liebt den minimalistischen Stil. Hier ging es ihm um den Ausdruck von Gelassenheit. ▲ Lorsqu'il a réalisé cette photo, Andy Thompson était encore étudiant au Blackpool College, où il préparait son diplôme de photographe professionnel. Il marque une prédilection pour le style minimaliste. Ici, il a choisi de donner une impression de décontraction.

PAGE 34 Photographer: MICHAEL BIONDO Client: FAIRCHILD PUBLISHING Camera: HASSELBLAD Film: KODAK T-MAX Art Director: KIM CIHLAR Designer: PAT NORDON Stylist: KIM CIHLAR Country: USA ■ The idea behind this fashion photo was to emphasize the studio environment. ● Die Idee bei dieser Modeaufnahme: die Betonung der Studioumgebung. ▲ Photo de mode prise en studio: le photographe désirait transmettre l'atmosphère particulière de son lieu de création.

PAGE 35 Photographer: LINDA BOHM Camera: HASSELBLAD Film: KODAK EPN Art Director: LINDA BOHM Country: USA ■ To avoid the baby upstaging the product, photographer showed only a portion of the face, thereby ensuring the attention would be drawn to the product, yet maintaining a human quality within the image. ● Damit das Baby dem darzustellenden Produkt nicht allzuviel Konkurrenz macht, zeigt die Photographin nur einen Teil des Gesichtes und erreicht damit, dass die Betonung auf dem Overall liegt, während die menschliche Qualität des Bildes erhalten bleibt. ▲ Afin de ne pas disperser l'attention sur des détails autres que le produit, la photographe a choisi de ne montrer qu'une partie du visage de l'enfant. L'accent est ainsi mis sur l'overall, sans que l'image ne perde de son humanité.

PAGE 36 Photographer: ROBERT QUICK Camera: BRONICA SQA Film: FUJI VELVIA Country: GREAT BRITAIN ■ The photographer, a senior in photography at Blackpool College, emphasized the aquatic theme by the predominant use of blue. ● Der Photograph, Student der Abschlussklasse für Photographie am Blackpool College, unterstreicht das Badethema durch das dominierende Blau. ▲ Le photographe, alors étudiant en dernière année de photographie au Blackpool College, a utilisé une dominante de bleu pour souligner son sujet, le bain..

PAGE 37 Photographer: MIKO LAJCZYK Camera: NIKON FE2 Film: FUJI VELVIA Country: FRANCE ■ Color and light were the elements that helped the photographer emphasize the radiance of his model. ● Der Photograph bediente sich elementarer bildnerischer Gestaltungsmittel: Farbe und Licht. ▲ Le photographe a su mettre en valeur le rayonnement de son modèle en utilisant les composantes fondamentales de toute création picturale: la couleur et la lumière.

PAGE 38 Photographer: GÜNTER PFANNMÜLLER Client: MESSE FRANKFURT Camera: SINAR 4x5" Film: KODAK EKTACHROME 64 Art Director: SABINE GASPER-MAUTES Designer: GÜNTER PFANNMÜLLER Stylist: KLAUS P. KRAUEL Agency: BEITHAN, HESSLER, MÄTTIG Country: GERMANY ■ Architecture served as a setting for the main subject, the fabric, which is accented by the lighting. The photo was used in an ad campaign for the home furnishing fair in Frankfurt. ● Architektur als Kulisse für den Hauptdarsteller, den Stoff, durch das Licht in Szene gesetzt. Die Aufnahme stammt aus einer Kampagne für die Heimtextilienmesse in Frankfurt. ▲ L'architecture sert de décor à l'étoffe, mise en scène au moyen de la lumière. Cette photo provient d'une campagne d'annonces pour la Foire du tissu d'ameublement à Francfort.

PAGE 39 Photographer: RODNEY SMITH Representative: ELIZABETH HARRISON Client: NAN A. TALESE/DOUBLEDAY PUBLISHERS Camera: LEICA M4 Film: KODAK TRIX-X Art Director: LESLIE SMOLAN Designer: JENNIFER DOMER Agency: CARBONE SMOLAN ASSOCIATES Country: USA ■ Photographer Rodney Smith dedicated a visual essay to the experience, the whimsy and the sense of style that a hat can bestow. It was published as *The Hat Book*. ● In einem Photoessay befasst sich der Photograph mit dem, was ein Hut bedeuten kann: mit der Erfahrung, der Verrücktheit und dem Gefühl von Stil. Er ist unter dem Titel *The Hat Book* als Buch erschienen. ▲ Le photographe Rodney Smith a consacré un petit album au chapeau, publié sous le titre *The Hat Book*. Il y parle de la sensation qu'apporte le fait de porter un couvre-chef, qui peut être aussi bien l'expression de la fantaisie que d'un sens de l'esthétique.

PAGE 40 Photographer: BERNHARD ANGERER Client: LUDWIG REITER Art Director: GERHARD PLAKOLM Designers: GERHARD PLAKOLM, UDO TITZ Agency: CZERNY, CELAND, PLAKOLM Country: AUSTRIA ■ Custom-made shoes, in the best Viennese shoe-making tradition. They were photographed under water, a rather unusual setting for shoes. ● Von Hand gefertigte Schuhe nach bester Wiener Schuhmachertradition. Sie wurden unter Wasser photographiert, einer eher ungewohnten Umgebung für Schuhe. ▲ Ces chaussures entièrement fabriquées à la main, selon la plus pure tradition des cordonniers viennois, ont été photographiées sous l'eau, une manière plutôt inattendue de présenter un tel produit.

PAGE 41 Photographer: CHRIS MEIER Camera: SINAR Film: FUJI RDP Country: GERMANY ■ In his series, "Photographic Paintings," Chris Meier searches for new photographic means of visual interpretation. The slight overlapping is obtained through a sandwiching technique. ● Um neue Wege, neue photographische Sehweisen geht es dem Photographen Chris Meier bei seiner Reihe «photographische Gemälde». Die geringfügigen Überlagerungen erreicht er durch Sandwich-Technik. ▲ Dans cette série intitulée «peintures photographiques», le photographe Chris Meier explore de nouvelle voies, de nouveaux modes de vision photographique. L'effet de superposition minime est obtenu à l'aide d'un montage en sandwich.

PAGE 42 Photographer: DANIEL WRESZIN Client: ASSOS OF SWITZERLAND Camera: HASSELBLAD Art Director: DANIEL WRESZIN Designer: PETER SARGENT Country: USA ■ A sense of mystery was used to set this image apart from conventional athletic fashion advertising: The photographer's goal was to create a sense of speed, style and authenticity. Real cyclists served as models. ● Etwas Geheimnisvolles sollte das Bild haben, um es von der üblichen Werbung für Sportkleidung zu unterscheiden. Dem Photographen ging es dabei um Geschwindigkeit, Stil und Authentizität. Als Modelle engagierte er Profiradfahrer. ▲ Cette image illustrant le catalogue d'un fabricant de vêtements de sports devait avoir quelque chose de mystérieux. Le photographe a engagé un cycliste professionnel pour la photo. Il a voulu exprimer avant tout la vitesse, le style et l'authenticité.

PAGE 43 Photographer: TAK KOJIMA Camera: BRONICA ETR Film: FUJICHROME RDP Country: USA ■ Colorful swimwear, effectively put into the proper light of ultraviolet rays causing fluorescent colors to glow, while non-fluorescent colors appear black or dark blue. Thus, working with strobe lighting and color filters, the photographer had full control over which portions of the picture he chose to intensify. ● Farbenfrohe Bademode, effektvoll ins rechte Licht gerückt. Während ultraviolette Strahlen die fluoreszierenden Farben reflektieren, erscheinen nicht-fluoreszierende Farben schwarz oder dunkelblau. Dadurch konnte der Photograph bestimmen, welche Teile hervorgehoben werden sollten. Er arbeitete mit einem Stroboskop und Farbfiltern. ▲ Maillot de bain dont les couleurs sont mises en valeur par des effets lumineux d'une grande efficacité. Les rayons ultraviolets reflètent les couleurs fluorescentes, les couleurs non fluorescentes devenant noires ou bleu foncé. Le photographe a donc pu déterminer sans peine quelle partie de la photo il voulait mettre en relief. Il a travaillé avec un éclairage stroboscopique et des filtres couleurs.

PAGES 44-45 Photographer: JOST WILDBOLZ Client: SCHNEIDERS BEKLEIDUNG Camera: PENTAX 6x7 Film: KODAK EKTACHROME 200 Art Director: FRANZ MERLICEK Designer: JUDITH MODL Agency: DEMNER & MERLICEK Country: AUSTRIA ■ People and fashion, the way one imagines them in real life: the right trench coat at the right time at the right place. The images were used in a catalog for an Austrian apparel maker. ● Menschen und Mode, wie sie im Alltag vorstellbar sind: der richtige Trenchcoat zur richtigen Zeit am richtigen Ort; die Harmonie von natürlichen Materialien. Die Bilder stammen aus einem Katalog für Schneiders Bekleidung. ▲ Une mode d'une élégance sobre, portée par des gens tels

qu'on se les imagine dans la vie de tous les jours. Ces photos sont tirées d'un catalogue de prestige et de vente par correspondance d'un fabricant de vêtements autrichien.

PAGES 46-47 Photographer: JOYCE TENNESON Client: DAYTON HUDSON Camera: POLAROID 20x24" Art Director: BILL THORBURN Country: USA ■ Images created for a limited-edition catalog presenting the designer collection of the Dayton Hudson department store. ● Bilder aus einem in limitierter Auflage hergestellten Katalog, in dem die Designerkollektion des Kaufhauses Dayton Hudson vorgestellt wird. ▲ Des images créées pour un catalogue, dans lequel sont présentés les modèles des grands designers de mode, vendus dans les grands magasins Dayton Hudson.

PAGES 48-49 Photographer: JOYCE TENNESON Client: DAYTON HUDSON Camera: POLAROID 20x24" Art Director: BILL THORBURN Country: USA ■ Feminine, elegant fashions by Thierry Mugler, Isaac Mizrahi, Romeo Gigli and Donna Karan photographed for a Dayton Hudson catalog. ● Feminine, elegante Mode von Thierry Mugler, Isaac Mizrahi, Romeo Gigli und Donna Karan, photographiert für einen Katalog ▲ Des modèles élégants de Thierry Mugler, Isaac Mizrahi, Romeo Gigli et Donna Karan. Joyce Tenneson a réalisé ces photos pour un catalogue des grands magasins Dayton Hudson.

PAGE 50 Photographer: MONICA ROSELLO Client: FIRA DE BARCELONA Camera: ARCA SWISS 4x5" Film: POLAROID 100 Art Director/Designer: RICARD BADIA Stylist: FERNANDO TORRENT Country: SPAIN ■ Pielespana, a leather fashion trade fair in Spain, needed a special visual interpretation. The photographer, therefore, concentrated on the Mediterranean spirit, sensuality and the sea as symbols for the city of Barcelona. ● Pielespana ist eine Ledermodemesse in Spanien. Der Kunde wollte eine besondere Interpretation des Themas. Die Photographin konzentrierte sich auf den mediterranen Geist, Sinnlichkeit und das Meer als Symbol der Stadt Barcelona. ▲ Pielespana est une foire du vêtement de cuir en Espagne; le mandant désirait une interprétation originale du sujet. La photographe a voulu faire ressortir la sensualité du tempérament méditerranéen, se concentrant sur la mer, symbole même de la ville de Barcelone.

PAGE 51 Photographer: JOHN HUET Representatives: MARILYN CADENBACH, ROBIN DICTENBERG Client: LOUIS Camera: LINHOFF 4x5" Film: KODAK TRI-X Designer: TYLER SMITH Country: USA ■ The 1940's were the subject of a new fall fashion collection and catalog. ● Die vierziger Jahre waren das Thema einer neuen Herbstkollektion für Damen und Herren und damit Thema der Aufnahmen für einen entsprechenden Katalog. ▲ Les années 40 – tel était le thème d'une nouvelle collection automne/hiver de vêtements hommes et femmes, et donc le sujet des photos du catalogue correspondant.

PAGE 52 Photographer: JEFFREY AARONSON Publisher: *TRAVEL HOLIDAY* Camera: NIKON F4S Film: FUJI VELVIA RVP Director of Photography: BILL BLACK Designer: LAURIE BAKER COHOE Country: USA ■ To capture the spirit of a new age of tolerance and freedom for the Roman Catholic Church in Russia, the photographer wanted to show the worshipers faces juxtaposed against the priests'. To accomplish this, he needed a high vantage point. Suddenly, a young woman approached and led him to the gallery where the choir performed, a place normally off limits to worshippers, not to mention foreigners. ● Der Beginn eines neuen Zeitalters der Toleranz und Freiheit für die orthodoxe Kirche Russlands. Um die Gesichter der Gläubigen, die in diese Moskauer Kathedrale strömten, der Prozession der Priester gegenüberzustellen, suchte der Photograph verzweifelt nach einem erhöhten Standpunkt. Eine junge Russin führte ihn zur Empore, ein Ort, zu dem Gläubige, geschweige denn Fremde, eigentlich keinen Zutritt haben. ▲ Interdite sous le régime communiste, l'église orthodoxe de Russie renaît aujourd'hui, plus puissante que jamais. Désirant photographier les fidèles qui se pressent devant l'autel lors d'une cérémonie dans une cathédrale de Moscou, le photographe cherchait désespérément un lieu surélevé pour prendre sa photo. C'est alors qu'une jeune Russe lui vint en aide, le conduisant vers la galerie, un endroit bien entendu interdit au public, et qui plus est aux étrangers!

PAGE 54 Photographer: DAVID POWERS Camera: MAMIYA RZ 67 Film: AGFA APX 120 Country: USA ■ This woman, a cancer patient, is a close friend of the photographer. The photo is meant to show her quiet strength and determination. ● Diese Frau, eine Krebspatientin, ist eine Freundin des Photographen. Ihre stille Stärke und Entschlossenheit haben ihn tief beeindruckt. ▲ Cette femme, malade du cancer, est une amie du photographe. Impressionné par sa force et sa volonté, le photographe désirait faire un portrait qui reflète les sentiments intérieurs de la personne.

PAGE 55 (all images) Photographer: ARTHUR MEYERSON Client: COCA COLA COMPANY Camera: NIKON F4 Film: Fuji Velvia Agency: CRITT GRAHAM & ASSOCIATES Country: USA ■ Darkness over Kuwait. These images of the burning oil fields were taken while on an assignment for Coca-Cola. The picture of the fire fighter was originally intended for the company's annual report but, due to its controversial nature, was not used. ● Ewige Nacht über Kuwait. Diese Bilder der brennenden Ölfelder Kuwaits entstanden während einer Auftragsarbeit des Photographen für Coca-Cola. Das Bild des Feuerlöschmannes wurde wegen des heiklen Themas schliesslich doch nicht im Jahresbericht der Firma verwendet. ▲ Obscurité sur le Koweit. Le photographe a réalisé ces images de champs pétrolifères en flammes alors qu'il travaillait pour une commande pour Coca-Cola. L'image du pompier ne fut pas utilisée en fin de compte dans le rapport annuel de la société, à cause de la controverse qui s'était déclenchée au sujet de la Guerre du Golf.

PAGES 56 Photographer: ANDY HERNANDEZ Publisher: *NEWSWEEK* Art Director: PATRICIA BRADBURY Country: USA ■ Events in Moscow, 1991: The people of Moscow pour into the streets in droves to show their solidarity with Russian President Boris Yeltsin. ● Ereignisse in Moskau, 1991, nach dem Putschversuch der alten Kommunisten gingen Tausende auf die Strassen Moskaus, um ihre Solidarität mit dem russischen Präsidenten Boris Jelzin zu demonstrieren. Die Aufnahme erschien in der Zeitschrift *Newsweek*. ▲ Moscou, 1991, juste après la tentative de putsch des anciens communistes. Dans les rues de Moscou, la foule manifeste sa solidarité au président Boris Eltsine.

PAGE 57 Photographer: BORIS YURCHENKO Publisher: *NEWSWEEK* Art Director: PATRICIA BRADBURY Country: USA ■ Soviet Army tanks line up near the Russian Parliment in a brief show of force, ending in a peaceful and rapid retreat. ● Aufnahme aus *Newsweek*: Eine kurze Machtdemonstration sowjetischer Panzer vor dem russischen Parlament im Jahre 1991 endete mit einem schnellen und friedlichen Rückzug. ▲ Les chars soviétiques, qui avaient pris place devant le Parlement russe en 1991 après la tentative de putsch, se retirent rapidement et dans le calme.

PAGE 58 Photographer: RAYMOND MEEKS Client: AMNESTY INTERNATIONAL Camera: GRAFLEX Film: KODAK TRI-X Art Director: JOHN DOYLE Agency: DOYLE ADVERTISING & DESIGN GROUP Country: USA ■ Hands that tell of suffering. This image, from a series of victims helped by Amnesty International was taken in Guatemala. Here, a father gently embraces his son who was paralyzed from the waist down by a sniper's stray bullet, which had been intended for the father. ● Raymond Meeks photographierte für Amnesty International Hände von Opfern, denen von AI geholfen wird. Hier die Hände eines Vaters, der seinen querschnittgelähmten Sohn umarmt. Er wurde von einer Kugel getroffen, die wahrscheinlich seinem Vater gegolten hatte. ▲ Raymond Meeks a photographié pour Amnesty International des mains de victimes auxquelles AI vient en aide. Ici, ces mains sont celles d'un père qui étreint son fils. Ce dernier a été atteint d'une balle qui était probablement destinée à son père et il est devenu paraplégique.

PAGE 59 (all images) Photographer: WILFRIED BAUER Client: *FAZ MAGAZIN* Art Director: HANS-GEORG POSPISCHIL Country: GERMANY ■ Scenes from Zagreb. (top) The wreckage of a Yugoslavian fighter brought from the East now serves as a memorial. (middle) The new Croatian emblem is already embossed on the holster of toy pistols. (bottom) Refugees from Eastern Croatia find shelter in this camp. ● Szenen aus Zagreb. Auf die Halfter der Kinderpistolen ist bereits das kroatische Wappen geprägt. Das zertrümmerte Leitwerk einer jugoslawischen Militärmaschine, die aus dem Osten herbeigeschafft wurde, wird zum Denkmal. Flüchtlinge aus dem Osten Kroatiens finden in diesem Lager Unterkunft. ▲ Scènes photographiées à Zagreb. Le blason croate était imprimé sur l'étui d'un revolver d'enfant, en vente sur le marché. L'épave d'un réacteur d'un avion militaire yougoslave, rapporté de l'Est, est devenue un monument. Les réfugiés de l'est de la Croatie sont hébergés dans un camp dont on voit ici une salle.

PAGE 60 Photographer: JOHN PAYNE Representative: KELLY CLEVELAND Client: CARL EMIL Camera: HORSEMAN 8x10" Film: 8x10 KODAK EKTACHROME EPP Designer: MORTEN THRONDSEN Agency: ANISDAHL/CHRISTENSEN Country: NORWAY ■ A Norwegian design company discovered images of this American photographer in an annual and wanted the same subject matter and feel in pictures to be used in advertising for a paper company. The photographer had an entirely free hand in this assignment. ● Eine norwegische Designfirma hatte Bilder des amerikanischen Photographen in einem Photojahrbuch entdeckt. Sie wollten in Thema und Stil ähnliche Aufnahmen für die Werbung eines Papierherstellers. ▲ Une firme de design norvégienne qui avait découvert les images de ce photographe américain dans un annuaire de la photo désirait quelque chose sur le même sujet et dans le même style pour la publicité d'un fabricant de papier.

PAGE 62 Photographer: MIKE RYAN Representative: MAUD GENG Camera: SINAR 8x10" Film: FUJICHROME Stylist: MARI QUIRK Country: USA ■ Working on a project for a computer software company, Mike Ryan was to photograph flowers, but by the time all was set for the shooting, the perfect tulips the stylist provided had begun to wilt. This, however, gave them an added beauty which became immediately apparent when the photographer adjusted the composition and lighting. ● Mike Ryan sollte für einen Computer-Software-Hersteller Blumenaufnahmen machen. Als alles für die Aufnahme bereit war, hatten die von der Stylistin besorgten perfekten Blumen bereits zu welken begonnen. Der Photograph veränderte Licht und Komposition, und plötzlich zeigte sich die besondere Schönheit ihres Welkens. ▲ Mike Ryan devait photographier de fleurs pour un fabricant de logiciels. Lorsque tout fut enfin prêt pour les prises de vues, les fleurs, qui avaient été soigneusement choisies par la styliste, commençaient déjà à se flétrir. Le photographe décida alors de modifier l'éclairage et la composition, et l'étrange beauté des fleurs mortes se révéla dans toute sa splendeur.

PAGE 63 Photographer: MARK WIENS Client: CATHOLIC DIOCESE OF WICHITA Camera: SINAR 4x5" Film: KODAK EKTACHROME EPY Art Director: GARY FREY Agency: MORRIS/FREY AGENCY Country: USA ■ "Donate your time and talents to the church instead of wasting them in self-indulgent pursuits" is the message of this poster for the Archdiocese of Wichita, Kansas. Tungsten lighting was used with a multiple exposure technique. Certain parts of the scene were exposed with diffusion filters so the photographer could control which areas were to be diffused and which were to be sharp. ● «Stellt Eure Zeit und Begabungen der Kirche zur Verfügung, statt sie eigennützig zu vertun» – so die Botschaft eines Plakates der katholischen Diözese von Wichita. Der Photograph arbeitete mit Mehrfachbelichtung, wobei für bestimmte Bereiche Streufilter verwendet wurden. Mit Hilfe der Beleuchtung und der Filter erscheinen bestimmte Bereiche der Aufnahme verschwommen. ▲ «Consacrez votre temps et vos talents à l'Eglise au lieu de les perdre inutilement» – tel était le message de l'affiche du diocèse catholique de Wichita. Le photographe a utilisé une technique d'expositions multiples; pour certaines zones, il a utilisé des filtres, afin de répartir la lumière.

PAGE 64 (both images) Photographer: HOLLY STEWART Camera: SINAR 4x5" Film: KODAK EPP Designer: JENNIFER MORLA Stylist: AMY NATHAN Country: USA ■ The photographer chose monochromatic subjects to bring out the subtleties of shape and shadow. (top) For the camisole she used natural light. (bottom) The oyster stew was shot with a soft box. ●

Die Photographin entschied sich für monochromatische Kompositionen, um Nuancen von Formen und Schatten herauszubringen. Für die Austernsuppe verwendete sie eine Soft Box, für die Wiederaufnahme natürliches Licht. ▲ La photographe a choisi de se limiter à des compositions monochromes, afin d'exprimer toutes les nuances des formes et des ombres. Pour la soupe aux huîtres, elle a utilisé une soft box, pour la photo du cintre, il a tiré parti de la lumière naturelle.

PAGE 65 Photographer: TERRY HEFFERNAN Client: RIDOMIL PC Camera: SINAR P Film: KODAK EKTACHROME 100 Art Director: JOHN DONAGHUE Agency: KETCHUM ADVERTISING Country: USA ■ The contrast between a lightbulb and its predecessor, the candle, was used in this advertisement for Ridomil to combine an old world feeling with a new age product. ● Die Aufnahme war für eine Anzeige bestimmt, in der ein Produkt des technischen Zeitalters mit der guten alten Zeit in Verbindung gebracht werden sollte. ▲ La photo a été réalisée pour une annonce dans laquelle un produit hautement technique devait être présenté comme au bon vieux temps.

PAGE 66 Photographer: ANDY LIVESEY Camera: SINAR F 8x10" Film: KODAK EKTACHROME 64T Country: GREAT BRITAIN ■ Andy Livesey, a student at Blackpool College, uses the beauty of everyday objects as subjects. Here he contrasts the vulnerability of the petals against the solid columns of the stamens; the texture and color of the vase are important elements in contrasting fragility with strength. ● Andy Livesey ist Student der Photoklasse am Blackpool College. Sein Thema: die Schönheit alltäglicher Dinge. Hier kontrastiert er die Verletzlichkeit der Blütenblätter mit den kräftigen Stempeln der Staubgefässe. Die Beschaffenheit und Farbe der Vase sind Ausdrucksmittel für Zartheit und Stärke. ▲ Andy Livesey est un étudiant de la classe de photographie au Blackpool College. Son sujet de prédilection: la beauté des choses quotidiennes. Ici, il met en contraste la fragilité des pétales de fleurs et la vigueur des étamines. La texture et la couleur du vase expriment également la vulnérabilité et la force.

PAGE 67 Photographer: PARISH KOHANIM Representative: ROSANNE KOHANIM Client: FLEXCO Camera: SINAR P 4x5" Film: KODAK EPP Art Director: KIM YOUNGBLOOD Agency: YOUNGBLOOD, SWEAT & TEARS Country: USA ■ The title of this ad for a flooring product, is "Wallflowers" something that goes unnoticed, blending in with the background. The intent was the opposite: to bring attention to the product. Playing on the pun, the photographer focused entirely on the flowers. ● «Mauerblümchen» war der Titel einer Anzeige für Bodenplatten. Gemeint war das Mauerblümchen im wahrsten Sinne des Wortes, aber die Absicht der Anzeige ist natürlich, Aufmerksamkeit auf das Produkt zu lenken. Der Photograph konzentrierte sich ganz auf die Schönheit der Blumen. ▲ Cette photo a été réalisée pour une annonce intitulée «Fleurs des murs», une publicité des dallages. Il s'agissait, tout en montrant ces petites fleurs qui poussent sur les murs, de souligner le côté naturel du produit. Le photographe s'est totalement concentré sur la beauté des fleurs.

PAGE 68 Photographer: DALE E. MCNEELY JR. Camera: DEARDORFF 4x5" Film: KODAK EPY Country: USA ■ Light and shadow, sharp and blurred areas were the elements used in composing this still life. ● Licht und Schatten, Schärfe und Unschärfe als Gestaltungselemente eines Stillebens. ▲ La lumière et l'ombre, la netteté et le flou comme éléments de composition d'une nature morte.

PAGE 69 Photographer: RON BAXTER SMITH Camera: SINAR 4x5" Film: POLAROID TYPE 55 Country: CANADA ■ The theme for this still life was all kinds of teeth. ● Zähne in verschiedenster Form als Thema eines Stillebens. ▲ Les formes de dents les plus diverses, sujet d'une nature morte.

PAGE 70 Photographer: GERRIT BUNTROCK Camera: CONTAX RTS II, 60MM ZEISS MACRO-PLANAR Film: Kodak P800/1600 Art Director: GERRIT BUNTROCK Country: GREAT BRITAIN ■ Inspiration for this image came from the great still life painters of the past. To show what can be achieved through composition and light, the photographer chose everyday objects and used a fiber-optic light guide to direct light onto the subject, while the camera shutter was open. The pushed, hence grainy, film helped to create the desired texture. ● Der Photograph liess sich von den Stilleben der grossen Meister der Vergangenheit inspirieren. Um zu zeigen, was er durch Komposition und Licht bewirken kann, wählte er schlichte Alltagsgegenstände. Bei offenem Verschluss wurde mit einer Glasfaseroptik-Lichtquelle Licht auf die Gegenstände gelenkt. Der grobkörnige Film sorgte für die gewünschte Textur. ▲ Le photographe s'est inspiré des grands maîtres de la nature morte pour cette composition. Il a choisi des éléments d'une grande simplicité de couleur et de forme, afin de montrer les subtils jeux de lumière et d'ombre sur les objets. Il a utilisé un système de Fibre Optic Light Guide pour diriger la lumière sur les objets tout en maintenant l'obturateur ouvert. La texture a été obtenue au moyen d'une pellicule à gros grain, poussée au développement.

PAGE 71 Photographer: MICHAEL NORTHRUP Representative: Robin Stevens Camera: BRONICA ETR Film: KODAK VERICHROME III Art Director: DAVE PLUNKERT Designer: JOYCE HESSELDERTH Country: USA ■ The photographer chose a simple subject to demonstrate the effects that can be obtained with varying degrees of focus. ● Der Photograph wählte ein altes Thema, um zu zeigen, welche Wirkung man mit verschiedenen Schärfen im Bild erreichen kann. ▲ Le photographe a choisi un sujet historique, afin de faire une démontration des effets que l'on peut obtenir sur une même image avec des focales variables.

PAGE 72 Photographer: SHEILA METZNER Publisher: *VOGUE PARIS* Editor in Chief: COLOMBE PRINGLE Stylist: SHEILA METZNER Country: FRANCE ■ For the new fragrance L'Eau d'Issey (Odyssey!) and a specially-shaped soap by Issey Miyake, characterized by clarity and purity, the photographer created a symbolic lake with symbolic water lilies. ● Für das Parfum L'Eau d'Issey (Odyssee) und eine speziell geformte Seife von Issey Miyake erdachte die Photographin einen symbolischen See mit symbolischen Seerosen.

Klarheit und Reinheit sind das Thema des Duftes. ▲ Pour le nouveau parfum L'Eau d'Issey (L'Odyssée) et un savon spécialement dessiné par Issey Miyake, la photographe Sheila Metzner a imaginé un étang symbolique avec des nénuphars artificiels. La limpidité et la pureté caractérisent ce parfum.

PAGE 73 Photographer: JENNIFER BAUMANN Camera: CONTAX RTS Film: AGFA 1000 Stylist: JENNIFER BAUMANN Country: USA ■ The soft shimmer of mother of pearl and the clarity of glass are caught in this still life, done to test a new film. The water is running to create a less stagnant moment. ● Der sanfte Glanz von Perlmutt und die Reinheit von Glas, eingefangen in einem Stilleben, das der Photographin dazu diente, einen neuen Film auszuprobieren. Das laufende Wasser bringt Bewegung in das Bild. ▲ Cette nature morte associe l'éclat mat des perles de culture à la pureté du verre et la transparence cristalline du verre et de l'eau. L'eau qui coule apporte un élément de mouvement dans cette image plutôt statique.

PAGE 74 Photographer: JIM DIVITALE Representative: SANDY DIVITALE Camera: HORSEMAN LX 4x5" Film: KODAK EKTACHROME 100 PLUS Stylist: SANDY DIVITALE Country: USA ■ The perfect proportions of the chambered nautilus, a classic symbol of beauty is accentuated by a softbox and strobe lighting as well as the Hosemaster Light Painting System to create a glowing effect from within. ● Der Nautilus mit seinen perfekten Proportionen ist eines der klassischen Symbole für Schönheit. Für diese Aufnahme verwendete der Photograph eine Softbox und Strobe-Licht sowie das Hosemaster-Light-Painting-System, um den Leuchteffekt im Inneren des Gehäuses zu erhalten. ▲ Le nautile, à cause de ses propotions parfaites, est l'un des symboles classiques de la perfection. Le photographe a utilisé ici une soft box et une lumière stroboscopique, ainsi qu'un système de lightpainting pour obtenir un effet d'éclairage de l'intérieur du coquillage.

PAGE 75 Photographer: JOHN PAYNE Client: CARL EMIL Camera: HORSEMAN 8x10" Film: KODAK EKTACHROME EPP Designer: MORTEN THRONDSEN Agency: ANISDAHL/CHRISTENSEN Country: NORWAY ■ A Norwegian design company had discovered images of this American photographer in a photography annual and wanted the same subject matter and feel in pictures which were to be used in advertising for a paper company. ● Eine norwegische Designfirma hatte Aufnahmen des amerikanischen Photographen John Payne in einem Photojahrbuch gesehen. Thema und Stil entsprachen genau ihrer Vorstellung im Zusammenhang mit Anzeigen für einen Papierhersteller. ▲ Ayant découvert les photos de John Payne dans un annuaire de la photo, une firme de design norvégienne lui avait demandé de travailler dans le même style sur le même sujet. La photo a été reproduite comme publicité pour un fabricant de papier.

PAGES 76-77 Photographer: ALEXANDER BAYER Client: VISION PHOTOSTUDIO Camera: SINAR P2 4x5" Film: AGFA RS 100 Country: SWITZERLAND ■ With the light painting technique demonstrated in these self-promotional images, the object is illuminated by means of a flexible fiber-optic wand while the shutter is open. ● Der Photograph arbeitete mit der Light-Painting-Technik, bei der das Objekt mit einer Glasfaseroptik-Lichtquelle bei offenem Verschluss beleuchtet wird. Die Bilder dienten als Eigenwerbung. ▲ Le photographe a travaillé avec la technique de la lightpainting, qui permet d'éclairer l'objet avec un tube lumineux flexible tout en gardant l'obturateur ouvert. Ces photos lui ont servi d'autopromotion.

PAGE 78 Photographer: CHRISTIAN VOGT Client: SCHWEIZERISCHE NATIONAL VERSICHERUNGSGESELLSCHAFT Camera: DIV. 35MM CAMERAS Film: KODAK EKTACHROME Art Director: CHRISTIAN VOGT Designer: SUSAN NASH Country: SWITZERLAND ■ Caring, security, calmness—Christian Vogt interprets an insurance company in his own special way. He was given carte blanche and he chose to let just a few elements carry the message. ● Fürsorge, Sicherheit, Ruhe – Christian Vogt lieferte seine Interpretation einer Versicherungsgesellschaft. Er hatte völlig freie Hand und entschied sich für einige wenige Elemente, um die Botschaft zu übermitteln. ▲ Assistance, sécurité, tranquillité – Christian Vogt propose ici une interprétation personnelle du rôle d'une société d'assurances. On lui avait laissé carte blanche pour cette commande et il décida de se limiter à quelques éléments porteurs du message.

PAGE 79 Photographer: CRAIG VAN DER LENDE Client: WOLVERINE WORLDWIDE Camera: CAMBO Films: POLAROID 809, KODAK EKTACHROME 8x10" Art Director/Designer: ELIZABETH BRANDT Agency: BURGLER & ASSOCIATES Country: USA ■ In this image, the photographer used a two-step process: first he made a Polaroid transfer to paper, then photographed the background and details. ● Das Bild entstand in zwei Arbeitsgängen; zuerst wurde ein Polaroid-Transfer auf Papier gemacht, dann der Hintergrund mit den Details photographiert. Die Aufnahme wurde als Plakat in Schuhläden verwendet. ▲ Cette photo a été réalisée en deux étapes: tout d'abord, le photographe a fait un transfert polaroïd sur papier, puis il a pris le fond et les détails. L'image a été utilisée comme affiche dans des magasins de chaussures.

PAGE 80 Photographer: ALFONS ISELI Camera: NIKON F4 Film: KODAK EKTACHROME 100 Country: SWITZERLAND ■ Soft daylight and a deep black background are responsible for the special impact of the "Figure with Flower Head." ● Weiches Tageslicht und nachtschwarzer Hintergrund sorgen für die spezielle Wirkung der «Figur mit Blumenkopf». ▲ L'atmosphère étrange de cette «figure à tête de fleur» résulte de la combinaison entre une lumière naturelle douce et un fond d'un noir profond.

PAGE 81 Photographer: KENRO IZU Representatives: JEAN CONLON, USA, MEGAPRESS AGENCY INC, JAPAN Client: YAMATOYA LTD. Camera: DEARDORF VIEW CAMERA Film: KODAK PLUS-X Art Director: KEIZO MATSUI Designer: YUKO ARAKI Country: Japan ■ Flowers were the subject for a calendar photographed in a 14"x20" format; afterwards platinum contact prints were made. ● Blumen waren das Thema eines Kalenders. Kenro Izu photographierte sie in einem Format von 14x20"; danach wurden Platinabzüge gemacht. ▲

Le thème des fleurs avait été retenu pour un calendrier. Kenro Izu les photographia dans un format de 14x20", puis il réalisa des tirages platine afin d'obtenir une plus grande subtilité dans les nuances.

PAGE 82 Photographer: LUZIA ELLERT Publisher: D+R-VERLAG, *A LA CARTE* Camera: SINAR 4x5" Film: KODAK EKTACHROME Art Director: USCHKA JESCHKO Stylist: LUZIA ELLERT Country: AUSTRIA ■ This image was used as an opener in the gourmet magazine *A la Carte.*, the theme of which was "Razor Sharp." The photographer was given a range of knives; the only stipulation being all of them should be shown. ● «Messerscharf» war das Thema. Verwendet wurde die Aufnahme als Aufmacher im Gourmetmagazin *A la Carte.* Die Photographin erhielt eine Reihe von Messern, und die einzige Auflage war, dass sie alle im Bild sein mussten. ▲ «Tranchant comme une lame», tel était le leitmotiv. L'image a été utilisée comme ouverture d'article dans un magazine des gourmets, *A la Carte.* La photographe avait reçu toute une série de couteaux et on lui avait demandé de les faire tous figurer sur l'image.

PAGES 84-85 Photographer: CHRISTIANE MAREK Client: CZERNY STYLING GMBH "BASSET" Camera: FUJI 680 Film: FUJICOLOR NSP Agency: WERBEAGENTUR ULI BARES Country: GERMANY ■ The feel of autumn was the subject for a series of still life photographs for a fashion firm. The small, seemingly minor things received the photographer's special attention. ● Herbststimmung war das Thema einer Reihe von Stilleben für eine Modefirma. Es sind die kleinen, scheinbar nebensächlichen Dinge, denen die Photographin besondere Aufmerksamkeit schenkte. ▲ Le sujet de cette série de natures mortes, réalisées pour un fabricant de vêtements, était l'atmosphère automnale. L'attention de la photographe se concentre en particulier sur des détails imperceptibles.

PAGE 86 Photographer: CAROL KAPLAN Representative: ROBIN FERNSELL Camera: NIKON Film: SCOTCH CHROMO 1000 Country: USA ■ Warm earthen colors, unpretentious shapes of pottery and subtle lighting evoke feelings of the quietness and peacefulness of simple life. ● Warme, erdige Töne, schlichte Formen und das Licht verleihen dem Bild Stille und Frieden einfachen Lebens. ▲ Des tons chauds, terreux, des formes simples et une belle lumière confèrent à cette image l'impression paisible de la vie simple.

PAGE 87 Photographer: RAMESH AMRUTH Representative: INGE METZGER Client: STEINBEISS TEMMING PAPIER Camera: SINAR 8"x10" Film: KODAK EPR Art Director: KLAUS BOSSERT Agency: CO & CO Country: GERMANY ■ In order to obtain the desired translucency of his images, the photographer worked with multiple exposure and a sandwich process on 8x10" transparencies. Printed on recycled paper, they were used in a calendar by paper maker Steinbeiss. ● Um die Transparenz seiner Bilder zu erreichen, arbeitete der Photograph mit Mehrfachbelichtungen und Sandwich-Prozess auf 8x10" Dias. Verwendet wurden sie in einem Kalender des Papierherstellers Steinbeiss, auf Recyclingpapier gedruckt. ▲ Pour obtenir la transparence de ces images qui, au premier coup d'œil ont l'air de peintures, le photographe a réalisé des expositions multiples et un processus de montage en sandwich de diapositives 8x10". Imprimées sur papier recyclé, elles ont été reproduites dans le calendrier d'un fabricant de papier.

PAGE 88 Photographer: ANDRÉ BARANOWSKI Client: GOLDEN CAPRICORN PUBLICATION Camera: NIKON F3 Film: KODACHROME 64/EKTACHROME Country: USA ■ A dynamic and stark composition, saturated with the tranquility of the moment and the awareness that the wonderful light will disappear at any second. ● Eine dynamische, strenge Komposition, durchdrungen von der Stille des Augenblicks und dem Bewusstsein, dass das wunderbare Licht jede Sekunde verschwinden kann. ▲ Une composition rigoureuse, non sans dynamisme, qui suggère la tranquillité de l'instant et la fugacité du temps, cette merveilleuse lumière pouvant changer d'un moment à l'autre.

PAGE 89 Photographer: GERRIT BUNTROCK Camera: SINAR P2 8x10", 180MM SYMMAR Film: KODAK EKTACHROME 100 Country: GREAT BRITAIN ■ "Food is beautiful in it's own right and should be shown without frills." With this in mind, the photographer relied on the strength of simple composition and lighting. He used a fiber optic light guide to control the light and to bring out the texture of the bread. ● «Lebensmittel an sich sind schön und sollten ohne überflüssiges Beiwerk gezeigt werden.» Von diesem Gedanken beseelt, verliess sich der Photograph ganz auf die Stärke der schlichten Komposition und der Beleuchtung. Um das Licht richtig zu dosieren und damit die Stofflichkeit des Brotlaibes herauszubringen, verwendete er eine Glasfaseroptik-Lichtquelle. ▲ «La nourriture est une belle chose en soi, il faudrait la montrer telle quelle.» En vertu de cette idée, le photographe s'est reposé complètement sur la puissance de cette forme simple et l'éclairage de la composition. Un système de fibre optic light guide lui a permis de doser la lumière et de mettre en valeur la texture de la miche de pain.

PAGE 90 Photographer: ANDRÉ BARANOWSKI Client: GOLDEN CAPRICORN PUBLICATIONS Camera: SINAR 4x5" Film: AGFA PROFESSIONAL 100 Country: USA ■ Stillness and motion are the components of this image. The sharpness of these contrasts is juxtaposed against the playful movement of the grapes and an overflowing cup of coffee ready to fall. ● Stille und Bewegung sind die Komponenten dieses Bildesaus einer Serie von Stilleben. Der Härte der Kontraste steht die spielerische Bewegung der Trauben und die Kaffeetasse, übergelaufen und im Begriff zu fallen, gegenüber. ▲ Le calme et le mouvement sont les deux éléments clé de cette image. Les contrastes nets s'opposent au mouvement des grains de raisin et de la tasse de café, trop remplie et prête à tomber de la table. Cette photo fait partie d'une série de natures mortes.

PAGE 91 Photographer: MICHAEL WISSING Camera: SINAR P Film: KODAK EPR 64 Art Directors: ERICH GRASDORF, MAX RINDLISBACHER Agency: ASGS EDITORIAL Country: GERMANY ■ "In a light landscape of green at its most versatile, the pears seem suffused with the sense of their future red blush." This image is meant as a protest against today's frenetic consumption. ● «In einer Lichtlandschaft des vielfältigsten Grüns legt sich die

Ahnung von kommendem Rot über die Birnen.» Der Photograph versteht seine Bilder als Protest gegen die allgegenwärtige Verkonsumierung. ▲ «Dans un lumineux paysage aux multiples nuances de vert, on devine que les poires vont bientôt se teinter de rouge.» Le photographe comprend ses images comme une protestation contre la consommation effrénée de notre époque.

PAGES 92-93 Photographer: CHRISTIAN VON ALVENSLEBEN Publisher: EDITION CHRISTIAN BRANDSTÄTTER Camera: UNIVERSAL PALMOS 275 (CA. 1915), WITH POLAROID BACK 669 Designers: PETER SCHMIDT, THOMAS NECHLEBA Country: GERMANY ■ "The Apocalyptic Menu," the book from which the images are taken, deals with the senseless wasting and poisoning of food. The sequence of the photographs follows that of a rich menu. It begins with knife and fork—the knife and fork of a soldier—and their position indicates it is four minutes to twelve. The photographer wanted to show the true face of today's food: the poisoning, the hidden brutality, the color enhancement. All photos were done with a flash in the studio using a Polaroid back on an old camera, then reproduced by means of a Kodak dye transfer procedure. ● *Das Apokalyptische Menu.* In dem Buch, aus dem diese Bilder stammen, geht es um die sinnlose Verschwendung und Vergiftung ursprünglicher Lebensmittel. Der Bildablauf entspricht dem eines anspruchsvollen Menus. Es beginnt mit dem Besteck, aber es ist ein Soldatenbesteck, und es zeigt an, dass es bereits vier Minuten vor zwölf ist. Dem Photographen Christian von Alvensleben ging es um das wahre Gesicht der heutigen Lebensmittel, Verseuchung, versteckte Brutalität und Schönfärberei. Alle Aufnahmen entstanden mit Blitzlicht im Studio, und zwar mit einer alten Kamera, auf die ein Polaroid-Back montiert wurde. Die Polaroids wurden im Kodak Dye-Transfer-Verfahren übertragen. ▲ Ces photos sont tirées d'un livre intitulé «Le menu apocalyptique», où il question du gaspillage des ressources alimentaires et de la pollution des aliments de base. L'ordre des images suit celui d'un menu. Il commence par le couvert, celui d'un soldat, qui indique qu'il est déjà «midi moins quatre», autrement dit qu'il est plus qu'urgent de réagir. Le photographe s'est efforcé de montrer sans aucune complaisance la nourriture que nous consommons aujourd'hui, la dégénérescence de produits qui sont devenus totalement artificiels et la violence cachée qu'un tel traitement de la nature suppose. Toutes les photos ont été prises en studio, avec flash, à l'aide d'un vieil appareil auquel avait été fixé un Polaroïd-back. Les tirages polaroïd furent ensuite transférés au moyen du procédé Kodak Dye-transfer.

PAGE 94 Photographer: MICHAEL O'BRIEN Publisher: *THE NEW YORK TIMES MAGAZINE* Camera: SINAR Film: KODAK EPP Art Director: JANET FROELICH Picture Editor: KATHY RYAN Country: USA ■ "An Eye for Danger"—this portrait of crime- and adventure-story author Robert Stone was taken for the cover of the *New York Times Magazine.* ● Robert Stone ist ein amerikanischer Autor, der sich mit Abenteuer- und Kriminalliteratur befasst. Sein Porträt erschien auf dem Umschlag vom *New York Times Magazine* mit der Headline: «Ein Auge für die Gefahr». ▲ Robert Stone est un auteur américain, spécialisé dans le livre d'aventures et le roman policier. Ce portrait a été publié en couverture du *New York Times Magazine* sous le titre «Un œil pour le danger».

PAGE 96 Photographer: HERB RITTS Representative: VISAGES Publisher: *ROLLING STONE* Art Director: FRED WOODWARD Director of Photography: LAURIE KRATOCHVIL Country: USA ■ "The New Elton John: Clean, Happy and in Love." *Rolling Stone* magazine used this photo on the cover of an issue containing the story of Elton John's drug and alcohol abuse and subsequent recovery. ● Der neue Elton John: sauber, glücklich und verliebt. *Rolling Stone* berichtete über den Popstar, der eine Drogen- und Alkoholentziehungskur hinter sich hat. ▲ Un nouvel Elton John: désintoxiqué, heureux et amoureux. Ce portrait introduisait un article dans *Rolling Stone* sur le chanteur pop, qui a réussi à se libérer de la dépendance de la drogue et de l'alcool.

PAGE 97 Photographer: HERB RITTS Representative: VISAGES Publisher: *ROLLING STONE* Camera: SINAR Film: POLAROID 55 Art Director: FRED WOODWARD Director of Photography: LAURIE KRATOCHVIL Country: USA ■ *Rolling Stone* used this photo on the cover of an issue featuring an interview with Tim Burton, the director of *Batman.* As Michael Keaton, who played Batman, would not pose in the costume, the cowl alone had to be used. It was then possible to treat it simply as a sculpture, lit accordingly and photographed. ● *Rolling Stone* brachte diese Aufnahme als Titel, um auf ein Interview mit dem Regisseur des Filmes *Batman* hinzuweisen. Der Hauptdarsteller Michael Keaton wollte nicht im Kostüm photographiert werden. So wurde das Batman-Thema nur durch das Kostüm dargestellt, das wie eine Skulptur beleuchtet wurde. ▲ Cette photo a été publiée en couverture de *Rolling Stone*, afin d'attirer l'attention sur une interview du metteur en scène du film *Batman.* L'acteur principal, Michael Keaton, ne voulait pas endosser le costume de Batman pour la photo. C'est pourquoi le héros du film est uniquement symbolisé par son déguisement, éclairé comme une sculpture.

PAGES 98-99 (all images) Photographer: TOM ZIMBEROFF Camera: HASSELBLAD, WISTA Film: KODAK Art Director: LISA LEVIN Agency: LISA LEVIN DESIGN Country: USA ■ These photos were selected from a promotional book for Tom Zimberoff. ● Porträts aus einem Promotionsbuch des Photographen Tom Zimberoff. ▲ Portraits tirés d'un livre promotionnel du photographe Tom Zimberoff.

PAGES 100-101 Photographer: MARC HAUSER Representative: RANDI FIAT & ASSOCIATES Publisher: MICHAEL GUNSELMAN Camera: ARCA-SWISS 4x5" Film: POLAROID TYPE 55 Art Director: MICHAEL GUNSELMAN Country: USA ■ These earnest, contemplative faces were among those used in a calendar. ● Ernste Gesichter, nachdenklich, versonnen. Die Porträts wurden für einen Kalender verwendet. ▲ Des visages sérieux, méditatifs, concentrés. Ces portraits ont été reproduits dans un calendrier.

PAGE 102 (left) Photographer: ALBERT WATSON Publisher: *ROLLING STONE* Art Director: FRED WOODWARD Director of Photography: LAURIE KRATOCHVIL Country: USA ■

American actor Tom Cruise, who is hard to pin down for an interview and ferociously protective of his private life, was portrayed by Albert Watson for a feature in *Rolling Stone.* ● Der amerikanische Schauspieler Tom Cruise, der schwer für ein Interview zu haben ist und sein Privatleben konsequent abschirmt, wurde von Albert Watson für einen Beitrag in *Rolling Stone* photographiert. ▲ L'acteur américain Tom Cruise, qui se laisse difficilement interviewer et protège farouchement sa vie privée, a été ici photographié par Albert Watson pour un article de *Rolling Stone.*

PAGE 102 (right) Photographer: ALBERT WATSON Publisher: *ROLLING STONE* Art Director: FRED WOODWARD Director of Photography: LAURIE KRATOCHVIL Country: USA ■ Canadian film maker David Cronenberg is not concerned with garden variety horror, but rather with the insidious horror of existential anguish: "I think, therefore I might not be." ● Der kanadische Filmemacher David Cronenberg befasst sich nicht mit der üblichen Form von Horror, sondern mit dem Horror des Gehemmtseins: «Ich denke, also bin ich vielleicht nicht.» ▲ Le réalisateur David Cronenberg ne traite pas de l'horreur d'une manière commune dans ses films: il met en scène l'angoisse existentielle de l'individu mal dans sa peau qui se dit: «Je pense, donc je ne suis pas.»

PAGE 103 Photographer: ALBERT WATSON Publisher: *ROLLING STONE* Art Director: FRED WOODWARD Director of Photography: LAURIE KRATOCHVIL Country: USA ■ Sharon Stone, a popular American actress was photographed for the cover of *Rolling Stone.* ● Sharon Stone, der heisseste Filmstar des Jahres 1992, für einen Umschlag von *Rolling Stone* photographiert. ▲ Sharon Stone, l'actrice la plus torride de l'année 92, photographiée pour une couverture du magazine *Rolling Stone.*

PAGE 104 Photographer: RON BAXTER SMITH Camera: POLAROID 20x24" Film: POLAROID 20x24" Art Director: DEL TERRELONGE Country: CANADA ■ Black impressions of America: The images are meant as a protest against the generalizations and stereotypes of African-Americans in the media. The late Malcolm X, American civil rights leader appears with raised arm in the background. ● Schwarze Impressionen aus Amerika. Diese Photographien sind ein Protest gegen die stereotype Darstellung der Amerikaner afrikanischer Herkunft in den Medien. Die Faust gehört Malcolm X. ▲ Impressions d'Amérique. Ces photos sont une protestation contre l'image stéréotypée des Américains d'origine africaine dans les médias.

PAGES 105 Photographer: AERNOUT OVERBEEKE Representatives: PIM MILO (NETHERLANDS), CHRISTA KLUBERT (GERMANY), HILARY BRADFORD (ITALY), FREDDY BRAZIL, (GREAT BRITAIN) Client: TELECOM GERMANY Camera: SINAR 4x5" Films: KODAK, FUJI Art Directors: GEORG KNICHEL, JOCHEN SMIDT, LUDGER HRUSCHKA Agency: TEAM BBDO Country: GERMANY ■ People and their work. This advertising campaign, is a series of photos of employees of Telcom's client companies. ● Menschen und ihre Arbeit. In einer Werbekampagne zeigt Telecom die Mitarbeiter seiner Kunden. ▲ Des hommes et des femmes sur leur lieu de travail. Telecom présente les collaborateurs de sa clientèle dans le cadre d'une campagne de publicité.

PAGE 106 (top left and right) Photographer: WULF-EIKE Camera: HASSELBLAD Film: KODAK PLUS-X Country: GERMANY ■ The images are part of the series on parties and guests. The photographer attempts to bring out the character of his subjects through their way of posing for the camera. Here he focused on (left) the competition between twins and (right) the way a girl and a boy handle their first romantic awareness. ● Aus der Serie «Hochzeiter-Bilder von Festen und Gästen». Der Photograph versuchte, durch die Selbstdarstellung seiner Sujets ihren Charakter herauszuarbeiten. Hier spielten Beziehungsmuster eine besondere Rolle: die Konkurrenz der Zwillinge (links) und der Umgang der Kinder mit ersten sexuellen Gefühlen. ▲ Ces images proviennent d'une série intitulée «Photos de mariage de fêtes et de leurs invités». Le photographe a voulu exprimer le caractère des personnages à travers leur façon de se présenter devant son objectif. Il met l'accent sur les relations entre modèles, ici la concurrence entre les jumelles ou le comportement d'enfants qui s'éveillent à la sexualité.

PAGE 106 (bottom left and right) Photographer: JUNJI FUTASHIMA Camera: MAMIYA RZ 67 Film: KODAK PLUS-X Country: JAPAN ■ The sadness and beauty of a former competitive swimmer: The photographer wanted an unusual setting for a swimmer and so he chose to take her portrait in the studio. ● Wehmut und Schönheit einer ehemaligen Leistungsschwimmerin. Junji Futashima photographierte sein Modell im Studio, um eine für das Sujet ungewöhnliche Situation zu schaffen. ▲ Tristesse et beauté d'une ancienne championne de natation. Junji Futashima a choisi de la photographier dans son studio, afin de la mettre dans une situation inhabituelle.

PAGE 107 Photographer: PHILIP ALAN POE Camera: NIKON F3, 50MM Film : FUJICHROME 100 Art Director: PHILIP ALAN POE Stylist: DANIELA KLIMPEL Country: GERMANY ■ This work concerns itself with the transformation of reality and the manipulation of color photographs. The photographer's tools: sharpness and blurriness, focus on movement, expression and lighting; he used a daylight film but only artificial light. ● Hier geht es dem Photographen um die Verschiebung der Wirklichkeit, um die Manipulation einer Farbaufnahme durch Schärfe, Unschärfe, Bewegungsschärfe, Ausdruck und Lichtführung. Er benutzte einen Tageslichtfilm, arbeitete jedoch ausschliesslich mit Kunstlicht. ▲ Le photographe s'intéressait à la manipulation de la réalité au travers d'une photo en couleurs. Il a utilisé des effets de netteté et de flou, la pose et l'éclairage. Il a travaillé avec une pellicule lumière naturelle dans un éclairage artificiel.

PAGE 108 (top left) Photographer: CLAUDIO ALESSANDRI Client: CASH FLOW ZEITSCHRIFTENVERLAG Camera: SINAR 8x10" Film: KODAK Art Director: CLAUDIO ALESSANDRI Stylist: ESTRELLA ELORDUY HERNANDEZ Country: AUSTRIA ■ The idea of showing athletes of the Austrian Olympic team from Barcelona in an unusual, "Spanish" way, was not accepted warmly by everybody. However, the 20 athletes who did agree were amused and very cooperative. The images were used in an editorial on sports and sponsoring. ● Mit seiner Idee, Athleten des österreichischen olympischen Teams von Barcelona einmal anders, nämlich «spanisch» darzustellen, stiess der Photograph nicht überall auf Gegenliebe. Aber die 20 Sportler, die mitmachten, waren amüsiert und zeigten sich sehr kooperativ. Die Bilder wurden in einem Artikel über Sponsoren und Sport verwendet. ▲ L'idée du photographe de présenter les athlètes de l'équipe olympique autrichienne à Barcelone autrement, c'est-à-dire «à l'espagnole», ne fut pas bien accueillie par tous. Mais les 20 sportifs qui décidèrent de jouer le jeu prirent la chose avec humour et ils furent très coopératifs. Ces images ont été reproduites dans un article sur le sponsoring sportif.

PAGE 108 (top right) Photographer: STEVE MARSEL Client: MATTHEW CARTER Camera: SINAR F 4x5" Film: KODAK T-MAX Designer: GARY KOEPKE Agency: KOEPKE DESIGN GROUP Country: USA ■ This photo of type designer Matthew Carter was used for a poster announcing a seminar in which he participated. A slide with letterforms he designed was projected on his face; as the characters conformed to the shape of his face, they distorted, making it even more interesting. ● Matthew Carter ist Schriftentwerfer. Dieses Porträt entstand für die Ankündigung eines Seminars über seine Schriften. Ein Dia mit von ihm entworfenen Schriften wurde auf sein Gesicht projiziert. Ein spezieller Effekt entstand durch die Verzerrung der Buchstaben, verursacht durch die Gesichtsform. ▲ Matthew Carter est créateur de polices. Ce portrait a été réalisé pour l'annonce d'un séminaire sur son travail. On décida de projeter une diapositive d'une de ses créations typographiques sur son visage; ceci produisit une déformation visuelle des caractères.

PAGE 108 (bottom left) Photographer: PETER LIEPKE Camera: CANON F Film: KODACHROME Country: USA ■ Although Philip Boscoe is a multi-faceted actor, the photographer chose to shoot this portrait with a Shakespearian flair. ● Philip Boscoe, ein vielseitiger Schauspieler, der in diesem Porträt eher als Shakespeare-Darsteller gezeigt wird. ▲ Dans ce portrait, Philip Boscoe, un acteur polyvalent, est présenté comme un interprète du répertoire shakespearien.

PAGE 108 (bottom right) Photographer: CHRISTIANE MAREK Camera: FUJI 680 Film: KODAK EKTACHROME 100 PLUS Country: GERMANY ■ Intensive color and double-exposed film were the stylistic devices used to achieve the unique look in this image. ● Durch die Farbintensität der Aufnahme, erreicht durch Doppelbelichtung, erhält diese Photographie den gewünschten Porträtcharakter. ▲ En accentuant l'intensité des couleurs à l'aide d'une double exposition, la photographe a réussi à créer un portrait très étrange, voire inquiétant, de ce personnage à lunettes.

PAGE 109 Photographer: FI MCGHEE Representative: SUZIE JOEL Publisher: TELEGRAPH MAGAZINE Camera: HASSELBLAD Film: FUJI Art Director: MICHAEL COLLINS Country: GREAT BRITAIN ■ A portrait of British actress Glenda Jackson. ● Die britische Schauspielerin Glenda Jackson. ▲ L'actrice anglaise Glenda Jackson.

PAGES 110-111 (Both images) Photographer: MARK SELIGER Publisher: *ROLLING STONE* Art Director: FRED WOODWARD Director of Photography: LAURIE KRATOCHVIL Country: USA ■ Photographs of the bands Red Hot Chili Peppers (left) and Skid Row (right) for *Rolling Stone*. ● Mark Seliger photographierte für *Rolling Stone* die Musiker der Gruppen Red Hot Chili Peppers und Skid Row. ▲ Mark Seliger a photographié les musiciens des groupes Red Hot Chili Peppers et Skid Row pour le magazine *Rolling Stone*.

PAGE 112 (both images) Photographer: MATTHEW ROLSTON Publisher: *ROLLING STONE* Art Director: FRED WOODWARD Director of Photography: LAURIE KRATOCHVIL Country: USA ■ "It is incredible what she can express with her eyes." Photographer Matthew Rolston said, referring to twenty-four year old actress Laura Dern, pictured here. ● «Es ist unglaublich, was sie mit ihren Augen ausdrücken kann.» Der Photograph Matthew Rolston spricht von der Schauspielerin Laura Dern. ▲ «C'est incroyable ce qu'elle peut exprimer avec ses yeux.» C'est ainsi que le photographe Matthew Rolston parle d'une jeune actrice de 24 ans, Laura Dern, dont il a fait le portrait.

PAGE 113 Photographer: MARY ELLEN MARK Publisher: *ROLLING STONE* Art Director: FRED WOODWARD Director of Photography: LAURIE KRATOCHVIL Country: USA ■ "It's not easy being evil in a world that's gone to hell" was the headline of an article about Anton LaVey, who earned a reputation as the Devil incarnate by establishing the Church of Satan in San Francisco, and through his writings, notably *The Satanic Bible*. ● «In einer Welt, die zum Teufel gegangen ist, ist es nicht leicht, teuflisch zu sein», so lautete die Headline zu einem Artikel in der Zeitschrift *Rolling Stone* über Anton La Vey, der sich als Inkarnation des Teufels einen Namen machte: er gründete in San Francisco die Kirche des Satans, und verfasste u.a. «Die satanische Bibel». ▲ «Dans un monde qui est devenu infernal, il n'est pas facile d'être diabolique», tel était le titre de l'article que *Rolling Stone* a consacré à Anton La Vey, un personnage qui s'est fait un nom en se faisant passer pour l'incarnation du diable. Il a fondé l'Eglise de Satan à San Francisco et il a rédigé notamment «La Bible satanique».

PAGE 114 Photographer: GILLES LARRAIN Client: AMERICAN BALLET THEATER Camera: SINAR C2 8x10" Film: KODAK EKTACHROME 64P Country: USA ■ Romeo and Juliet: As the picture was to be used for a life-size poster, Gilles Larrain took the action photograph with a large-format camera. The satin cloth was used as an additional element to add motion. The falling cloth, expression and movement of the dancers, had to be exactly planned and timed. ● Romeo und Julia. Gilles Larrain benutzte eine Grossformat-Kamera, weil die Aufnahme für ein lebensgrosses Plakat verwendet werden sollte. Das Satintuch sorgt für mehr Bewegung im Bild. ▲ Roméo et Juliette. Gilles Larrain a utilisé un appareil grand format, car les clichés devaient être utilisés pour une affiche grandeur nature. L'étoffe de satin devait donner une certaine dynamique à l'image.

PAGE 115 Photographer: RON BAXTER SMITH Camera: SINAR 4x5" Film: POLAROID TYPE 55 Country: CANADA ■ Nude. ● Akt. ▲ Nu.

PAGES 116-117 (all images) Photographer: MARC NORBERG Client: BLUES HEAVEN FOUNDATION Camera: HASSELBLAD ELX Film: KODAK PLUS-X Country: USA ■ In an ongoing assignment, Marc Norberg portrays blues and jazz musicians for the archives of the Blues Heaven Foundation. ● Für das Archiv der Blues-Heaven-Stiftung porträtiert Marc Norberg Blues- und Jazz-Musiker. ▲ Marc Norberg a fait les portraits de ces musiciens de blues pour les archives de la Fondation Blues Heaven.

PAGE 118 Photographer: RINGO TANG Country: HONG KONG ■ Nude with veil. ● Akt mit Schleier. ▲ Nu au voile.

PAGE 119 (both images) Photographer: TOSHIAKI TAKEUCHI Representative: YUKO TEI Cameras: HASSELBLAD 500C, SONNAR CF1 50MM, PENTAX 645 Film: KODAK T-MAX Country: JAPAN ■ The photographer tries to create his images without any preconceived ideas; they evolve during the process. Monochrome negatives are printed as color prints to create an unusual effect through color manipulation. ● Losgelöst von den Grenzen der Realität sucht der Photograph nach neuen Ausdrucksformen. Er geht ohne feste Vorstellung an die Arbeit, seine Bilder entwickeln sich während des Aufnahmeprozesses. Monochrome Negative werden in Farbe gedruckt, um durch Farbmanipulation eine besondere Wirkung zu erzielen. ▲ Le photographe cherche de nouvelles formes d'expression, essayant de se libérer complètement des limites de la réalité. Il procède sans idée préconçue, ses images s'élaborant au cours du processus de prise de vues. Les négatifs monochromes sont imprimés en polychromie, des effets spéciaux étant obtenus grâce à des manipulations de couleurs.

PAGE 120 (top) Photographer: DIETER BLUM Client: GRUNER & JAHR VERLAG Camera: LEICA R5 Film: KODAK EKTACHROME 400 Art Director: WOLFGANG BEHNKEN Country: GERMANY ■ A scene from John Neumeier's ballet version of Johann Sebastian Bach's "Magnificat," commissioned by *Stern* magazine. For 1½ years photographer Dieter Blum followed the work of John Neumeier and the Hamburg ballet. In order to most effectively show the drama in this image, he stood on the lighting walkway. ● Eine Szene aus John Neumeiers Bühneninterpretation des geistlichen Werkes Magnificat von Johann Sebastian Bach. Über einen Zeitraum von 1½ Jahren verfolgte der Photograph Dieter Blum die Arbeit von John Neumeier mit dem Hamburger Ballett. Um die Dramaturgie wirksam darstellen zu können, photographierte er von der Beleuchtungsbühne aus. Es handelte sich um eine Auftragsarbeit für den *Stern*. ▲ Une scène du Magnificat de Johann Sebastian Bach, mis en scène par John Neumeier. Afin d'exprimer pleinement la dramaturgie, Dieter Blum a pris les photos du haut de la rampe des projecteurs. Il a suivi le travail de mise en scène de John Neumeier avec le Ballet de Hambourg pendant un an et demi. Il s'agissait d'une commande du magazine *Stern*.

PAGE 120 (bottom left) Photographer: ROSANNE OLSON Representative: LEHMEN DABNEY, INC. Camera: CAMBO 4x5" Film: POLAROID TYPE 55 Country: USA ■ Richard Dizon, masseur. The premis was to capture the dignity and caring nature of the subject. ● Richard Dizon, Masseur. Rosanne Olson wollte die Würde und Fürsorglichkeit ihres Modells zum Ausdruck bringen. ▲ Richard Dizon, masseur. Rosanne Olson s'est efforcée d'exprimer la dignité et la personnalité pleine de sollicitude de son sujet.

PAGE 120 (bottom right) Photographer: ROSANNE OLSON Representative: LEHMEN DABNEY, INC. Camera: CAMBO 4x5" Film: POLAROID TYPE 55 Country: USA ■ "Sacrifice," a statement of the sacrifices of women in every culture throughout the centuries. ● «Sacrifice» – gemeint sind die Opfer der Frauen in allen Kulturen und in allen Zeiten. ▲ «Sacrifice», un témoignage sur les sacrifices auxquels ont dû se soumettre les femmes de toutes les cultures à toutes les époques.

PAGE 121 Photographer: WALTER FOGEL Camera: NIKONOS V Film: AGFA CT 21 Country: GERMANY ■ Under water, man loses his shyness of the camera and moves freely, weightlessly. The photographer used colored gel sheets, positive film developed as negative film, and a self-devised flash in combination with his camera. ● Unter Wasser verliert der Mensch die Scheu vor der Kamera, er bewegt sich schwerelos und frei. Der Photograph benutzte farbige Lackfolien, einen Diafilm, der als Negativfilm entwickelt wurde, und eine von ihm konstruierte Blitzanlage. ▲ Sous l'eau, l'individu perd toute inhibition devant l'appareil photo; il se meut en apesanteur, librement. Walter Fogel a utilisé ici de la toile cirée, un film positif développé comme un négatif et une installation de flash qu'il a construite spécialement.

PAGE 122 (top left) Photographer: MAX AGUILERA-HELLWEG Representative: ONYX Publisher: *ENTERTAINMENT WEEKLY* Camera: EBONY SV 4x5" Film: KODAK EPP 100 Photo Editors: MARY DUNN, DORIS BRAUTIGAN Country: USA ■ Thirty minutes was all American film director Martin Scorsese would allow for this portrait for *Entertainment Weekly*. Furthermore, it had to be done right next to his appartment. This resulting picture was taken at Josef Astor's breakfast nook. ● Gerade 30 Minuten gab der amerikanische Filmregisseur Martin Scorsese dem Photographen für die Porträtaufnahmen, die in einem Artikel der Zeitschrift *Entertainment Weekly* erscheinen sollten. Ausserdem mussten die Aufnahmen gleich neben seiner New Yorker Wohnung stattfinden. ▲ Le photographe ne disposait que de 30 minutes pour faire un portrait du cinéaste Martin Scorsese, qui devait illustrer un article du magazine *Entertainment Weekly*. En plus, il lui fallut prendre ces photos à proximité de l'appartement new-yorkais du réalisateur.

PAGE 122 (top right) Photographer: MICHAEL LLEWELLYN Representative: ONYX Publisher: CONDÉ NAST PUBLICATIONS, *DETAILS* Camera: SINAR F, 150MM Film: KODAK T-MAX 100, EKTACHROME PLUS 4x5" Art Director: GREG POND Country: USA ■ The assignment was to portray Tim Burton in relation to his movie *Batman Returns*. ● Der Auftrag von *Details* war ein Porträt des Regisseurs Tim Burton, das auf seinen Film *Batman Returns* anspielen sollte. ▲ Le photographe avait reçu mandat de faire un portrait du cinéaste Tim Burton qui évoque son film, «Le retour de Batman».

PAGE 122 (bottom left) Photographer: MARK HANAUER Representative: ONYX Publisher: *ENTERTAINMENT WEEKLY* Photo Editors: MARY DUNN, DORIS BRAUTIGAN Camera: SINAR Film: POLAROID TYPE 55 Country: USA ■ The image, destined for the cover of *Entertainment Weekly*, merely had to say "Batman." ● Das für den Umschlag der Zeitschrift *Entertainment Weekly* bestimmte Bild sollte schlicht «Batman» sagen. ▲ Cette image pour *Entertainment Weekly* devait tout simplement représenter «Batman».

PAGE 122 (bottom right) Photographer: MICHELE CLEMENT Representative: NORMAN MASLOV Publisher: *NEW YORK TIMES MAGAZINE* Camera: MAMIYA RZ 67 Film: ILFORD FP 4 Art Director: KATHY RYAN Country: USA ■ Daniel Day-Lewis is known as an actor who portrays a role with such devotion that he can suffer physically and mentally from it. This portrait had to reflect this intensity, so photographer Michele Clement prepared three different situations to be ready to shoot when the actor arrived. Despite warnings to the contrary by the public relations representative, Day-Lewis proved to be an excellent model. ● Daniel Day-Lewis ist als ein Schauspieler bekannt, der sich so in seine Rollen hineinversetzt, dass er physisch und psychisch darunter leidet. Sein Porträt für das *New York Times Magazine* musste seiner Intensität gerecht werden. Entgegen den Warnungen der PR-Person erwies sich Day-Lewis als hervorragendes Modell. ▲ L'acteur américain Daniel Day-Lewis est connu pour sa faculté de s'investir dans les rôles qu'il interprète, au point de mettre en jeu sa santé physique et mentale. Michele Clement avait préparé trois mises en scène avant que l'acteur n'arrive. Contrairement aux avertissements des responsables en relations publiques, Day-Lewis s'avéra un modèle exceptionnel.

PAGE 123 Photographer: SANDRA EISNER Client: JAMIE BAUM Camera: NIKON F3 Film: KODAK EES Country: USA ■ The photographer focused on the connection that flutist and composer Jamie Baum has with her instrument and her music. ● Der Photographin ging es um die fast organische Verbundenheit der Flötistin und Komponistin Jamie Baum mit ihrem Instrument und ihrer Musik. ▲ La photographe a voulu montrer ici la symbiose entre l'intrument et son interprète, la flûtiste et compositrice Jamie Baum.

PAGE 124 Photographer: TIMOTHY WHITE Representative: ONYX Publisher: *AMERICAN FILM MAGAZINE* Camera: MAMIYA RZ 67 Film: POLAROID TYPE 665 Art Director: FRANCINE HILL Stylists: DEBRA WAKNIN, STEFAN ERICKSON Country: USA ■ In order to obtain cool tones in important portions and warmer tones in other areas, the prints of this portrait of Jeremy Irons were first produced 2-3 stops too dark, selenium toned, then bleached back to the level the photographer desired. ● Porträt des Schauspielers Jeremy Irons. Um im wichtigsten Bereich kühle Töne zu erhalten, während die Töne in den anderen Bereichen wärmer sein sollten, wurden die Bilder zuerst zwei bis drei Stufen zu dunkel gedruckt, dann erhielten sie eine Selentönung und wurden schliesslich aufgehellt. ▲ Portrait de l'acteur Jeremy Irons. Afin d'obtenir des teintes froides dans les parties les plus importantes de la photo, tout en conservant des tons plus chauds dans d'autres, les tirages furent d'abord imprimés trop foncé, puis teintés au sélénium et éclaircis conformément aux instructions du photographe.

PAGE 125 Photographer: MARK SELIGER Publisher: *ROLLING STONE* Art Director: FRED WOODWARD Director of Photography: LAURIE KRATOCHVIL Country: USA ■ This image was used for a story on the band Metallica. ● *Rolling Stone* brachte einen Artikel über die Gruppe Metallica. ▲ Cette photo a été utilisée pour un article de *Rolling Stone* sur le groupe Metallica.

PAGE 126 (top left) Photographer: JEFF SOWARDS Camera: PENTAX 6x7" Film: KODAK TRI-X PAN Country: USA ■ This surreal image shows the back of a man's head with intriguing structures. ● Dieses surreal wirkende Bild zeigt den Hinterkopf eines Mannes. Der Photograph war fasziniert von den Strukturen. ▲ Ce que l'on voit en réalité sur cette image absolument surréaliste n'est autre que la nuque d'un homme. Le photographe était fasciné par les effets de structures.

PAGE 126 (top right) Photographer: DAVID HOLT Stylist: STEVE POLINSKY Country: USA ■ Even after having finished seven photographs on the theme of Christ's crucifixion, the photographer felt that he had just touched the surface of this extraordinary subject and decided to do an entire book. ● Nachdem er sieben Bilder fertiggestellt hatte, wurde sich der Photograph bewusst, dass er gerade die Oberfläche des aussergewöhnlichen Themas der Kreuzigung Christi berührt hatte, und er beschloss, ein ganzes Buch zu machen. ▲ Après avoir terminé sept photos sur le thème de la Crucifixion, le photographe se rendit compte qu'il n'avait fait qu'effleurer le sujet; il décida en conséquence d'y consacrer un livre tout entier.

PAGE 126 (bottom left) Photographer: HOWARD SCHATZ Publisher: PACIFIC PHOTOGRAPHIC PRESS Camera: HASSELBLAD Film: KODAK PXP Art Director: HOWARD SCHATZ Country: USA ■ *Gifted Women* is the title of a book that celebrates talented, successful women from the San Francisco Bay area. They are artists, musicians, scientists, dancers, writers, managers, etc. whose passionate efforts to achieve interested the photographer the most. This is a portrait of Amy McCombs, President and General Manager of KRON-TV in San Francisco. ● *Gifted Women* ist der Titel eines Buches, das begabten, erfolgreichen Frauen aus der Gegend von San Francisco gewidmet ist. Es sind Künstlerinnen, Musikerinnen, Wissenschaftlerinnen, Tänzerinnen, Schriftstellerinnen, Managerinnen, etc. Es ging dem Photographen dabei um ihr leidenschaftliches Bemühen, ihr Ziel zu erreichen. Gezeigt ist ein Porträt von Amy McCombs, die seit April 1988 Direktorin und Geschäftsführerin von KRON-TV in San Francisco ist. ▲ *Gifted Women* est un livre qui rassemble des portraits de femmes de la région de San Francisco qui ont réussi. Elles sont artistes, musiciennes, scientifiques, danseuses, écrivaines, directrices d'entreprises. Le photographe ne désirait pas tant représenter leur succès que la passion qui les anime chacune dans leur domaine. Nous voyons ici un portrait d'Amy McCombs, qui occupe depuis 1988 le poste de directrice de KRON-TV, à San Francisco.

PAGE 126 (bottom right) Photographer: STEVE MARSEL Camera: SINAR F 4x5" Film: KODAK T-MAX 100 Country: USA ■ Steve Marsel likes humor in his self-portraits, which he considers an excellent means of self-examination. ● Steve Marsel mag Selbstporträts mit Humor. Für ihn sind sie ein gutes Mittel, über sich selbst nachzudenken. ▲ Le photographe Steve Marsel aime créer des autoportraits plein d'humour. Il les considère comme une excellente méthode d'introspection.

PAGE 127 Photographer: HOWARD SCHATZ Publisher: PACIFIC PHOTOGRAPHIC PRESS Camera: HASSELBLAD Film: KODAK PXP Art Director: HOWARD SCHATZ Country: USA ■ *Gifted Women* is the title of a book that celebrates talented, successful women from the San Francisco Bay area. ● *Gifted Women* ist der Titel eines Buches, das begabten, erfolgreichen Frauen aus der Gegend von San Francisco gewidmet ist. ▲ *Gifted Women* est un livre qui rassemble des portraits de femmes de la région de San Francisco qui ont réussi.

PAGE 128 Photographer: SUE BENNETT Country: USA ■ A Native American, photographed with natural light. ● Indianerin, mit natürlichem Licht photographiert. ▲ Une autochtone de l'Amérique, photographié sous une lumière naturelle.

PAGE 129 Photographer: GREG BOOTH Client: GREG BOOTH Camera: NIKON F4 Film: AGFAPAN 25 Art Directors: GREG BOOTH/DICK MITCHELL Designer: DICK MITCHELL Agency: RBMM/THE RICHARDS GROUP Country: USA ■ A young Indian guide brought the photographer, Greg Booth, to the ancient cliff dwellings of the Navaho Indians in Canyon De Chelly, Arizona. Even more than the mystical landscape, the faces of its inhabitants fascinated him, so the grandparents of his guide agreed to serve as his models. The cowboy hat of the grandfather, which he instisted on wearing despite his Indian-style clothing, cast a shadow on his figure, providing a perfect backdrop for his wife's leathery face which seemed to echo the striations of the ancient cliff beyond. ● Ein junger indianischer Führer brachte den Photographen Greg Booth zu den alten Felsbehausungen der Navajo-Indianer im Canyon De Chelly, Arizona. Noch mehr als die fast mystische Landschaft interessierten ihn die Gesichter ihrer Bewohner. Die Grosseltern des Führers waren bereit, sich photographieren zu lassen. Der Cowboyhut des Grossvaters, von dem er sich trotz indianischer Tracht nicht trennen wollte, warf Schatten auf seine Gestalt. Er wurde zum perfekten Hintergrund für das sonnengegerbte Gesicht seiner Frau, auf dem sich die Furchen des Felsens zu wiederholen scheinen. ▲ Un jeune guide indien avait conduit le photographe Greg Booth sur le site des anciennes habitations troglodytiques des Indiens Navajo, dans le Canyon De Chelly, en Arizona. Plus encore que le paysage, ce furent les visages des habitants de cette contrée qui le fascinèrent. Les grands-parents du guide acceptèrent de se faire photographier. Malgré son costume indien, le grand-père ne voulut pas ôter son chapeau de cow-boy; l'ombre de sa sihouette constitue un fond idéal, contre lequel se détache le visage buriné de soleil de sa femme; les sillons des roches séculaires semblent s'y refléter.

PAGE 130 Photographer: MICHAEL BIONDO Clients: KRIS KROSS, SONY MUSIC Camera: HASSELBLAD Film: FUJI, KODAK Art Director/Designer: STACY DRUMMOND Stylist: TANJA TWIST Country: USA ■ This photograph of the rap group Kris Kross by Michael Biondo was used for an album cover. ● Michael Biondo photographierte die Rap-Gruppe Kris Kross für eine Schallplattenhülle. ▲ Michael Biondo a photographié le groupe de rap Kris Kross pour une couverture d'album.

PAGE 131 Photographer: ROLAND FISCHER Representative: GALERIE SCHNEIDER Publisher: *FAZ MAGAZIN* Camera: MAMIYA RB67 Film: VPS 120 Art Director: HANS-GEORG POSPISCHIL Country: GERMANY ■ Concentrated but absent, close and yet far away—Roland Fischer photographs his models in swimming pools. Normally they stand in the water for an hour, clad in divers' suits, held down by weights, their arms crossed on their backs. He is interested in the model's look, the personality of the model is immaterial; some did not even recognize themselves afterwards. ● Konzentriert sollen sie sein, aber ohne Anteilnahme, ganz nah und doch entrückt. Roland Fischer photographiert seine Modelle im Swimmingpool. Meistens stehen sie eine Stunde im Wasser, eingezwängt in Taucheranzüge, mit Gewichten nach unten gezogen, die Arme auf dem Rücken verschränkt. Der Blick seiner Modelle interessiert ihn, die Persönlichkeit ist ihm gleichgültig. Manche haben sich nicht einmal wiedererkannt. ▲ Totalement concentrée, à la fois proche et lointaine, la femme vue par Roland Fischer. Il fait poser ses modèles dans une piscine. La plupart du temps, elles sont obligées de rester une heure entière dans l'eau, le corps emprisonné dans un vêtement de plongée, les mains dans le dos, complètement immobiles. Leur personnalité lui importe peu, seul l'intensité du regard l'intéresse. Certaines ont eu de la peine à se reconnaître lorsqu'elles découvrent leur photo.

PAGES 132-133 (all images) Photographer: MICHEL DUBOIS Representative: PAUL FRIEDLAND Publisher: LES ÉDITIONS LOUISE Camera: SINAR P 4x5" Film: KODAK T-MAX AND INFRARED Art Director: MICHEL DUBOIS Country: FRANCE ■ *Mnemosyne* is the title Michel Dubois gave to his book of images of women with poetic texts by Jean-David Jumeau-Lafond. Mnemosyne is the goddess of memory, mother of the nine Muses, and this work concerns itself with unreal memories, with which the observer feels acquainted. ● *Mnemosyne* nennt Michel Dubois seinen Photoband mit Frauenbildern und Texten von Jean-David Jumeau-Lafond. Mnemosyne ist die Göttin des Gedächtnisses, Mutter der neun Musen, und in diesem Band geht es um Erinnerungen, nicht real aber möglich. ▲ Ces photos de Michel Dubois figurent dans un livre au titre évocateur de *Mnemosyne*, personnification de la Mémoire dans la mythologie grecque, qui engendra les neuf Muses. Les images des femmes sont accompagnées d'un texte de Jean-David Jumeau-Lafond. L'ouvrage met en scène des souvenirs imaginaires, qui peuvent toutefois paraître familiers au spectateur.

PAGE 134 Photographer: MICHAEL HOGREFE Camera: SINAR P2 8x10" Film: AGFACHROME 100 RS PROFESSIONAL Country: GERMANY ■ How does a photographer handle extreme conditions such as photographing metal parts in a dark area, liquid with colorless objects arrranged in a color photograph, with a certain plasticity and absolute sharpness? The photographer succeeded in making a colorful, pliant image out of this monochrome composition. ● Wie kommt man mit extremen Aufnahmebedingungen zurecht, zum Beispiel mit Metallteilen auf/in dunkler Fläche, Flüssigkeit und farblosen Sujets, arrangiert in einer Farbaufnahme mit Plastizität und absoluter Schärfe? Diese monochrome Komposition spricht für sich. ▲ Comment faire pour résoudre des conditions de prises de vues extrêmes: clés anglaises, écrous et vis flottant sur une flaque de pétrole noirâtre? Le photographe a relevé le défi, faisant de cet arrangement monochrome une image en couleurs d'une grande plasticité et d'une netteté absolue.

PAGE 136 (top) Photographer: RON FEHLING Representative: WESTSIDE STUDIO Camera: CAMBO 4x5" Film: FUJI-RDP 100 Country: CANADA ■ Honey: the essense of purity and nature, of tradition. The accentuating light and warm, monochromatic tones of the objects, as well as the blurred background, lend the desired mood to this photograph, which was exposed separately with greatly diffused lighting. ● Honig, das Gefühl von Reinheit und Natürlichkeit, von Althergebrachtem. Die gewünschte Stimmung erreichte der Photograph durch das akzentuiert gesetzte Licht, die warmen Töne der Gegenstände und den verschwommenen Hintergrund, den er separat mit starker Überstrahlung belichtete. ▲ La pureté d'un produit traditionnel naturel, le miel. Le photographe a obtenu l'atmosphère souhaitée en dirigeant la lumière sur les objets aux teintes chaudes. Il a en outre éclairé l'arrière-plan à l'aide d'une lumière diffuse.

PAGE 136 (middle) Photographer: TERRY HEFFERNAN Client: BATTLE MOUNTAIN GOLD Camera: SINAR P Film: EKTACHROME 100 Designer: KENNY RAGLAND Agency: SAVAGE DESIGN GROUP Country: USA ■ This image is part of a photographic essay on the "Beauty of Gold" and was used in the Battle Mountain Gold Annual Report. ● Dieses Bild gehört zu einem Photoessay über die Schönheit des Goldes. Es wurde im Jahresbericht von Battle Mountain Gold verwendet. ▲ Cette image est tirée d'un reportage photo sur la beauté de l'or. Elle a été reproduite dans un rapport annuel.

PAGE 136 (bottom) Photographer: LAURIE RUBIN Representative: RANDI FIAT & ASSOCIATES Client: WACE USA Camera: CAMBO Film: KODAK EKTACHROME Art Director/Designer: DON MORAVICK Agency: ART IN PROGRESS Country: USA ■ The client was a conglomeration of companies in the graphic industry whose intent was to demonstrate their capabilities in a brochure. First you see the woman, then the unexpected rest, the photographs of single elements were then combined electronically. ● Die Aufnahme entstand im Auftrag eines Konglomerats von Firmen im Bereich der graphischen Industrie. Erst sieht man die Frau, dann das unerwartete Ende. Die einzelnen Elemente wurden elektronisch zusammengefügt. ▲ Il s'agissait ici d'une commande d'une association d'entreprises spécialisées dans le secteur de l'industrie graphique. Au premier coup d'œil, on voit la femme – puis on découvre la femme-objet. Cette image surréaliste a été composée grâce à un processus d'intégration électronique.

PAGE 137 (all images) Photographer: STEFAN KIRCHNER Client: DENHALI/ROMEO GIGLI PROFUMO Camera: DEARDORFF 8x10" Film: KODAK EKTACHROME Art Director: CHRISTOPH RADL Stylist: NADINE ASIOLI Agency: ITALIANA DI COMMUNICAZIONE Country: ITALY ■ The African and Indian style windows were reconstructed in the studio, then the perfume bottle was photographed in as natural a light as possible. ● Die drei Fenster wurden im Studio nachgebaut. Dann wurde der Parfumflakon in möglichst natürlich wirkendem Licht photographiert. ▲ Les fenêtres de styles africain et indien ont été construites en studio. Ensuite, le flacon de parfum a été photographié dans une lumière qui devait avoir l'air aussi naturelle que possible.

PAGE 138 Photographer: ALEXANDER BAYER Client: VISION FOTOSTUDIO Camera: SINAR P2 Film: AGFA RS 100 4/5" Art Director: ALEXANDER BAYER Country: SWITZERLAND ■ A new lighting technique in car photography: by means of light painting (Hosemaster) the photographer obtained the extreme contrasts between the Corvette and the cloth. The photo was used as promotion for the photographer's book *Portraits*. ● Eine neue Lichtführung in der Autophotographie: mit Hilfe von Lightpainting (Hosemaster) erreichte der Photograph die übersteigerten Kontraste auf der Corvette und dem Tuch. Die Aufnahme diente als Eigenwerbung für das Buch *Portraits*. ▲ Une révolution dans la photographie de voitures: à l'aide de la lightpainting (Hosemaster), le photographe a créé des effets de contraste lumineux extrêmes sur la Corvette et sur l'étoffe. Cette image a été utilisée comme publicité pour le livre *Portraits*.

PAGE 139 Photographer: RODNEY RASCONA Representative: RITA HOLT Client: AUDI OF AMERICA Camera: SINAR 4x5" Film: KODAK EKTACHROME Art Director/Designer: BARRY SHEPARD Agency: SHR DESIGN COMMUNICATIONS Country: USA ■ This Horch 853, an Audi from 1930, is exhibited in the Deutsche Museum in Munich. The purpose of this photograph was to show the traditional design heritage of the current Audi V8 Quatro. ● Dieser Horch 853, ein Audi aus dem Jahre 1930, steht im Deutschen Museum in München. Rodney Rascona photographierte ihn für Audi of America. Es ging dabei um die Designtradition des heutigen Audi V8 Quatro. ▲ Ce modèle de Horch 853, une Audi de l'année 1930, est exposé au Deutsche Museum de Munich. Rodney Rascona l'a photographié pour Audi of America. Il s'agissait ici de mettre l'accent sur le design de tradition de la Audi V8 Quatro.

PAGE 140 (right) Photographer: DANIEL HARTZ Client: DURAVIT AG Camera: SINAR PII Film: KODAK EPP Creative Director: DIETER BRUCKLACHER Art Director: DANIEL HARTZ Designer: SIEGER DESIGN (PRODUCT) Agency: WERBUNG etc. Country: GERMANY ■ The location was chosen in accordance with the "deconstructivist" style of the washstand: the Parc de la Villette, in Paris. ● Dem «dekonstruktivistischen» Stil des Waschtisches entsprechend wurde die Location ausgewählt: der Parc de la Villette in Paris. ▲ La pho-

tographie a été prise dans le cadre du Parc de la Villette, un lieu qui va bien avec le style «déconstructiviste» de ce lavabo.

PAGE 141 (both images) Photographer: EMILIO TREMOLADA Client: DRIADE SpA Camera: SINAR Art Director: ADELAIDE ACERBI Country: ITALY ■ A dramatic play of light and shadows with canvasses that capture the silhouettes and show elements of the furniture—with these stylistic tools the photographer produced images that set themselves apart from the conventional presentation of furniture. These photographs were used in a catalog of Driade. Shown are designs by (top) Elliott Littman and (bottom) Borek Sipek. ● Ein dramatisches Spiel von Licht und Schatten mit Leinwänden, die Silhouetten aufnehmen oder Elemente der Möbel zeigen – mit diesen Stilmitteln wurden Photographien inszeniert, die nichts mit der üblichen Darstellung von Möbeln zu tun haben. Verwendet wurden diese Aufnahmen in einem Katalog von Driade. Die Designs sind von Elliott Littman und Borek Sipek. ▲ Un éclairage contrasté et un arrière-plan de toiles, sur lesquelles sont projetées les silhouettes ou des détails des meubles. Cette mise en scène a permis au photographe de créer des images qui sont différentes des représentations habituelles de ce sujet. Les meubles ont été dessinés par Elliott Littman et Borek Sipek, et reproduits dans un catalogue de Driade.

PAGES 142-143 Photographer: MICHAEL SIEGER Client: MARSBERGER GLASWERKE RITZENHOFF GMBH Camera: MAMIYA 645, CANON EOS 600 Art Director: MICHAEL SIEGER Designer: SIEGER DESIGN (PRODUCTS) Stylists: MICHAEL AND CHRISTIAN SIEGER Agency: SIEGER DESIGN CONSULTING GMBH Country: GERMANY ■ The location chosen for these images was castle Harkotten, headquarters of Sieger Design, the creators of a new collection for Marsberger Glassworks. Abstraction and ambiance reinforce the philosophy of the products. ● Location für diese Aufnahmen war Schloss Harkotten, der Sitz von Sieger Design, Gestalter einer neuen Kollektion für die Marsberger Glaswerke. Abstrahierung und stimmungsvolles Ambiente unterstützen den Anspruch der Produkte. ▲ Ces photos dont été prises au château de Harkotten, le siège de la firme Sieger Design, pour le lancement d'une nouvelle collection d'objets de verre. L'abstraction et le cadre ambiant soulignent les exigences du produit.

PAGE 144 (top) Photographer: AK WERBEFOTOGRAFIE Client: ROSENTHAL Camera: PLAUBEL 13x18" Film: KODAK EPN Country: GERMANY ■ Exclusive products made by Rosenthal were placed on a platform coated with roofing felt and photographed with a low camera angle. ● Exklusive Produkte der Firma Rosenthal, von einem tiefen Kamerastandpunkt aus auf einem Podest photographiert. Dachpappe diente als Untergrund. Die Aufnahme wurde in einem Möbelprospekt verwendet. ▲ Des produits exclusifs de la firme Rosenthal disposés sur une plate-forme et photographiés dans une perspective à ras de terre sur un sol de carton-pierre.

PAGE 144 (bottom) Photographer: SUE STAFFORD Client: POWERHOUSE MUSEUM Camera: SINAR 4x5" Film: KODAK EKTACHROME 100 PLUS Designer: MARC NEWSON (PRODUCT) Country: AUSTRALIA ■ The "Lockheed Lounge," designed by Marc Newson, was photographed for a book and permanent exhibition on "Success and Innovation in Australia's Industries." The lounge was lit from above by a large soft light source with several reflectors strategically placed. ● Die «Lockheed Lounge», eine von Marc Newson entworfene Chaiselongue, wurde für das Buch und die permanente Ausstellung «Erfolg und Innovation in der australischen Industrie» aufgenommen. Beleuchtet wurde sie von oben mit weichem Licht aus einer grossen Lichtquelle und diversen strategisch plazierten Reflektoren. ▲ Cette chaise-longue, dessinée par Marc Newson, a été photographiée pour le livre et l'exposition permanente «Succès et innovation dans l'industrie australienne». Elle a été éclairée d'en haut par une source lumineuse diffuse, renforcée de réflecteurs judicieusement disposés.

PAGE 145 Photographer: KRIS RODAMMER Camera: NIKON F3 Film: KODACHROME 64 Country: USA ■ This chair was constructed and painted by an elderly gentleman who had a fondness for this particular shade of green, a color he actually used in painting his entire house. The photographer was concerned with the intriguing and surprising use of color in everyday things. ● Ein alter Mann mit einer besonderen Vorliebe für diesen speziellen Grünton hat den Stuhl gebaut und angestrichen. Sein ganzes Haus hat diesen Farbton. Dem Photographen geht es um den eigenartigen, oft überraschenden Gebrauch von Farben für ganz alltägliche Dinge. ▲ Cette chaise a été construite et peinte par un vieux monsieur qui aime tout particulièrement cette nuance de vert, au point qu'il en a fait recouvrir tous les murs de sa maison. Le photographe a voulu mettre en relief le rôle de la couleur, qui peut transformer les objets les plus quotidiens de manière surprenante.

PAGE 146 Photographer: MICHAEL FURMAN Representative: VICTORIA SATTERTHWAITE Client: POTLATCH PAPER COMPANY Camera: NIKON Film: KODACHROME Designer: KERRY POLITE Agency: POLITE DESIGN Country: USA ■ Michael Furman took a series of detailed photographs of bicyles for a variety of purposes, including promoting a special edition bicycle, the Quest. The images were used in a book produced by Potlatch Paper Corporation to demonstrate the print quality of their Eloquence line of paper. ● Diese Detailaufnahme diente der Verkaufsförderung von Quest, einer Sonderreihe von Fahrrädern, die von Spectrum lanciert wurde. Das Bild wurde auch in einer Broschüre des Papierherstellers Potlatch verwendet. ▲ Ce détail a été utilisé pour la promotion de Quest, une nouvelle ligne de vélos lancée par Spectrum. L'image a été reproduite dans une brochure du fabricant de papier Potlatch.

PAGE 147 (all images) Photographer: CLINT CLEMENS Representative: ART + COMMERCE Camera: SINAR P 4x5" Film: KODAK F 100 Art Director: WARREN JOHNSON Backdrop: PATTY BURNS Agency: CARMICHAEL LYNCH Country: USA ■ These shots of Harley Davidson motorcycles were made with available light in abondoned warehouses, allowing each detail to receive the attention it deserves. ● Porträtaufnahmen der Harley Davidson, in verlassenen Lagerhäusern mit natürlichem Licht aufgenommen. Jedem Detail sollte die ihm gebührende Aufmerksamkeit zukommen. ▲ Des photos de motos Harley Davidson mises en scène comme des portraits de studio! Elles ont été prises à la lumière du jour dans des entrepôts abandonnés. Les plus infimes détails ont été rendus avec le même souci de précision.

PAGE 148 (top) Photographer: CLAUDIO LAZI Client: LORIS AZZARO Art Director: ALBERT VELLI Country: FRANCE ■ "Acteur," Eau de Toilette by Loris Azzaro for men. ● Werbung für Loris Azzaros Herren-Eau-de-Toilette «Acteur». ▲ Publicité pour «Acteur», l'eau de toilette pour hommes de Loris Azzaro.

PAGE 148 (bottom) Photographer: JIM DIVITALE Representative: SANDY DIVITALE Camera: HORSEMAN 4x5" Film: KODAK EKTACHROME 100 PLUS Country: USA ■ Because of their small size, glass packaging and transparency of the liquid itself, perfume bottles are a particular challenge. Here, the composition emphasizes the special shape of the bottle and was lit with only one light source—the Hosemaster Light Painting System. ● Aufnahmen von Parfumflaschen bedeuten wegen ihrer kleinen Grösse, der Glasverpackung und der Transparenz der Flüssigkeit eine besondere Herausforderung für den Photographen. Die Komposition betont hier die spezielle Form der gewählten Flasche. Beleuchtet wurde nur mit einer Lichtquelle, dem Hosemaster-Light-Painting-System. ▲ La taille de ces flacons de parfum, leur emballage de verre et la transparence du liquide représentaient une véritable gageure pour le photographe. La composition souligne ici la forme particulière de la bouteille. Elle a été éclairée au moyen d'un système de lightpainting Hosemaster.

PAGE 149 Photographer: DETLEF ODENHAUSEN Camera: HORSEMAN 4x5" Film: KODAK EPP Country: GERMANY ■ A medium blue filter lends to this image a sense of coolness that a fan provides. ● Ein mittlerer Blaufilter sorgte bei dieser Aufnahme für das Gefühl von Kühle, die ein Ventilator spendet. ▲ L'effet rafraîchissant d'un ventilateur a été rendu au moyen d'un filtre bleu moyen.

PAGE 150 Photographer: PAULO GREUEL Publisher: DONNA MAGAZINE Camera: NIKON F3 Film: POLACHROME CS 135 Art Director: GIANNI BRANCACCIO Country: ITALY ■ "Art and fashion." Italian magazine *Donna* presented shoes and accessories like art. ● «Kunst und Mode». Die italienische Zeitschrift *Donna* präsentierte Schuhe und Accessoires wie Kunst. ▲ «Art et Mode». Des chaussures et des accessoires présentés comme des peintures dans le magazine italien *Donna*.

PAGE 151 Photographer: VICTORIA HUBER Camera: NIKON F4 Film: AGFACHROME 1000 RS Country: GERMANY ■ Form and dream, reality and vision. Beautiful things, depicted in soft, monochrome color. ● Gestalt und Traum, Realität und Vision. Schöne Dinge, inszeniert in sanfter Farbstimmung. ▲ La forme et le rêve, la vision et la réalité. De beaux objets, mis en scène dans une atmosphère douce.

PAGE 152 (top left) Photographer: AXEL DÖHLER Camera: SINAR F 4x5" Film: KODAK EKTACHROME 100 PLUS Art Director: JOSEPH DUFFY Country: USA ■ The photographer constructed the rusty, industrial-looking set in his studio in juxtaposition to the modern athletic shoes, conveying strength and endurance. A low camera angle was chosen to make the shoe look majestic and add drama. The set was lit with 6 individual lightsources, diffused in certain areas. ● Die Aufbauten mit dem rostigen, industriellen Look konstruierte der Photograph im Studio, als Kontrast zu den modernen Sportschuhen, die Kraft und Ausdauer bedeuten. Er entschied sich für einen tiefen Kamerastandort, um dem Schuh etwas Majestätisches zu verleihen und Spannung zu erzeugen. Die Beleuchtung erfolgte durch sechs Lichtquellen. ▲ Le photographe a construit en studio les superstructures rouillées, qui créent un look industriel, en contraste avec les chaussures de sport, symboles d'énergie et d'endurance. Il a choisi un angle de vue assez bas, afin de donner plus de majesté à la chaussure et susciter une certaine tension. L'éclairage a été obtenu au moyen de six sources lumineuses.

PAGE 152 (top right) Photographer: CHRIS AIREY Camera: SINAR 8x10" Film: KODAK EKTACHROME 64T Country: GREAT BRITAIN ■ The photographer was a student at Blackpool College when he took this photograph. He makes it look like a painting by using a sheet of clear glass in front of the camera lens, then painting dark colors and vaseline onto certain areas of the glass and with a slight camera movement, the desired effect was created. ● Chris Airey war Student der Photoklasse am Blackpool College in London, als er diese Aufnahme machte. Er arbeitete mit einer klaren Glasscheibe vor dem Kameraobjektiv, die er stellenweise mit dunklen Farben und Vaseline bemalte. Mit einer leichten Bewegung der Kamera wurde der gewünschte Effekt erzielt. ▲ Chris Airey était encore étudiant en photographie au Blackpool College au moment où il a réalisé cette photo. Il a fixé une plaque de verre devant l'objectif de son appareil, la recouvrant par endroits de couleur foncée et de vaseline. Il a obtenu l'effet souhaité grâce à un léger mouvement de la caméra.

PAGE 152 (bottom left) Photographer: JODY DOLE Client: PHILIPS LIGHTING Camera: NIKON F4s Art Director: LARRY BENNETT Designer: JODY DOLE Agency: McKINNEY + SILVER Country: USA ■ The transparency of a lightbulb, captured in a practically monochrome photograph. The background was created by Jody Dole using custom built lighting and a lenticular screen film. ● Die Transparenz einer Glühbirne, interpretiert in einem fast monochromen Bild. Der Photograph verwendete eine spezielle Beleuchtungsanlage und einen Linsenrasterfilm. ▲ La transparence d'une ampoule électrique, exprimée dans une image presque monochrome. Pour le fond, le photographe a utilisé un éclairage spécial et un film lenticulaire tramé.

PAGE 152 (bottom right) Photographer: JODY DOLE Client: KPMG PEAT MARWICK Camera: NIKON F3 Film: 3M 1000 Art Director/Designer: DONNA M. BONAVITA Country: USA ■ The principles of quality measurement were the subject of an issue of the client's customer magazine *World*. Antique scientific measuring devices served as a visual metaphor. ● Prinzipien der Qualitätsmessung war das Thema der Kundenzeitschrift des Auftraggebers. Alte wissenschaftliche Messgeräte dienten dabei als visuelle Metapher. ▲ Les principes qui régissent une production de qualité étaient le sujet d'un numéro du magazine d'information publié par le mandant. D'anciens instruments de mesure servent de métaphores visuelles.

PAGE 153 Photographer: ZAFER & BARBARA BARAN Camera: MAMIYA RB 67 Film: KODAK EKTACHROME EPY 120 Country: GREAT BRITAIN ■ The photographers almost exclusively used Tungsten back lighting to emphasize their subject. ● Die Photographen arbeiteten fast ausschliesslich mit Tungsten-Hintergrundbeleuchtung, um den Gegenstand zu betonen. ▲ Les photographes ont presque exclusivement utilisé l'éclairage tungstène de l'arrière-plan, afin de mettre en relief l'objet.

PAGE 154 Photographer: NOB FUKUDA Client: KNOLL INTERNATIONAL JAPAN Camera: TOYO VIEW 4x5" Film: KODAK PLUS-X Country: JAPAN ■ The harmony of a traditional Japanese temple (Daikakuji in Kyoto) and modern furniture. Knoll International used this photograph for advertising purposes. ● Harmonie zwischen der Architektur eines traditionellen japanischen Tempels, dem Daikakuji in Kyoto, und modernen Möbeln. Knoll International verwendete die Aufnahme für Werbezwecke. ▲ L'harmonie entre l'architecture d'un temple japonais et la ligne d'un meuble contemporain. Cette photo a été utilisée comme publicité par Knoll International.

PAGE 155 Photographer: WILLIAM SHARPE Client: SHARPE NICHOLS CO. Camera: SINAR C Film: KODAK 64T Country: USA ■ The end of a workday, a time to relax in the comfort of a timeless piece of furniture: the Paris Club Chair. The reader was to experience a quiet moment. The photographer decided on a precise time of day for shooting, and used all natural light with white reflectors. ● Das Ende eines Arbeitstages, Zeit zum Entspannen in einem zeitlosen, bequemen Sessel, einem Klassiker. Der Leser der Anzeige sollte diesen Moment der Ruhe miterleben. Der Photograph hatte die Tageszeit für die Aufnahme genau geplant, wobei er das vorhandene Tageslicht und weisse reflektierende Flächen benutzte. ▲ Une journée de travail s'achève: voici venu le moment de se détendre dans un bon fauteuil, un classique. C'est ainsi que le lecteur était invité à lire l'annonce qu'illustrait cette photo. Le photographe avait planifié exactement le moment de la prise de vues, tirant parti de la lumière naturelle et des surfaces réfléchissantes blanches.

PAGE 156 (left) Photographer: ANDREAS MARX Client: HOFFMANN SONAX KG Camera: SINAR P 2 13x18" Film: KODAK EPP 100 Agency: IN HOUSE Country: GERMANY ■ The assigment was to create a corporate image photograph for use in the annual report of Sonax, makers of car care products. The special perspective, lighting and pearls of water on the lacquer of a Mercedes Benz, all speak for care and quality. ● Aufnahme für den Jahresbericht der Firma Sonax, Hersteller von Autopflegemitteln. Die spezielle Perspektive, die Lichtführung und die Wasserperlen auf dem Lack eines Mercedes, das alles spricht von Sorgfalt und Qualität. ▲ La photo était une commande de Sonax, un fabricant de produits haut de gamme pour l'entretien des carosseries, et devait illustrer le rapport annuel de cette firme. Les gouttelettes d'eau sur la vitre et le capot d'une voiture prestigieuse symbolisent les propriétés de ces produits.

PAGE 156 (right) Photographer: DOUG TAUB Client: LEXUS Designer: TOM SAPUTO Agency: TEAM ONE ADVERTISING Country: USA ■ "The relentless pursuit of perfection." The camera had to see the Lexus as it would be seen by a normal observer. The photograph was taken at dawn using natural light. ● «Das unablässige Bemühen um Perfektion». Die Kamera sollte den Lexus wie ein gewöhnlicher Betrachter sehen. Die Aufnahme wurde in der Morgendämmerung mit natürlichem Licht gemacht. ▲ «L'inlassable recherche de la perfection.» Il fallait montrer le Lexus dans la perspective d'un spectateur ordinaire. La photo a été prise à la lumière de l'aube.

PAGE 157 (top) Photographer: RICK RUSING Representative: JEAN GARDNER Client: BEECHCRAFT Camera: SINAR 8x10" Film: KODAK 100 PLUS Art Director: JOHN BOONE Agency: TEAM ONE Country: USA ■ The assignment was to depict the contrast between a modern Beechcraft Starship and a 50 year-old aircraft hangar. The photographer took the approach of working with dramatic rim lighting of the aircraft, a technique normally used in car photography. ● Die Aufgabe bestand darin, den Kontrast zwischen dem modernen Beechcraft Starship und dem alten Hangar herauszuarbeiten. Die Lösung des Photographen ist die dramatische Beleuchtung des Flugzeuges, wie sie bei Autoaufnahmen üblich ist. ▲ On avait demandé au photographe de faire une image du tout nouveau Beechcraft Starship dans un vieux hangar à avions. L'éclairage dramatique, semblable à celui qu'on utilise pour mettre en relief la carosserie dans les photos de voitures, renforce l'impression de contraste.

PAGE 157 (bottom) Photographer: DEBORAH ROUNDTREE Representative: DAVID ZAITZ Client: TOYOTA USA Camera: MAMIYA RZ 6x7" Film: FUJI RDP Art Director: KAREN KNECHT Stylist: BRIGITTE FAULANT Agency: SAATCHI + SAATCHI Country: USA ■ Deborah Roundtree worked with a photograph and subsequent oil painting of the image to depict cars in an unusual way. These were for use in a Toyota automobile catalog. ● Deborah Roundtree arbeitete mit Photographie und anschliessender Bemalung mit Ölfarbe, um Autos auf ungewöhnliche Art darzustellen. Ihre Bilder waren für einen Toyota-Autokatalog bestimmt. ▲ Deborah Roundtree a retravaillé sa photo à la peinture à l'huile, afin de présenter les voitures de manière tout à fait originale. L'image a été publiée dans un catalogue des voitures Toyota.

PAGE 158 (top row) Photographer: CHRISTOPHER THOMAS Representative: DAGMAR STAUDENMEIER Client: GETRÄNKEVERTRIEB VETTER Camera: SINAR 13x18" Film: KODAK EPY Art Director: EDITH KILGER Agency: HEYE + PARTNER Country: GERMANY ■ A touch of jungle atmosphere, without being too severe, was required for an ad campaign for this

Brazilian liquor. The photographer concentrated on the texture of the background and the lighting. ● Etwas Dschungelatmosphäre war gefragt für diesen Schnaps aus Brasilien, ohne zu konkret zu werden. Der Photograph hat sich daher auf das Licht und die Hintergrundstruktur konzentriert. ▲ Ces images pour des liqueurs brésiliennes devaient seulement suggérer l'atmosphère de la jungle. Le photographe s'est donc concentré sur la lumière et la texture du fond.

PAGE 158 (bottom row) Photographer: CRAIG CUTLER Representative: MARZENA Camera: TOYO 4x5 Film: KODAK VERICOLOR TYPE L Country: USA ■ In his studies of glass objects, the photographer blended their form and color. As a result, it is hard to distinguish between the object and the background. The photographs were then hand printed to achieve the subtle nuances in color. ● Dem Photographen Craig Cutler ging es bei diesen persönlichen Studien um die Verschmelzung von Farbe und Form, so dass Objekt und Hintergrund sich miteinander verbinden. Um die Farbnuancen zu erhalten, wurden alle Aufnahmen von Hand abgezogen. ▲ Ces photos sont des études personnelles. Le photographe Craig Cutler a traité les objets en verre comme des formes colorées abstraites en intégrant les espaces «vides». La courte distance focale lui a permis d'obtenir un fondu des couleurs et de l'arrière-plan.

PAGE 159 Photographer: CONNY J. WINTER Client: BERTSCH-WINTER Camera: NIKON Film: KODAK EKTACHROME 64 Country: GERMANY ■ In a calendar on "Design in Europe," Spain is represented with the Toledo chair of designer Jorge Pensi. The photograph was first taken with positive film, then it was exposed on Polaroid film and transfered on gelatine material. ● In einem Kalender über Design in Europa ist Spanien durch den Toledo-Stuhl des Designers Jorge Pensi vertreten. Das Photo wurde auf Diafilm gemacht, dann auf Sofortbildmaterial belichtet und auf Gelatine transferiert. ▲ Dans un calendrier sur le design en Europe, l'Espagne est représentée par la chaise Toledo du designer Jorge Pensi. Le photographe a d'abord pris une diapositive, qui a été exposée sur film polaroïd, le résultat étant transféré sur gélatine.

PAGE 160 (top & middle) Photographers: SHEILA METZNER, KEIICHI TAHARA Clients: MERCEDES-BENZ AG, KODAK AG Publisher: EDITION CANTZ Film: KODAK Country: GERMANY ■ These studies of the new S-class Mercedes are part of a book entitled *An Image of Class*; it contains the freestyle interpretation of this theme by 18 international photographers, and was a joint project of Mercedes-Benz and Kodak. Sheila Metzner (top) devoted her efforts to futuristic form. (bottom) With his monochrome image, Keiichi Tahara achieved the abstraction he desired. ● Diese Bilder des neuen S-Klasse von Mercedes sind Teil des Buches *An Image of Class* mit freien Interpretationen des Themas von 18 internationalen Photographen – ein Projekt von Mercedes-Benz und Kodak. Sheila Metzner ging es um die futuristische Form, Keiichi Tahara um Abstraktion und Visualisierung von Schnelligkeit. ▲ Ces images de la nouvelle Mercedes font partie d'un choix d'interprétations personnelles de 18 photographes internationale, réunies dans le livre *An Image of Class*. Le projet a été sponsorisé par Mercedes-Benz et Kodak. La photo de Sheila Metzner met en relief la noblesse de la ligne. Keiichi Tahara s'est efforcé d'exprimer l'abstraction des formes et de visualiser la vitesse.

PAGE 160 (bottom) Photographer: RICK RUSING Representative: JEAN GARDNER Client: INFINITI Camera: SINAR 8x10" Film: FUJI RTP 64 Art Director: BRUCE RITTER Agency: HILL HOLIDAY Country: USA ■ For the launch of the Infiniti J30, a classical portrait of the car was desired. The photographer's solution: dramatic lighting and a painted backdrop. ● Für die Einführungskampagne des Infiniti J30 war vom Kunden ein «klassisches Porträt» gewünscht. Die Lösung des Photographen: dramatische Beleuchtung und ein gemalter Hintergrund. ▲ Le photographe avait reçu mandat de créer une image «classique» de l'Infiniti J30. Il a donc choisi de présenter la voiture sous un éclairage dramatique et contre un décor peint.

PAGE 161 Photographer: DIETMAR HENNEKA Publisher: EDITION CANTZ Clients: MERCEDES-BENZ AG, KODAK AG Camera: SINAR P2 Film: KODAK EKTACHROME 200 Designers: ENRICO CASPARI, DIETER NASS, TATJANA WOLFENSBERGER Country: GERMANY ■ For his "Hommage à Edward Hopper," photographer Dietmar Henneka constructed this lifesize mock-up of a Western Hotel in a studio and painted it like a stage decor. In order to reinforce the Hopper feel, the depth was taken out during scanning and the sharpness exaggerated. ● Für seine «Hommage an Edward Hopper» baute Dietmar Henneka sein Western Hotel 1:1 in einem Studio auf, wobei die Aufbauten wie ein Bühnenbild behandelt wurden. Um dem Hopper-Vorbild näher zu kommen, wurden im Scanner die Tiefe herausgenommen und die Schärfe überzeichnet. ▲ L'image de Dietmar Henneka, intitulée «Hommage à Edward Hopper», mêle la réalité et le rêve. Le décor de cette toile a été reconstitué grandeur nature en studio et coloré à grands coups de pinceau, afin de donner l'illusion d'une peinture. Les effets de profondeur ont été gommés et la netteté accentuée au moyen du scanner.

PAGES 162 (top)-**163** (both images) Photographer: MICHAEL FURMAN Representative: VICTORIA SATTERTHWAITE Client: POTLATCH PAPER COMPANY Camera: SINAR P2 4x5" Film: KODAK PLUS-X Designer: KERRY POLITE Agency: POLITE DESIGN Country: USA ■ Cars were the subject of a catalog entitled "Michael Furman on Eloquence" (a grade of paper). The Porsche 917 K, the Hispano Suiza and the Porsche 718 RSK were photographed at the Collier Museum in Naples Florida. ● Autos waren das Thema des Katalogs «Michael Furman auf Eloquence» (eine Papierqualität). Der Porsche 917 K, der Hispano Suiza und der Porsche 718 RSK wurden im Collier-Museum in Naples, Florida, photographiert. ▲ Ces photographies ont été réalisées pour un catalogue intitulé «Michael Furman sur Eloquence» (une qualité de papier). Les trois modèles, une Porsche 917K, une Hispano Suiza et une Porsche 718 RSK, ont été photographiés au Collier Museum de Naples, en Floride.

PAGE 162 (bottom) Photographer: RON BAXTER SMITH Client: LA CURE Camera: FUJI 6x17 Film: AGFACHROME 1000 Art Director/Designer: DEL TERRELONGE Country: CANADA ■ This panoramic image suggests escape from everyday life and was used in a travel agency brochure. ● In diesem Panoramabild geht es um das Entkommen aus dem Alltag. Es wurde in der Broschüre eines Reisebüros verwendet. ▲ Cette photo suggère l'évasion. Elle a été reproduite dans le catalogue d'une agence de voyages.

PAGE 164 Photographer: RICHARD HAMILTON SMITH Representative: MARY ATOLS/JOHN HOFFMAN Publisher: GRAPHIC ARTS CENTER PUBLISHING Camera: Nikon F3 Film: KODACHROME 25 Art Director: DOUG PFEIFFER Country: USA ■ This photo was taken for the book *Minnesota II*. These corrugated metal boat houses are located in a small backwater area along the Mississippi River in Red Wing, Minnesota. They actually float on the river, anchored by long poles driven into the river bottom. Predawn hours in May offered the best conditions for a photograph and an exposure time of 20 minutes was required to achieve the desired effect. ● Die Aufnahme entstand für das Buch *Minnesota II*. Diese Bootshäuser aus Wellblech befinden sich in einem Seitenarm des Mississippi in Red Wing, Minnesota. Sie sind an langen, in den Flussgrund gerammten Stangen verankert und treiben förmlich auf dem Wasser. Ein früher Morgen im Mai kurz vor Dämmerung schien sich am besten für die Aufnahme zu eignen. Der Photograph belichtete ganze 20 Minuten, um den gewünschten Effekt zu erzielen. ▲ Richard Hamilton Smith a réalisé ces photos de maisons flottantes en tôle du Mississippi (à Red Wing, Minn.) aux premières heures de l'aube d'une journée de mai. L'exposition a duré vingt bonnes minutes.

PAGE 166 Photographer: ARTHUR MEYERSON Client: KPMG PEAT MARWICK (WORLD MAGAZINE) Camera: NIKON F4 Film: FUJI VELVIA Designer: DONNA M. BONAVITA Country: USA ■ The destruction of the Amazon rain forest was the subject of an article in the client's company magazine. The project was supported by Wildlife Conservation International. ● Die Zerstörung des tropischen Regenwaldes der Amazonasregion war das Thema eines Beitrags in der Firmenzeitschrift des Auftraggebers. ▲ Réalisée pour une publication d'entreprise, cette photo, prise au Brésil, illustre un article concernant la destruction de la forêt tropicale amazonienne.

PAGE 167 (both images) Photographer: Mercier/Wimberg Camera: HASSELBLAD 500C/M, ROLLEIFLEX Film: KODAK EKTACHROME Art Director: KEN WHITE Designer: BOB DINETZ Country: USA ■ Photographers Mark Mercier and Jim Wimberg grew up by the ocean and love it; their treasures are the washed-up artifacts they find on the beach. ● Die Photographen Mark Mercier und Jim Wimberg wuchsen am Meer auf, und sie lieben es. Ihre Schätze sind die Dinge, die sie am Strand finden, vom Meer verwaschen und geformt. ▲ Les photographes Mark Mercier et Jim Wimberg ont grandi au bord de la mer et ils aiment l'océan. Leurs trésors sont ces choses que l'on trouve sur la plage, délavés par l'eau de mer et transformés par les ans.

PAGE 168 (top) Photographer: KAI MUI Client: EASTMAN KODAK Co. Camera: NIKON F4 Film: KODAK EKTAR 25 Art Director: KAI MUI Stylist: MICHELLE SAUNDERS Agency: MUI + GRAY Country: USA ■ "American West" This previously unpublished photograph demonstrates the exposure latitude of Kodak Ektar 25 films, going from dark to light without sacrificing any detail. ● «American West», eine unveröffentlichte Aufnahme, die den Belichtungsspielraum der Kodak-Ektar-25-Filme demonstriert. ▲ «L'Ouest américain». Cette photo inédite avait été réalisée pour démontrer les qualités d'exposition des films Kodak Ektar 25, qui peut rendre toutes les nuances.

PAGE 168 (bottom) Photographer: JAMEY STILLINGS Client: INTERMOUNTAIN CANOLA COMPANY Camera: OLYMPUS OM4 Film: FUJI VELVIA 35MM Art Director: RAY BATHEA Agency: RUMRILL HOYT INC. Country: USA ■ The assignment was to create beautiful images of rapeseed. On the evening of his first scouting day, the photographer saw this corn elevator in such a magical light that he ran out into the field and worked furiously with his assistant to capture the beautiful but fleeting scene. No filters were used. ● Der Auftraggeber wollte eine schöne Aufnahme von Rapssaat. Am Abend des ersten Erkundungstages sah der Photograph diesen Getreidesilo in einem so speziellen Licht, dass er aufs Feld rannte und mit seinem Assistenten wie besessen arbeitete, um die schöne und doch so vergängliche Stimmung einzufangen. Bei den Aufnahmen wurden keinerlei Filter benutzt. ▲ On avait demandé au photographe de faire de belles images de cultures de canola (graines de colza) pour une publicité. Le silo à grains se présenta dans un éclairage si extraordinaire dans la soirée qu'il courut le plus vite possible vers la colline d'en face, afin de trouver le bon point de vue et saisir cette lumière magique, mais ô combien éphémère. Il n'a utilisé aucun filtre.

PAGE 169 Photographer: STUART DEE Camera: CANON EOS-1 Film: FUJI VELVIA Country: CANADA ▼ Vacation on the beach—a graphic, surreal and somewhat whimsical photograph. The intent was to convey a feeling of freedom and lightness, suggesting leisure time and carefree holidays. ● Ferien am Meer – es ging um das Gefühl von Freiheit und Leichtigkeit, von Freizeit und sorglosen Ferien. ▲ Le photographe désirait faire une image un peu délirante sur le thème des vacances au bord de la mer et du temps libre. Il voulait exprimer le plaisir de l'insouciance et la joie de vivre.

PAGE 170 (top) Photographer: TERRY HUSEBYE Client: PACIFIC BELL DIRECTORY Camera: NIKON F4 Film: FUJI RDP Art Director: STEVE POWELL Agency: SMART CREATIVE SERVICES Country: USA ■ Kern County Fair. The image was an assignment for the cover of the regional telephone directory. Due to the length of exposure after dusk, this strange interplay of real and surreal was achieved—the excitement of a wild ride on the "Wave Swinger" in contrast to the rather stoic calm of the ride's operator. ● Jahrmarkt in Kern County. Aufnahme für den Umschlag des Telephonbuches der Region. Dank der langen Belichtungszeit nach Sonnenuntergang entstand diese eigenartige Mischung von Realem und Surrealem; das aufregende Erlebnis der wilden Fahrt mit dem «Wave Swinger» im

Kontrast zur stoischen Ruhe des Karussellbedieners. ▲ Ce manège tournoyant à folle allure a été photographié à la foire annuelle de Kern County, en Californie, pour la couverture de l'un des annuaires téléphoniques. La photo a été prise au coucher du soleil, avec un temps d'exposition très long. L'image a quelque chose de magique. Le plus étonnant, c'est le contraste avec l'attitude impassible du responsable du manège en question, le «Wave Swinger».

PAGE 170 (bottom row) Photographer: PETER ECKERT Camera: KONI OMEGA 6X7 Film: AGFA PAN 100 Country: USA ■ Night is the time for Peter Eckert, it provides him with the best conditions for images of the industrial sections of Portland, Oregon, and the long exposure times create unexpected effects. The Blitz Weinhardt Brewery with its railroad cars, modern holding tanks and turn-of-the-century buildings was especially intriguing. ● Die Nacht ist die Zeit für Peter Eckert, die ihm die besten Voraussetzungen für seine Bilder aus Industrievierteln der Stadt Portland liefert, und oft ergeben die langen Belichtungszeiten unerwartete Effekte. Die Blitz-Weinhardt-Brauerei mit ihren Eisenbahnwaggons, modernen Tanks und Gebäuden aus der Jahrhundertwende war ein besonders verlockendes Objekt. ▲ Peter Eckert a trouvé que le moment idéal pour prendre des photos des quartiers industriels de Portland, dans l'Oregon, était la nuit. Les temps d'exposition particulièrement longs produisent parfois des effets surprenants. Avec ses wagons de chemins de fer, ses réservoirs modernes et ses bâtiments du début du siècle, la brasserie Blitz-Weinhardt offrait un sujet particulièrement intéressant.

PAGE 171 Photographer: RON BAMBRIDGE Camera: WISTA FIELD CAMERA Film: Kodak Ektachrome 64 Country: GREAT BRITAIN ■ The photographer searched for an unusual landscape, which he found in Iceland with its black volcanic sand beaches, huge glaciers and icy peaks. This geothermal power station is set in a blue lagoon with hot springs where people swim. ● Eine ungewöhnliche Landschaft hatte der Photograph gesucht. Er fand sie in Island mit seinen schwarzen Lavastränden, riesigen Eiskappen und Bergkuppen. Dieses geothermische Kraftwerk befindet sich in einer Lagune mit heissen Quellen. ▲ Le photographe désirait faire des vues de paysages hors du commun. C'est ainsi qu'il se retrouva en Islande, pays où l'on peut voir des plages de sable volcanique noir, des glaciers, des coulées de lave refroidies et des icebergs. Ici, les habitants se baignent dans les eaux réchauffées par une centrale géothermique.

PAGE 172 Photographer: GEORGE SIMHONI Representatives: ROBIN DICTENBERG (USA), WESTSIDE STUDIO (CANADA), DAVID GARDINER (GREAT BRITAIN) Camera: HASSELBLAD Film: KODAK EKTACHROME HIGH SPEED Country: CANADA ■ The similarity to Millet's famous painting "The Gleaners" is no coincidence. In order to obtain the desired atmosphere, the photographer used flash lighting directed towards the heads. ● Die Ähnlichkeit mit Millets berühmtem Bild «Die Ährenleserinnen» ist nicht zufällig. Um die gewünschte Atmosphäre zu erreichen, richtete der Photograph Blitzlicht auf die Köpfe. ▲ Cette photo est inspirée du célèbre tableau de Millet «Les Glaneuses». Bien que le photographe ait voulu un effet pictural, la scène n'a pas été prise en lumière naturelle, mais avec un flash dirigé sur les têtes.

PAGE 173 Photographer: NIKOLAY ZUREK Client: ICF INTERNATIONAL INC. Camera: NIKON F2 Film: POLAROID POLAPAN Art Director: NIKOLAY ZUREK Country: USA ■ To contrast the old with the rebuilt portions of a steel mill in Ohio, black-and-white film was most suitable. The assignment was to generate art photographs of renovated plants, in color, for office walls and the annual report of the client. This black-and-white image was taken "on the side." ● Der alte und der neue Teil einer Stahlfabrik in Ohio. Der Kontrast liess sich am besten in Schwarzweiss herausarbeiten. Der Auftrag, bei dem es um die Modernisierung von Fabriken ging, verlangte Farbaufnahmen für die Büros und den Jahresbericht des Kunden. Dieses Schwarzweissbild entstand am Rande. ▲ L'ancien et le nouveau bâtiment d'une aciérie dans l'Ohio. Le noir et blanc était particulièrement indiqué pour rendre le constraste. Le photographe devait faire des photos en couleurs de tous les sites rénovés de cette firme, afin de décorer ses bureaux ainsi que le rapport annuel. Cette photo a été prise en marge de cette commande.

PAGE 174 (all images) Photographer: INTAE KIM Clients: COLOR HOUSE, PRISM STUDIO Camera: MAMIYA RB 67, ASHANI PENTAX Film: KODAK EPR 120, KODAK PANATOMIC-X Country: USA ■ Dunes at the Death Valley National Monument. The photographer waited patiently for the right light. The images are titled "Death Valley at Dawn" (top), "Dream in the Desert" (middle), and "Light of Symphony" (bottom). ● Dünen im Death Valley National Monument. Der Photograph wartete geduldig auf das richtige Licht. Er nannte seine Bilder «Das Tal des Todes im Morgengrauen» (oben), «Traum in der Wüste» (unten links), «Das Licht der Symphonie» (unten rechts). ▲ Ces photos de dunes ont été prises sur le site du Death Valley National Monument. En haut: «La Vallée de la Mort à l'aube»; en bas à gauche: «Le rêve dans le désert»; en bas à droite: «La lumière de la symphonie». Pour chacun de ces clichés, le photographe dut attendre le moment où la lumière dessinait les formes les plus intéressantes.

PAGE 175 Photographer: LOU JONES Publisher: RIZZOLI Camera: NIKON FE Film: KODACHROME 200 Country: ITALY ■ Schooners in Bartlett Harbor, Maine. The assignment was to generate a photographic illustration of Moby Dick, for *Dove* magazine. ● Schoner in Bartlett Harbor, Maine. Das Bild war ein Auftrag der Zeitschrift *Dove*, bei dem es um die photographische Illustration von Moby Dick ging. ▲ Une goélette à Bartlett Harbor, dans le Maine. L'image était une commande du magazine *Dove*, pour lequel le photographe devait illustrer Moby Dick au moyen de photos.

PAGE 176 Photographer: HARRY DE ZITTER Client: FRIESLAND TOURISM Camera: LINHOF TECHNORAMA Film: FUJI VELVIA 120 Art Director: BERT RORIJE Agency: VOSKAMP RORIJE & ROS Country: NETHERLANDS ■ Vlieland Island, the North Sea, this region of Friesland has stretches of countryside that have remained completely untouched. This image was intended to mimic the style of the landscapes done by the Dutch masters. ● Die Insel Vlieland, Nordsee. In Friesland gibt es Landschaftsstriche, die völlig unberührt geblieben sind. Die Bildserie sollte an den Stil der Landschaftsbilder der alten niederländischen Meister erinnern. ▲ Une vision féerique de l'île de Vlieland sur la mer du Nord. Cette image exprime la beauté encore intacte des paysages de la Frise, rappelant le style des peintures des grands maîtres hollandais.

PAGE 177 (all images) Photographer: NADAV KANDER Publisher: *CONDÉ NAST TRAVELER* Camera: 4x5" Film: KODAK EPR Country: USA ■ Landscapes in Iceland, photographed at midnight in early June, when the sun never sets. ● Isländische Landschaft. Diese Bilder entstanden im Juni gegen Mitternacht, wenn die Sonne in Island nicht untergeht. ▲ Le paysage de l'Islande. Ces photos ont été réalisées au mois de juillet, vers minuit, le soleil ne se couchant pas à cette période de l'année dans ce pays.

PAGE 178 Photographer: TERRY VINE Client: MAGUIRE THOMAS PARTNERS Camera: NIKON F3 Film: KODACHROME Art Director: LOWELL WILLIAMS Designer: LOWELL WILLIAMS DESIGN Country: USA ■ The swimmer and the water are part of the perfect symmetry of the composition, becoming an integral part of the architecture. This photo, in which a person interacts with architecture, was shot for an introductory brochure of a Dallas building complex. ● Die Schwimmerin und das Wasser sind Teil der perfekten Symmetrie dieser Komposition, sie werden quasi Bestandteil der Architektur. Die Bilder für eine Broschüre, in der ein Gebäudekomplex vorgestellt wurde, sollten Menschen in Verbindung mit der Architektur zeigen. ▲ La parfaite symétrie de la composition confère à cette image une dimension surréelle, l'eau et la nageuse étant en quelque sorte partie intégrante de l'architecture. Cette photo illustrait une brochure pour un centre abritant des bureaux, dans laquelle il fallait montrer des individus en relation avec l'architecture.

PAGE 180(both images)**-181** (both images) Photographer: JIM HEDRICH Client: MAGUIRE THOMAS PARTNERS Art Director/ Designer: LOWELL WILLIAMS Agency: PENTAGRAM DESIGN Country: USA ■ Interplay between shapes and colors—these images display the beauty of a mixed-use building complex. Used in a leasing brochure, they were intended to attract lessees from a wide range of businesses. ● Ein Spiel von Formen und Farben – Bilder, die die Schönheit eines Gebäudekomplexes zeigen. Sie wurden in einer Broschüre verwendet, mit der mögliche Mieter angesprochen werden sollen. ▲ Des jeux de formes et de couleurs – des images qui montrent la beauté de l'architecture d'un complexe de bâtiments de bureaux. Elles ont été reproduites dans une brochure visant à attirer des locataires potentiels des branches d'activité les plus diverses.

PAGE 182 (both images) Photographer: MIQUEL GONZALEZ Publisher: *ZEIT MAGAZIN* Camera: NIKON FM2 Film: KODAK INFRARED HS Country: SPAIN ■ Barcelona, one year before the Olympic Games of 1992. Miquel Gonzales was fascinated by the architectural changes in his home town. Shown are (top) the bridge "Bach de Roda" by architect Calatrava and (bottom) the Olympic Stadium. ● Barcelona, ein Jahr vor der Olympiade 1992. Miquel Gonzales war fasziniert von der architektonischen Erneuerung seiner Heimatstadt. Hier abgebildet sind die Brücke «Bach de Roda» des Architekten Calatrava und das Olympiastadion. ▲ Ces vues du site des Jeux Olympiques 1992 de Barcelone ont été prises un an avant l'événement. Miquel Gonzales, qui est né dans cette ville, avait été frappé par les transformations qu'elle avait subies. On peut voir le pont «Bach de Roda» de l'architecte Calatrava et le stade olympique.

PAGE 183 Photographer: GREG PEASE Camera: HASSELBLAD SUPERWIDE Film: FUJI VELVIA Country: USA ■ Four young Japanese sculptors went to Baltimore to create a 33 foot high sculpture of the Fudo Myoh-oh, the incarnation of Buddha. American students of the Maryland Institute, College of Arts were involved in this two-year project and photographer Greg Pease recorded the sculptors' progress as the grim, warrior-like Fudo Myoh-oh gradually emerged from the layers of wood. ● Vier junge japanische Bildhauer waren nach Baltimore gekommen, um am Maryland Institute, College of Arts, eine ca. zehn Meter hohe Skulptur des Fudo Myoh-oh, einer Buddha-Inkarnation, zu schaffen. Amerikanische Studenten beteiligten sich an den zwei Jahre dauernden Arbeiten, und der Photograph Greg Pease dokumentierte, wie sich der grimmige, kriegerische Fudo Myoh-oh nach und nach aus den Holzschichten herausschälte. ▲ Quatre jeunes sculpteurs japonais étaient venus spécialement à Baltimore pour créer une sculpture de presque 10 m de haut de Fudo Myoh-oh, l'une des incarnations de Bouddha. Des étudiants américains du Maryland Institute, College of Art participèrent à sa fabrication qui dura deux ans. Le photographe Greg Pease documenta les phases de ce travail, comment la figure guerrière de la divinité grimaçante surgit petit à petit du bois.

PAGE 184 (both images) Photographer: CHRISTOPH SEEBERGER Camera: LEICA M Film: POLAROID POLAPAN Country: GERMANY ■ For these images, a small format camera aided the photographer in creating atmospheric, graphically reduced images, which reflect their own special reality. ● Bei diesen Bildern erwies sich die Kleinbildkamera als sehr geeignet. Christoph Seeberger ging es um atmosphärische, graphisch reduzierte Aufnahmen, die eine eigene Realität zeigen. Sie entstanden als zusätzliche Arbeiten bei einem Industrieauftrag. ▲ Pour ces photos, l'usage d'un appareil petit format s'imposait. Christoph Seeberger voulait rendre l'atmosphère, créer des images graphiques d'une grande simplicité, qui aient leur propre réalité.

PAGE 185 Photographer: RICHARD EASTWOOD Client: FORWARD VINEY WOOLAN Camera: HASSELBLAD 2000 FCW Film: FUJICHROME Art Director: RICHARD EASTWOOD Country: AUSTRALIA ■ Sometimes certain aspects of a building can create startling illusions of two-dimensionality, as emphasized by this staircase with its repetitive elements and color combinations. The assignment was to photograph a new university building. ● Manchmal erzeugen besondere Blickwinkel Illusionen, wie hier die Illusion von Zweidimensionalität, hervorgerufen durch die Treppe mit den sich wiederholenden Elementen und speziellen

Farbkombinationen. ▲ Certains angles de vue suscitent des effets particuliers: c'est ainsi que cette photo d'un escalier, avec ses éléments qui se répètent et ses combinaisons de couleurs particulières, donne l'illusion d'un tableau, toute profondeur étant abolie.

PAGE 186 Photographer: MEINRAD FALTNER Representative: ZEFA (ZENTRALE FARBBILD AGENTUR) Camera: SINAR F2 Film: KODAK EPN 100/120 Country: AUSTRIA ■ The Haas building by architect Hans Hollein, in Vienna. The photographer was concerned with optically reducing the building to its graphical structures. ● Das Haas-Haus des Architekten Hans Hollein am Stephansplatz in Wien. Dem Photographen ging es um Reduktion auf die graphischen Strukturen des Hauses. ▲ La Maison Haas de l'architecte Hans Hollein à Vienne. Le photographe s'est efforcé de rendre les lignes essentielles de la structure du bâtiment, d'une grande rigueur.

PAGE 187 (both images) Photographer: LONNIE DUKA Client: FLUOR CORPORATION (left), WAHLCO ENVIRONMENTAL (right) Camera: NIKON F3 Film: Fuji Velvia Designers: JOHN TOM (left), LARRY PAO (right) Agency: THE JEFFERIES ASSOCIATION (left), LARRY PAO DESIGN (right) Country: USA ■ Power plants photographed for the annual reports of the clients. The photographer focused on symbolic, sculptural elements inherent in these facilities with mixed colorations enhancing the concept. ● Kraftwerke, aufgenommen für die Jahresberichte der Auftraggeber. Die Photographin konzentrierte sich bei diesen Photos auf symbolhafte, skulpturartige Elemente der Anlagen. Die spezielle Farbgebung unterstützt das Konzept. ▲ Les photos de ces centrales électriques ont été reproduites dans un rapport annuel. La photographe s'est concentré sur les éléments symboliques, sculpturaux, de ces sites industriels. Le coloris particulier renforce son intention.

PAGE 188 Photographer: TIM GRIFFITH Camera: CAMBO WIDE Film: FUJI NEOPAN 4x5" Country: AUSTRALIA ■ In a personal project, Tim Griffith explored the forms of contemporary Japanese architecture. This interior is from the Tokyo Budokan, a building dedicated to Japanese martial arts, designed by architect Rokkaku. ● Der Photograph befasste sich in einem persönlichen Projekt mit der zeitgenössischen japanischen Architektur. Der Raum gehört zum Budokan von Tokio (den japanischen Kampfsportarten gewidmetes Gebäude) des Architekten Rokkaku. ▲ Dans un projet personnel, le photographe s'était consacré aux formes de l'architecture contemporaine japonaise. Cette salle fait partie du Budokan à Tokyo (un bâtiment consacré à la pratique du budo), qui a été dessiné par l'architecte Rokkaku.

PAGE 189 (both images) Photographer: RICHARD FISCHER Publisher: GRUNER & JAHR, *ART* Camera: TOYO VIEW 4x5" Film: KODAK EKTACHROME EPP Art Director: DETLEF CONRAD Country: GERMANY ■ Near the French city of Poitiers, a leisure and technolgy park with spectacular architecture was built. Shown here are (top) the International Institute for Innovate Research, inspired by a lotus flower and (bottom) a "rock crystal," housing the "Kinémax" theater with Europe's largest screen. All buildings were designed by Parisian architect Denis Laming. ● In der Nähe der Stadt Poitiers in Frankreich entstand ein Freizeit- und Technologiepark mit spektakulärer Architektur. Hier abgebildet sind das Internationale Institut für innovative Forschung als Zelle und «der Bergkristall», der das «Kinémax»-Theater mit der grössten Kinoleinwand Europas beherbergt. Alle Bauten sind von dem Pariser Architekten Denis Laming. ▲ Le Futuroscope, un parc de loisirs et de technologie d'une architecture spectaculaire, se trouve non loin de Poitiers, en France. La forme de l'Institut international pour la recherche fondamentale rappelle celle d'une cellule. Celle du «Kinémax», qui abrite le plus grand écran de cinéma d'Europe, le «Cristal de roche». Tous les bâtiments ont été créés par l'architecte parisien Denis Laming.

PAGE 190 Photographer: HARA Publisher: HARRY N. ABRAMS Camera: NIKON F3 Film: KODACHROME 64 Art Director: HARA Designer: TOM LEWIS Stylist: HARA Country: USA ■ White Pelicans living amongst the flamingos on the shores of the Rift Valley of East Africa preparing for flight. Intrigued by the beauty of the birds, the photographer made an expedition into the harshest part of desolate Rift Valley, where temperatures averaged 125°F. This is one of the photographic illustrations from a book entitled *Flamingo: A Photographer's Odyssey.* ● Weisse Pelikane beim Kampfritual. Sie leben mit den Flamingos an den Ufern der Seen im ostafrikanischen Grabensystem. Überwältigt von der Schönheit der Vögel unternahm die Photographin eine Expedition in den rauhesten Teil des Grabensystems, wo Durchschnittstemperaturen von 45°C herrschten. Diese Aufnahme stammt aus dem Buch *Flamingo: A Photographer's Odyssey.* ▲ Des pélicans blancs au cours d'un combat rituel. Ils vivent avec des flamands roses sur les rives des lacs de la Rift Valley en Afrique orientale. Fasciné par la beauté de ces oiseaux, la photographe entreprit une expédition dans les recoins les plus sauvages de cette contrée, dont les températures moyennes sont de 45°C. Il s'agit de l'une des photos illustrant un livre intitulé *Flamingo: A Photographer's Odyssey.*

PAGE 192 (both images) Photographer: BRITTA JASCHINSKI Camera: NIKON Film: KODAK TRI-X Country: GERMANY/GREAT BRITAIN ■ A personal view of vanishing nature. These pictures were taken in the London Zoo. ● Eine persönliche Sicht bedrohter Tiere. Diese Aufnahmen der Photographin Britta Jaschinski entstanden im Londoner Zoo. ▲ Une vision personnelle des espèces animales menacées d'extinction. Ces photos ont été prises au zoo de Londres.

PAGE 193 Photographer: SATISH SREEDHARAN Publisher: *MINOLTA MIRROR* Camera: MINOLTA Film: KODAK EKTACHROME EPP Art Director: FRED. O. BECHLEN Country: MALAYSIA ■ This shot was a stroke of luck. Satish Sreedharan was on a Malaysian photobook assignment at the Bako National Park in Sarawak when a fluttering bird drew his attention to this oriental snake devouring his prey. He began to shoot from about a yard

away, finally ending up as close as 6 inches. ● Satish Sreedharan befand sich im Bako National Park in Sarawak wegen eines Photobandes über Malaysia, als er durch des Aufflattern eines Vogels diese orientalische Schlange entdeckte, die ihre Beute verzehrte. Er wagte sich bis auf 15cm heran, um seine Aufnahme zu machen. ▲ Satish Sreedharan était en train de prendre des photos au Bako National Park de Sarawak pour un album sur la Malaisie, lorsque son attention fut attirée par un oiseau battant des ailes. C'est ainsi qu'il découvrit ce serpent qui dévorait avidement sa proie. Il finit par s'aventurer jusqu'à environ 15 cm de l'animal pour faire cette photo.

PAGE 194 (top) Photographer: CLINT CLEMENS Representative: ART + COMMERCE Client: RALSTON PURINA Camera: FUJI 680 Film: KODAK EPP 120 Art Director: MARK ARNOLD Agency: TBWA KERLICK SWITZER Country: USA ■ An animal food company commissioned this photograph, intended to show the liveliness and healthiness of the dog. ● Diese Aufnahme entstand im Auftrag eines Tierfutterherstellers. ▲ Cette photo a été réalisée à la demande d'un fabricant d'aliments pour chiens.

PAGE 195 (bottom) Photographer: ELKE RITSCHEL Camera: NIKON F4s Film: KODAK EPP Country: GERMANY ■ Death of a pet. In order to help her overcome the loss of her dog Fritz, the photographer took this last photo of him. ● Tod eines Haustieres. Um den Verlust ihres Hundes Fritz besser verarbeiten zu können, machte die Photographin ein letztes Photo von ihm. ▲ La mort d'un animal familier. Pour se consoler de la perte de son chien, Fritz, Elke Ritschel fit une dernière photo de lui.

PAGE 195 (top) Photographer: FRIEDRICH K. RUMPF Publisher: *SÜDDEUTSCHE ZEITUNG MAGAZIN* Camera: NIKON F3 Film: KODAK TECHNICAL PAN Art Director: ANDREA HINRICH Country: GERMANY ■ An artificial scene on the Nile with two crocodiles, which can be seen in the Museum König in Bonn. The photographer was fascinated by the surreal character of the diorama. ● Eine künstliche Nillandschaft mit zwei Krokodilen im Bonner Museum König. Es ging dem Photographen um den surrealen Charakter von Dioramen. ▲ Une reconstitution des rives du Nil avec deux crocodiles au Musée König de Bonn. Le photographe souhaitait retrouver l'atmosphère surréaliste du diorama.

PAGE 195 (bottom) Photographer: ADRIAN BURKE Representative: RENATA JACK Camera: DEARDORFF 8x10" Film: FUJI VELVIA Designer: JOE HOZA Country: GREAT BRITAIN ■ These frogs were obtained from an agency that supplies animals for photo purposes. They were carefully placed on top of each other, and remained so just long enough for the picture to be taken. ● Die Frösche kamen von einer Agentur, die Tiere für Photos liefert. Vorsichtig wurden sie aufeinandergesetzt, und sie blieben gerade lange genug in dieser Position für die Aufnahme. ▲ Les grenouilles de cette image ont été fournies par une agence spécialisée à laquelle les photographes s'adressent quand ils ont besoin d'un animal pour une photo. Empilées précautionneusement les unes sur les autres, elles restèrent immobiles juste le temps que le photographe fasse son cliché.

PAGE 196 Photographer: STEFAN WARTER Publisher: GRUNER & JAHR, *SPORTS* Camera: NIKON F4s Film: KODAK EKTACHROME 200 Art Director: DETLEF SCHLOTTMANN Country: GERMANY ■ An evening training session prior to the European Championship in 2-man bobsled. The course was illuminated with sodium vapor lamps which created the shimmering stripes on the ice and caused the bobsled to appear as a silhouette. The intent was to capture the atmosphere, not the news. ● Abendtraining vor den Europameisterschaften im Zweierbob. Die Streckenbeleuchtung mit Natriumdampfleuchten erzeugte den Glanzstreifen auf dem Eis. Der Bob erscheint nur noch als Silhouette. Es ging nicht um aktuelle Berichterstattung, sondern um das Einfangen der Atmosphäre. ▲ L'entraînement du soir avant les championnats d'Europe de bob à deux. La bande lumineuse sur la glace a été produite par l'éclairage du parcours au moyen de lampes à la vapeur de sodium. Le bob n'est plus qu'une silhouette.

PAGE 198 Photographer: ANDREW ECCLES Representative: OUTLINE Publisher: *AMERICAN HEALTH* Camera: MAMIYA RZ 67 Film: KODAK EPR 64 Art Director/Designer: MARK DANZIG Photo Editor: KATE SULLIVAN Country: USA ■ Olympic Athletes 1992— Andrew Eccles wanted images that were as powerful and beautiful as the atheletes themselves, while showing the beauty of their countries. ● Olympische Athleten 1992 – Andrew Eccles wollte Bilder, die so kraftvoll und schön sind wie die Athleten selbst und gleichzeitig die Schönheit des von ihnen vertretenen Landes zeigen. ▲ Les athlètes olympiques de 1992 – Andrew Eccles désirait faire des images qui soient aussi puissantes et fascinantes que les sportifs eux-mêmes, tout en montrant la beauté du pays qu'ils représentaient.

PAGE 199 (top) Photographer: OLIVER RECK Representative: ATP ARTHUR THILL PRODUCTION Publisher: FALKEN VERLAG GMBH Camera: NIKON F4 Film: KODAK EKTACHROME EPP Country: GERMANY ■ Team competition in show jumping at the Olympic Games 1992. The photographer chose an elevated vantage point in order to capture this spectacular obstacle amidst a static background from an unusual perspective. ● Mannschaftswettbewerb im Springreiten an den Olympischen Spielen 1992. Der Photograph wählte einen erhöhten Standpunkt, um dieses spektakuläre Hindernis aus ungewöhnlicher Perspektive und mit ruhigem Hintergrund zeigen zu können. ▲ Le saut d'obstacles aux Jeux Olympiques de 1992. Le photographe avait cherché un point de vue surélevé, afin de prendre cette course hippique spectaculaire dans une perspective inhabituelle et sur un fond plus calme que celui des tribunes.

PAGE 199 (bottom row) Photographer: SUSAN ALINSANGAN Camera: LEICA Film: KODAK TRI-X Country: USA ■ The transformation of the human body in water. The photographer had a difficult time staying dry. ● Die Veränderung des menschlichen Körpers im Wasser. Die Photographin hatte alle Mühe, nicht völlig durchnässt zu werden. ▲ Les transformations du corps humain sous l'eau. La photographe eut toutes les peines du monde à ne pas être éclaboussée.

PAGE 200 Photographer: JOHN HUET Representatives: MARILYN CADENBACH, ROBIN DICTENBERG Camera: PENTAX 6x7 Film: KODAK TRI-X Photogravure: JON GOODMAN Country: USA ■ Image (hand-pulled photogravure) of a street basketball player. ● Bild (Handabzug) eines Strassen-Basketballspielers. ▲ Image (photogravure tirée à la main) d'un joueur de basket de la rue.

PAGE 201 (left) Photographer: NEIL LEIFER Publisher: *TIME MAGAZINE* Art Directors: RUDOLPH C. HOGLUND, ARTHUR HOCHSTEIN Country: USA ■ The Chinese diving gold medalist, Fu Mingxia, was shown on the cover of a special issue of *Time* magazine featuring Olympic highlights of Barcelona 1992. ● Fu Mingxia aus China, Gewinnerin der Goldmedaille im Kunstspringen. Ihr Bild erschien auf dem Umschlag einer Spezialnummer von *Time* zur Olympiade in Barcelona 1992. ▲ Cette photo de la Chinoise Fu Mingxia, médaille d'or de plongeon aux Jeux Olympiques de Barcelone 1992, a été reproduite en couverture du magazine *Time*.

PAGE 201 (right) Photographer: GREGORY HEISLER Publisher: *TIME MAGAZINE* Art Directors: RUDOPH C. HOGLUND, ARTHUR HOCHSTEIN Country: USA ■ The Kenyan marathon runner Ibrahim Hussein during training. This image was used on the cover of a special Olympics edition of *Time* covering the 1992 games in Barcelona. ● Der kenyanische Marathonläufer Ibrahim Hussein beim Training. Das Bild erschien auf dem Umschlag einer Sondernummer des Magazins *Time* zu den Olympischen Spielen 1992 in Barcelona. ▲ Le marathonien kényan Ibrahim Hussein au cours d'un entraînement. Cette image a été publiée en couverture d'une édition spéciale du magazine *Time*, consacrée aux Jeux Olympiques 1992 de Barcelone.

PAGE 202 Photographer: HUGH KRETSCHMER Representative: JOHN SHARPE Client: SPINDLETOP RECORDS Camera: TOYO 45G Film: FUJI RDP Art Director: LARRY VIGON Country: USA ■ Various mediums of communication arranged to look like a face. The image, which also alludes to the fact that the artist plays a saxophone, served as the cover for an album with the title "Talk To Me." ● Kommunikationsmittel, so arrangiert, dass daraus ein Gesicht entsteht. Das Bild, das auch ausdrücken sollte, dass es sich um einen Saxophonspieler handelt, wurde für die Hülle einer Schallplatte verwendet. ▲ Des moyens de communication disposés de manière à évoquer un visage. Cette image a servi à illustrer la couverture d'un album.

PAGE 204 (both) Photographer: MICHAL MACKU Camera: PENTACON SIX Film: FOMAPAN F-17 Art Director: DR. HANA MYSLIVECKOVA Country: Czech Republic ■ Parts of the human body, in a new context, questioning reality. The photographer uses a special technique he developed which he calls "gellage" (gelatin and collage), based on removing the light sensitive emulsion and putting it layer by layer on paper, offering unlimited possibilities in composition. ● Teile des menschlichen Körpers, in neuen Zusammenhängen, verfremdet, Realität in Frage stellend. Der Photograph arbeitet mit einer speziell von ihm entwickelten Technik, die er Gellage (Gelatine + Collage) nennt. Er entfernt die lichtempfindliche Emulsion, um sie in mehreren Schichten auf Papier aufzutragen. Das bedeutet unbegrenzte Möglichkeiten der Komposition. ▲ Des fragments du corps humain représentés de manière inattendue. Le photographe a travaillé au moyen d'une technique qu'il a lui-même mis au point et qu'il appelle «gellage» (gélatine + collage). Elle consiste à extraire d'une matrice l'émulsion de sels d'argent, sensible à la lumière, afin de la déposer en plusieurs couches sur le papier. Cela permet de varier la composition à l'infini.

PAGE 205 (all images) Photographer: FULTON DAVENPORT Camera: SINAR F Film: POLAROID 55, KODAK VERICOLOR HC Country: USA ■ This work is about the signs, symbols, and myths of our culture. Through the juxtaposition of images, their meaning is brought into question. The process begins with photographing the subjects and scenes and ends with the construction of a new constellation of the original images. ● Hier geht es um Zeichen, Symbole und Mythen unserer Kultur. Die Gegenüberstellung der Bilder stellt ihre Bedeutung in Frage. Der Prozess beginnt mit Aufnahmen der Objekte und Szenen und endet mit der Konstruktion eines neuen Umfeldes für die ursprünglichen Bilder. ▲ Cette photo parle des signes, des symboles et des mythologies de la culture contemporaine. Le contraste entre les images permet de remettre en cause leur sens. Les objets et les scènes sont tout d'abord photographiés; le processus s'achève avec la création d'un nouveau décor pour les images originales.

PAGE 206 (all images) Photographer: NANCY R. COHEN Country: USA ■ Poses of isolation and desparation. The bare room and the lighting enhance the impression of desolation. ● Gebärden der Isolation und Verzweiflung. Der kahle Raum und die Beleuchtung unterstützen die gewünschte Wirkung. ▲ Des attitudes qui suggèrent l'isolation et le désespoir. L'espace et l'éclairage contribuent à renforcer l'atmosphère.

PAGE 207 (both images) Photographer: HANS NELEMAN Camera: SINAR P 8x10" Film: KODAK EKTACHROME Country: USA ■ (left) Portrait of a lizard, spotted in Chinatown, and (right) a portrait of the photographer himself, inspired by Rembrandt's self-portraits. ● Porträt einer in Chinatown entdeckten Eidechse und ein Porträt des Photographen selbst, von Rembrandts Selbstporträts inspiriert. ▲ L'image d'un lézard découvert à Chinatown et un portrait du photographe lui-même, inspiré des autoportraits de Rembrandt.

PAGE 208 Photographer: JEAN-LOUIS LEIBOVITCH Client: MUSÉE AUTOMOBILE DE LA SARTHE Camera: SINAR Film: KODAK EKTACHROME Country: FRANCE ■ The assignment required a representation of all the professions connected with the automobile industry. All subjects were photographed in the studio, then the photographer mounted the cut out black-and-white images on a full-color street scene and then photographed it. ● Der Auftrag verlangte eine Darstellung von Menschen aus allen mit der Automobilindustrie verbundenen Berufen. Die Personen wurden im Studio photographiert, dann setzte der Photograph die ausgeschnittenen Schwarzweissbilder in eine farbige, strassenähnliche Dekoration und photographierte diese Montage. ▲ On avait demandé au photographe de représenter les différents métiers de l'industrie automobile. Tous les personnages ont été photographiés en studio; les tirages noir et blanc furent ensuite découpés et intégrés dans le décor en couleurs; enfin, le photographe prit une photo du montage.

PAGE 209 Photographer: MICHELE CLEMENT Representative: NORMAN MASLOV Client: ADLA Camera: NIKON F2 Film: POLAROID POLAPAN Art Director: SCOTT MILLER Model Builder: DAVE BIAGINI Country: USA ■ "Reality check"—the Art Directors' Club of Los Angeles used this image in its call for entries. Designer Scott Miller sent a huge box of articles to Clement. He and a model maker then experimented with them on a mannequin head. After seeing the results on a human model, they changed the whole concept. The model remained motionless for hours, and Polapan film helped document each step. ● «Überprüfung der Realität» – der Art Directors Club von Los Angeles verwendete dieses Bild als Einladung zu seinem Kommunikationswettbewerb. Designer Scott Miller schickte dem Photographen eine riesige Schachtel voller Gegenstände, mit denen dieser zusammen mit dem Modellbauer an einem Puppenkopf experimentierte. Nachdem sie das menschliche Modell sahen, wurden alle Konzepte umgeworfen. Dank des Polapan-Films konnte jeder Fortschritt registriert werden. ▲ «Examiner la réalité» – cette image a été utilisée par l'Art Directors Club de Los Angeles pour l'invitation à son concours de communication visuelle. Le designer Scott Miller avait envoyé au photographe une boîte énorme, remplie d'objets; ce dernier fit des expériences avec le modéliste en utilisant une tête de mannequin. Lorsque le modèle véritable se présenta, il fallut complètement transformer le projet. Toutes les étapes du concept purent être documentées grâce à un film Polapan.

PAGE 210 (all images) Photographer: MARCEL RITSCHEL Publisher: *AUSTRALIAN CAMERA* Camera: MAMIYA C330 S / PENTAX 6x7" Film: KODAK T-MAX 100 / KODAK TECHNICAL PAN Country: AUSTRALIA ■ "Altered States"—profound subjectivity is what these images attempt to convey. Through its expression of movement, each image maintains a certain metamorphic quality. ● «Veränderte Zustände» – absolute Subjektivität wollen diese Bilder vermitteln. Durch den Ausdruck von Bewegung bewahrt sich jedes Bild eine metamorphische Qualität. ▲ «Transformations» – ces images doivent donner une impression de subjectivité absolue. L'expression du mouvement suggère la métamorphose de l'image.

PAGE 211 Photographer: POBY Camera: HASSELBLAD 553 ELX Film: FUJI VELVIA Country: GERMANY ■ The dancer stood behind a sandblasted, matte glass pane. The translucence was obtained by brushing the pane with a mixture of water and oil. ● Die Tänzerin steht hinter einer sandgestrahlten, sogenannten Mattglasscheibe. Die Durchsicht wird durch Bestreichen der Scheibe mit einem Wasser-Öl-Gemisch erreicht. ▲ La danseuse se tient devant une plaque de verre dépoli. L'effet de transparence a été obtenu en passant sur le panneau un mélange d'eau et d'huile.

PAGE 212 (both images) Photographer: DEAN BURTON Camera: KOWA SIX Film: KODAK VERICOLOR HC Country: USA ■ Coming to Tucson from a rural town on the coast of Maine, one of the major themes the photographer uses is the collision of nature and urban industrial expansion in the Arizona desert. ● Der Photograph kam aus einer ländlichen Küstenstadt in Maine nach Tucson. Seither befasst er sich mit dem Aufeinanderprallen von Natur und Industrie in der Wüste Arizonas. ▲ Lorsqu'il arriva à Tucson, le photographe venait d'une petite ville côtière du Maine. Le choc entre la nature et l'expansion industrielle dans le désert de l'Arizona est depuis lors l'un des principaux sujets de ses photos.

PAGE 213 (both images) Photographer: ELIE BERNAGER Camera: HASSELBLAD Country: FRANCE ■ "*The world is about to vanish. You have to rush if you still want to see something,*" Paul Cezanne. Simple, abandoned objects, found by coincidence speak a silent language. Amidst the vanity of cities, the photographer searches for a bit of poetry. ● «Die Welt ist dabei zu verschwinden. Man muss sich beeilen, wenn man noch etwas sehen will», Paul Cézanne. Einfache, fortgeworfene Objekte, per Zufall gefunden, sprechen eine stumme Sprache. Inmitten der Eitelkeit der Städte sucht der Photograph ein wenig Poesie. ▲ «Le monde est en train de disparaître. Il faut se dépêcher si l'on veut encore voir quelque chose.» Paul Cézanne. Ces «objets bruts», trouvés par hasard, suggèrent le langage muet des choses. Il s'agissait pour le photographe de «retrouver un peu de poésie au milieu de la vanité des villes».

PAGE 230 Photographer: MICHAEL NORTHRUP Representative: ROBIN STEVENS Camera: BRONICA ETR Film: KODAK VERICHROME Art Director: DAVE PLUNKERT Designer: JOYCE HELLDERTH Country: USA ■ Color is isolated on different surfaces, and the spread of color is prevented, objects on the same plane show a different focus, objects on different planes are either fragmented or whole. The photographer is demonstrating the possibilites of this special process. ● Farbe wird auf verschiedenen Oberflächen isoliert, das Verfliessen von Farben wird verhindert, Gegenstände auf der gleichen Ebene sind unterschiedlich scharf, Objekte auf verschiedenen Ebenen sind ganz oder Fragmente – ein Photográph demonstriert die Möglichkeiten eines besonderen Verfahrens. ▲ Les couleurs sont isolées sur diverses surfaces, les objets situés sur le même plan ne présentent pas tous la même netteté, les éléments appartenant à des surfaces différentes sont rendus intégralement ou sous forme de fragments – le photographe a voulu faire la démonstration des effets spéciaux que l'on peut obtenir en utilisant une technique particulière.

PAGE 240 Photographer: ALFONS ISELI Camera: NIKON F4 Film: KODAK EKTACHROME 100 Country: SWITZERLAND

C A L L   F O R   E N T R I E S

GRAPHIS DESIGN 95

ENTRY DEADLINE: NOVEMBER 30, 1993

ADVERTISING: Newspaper and magazine. **DESIGN**: Promotion brochures, catalogs, invitations, record covers, announcements, logos, corporate campaigns, calendars, books, book covers, packaging (single or series, labels or complete packages). **EDITORIAL**: Company magazines, newspapers, consumer magazines, house organs, annual reports. **ILLUSTRATION**: All categories, black-and-white or color. **ELIGIBILITY**: All work produced between December 1, 1992 and November 30, 1993, including unpublished work by professionals or students.

GRAPHIS PHOTO 94

ENTRY DEADLINE: AUGUST 31, 1993

ADVERTISING PHOTOGRAPHY: Ads, catalogs, invitations, announcements, record covers and calendars on any subject. **EDITORIAL PHOTOGRAPHY**: Photos subject for journals, books and corporate publications. **FINE ART PHOTOGRAPHY**: Personal studies on any subject. **UNPUBLISHED PHOTOGRAPHS**: Experimental or student work on any subject. **ELIGIBILITY**: All work produced between Sept. 1, 1992 and Aug. 31, 1993.

GRAPHIS POSTER 95

ENTRY DEADLINE: APRIL 30, 1994

CULTURAL POSTERS: Exhibitions, film, music and theater. **ADVERTISING POSTERS**: Consumer goods and self-promotion. **SOCIAL POSTERS**: Education, conferences, political issues. **ELIGIBILITY**: All work produced between May 1, 1993 and April 30, 1994.

GRAPHIS ANNUAL REPORTS 5

ENTRY DEADLINE: APRIL 30, 1995

All annual reports, brochures, and other corporate collateral material. **ELIGIBILITY**: Work published between May 1, 1993 and April 30, 1995.

RULES

By submitting work, the sender grants permission for it to be published in any Graphis book, any article in Graphis magazine, or any advertisement, brochure or other printed matter produced specifically for the purpose of promoting the sale of these publications.

■ **ELIGIBILITY**: All work produced in the 12-month period previous to the submission deadline, including unpublished work by professionals or students, is eligible.

■ **WHAT TO SEND**: Please send the printed pieces or duplicate transparencies (please mark the dupes with your name) accompanied by a completed entry label. ALL 35MM SLIDES MUST BE CARDBOARD-MOUNTED, NO GLASS! *We regret that entries cannot be returned.*

■ **HOW AND WHERE TO SEND**: Please tape (do not glue) the completed entry form (or a copy) to the back of each piece. Entries can be sent by air mail, air parcel post or surface mail. Please do not send anything by air freight. Write "No Commercial Value" on the package, and label it "Art for Contest." The number of photographs and transparencies enclosed should also be marked on the parcel. (If sending by air courier—Federal Express or DHL, for instance—label the package "Doc-uments, Commercial Value $00.00".) For entries from countries with exchange controls, please contact us.

■ **SINGLE ENTRIES**: North America, U.S. $15; Germany, DM 15, All other countries, SFr 15.

■ **FOR AN ENTRY OF THREE OR MORE PIECES IN A SINGLE CONTEST**: North America, U.S. $35, Germany DM 40, All other countries SFr 40.

■ **STUDENTS' ENTRIES**: Free with copy of student identification. Please make checks payable to **GRAPHIS PRESS CORP., ZÜRICH**, and include in parcel. A confirmation of receipt will be sent to each entrant, and all entrants will be notified whether their work has been accepted for publication. By submitting work, you qualify for a 25 percent discount on the purchase of the published book. Please send entries to:

GRAPHIS PRESS CORP., 107 DUFOURSTRASSE CH-8008 ZÜRICH, SWITZERLAND

E I N L A D U N G

GRAPHIS DESIGN 95

EINSENDESCHLUSS: 30. NOVEMBER 1993

WERBUNG: In Zeitungen und Zeitschriften. **DESIGN**: Werbeprospekte, Kataloge, Einladungen, Schallplattenhüllen, Anzeigen, Signete, Image-Kampagnen, Kalender, Bücher, Buchumschläge, Packungen. **REDAKTIONELLES DESIGN**: Firmenpublikationen, Zeitungen, Zeitschriften, Jahresberichte. **ILLUSTRATIONEN**: Alle Kategorien, schwarzweiss oder farbig. **IN FRAGE KOMMEN**: Alle Arbeiten von Fachleuten und Studenten – auch nicht publizierte Arbeiten –, die zwischen Dezember 1992 und November 1993 entstanden sind.

GRAPHIS PHOTO 94

EINSENDESCHLUSS: 31. AUGUST 1993

WERBEPHOTOGRAPHIE: Anzeigen, Kataloge, Einladungen, Plattenhüllen, Kalender. **REDAKTIONELLE PHOTOGRAPHIE**: Pressephotos, Firmenpublikationen usw. **KÜNSTLERISCHE PHOTOGRAPHIE**: Persönliche Studien. **UNVERÖFFENTLICHTE PHOTOS**: Experimentelle Photographie und Arbeiten von Studenten. **IN FRAGE KOMMEN**: Arbeiten, die zwischen September 1992 und August 1993 entstanden sind.

GRAPHIS POSTER 95

EINSENDESCHLUSS: 30. APRIL 1994

KULTUR: Plakate für Ausstellungen, Film-, Theater-, Ballettaufführungen etc. **WERBUNG**: Plakate für Konsumgüter, Eigenwerbung **GESELLSCHAFT**: Ausbildung, Politik, Umwelt **IN FRAGE KOMMEN**: Arbeiten, die zwischen Mai 1993 und April 1994 entstanden sind.

GRAPHIS ANNUAL REPORTS 5

EINSENDESCHLUSS: 30. APRIL 1995

IN FRAGE KOMMEN: Jahresberichte einer Firma oder Organisation, die zwischen Mai 1993 und April 1995 publiziert wurden.

TEILNAHMEBEDINGUNGEN

Durch Ihre Einsendung erteilen Sie dem Graphis Verlag die Erlaubnis zur Veröffentlichung der Arbeiten in den Graphis-Büchern und in der Zeitschrift Graphis oder für die Wiedergabe im Zusammenhang mit Besprechungen und Werbematerial für Graphis-Publikationen.

■ **IN FRAGE KOMMEN**: Alle Arbeiten von Fachleuten und Studenten – auch nicht publizierte Arbeiten –, die in der angegebenen Periode vor Einsendeschluss entstanden sind.

■ **WAS EINSENDEN**: Senden Sie uns das gedruckte Beispiel oder Duplikatdias (bitte Dias mit Ihrem Namen versehen) zusammen mit dem ausgefüllten Etikett. KLEINBILDDIAS BITTE IM KARTONRAHMEN, KEIN GLAS! *Bitte beachten Sie, dass Einsendungen nicht zurückgeschickt werden können.*

■ **WIE SCHICKEN**: Befestigen Sie das ausgefüllte Etikett (oder eine Kopie) mit Klebstreifen (nicht mit Klebstoff) auf der Rückseite jeder Arbeit. Bitte per Luftpost oder auf normalem Postweg einsenden. Keine Luftfrachtsendungen. Deklarieren Sie «ohne jeden Handelswert» und «Arbeitsproben». Die Anzahl der Dias und Photos sollte auf dem Paket angegeben werden. Bei Luftkurier-Sendungen vermerken Sie «Dokumente, ohne jeden Handelswert».

■ **GEBÜHREN**: SFr. 15.–/DM 15,– für einzelne Arbeiten; SFr. 40.–/DM 40,– pro Kampagne oder Serie von mehr als drei Stück.

■ **STUDENTEN**: Diese Gebühren gelten nicht für Studenten. Senden Sie uns bitte eine Kopie des Studentenausweises.

Bitte senden Sie uns einen Scheck (SFr.-Schecks bitte auf eine Schweizer Bank ziehen) oder überweisen Sie den Betrag auf PC Zürich 80-23071-9 oder PSchK Frankfurt 3000 57-602 (BLZ 50010060. Jeder Einsender erhält eine Empfangsbestätigung und wird über Erscheinen oder Nichterscheinen seiner Arbeit informiert. Durch Ihre Einsendung erhalten Sie 25% Rabatt auf das betreffende Buch. Bitte senden Sie Ihre Arbeit an folgende Adresse:

GRAPHIS VERLAG, DUFOURSTRASSE 107, CH-8008 ZURICH, SCHWEIZ

APPEL D'ENVOIS

GRAPHIS DESIGN 95

DATE LIMITE D'ENVOI: 30 NOVEMBRE 1993

PUBLICITÉ: journaux, magazines. **DESIGN**: brochures, catalogues, invitations, pochettes de disque, annonces, logos, campagnes d'identité visuelle, calendriers, livres, jaquettes, packaging (spécimen ou série, étiquettes ou emballages complets). **DESIGN ÉDITORIAL**: magazines de sociétés, journaux, revues, publications d'entreprise, rapports annuels. **ILLUSTRATION**: toutes catégories noir et blanc ou couleurs. **ADMISSION**: tous travaux réalisés entre le 1er décembre 1992 et le 30 novembre 1993, y compris les inédits de professionnels ou d'étudiants.

GRAPHIS PHOTO 94

DATE LIMITE D'ENVOI: 31 AOUT 1993

PHOTO PUBLICITAIRE: publicités, catalogues, invitations, annonces, pochettes de disque et calendriers sur tous sujets. **PHOTO RÉDACTIONNELLE**: reportages pour périodiques, livres et publications d'entreprise. **PHOTO D'ART**: études personnelles. **PHOTOS INÉDITES**: travaux expérimentaux ou projets d'étudiants. **ADMISSION**: tous travaux réalisés entre le 1er septembre 1992 et le 31 août 1993.

GRAPHIS POSTER 95

DATE LIMITE D'ENVOI: 30 AVRIL 1994

AFFICHES CULTURELLES: expositions, films, musique, théâtre etc. **AFFICHES PUBLICITAIRES**: produits de consommation, autopromotion. **AFFICHES SOCIALES**: formation, conférences, politique. **ADMISSION**: tous travaux réalisés entre le 1er mai 1993 et le 30 avril 1994.

GRAPHIS ANNUAL REPORTS 5

DATE LIMITE D'ENVOI: 30 AVRIL 1995

Rapports annuels, brochures et tout matériel d'identité corporate. **ADMISSION**: travaux publiés entre le 1er mai 1993 et le 30 avril 1995.

REGLEMENT

Par votre envoi, vous donnez aux Editions Graphis l'autorisation de publier les travaux reçus dans nos livres Graphis, dans tout article du magazine Graphis ou toute publicité, brochure ou autre matériel publicitaire destiné à promouvoir la vente de ces publications.

■ **ADMISSION**: sont acceptés tous les travaux de professionnels et d'étudiants – même inédits – réalisés pendant les douze mois précédant le délai limite d'envoi.

■ **QUE NOUS ENVOYER**: un exemplaire imprimé ou un duplicata de la diapositive (n'oubliez pas d'inscrire votre nom dessus) avec l'étiquette ci-jointe, dûment remplie. NE PAS ENVOYER DE DIAPOSITIVES SOUS VERRE! *Les travaux ne peuvent pas être retournés.*

■ **COMMENT ET OÙ ENVOYER**: veuillez scotcher (ne pas coller) au dos de chaque spécimen les étiquettes (ou photocopies) dûment remplies. Envoyez les travaux par avion ou par voie de surface. Ne nous envoyez rien en fret aérien. Indiquez «Sans aucune valeur commerciale» et «Echantillons pour concours». Inscrire le nombre de diapositives et photos sur le paquet. (Pour les envois par courrier, indiquer «Documents, sans aucune valeur commerciale). Pour les envois en provenance de pays soumis au contrôle des changes, veuillez nous contacter.

■ **ENVOI D'UN SEUL TRAVAIL**: droits d'admission, SFr 15.– /US$ 15.00

■ **ENVOI D'UNE SÉRIE DE TROIS TRAVAUX OU PLUS POUR UN SEUL CONCOURS**: SFr 40.–/US 35.00

■ **ÉTUDIANTS**: les étudiants sont exemptés de la taxe d'admission. Prière de joindre une photocopie de la carte d'étudiant.

Veuillez joindre à votre envoi un chèque tiré sur une banque suisse ou verser ce montant au compte chèque postal Zurich, 80.23071.9. Nous vous ferons parvenir un accusé de réception. Tous les candidats seront informés de la parution ou non-parution de leurs travaux. Votre envoi vous vaudra une réduction de 25% sur l'annuel en question. Veuillez envoyer vos travaux à l'adresse suivante:

EDITIONS GRAPHIS, DUFOURSTRASSE 107, CH-8008 ZURICH, SUISSE

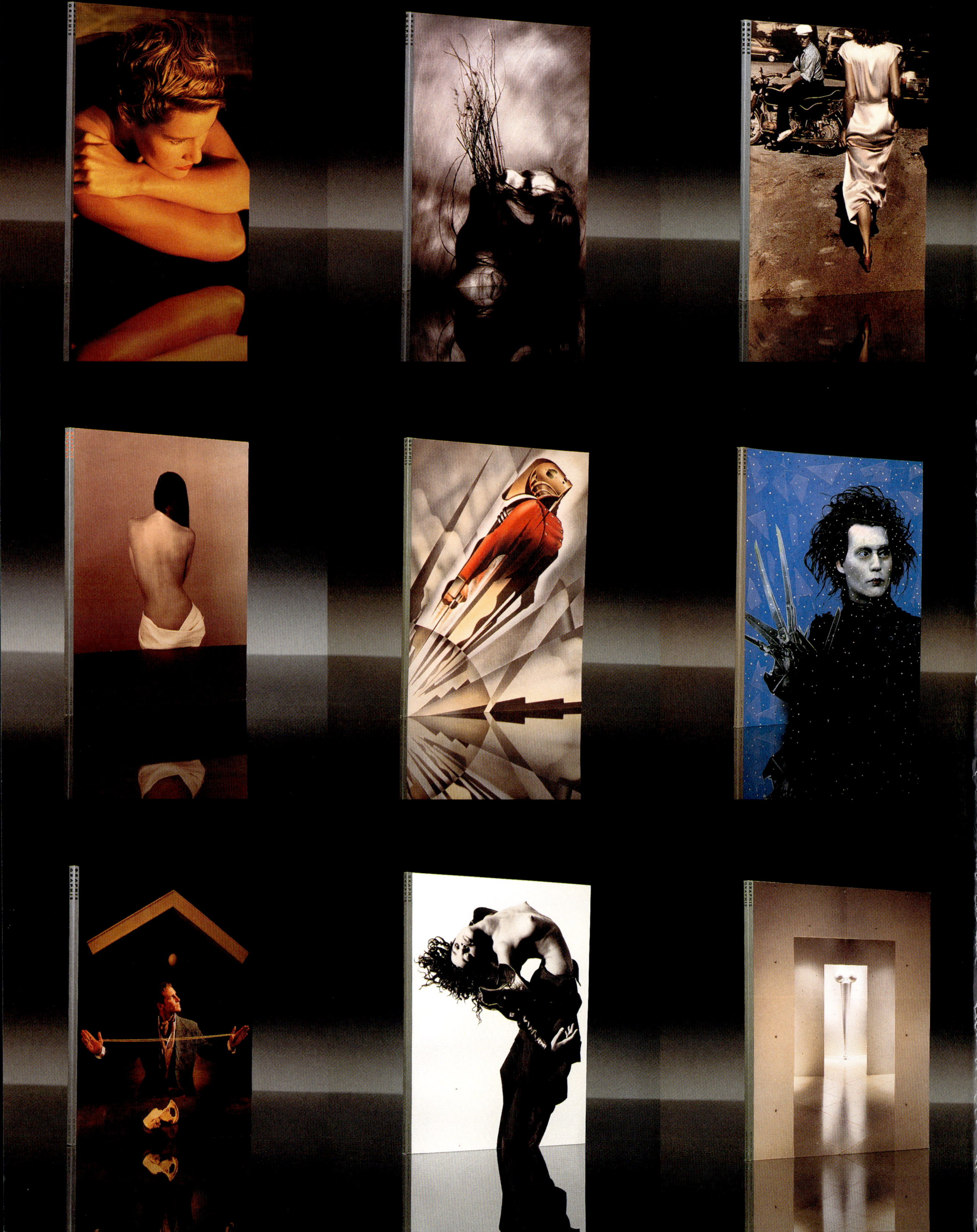

SUBSCRIBE TO GRAPHIS: USA AND CANADA

MAGAZINE USA CANADA

☐ NEW   ☐ RENEW
☐ GRAPHIS (TWO YEARS/12 ISSUES) US $149.00 US $166.00
☐ GRAPHIS (ONE YEAR/6 ISSUES) US $79.00 US $88.00
IMPORTANT! CHECK THE LANGUAGE VERSION DESIRED:
☐ ENGLISH   ☐ GERMAN   ☐ FRENCH
☐ CHECK ENCLOSED
☐ PLEASE BILL ME
☐ 25% DISCOUNT FOR STUDENTS WITH COPY OF VALID,
   DATED STUDENT ID AND PAYMENT WITH ORDER
FOR CREDIT CARD PAYMENT:
☐ VISA   ☐ MASTERCARD

ACCT. NO **EXP. DATE**

SIGNATURE

PLEASE PRINT

NAME **DATE**

TITLE

COMPANY

ADDRESS

CITY **POSTAL CODE**

COUNTRY

SEND ORDER FORM AND MAKE CHECK PAYABLE TO:
GRAPHIS US, INC.,
141 LEXINGTON AVENUE
NEW YORK, NY 10016-8191
SERVICE WILL BEGIN WITH ISSUE THAT IS CURRENT
WHEN ORDER IS PROCESSED. (PHOTO 93)

REQUEST FOR CALL FOR ENTRIES
PLEASE PUT ME ON THE "CALL FOR ENTRIES" LIST FOR THE
FOLLOWING TITLES:

☐ GRAPHIS DESIGN ☐ GRAPHIS ANNUAL REPORTS
☐ GRAPHIS DIAGRAM ☐ GRAPHIS CORPORATE IDENTITY
☐ GRAPHIS POSTER ☐ GRAPHIS PACKAGING
☐ GRAPHIS PHOTO ☐ GRAPHIS LETTERHEAD
☐ GRAPHIS LOGO ☐ GRAPHIS TYPOGRAPHY

SUBMITTING MATERIAL TO ANY OF THE ABOVE TITLES QUALIFIES
SENDER FOR A 25% DISCOUNT TOWARD PURCHASE OF THAT TITLE.

SUBSCRIBE TO GRAPHIS: EUROPE AND WORLD

MAGAZINE GERMANY U.K. WORLD

☐ NEW   ☐ RENEW
☐ GRAPHIS (TWO YEARS/12 ISSUES) DM 326,– £ 113.00 SFR 280.–
☐ GRAPHIS (ONE YEAR/6 ISSUES) DM 181,– £ 63.00 SFR 156.–
IMPORTANT! CHECK THE LANGUAGE VERSION DESIRED:
☐ ENGLISH   ☐ GERMAN   ☐ FRENCH
☐ SUBSCRIPTION FEES INCLUDE POSTAGE TO ANY
   PART OF THE WORLD
☐ AIRMAIL SURCHARGES (PER YEAR) DM 75,– £ 26.00 SFR 65.–
☐ REGISTERED MAIL (PER YEAR) DM 24,– £ 8.50 SFR 20.–
☐ CHECK ENCLOSED (PLEASE MAKE SFR.–CHECK PAYABLE
   TO A SWISS BANK.
☐ STUDENTS MAY REQUEST A 25% DISCOUNT BY SENDING STUDENT ID
FOR CREDIT CARD PAYMENT (ALL CARDS DEBITED IN SWISS FRANCS):
☐ AMERICAN EXPRESS ☐ DINER'S CLUB
☐ EURO/MASTERCARD ☐ VISA/BARCLAY/CARTE BLEUE

ACCT. NO **EXP. DATE**

SIGNATURE

PLEASE PRINT

NAME **DATE**

TITLE

COMPANY

ADDRESS

CITY **POSTAL CODE**

COUNTRY

SEND ORDER FORM AND MAKE CHECK PAYABLE TO:
GRAPHIS PRESS CORP.,
DUFOURSTRASSE 107
CH-8008 ZÜRICH, SWITZERLAND
SERVICE WILL BEGIN WITH ISSUE THAT IS CURRENT
WHEN ORDER IS PROCESSED. (PHOTO 93)

REQUEST FOR CALL FOR ENTRIES
PLEASE PUT ME ON THE "CALL FOR ENTRIES" LIST FOR THE
FOLLOWING TITLES:

☐ GRAPHIS DESIGN ☐ GRAPHIS ANNUAL REPORTS
☐ GRAPHIS DIAGRAM ☐ GRAPHIS CORPORATE IDENTITY
☐ GRAPHIS POSTER ☐ GRAPHIS PACKAGING
☐ GRAPHIS PHOTO ☐ GRAPHIS LETTERHEAD
☐ GRAPHIS LOGO ☐ GRAPHIS TYPOGRAPHY

SUBMITTING MATERIAL TO ANY OF THE ABOVE TITLES QUALIFIES
SENDER FOR A 25% DISCOUNT TOWARD PURCHASE OF THAT TITLE.

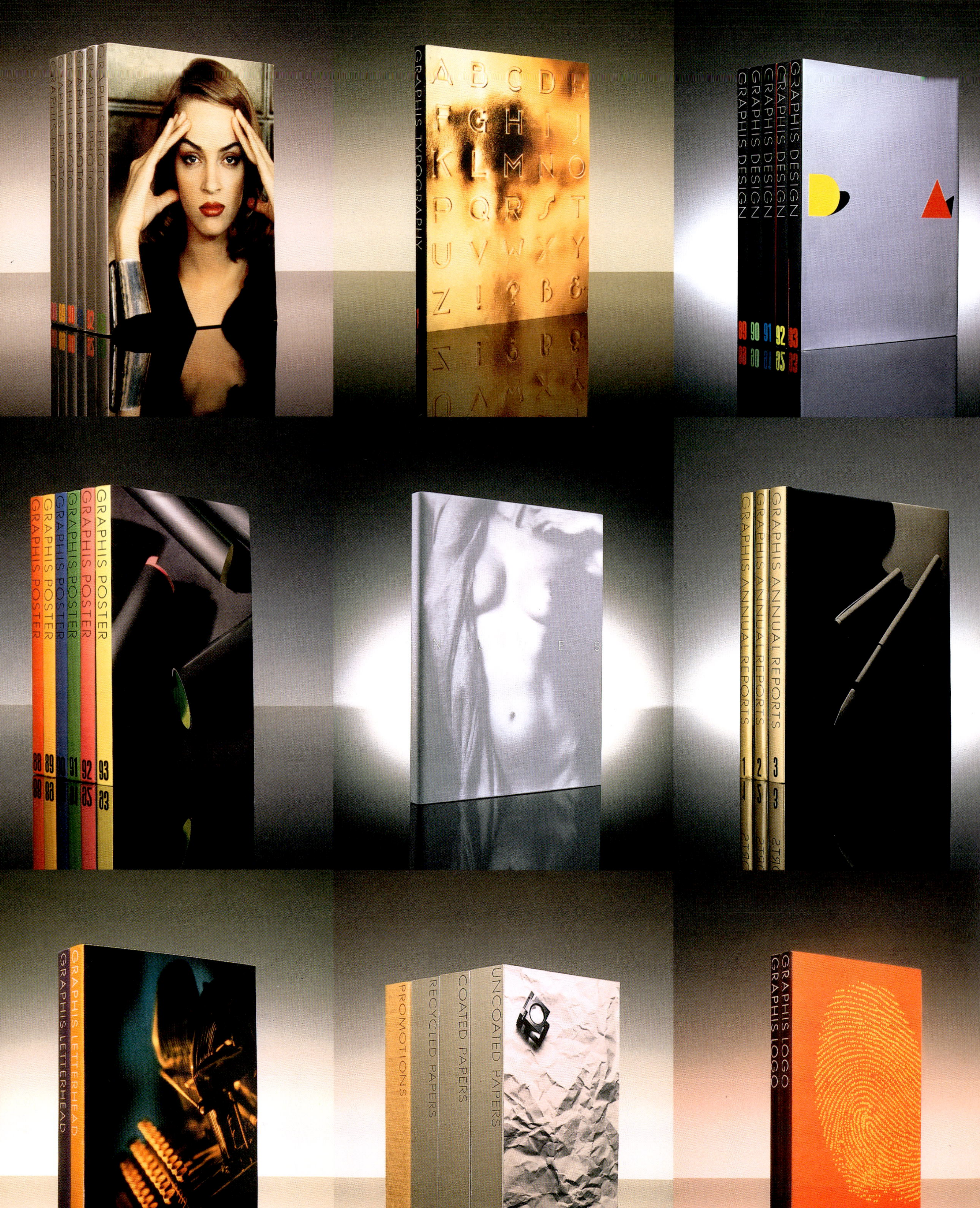

GRAPHIS PHOTO
GRAPHIS TYPOGRAPHY
GRAPHIS DESIGN
GRAPHIS POSTER
NUDES
GRAPHIS ANNUAL REPORTS
GRAPHIS LETTERHEAD
PROMOTIONS
RECYCLED PAPERS
COATED PAPERS
UNCOATED PAPERS
GRAPHIS LOGO

BOOK ORDER FORM: USA AND CANADA

BOOKS	USA	CANADA
☐ GRAPHIS PHOTO 93	US $69.00	US $94.00
☐ GRAPHIS PHOTO 92	US $69.00	US $94.00
☐ GRAPHIS POSTER 93	US $69.00	US $94.00
☐ GRAPHIS POSTER 92	US $69.00	US $94.00
☐ GRAPHIS DESIGN 93	US $69.00	US $94.00
☐ GRAPHIS DESIGN 92	US $69.00	US $94.00
☐ GRAPHIS ANNUAL REPORTS 3	US $75.00	US$100.00
☐ GRAPHIS LETTERHEAD 1	US $69.00	US $94.00
☐ GRAPHIS LOGO 1	US $50.00	US $70.00
☐ THE GRAPHIC DESIGNER'S GREENBOOK	US $25.00	US $41.00
☐ GRAPHIS PUBLICATION 1/MAGAZINDESIGN 1 ☐ ENGLISH ☐ GERMAN	US $75.00	US$100.00
☐ ART FOR SURVIVAL: THE ILLUSTRATOR AND THE ENVIRONMENT	US $40.00	US $60.00
☐ GRAPHIS NUDES	US $75.00	US$100.00
☐ GRAPHIS PACKAGING 5	US $75.00	US$100.00
☐ GRAPHIS DIAGRAM 1	US $69.00	US $94.00

☐ CHECK ENCLOSED (GRAPHIS AGREES TO PAY MAILING COSTS)

☐ PLEASE BILL ME (MAILING COSTS IN ADDITION TO ABOVE BOOK
PRICES WILL BE CHARGED). BOOK(S) WILL BE SENT WHEN
PAYMENT IS RECEIVED)

PLEASE PRINT

NAME   DATE

TITLE

COMPANY

ADDRESS

CITY   POSTAL CODE

COUNTRY

DATE   SIGNATURE

SEND ORDER FORM AND MAKE CHECK PAYABLE TO:
GRAPHIS US, INC.,
141 LEXINGTON AVENUE,
NEW YORK, NY 10016, USA

REQUEST FOR CALL FOR ENTRIES
PLEASE PUT ME ON YOUR "CALL FOR ENTRIES" LIST FOR THE
FOLLOWING TITLES:

☐ GRAPHIS DESIGN   ☐ GRAPHIS ANNUAL REPORTS
☐ GRAPHIS DIAGRAM   ☐ GRAPHIS CORPORATE IDENTITY
☐ GRAPHIS POSTER   ☐ GRAPHIS PACKAGING
☐ GRAPHIS PHOTO   ☐ GRAPHIS LETTERHEAD
☐ GRAPHIS LOGO   ☐ GRAPHIS TYPOGRAPHY

SUBMITTING MATERIAL TO ANY OF THE ABOVE TITLES QUALIFIES
SENDER FOR A 25% DISCOUNT TOWARD PURCHASE OF THAT TITLE.

BOOK ORDER FORM: EUROPE AND WORLD

BOOKS	GERMANY	U.K.	WORLD
☐ GRAPHIS PHOTO 93	DM 149,–	£ 49.00	SFR. 123.–
☐ GRAPHIS PHOTO 92	DM 149,–	£ 49.00	SFR. 123.–
☐ GRAPHIS POSTER 93	DM 149,–	£ 49.00	SFR. 123.–
☐ GRAPHIS POSTER 92	DM 149,–	£ 49.00	SFR. 123.–
☐ GRAPHIS DESIGN 93	DM 149,–	£ 49.00	SFR. 123.–
☐ GRAPHIS DESIGN 92	DM 149,–	£ 49.00	SFR. 123.–
☐ GRAPHIS ANNUAL REPORTS 3	DM 162,–	£ 52.00	SFR. 137.–
☐ GRAPHIS LETTERHEAD 1	DM 149,–	£ 49.00	SFR. 123.–
☐ GRAPHIS LOGO 1	DM 108,–	£ 36.00	SFR. 92.–
☐ THE GRAPHIC DESIGNER'S GREENBOOK	DM 54,–	£ 18.00	SFR. 46.–
☐ GRAPHIS PUBLICATION 1/MAGAZINDESIGN 1 ☐ ENGLISH ☐ GERMAN	DM 162,–	£ 52.00	SFR. 137.–
☐ ART FOR SURVIVAL: THE ILLUSTRATOR AND THE ENVIRONMENT	DM 89,–	£ 33.00	SFR. 79.–
☐ GRAPHIS NUDES	DM 148,–	£ 59.00	SFR. 148.–
☐ GRAPHIS PACKAGING 5	DM 160,–	£ 48.00	SFR. 132.–
☐ GRAPHIS DIAGRAM 1	DM 138,–	£ 49.00	SFR. 112.–

☐ PLEASE BILL ME (MAILING COSTS IN ADDITION TO ABOVE BOOK
PRICES WILL BE CHARGED).

PLEASE PRINT

NAME   DATE

TITLE

COMPANY

ADDRESS

CITY   POSTAL CODE

COUNTRY

DATE   SIGNATURE

PLEASE SEND ORDER FORM TO:
GRAPHIS PRESS CORP.,
DUFOURSTRASSE 107,
CH–8008 ZÜRICH, SWITZERLAND

REQUEST FOR CALL FOR ENTRIES
PLEASE PUT ME ON YOUR "CALL FOR ENTRIES" LIST FOR THE
FOLLOWING TITLES:

☐ GRAPHIS DESIGN   ☐ GRAPHIS ANNUAL REPORTS
☐ GRAPHIS DIAGRAM   ☐ GRAPHIS CORPORATE IDENTITY
☐ GRAPHIS POSTER   ☐ GRAPHIS PACKAGING
☐ GRAPHIS PHOTO   ☐ GRAPHIS LETTERHEAD
☐ GRAPHIS LOGO   ☐ GRAPHIS TYPOGRAPHY

SUBMITTING MATERIAL TO ANY OF THE ABOVE TITLES QUALIFIES
SENDER FOR A 25% DISCOUNT TOWARD PURCHASE OF THAT TITLE.

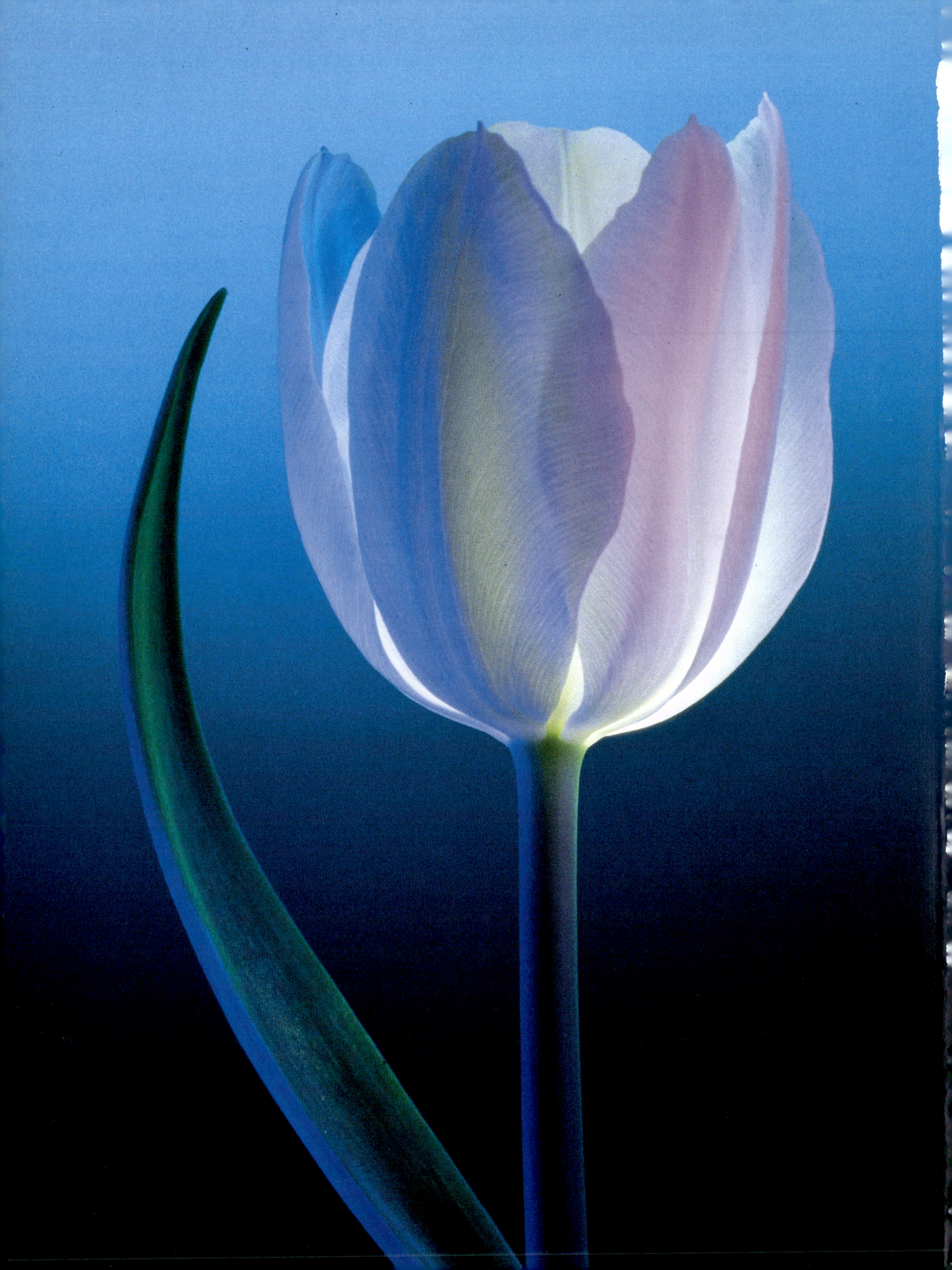